Lecture Notes in Computer Science 4743

Commenced Publication in 1973
Founding and Former Series Editors:
Gerhard Goos, Juris Hartmanis, and Jan van Leeuwen

T0180860

Parimala Thulasiraman   Xubin He
Tony Li Xu   Mieso K. Denko
Ruppa K. Thulasiram   Laurence T. Yang (Eds.)

Frontiers of High Performance Computing and Networking – ISPA 2007 Workshops

ISPA 2007 International Workshops
SSDSN, UPWN, WISH, SGC, ParDMCom,
HiPCoMB, and IST-AWSN
Niagara Falls, Canada, August 29-31, 2007
Proceedings

 Springer

Volume Editors

Parimala Thulasiraman
University of Manitoba, Winnipeg, MB, Canada
E-mail: thulasir@cs.umanitoba.ca

Xubin He
Tennessee Technological University, Cookeville, TN, USA
E-mail: hexb@tntech.edu

Tony Li Xu
St. Francis Xavier University, Antigonish, NS, Canada
E-mail: tonylixu@gmail.com

Mieso K. Denko
University of Guelph, Guelph, ON, Canada
E-mail: denko@cis.uoguelph.ca

Ruppa K. Thulasiram
University of Manitoba, Winnipeg, MB, Canada
E-mail: tulsi@cs.umanitoba.ca

Laurence T. Yang
St. Francis Xavier University, Antigonish, NS, Canada
E-mail: lyang@stfx.ca

Library of Congress Control Number: 2007933704

CR Subject Classification (1998): F.1, F.2, D.1, D.2, D.4, C.2, C.4, H.4-5

LNCS Sublibrary: SL 1 – Theoretical Computer Science and General Issues

ISSN   0302-9743
ISBN-10   3-540-74766-4 Springer Berlin Heidelberg New York
ISBN-13   978-3-540-74766-6 Springer Berlin Heidelberg New York

Springer is a part of Springer Science+Business Media

springer.com

© Springer-Verlag Berlin Heidelberg 2007
Printed in Germany

Typesetting: Camera-ready by author, data conversion by Scientific Publishing Services, Chennai, India
Printed on acid-free paper   SPIN: 12118182   06/3180   5 4 3 2 1 0

Preface

This proceedings volume contains the refereed and revised papers presented at the seven workshops held in conjunction with the Fifth International Symposium on Parallel and Distributed Processing and Applications (ISPA 2007), in Niagara Falls, Ontario, Canada, August 29–31, 2007. The objective of the workshops is to provide an outstanding international forum for academics, educators, engineering, and industrial professionals to contribute and to disseminate innovative and state-of-the-art research, to report, discuss and exchange experimental or theoretical results, experience, work-in-progress, and case studies on high-performance computing and networking. These workshops are:

1) SSDSN 2007: The 2007 International Workshop on Security and Survivability in Distributed Sensor Networks
2) UPWN 2007: The 2007 International Workshop on Ubiquitous Processing for Wireless Networks
3) WISH 2007: The 2007 International Workshop on Intelligent Systems and Smart Home
4) SGC 2007: The 2007 International Workshop on Semantic and Grid Computing
5) ParDMCom 2007: The 2nd International Workshop on Parallel and Distributed Multimedia Computing
6) HiPCoMB 2007: The 3rd Workshop on High-Performance Computing in Medicine and Biology
7) IST-AWSN 2007: The 2nd International Workshop on Intelligent Systems Techniques for Ad Hoc and Wireless Sensor Networks

Each of the workshops focuses on a particular theme of high-performance computing and networking and complements the spectrum of the main conference.

We would like to thank the ISPA 2007 General and Steering Co-chairs, Laurence T. Yang, Ruppa K. Thulasiram, Jie Wu, and Minyi Guo, for their guidance and vision, and the Program Co-chairs, Ivan Stojmenovic and Weijia Jia, for their support and encouragement. We deeply appreciate the tremendous efforts and contributions of the Chairs of individual workshops. Our thanks also go to all authors for their valuable contributions and to all Program Committee members and reviewers for providing timely and in-depth reviews. Last but not least, we deeply appreciate Tony Li Xu for his great help and hard work with editing the proceedings.

August 2007

Xubin (Ben) He
Parimala Thulasiraman

Preface

International Workshop on Security and Survivability in Distributed Sensor Networks (SSDSN 2007)

Sensor networks have been widely applied in many practical problems. And sensor networks are expected to become a more significant part of the future ubiquitous computing era. However, sensor networks introduce new security and survivability challenges due to their severe resource constraints and absence of a trusted infrastructure. During the last few years, novel research has been performed in all aspects of security and survivability for sensor networks, as well as experimental studies of fielded systems.

This workshop aims to bring together the technicians and researchers who share interest in the field of security and survivability in sensor networks. The main purpose is to promote discussions of research and relevant activities in security and survivability-related topics in distributed and mobile sensor networks. It also aims at increasing the synergy between academic and industry professionals working in this area.

This year we were pleased to have received a number of high-quality submissions. We conducted a rigorous peer-review process for each submission, with the support of all Program Committee members as well as external reviewers. Based on the reviews, we selected five papers to be presented at the workshop. We regret that many quality submissions could not be included. We would like to thank all the authors of the submissions for their contribution. We would also like to thank the Program Committee members for their efforts in reviewing the submissions.

We would also like to thank the ISPA workshop Chairs Xubin He and Parimala Thulasiraman for their excellent work in driving and supporting us in the numerous phases of workshop development.

Jong Sou Park
Jang-Se Lee
Dong Seong Kim

Executive Committee

General Chair	Jong Sou Park, Korea Aerospace University, Korea
Program Chairs	Jang-Se Lee, Korea Maritime University, Korea
	Dong Seong Kim, University of Maryland College Park, USA

Program Committee

Alvaro Crdenas	University of California, Berkeley, USA
DaeHun Nyang	Inha University, Korea
Dong Seong Kim	University of Maryland College Park, USA
Hiroaki Kikuchi	Tokai University, Japan
Jang-Se Lee	Korea Maritime University, Korea
Jong Sou Park	Korea Aerospace University, Korea
Nan Zhang	University of Texas at Arlington, USA
Sang-Soo Yeo	Kyushu University, Japan
Shiqun Li	Shanghai Jiao Tong University, China
Tieyan Li	Institute for Infocomm Research, Singapore
Junyang Zhou	Hong Kong Baptist University, Hong Kong
Zinaida Benenson	University of Mannheim, Germany

International Workshop on Ubiquitous Processing for Wireless Networks (UPWN 2007)

Traditionally, wireless systems are considered for voice communication. However, wireless networks are becoming more popular for data processing. Since wireless communication guarantees freedom of movement, it can provide easier access from anywhere. Hence, wireless networks are a vital element for ubiquitous processing.

The Ubiquitous Processing for Wireless Networks workshop aims to cover the topics of seamless, secure, and intuitive access for distributed processing of various ubiquitous computing networks. Grid is a good example of distributed processing for a ubiquitous network environment. Since the technology is evolving into the direction of wireless, and the fast processing speed is also getting more attention, there has been much effort to support ubiquitous computing through distributed and parallel processing over scattered networks.

This conference provides an international forum for the presentation and showcase of recent advances in various aspects of ubiquitous processing over wireless networks. It reflects the state of the art of the computational methods, involving theory, algorithm, numerical simulation, error and uncertainty analysis and/or novel application of new processing techniques in engineering, science, and other disciplines related to ubiquitous computing networks. In the conference, several topics on the specific themes for intensive discussions were included according to the areas of interest. This workshop is a unique opportunity for developers, administrators, researchers, and service providers in ubiquitous computing to meet to discuss the wireless data communication technology. It can provide an inside view of new paradigms of parallel and distributed processing for ubiquitous networks over wireless networks.

We are very proud to have received a large number of high-quality submissions. Based on the reviews, with the great support of all Program Committee members as well as a group of external reviewers, we selected 8 out of 32 submitted papers to be included in these proceedings. We regret that many quality submissions could not be included. Once again, we would like to thank all the authors of all the submissions for their contribution and all the ISPA 2007 committee members.

Keecheon Kim

Executive Committee

Steering Chair   Keecheon Kim, Konkuk University, Korea
General Co-chairs   Jongwon Choe, Sookmyung University, Korea
                        Hyunseung Choo, Sungkyunkwan University, Korea
Program Co-chair   Jinsung Choi, LG Electronics, Seoul, Korea

Program Committee

Koji Okamura   Kyushu University, Japan
Jianping Wu   Tshingwha University, China
Vicent Tang   NUS, Singapore
Yan Ma   Beijing University of Post and Telecommunication,
                      China
Michael Ha   Sprint Nextel Communications, USA
Sang Lee   Microsoft, USA
Oshiito Oyama   Tsukuba University, Japan
Jaepil Yoo   Konkuk University, Korea

International Workshop on Intelligent Systems and Smart Home (WISH 2007)

We are proud to present the proceedings of the 2007 International Workshop on Intelligent Systems and Smart Home, held at Niagara Falls, Canada during August 29–31.

Smart home environments (SHE) are emerging rapidly as an exciting new paradigm including ubiquitous, grid, and peer-to-peer computing to provide computing and communication services any time and anywhere. In order to realize such advantages, intelligent systems need to be suitable for SHE. WISH 2007 was intended to foster the dissemination of state-of-the-art research in the area of SHE including intelligent systems, security services, business models and novel applications associated with their utilization. The aim of WISH 2007 was to be the premier event in intelligent theories and practical applications, focusing on all aspects of SHE and providing a high-profile, leading-edge forum for researchers and engineers alike to present their latest research.

In order to guarantee high-quality proceedings, we put extensive effort into reviewing the scientific papers. We received 58 papers from Korea, USA, China, Taiwan, Mexico, UK, France, Thailand, Japan and the Czech Republic, representing more than 45 universities or institutions. All submissions were peer reviewed by two to three Program or Technical Committee members or external reviewers. It was extremely difficult to select the presentations for the workshop because there were so many excellent and interesting ones. In order to allocate as many papers as possible and keep the high quality of the workshop, we finally decided to accept 13 papers for oral presentations. We believe all of these papers and topics will not only provide novel ideas, new results, work in progress and state-of-the-art techniques in this field, but will also stimulate future research activities.

This workshop would not have been possible without the support of many people who made it a success. First of all, we would like to thank the Steering Committee Co-chairs, Laurence T. Yang and Minyi Guo, for nourishing the workshop and guiding its course. We thank the Program Committee members for their excellent job in reviewing the submissions and thus guaranteeing the quality of the workshop under a very tight schedule. We are also indebted to the members of the Organizing Committee. Particularly, we thank Ching-Hsien Hsu, JongHyuk Park, Cho-Li Wang and Gang Pan for their devotion and effort to make this workshop a real success. Finally, we would like to take this opportunity

to thank all the authors and participants for their contributions, which made
WISH 2007 a grand success.

Laurence T. Yang
Minyi Guo
Ching-Hsien Hsu
Jong Hyuk Park
Cho-Li Wang
Gang Pan

Executive Committee

Steering Chairs	Laurence T. Yang, St. Francis Xavier University, Canada
	Minyi Guo, University of Aizu, Japan
General Co-chairs	Ching-Hsien Hsu, Chung Hua University, Taiwan
	Jong Hyuk Park, Hanwha S & C Co., Ltd., Korea
Program Co-chairs	Cho-Li Wang, The University of Hong Kong, Hong Kong
	Gang Pan, Zhijiang University, China
Publicity Co-chairs	Jong Wook Han, ETRI, Korea
	David Simplot-Ryl, University of Lille 1, France
	Jiang (Linda) Xie, Georgia State University, USA
International Advisory Committee	Jiannong Cao, Hong Kong Polytechnic University, Hong Kong
	Zhi-Hua Zhou, Nanjing University, China
	Edwin H-M. Sha, University of Texas at Dallas, USA
	Yi Pan, Georgia State University, USA

Program Committee

Aaron Quigley	University College Dublin, Ireland
Akira Namatame	National Defense Academy, Japan
Alex Zhaoyu Liu	University of North Carolina at Charlotte, USA
Ali Shahrabi	Glasgow Caledonian University, UK
Anthony Jameson	DFKI, Germany
Arjen Lenstra	EPFL, Switzerland
Biplab Kumer Sarker	University of New Brunswick, Canada
Byoung-Soo Koh	DigiCAPS Co., Ltd, Korea
Carlo Blundo	Università di Salerno, Italy
Ce-Kuen Shieh	National Cheng Kung University, Taiwan
Christophe Bidan	Supelec, France
Deok-Gyu Lee	ETRI, Korea
Dingzhu Lu	City University of Hong Kong, Hong Kong
Elhadi Shakshuki	Acadia University, Canada
George Roussos	University of London, UK
Gerd Kortuem	Lancaster University, UK
Han-Chieh Chao	National Ilan University, Taiwan
Jianhua Ma	Hosei University, Japan
Jin Wook Lee	Samsung Advanced Institute of Technology, Korea
Jingling Xue	The University of New South Wales, Australia
Karen Henricksen	NICTA, Australia

International Workshop on Semantic and Grid Computing (SGC 2007)

As extensions of current Web and grid computing, semantic computing and semantic grid systems are characterized as open systems in which information, software, computing resources and services are given well-defined and standardized meaning at a semantic level. They provide a detailed semantic structure of all components in the computing world. This approach helps bring resources virtually together and makes it easier for resources to be discovered and processed automatically.

This workshop aims to provide a forum for researchers to discuss and share their findings and ideas in semantic and grid computing, and to envision the future work in this area.

This year we were very proud to receive a number of high-quality submissions. We conducted a rigorous peer-review process with the great support of all Program Committee members. We congratulate the authors of accepted papers and regret many quality submissions could not be included, due to the time and space limit.

We would like to take this opportunity to extend our sincere gratitude to all authors for their contributions to the program and to all Program Committee members for their dedication and care in reviewing this years submissions. We would also like to express our gratitude and appreciation to the ISPA 2007 Workshop Chairs Xubin He and Parimala Thulasiraman for their excellent work in driving and supporting us in the various phases of workshop development.

We hope that all readers will enjoy the workshop proceedings.

Beniamino Di Martino
Laurence T. Yang
Hai Jiang
Xubin He
Young-Sik Jeong

Executive Committee

Steering Chairs   Laurence T. Yang, St. Francis Xavier University,
                           Canada
                         Beniamino Di Martino, Second University of Naples,
                           Italy
General Chairs   Xubin He, Tennessee Technological University, USA
                         Young-Sik Jeong, Wonkwang University, Korea
Program Chairs   Beniamino Di Martino, Second University of Naples,
                           Italy
                         Hai Jiang, Arkansas State University, USA

Program Committee

Huajun Chen   Zhejiang University, China
Xiaowu Chen   Beihang University, China
Orlando De Pietro   University of Calabria, Italy
Aldo Di Russo   Unicity, Italy
Christian Engelmann   Oak Ridge National Laboratory, USA
Aldo Gangemi   Italian National Research Council, Italy
Carol Goble   University of Manchester, UK
Daniel Grosu   Wayne State University, USA
Jizhong Han   Chinese Academy of Sciences, China
Youn-Hee Han   Korea University of Technology and Education,
                           Korea
Dongwon Jeong   Kunsan National University, Korea
Wenbin Jiang   Huazhong University of Science and Technology,
                           China
Li Ou   Dell Inc., USA
Marcin Paprzycki   SWPS and IBSPAN, Poland
Dana Petcu   Western University of Timisoara, Romania
Omer Rana   Cardiff University, UK
David De Roure   University of Southampton, UK
Marta Sabou   Open University, UK
Haiying Shen   University of Arkansas, USA
Domenico Talia   University of Calabria, Italy
Flavio Tariffi   SPACE, Italy
Juan Tourino   University of A Coruna, Spain
Paola Velardi   University "La Sapienza" of Rome, Italy
Zhiyong Xu   Suffolk University, USA
Yifeng Zhu   University of Maine, USA

The 2nd International Workshop on Parallel and Distributed Multimedia Computing (ParDMCom 2007)

In recent years, multimedia computing has become an increasingly popular technology. Together with significant development in high-speed networks, multimedia computing has opened a wide range of new applications by combining a variety of information sources such as voice, graphics, animation images, audio and text. The latest introduction of high-definition and interactive television has generated important issues in relation to the creation, processing and management of multimedia content. This new technology requires a huge amount of data processing, which naturally leads to parallel and distributed computing.

Considering the emergence of multimedia computing as a major area of research, the second consecutive edition of ParDMCom was held to provide opportunities for the scientists, engineers, developers and other experts to share the recent research developments in theories, algorithms, architectures, systems and integrated multimedia platforms that exploit parallel and distributed computing.

ParDMCom 2007 attracted high-quality submissions from Asia, Middle East, Europe, and America. Thanks to the great efforts of our technical Program Committee, we maintained a stringent peer-review process for each submission. Every paper had two to four independent reviews.

We would like to extend our appreciation to each member of the ParDMCom 2007 and ISPA 2007 Organizing Committees, and anyone involved in helping ensure the success of ParDMCom 2007. Last but not least, we would like to thank and congratulate authors of the accepted papers.

Agustinus Borgy Waluyo
Rong-Chi Chang

Executive Committee

Steering Co-chairs	Laurence T. Yang, St. Francis Xavier University, Canada
	Jianhua Ma, Hosei University, Japan
General Co-chairs	Shu-Ching Chen, Florida International University, USA
	Hui-Huang Hsu, Tamkang University, Taiwan
Program Co-chairs	Agustinus Borgy Waluyo, Institute for Infocomm Research, Singapore
	Rong-Chi Chang, Asia University, Taiwan

Technical Program Committee

Alex Zhaoyu Liu	University of North Carolina at Charlotte, USA
Bernady O. Apduhan	Kyushu Sangyo University, Japan
Chengcui Zhang	University of Alabama at Birmingham, USA
Chih-Hao Lin	Asia University, Taiwan
Chuan-Ho Kao	Tak-Ming College, Taiwan
Daniel C Doolan	National University of Ireland at Cork, Ireland
Dorin Bocu	Transylvania University of Brasov, Romania
Guojun Wang	Central South University, China
Hong-Va Leong	Hong Kong Polytechnic University, Hong Kong
Hongli Luo	Indiana University-Purdue University Fort Wayne, USA
Hung-Kuang Chen	National Chin-Yi Institute of Technology, Taiwan
Ismail Khalil Ibrahim	Johannes Kepler University Linz, Austria
James Joshi	University of Pittsburgh, USA
Jason C. Hung	Northern Taiwan Institute of Science and Technology, Taiwan
Lawrence Y. Deng	St. John's University, Taiwan
Mei-Ling Shyu	University of Miami, USA
Michael Ditze	University of Paderborn, Germany
Qun Jin	Waseda University, Japan
Shih-Nung Chen	Asia University, Taiwan
Te-Hua Wang	Chihlee Institute of Technology, Taiwan
Wenbin Jiang	Huazhong University of Science and Technology, China
Wen-Chih Chang	Chung Hua University, Taiwan
Rong-Ming Chen	National University of Tainan, Taiwan
Xiaochuan Yi	AT & T, USA
Yi-Chun Liao	China University of Technology, Taiwan
Zhiwen Yu	Kyoto University, Japan
Zhiyong Xu	Suffolk University, USA

International Workshop on High-Performance Computing in Medicine and Biology(HiPCoMB 2007)

Medical applications and biological data require special processing resources, while guaranteeing privacy and security.

High-performance computing becomes crucial in dealing with huge sensitive data for special medical activities, such as diagnosis, therapy, e-health, tele-surgery, as well in supporting requirements of specific domains, such as phylogenetics, genomics and proteomics. Moreover, novel biomedical applications require the integration and sharing of huge amounts of data.

The grid paradigm offers great computing power and flexible data handling capabilities, thus allowing users and laboratories to share their facilities (computing and data storage resources, instruments, knowledge, etc.) through high bandwidth networks among dynamically formed virtual organizations.

Current grid middleware offers basic services for grid management, applications development and deployment. To face the complexity of novel, cooperative, distributed health and bioinformatics applications, new specialized grid services have to be developed in such a way that grids can be deployed to specifically address the needs of the biomedical community.

This workshop aims to provide a forum for researchers to discuss and share their findings and ideas in the application of high-performance and grid applications in biomedical and bioinformatics areas and to envision the future work in this area.

This year we were proud to receive many high-quality submissions. We conducted a rigorous peer-review process for each submission, with the great support of all Program Committee members. Based on the reviews, we selected four papers to be included in this program. We congratulate the authors of accepted papers, and regret many quality submissions could not be included, due to the time and space limit.

Taking this opportunity, we would like to thank all the authors for their contributions to the program. We would also like to thank the Program Committee members for their efforts in reviewing the submissions.

We would like to thank the ISPA 2007 Steering Committee Co-chair, Laurence T. Yang, and the HiPCoMB 2007 General Co-chairs, Vipin Chaudhary and Panos M. Pardalos.

Giovanni Aloisio
Maria Mirto
Almerico Murli
Hans De Sterck

XX   Organization

Executive Committee

General Co-chairs   Vipin Chaudhary, Wayne State University, USA
                          Panos M. Pardalos, University of Florida, USA
                          Laurence T. Yang, St. Francis Xavier University,
                             Canada
Program Co-chairs   Giovanni Aloisio, University of Salento, Italy
                          Maria Mirto, University of Salento, Italy
                          Almerico Murli, University of Naples Federico II, Italy
                          Hans De Sterck, University of Waterloo, Canada

Program Committee

Vincent Breton   CNRS/IN2P3, LPC Clermont-Ferrand, France
Rita Casadio   Biocomputing Lab, University of Bologna, Italy
Giuliano Laccetti   University of Naples Federico II, Italy
Alfredo Tirado-Ramos   University of Amsterdam, The Netherlands
Cecilia Saccone   ITB/CNR Institute of Biomedical Technologies of
                             Bari, Italy
Peter M.A. Sloot   University of Amsterdam, The Netherlands
Tony Solomonides   University of West of England, UK

2nd International Workshop on Intelligent Systems Techniques for Ad Hoc and Wireless Sensor Networks (IST-AWSN 2007)

Recent advances in silicon technology in wireless ad hoc and sensor networks have dramatically changed the way their applications are used and managed. These technologies offer exciting ways of deploying and maintaining AWSN applications. Consequently, new challenges and opportunities have been provided to the artificial intelligence research community. This workshop aims to bring together researchers and practitioners working on different artificial intelligence techniques associated with ad hoc and wireless sensor networks in an effort to highlight the state of the art, discuss challenges and opportunities, and to explore new research directions.

We received many high-quality papers and each paper underwent a rigorous peer-review process with at least two reviewers per paper. We selected nine papers for presentation and publication in the workshop proceedings. We would like to thank the Program Committee members for their support and professional comments which made this workshop a success. We thank all the authors who submitted papers to this workshop. We are also grateful to the ISPA 2007 workshop Co-chairs for their continuous support and cooperation. Moreover, we would like to thank the Jodrey School of Computer Science, Acadia University for their continued support in maintaining the workshop Web site and allowing us the opportunity to organize the IST-AWSN workshop.

Elhadi Shakshuki
Darcy Benoit
Mieso K. Denko

Executive Committee

General Co-chairs	Makoto Takizawa, Tokyo Denki University, Japan
	Leonard Barolli, Fukuoka Institute of Technology, Japan
	Laurence T. Yang, St. Francis Xavier University, Canada
Advisory Committee	Arjan Durresi, Louisiana State University, USA
	David Taniar, Monash University, Australia
	Ismail Khalil Ibrahim, Johannes Kepler University of Linz, Austria
	Qiang Yang, Hong Kong University of Science and Technology, Hong Kong
	Zakaria Maamar, Zayed University, UAE
Workshop Co-chairs	Elhadi Shakshuki, Acadia University, Canada
	Darcy Benoit, Acadia University, Canada
	Mieso Denko, University of Guelph, Canada

Program Committee

Abdel Obaid	University of Quebec, Canada
Agustinus Borgy Waluyo	Institute for Infocomm Research, Singapore
Ahmed Khoumsi	University of Sherbrooke, Canada
Alexander Ferworn	Ryerson University, Canada
Ali M. El Kateeb	University of Michigan-Dearborn, USA
Christel Kemke	University of Manitoba, Canada
Haidar Safa	American University of Beirut, Lebanon
Hisham Al-Mubaid	University of Houston-Clear Lake, USA
Iker Gondra	St. Francis Xavier University, Canada
Jamal Bentahar	Concordia University, Canada
Javier Garca-Villalba	Universidad Complutense de Madrid, Spain
Jiang (Leo) Li	Howard University, USA
Jianhua Ma	Hosei University, Japan
Jim Diamond	Acadia University, Canada
John Anderson	University of Manitoba, Canada
Kuo-Ming Chao	Coventry University, UK
Mohamed Ould-Khaoua	University of Glasgow, UK
Mounir Boukadoum	University of Quebec, Canada
Muhammed Younas	Oxford Brookes University, UK
Pratik K. Biswas	Avaya Labs, USA
Rasit Eskicioglu	University of Manitoba, Canada
S.M.F.D Syed Mustapha	University of Malaya, Malaysia
Soraya Kouadri Mostfaoui	Oxford Brookes University, UK
Soumaya Cherkaoui	University of Sherbrooke, Canada
Tarek Sheltami	King Fahd University, Saudi Arabia

Table of Contents

Workshop on Intelligent Systems and Smart Home

Workshop on Semantic and Grid Computing

Workshop on Parallel and Distributed Multimedia Computing

Workshop on High Performance Computing in Medicine and Biology

Workshop on Intelligent Systems Techniques for Ad Hoc and Wireless Sensor Networks

To Increase Survivability with Software Rejuvenation by Having Dual Base Station in WSN Environment

Su Thawda Win[1], Thandar Thein[1], and Jong Sou Park[2]

[1] University of Computer Studies, Yangon, Myanmar
Ucsy23@most.gov.mm, tdt@wwlmail.com
[2] Korea Aerospace University, Seoul, Korea
jspark@hau.ac.kr

Abstract. In a near future, our use of computer technology will increasingly depend on Wireless Sensor Network (WSN) system consists of plethora of nodes. This WSN's survivability will depend most critically on base station that attaches WSN to outside network including Internet. The need for survivability is most pressing for mission critical systems. To increase the survivability, we show up the detection model with proactive rejuvenation and reactive recovery through a Continuous Time Markov Chain (CTMC) process, where it is designed to provide continued useful service in face of attacks, failures, or accidents and to prevent the intruders' attempts in their tracks. Afterwards, we focus on downtime analysis. This is a general model which can be applicable to any nodes in a WSN environment. But this model can be more critically used for base station since base station is almost a single point of failure in a WSN.

1 Introduction

Our social infrastructure has grown to become a critical enabling agent in business, industry, government and defense provided over distributed network systems operating on local, national and global scales. Research into reliable and survivable systems is important due to the increasing number of information systems and society's increasing dependence on these systems for service. Disruption and loss of services have resulted in huge financial losses, time and exposure of confidential data. This becomes more and more important on WSN case since WSN usually collects and store very personal and real time data [15].

Traditional security approaches that provide guarantees related to confidentiality, integrity, and authenticity enhance security, are primarily focused on the prevention and detection of attacks and intrusions rather than on continued correct operation while under attack. But, they are inadequate to deal with the modern security problems associated with highly distributed systems, which have neither central administrative control nor global visibility.

This critical network system must be robust and able to survive in face of attacks, failures or accidents.

Survivable network systems need not only detect correctly and accurately in the presence of attacks or intrusion faults, but also keep security in face of such kinds of

P. Thulasiraman et al. (Eds.): ISPA 2007 Workshops, LNCS 4743, pp. 1–10, 2007.

attacks or faults, especially WSN [15]. In addition to, the criticality of real-time attack detection and recovery is the main motivation for employing survivability. As a result, network survivability is an essential aspect of reliable communication services, especially military applications of WSN [1].

Survivability is the capacity of a system, to fulfill its mission in a timely manner, in the presence of attacks, failures, or accidents [10]. The emphasis of survivability is on continuity of operations, with the understanding that security precautions cannot guarantee that systems will not be penetrated and compromised. In particular, survivability refers to the capability of a system to provide essential services in the presence of successful intrusion, and to recover compromised services in a timely manner after intrusion occurs.

A survivable system should resist in face of cyber attacks (e.g., denial of service), internal failures (e.g., human errors, software design errors, hardware malfunctions, etc.), and external accidents (e.g., natural disasters). A survivability strategy can be set up in three steps: protection, detection and response, and recovery [11]. However, the realities of survivable network system design impose a balance of cost and acceptable levels of risk. A good survivability solution covers not only what happens when an anticipated damage occurs but also what might happen in response to unanticipated events.

Recently, a proactive fault management approach, called software rejuvenation, is proposed [9]. Software rejuvenation is a cost effective technique for dealing with software faults that include protection not only against hard failures, but against performance degradation as well. It involves stopping the running software occasionally, terminating an application gracefully, cleaning its internal state and restarting it. Cleaning the internal state of software might involve garbage collection, flushing operating system kernel tables, and reinitializing internal data structures, etc. [8]. Or it could be a very simple sleep which can help not only security but also saving energy in a WSN environment.

Moreover, it can be regarded as a preventive and proactive solution that is particularly useful for counteracting the phenomenon of software aging. If any attacks or intrusions could not be solved yet, those will be security-aging problems.

In a client-server type of application where the server is intended to run perpetually for providing a service to its clients, rejuvenating the server process periodically during the biggest idle time of the server increases the availability of that service [9].

Software Rejuvenation has been used in high availability and mission critical systems [12, 13] to increase the survivability level or to survive despite ongoing attacks.

Although the fault in the program still remains, performing the rejuvenation occasionally or periodically prevent failures due to that fault. Any rejuvenation typically involves an overhead, but it prevents more sever crash failures from occurring. Hence, an important issue in analyzing rejuvenation policies is to determine their usefulness in terms of availability, downtime, and cost and to provide an optimal criterion to decide when and how often to recover the system from the degraded state [2].

Existing rejuvenation architectures mainly profit from the information, when a crash occurs. Proactive rejuvenation is the preferred solution when faults can be efficiently avoided using a realistic rejuvenation schedule. We will utilize the advantages of software rejuvenation method in security field as a preventing and renewal method to ensure survivability. There were many research works on cluster based availability analysis using software rejuvenation. Here, we try to apply this concept for WSN environment to enhance survivability of WSN.

The rest of this paper is organized as follows. In section 2, we discuss previous related work and outline the novel aspects of our work. Section 3 describes the proposed system architecture for providing more survive and robust in WSN. Section 4 deals with an overview of survivability model based on rejuvenation and recovery; afterwards we focus the effects of rejuvenation on downtime and unavailability. Finally, we conclude with a summary of our results in section 5.

2 Related Works

The community of high-speed network users and providers find survivability important. In [4], the author developed a tool to access survivability by evaluating reliability, availability, and restorability of SONET networks using a Parametric State Reward Markov (SRMM/p). Survivability of a network is affected by the restoration time and the amount of recovery after restoration.

Although rejuvenation has been informally used for years, the first formalized publication dates back to 1995 [9]. Huang *et al.* have proposed the technique of software rejuvenation, which is periodic preemptive restart of a running system to prevent future failures. The model is also useful to find optimal trigger rates/frequencies for rejuvenation.

Garg *et al.* [7] introduced the idea of periodic rejuvenation and extend the original Huang *et al.* model [9]. To deal with deterministic interval between successive rejuvenations the system behavior is represented through a Markov Regenerative Stochastic Petri net.

In [6], a methodology is proposed for detecting and estimating software aging in a UNIX operating system. If the monitoring tool does not receive a response from a machine after a fixed amount of time, it is rejuvenated. In this paper, we will perform rejuvenation according to condition triggered schemes if it is necessary.

Candea *et al.* [3] presented a rejuvenation technique in Recovery Oriented Computing. In our recovery approach, we emphasize on survivability of the distributed system by means of rejuvenation for preventive manner and recovery with redundant component for achieving survivability.

3 Overall Structure of Proposed System

The architecture of proposed system is depicted in figure 1. In this model, we consider failure detection and recovery from adverse conditions in a timely fashion by combining proactive rejuvenation and reactive recovery.

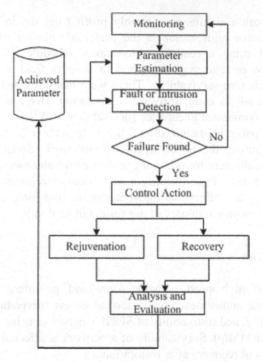

Fig. 1. The Structure of Proposed System

Proactive rejuvenation restricts the intruders' processes in their tracks, halting abuse before it happens and can reduce downtime of the system. Reactive recovery with redundant component achieves continued service. This is a way of survivability.

A significant impediment to the development of large-scale survivable distributed systems is the ability to accurately monitor these systems in real-time. More powerful monitoring mechanisms support more accurate decisions about the abnormality. By combining visualization and intrusion detection, we can more easily monitor large-scale systems in real-time for malicious or mal functional behavior. Through useful graphical monitoring, we can more quickly react to undesirable events and therefore increase the survivability of these systems [14].

The detection has to be as accurate and timely as possible. It is essential in all phases of attack because reaction or adaptation is impossible without form of exact recognition. Especially, to counteract the malicious attacks, countermeasures the successful attacks should be planned and deployed in advance. Moreover, rapid detection is a critical ingredient of fast recovery and is therefore an integral part of any recovery-oriented approach to system dependability. Of course, there can be debates on where and how we implement this proposed structure, since WSN is very resource limited. We can assume distributed implementation to reduce each node burden on communication that is the biggest source of energy consumption. We also can assume base station to take care of this burden. We do not involve in this detailed discussion and implementation issues here, but we will leave it as a future research. Here basically we are assuming dual base station architecture for our WSN. If one base station fails then other one switches over. The role of base station is very important not only its function to connect WSN to out side world but also its security with single point of failure [5].

When we found that there is an intrusion or failure on a base station, it asks the corresponding control actions to rejuvenate the infected component and recover it with immunized component which provides more robust services. The redundant component is used as a temporary buffer base station until the generation of immunized component.

4 Rejuvenation Based Survivability Model

The basic idea of rejuvenation based survivability model will be described. To support critical services continuously to the nodes in a wireless sensor network environment, the recovery scheme is based on redundant base station, prepared before the operation and immunized base station which are dynamically generated on the fly. This redundant base station will be used as a buffer while a more robust node is ready and deployed. The buffer base station will take over the service for a brief period until the immunized base station is ready. Here we are assuming dual base stations with wireless capability, and these dual base stations can be connected to directly to sensor nodes. And more than one buffer base stations with temporary back off capability without direct wireless connection with sensor nodes. The reason why we assume this rather complex switch over from one base station to buffer base station and other dual base station is that we can get more time and analysis on failure while in buffer base station. If we switch directly from one base station to other dual base station then we may face same failure or attack for the second dual base station before we have time to analyze the reason for failure or attack. Therefore we call the dual base station as "immunized base station".

This dual base station concept will help survive the WSN system under normal failure and attack as shown in Figure 2.

The Control Manager, Preventive Mechanism, and Base station immunization work load can be distributed among other computers connected to base station.

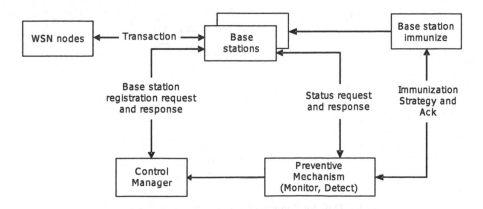

Fig. 2. Dual base station with security enhancement

This dual base station concept will help survive the WSN system under normal failure and attack as shown in Figure 2.

The survivability model with rejuvenation consists of six major components, sensor nodes, base stations, Control Manager, Preventive Mechanism, and base station immunization. Before the operation starts, the redundant server components are generated and deployed into a safe area. Isolated redundancy usually provides higher survivability, because the replaced base station can be running in an uninfected area.

By doing base station registration or requesting base station information from sensor nodes, the registry provides a formal naming service in a WSN environment.

The preventive mechanism consists of three components: monitoring process, detecting process, and rejuvenation process. The monitoring process maintains a list of available base station components, checks the base station's operating status, and responds to the control manager's request. Furthermore, it is responsible to communicate with other monitors to check other monitor's status that is located in a safe place or unsafe. When we find the situation that is unavailable because of internal failures or cyber attacks, it informs to other monitors.

The monitoring process helps a detecting process in the detection of rejuvenations of the base station. The detecting process has to weigh the risk of policy with further damage against the policy of shutting the system in an emergency stage or rejuvenation or to inform the detection strategy for generation of immunized base station. The detection process is responsible to analyze the reason for failure and the type of attacks in order to find out possible immunization methods.

When the event of any failures (component, system, or network), or attacks on the system, degradation of the node are found, the recovery operation starts with sending a shutdown message to the infected base station. While the infected base station is performing rejuvenation, it is required to have the proper continued service from the redundant (buffer) base station until the immunized base station is allocated.

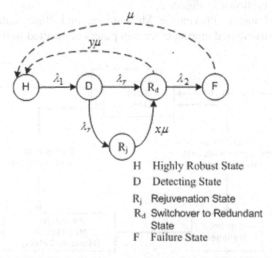

H   Highly Robust State
D   Detecting State
R_j Rejuvenation State
R_d Switchover to Redundant State
F   Failure State

Fig. 3. CTMC for Rejuvenation Based Survivability Model

4.1 Model Description

Let the probabilities of the system being in states:

- Highly Robust (H), when at least one node is functioning properly;
- Detecting (D), when detection is triggered;
- Rejuvenation (R_j), when infected or failed node is performing rejuvenation;
- Switchover to Redundant (R_d), when redundant or immunized component is temporarily used to provide continued service; and
- Failure (F), when all nodes stop running

be $\pi_h, \pi_d, \pi_{rj}, \pi_{rd}$, and π_f respectively.

Assumptions:

- Time to repair is exponentially distributed with a rate μ.
- Time to carry out repair is $y\mu$ times the time to carry out redundancy and $x\mu$ times the time to carry out rejuvenation preventive maintenance.

We denote as,

λ_1 = detection rate of fault

λ_r = rejuvenation rate or redundant rate

λ_2 = failure rate

μ = repair rate of failure

$x\mu$ = rejuvenation service rate where (x>1)

$y\mu$ = recovery rate of redundancy where (y>x)

Our state transition diagram in Figure 3 can be described as Markov process class. Writing down steady-sate balance equations by using principle rate in is equal to rate out, we have

$$\lambda_1 \pi_h = \mu \pi_f + y\mu \pi_{rd}$$
$$\lambda_1 \pi_h = \lambda_r \pi_d + \lambda_r \pi_d$$
$$\lambda_r \pi_d = x\mu \pi_{rj}$$
$$\lambda_r \pi_d + x\mu \pi_{rj} = \lambda_2 \pi_{rd} + y\mu \pi_{rd}$$
$$\lambda_2 \pi_{rd} = \mu \pi_f$$

Solving the above equations, we obtain the following expressions for the steady-state probabilities:

$$\pi_d = \frac{\lambda_1}{2\lambda_r}\pi_h$$

$$\pi_{rj} = \frac{\lambda_1}{2x\mu}\pi_h$$

$$\pi_{rd} = \frac{\lambda_1}{(\lambda_2 + y\mu)}\pi_h$$

$$\pi_f = \frac{\lambda_1\lambda_2}{\mu(\lambda_2 + y\mu)}\pi_h$$

where

$$\pi_h = \frac{1}{1+\dfrac{\lambda_1}{2\lambda_r}+\dfrac{\lambda_1}{2x\mu}+\dfrac{\lambda_1}{\lambda_2 + y\mu}+\dfrac{\lambda_1\lambda_2}{\mu(\lambda_2 + y\mu)}}$$

Detection delay in state, switch over delay to redundant state and rejuvenation state is a system down state, then the steady state unavailability for unavailable service (S_r) can be written as

Unavailability factor

$$\cup(S_r) = \pi_d + \pi_{rd} + \pi_{rj} + \pi_f$$

$$= \pi_h\left[\frac{\lambda_1}{2\lambda_r}+\frac{\lambda_1}{2x\mu}+\frac{\lambda_1}{\lambda_2 + y\mu}+\frac{\lambda_1\lambda_2}{\mu(\lambda_2 + y\mu)}\right]$$

4.2 Downtime Analysis

Let us now analyze how the downtime change when the switchover to redundant and rejuvenation rate λ_r changes. The expected total downtime of the service (S_r) with support for detection, redundancy and rejuvenation in an interval of L time unit is:

$$Downtime\ S_r(L) = \text{Unavailability factor} \times L$$
$$= \cup(S_r)\times L$$

$$= \pi_h\left[\frac{\lambda_1}{2\lambda_r}+\frac{\lambda_1}{2x\mu}+\frac{\lambda_1}{\lambda_2 + y\mu}+\frac{\lambda_1\lambda_2}{\mu(\lambda_2 + y\mu)}\right]\times L$$

We need to differentiate the above equation with respect to λ_r to examine the behavior of downtime when λ_r changes.

$$\frac{d}{d\lambda_r}Downtime\ S_r(L) =$$

$$L\times\left[\frac{-\lambda_1}{2\lambda_r^2}\times\frac{1}{\left[1+\dfrac{\lambda_1}{2\lambda_r}+\dfrac{\lambda_1}{2x\mu}+\dfrac{\lambda_1}{\lambda_2+y\mu}+\dfrac{\lambda_1\lambda_2}{\mu(\lambda_2+y\mu)}\right]}\right]\ \frac{d}{d\lambda_r}Downtime\ S_r(L)<0$$

$\Rightarrow\ S_r$ is decreasing with respect to λ_r

It can be noticed that the value of the above derivative is always negative. In other words, the downtime always decreases when the value of λ_r increases.

This means that reducing the total downtime of a system can stay in a state H (Highly Robust State) more often and the chance of a failure becomes smaller and the survivability would be up.

Here, we calculated the effects of rejuvenation on downtime and unavailability respectively. Downtime in minutes per year is

$$Downtime \ S_r(L) \ = \cup (S_r) \times 8760 \times 60$$

In figure 4, we have plotted the downtime as a function of the mean time between rejuvenation service rates

$\dfrac{1}{\lambda_r}$ (in seconds) for

$$\frac{1}{\lambda_1} = 5,000 \ h, \frac{1}{\lambda_2} = 10,000 \ h, \frac{1}{\mu} = 2h, \frac{1}{x\mu} = 2 \ \text{min}, \ \frac{1}{y\mu} = 1 \ \text{min}$$

$$(h = \text{hour, min} = \text{minute})$$

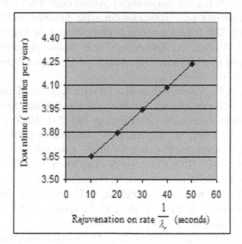

Fig. 4. Downtime change due to rejuvenation rate

Our results indicate that preventive rejuvenation and recovery approach have a significant impact on reducing downtime and availability improvement. Therefore, our system will increase survivability of WSN with dual base station.

5 Conclusion

In this paper, we have applied the concept of software rejuvenation methodology as additional security measures to enhance survivability. More precisely, the rejuvenation methodology prevents the intruders' attempts in ways of attack and the anticipated intrusion and protects unpredictable whole system failure by detecting and monitoring the server in a timely fashion. Our recovery model with rejuvenation is intended to improve the availability of the WSN and to reduce downtime of base station. Already, we have presented some discussion of downtime analysis. Our model can be applied to support the pressing requirements for survivability in mission-critical systems. Since base station's security is very important due to its single point of failure characteristic in a WSN structure, we proposed a method of rejuvenation to increase the survivability of base station which will directly increase the survivability of our WSN. This concept of applying rejuvenation to base station can be easily applied to distributed sensor nodes with minor modification and scaling of parameters like down time, failure rate, etc. This will be our future research.

References

1. Akyildiz, I.F., Su, W., Sankarasubramaniam, Y., Cayirci, E.: A Survey on Sensor Networks. IEEE Communications Magazine , 102–114 (2002)
2. Bobbio, A., Sereno, M., Anglano, C.: Fine Grained Software Degradation Models for Optimal Software Rejuvenation Policies. Performance Evaluation 46, 45–62 (2001)
3. Candea, G., Cutler, J., Fox, A.: Improving Availability with Recursive Microreboots: A Soft-State System Case Study. Performance Evaluation Journal 56 (2004)
4. Cankaya, H.C., Nair, V.S.S.: A Survivability Assessment Tool for Restorable Networks. In: 3rd IEEE Symposium on Application-Specific Systems and Software Engineering Technology, pp. 319–324. IEEE Computer Society Press, Los Alamitos (2000)
5. Deng, J., Han, R., Mishra, S.: Enhancing Base Station Security in Wireless Sensor Networks, University of Colorado, Department of Computer Science Technical Report CU-CS-951-03 (2003)
6. Garg, S., Moorsel, A.V., Vaidyanathan, K., Trivedi, K.S.: A Methodology for Detection and Estimation of Software Aging. In: Proc. of the 9th Int. Symposium on Software Reliability Engineering, Paderborn, Germany, pp. 283–292 (1998)
7. Garg, S., Puliafito, A., Telek, M., Trivedi, K.S.: Analysis of Software Rejuvenation using Markov Regenerative Stochastic Petri net. In: Proc. of the 6th Int. Symposium on Software Reliability Eng., pp. 24–27. IEEE Computer Society Press, Los Alamitos (1995)
8. http://shannon.ee.duke.edu/Rejuv/software-rejuvenation.html
9. Huang, Y., Kintala, C., Kolettis, N., Fulton, N.D.: Software Rejuvenation: Analysis, Module and Applications. In: Proc. of the 25th Symposium on Fault Tolerant Computer Systems, Pasadena, California, pp. 381–390 (1995)
10. Knight, J.C., Sullivan, K., Elder, M.C., Wang, C.: Survivability Architectures: Issues and Approaches. In: Proc. of the DARPA Information Survivability Conference and Exposition, Los Alamitos, California, pp. 157–171 (2000)
11. Park, J.S., Froscher, J.N.: A Strategy for information Survivability. In: 4th IEEE/CMU/SEI Information Survivability Workshop (ISW), Vancouver, Canada, pp. 18–20 (2002)
12. Tai, A.T., Alkalai, L., Chau, S.N.: On-Board Preventive Maintenance for Long-Life Deep Space Missions: A Model-Based Analysis. In: Proc. of the 3rd IEEE Int. Computer Performance and Dependability Symp, pp. 166–205. IEEE CS Press, Los Alamitos (1998)
13. Tai, A.T., Alkalai, L., Chau, S.N.: On-Board Preventive Maintenance: A Design-Oriented Analytic Study for Long-Life Applications. Performance Evaluation 35, 215–232 (1999)
14. Varner, P.E., Knight, J.C.: Security Monitoring, Visualization, and System Survivability, A Position Paper for ISW-2001, Information Survivability Workshorp (2001)
15. Wood, A.D., Stankovic, J.A.: Denial of Service in Sensor Networks. IEEE Computer Magazine , 54–62 (2002)

DoS Attack Mining in Sensor Node Replacement

Hnin Yu Shwe[1], Bong Jae Lee[2], and Jang-See Lee[3]

[1] University of Computer Studies, Yangon, Myanmar
hninyushwe@gmail.com
[2] Korea Aerospace University, Seoul, Korea
leebj2200@paran.com
[3] The Division of Information Technology Engineering, Korea Maritime University, Korea
jslee@bada.hhu.ac.kr

Abstract. Sensor node repairing is important for providing continuous sensing services. However, sometimes sensor nodes fail due to environmental interference such as attacks. Automatically replacing faulty sensor nodes in a sensor network may not be the course of action if the sensor network is under attack, because the attack will most likely disable the new nodes as well. In the extent of our knowledge, existing approaches tried to replace failed nodes with functional ones without examining whether the nodes failed due to some attacks. In order to study the efficient strategies for monitoring and repairing network behavior, we propose a framework for sensor nodes replacement that uses the mining technique in monitoring and repairing sensor nodes in wireless sensor network.

1 Introduction

Due to many attractive characteristics of sensor nodes such as small size and low cost, wireless sensor networks are expected to be intensively utilized in the future. However, one common characteristic of nodes in wireless sensor networks is that they are prone to failure. Sensor nodes carry limited, generally irreplaceable, power sources. Nodes in sensor networks can fail for many different reasons: their batteries may be depleted, they may be accidentally destroyed, and a malicious adversary may deliberately incapacitate them [6]. Upon sensor node failures, holes may appear in the sensing coverage. Network performance may be greatly degraded upon a loss of some constituent nodes. Seriously, network may fail to deliver its functionalities required by applications because of numerous faulty nodes. Therefore, to overcome sensor node failure, faulty nodes should be detected and replaced promptly [5].

Recent wireless sensor networks' research areas mainly focus on routing protocols, energy efficiency and localization, and there exists little work that has attempted to repair sensor nodes in wireless sensor networks. Mei et al. [7] propose to use a small number of mobile robots to replace failed sensor nodes. However, in their study, whenever a sensor node fails, mobile robot moves to that location and simply changes the failed nodes with the functional ones. In case where sensor network is under attack, the attack should be dealt with and disabled before replacing the sensor nodes

P. Thulasiraman et al. (Eds.): ISPA 2007 Workshops, LNCS 4743, pp. 11–19, 2007.

that were affected by it. Otherwise, replacing a new node will simply be the waste of functional one. Within a short period of time, backup nodes will run out in this manner.

In this paper, we propose the use of attack classifier in sensor node replacement. We use robots to assist sensor replacement. As in [7], all robots are mobile and can pick, carry and unload sensor nodes. Initially, the robots carry a certain amount of functional sensor nodes. When sensor nodes fail, the robots inform the base station about the node failure. Intrusion detector residing at the base station then checks whether there is an attack in that location. This paper addresses a particular class of DoS attacks that overwhelm resources along a multi-hop data delivery path. If there is a DoS attack, the base station deals with it and then sends the response message to the relevant robot. After receiving the response message from base station, the robots move to the locations of the failed nodes and unload functional sensor nodes.

Figure 1 presents an overview of the robot assisted sensor repair system. Since the number of robots is much smaller than the number of sensor nodes, the cost is expected to be lower the requiring most of sensor nodes to have mobility.

The rest of the paper is organized as follows. In section II, we propose a node replacement architecture for sensor network. We discuss the related work in Section III. Section IV describes sensor nodes replacement algorithm. Performance evaluation is given in Section V. Section VI discusses some of the future work and concludes the paper.

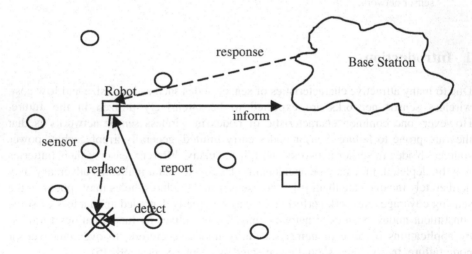

Fig. 1. An overview of sensor replacement using robots. The circles represent sensor nodes and squares represent robots. A node detects a dual node's failure (shown by a cross over the circle) and then reports a failure to a robot. A robot forwards the failure message to the base station. After detecting and clearing attack, if it exists, base station response to the robot. Then the robot moves to the failure location and replaces the failed node.

2 Nodes Replacement Architecture

The key objective of node replacement in sensor network is to increase the network survivability. Assume that a sensor network is deployed to monitor a certain target area, which is divided into square equal-size sub-areas as shown in Fig2. The number of sub-areas is the same as the number of robots and each robot is assigned with an equal-size sub-areas. We make the following assumptions in this study:

  i.) Sensor nodes are randomly uniformly distributed into a 2-dimensional field. Their locations are known by themselves according to the initial deployment informa-tion. Sensor nodes have limited lifetime.

  ii.) Robots are initially randomly uniformly distributed inside the field where the sensor nodes are deployed. Each robot carries a certain number of functional nodes. The robots travel at a constant speed v. Robots can localize themselves. The number of robots is much smaller than the number of sensor nodes.

  iii.) All the sensor nodes and the mobile robots communicate via wireless links. When a failure is detected, an appropriate robot should receive the failure report and should replace the failed node. The work can be done by the following four stages:

  i.)   Initialization
  ii.)   Failure detection and reporting
  iii.)   Intrusion detection
  iv.)   Failure handling

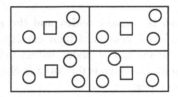

Fig. 2. Partition an area into square equal-size sub-areas. The small squares represent the robots in each sub-area and the small circles indicate sensors.

3 Related Work

Repairing sensor network using mobile robots has been proposed in [7]. In their study, they used a small number of mobile robots to replace failed sensor nodes. Robots are mobile and can pick, carry and unload sensor nodes. When sensor nodes detect failures of their neighbors, they report to manager robot. Manager robot then determines which maintainer robot should handle a specific failure. Then the maintainer robots move and replace failed nodes with functional ones.

To repair a faulty sensor, the work in [5] proposed a replacement protocol for hybrid sensor networks composed of mobile and static sensors. A static sensor node can check its energy status and seek for replacement when its current energy falls below a certain threshold. If a redundant static sensor is located close to a dying sensor and can fulfill the coverage requirement, it can be used for substitution. However, if the redundant sensor is mobile node and is located far away from the dying sensor, the mobile sensor moves to the dying sensor according to the available location information.

The work in [9] proposed a Grid-Quorum solution to locate the closest redundant sensor with low message complexity, and propose to use cascaded movement to relocate the redundant sensor in a timely, efficient and balanced way. Cascading movement will cause sensors to move several times, wasting energy.

Wang et al. [10] proposed deploying redundant static nodes and the redundant nodes can be turned off initially and be turned on later when coverage holes appear upon sensor failures. This technique is insufficient to handle the case where a coverage hole exists even if turning on all the remaining sensor nodes around the hole.

There have been several research efforts on node replacement in sensor networks. To the best of our knowledge, there is no existing node replace architecture using mining technology in wireless sensor networks. Our proposed architecture provides scalability. The key advantage of proposed architecture is the achievement of longer network survivability life time than the existing approaches.

4 Sensor Nodes Replacement Algorithm

4.1 Initialization

Initial relationship between the sensor nodes and the robot. In the initialization stage, the robots first move to the centers of their corresponding sub-areas and then broadcast their location to all the sensor nodes within their sub-areas. Each sensor node then selects the closest robot, which is the robot in charge of the node's sub-area, as its *myGuardian* for failure report.

Initial relationship among sensor nodes. The sensor nodes broadcast their locations to their neighbor sensor nodes within one-hop distance in the same sub-area for establishing dual relationship for failure detection. Every sensor receives one message from each of its neighbors, picks its closest neighbor as its dual node, and then sends a confirmation message to the dual node to establish the dual relationship.

After initialization, all the sensor nodes and robots know their location, and the dual relationship between sensor nodes is established. In the subsequent stages, when a robot moves, it needs to update some sensor nodes of its new location.

4.2 Failure Detection and Reporting

After initialization, each sensor node periodically sends hello messages to its dual node. If a node has not received any hello message from its dual node for a certain amount of time, the node conceives that its dual node has failed and sends a failure message with the failed node's location to the *myGuardian* robot. And then it selects a new dual node from its one-hop neighbors in the same fashion as during the initialization stage.

4.3 Intrusion Detection

Upon a failure report from sensor nodes, *myGuardian* robot forwards the failure message to the base station to determine there has an attack. Intrusion detector residing at the base station has the ability to determine whether the sensor failure is the cause of an attack. Base station then, if there is a DoS attack, dealt with and disable it. After-ward, the base station sends response message to the *myGuardian* robot.

4.4 Failure Handling

Upon receiving the response message to repair a failure from the base station, the robot moves to the failed node's location and replaces the failed node with a functional one. When the robot is moving towards a failed sensor node, it still can receive failure repair request forwarding from the base station. The robot queues such requests and handles the failures in a first-come-first-serve fashion.

SENSOR NODE

```
 1. Receive all the robot's initial location broadcasts
 2. Set the closest robot as myGuardian
 3. Broadcast the location to its neighbor nodes
 4. Receive broadcasting message from all its neighbors
 5. Setup dual relationships with its closest neighbor
 6. Set a timeout T
 7. while (TRUE)
 8.  do if (receive a new location update message)
 9.      then if (message.robot = = myGuardian)
10.           then Update the robot's location
11.       else do nothing
12.       if (timeout)
13.       then Reset the timeout T
14.         Send a hello message to its dual node
15.             Check the last time receiving a hello
                message
16.             if the time duration is too long
                (>threshold)
17.                then Detect a failure
18.         Send the failure to myGuardian
```

Fig. 3. A sensor node's behavior

ROBOT

```
1. Broadcast its location to all sensors
2. while (TRUE)
3. do if (receive a failure message from a sensor)
4.   Forward the fail message to the base station
5.   Receive the response message from the base
     station
6.   Move to the failure location
7.   Stop and replace the failed node
8.   Broadcast its new location
```

Fig. 4. A robot behavior

5 Performance Evaluation

To evaluate the feasibility of our mechanism in current WSN platforms, we need to measure the performance of our proposed architecture for sensor nodes replacement. To do this, we used See-5 classification tool on the KDD data set. See-5 is a data-mining tool for classification of data and prediction of new cases using automatically generated decision trees. Using this tool and the KDD data set, we created a set of locally optimal decision trees from which optimal subset of trees was selected for predicting new cases (attacks).

5.1 Denial of Service (DoS) Attack

In contrast to resource-rich networks such as the internet, a WSN is less stable, more resource limited, subject to open wireless communication and prone to the physical risks of in site deployment [2]. These factors increase the susceptibility of WSNs to DoS attacks.

A denial of service attack is any event that diminishes or eliminates a network's capacity to perform its expected function [8]. Hardware failures, software bugs, resource exhaustion, environmental conditions, or any complicated interaction between these factors can cause a DoS.

Table 1. DoS attack in sensor network

DoS Attack	Defense Strategy
Radio interference	Use spread-spectrum
Physical tampering	Make nodes tamper-resistant
Denying channel	Use error correction code
Black holes	Multiple routing paths
Misdirection	Source authorization
Flooding	Limit the connections

In DoS attacks, the attacker's objective is to make target destinations inaccessible by legitimate users [3]. A sensor network without sufficient protection from DoS attacks may not be deployable in many areas [1]. Nodes of a sensor network cannot be trusted for the correct execution of critical network functions.

DoS attacks can happen in multiple sensor network protocol layers. Table 1 depicts the typical DoS attacks and the corresponding defense strategies.

Among there exist many types of DoS attack, here we simulate four common attacks.

1. Routing request flooding attack (RREQ flooding): the malicious node deliberately floods the whole network with meaningless route discovery messages in order to exhaust the network bandwidth and effectively paralyze the network.

2. SMURF attack: In one variant of misdirection, the attacker forges the victim's address as the source of many broadcast Internet control-message-protocol echoes. The attacker directs all the echo replies back to the victim, flooding its network link. By misdirecting many traffic flows in one direction, the DoS attack can target an arbitrary victim.

3. HELLO flood attack: In a HELLO flood attack a malicious node can send, record or replay HELLO-messages with high transmission power. It creates an illusion of being a neighbor to many nodes in the networks and can confuse the network routing badly [4].

4. Acknowledgement spoofing: If a protocol uses link-layer acknowledgements, these acknowledgements can be forged, so that other nodes believe a weak link to be strong or disabled nodes alive.

5.2 Simulation Environment

For simplicity we assume the following in our simulation: (1) the sensors are static in the field, (2) in the beginning each battery has the same maximum energy, (3) robots move around to replace sensor nodes, (4) two sensor nodes which have dual relationship periodically check each other, (5) when failure occur, dual node sends failure report to manager robot, (6) IDS is present at the base station and constantly monitors all nodes in sensor network. The sensor network consists of some malicious nodes which occasionally launch DoS attacks.

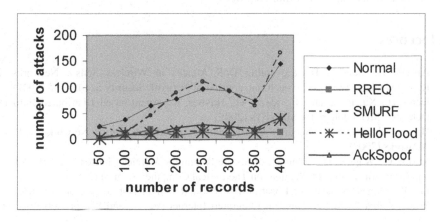

Fig. 5. Number of attacks

Fig 5 depicts the number of various attacks for each different number of records. We run the experiments for different number of records and count up the number of detected attacks.

Table 2 shows the intrusion detection results of See-5 classification tool. We observed that See-5 classifier has achieved over 90% detection performance for the AckSpoof attack. For SMURF and HelloFlood attack, the See-5 approach achieves a detection rate of 100%. See-5 approach obtains 75% accuracy for RREQ attack and 94.67% accuracy for identifying normal data types.

Table 2. Detection results of See-5

	Normal	RREQ	SMURF	Hello Flood	Ack Spoof
Normal	94.67%	0.00%	2.67%	1.33%	1.33%
RREQ	25.00%	75.00%	0.00%	0.00%	0.00%
SMURF	0.00%	0.00%	100.00%	0.00%	0.00%
HelloFlood	0.00%	0.00%	100.00%	0.00%	0.00%
AckSpoof	9.09%	0.00%	0.00%	0.00%	90.01%

6 Future Work and Conclusion

Sensor node replacement is a very interesting and popular field. Many researchers are still developing the various issues for this architecture. In this paper, we have presented the DoS attack mining in sensor nodes replacement. We believe that our pro-posed mechanism will be efficient for sensor network survivability. As part of our future work, we shall be studying the impact of our proposed methodology in surveillance WSNs such as military services.

References

1. Afrand, A., Sajal, K.D.: Preventing DoS Attacks in Wireless Sensor Networks: A Repeated Game Theory Approach. Int. Journal of Network Security 5, 145–153 (2007)
2. Deng, H., Xu, R., Zhang, F., Kwan, G., Haynes, K.: Agent-based Distributed Intrusion Detection Methodology for MANETs (2005)
3. Hu, F., Sharma, N.K.: Security Considerations in Ad hoc Sensor Networks. Ad Hoc Networks (2003)
4. Karlof, C., Wagner, D.: Summary of Secure Routing in Wireless Sensor Network: Attacks and Countermeasures. In: Seminar on Theoretical Computer Science (2005)
5. Le, T., Ahmed, N., Jha, S.: Location-free Fault Repair in Hybrid Sensor Networks. In: Proc. of First ACM Int. Conf. on Integrated Internet Ad hoc and Sensor Networks, vol. 138 (2006)

6. Le, T., Ahmed, N., Parameswaran, N., Jha, S.: Fault Repair Framework for Mobile Sensor Networks. In: IEEE COMSWARE (2006)

7. Mei, Y., Xian, C., Das, S., Hu, Y.C., Lu, Y.H.: Repairing Sensor Network Using Mobile Robot. In: Proc. of the ICDCS Int. Workshop on Wireless Ad hoc and Sensor Networks, Lisboa, Portugal (2006)

8. Walters, J.P., Liang, Z., Shi, W., Chaudhary, V.: Wireless Sensor Network Security: A Survey, Security in Distributed, Grid, and Pervasive Computing (2006)

9. Wang, G., Cao, G., Porta, T., Zhang, W.: Sensor Relocation in Mobile Sensor Networks. In: the 24th Conf. of the IEEE Communications Society (2005)

10. Wang, X., Xing, G., Zhang, Y., Lu, C., Pless, C., Gill, C.: Integrated Coverage and Connec-tivity Con_guration in Wireless Sensor Networks. In: ACM SenSys, pp. 28–29. ACM, New York (2003)

Secure Cluster Header Election Techniques in Sensor Network

Pungho Lee[1], Jimmook Kim[2], Insung Han[1], Hwangbin Ryou[1], and Woo Hyun Ahn[1]

[1] Dept, Of Computer Science, Kwangwoon University, Korea
{aiki,ishan78,ryou,whahn}@kw.ac.kr
[2] Dept, of Computer Information, Sun Moon University, Korea
calf0425@kw.ac.kr

Abstract. Distributed wireless sensor network in various environment have characteristic that is surveillance of environment-element and offering usefully military information but there is shortcoming that have some secure risks. Therefore secure service must be required for this sensor network safety. More safe and effective techniques of node administration are required for safe communication between each node. This paper proposes effective cluster-header and clustering techniques in suitable administration techniques of group-key on sensor network.

In this paper, first each node transmit residual electric power and authentication message to BS(Base-Station). BS reflects *"Validity Authentication Rate"* and residual electric power. And it selects node that is more than these regularity values by cluster header. After BS broadcasts information about cluster header in safety and it transmits making a list of information about cluster member node to cluster header. Also, Every rounds it reflects and accumulates *"Validity Authentication Rate"* of former round. Finally, BS can select more secure cluster header.

Keywords: Sensor Network, Cluster Header, Security, Group Key, LEACH.

1 Introduction

Wireless sensor networks are quickly gaining popularity due to the fact that they are potentially low cost solutions to a variety of real-world challenges[1]. Sensor networks usually consist of a large number of ultra small autonomous devices. Each device, called a sensor node, is battery powered and equipped with integrated sensors, data processing capabilities, and short-range radio communications. In typical application scenarios, sensor nodes are spread randomly over the terrain under scrutiny and collect sensor data. Also, sensor network is a typically an ad hoc network, which requires every sensor node be independent and flexible enough to be self-organizing and self-healing according to different situations. There is no fixed infrastructure available for the purpose of network management in a sensor network. So, Sensor networks are being deployed for a wide variety of applications , including military sensing and tracking, environment monitoring, patient monitoring and tracking, smart environments, etc. But, When sensor networks are deployed in a

P. Thulasiraman et al. (Eds.): ISPA 2007 Workshops, LNCS 4743, pp. 20–31, 2007.

hostile environment, security becomes extremely important, as they are prone to different types of malicious attacks. For example, an adversary can easily listen to the traffic, impersonate one of the network nodes, or intentionally provide misleading information to other nodes. However, due to inherent resource and computing constraints, security in sensor networks poses different challenges than traditional network/ computer security. One security aspect that receives a great deal of attention in wireless sensor networks is the area of key management. Wireless sensor networks are unique (among other embedded wireless networks) in this aspect due to their size, mobility and computational/power constraints.

However, due to inherent resource and computing constraints, security in sensor networks poses different challenges than traditional network key management security. The problem is known as the key agreement problem, which has been widely studied in general network environments. There are three types of general key agreement schemes: trusted-server scheme, self-enforcing scheme, and key pre-distribution scheme. The trusted-server scheme depends on a trusted server for key agreement between nodes, e.g., Kerberos [9]. This type of scheme is not suitable for sensor networks because there is no trusted infrastructure in sensor networks. The self-enforcing scheme depends on asymmetric cryptography, such as key agreement using public key certificates. However, limited computation and energy resources of sensor nodes often make it undesirable to use public key algorithms, such as Diffie-Hellman key agreement [6] or RSA [12], as pointed out in [11]. The third type of key agreement scheme is key pre-distribution, where key information is distributed among all sensor nodes prior to deployment. If we know which nodes will be in the same neighborhood before deployment, keys can be decided a priori. However, most sensor network deployments are random; thus, such a priori knowledge does not exist. These approach allow a great deal of security, but restricts the types of communication and is expensive to update any of the keys in sensor network. In practice, it is usually very difficult, and sometimes impossible, to guarantee the knowledge of sensors' expected locations. Moreover, this assumption severely limits the deployment of sensor networks. In this sense, group key establishment is potentially more suitable than pair-wise key establishment as sensors do not waste energy every time they wish to communicate with another device by establishing a new shared secret key[9].

Group key management mainly includes activities for the establishment and the maintenance of a group key. Secure group communication requires scalable and efficient group membership with appropriate access control measures to protect data and to cope with potential compromises. A secret key for data encryption must be distributed with a secure and efficient way to all members of the group. Another important requirement of group key management protocols is key freshness. A key is fresh if it can be guaranteed to be new. Moreover, the shared group key must be known only to the members of the group. Third important cryptographic properties must be encountered in group key agreement. Assume that a group key is changed m times and the sequence of successive keys is K=$\{K_0, \ldots, K_m\}$. First, Computational group key secrecy: It guarantees that it is computational infeasible for any passive adversary to discover any group key $K_i \in K$ for all I. Second, Decisional group key secrecy: It ensures that there is no information leakage other that public blinded key information. Third, Key independence: It guarantees that a passive adversary who knows a proper subset of group keys can not discover any other of the remaining keys. Key independence can be decomposed into forward secrecy and backward secrecy. Forward secrecy guarantees that a passive adversary who knows a contiguous subset of old group keys cannot discover any subsequent group key. Backward secrecy guarantees that a passive adversary who knows a contiguous subset of group keys cannot discover preceding group key. Group key establishment can be either centralized or distributed. In the first case, a member of the group is responsible for the generation and the distribution of the key. In distributed group key establishment all group members contribute to the generation of the key. Clearly, the second approach is suited for sensor networks because problems with centralized trust and the existence of single point of failure can be avoided.

In this paper, We propose novel cluster header election mechanism that effective and stable sensor node can be selected, before using above group key management. Proposed mechanism is choosing cluster header by sensor node of standard number excess that reflecting "*Security*" , "*Authentication Rate*", "*Power*", etc. And after cluster can delegate part of authority of administration to other member sensor node. It reflects values of select-standards used choice of cluster header during every time to next round and distinguish stable sensor node through accumulate data.

The remainder of this chapter is organized as follows. In Section 2, we summarize the related work for the sensor network security. Continuously we introduce secure sensor network mechanism in Section 3 and describe our implementation result that compared to exist mechanism in Section 4. Finally, we conclude this paper in Section 5.

1.1 LEACH Security Mechanism Based on LEAP

Kindly LEAP/LEACH[7] is devoted to propose LEACH security method that induces balanced energy consumption by fair clustering mechanism and extends the life time of sensor network, and security method that minimizes power usage and processing overhead by using LEAP[9] and can apply to sensitive sensor network system. LEACH[3][4] is a communication protocol for micro-sensor networks. It collects data from distributed micro-sensors and transmits it to a base station. So, LEACH uses the following clustering-model: Some of the nodes elect themselves as cluster-heads. These cluster-heads collect sensor data from other nodes in the vicinity and transfer the aggregated data to the base station. Since data transfers to the base station dissipate much energy, the nodes take turns with the transmission – the cluster-heads "rotate". This rotation of cluster-heads leads to a balanced energy consumption of all nodes and hence to a longer lifetime of the network.

For security of the LEACH, LEAP/LEACH use LEAP protocol for secure key management. LEAP protocol provides various types of key management methods such private key, pair-wise key, cluster key, and group key. Firstly, All nodes include master key from manufacturing phase, and all keys is not submitted during communication. Communication between nodes is a general type and pair-wise key is needed for this. Node u and v generate pair-wise key and each node does using key generation function. And cluster head and cluster nodes must share cluster key for communicating. Cluster head u and all cluster node v_1, v_2, v_3, ... , v_m generate cluster key and share it. Cluster u generates random value r and generates cluster key by key generation function. Generated cluster key is transmitted to all cluster nodes after encrypting it with pair-wise key. By using this method, LEAP/LEACH use dynamic clustering method to increase energy efficiency by data integration. For fair energy consumption, each node is randomly elected as a cluster head likely LEACH.

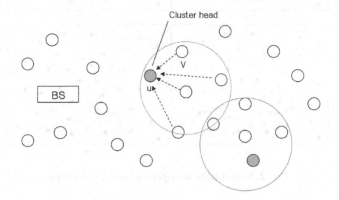

Fig. 1. LEACH security mechanism based on LEAP

After all, LEAP/LEACH needs the secure communication between node and BS, and nodes for clustering. Also, This mechanism propose various key management schemes according to the communication type such as unicast, multicast, and broadcast. Also, proposed protocol can encrypt and authenticate all processes of clustering and data transmission. So, For eliminating spoiled node and adding new node, secure protocol must provide broadcasting service. This method can prevent an attacker from disguising as BS through time slot, and can securely add a new node.

But, When received key was leaked to attacker, the whole network was dangerous because all nodes receive the same key from BS. And authentication and creation of key are as necessary as the number of vicinity nodes for sharing of cluster-key. Also, there is the problem with demanding of additory spaces that save these keys.

1.2 SLEACH[2]

Performing clustering on a sensor network deployment prior to localization has several advantages. For example, it creates a regular pattern from which location information can be extracted. And it helps reduce the amount of communication overhead since only the cluster-heads need to be involved in the initial phase of the localization. Also, Base-station can make management of distributed sensor nodes easily. For this method, there is some of studies. For practical deployment model, where sensor nodes are only required to be deployed in groups. The knowledge used to improve the performance of key pre-distribution is the assumption that the sensor nodes belonging to the same group are deployed close to each other.

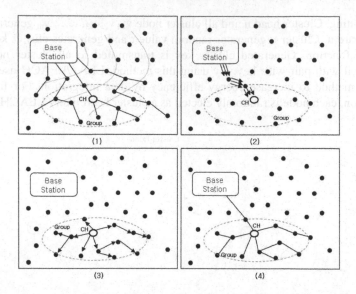

Fig. 2. Sensor node management using Clustering

In SLEACH propose a solution that divides this authenticated broadcast into two smaller steps, leveraging on the BS, which is trusted and has more resources. In a nutshell, assuming that each sensor node shares a secret symmetric key with the BS, each cluster header can send a slightly modified adv message, including the id of the cluster header in plaintext (which will be used by the ordinary nodes as usual) and a message authentication code (MAC) generated using the key the cluster header shares with the BS (the MAC will be used by the BS for the purpose of authentication). Once all these (modified) *adv* messages have been sent by the cluster headers, the BS will compile the list of legitimate cluster headers, and send this list to the network using the µTESLA broadcast authentication scheme. Ordinary nodes now know which of the (modified) *advs* they received are from legitimate nodes, and can proceed with the rest of the original protocol, choosing the cluster header from the list broadcast by the BS.

However, this would require that BS to authenticate each and all nodes of the network at the beginning of each round, which is not only prohibitively expensive, but also makes BS a bottleneck of the system.

2 Proposed Techniques

In this paper, we present the proposal on cluster header election mechanism that improves LEACH-C mechanism required in previous studies in group key mechanism. As for the proposed techniques, BS receives AREP(Authentication Reply) message from sensor nodes, broadcasting AREQ(Authentication Request) message to sensor node for the constant period. After that, BS calculates "*Validity Authentication Rate*" for each node, by filtering collected AREP messages. At this time, "*Validity Authentication Rat*" is about the matter whether there is integrity for sensor nodes and is the intensity of the confidentiality, and BS selects cluster header, reflecting " *Validity Authentication Rate* " as well as residual power value for sensor nodes when selecting cluster header. After completing its cluster header selection performance, BS creates the member list to which belongs to for each cluster header in order to safely broadcast. After receiving this member list, nodes performs the clustering based on the data stated on the list and conveys the data to cluster header. Cluster header ignores all data from nodes other than members it controls. In other words, in consideration into the security when selecting cluster header as the starting point of cluster, this technique is designed to increase the local security and efficiency of sensor node management by classifying the created cluster into each group and providing different group keys.

2.1 Assumption

Each sensor nodes share $K_{Pair}{}^i$ in different BS-to-Node key pairs, having $Key_{MAC}{}^i$, the authenticated value additionally to create MAC. Like the key pairs, this value is different in each sensor node, sharing with BS and receiving the allocation from BS before the sensor node distribution. In addition, another assumption is that BS has the security itself and has the sufficient computation capabilities.

2.2 Sensor Node Authentication

In order to process the authentication for the distributed sensor nodes, BS broadcasts AREQ Message containing R_Value^i, random number value R_Value^i that has been randomly created. At this time, the time value measurement at the time of transfer is recorded, and this process is continuously transferred by up to certain n times. In this case, the random values contained in these messages are different with each other.

$$R\_Value^i = Random\_Value\_Generator()$$

$$BS \rightarrow * : AREQ \mid R\_Value^i \ (i = 0,,,,,n)$$

Sensor node received AREQ message measures its own residual power value in residual power value measurement method in LEACH technique. Residual power value measured this time is assumed as P_Value^i.

Assuming there is A, the discretional sensor node, A performs the XOR computation between R_Value^i the random value continued in AREQ and $Key_{MAC}{}^i$, the value to create MAC.

Then, it performs the XOR computation between the result value and P_Value^i, the Residual power value A measured. After that, this value is encrypted in One-way Hash method and then transformed MAC for Residual power value.

$$MAC_A{}^i$$

$$= Hash(S_A{}^i)$$

$$= Hash((R\_Value^i \oplus Auth\_Value^A) \oplus Key_{MAC}{}^A)$$

The node A prepares authentication message by encrypting MAC value for residual power value and residual power value measured in the in the entire process, and then responses by transferring them to key pair shared with BS.

$$M_i = EK(K_{Pair}{}^A, Power_A \mid MAC_A{}^i)$$

$$Node_i \rightarrow BS : AREP \mid M_i$$

BS receives and checks the total m of AREP message $(0 \le m \le n)$ for up to n times of AREQ message, from sensor node A. In other words, it creates MAC in the same process as A, sensor node by using Authentication Value, Random Value and residual power value whose BS itself has MAC value acquired after the decryption to key pair, and checks the integrity by comparing MAC of A, sensor node. If there is any problem in the integrity, the corresponding authentication message is ignored and the list is made. At this time, if the authentication fails to a certain degree of proportion, it is excluded from the network or the cluster header priority selection criteria.

2.3 Sensor Node Authentication

The response time means the time from BS broadcasting AREQ message till receiving the response to AREP message, and this value becomes essentially necessary in order to create "*Validity Authentication Time*" necessary to measure " *Validity Authentication Time* " afterwards.

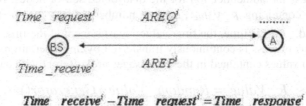

$$Time\_receive^i - Time\_request^i = Time\_response^i$$

Fig. 3. Response time against the AREQ/AREP

The process is illustrated in the Fig 3 BS measures and stores the time of when broadcasting AREQ message, and then measures the time receiving Authentication Reply Message from sensor node to calculate the differences. Such calculated response time $Time\_response^i$ is enlisted with about whether AREP message is authenticated to be used for the filtering necessary for the "*Validity Authentication Rate*" calculation afterwards.

2.4 Cluster Header Election Reflecting Validity Authentication Rate

Among the response time information list created through the process described in 2.3, the least time information, namely the shortest response time $Time\_response^i$ is added to the threshold time value $Time\_stamp$ to make "*Validity Authentication Time*", and then the excessive response time value is deleted with the corresponding "*Authentication Reply Message*".

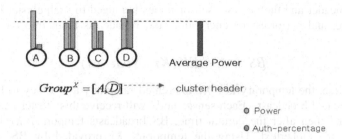

Fig. 4. Cluster election based on considering security

Namely, it accepts only authentication message that received within the certain interval as effective, but in case of the excess of *"Validity Authentication Time"* value, it nullifies AREP message recorded together with the response time value on the list, determining the malicious attacker reply/delay attack and link as unstable. At this time, it is assumed that the threshold time value is predetermined, and it may be different depending on the amount of sensor node distributed to sensor network.

BS calculates *"Validity Authentication Rate"* by reflecting n, the number of entire AREQ messages transferred as described in 2.2 together with the number of AREP message which has gone through the filtering through the "Validity Authentication Time" value as above. In addition, reflecting this "Validity Authentication Rate" and residual power value of sensor node, BS selects sensor node having more than certain degree of the power energy value and "Validity Authentication Rate" of sensor nodes as cluster header. In this context, even when with the slightly smaller residual power value, if authentication rate of AREP messages for AREQ message is the highest, they are selected as cluster header as in Fig 5.

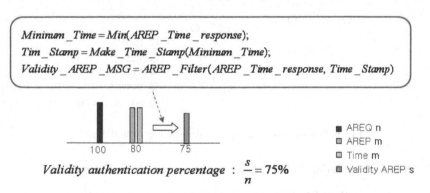

Fig. 5. Measurement algorithm of *Validity Authentication Rate*

2.5 Cluster Header Selection and Group Formation

Each sensor node simply stores the information on its own vicinity sensor nodes, which is closest to it, through the communications, while BS prepares information on the cluster header and the member sensor nodes belonged to such cluster header into the message, and performs the encryption and broadcasts them into the temporary K_T.

$$BS \rightarrow * : EK(K_T, Node^D{}_{CH})$$

At this time, the temporary key K_T is created randomly as the key to be used for the authenticated broadcast. Each sensor node will receive this cluster header sensor node list and then after the certain time, BS broadcasts temporary K_T in order to decryption this ciphertext. Using the temporary K_T provided by BS, each node interprets the stored ciphertext, check the cluster header information and may know the cluster information to which it belongs.

2.6 Assignment of Administration

After the creation of the cluster header election and cluster, BS will assign some parts of the management authority from sensor node to cluster header. Cluster header collects the information on the vicinity sensor node to transmit to BS, and then BS finally receives the data of sensor nodes. In this case, cluster header receives only data of sensor node specified on the member list it owns, ignoring the data sent from other sensor node as in Fig 6. The nodes unauthenticated by BS through the AREQ/AREP message in the initial phase will be disqualified to perform the tasks in the cluster because they are excluded from the member list provided by cluster header afterwards, so that the malicious sensor node may avoid the data transmitted by the internal cluster.

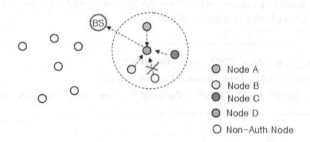

Node A
Node B
Node C
Node D
Non−Auth Node

Fig. 6. Sensor node filtering by using management delegating

2.7 Data Accumulation Style *Validity Authentication Rate* Estimation

When measuring *"Validity Authentication Rate"*, BS transmits AREQ messages by n numbers in total, and sensor node should transmit AREP messages by n numbers for these AREQ messages. This property may cause the excessive energy consumption of sensor node. Accordingly, this technique will reflect the measured *"Validity Authentication Rate"* to the cluster header selection criteria, and make the estimation on *"Validity Authentication Rate"* of each sensor node based on the " *Validity Authentication Rate* " information accumulated in every round. BS first calculates the average value on " *Validity Authentication Rate* " accumulated during the certain rounds. From the next round, BS broadcasts only one AREQ message to request residual power value of sensor node, and replaces the average "*Validity Authentication Rate* " value to " *Validity Authentication Rate* " to use.

2.8 Use Cycle of Average Validity Authentication Rate

Malicious attacker in sensor network may perform the malicious behavior by intruding into sensor network in the irregular cycle or time, or may be unstable in its traffic due to the sensor network properties. Thus, forecasting "*Validity Authentication Rate*" through the average "*Validity Authentication Rate*" may cause the error. There is need for the synchronization by repeating the procedure 2.6 periodically so that such accumulated error may not make bad influence.

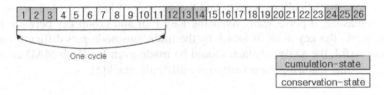

Fig. 7. "Validity Authentication Rate" pre-sumption and accumulating period

As in Fig., BS measures and accumulates "Validity Authentication Rates" for each sensor node every round from Round 1 ~ Round 3, and then from Round 4, estimates "*Validity Authentication Rate*" of nodes as the accumulated "*Validity Authentication Rate* " average value to use the cluster header selection criteria. That is, Round 4, 5, 6 through..., 11 does not require the task to measure the separate "*Validity Authentication Rate*", calculating the average "*Validity Authentication Rate*" to be used for Round 15~23 by measuring and accumulating "*Validity Authentication Rate*" in Round 12 ~ Round 14 after Round 11. Like this, during the certain period, it measures and accumulates "*Validity Authentication Rate*", and then by calculating and using the value based on the accumulated data during another constant period, it minimizes the energy consumption caused by the excessive authentication.

3 Analysis

In the proposed technique in this paper, we presented how to select the sensor node secure from the security attack as cluster header, group leader of the grouping standard when performing the cluster header election appropriate to group key and grouping. In addition, Table 1 summarizes the security weakness and how to attack in sensor network, and the proposed technique shows the applications as to whether there is the response or not to such security weakness and attack[8].

In this paper, SKA supports RC5. Unlike in other cryptography algorithm, RC5 features that the key attack is quite difficult. For example, if RC5 of 12 rounds in 64bit key, the search should be made for all keys of total 1.84467×10^{19}, and it would

Table 1. Ability of sensor network attack

Attack Types		LEACH-C	LEAP/LEACH	Proposed
Routing related	Hello attack	X	O	O
	Bogus routing info. attack	△	O	O
	Sybil attack	X	O	O
Data forwarding related	Message delay attack	X	X	△
	Message alteration attack	X	O	O
	Message replay attack	X	O	O
Physical related	Byzantine attack	X	X	X

take about 3 years even under the assumption that 1.5138% of the entire keys for 263 days have been statistically processed and the number of key processed per second is linearly increasing. If periodically replacing Key Pair and group key between BS and sensor network, the key analysis attack by the malicious node gets difficult, and even if it is successful, the analysis/attach should be made even for Hash MAD combining with Key_{MAC}, thus featuring the actually very difficult attack[5].

4 Conclusion

In this paper, we presents cluster header and grouping techniques appropriate to group keys that solves the weak security problem in sensor network. The proposed technique enables the cluster header selection and grouping, by comprehensively reflecting the validity authentication rate that reflects the residual electricity amount, data integrity and confidentiality intensity through the communications between the initial BS. It is designed to minimize the electricity consumption by measuring the validity authentication rate node with the data accumulation technique and simply requiring the authentication, which maximizes the compatibility with the existing technique because it may be applicable to the existing group key technique.

References

1. Akyildiz, I.F., Su, W., Sankarasubramaniam, Y., Cayirci, E.: A survey on sensor networks. IEEE Communications Magazine (2002)
2. Deng, J., Han, R., Mishra, S.: Security Support for In-Network Processing in Wireless Sensor Networks. In: Proceedings of the 1st ACM Workshop on the Security of Ad Hoc and Sensor Networks, ACM Press, New York (2003)
3. Heinzelman, W., Chandrakasan, A., Balakrishana, H.: Energy Efficient Communication Protocol for Wireless Microsensor Networks. In: Proceedings of the 33rd Annual Hawaii International Conference on system Sciences (2000)
4. Dasgupta, K., Kalpakis, K., Namjoshi, P.: An Effcient Clustering-based Heuristic for Data Gathering and Aggregation in Sensor Networks. In: Wireless Communication and Networking (2003)

5. Karlof, C., Wagner, D.: Secure routing in wireless sensor networks: Attacks and countermeasures. In: Proceedings of the 1st IEEE International Workshop on Sensor Network Protocols and Applications, Anchorage AK, May 11, 2003, IEEE, Los Alamitos (2003)
6. Diffie, W., Hellman, M.E.: New directions in cryptography. In: IEEE Transactions on Information Theory, IEEE Computer Society Press, Los Alamitos (1976)
7. Jang, K.-W., Jung, W.-s., Shin, D.-k., Jun, M.-S.: Design of Secure Clustering Routing Protocol using SNEP and μTESLA on Sensor Network Communication" in IJCSNS International Journal of Computer Science and Network Security (2006)
8. Ren, K., Lou, W., Moran, P.J.: A proactive data security framework for mission-critical sensor networks. In: IEEE Military Communication Conference (MILCOM 2006), Washington, DC (2006)
9. Zhu, S., Setia, S., Jajodia, S.: LEAP: Efficient Security Mechanisms for Large-Scale Distributed Sensor Networks. In: Proceedings of the 10th ACM Conference on Computer and Communication Security (2003)
10. Neuman, B.C., Tso, T.: Kerberos: An authentication service for computer networks. IEEE Communications (1994)
11. Perrig, A., Szewczyk, R., Wen, V., Cullar, D., Tygar, J.D.: SPINS: Security protocols for sensor networks. In: Proceedings of the 7th Annual ACM/IEEE Internation Conference on Mobile Computing and Networkin (MobiCom), IEEE Computer Society Press, Los Alamitos (2001)
12. Rivest, R.L., Shamir, A., Adleman, L.M.: A method for obtaining digital signatures and public-key cryptosystems. In: Communications of the ACM, ACM Press, New York (1978)
13. RC5 Cracking Project, http://www.distributed.net/rc5/ (1997)

A Secure Data Aggregation Scheme for Wireless Sensor Networks

Shu Qin Ren, Dong Seong Kim, and Jong Sou Park

Computer Engineering Dept., Korea Aerospace University,
200-1 Huajun-Dong, Dukyan-Gu, Koyang-shi, Geyonggi-Do, 412-791, South Korea
{sqren,dskim,jspark}@hau.ac.kr

Abstract. The proliferation of sensor networks provides a promising solution for a variety of ubiquitous data services, but it challenges the data security and privacy because of its unfavorable deployment nature of being prone to physical attacks with circumscribed source available. Considering the data redundancy, energy constraint, and security requirement, this paper proposed a secure data aggregation scheme which supports end-to-end encryption using privacy homomorphism as well as hop-by-hop verification using ECC based MAC in cluster based sensor networks. The analytic comparing results show that our scheme has higher resistance against eavesdropping and fabricating attacks at a little additional computational cost with higher connectivity.

1 Introduction

Wireless sensor networks which consist of large scale of tiny sensor nodes with low cost, low power, limited computation, smaller memory and low bandwidth, are emerging as a popular solution to many challenging domestic, commercial and military applications. These sensor nodes collectively monitor the area, which generates a substantial amount of data to transfer. The data redundancy and limited energy constraint characteristics in WSN raise challenge to the traditional security measures.

The energy-efficient data access mechanism such as clustering, in which the data can be preprocessed before submission, is commonly accepted as an option to increase scalability, reduce delay and prolong the network lifetime for wireless sensor network. Several studies [1 2 3] have addressed the security issues focusing on the peer-to-peer communication, not considering about energy reduction with data aggregation. Przydatek, B et al. discussed about the secure information aggregation (SIA) within the sensor networks using Merkle hash tree verification [5], which provides authentication on the root or aggregator without considering about the intermediate relay attack. Tanveer Z. et al. proposed a security scheme for clustering WSN by using a hierarchical key management scheme [14]. But the network key shared by the entire sensor network makes the network apt to leak this key easily, which will lead to the complete control of the whole network by the attacker.

P. Thulasiraman et al. (Eds.): ISPA 2007 Workshops, LNCS 4743, pp. 32–40, 2007.

In order to keep the sensitive data privacy and security, and also reduce the load traffic as early as possible simultaneously, we propose a secure communication scheme in the clustering WSN combining privacy homomorphism (PH) based end-to-end encryption and ECC-MAC based hop-by-hop authentication. In this scheme, the data is just encrypted once on the collecting nodes, and decrypted once on the base station. The relaying nodes, including the aggregator just authenticate the concealed data without decryption. In addition, the aggregator needs aggregation operation.

The rest of the paper is organized as follows. Section 2 gives the system architecture. Section 3 details the secure data transmit scheme within clustering WSN, which combining PH based end-to-end encryption and ECC-MAC based hop-by-hop authentication. Section 4 analyzes the security performance of this scheme. At last, we give the conclusion in section 5.

2   System Architecture

We assume all the data query requests are from data base, other requests from other place will be ignored by sensor nodes; the query results will be sent back to the base station after aggregation. And if the node is compromised, the pre-loaded key will be removed automatically. The attacker cannot fabricate query request without the signature of the base station, but it can snoop the message transferred on the link and it can also inject message intended to send to the base station.

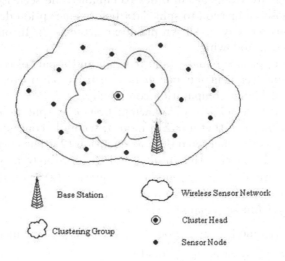

Fig. 1. The infrastructure of the data query framework

Our design goal is to protect the sensitive message from leaking to the snooper, and to detect the injected or fabricated message and drop it as early as possible. For the first goal, we adopted PH based encryption to conceal the original data from the overhearing; for the second goal, hop-by-hop authentication is adopted to verify the message through message authentication code (MAC).

For a secure data communication, there are 4 steps needed in this scheme: First, the collecting nodes will encrypt the sensitive data and encrypt using PH, and the encrypted data and its authentication will be sent to the aggregator. During the transmission, the concealed data is checked through hop-by-hop authentication with MAC of the encrypted data on the pairwise key. Second, the aggregator will check the data validity from the sensor nodes and calculate the aggregation of the valid data. At last, the aggregator will send back the aggregation to the base station. This aggregated result is still authenticated hop-by-hop using MAC. At last, the base station will check the authentication of the aggregator and extract the real aggregation data.

3   Secure Data Aggregation in Cluster Based WSN

3.1   Privacy Homomorphism (PH)

Suppose A is a domain of plaintext value $A = \{a_1, a_2, ..., a_m\}$, B is the domain of the ciphertext value $B = \{e_1, e_2, ..., e_n\}$. $E_k(a_i)$ is an encrypted function using k, and $D_k(e_i)$ is the corresponding decryption function. And Δ is an operation. (E_k, D_k, A, B) is defined as a PH if it meets the equation (1).

$$D_k(E_k(a_i) \, \Delta \, E_k(a_j)) = D_k(e_i \, \Delta \, e_j) = a_i \, \Delta \, a_j \tag{1}$$

It means the operation Δ can be executed on the deciphered data, which will not affect the ultimate result [6]. In order to enhance the security level of PH, the new PH proposed a method to split data before encryption data, which can prevent the ciphertext-only or known-plaintext attacks [7]. In our model, this new PH is adopted as following:

Selecting two big primes p and q, and $n = pq$, and a pair of constants $r_p \epsilon Z_p$ and $r_q \epsilon Z_q$. The split segment number m is a security parameter, higher value higher security, but higher computation complexity.

Encryption of a data $a \epsilon Z_n$ is as following: first, a is split randomly into m sections: $a_1, a_2, ..., a_m$ such that $a = \Sigma a_i \bmod n$; secondly compute each section modulo to p and q as the encrypted data as equation (2). The encryption key is key $= (p, q, r_p, r_q)$. To decrypt this result, the i-th coordinate is by $[r_p^{-i} \bmod p, r_q^{-i} \bmod q]$ to retrieve $[a_i \bmod p, a_j \bmod q]$ as equation (3) and (4), then adding up all the shares to get $[a \bmod p, a \bmod q]$ as equation (5); at last, the data can be extracted using Chinese remainder theorem.

$$E_k(a) = ([a_1 r_p \bmod p, \ a_1 r_q \bmod q], \ [a_2 r_p^2 \bmod p, \ a_2 r_q^2 \bmod q], \ ...,$$
$$[a_m r_p^m \bmod p, \ a_m r_q^m \bmod q])$$
$$= ([e_{11}, \ e_{12}], \ [e_{21}, \ e_{22}], \ ..., \ [e_{m1}, \ e_{m2}]) \tag{2}$$

$$D_k(e_{i1}) = e_{i1} r_p^{-i} \bmod p \tag{3}$$

$$D_k(e_{i2}) = e_{i2} r_q^{-i} \bmod q \tag{4}$$

$$D_k(E_k(a)) = \Sigma D_k ey(e_{ij}) \bmod n, \ j = 1, 2 \tag{5}$$

3.2   ECC-MAC Based Pairwise Key

Node i has the private-public key pair as: $\{k_i,\ k_iP\ \}$; node j has the private-public key pair as: $\{k_j,\ k_jP\ \}$; and node v has the private-public key pair as: $\{k_v,\ k_vP\ \}$. The shared pairwise key between adjacent nodes can be built as Fig 2. ECC is a public-key cryptosystem operating over points on an elliptic

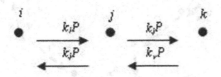

Fig. 2. Establishing shared secret using ECC

curve. Some studies claimed that ECC seemed to be a good candidate for the key distribution in wireless sensor network [13,15], with smaller key size and promising performance, the cost for generating a 163-bit shared key is 34.16sec for 100 trials, with a standard deviation of 0.934sec, and 1410 B of SRAM, 34342 B of ROM [15]. The main cryptographic operation in ECC is scalar point multiplication which computes $Q = kP$, a point P is multiplied by an integer k resulting another point Q on the curve. We use this point multiplication to generate a shared key between any two adjacent nodes. Suppose node i and node j are neighbor nodes, with the private and public key pair k_i, k_iP and k_j, k_jP respectively. Each node sends its public key to the neighbor node, and multiplies its private key with the received public key to generate a shared key between these two nodes, as Figure 2. This shared key is used for message authentication through MAC of the message on this shared key, which is used for hop-by-hop message authentication. In addition, this authentication is executed on the relayed encrypted message which is generated on the sensing node, with addition homomorphism characteristic.

3.3   Secure Data Aggregation with PH and ECC-MAC

Encrypting Sensitive Data Based on PH. Based on the above PH, each sensor node has pre-loaded key (p, q, r_p, r_q). Considering the computation complexity and power consumption, our model set the split section number m as 2. And the sensitive data s_i from the node S_i will first be split randomly into two part s_{i1} and s_{i2}, where $s_i = (s_{i1} \bmod n) + (s_{i2} \bmod n)$; and secondly the split data is encrypted as following:

$$E_k(s_{i1}) = ([s_{i1}r_p \ mod \ p, \ s_{i1}r_q \ mod \ q] = e_{11} \tag{6}$$

$$E_k(s_{i2}) = ([s_{i2}r_p \ mod \ p, \ s_{i2}r_q \ mod \ q] = e_{12} \tag{7}$$

$$E_k(s_i) = (e_{i1} \ e_{i2}) = e_i \tag{8}$$

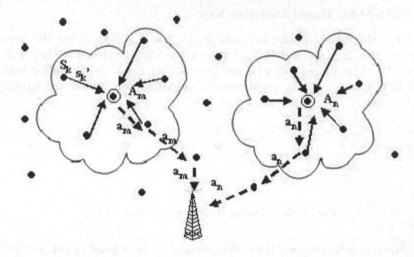

Fig. 3. Secure Data Aggregation in Clustering WSN

These encrypted data is sent to the aggregator, which is in charge of the aggregation. During the transmission, the data is checked hop-by-hop through a shared secret between adjacent nodes.

Data Verification through Hop-by-hop Authentication. The data collected from collecting nodes is split and encrypted as above before arriving to the aggregator through single hop or multi hop. During the transmission, hop-by-hop authentication of the cipher text is used to block DOS attack.

Suppose node i collects a sensitive data, and encrypts the data as e_i using PH encryption function, and then sending the concealed data e_i to the aggregator through next hop node j. The authentication between i and j is operated on the shared secret on the communication channel through MAC as equation (9).

$$M_{ij} = MAC(K_{ij}, \ m) = MAC(k_i(k_jP), \ e_i) \qquad (9)$$

Here, K_{ij} is the shared secret between node i and node j based on ECC: K_{ij} = $k_i \ (k_jP)$ = $k_j \ (k_iP)$, as in Figure 2. And M_{ij} is the authentication. So the complete message transferred from node i to node j can be expressed as $i \rightarrow j$: me_i, M_{ij}. Node j receiving message m, it will compute $MAC(e_i|k_j(k_iP))$ and compare with the received Mij; if the comparing result is equal, it will relay it to the next hop, or else, it just drops the package.

Data Authentication and Aggregation. For some specific application, the pre-fixed clustering architecture is accessible; but for most application, self-configure and dynamic are two most important characteristics. And also this kind of dynamic clustering is beneficial to extend the lifetime of the whole network. Leader selection algorithm in [8] is the basis for the aggregator selection. And [4] added the willingness of a node using a coefficient to select leader, this coefficient is calculated as a function of the amount of available resources. V. Mittal proposed a local clustering algorithm for wireless sensor network, in which O(R4) time is needed to build cluster, and each node only needs information about nodes that are most 2R away [9]. In our model, we will borrow this methodology for selecting aggregator.

For the query group, in which the aggregator is selected according to the algorithm in [9], each sensor node has its own private key k_i and public key $Q_i = k_i P$, which are pre-loaded on the sensor node according to the ECC parameters. A selected aggregator has its own private key k_a and public key $Q_a = k_a P$. The sensitive data s_i is first encrypted with an privacy homomorphism encryption function as $e_i = E_k(s_i)$, and then the encrypted data and its authentication on the shared secret with the adjacent node $MAC(e_i|k_i(k_v P))$ are sent to the aggregator through adjacent node v. When node v receives the data and MAC, it will verify the authentication and drop the forge message. If the message passes the authenticity check, it will be relayed to the next hop to the aggregator with new authentication code by the shared secret between current node and next hop node. Here the next hop is the cluster head, the sent message is $e_i, MAC(e_i|k_v(k_h P))$.

The aggregator can authenticate the data package from a specific sensor node as above. Suppose the aggregation function is f_A, , and the operation set is $\Delta 1, \Delta 2, , \Delta n$, the aggregation is only executed on the authenticated encryption data as equation (10), which prevent the malicious data from impersonated sensor node. But it cannot prevent the compromised attack. In our current scheme, we just consider the sum/average aggregation operation.

$$f_A(\{e_1, e_2, ..., e_m\}, \{\Delta 1, \Delta 2, , \Delta n\}) = ([a_{11} \ a_{12}], [a_{11} \ a_{12}]) \qquad (10)$$

Data Extract on the Base Station. The base station collects the aggregation result from all the aggregators with the corresponding authenticated signature. The base station and the relay nodes can authenticate the aggregation using a symmetric key between adjacent nodes, as section 3.3.2, which ensures to drop forge message as early as possible. And then the base station extracts the real data value using decryption function. In our model, the first and second coordinates are by $[r_p^{-1} \bmod p, r_q^{-1} \bmod q]$ and $[r_p^{-2} \bmod p, r_q^{-2} \bmod q]$ respectively as equation (11), the original value can be extracted by modulating the sum of these vector to n, as equation (5).

$$D_k([a_{11} \ a_{12}], [a_{11} \ a_{12}]) = ([a_{11} r_p^{-1} \ mod p \ a_{12} r_q^{-1} \ mod q],$$
$$[a_{21} r_p^{-2} \ mod p \ a_{22} r_q^{-2} \ mod q]) \qquad (11)$$

4   Performance Analysis of Our Scheme

We employed PH not only for privacy but also for security because the real data is hidden in the forwarding procedure. And the data freshness is kept through random splitting before encryption. It is an efficient way to prevent eavesdropping attack. In addition, we employed pairwise authentication to block the fabricated message as soon as possible. Due to the shared key is established using ECC based point multiplication, the difficulty to get the key is a discrete logarithm problem. This scheme is suitable for hierarchical WSN with a little additional computation cost.

We can regard the whole system as three steps: the first is pre-configuration, the selected curve parameters are preloaded in each sensor node; the second step is the bootstrapping. The pairwise keys between nodes are built and the role of each node is decided as collecting node, relaying node or cluster header; and the third is the data transfer with PH and hop-by-hop authentication. Step 1 is just operated once before deployment, step 2 runs only once for pairwise key establishment, and the cluster head selection depends on the transaction. In this section, we just analyze the computation complexity, communication complexity, and then give the overall of energy consumption in step 2 and step 3.

The energy consumption E can be calculated by $E = UIt$, where U is the voltage, I is the current, and t is the time duration. We used 2 AA batteries to power Micaz mote, so U is about 3.0 volts. The current value varies in MCU on/Radio off, MCU on/Radio Rx, and MCU Tx/Radio operations as 1.8mA : 21.8mA : 19.5mA, which is abstracted from [12].

For step 2, assume sensor node S_i has N_{ei} neighbor nodes, and it belongs to cluster c_k, cluster size is Nck. The communication for pairwise key establishment is $o(2N_{ei})$ in transfer, $o(2N_{ei})$ in receive; the communication message for header selection in the cluster is $o(Nck2)$. So the energy consumption for key setting up and cluster head selection at one node is as equation (12) (13) respectively. From the equations, E_1 is the biggest, however it is just operated once at bootstrapping. E_2 is consumed when aggregators are changed.

For step 3, suppose there are N_c nodes for collecting data, N_r for relaying, and N_a aggregators. Given packet 38 bytes in each packet, and 250kbps for the transfer radio, the transfer time for each packet is 38 * 8 / 250kbps = 1.2ms. The energy for transferring a packet is 3.0(v)19.5(mA)1.2(ms) = 70.2(μJ) , the energy for receiving a packet is 3.0(v)21.8(mA)1.2(ms) = 78.5(μJ). For authentication, two point multiplications and two MAC are required for local computation in sender and receiver respectively. It takes about 0.81s to perform a point multiplication on a 160-bit elliptic curve [13], and 75ms for MAC computation [12]. The computation time of PH at the sensing node is t_e, the aggregation time period is t_a. Equation (14) gives the energy consumption for the collecting sensor node; and equation (15) for the relaying node; and equation (16) for aggregator.

$$E_1 = 3v \times 21.8mA \times 1.2ms \times 2N_{ei} + 3v \times 19.5mA \times 1.2ms \times 2N_{ei}$$
$$+3v \times 1.6mA \times 75ms \times N_{ei} + 3v \times 1.6mA \times 0.81s \times N_{ck} \quad (12)$$

$$E_2 = 3v \times 21.8mA \times 1.2ms \times N_{ck}^2 = 78.49N_{ck}^2(\mu J) \quad (13)$$

$$E_{31} = 3v \times 1.8mA \times t_e + 3v \times 21.8mA \times 1.2ms = 78.48 + 5.4t_e(\mu J); \quad (14)$$

$$E_{32} = 3v \times 21.8mA \times 1.2ms + 3v \times 19.5mA \times 1.2ms + 3v \times 1.6mA \times 75ms$$
$$= 508.68(\mu J); \quad (15)$$

$$E_{33} = 3v \times 21.8mA \times 1.2ms \times N_c + 3v \times 1.6mA \times 75ms \times N_c$$
$$+3v \times 1.8mA \times t_a + 3v \times 19.5mA \times 1.2ms$$
$$= 438.48N_c + 5.4t_a + 70.2$$
$$= 78.48 + 5.4t_e(\mu J) \tag{16}$$

From the above, we can see the local computation cost is expensive for key setting up (equation (12)), yet it is just executed once. And the gain is less computation and communication cost in data transfer as (14) (15) (16), because no encryption or no decryption for data transfer, and high level secure authentication.

For key pre-distribution system, if hop-by-hop encryption is used, E_1 maybe less than the value in our scheme, no point multiplication needed. E2 is about same. Yet the cost for data transfer E_{31}, E_{32}, E_{33} will be more expensive than ours, because of more encryption and decryption operations, which is needed for each packet.

For pure ECC based scheme, even though the security level can be ensured with less key size, encryption, decryption and digital signature is too expensive for local computation, as most researchers' view.

And if we adopted the PH end-to-end encryption with key distribution scheme for authentication, the computation cost for pairwise key establishment will be reduced at the cost of bigger key size on each sensor nodes, and also the secure connectivity depends on the key ring distribution. The secure link in our scheme is established as the real physical links with a little additional communication once at the deployment time. From the equations aforementioned, we can extract this computation cost is worthy when more than 10 packets are transferred from same node, which is less than the communication cost. So our scheme performs better when the traffic load is heavier.

5 Conclusion

This paper proposed a scheme for clustering WSN with security and privacy. We used the PH to ensure data aggregation without leaking the data privacy; and we established the pairwise key with ECC to get higher security level, shunning the expensive encryption, decryption and signature cost with ECC. Because of the PH property, we just encrypt message and decrypt message only once on the collecting nodes and the base station respectively, with less computation cost on the relaying nodes. And the encrypted key is pre-loaded before deployment, without additional communication cost for the encryption key exploring. And for the hop-by-hop ECC-MAC authentication, 1 point multiplication and 2 MAC are the local communication. Our scheme provides a secure and efficient way for clustering WSN with a little additional computation complexity and less communication complexity, comparing with other schemes.

Our ongoing work is to implement the proposed scheme and to evaluate the performance of the scheme on the real testbed. In addition, the optimization of point multiplication will be further explored in our research.

40   S.Q. Ren, D.S. Kim, and J.S. Park

Acknowledgments. We would like to thank Ms. Khin Mi Mi Aung for her valuable comments and suggestion during the manuscript preparation of the first draft. This research is supported by the MIC (Ministry of Information and Communication), Korea, under the ITRC (Information Technology Research Center) support program supervised by the IITA (Institute of Information Technology Assessment).

References

1. Perrig, A., Szewczyk, R.: SPINS: Security protocols for sensor networks. Journal of Wireless Networks 8, 521–534 (2002)
2. Chan, H., Perrig, A., Song, D.: Random Key Predistribution Schemes for Sensor Networks. In: Proc. of the 2003 IEEE Symp. on Security and Privacy, Berkeley, pp. 197–213. IEEE Computer Society Press, Los Alamitos (2003)
3. Gupta, V., Millard, M., Fung, S., Zhu, Y., et al.: Sizzle: A standards-based end-to-end security architecture for the embedded internet. In: Proc. PerCom 2005, Kauai, March, 2005, pp. 247–256 (2005)
4. Dulman, S., Havinga, P., Jurink, J.: Wave leader election protocol for wireless sensor networks. In: MMSA Workshop, Delft, the Netherlands, December, 2002 (2002)
5. Przydatek, B., Song, D., Perrig, A.: SIA: Secure information aggregation in sensor networks. In: Proc. of SenSys'03, NewYork, November, 2003, pp. 255–265 (2003)
6. Domingo-Ferrer, J.: A New Privacy Homomorphism and Applications. Information Processing Letters 60(5), 277–282 (1996)
7. Girao, J., Schneider, M., Westhoff, D.: CDA: Concealed data aggregation in wireless sensor networks. In: Proc. of the ACM Workshop on Wireless Security, ACM Press, New York (2004)
8. Lynch, N.: Distributed algorithms. Morgan Kaufmann, San Francisco (1997)
9. Mittal, V., Demirbas, M., Arora, A.: LOCI: Local Clustering Service for Large Scale Wireless Sensor Networks. Technical Report OSU-CISRC-2/03-TR07 (2003)
10. An, L., Panos, K., Ning, P.: TinyECC: Elliptic Curve Cryptography for Sensor Networks (Version 0.3) (Febraury 2007), http://discovery.csc.ncsu.edu/software/TinyECC/
11. Malan, D.J., Welsh, M., Smith, M.D: A public-key infrastructure for key distribution in tinyos based on elliptic curve cryptography. In: Proc. of the First IEEE International Conference on Sensor and Ad Hoc Communications and Networks, Santa Clara, CA, October, 2004, pp. 71–80. IEEE Computer Society Press, Los Alamitos (2004)
12. Haodong, W., Bo, S., Qun, L.: Elliptic Curve Cryptography Based Access Control in Sensor Networks. International Journal of Security and Networks , 127–137 (2006)
13. Gura, N., Patel, A., Wander, A.: Comparing elliptic curve cryptography and RSA on 8-bit CPUs. In: Proc. of the 2004 Workshop on Cryptographic Hardware and Embedded Systems, pp. 119–132 (2004)
14. Tanveer, Z., Albert, Z.: A Security Framework for Wireless Sensor Networks. In: SAS 2006, pp. 49–53 (2006)
15. Malan, D., Welsh, M., Smith, M.: A public-key infrastructure for key distribution in tinyos based on elliptic curve cryptography. In: Proc. of the 2nd IEEE International Conference on Sensor and Ad Hoc Communications and Networks (SECON 2004), pp. 71–80. IEEE Computer Society Press, Los Alamitos (2004)

A Key Revocation Scheme for Mobile Sensor Networks

Dong Seong Kim, Mohammed Golam Sadi, and Jong Sou Park

Network Security and System Design Lab., Korea Aerospace University, Republic of Korea
{dskim,sadi,jspark}@kau.ac.kr

Abstract. Mobile Sensor Network (MSN) imposes challenges to apply security schemes for mobility and free joining and leaving in the network. Key predistribution scheme used for Wireless Sensor Network (WSN) is a potential candidate applicable to MSN as it is a brach of WSN with some additional features. In this paper, we evaluate the feasibilty of a key predistribution scheme named Randomized Grid Based (RGB) scheme proposed for WSN in the context of MSN. We propose a key revocation scheme applying redundancy on RGB scheme to ensure best connectivity and resiliency. The analysis proves the effectiveness of the scheme in terms of connectivity and resiliency.

Keywords: sensor networks, key revocaction, key predistribution, randomized grid based scheme.

1 Introduction

Recent advances in wireless communication and electronics have enabled the development of low-cost, low-power, multifunctional sensor nodes that are small in size and communicate in short distance. This tiny sensor node, which consists of sensing, data processing and communication components leverage the idea of wireless sensor networks (WSN). For a wide variety of military and civilian applications WSN received a lot of attention. This brings out several issues for WSN and at the same time several studies [1, 3-5, 7, 10, 16] have been proposed to resolve the issues. Mobility of the sensor node broadens new issues for the Mobile Sensor Networks (MSN).

We know that sensor nodes are constrained device in terms of computation and communication, memory, energy etc. this makes public key cryptography unsuitable for the MSN as well as WSN. Moreover lacking of any server based infrastructure and mobile ad-hoc nature of the MSN makes improper to use any online server based solution. Key management based on key predistribution scheme (KPS) is pioneer candidate for MSN. In difference to WSN, nodes in the MSN have the ability to move frequently and can leave or join in the network independently. These additional operational requirements enforce more constraints on security design for designing the MSN. So special care need to be taken to use the security schemes proposed for WSN. Sanchez and Baldus [15] evaluated several popular key management scheme for MSN and proposed a novel approach to control and replace pool-based pre-distributed keys.

P. Thulasiraman et al. (Eds.): ISPA 2007 Workshops, LNCS 4743, pp. 41–49, 2007.

In this paper we discuss the eligibility to use keys by applying Randomized Grid Based (RGB) scheme [14] for MSN instead of using distributed polynomial shares to the sensor nodes. Finally we propose a revocation scheme applying redundancy on the RGB scheme so that we can obtain steady connectivity and high resiliency for the MSN.

2   Background of WSN and MSN

Wireless Sensor Networks (WSN) can be categorized in to two depending on the network size and mobility of the sensor node. We can define Distributed Sensor Network (DSN) (Fig-1(a)) to be a large-scale, wireless, ad hoc, multi-hop unpartitioned network of immobile sensor nodes. The scale of nodes in DSN can range up to thousands or more. DSN-wide connectivity is not required or cannot be guaranteed. In a system of N nodes, there may be multiple independent WSN connecting different subsets of the N nodes.

On the other hand MSN (Fig-1(b)) can be defined as a small, medium or large scale WSN of mobile sensor nodes. Mobility of sensor nodes allows them to join or quit the MSN spontaneously. Thus the size and membership of a MSN is unpredictable. For comparison, a number of MSN can be seen as multiple disconnected partition of a large scale DSN.

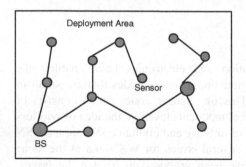

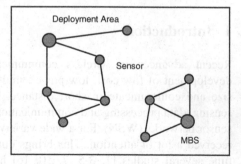

Fig. 1(a). Large Scale DSN   **Fig. 1(b).** Mobile Sensor Network

In MSN application, a large group of interoperable mobile nodes (thousands of nodes) are initially deployed in an area and then, by different means, spontaneously join to form different MSN, i.e. the MSN is typically composed of a subset of the N nodes. New nodes may be deployed in subsequent phases to the initial deployment. We assume that Base Stations (BS) in MSN which collect sensor data, are also typically mobile. The Mobile Base Stations (MBSs) can also regularly connect to the MSN at given intervals in time so that MBSs do not need to be continuously available at the MSN.

3   Key Management Scheme for MSN

In this section, we tried to focus on the adaptability of Randomized Grid Based (RGB) scheme for MSN. Usually it is almost impossible to foresee the size and membership of an MSN (typical two to tens or hundreds of nodes) but we can get the total number of nodes N in the system during security design of the network. We assume that the sensor nodes are not tamper resistant. Based on the following factors, we will evaluate acceptability of RGB scheme for MSN.

- Scalability
- Robustness (resistance to node captures and other security attacks)
- Computational and communication performance and storage needs
- Feasibility for ad hoc networking
- Connectivity properties in small/medium MSNs
- Security services enabled (confidentiality, integrity and authentication)

RGB scheme [14] is a hybrid approach that combines basic probabilistic scheme [7] on the basis of grid-based scheme [10] and ensures high resiliency in the network. The main idea of RGB scheme is that for a network of size N a virtual grid of m x m is constructed where each row and column of the grid is assigned a distinct group of bivariate polynomials. Then the setup server assigns each sensor a unique intersection in the grid and randomly allocates total of $2t$ numbers of polynomial shares to the sensor node from the polynomial groups assigned to the corresponding row and column of that intersection.

Scalability. Having the network size N larger than the actual sensor nodes in the network allows to add more nodes in the MSN in future whenever it is required to expand the network. As such sensor nodes can be added dynamically without having to contact with the previously deployed sensor nodes.

Robustness. This scheme provides significant resiliency over a large number of node capture. This scheme establishes unique pairwise keys between sensor nodes in the network. To compromise a key between any two pair of sensor nodes without compromising them physically it is necessary to compromise the common bivariate polynomial they share. To do this, the attacker needs to compromise $t+1$ number of sensors that have polynomial shares of same bivariate polynomial. Selectively to compromise such nodes among the pool of nodes is almost difficult. Thus RGB ensures robustness for key compromise in the MSN.

Computation, communication and memory requirement. RGB scheme uses polynomial shares to evaluate pairwise keys and most of the computations are to evaluate keys. Liu and Ning [10] developed an efficient technique to evaluate these polynomials with the limited processing capabilities that is feasible to apply it to the sensor node of the MSN. As like other key distribution scheme sensor nodes have to do several communications during the key setup phase of the network. Path key setup requires additional communication overhead but this may be required only during the initialization period of the network. RGB scheme needs additional memory overhead compare to the other existing scheme but this is not a very significant factor, as technological improvement of sensor node for MSN will pave an easy solution.

Authentication. In RGB scheme each sensor node is provided a sensor ID issued by the setup server. As though the mobile nodes may spontaneously join or quit the network the MSN, these unique ID will provide the facility to authenticate between the sensor nodes of the MSN.

4   Key Revocation and Replacement Using RGB

Base station initiated revocation mechanisms proposed by Eschenauer and Gligor[7] may slow the node revocation process due to the potential high latency between the nodes and the base station.

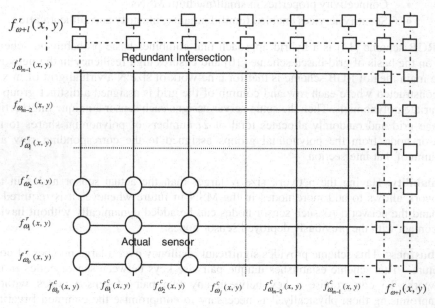

Fig. 2. Polynomial allocation and key revocation scheme for MSN

In such case distributed revocation protocol is well suited to MSN that ensures fast response to seal off compromise node after an attack detection to prevent more significant harm in the network. To effectively apply our revocation scheme we follow the following assumptions proposed by Sanchez and Baldus [15].

- We assume that there are M MBSs in network which does not necessarily reside at the MSN, where M<<N.
- MBSs are not limited to computing power and memory. Further more they have tamper proof hardare and usually they are not left unattended and they are typically only present at the MSNs deployment area sporadically.
- MBSs have larger wireless communication range than sensor nodes.
- MBS can use public key cryptography to secure MBS to MBS
- Sensor nodes and MBSs have a mechanism to easily and efficiently identify the key or polynomial share associated with the node.
- Each sensor node will be distributed pairwise keys for communicating wih the MBSs securely.

To apply key revocation scheme we need to have intrusion detection systems in the network. Several intrusion detection systems [2, 8, 11, 17, 18] have been proposed for sensor network. In our scheme we assume that one of these efficient detection techniques is adapted to detect compromised node in the mobile sensor network.

4.1 Extending RGB Scheme for Revocation

To make the key revocation simple and cost effective in terms of communication and connectivity, we propose redundancy to the grid structure of RGB scheme [14], depicted in Figure 2. The redundancy will be enforced during initialization period of the sensor nodes. Here we will extend the size of the grid structure from m x m to $(m+l)$ x $(m+l)$. The setup server will allocate polynomial shares to these additional intersections of the grid but will not assign them to any sensor nodes. Then the setup server will store this intersection IDs and their allocated polynomial shares and provide this information to all of the MBSs in the network so that revocation of polynomials can be done locally as soon as compromise of node is detected.

4.2 Core Revocation Protocol

If a node is captured by the adversary then there is no way to recover it but if some of keys of the node are compromised then we can apply key revocation process to encounter this problem. In our scheme, when IDS detects a compromised node in the network, MBS will immediately broadcast a message along with the compromised sensor ID to block all the communication with that node. Then the MBS will initiate revocation of polynomial shares of that sensor node through sending revocation message using a secure link. Upon getting proper response from the node MBS will assign a redundant intersection of the grid and with the corresponding allocated polynomials so that the node will have new ID and polynomial shares. Then the sensor node will initiate polynomial share discovery and path discovery method again to establish pairwise key with its neighbors. Thus the sensor node will have opportunity to restrain its connectivity to its neighbors.

If the sensor node is captured by the adversary the MBS will block all the links with that node and calculate the connectivity probability $\rho_{current}$ for each sensor node in the network. If the connectivity probability reaches less than a certain threshold value ρ_{th}, the MBS will initiate the same revocation for the sensor node as described before. MBS can also perform this task in random time to ensure that the network connectivity always remains at a satisfactory level.

Bivariate polynomials are t degree collision resistant that indicates, to compromise a bivariate polynomial it is necessary to compromise t+1 shares of that polynomial. If a bivariate polynomial is compromised then all the keys generated from that polynomial shares will be in threat. To encounter this MBS will maintain an efficient compact database that will keep the information about the compromise number of a bivariate polynomial. Whenever a sensor node is compromised MBS will also update its database of the compromised polynomial list. If the count number for a bivariate polynomial reaches to t, then it is necessary to revoke that polynomial form the network. To perform this MBS will broad cast a signed revocation message with the id of the bivariate polynomial. After receiving the signed message from the MBS, sensor nodes containing the polynomial share will erase the polynomial share and will request the MBS to provide a new polynomial share. In the mean time the MBS will communicate to the setup server to get new bivariate polynomial and then provide it to the sensor nodes that erases polynomial share from their memory. This will prevent compromise of any key that is used to have a secure link between uncompromised nodes and the connectivity of the network.

Each time after modification of any local database of the MBS it will communicate to the other database to keep database information global and thus make it in a consistent state all the time.

5 Security Analysis

Here in this section we analyze the acceptability of revocation and replacement of keys in terms of network connectivity and resiliency. We have not provided any performance analysis of the underlying IDS system as it is beyond of our research scope. This may be found in the corresponding papers [8, 11, 12, 17]. For the IDS we assume that the global IDS attack detection ratio r ($0 < r < 1$) as an input parameter that can be measured and quantified in different MSN configuration [22].

5.1 Restoring the Connectivity

Based on Erdos and Renyi model [6] and Eschenauer and Gligor [7] showed that for large number of N nodes, to have almost connected random graph the required degree of a sensor node varies insignificantly. Applying the same method we can estimate the connectivity to ensure a secure MSN using RGB scheme. Thus RGB scheme shows the feasibility to MSNs of sizes from 1000 to 10000 nodes with required network connectivity.

When a sensor node is captured the links with its neighbors are compromised. In key distribution scheme (KPS) other links between uncompromised has chances to be compromised as several nodes can possess same keys. But the usage of distinct keys used for each link prevents the compromise of other links immediately. But the adversary can be able to compromise key between uncompromised nodes if they can grab the bivariate polynomial used to calculate the pairwise key between them. This is possible only when an adversary can compromise at least t numbers of polynomial shares of that particular bivariate polynomial. Practically it is almost impossible to compromise selective nodes that share the common polynomial. To prevent this situation our revocation scheme has a technique to find the compromised polynomial and replace it by a new one to all of the sensor nodes in the MSN which have polynomial shares of that compromised polynomial and keep alive the initial connectivity.

Another important issue to compromise of nodes is that neighborhood connectivity decreases and the MSN may loose several paths at each compromise of nodes. It may affect routing of data transmission or may make a path key discovery expensive in terms of communication. Continuous monitoring of network connectivity after each compromise encounters this problem. After detection of each capture or compromise of sensor nodes the MBS calculates the connectivity probability $\rho_{current}$ and check with the threshold probability $p_{Threshold}$ which is set during the design time of the MSN. So whenever the connectivity goes below the threshold value the MBS will initiate the revocation to replace polynomial shares from the extended intersection of the grid to maintain the network connectivity to a satisfactory condition.

5.2 Resiliency Enhancement

Resiliency is very important security requirements for either WSN or MSN. Resiliency of RGB scheme is calculated as the fractions of the total network communications that are compromised when N_c nodes are compromised. RGB scheme provides high degree of resiliency for Wireless sensor network. Here we will explain the effectiveness of resiliency by applying the revocation scheme to MSN. We stated that adversary can not compromise any key of uncompromised node until they compromise the bivariate polynomial used to generate that key. But in our scheme we have a method to detect the bivariate polynomial when it is in approaching to be compromised and at that moment we replace it by a new one and it helps to use the   previous connectivity with secure links. IDS has the most important rule to get this achievement for the MSN. If we assume that, no IDS is introduced in the MSN and these captured nodes contributes to increase in compromised communication by compromising bivariate polynomial. Let the total number of captured node is N_c. According to GBR scheme the expected fraction of compromised communication without any IDS is

$$P_{N_c} = 1 - \sum_{t=0}^{k} P(k) \quad \text{where} \quad P(k) = \frac{N_c!}{(N_c-k)!k!}(\frac{\tau}{m\omega})^k(1-\frac{\tau}{m\omega})^{N_c-k}$$

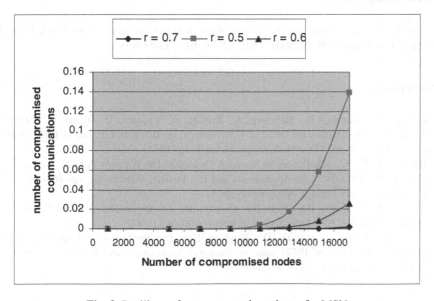

Fig. 3. Resiliency for our revocation scheme for MSN

Suppose an IDS with an attack detection ration r is used and the detected compromised polynomial shares are revoked according to the scheme stated earlier. If we assume that each N_c captured node runs one attack then exactly (1-r) N_c captured sensors are undetected and the expected fraction of the total undetected compromised polynomial is $P_{(1-r)N_c}$. Figure 3 shows graphical presentation of compromised communication link with regard to compromised sensor node in the MSN for different detection ratio. Graph shows that for higher detection ration the MSN work almost perfect.

6 Conclusion

We have presented a brief review of a key predistribution scheme called Randomized Grid Based (RGB) scheme, proposed for WSN in the context of MSN. We then pro posed a key revocation scheme by applying redundancy to the RGB scheme. The analysis showed that the revocation process ensures excellent resiliency for the MSN maintaining the network connectivity even when a large number of nodes are compromised. Most of the overhead for the revocation process goes to the MBSs which we assumed that are expensive nodes. But this scheme also introduces additional memory overhead to store additional keys for communicating with the MBSs. A trade off with memory overhead and other features will pave the way to adapt this scheme for the MSN. As for future works we would like to do more detailed analysis for the revocation scheme and quantitative comparison with other schemes.

Acknowledgement

This work was supported by the Korea Research Foundation Grant funded by the Korean Government (MOEHRD)" (KRF-2006-612- D00085).

References

1. Blundo, C., Santis, A.D., Herzberg, A., Kutten, S., Vaccaro, U., Yung, M.: Perfectly-Secure Key Distribution for Dynamic Conferences. In: Brickell, E.F. (ed.) CRYPTO 1992. LNCS, vol. 740, pp. 471–486. Springer, Heidelberg (1993)
2. Brutch, P., Ko, C.: Challenges in Intrusion Detection for Wireless Ad-hoc Networks. In: Proc. of the 2003 Sym. on Applications and the Internet Workshops, pp. 368–373. IEEE Computer Society Press, Los Alamitos (2003)
3. Carman, D.W., Kruus, P.S., Matt, B.J.: Constraints and Approaches for Distributed Sensor Network Security. NAI Labs Technical Report #00-010 (2000)
4. Chan, H., Perrig, A., Song, D.: Random Key Predistribution Schemes for Sensor Networks. In: Proc. of IEEE Sym. on Research in Security and Privacy, pp. 197–213. IEEE Computer Society, Los Alamitos (2003)

5. Du, W., Deng, J., Han, Y.S., Chen, S., Varshney, P.K.: A Pairwise key Predistribution Scheme for Wireless Sensor Networks. In: Proc. of the 10th ACM Conf. on Computer and Communications Security, pp. 42–51 (2003)
6. Erdos, P., Renyi, A.: On random graphs. I. Publ. Math. Debrecen 6, 290–297 (1959)
7. Eschenauer, L., Gligor, V.D.: A Key-Management Scheme for Distributed Sensor Networks. In: Proc. of the 9th ACM Conf. on Computer and Communications Security, pp. 41–47. ACM Press, New York (2002)
8. Ganeriwal, S., Srivastava, M.B.: Reputation-based Framework for High Integrity Sensor Networks. In: Proc. of the 2nd ACM workshop on Security of Ad-Hoc and Sensor Networks, pp. 66–77. ACM Press, New York (2004)
9. Nadkarni, K., Mishra, A.: A Novel Intrusion Detection Approach for Wireless Ad hoc Networks. Proc. of the IEEE Wireless Communications and Networking Conf. IEEE Computer Society 2, 831–836 (2004)
10. Nesome, J., Shi, E., Song, D., Perrig, A.: The Sybil Attack in Sensor Networks: Analysis & Defenses. In: Proc. of IEEE Int. Conf. on Information Processing in Sensor Networks, pp. 259–268. IEEE Computer Society Press, Los Alamitos (2004)
11. Perrig, A., Szewczyk, R., Wen, V., Culler, D., Tygar, J.D.: SPINS: security protocols for sensor netowrks. In: Proc. of the 7th Annual ACM/IEEE Int. Conf. on Mobile Computing and Networking, pp. 189–199. IEEE Computer Society Press, Los Alamitos (2001)
12. Sadi, M.G., Park, J., Kim, D.: Randomized Grid Based Scheme for Wireless Sensor Network. In: Wang, J., Liao, X.-F., Yi, Z. (eds.) ISNN 2005. LNCS, vol. 3498, pp. 415–420. Springer, Heidelberg (2005)
13. Sanchez, D., Baldus, H.: Key Management for Mobile Sensor Networks. In: Burmester, M., Yasinsac, A. (eds.) MADNES 2005. LNCS, vol. 4074, pp. 14–26. Springer, Heidelberg (2006)
14. Stallings, W.: Cryptography and Network Security: Principles and Practice, 2nd edn. Prentice-Hall, Englewood Cliffs (1999)
15. Watkins, D., Scott, C.: Methodology for evaluating the effectiveness of intrusion detection in tactical mobile ad-hoc networks. Proc. of IEEE Wireless Communications and Networking Conferences 1, 622–627 (2004)
16. Zhang, Y., Lee, W.: Intrusion detection in Wireless Ad-Hoc Networks. In: Proc. of The 6th Int. Conf. on Mobile Computing and Networking, pp. 275–283 (2000)

Adaptive Binding Update Schemes in NEMO*

Sun Ok Yang[1] and SungSuk Kim[2,**]

[1] Institute of Information and Communications, Seoul, S. Korea
soyang@disys.korea.ac.kr
[2] Dept. of Electronic Business,
Seokyeong University, Seoul, S. Korea
sskim03@skuniv.ac.kr

Abstract. When a mobile network moves from one place to another, it changes the reachability of the mobile network in the Internet topology. Network Mobility (NEMO) is concerned with the management of this movement of the mobile network. It is necessary to exchange binding update messages frequently for seamless mobility. However, it incurs both the increase of network overhead and poor usage of mobile router energy efficiency. Our main concerns focus on binding update message management to support efficient network mobility. Thus, this paper proposes an adaptive binding lifetime according to the duration for which mobile router resides in each network under the condition that the mobility type of the mobile router is known in advance. By introducing this algorithm, the number of binding update messages for refreshing the binding could be reduced compared to the default behavior of NEMO, which is defined in RFC3963. Simulation results are shown to prove the effectiveness of the proposed schemes.

1 Introduction

Network mobility (NEMO) is concerned with the management of this movement of the mobile network. It includes one or more mobile routers (MRs) that connect to the global Internet. Typical examples of a mobile network are personal area network (PAN) and a network inside vehicles [1]. Network mobility example is shown in Fig. 1. NEMO basic support protocol is a solution for preserving session continuity by means of bidirectional tunnelling between home agent (HA) and a mobile network. A MR sends a binding update message (BU) to its HA and correspondent nodes (CNs) each time it changes its point-of-attachment. At this time, if the lifetime in BU is set to be short, HA quickly detects that the MR is disconnected from the network. It, however, needs a lot of BU messages transmission over which overburden processing overload on HA and deteriorates wireless bandwidth utilization. And moreover, transmission of BUs from MR to

---

* This work was supported by the Korea Research Foundation Grant funded by the Korean Government (MOEHRD, Basic Research Promotion Fund) (KRF-2006-311-B00775).
** Corresponding author.

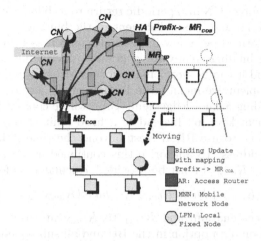

Fig. 1. Network Mobility example

a large number of CNs would cause a BU explosion. To suppress those BUs, only multicast delivery BUs have been proposed. This is an innovative trend for large mobile networks. However, MR should still send multicast delivery BU frequently to the number of CNs. Conversely, if lifetime in BU is set to be long, HA and CNs keep it in a binding cache until the lifetime expires. Therefore, the number of BUs decreases and overhead for the messages is reduced. However, if a long lifetime, the time shifting vulnerability in [2] would increase in exposure to on-path attackers. It would allow the attacker to continue its attack even after the attacker is no longer able to eavesdrop on the path. Also, it is vulnerable to on-path denial-of-service attacks [2]. Hence, it is necessary to obtain the proper lifetime value considering both the cases. Thus, we take an interest in a BU management which MR transmits to its HA and relevant CNs.

Let us consider some kinds of vehicle (e.g. bus, train, airport etc.). They have uniform movement pattern for some networks. If the information related with each vehicle's past movements is maintained locally and available, we can guess the current resident time considering its mobility type. Thus, this paper presents an adaptive binding lifetime according to the duration for which the MR resides in each network under the condition that the moving pattern of the MR is known in advance. As you know, the proposed schemes require extra cost to maintain profile on the MR side. But the cost is not significant. In contrast, a MR can reduce the number of messages and thus can solve the BU explosion. In addition, the traffic load for CNs is also reduced. This can be very valuable result in NEMO.

2   Adaptive Binding Update Algorithm

Return Routability with Network Prefix procedure: With route optimization for NEMO [3], if no appropriate precautions are taken, mobile network nodes (MNNs) could use the bidirectional tunnel to launch IP spoofing attacks.

Therefore, NEMO forces CN into periodic return routability with network prefix (RRNP) procedure [4] and reestablishment of the binding [5]. This authorization should be performed per a few minutes. It can represent a burden for MRs that just have the bindings ready for a possible packet but are not currently communicating, and it can be problematic for an MR in standby mode.

To solve the problem, we include the lifetime credit authorization option [5] in the BU and binding acknowledgement (BA), whose content is based on K_{bm} (binding management key) [6]. Instead of a fixed limit (1 second 7 minutes), the MR can continue to use RRNP test beyond the time it has already been reachable at this address. To authorize this continued use, a keyed hash using the next key credit (K_{credit}) must be provided, calculated as follows [3]:

$$K_{credit} = hash(K_{bmN} \mid hash(K_{bmN-1} \mid hash(K_{bmN-2} \mid ...K_{bm1})))$$

Here | denotes concatenation, and K_{bm1} to K_{bmN} are used to calculate the binding authorization data option in the BU and all subsequent BUs. The next K_{credit} is calculated on the basis of the previous K_{credit} and the latest K_{bm}. The MR and CNs should hold some state in the binding cache entries related to credit authorization. The following conceptual information must be retained: the total time of binding for MR's home address, the current K_{credit} value, and the number of K_{bm} values is included in the K_{credit} value.

In this paper, these values which are computed on the basis of local profile. The total time for MR's home address is expected resident time from profile. The number of K_{bm} is the expected resident time divided by the lifetime of the router advertisement (3.5 minutes) [6]. The sending of K_{credit} determined in this way, has an effect on sending the number of K_{bm} once, which requires expected resident time. Thus, it can reduce the number of messages.

Binding Update Messages: If the information regarding each vehicle's past movements is maintained locally and is available, the proper BU lifetime can be provided whenever the MR enters a network. In this paper, three kinds of BU messages are used according to the lifetime.

- BU_α has a default lifetime (LT_α) of BU, which is used in existing MIPv6 [6]. When a MR moves into a new network, it should transmit BU_α to its HA and CNs after forming new CoA.
- BU_β has an adaptive lifetime (LT_β) and K_{credit} of BU, which is computed on the basis of local profile. A MR has to transmit it to its CNs. K_{credit} is calculated with values stated before.
- BU_0 contains zero lifetime value (LT_0). When MR migrates to a network in another domain before BU_β has expired, it will be used to notify both the HA and the external CNs that the cached data regarding BU has become stale and must be removed.

Only BU_β is newly devised in this paper; the other two BUs were originally used in MIPv6. If a MR does not migrate out of the network after the expiry of LT_β, BU_α will be used thereafter. It is important to note that the proposal does not incur additional search cost even though the MR leaves the current network before the lifetime expires.

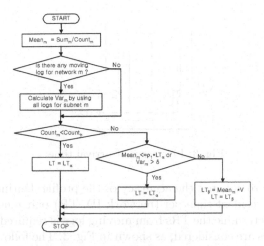

Fig. 2. Adaptive lifetime determination algorithm

Adaptive Lifetime Determination Algorithm: Generally, a vehicle such as bus, train etc. arrives, stays, and leaves each network very regularly. Although there is a little difference among the visits in each network, arrival and departure time are almost same. Using these values, MR's mobility type can be determined.

At fist, When a MR leaves a network, information (a moving log) about the visit is recorded. The log contains an ordered triplet (1, AT, DT) that represents location identifier, arrival time, and departure time. The resident time (t_n) for the n-th visit is computed by simply subtracting AT_n from DT_n. If $t_n < \rho_1 * LT_\alpha$, this log excludes a moving log of which the resident time is very short. Here, ρ_1 is a constant (≥ 1) and $\rho_1 * LT_\alpha$ is a threshold value to determine whether a current moving log is meaningful. t_n adds to total resident time (Sum_m) and total number of visits $(Count_m)$ increases by 1.

LT_β is periodically calculated using the average resident time and the frequency of logs. An Adaptive lifetime (LT_β) algorithm is described in Fig. 2. In the algorithm, the variance rate as well as the average resident time $(Mean_m)$ is considered. To quantify the degree of accuracy of the profile, the variance (Var_m) is calculated for all networks as follows:

$$Var_m = \frac{1}{n} \sum_{i=1}^{n} (t_i - Mean_m)^2 \qquad (1)$$

If the number of visits to network m is less than a constant value $(Count_b)$, LT_α will be used since network m may not give a reliable information from moving logs. If Var_m is greater than constant δ or $Mean_m$ less than $\rho_1 * LT_\alpha$, LT_α will also be used; otherwise, the LT_β is calculated by multiplying the mean resident time by the constant V, and then, it is used as the lifetime for BU, when the MR visits network m after creating the profile.

In addition the resident time for some networks often depends on the arrival time. Based on this observation, we also take into account the time region (TR)

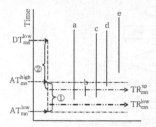

Fig. 3. Five cases of arrival time

of the arrival time to enhance the accuracy of the profile. During periodic calculations, the mean resident time per (network ID, TR) pair must be considered. An algorithm to determine the TRs from moving logs is required for the purpose. Five different cases are considered, as shown in Fig. 3. The following information is also maintained in the profile per TR:

- AT_{mn}^{high} : the highest (or latest) arrival time
- AT_{mn}^{low} : the lowest (or earliest) arrival time
- DT_{mn}^{low} : the lowest (or earliest) departure time
- $Count_{mn}$: the number of visits included in TR_{mn}
- $TotalCount_{mn}$: the total number of visits considered in TR_{mn}
- TR_{mn}^{up} : the upper boundary of the TR_{mn}
- TR_{mn}^{low} : the lower boundary of the TR_{mn}

where subscriptions n and m represent n-th TR to network m. Since the TR is considered along with the visiting network, each TR_{mn} maintains its visiting number ($TotalCount_{mn}$, $Count_{mn}$) separately. These values are used algorithm to determine mobility type in Figs. 3 and 4.

In Fig. 3, the first and the second vertical dotted lines represent the arrival time interval($Interval_{mn}^{AT}$) and resident time interval ($Interval_{mn}^{RT}$), respectively, which are calculated as shown in Fig. 4. The solid lines present the current visiting time in Fig. 3. In the case of Fig. 3(e), it is natural to exclude a new visit from the arrival TR_{mn}.

The visits in Figs. 3(a) or 3(b) require to verification as to whether the MR resides too long or too briefly in the network. If the resident time (t_{mn}) is longer than $\frac{1}{2} \times \rho_2 \times Interval_{mn}^{RT}$ and shorter than $\frac{3}{2} \times \rho_2 \times Interval_{mn}^{RT}$, the current visiting log is used in periodic calculations since it can provide reliable information; otherwise, the log is completely excluded (Fig. 3(b)). Here, ρ_2 is a constant ($0 < \rho_2 \leq 2$).

At first glace, Figs. 3(c) and 3(d) initially appear to be similar cases. However, if two cases are considered, the TR_{mn} does not provide useful information. Thus, the process is required for an accurate determination. If AT of the visit is greater than TR_{mn}^{low} and less than TR_{mn}^{up}, the log includes the TR_{mn} and both $Count_{mn}$ and $TotalCount_{mn}$ increase by 1 since this variable will be used to determine the accuracy of the profile (Fig. 3(c)); otherwise, the case shown in Fig. 3(d), excluded and only $TotalCount_{mn}$ increases by 1. It will be used to form another

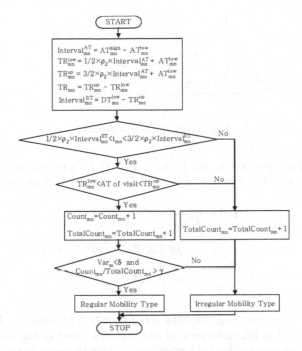

Fig. 4. Mobility type determination algorithm

arrival TR. After arrival TRs are determined by means of this method, the comparisons between $\frac{Count_{mn}}{TotalCount_{mn}}$ and Var_m are both required to evaluate the usefulness of the information regarding the TR. In other words, if Var_m is smaller than δ and $\frac{Count_{mn}}{TotalCount_{mn}}$ is larger than γ, the TR_{mn} is classified as *Regular Mobility Type*; otherwise, it is classified as *Irregular Mobility type*(see Fig. 4). In the above comparison, it is assumed δ and γ have proper constant values, respectively .

3   Performance Analysis

Simulation Scenario: The simulation scenario for the schemes is depicted in Fig. 5. Each MR collects log data that contain (l, AT_n, DT_n) whenever it leaves a visited network. It is assumed that the resident time at any network follows gamma distribution [7] with shape parameter α. As it is generally known, gamma distribution is selected because it can be shaped to represent various distributions as well as measured data that cannot be characterized by a particular distribution.

Equations (2), (3), and (4) describe the density function for resident time, the mean resident time at a visited network and the variance for the resident time distribution, respectively, where t is the resident time at each visited network. It is important to note, however, that the resident time follows an exponential

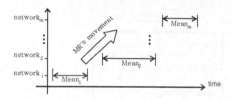

Fig. 5. Simulation scenario

distribution where parameter $\alpha=1$, $\lambda = 1/E(t)$ in gamma distribution. The results are shown as the amount of bandwidth allocated by those messages.

$$f(t) = \frac{\lambda^\alpha}{\Gamma(\alpha)}(\lambda t)^{\alpha-1}e^{-\lambda t}, t \geq 0 \tag{2}$$

$$E(t) = \frac{\alpha}{\lambda} \tag{3}$$

$$V(t) = \frac{\alpha}{\lambda^2} \tag{4}$$

All parameters of our experiments are presented in table 1. The constant parameters defined in previous section are first described in the table where ρ_1, ρ_2 and $Count_b$ are used to check whether to consider the current movement log or not, and δ and γ to determine mobility type of the network. V mean the weight value for the calculated lifetime of regular mobility type. The disconnection rate (ζ) is set 0.001 but scarcely affects overall performance since the proposed schemes and NEMO treat disconnection in the same manner.

Table 1. Parameter Settings

parameter	value	meaning
ρ_1	2	constant (≥ 1)
ρ_2	2	constant ($0<\rho_2\leq 2$)
$Count_b$	10	threshold of Count
δ	10	constant to determine mobility type
γ	0.8	constant of $\frac{Count_{mn}}{TotalCount_{mn}}$
V	1.0	constant for variance
κ	0.3	intra-domain moving rate
ζ	0.001	disconnection rate

The Results: In Eqs. (5) and (6), BW_{NEMO} and BW_{PRO} mean the amounts of the allocated bandwidth for BUs in NEMO and the proposed scheme (PRO), respectively. $Size_{BU}$ is defined as the size of a BU (88bytes=IPv6 header (40bytes)+ Binding Update Extension Header(28bytes)+Mobile Network Prefix Option 20bytes)) [4][8]. f_{HA} is denoted as the BU emission frequency from the MR to its HA and f_{CN} is the average BU emission frequency from the MR to its CNs. When a MR migrates, κ represents the intra-domain moving rate. The

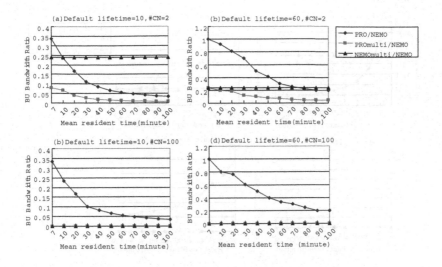

Fig. 6. Comparison of BU bandwidth in gamma distribution

MR transmits M consecutive BUs to its external CNs, and transmits another BU to its HA, receiving a BA from HA.

$$BW_{NEMO} = Size_{BU} \times \{\kappa \times (f_{CN} \times (\sharp CN + 1) + f_{HA})$$
$$+(1 - \kappa) \times (M \times \sharp CN + 2)\} \qquad (5)$$

$$BW_{PRO} = Size_{BU} \times \{\kappa \times f_{PRO} \times (\sharp CN + 1)$$
$$+(1 - \kappa) \times (M \times \sharp CN + 2)\} \qquad (6)$$

$$BW_{NEMOmulti} = Size_{BU} \times f_{NEMOmulti} \qquad (7)$$

$$BW_{PROmulti} = Size_{BU} \times f_{PROmulti} \qquad (8)$$

In Eq. (5), #CN is the number of the current CNs which are not on the MR's home network. When a MR migrates along networks, it transmits a BU to each CN and to its HA equal to f_{CN} and f_{HA}. In Eq. (6), if the profile information proposed in this paper can be used, the refreshment frequency may be reduced to f_{PRO}. In Eqs. (7) and (8), $BW_{NEMOmulti}$ and $BW_{PROmulti}$ show the amounts of the allocated bandwidth for multicast delivery of BUs in NEMO and PRO. Multicast refreshment frequency in NEMO and PRO are $f_{NEMOmulti}$ and $f_{PROmulti}$, respectively.

Figures 6 and 7 represent the comparison between the existing schemes (NEMO, NEMOmulti)and the proposed schemes (PRO, PROmulti) in gamma and an exponential distribution where the mean resident time varies from 7 to 100 minutes and variance is set to 0.01. When LT_α is set to 10 and 60 seconds, #CN is set to 2 and 100, respectively. It is assumed that a MR migrates as

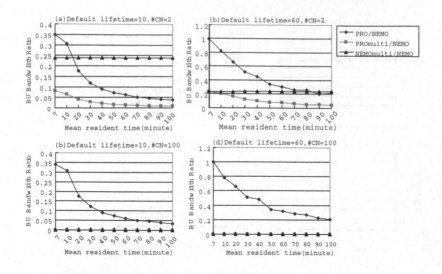

Fig. 7. Comparison of BU bandwidth in exponential distribution

regular mobility type in 30% of the all networks recorded in the profile, irregular mobility type in the remaining 70%. BU bandwidth depends on #CN, f_{HA}, f_{CN}, f_{PRO}, $f_{NEMOmulti}$, and $f_{PROmulti}$.

Since the behaviors of the BU bandwidth are almost same, when variance is 0.01 and 0.1, Fig. 6 represents the results where variance is 0.01. In Figs. 6(a) and 6(b), $\frac{PRO}{NEMO}$ decreases as the mean resident time increases. In the case of mean resident time=50 in Fig. 6(a), PRO requires only 7% of messages that NEMO needs. As the mean resident time increases, $\frac{NEMOmulti}{NEMO}$ shows a fixed value but $\frac{PROmulti}{NEMO}$ decreases near to 0 since only PROmulti is benefited from the profile. Figures 6(c) and 6(d) show the results when LT_α is set to 60 seconds. In the figures, $\frac{PRO}{NEMO}$ decreases less than that in Figs. 6(a) and 6(b). This indicates that the BU bandwidth ratio is affected by the longer LT_α. Namely, the amount of BU for all schemes generated much less than that in Figs. 6(a) and 6(b) as the result of that the lifetime of BU is set long.

Thus, we come to know that bandwidth usage in the PRO is the more efficient than the NEMO from Fig. 6. The reason is that existing schemes transmits BUs its CNs whenever the default lifetime expires, whereas the PRO only transmits the BUs to refresh time when LT_β expires. That is, this results from that LT_β is lengthened more than default lifetime in NEMO if a long resident time is computed for the current location from the profile. There may be differences between the computed lifetime and real resident time. In spite of this, the level of reduced bandwidth is substantial, in networks where MRs are determined as consisting mainly of regular mobility type. In particular, when a MR does not migrate across domains frequently, most of the signaling load is generated by the refreshing BUs. The central improvements proposed in this paper, are achieved by decreasing the number of periodic refreshing BUs.

Figure 7 also represents the comparison between existing schemes and the proposed schemes in an exponential distribution where the mean resident time varies from 7 to 100 minutes. The behaviors of BU bandwidth ratio in Fig. 7 is almost same with those in Fig. 6. That is, the function of the resident time distribution rarely has an influence on the overall performance. It is important to note here that the mean resident time can be much longer than LT_α in reality in case of the MR has a regular mobility type. The MRs, therefore, will only transmit a small number of messages. Although the MR migrates regular, the default mechanism in NEMO will be used and thus there is little additional overhead. Thus, the efficiency of the proposed schemes can improve over the results presented in this paper.

4   Conclusion

In this paper, binding update schemes on the basis of mobility type are proposed to support efficient network mobility. By capturing some regularity in movement patterns of each MR, this approach can reduce the amount of the overhead incurred by frequent binding updates, all without exposing nodes to significant new vulnerabilities. From the MR's resident time at visited networks, the adaptive lifetime is determined dynamically. As its primary purpose is to reduce signaling, it can be used in NEMO to assist in reducing the frequency of care-of tests and expand the applicability of the solution, to provide both reduced signaling and reduced latency upon movements. However, we still have to dig further at the correctness of the profile and ascertain the effects of each parameter through data mining algorithms since our scheme are based on local profiles.

References

1. Lamsal, P.: Network Mobility:
   https://www.cs.helsinki.fi/u/kraatika/Courses/IPsem04s/nemo.pdf
2. Nikander, P., Arkko, J., Aura, T., Montenegro, G., Nordmark, E.: Mobile IP Version 6 Route Optimization Security Design Background, RFC 4225 (2005)
3. Ng, C., Thubert, P., Ohnishi, H., Paik, E.: Taxonomy of Route Optimization models in the NEMO Context. IETF Internet Draft, draft-thubert-nemo-ro-taxonomy-04.txt (2005)
4. Devarapalli, V., Wakikawa, R., Petrescu, A., Thubert, P.: Network Mobility (NEMO) Basic Support Protocol, RFC 3963 (2005)
5. Arkko, J., Vogt, C.: Credit-Based Authorization for Binding Lifetime Extension, draft-arkko-mipv6-binding-lifetime-extension-00 (2004)
6. Johnson, B., Perkins, C., Arkko, J.: Mobility Support in IPv6, RFC 3775 (2004)
7. Lin, Y.B., Lai, W.R., Chen, R.J.: Performance Analysis for Dual Band PCS Networks. IEEE Journal on Trans. on Computers 49(2), 148–159 (2000)
8. Soliman, H., Castellucia, C., Malki, K.E., Bellier, L.: Hierarchical MIPv6 mobility management (HMIPv6), RFC 4140 (2005)

An Information Aggregation Scheme of Multi-node in Ubiquitous Sensor Networks

Haeryong Park[1,*], Seongan Lim[2], Ikkwon Yie[2], Hyun Kim[1],
Kilsoo Chun[1], and Jaeil Lee[1]

[1] KISA (Korea Information Security Agency),
78, Garak-Dong, Songpa-Gu, Seoul, Korea, 138-803
{hrpark,hkim,kschun,jilee}@kisa.or.kr
[2] Department of Mathematics, Inha University,
Incheon, Korea, 402-751
{seongannym,ikyie}@inha.ac.kr

Abstract. Mobile networking, mobile systems and applications and ubiquitous computing infrastructures are of strongly growing importance in the IT sector in general, and for the parallel and distributed computing community. Particularly, when an signed(authenticated) information of multi-node is aggregated in ubiquitous sensor networks, the number of the signing information is very small. Thus, signature scheme which signs information has strong unforgeability. In 2005 Yu and Chen proposed threshold signature scheme [12]. Their scheme has a high efficiency. But, their scheme is not suitable for ubiquitous sensor networks because their scheme has no strong unforgeability. In this paper, we modify their scheme so that modified scheme is suitable for ubiquitous sensor networks. Also, our scheme has a good efficiency, and a smaller secret key than other cryptosystems with a similar security level.

1 Introduction

Mobile networking, mobile systems and applications and ubiquitous computing infrastructures are of strongly growing importance in the IT sector in general, and particularly for the parallel and distributed computing community. Mobile internet access has become a commonplace service. Many conventional software products such as e-mail systems, databases, or enterprise resource planning have been adapted towards mobile usage patterns. The world of ubiquitous information processing will soon be revolutionizing our day-to-day routines. Major components are sensor networks, radio frequency identification technology, and whole new layers of data management assembling their low-level signals to high-level knowledge. While there has been tremendous progress during the last decade in the networking sector and at the mobile computing software level, many challenging research and development issues remain. Examples include the optimization of mobile communication channels, the automated planning of scalable mobile

---

* Corresponding author.

P. Thulasiraman et al. (Eds.): ISPA 2007 Workshops, LNCS 4743, pp. 60–68, 2007.

networks or the inherent support of ad-hoc routing and computing. For parallel and distributed processing, these trends also mean that new, more flexible techniques of accessing global grid infrastructures are becoming available. However, mobile systems are not only access technologies but can also build the core of loosely-coupled parallel processing scenarios, even in an ad-hoc fashion. Moreover, the whole area of ubiquitous computing will yield a tremendous increase of information, for example based on the output of thousands of sensors, challenging the capacity of parallel processing architectures at the higher layers.

Elliptic Curve Cryptosystem. The opportunity to conveniently use elliptic curve cryptosystems within commercial applications is only now becoming a reality. There are however many issues to consider when making the choice between an application based on an elliptic curve cryptosystem and one based on RSA. We have found some of the issues (security, performance, standards and interoperability) that are perhaps most pertinent when making such a choice. However, the comparisons are made under the premise that an elliptic curve cryptosystem with 160 bits key offers the same security as RSA with 1024 bits key. Thus, signature scheme based on elliptic curve cryptosystem instead of RSA signature scheme is mainly used in wireless networking environment because of this advantage. Furthermore, this signature can be used in Ubiquitous Sensor Networks.

Threshold Cryptosystem. The notion of secret sharing scheme [8] was introduced by Shamir in 1979. Secret sharing can be used for the distribution of a sensitive information among different nodes. The drawback of this solution is the failure for the reconstruction. To solve this problem the notion of threshold cryptosystems was suggested, most notably by Desmedt and Frankel [4] in 1989. A threshold $t < n$ is set, such that more than t nodes are required to cooperate to retrieve a sensitive information while the cooperation of no more than t nodes will find no information about a sensitive information. Note that secret sharing scheme and threshold cryptosystem are parallel and distributed processing.

Strong Unforgeability. Very recently, Boneh et al. introduced the security notion "strong unforgeability" that means unforgeability of another valid signatures of any message, including m, when a valid signature of m is given [2]. Particularly, when an signed(authenticated) information of multi-node is aggregated in ubiquitous sensor networks, the number of the signing information is very small. We consider sensor network detects a water level(low, middle, high) of the river. When a water level is a high, if attacker $\mathcal{A}$ forge the low level information by using the low level signatures which multi-node signed, then it may result in many the killed and the injured. Thus, signature scheme which signs information in ubiquitous sensor networks has strong unforgeability.

Our Result. Recently, Yu and Chen proposed the (t, n) threshold signature scheme using the short secret key characteristic and good efficiency characteristic of the elliptic curve cryptosystem. Their scheme has a high efficiency. But, their scheme is not suitable for ubiquitous sensor networks because their scheme has no strong unforgeability. In this paper, we modify their scheme so that modified scheme is suitable for ubiquitous sensor networks. Also, we prove the security of our scheme.

The remainder of this paper is structured as follows. In Section 2 we review the Yu-Chen's threshold signature scheme. In section 3, we analyze Yu-Chen's scheme. In section 4, we modify their scheme so that modified scheme is suitable for ubiquitous sensor networks. Section 5 offers security analysis of our scheme. In section 6, we offer the performance analysis of our scheme. Finally, Section 7 is a conclusion.

2 Review of Yu-Chen's Threshold Signature Scheme

In this section, we review Yu-Chen's threshold signature scheme. Yu-Chen's scheme consists of two system setup steps(**Setup, KeyGen**) and four signature steps(**IndSignGen, VerIndSign, SignGen, VerSign**). Suppose in **IndSignGen** step, there is a subgroup that needs to sign message m and consists of $U_1, U_2, \cdots, U_t(t$ nodes of n nodes). Yu-Chen's scheme is as follows:

Setup. The trust party $\mathcal{CA}$ chooses a large prime number p and a base point $G \in E(GF(p))$ with prime order N. The $\mathcal{CA}$ chooses one-way hash function $h : \{0,1\}^* \to Z_N$ and publishes p, N, G and h.

KeyGen. The $\mathcal{CA}$ chooses t random numbers $a_i(i = 0, 1, \ldots, t-1)$ and generates $f(x) = a_{t-1}x^{t-1} + \cdots + a_1 x + a_0 \bmod N$ where $a_i \in Z_N$ is a random integer. The $\mathcal{CA}$ computes the group secret key $f(0) = a_0$ and secret key $f(x_j)$ of individual node U_j. The $\mathcal{CA}$ chooses n integers $x_1, x_2, \cdots, x_n$ in Z_N and computes:

$$Y = f(0)G, \ X = -Y, \ Y_j = f(x_j)G, \ X_j = -Y_j$$

The $\mathcal{CA}$ publishes X and X_j. The $\mathcal{CA}$ sends $f(x_j)$ and x_i $(i = 1, 2 \cdots, n)$ securely to individual node U_j $(j = 1, 2 \cdots, n)$. Also, the $\mathcal{CA}$ sends x_i $(i = 1, 2, \cdots, n)$ to the dealer node.

IndSignGen. Each node U_i uses his secret key $f(x_i)$ and a random integer k_i $(1 \le k_i \le N - 1)$ to compute his signature (r_i, s_i) for message m:

$$R_i = (x_{R_i}, y_{R_i}) = k_i G, \ r_i = x_{R_i} \bmod N,$$
$$r_i s_i = k_i + f(x_i)\Delta_i h(m) \bmod N, \text{ where } \Delta_i = \prod_{j=1, j \neq i}^{t} \frac{-x_j}{x_i - x_j}.$$

Node U_i sends his individual digital signature (r_i, s_i) and R_i to the dealer node.

VerIndSign. After receiving all digital signatures (r_i, s_i) of U_i $(i = 1, 2, \cdots, t)$, the dealer node uses the following equation to verify the validity of each individual signature.

$$D_i = (x_{D_i}, y_{D_i}) = r_i s_i G + h(m)\Delta_i X_i,$$
$$d_i = x_{D_i} \bmod N$$

Check whether $d_i = r_i$ is satisfied. If yes, then (r_i, s_i) on message m is a valid signature of U_i. Otherwise, the signature is invalid and the secretary sends an error message to U_i.

SignGen. The dealer node computes and publishes the signature (r, s) and (r_i, s_i) $(i = 1, 2, \cdots, t)$ on message m:

$$R = \sum_{i=1}^{t} R_i = (x_R, y_R),$$
$$r = x_R \bmod N, \ s = \sum_{i=1}^{t} r_i s_i \bmod N$$

VerSign. The verifier of (r, s) and (r_i, s_i) $(i = 1, 2, \cdots, t)$ calculates the following equation:

$$S = \sum_{i=1}^{t} r_i s_i \bmod N$$

Then, the verifier determines whether $S = s$ is satisfied. If no, the signature is invalid. Otherwise, the following equation is calculated:

$$Q = (x_Q, y_Q) = sG + h(m)X, \ q = x_Q \bmod N$$

Then, the verifier determines whether $q = r$ is satisfied. If satisfied, (r, s) is a valid signature for message m. Otherwise, the signature is invalid.

3 Cryptanalysis of Yu-Chen's Threshold Signature Scheme

In this section, we analyze Yu-Chen's threshold signature scheme. In particular, we describe two strong unforgeability attacks for Yu-Chen's scheme.

[Attack 1]
Suppose that an attacker $\mathcal{A}$ has R_i $(i = 1, 2, \cdots, t)$ and a valid signature on message m, that is, (r, s) and (r_i, s_i) for $i = 1, 2, \cdots, t$. In this case, the dealer node can be an attacker $\mathcal{A}$.

Step 1. $\mathcal{A}$ chooses t numbers $k_i' \in Z_n$ for $i = 1, 2, \cdots, t$. $\mathcal{A}$ computes:

$$R_i' = R_i + k_i'G = (x_{R_i'}, y_{R_i'}), \ r_i' = x_{R_i'} \bmod N,$$
$$r_i's_i' = k_i' + r_i s_i \bmod N$$

Step 2. $\mathcal{A}$ computes:

$$R' = \sum_{i=1}^{t} R_i' = \sum_{i=1}^{t} k_i G + \sum_{i=1}^{t} k_i'G = (x_{R'}, y_{R'}),$$
$$s' = \sum_{i=1}^{t} r_i's_i' \bmod N, \ r' = x_{R'} \bmod N$$

$\mathcal{A}$ generates a valid signature of m, that is, (r', s') and (r_i', s_i') $(i = 1, 2, \cdots, t)$.

Verification. The following equations are satisfied:
$S = \sum_{i=1}^{t} r_i's_i' \bmod N = s'$,

$$Q = (x_Q, y_Q) = s'G + h(m)X = (\sum_{i=1}^{t} r_i' s_i')G + h(m)X$$
$$= \sum_{i=1}^{t}(k_i' + k_i + f(x_i)\Delta_i h(m))G + h(m)X$$
$$= \sum_{i=1}^{t}(k_i' + k_i)G + \sum_{i=1}^{t} f(x_i)\Delta_i h(m)G - f(0)h(m)G$$
$$= (\sum_{i=1}^{t}(k_i' + k_i))G + f(0)h(m)G - f(0)h(m)G = R'.$$

Thus $q = x_Q \bmod N = x_{R'} \bmod N = r'$.

[Attack 2]

Suppose that an attacker $\mathcal{A}$ has a valid signature on message m, that is, (r, s), and (r_i, s_i) $(i = 1, 2, \cdots, t)$. In this case, all entities except for $\mathcal{CA}$ can be an attacker $\mathcal{A}$.

Step 1. $\mathcal{A}$ chooses t random numbers $l_i \in Z_n$ with $\sum_{i=1}^{t} l_i \bmod N = 0$ $(i = 1, 2, \cdots, t)$. $\mathcal{A}$ computes $s_i' = s_i + r_i^{-1} l_i \bmod N$, that is, $r_i s_i' = r_i s_i + l_i \bmod N$. $\mathcal{A}$ generates a valid signature of m, that is, (r, s) and (r_i, s_i') $(i = 1, 2, \cdots, t)$.

Verification. The following equation is satisfied:
$$S = \sum_{i=1}^{t} r_i s_i' \bmod N = \sum_{i=1}^{t} r_i s_i + \sum_{i=1}^{t} l_i \bmod N$$
$$= \sum_{i=1}^{t} r_i s_i \bmod N = s,$$
$$Q = (x_Q, y_Q) = sG + h(m)X = (\sum_{i=1}^{t} r_i s_i')G + h(m)X$$
$$= (\sum_{i=1}^{t} k_i + f(x_i)\Delta_i h(m) + l_i)G + h(m)X$$
$$= (\sum_{i=1}^{t} k_i)G + (\sum_{i=1}^{t} f(x_i)\Delta_i h(m))G + (\sum_{i=1}^{t} l_i)G - f(0)h(m)G$$
$$= \sum_{i=1}^{t} k_i G + f(0)h(m)G - f(0)h(m)G = \sum_{i=1}^{t} k_i G = R.$$

Thus $q = x_Q \bmod N = x_R \bmod N = r$.

4 Proposed Information Aggregation Scheme

In this section, we propose information aggregation scheme. Our scheme consists of two system setup steps(**Setup**, **KeyGen**) and four signature steps (**IndSignGen**, **VerIndSign**, **SignGen**, **VerSign**). Suppose in **IndSignGen** step, there is a subgroup that needs to sign message m and consists of $U_1, U_2, \cdots, U_t$ (t nodes of n nodes). Our scheme is as follows:

Setup. The $\mathcal{CA}$ chooses a large prime number p and a base point $G \in E(GF(p))$ with prime order N. The $\mathcal{CA}$ chooses one-way hash function $h : \{0, 1\}^* \to Z_N$ and publishes p, N, G and h.

KeyGen. The $\mathcal{CA}$ chooses t random numbers a_i $(i = 0, 1, \ldots, t-1)$ and generates $f(x) = a_{t-1}x^{t-1} + \cdots + a_1 x + a_0 \bmod N$ where $a_i \in Z_N$ is a random integer. The $\mathcal{CA}$ computes the group secret key $f(0) = a_0$ and secret key $f(x_j)$ of individual node U_j. The $\mathcal{CA}$ chooses n integers $x_1, x_2, \cdots, x_n$ in Z_N and computes:

$$Y = f(0)^{-1}G, \quad X = f(0)G, \quad Y_j = f(x_j)^{-1}G, \quad X_j = f(x_j)G$$

The $\mathcal{CA}$ publishes Y, X, Y_j and X_j $(j = 1, 2 \ldots, n)$. The $\mathcal{CA}$ sends $f(x_j)$ and x_i $(i = 1, 2 \ldots, n)$ securely to individual node U_j $(j = 1, 2 \ldots, n)$. Also, the $\mathcal{CA}$ sends x_i $(i = 1, 2, \cdots, n)$ to the dealer node.

IndSignGen. Each member U_i uses his secret key $f(x_i)$ and a random integer k_i $(1 \le k_i \le N - 1)$ to compute his signature (r_i, s_i) for message m:

$$R_i = (x_{R_i}, y_{R_i}) = k_i G, \; r_i = x_{R_i} \bmod N,$$
$$r_i s_i = k_i f(x_i) + f(x_i)^2 \Delta_i h(m) \bmod N$$

Member U_i sends his individual digital signature (r_i, s_i) and R_i to the dealer node.

VerIndSign. After receiving all digital signatures (r_i, s_i) of U_i $(i = 1, 2, \cdots, t)$, the dealer node uses the following equation to verify the validity of the signature.

$$D_i = (x_{D_i}, y_{D_i}) = r_i s_i Y_i - \Delta_i h(m) X_i,$$
$$d_i = x_{D_i} \bmod N$$

Check whether $d_i = r_i$ is satisfied. If yes, then (r_i, s_i) on message m is a valid signature of U_i. Otherwise, the signature is invalid and the dealer node sends an error message to U_i.

SignGen. The dealer node computes and publishes the signature (r, s) and (r_i, s_i) $(i = 1, 2, \cdots, t)$ on message m:

$$R = \sum_{i=1}^{t} R_i = (x_R, y_R),$$
$$r = x_R \bmod N, \; s = \sum_{i=1}^{t} r_i s_i Y_i$$

VerSign. The verifier of (r, s) and (r_i, s_i) $(i = 1, 2, \cdots, t)$ calculates the following equation:

$$S = \sum_{i=1}^{t} r_i s_i Y_i$$

Then, the verifier determines whether $S = s$ is satisfied. If no, the signature is invalid. Otherwise, the following equation is calculated:

$$Q = (x_Q, y_Q) = s - h(m)X, \; q = x_Q \bmod N$$

Then, the verifier determines whether $q = r$ is satisfied. If satisfied, (r, s) is a valid signature for message m. Otherwise, the signature is invalid.

VerIndSign Correctness
$$
\begin{aligned}
D_i &= (x_{D_i}, y_{D_i}) = r_i s_i Y_i - \Delta_i h(m) X_i \\
&= (k_i f(x_i) + f(x_i)^2 \Delta_i h(m)) Y_i - \Delta_i h(m) X_i \\
&= k_i G + f(x_i) \Delta_i h(m) G - \Delta_i h(m) X_i \\
&= k_i G + \Delta_i h(m) X_i - \Delta_i h(m) X_i = k_i G = R_i
\end{aligned}
$$

VerSign Correctness
$$
\begin{aligned}
Q &= (x_Q, y_Q) = s - h(m)X \\
&= \sum_{i=1}^{t} (k_i f(x_i) + f(x_i)^2 \Delta_i h(m)) Y_i - h(m)X \\
&= \sum_{i=1}^{t} (k_i G + f(x_i) \Delta_i h(m) G) - h(m)X \\
&= \sum_{i=1}^{t} k_i G + \sum_{i=1}^{t} f(x_i) \Delta_i h(m) G - h(m)X \\
&= \sum_{i=1}^{t} k_i G + h(m)X - h(m)X = \sum_{i=1}^{t} k_i G = R
\end{aligned}
$$

5 Security Analysis of Our Scheme

In this section, we describe the security analysis of our scheme. Our scheme is secure against a group secret key recovery attack, forgery attack for individual signature, and our two attacks in section 3.

Attack 1. The attacker $\mathcal{A}$ adopts a group secret key recovery attack. $\mathcal{A}$ can obtain the group public key $X = f(0)G$. To succeed this attack $\mathcal{A}$ must obtain the group secret key $f(0)$ from X. But, it is impossible because it means to solve the ECDLP problem.

Attack 2. The attacker $\mathcal{A}$ (the dealer node) adopts an attack to generate a valid individual signature. $\mathcal{A}$ chooses a random number $k_i \in Z_N$ and $R_i = (x_{R_i}, y_{R_i}) = k_i G$. Then $\mathcal{A}$ computes $r_i = x_{R_i} \bmod N$. To compute $r_i s_i$ $\mathcal{A}$ must obtain $f(x_i)$ from $X_i = f(x_i)G$. However, it is impossible because it means to solve the ECDLP problem.

Attack 3. The attacker $\mathcal{A}$ (the dealer node) knows a valid signature with R_i and (r_i, s_i) $(i = 1, 2, \cdots, t)$, and tries to attack by modifying R_i and (r_i, s_i) $(i = 1, 2, \cdots, t)$. $\mathcal{A}$ chooses a random number $k_i' \in Z_n$ and computes $R_i' = R_i + k_i'G = k_i G + k_i'G = (x_{R_i'}, y_{R_i'})$, $r_i' = x_{R_i'} \bmod N$. To generate $r_i's_i'$ $\mathcal{A}$ must compute $k_i'f(x_i) \bmod N$. But, it is impossible because $\mathcal{A}$ does not know $f(x_i)$.

Attack 4. The attacker $\mathcal{A}$ adopts our attack [Attack 2] for Yu-Chen's scheme. $\mathcal{A}$ must choose t numbers $l_i \in Z_N$ with $\sum_{i=1}^{t} l_i f(x_i) \bmod N = 0$, because $s = \sum_{i=1}^{t}(r_i s_i)Y_i = \sum_{i=1}^{t}(r_i s_i + l_i)Y_i = \sum_{i=1}^{t}(r_i s_i)Y_i + \sum_{i=1}^{t} l_i Y_i$ is satisfied. However, it is impossible because $\mathcal{A}$ does not know $f(x_i)(i = 1, 2, \cdots, t)$.

6 Performance Analysis of Our Scheme

The **SignGen** and **VerSign** of our scheme need not the multiplication inverse operation. Thus, the performance for the **SignGen** and **VerSign** of our scheme is superior to that of more ElGamal signature scheme and the DSA signature scheme. Though most of the current digital signature schemes are built on the RSA signature scheme or ElGamal signature scheme, our scheme is built on the elliptic curve discrete logarithm problem. Our scheme requires only 160 bits to achieve the same level of security as an RSA with 1024 bits key. As signature scheme based on elliptic curve discrete logarithm problem is compared with RSA signature scheme or ElGamal signature scheme, advantages of our scheme on the similar security level are short secret key, small memory space, and fast operating speed. Thus, our scheme is suitable for ubiquitous sensor networks. To analyze the performance of our scheme, the definitions are as follows:

- T_H : The time cost of the hash function operation.
- T_I : The time cost of modulus opposite element operation.
- T_M : The time cost of executing modulus operation.
- T_{EM} : The time cost of elliptic curve multiplication operation.
- T_{EA} : The time cost of elliptic curve addition operation.

If our scheme has 160-bits prime number p and N, in [5] the time complexity is evident in the following relationship:

$$T_{EA} \approx 0.12 \; T_M, \; T_{EM} \approx 29 \; T_M$$

Time complexity of our scheme is as shown in Table 1. Because integer addition and multiplication operation are low time complexity, total time complexity does not contain their time complexity.

Table 1. Time complexity of our scheme

Items	Time complexity	Rough estimation
Our scheme signature generation	$(3t+1)T_M + tT_I$ $+(t+1)T_H + (3t-2)T_{EA}$	$(119.36t + 0.76)T_M$ $+tT_I + (t+1)T_H$
Our scheme signature verification	$(t+1)T_{EM} + tT_{EA}$ $+T_H + T_M$	$(29.12t + 30)T_M + T_H$

7 Conclusion

We reviewed Yu-Chen's (t,n) threshold signature scheme. Their scheme uses the short secret key characteristic and has a good efficiency characteristic of the elliptic curve cryptosystem. Thus, Their scheme has a high efficiency. But, their scheme is not suitable for ubiquitous sensor networks because their scheme has no strong unforgeability. We modified their scheme so that modified scheme is suitable for ubiquitous sensor networks. Also, we proved the security of our scheme.

Acknowledgments. This work was supported by MIC and the KRF Grant (KRF-2004-R03-10023) funded by the Korean Government(MOEHRD).

References

1. Beresford, A., Stajano, F.: Location Privacy in Pervasive Computing. In: IEEE Pervasive Computing 2003, pp. 46–55. IEEE Computer Society Press, Los Alamitos (2003)
2. Boneh, D., Shen, E., Waters, B.: Strongly Unforgeable Signatures on Computational Diffie-Hellman. In: Yung, M., Dodis, Y., Kiayias, A., Malkin, T.G. (eds.) PKC 2006. LNCS, vol. 3958, pp. 229–240. Springer, Heidelberg (2006)
3. Chen, T.S., Hsiao, T.C., Chen, T.L.: An efficient threshold group signature scheme. In: IEEE Region 10 Conference(TENCON), pp. 13–16. IEEE Computer Society Press, Los Alamitos (2004)
4. Desmedt, Y., Frankel, Y.: Threshold cryptosystems. In: Brassard, G. (ed.) CRYPTO 1989. LNCS, vol. 435, pp. 307–315. Springer, Heidelberg (1990)
5. Jurisic, A., Menezes, A.J.: Elliptic curves and cryptography, available from http://www.certicom.com

68   H. Park et al.

6. Robshaw, M., Yin, Y.: Elliptic Curve Cryptosystems. An RSA Laboratories Technical Note (1997)
7. Sarma, S., Weis, S., Engels, D.: RFID systems and security and privacy implications. In: Kaliski Jr., B.S., Koç, Ç.K., Paar, C. (eds.) CHES 2002. LNCS, vol. 2523, pp. 454–469. Springer, Heidelberg (2003)
8. Shamir, A.: How to share a secret. Communications of the ACM 22, 612–613 (1979)
9. Stajano, F.: Security fot Ubiquitous Computing. Halsted Press (2002)
10. Vanstone, S.A., Zuccherato, R.J.: Elliptic curve cryptosystems using curves of smooth order over the ring Z_n. IEEE Trans. on Information Theory 43(4), 1231–1237 (1997)
11. Weiser, M.: Some Computer Science Problems in Ubiquitous Computing. Communications of the ACM (1993)
12. Yu, Y.L., Chen, T.S.: An efficient threshold group signature scheme. The Journal of Applied Mathematics and Computation 167, 362–371 (2005)

QLP-LBS: Quantization and Location Prediction-Based LBS for Reduction of Location Update Costs*

In Kee Kim, Sung Ho Jang, and Jong Sik Lee

School of Computer Science and Information Engineering
Inha University
#253, Yonghyun-Dong, Nam-Ku,
Incheon 402-751, South Korea
md10002@naver.com, ho7809@hanmail.net, jslee@inha.ac.kr

Abstract. This paper proposes the QLP-LBS (Quantization and Location Prediction-based LBS). This QLP-LBS system is based on quantization theory and
uses statistical location prediction mechanism. This LBS applies the quantum
range of quantization theory to each mobile user and reduces location update
costs by comparing results between moving distance of mobile user and quantum range. But, this LBS system generates location errors from the quantization. In order to solve this problem, we apply statistical location prediction
mechanism to LBS system. This prediction mechanism predicts location of mobile user using its historical path and decrease location errors by quantization
and makes more reliable LBS system. For performance evaluation, this paper
measures location accuracy and reduction rate of location update costs with
various quantum ranges. This experiments show that QLP-LBS effectively reduces location update costs of LBS system. Also, QLP-LBS solves problem of
location errors using location prediction mechanism which is problem of general quantized system. Therefore, QLP-LBS is solution for reduction of location
update costs and has reliable location accuracy.

1 Introduction

Recently, the telematics [1]-based services have been strongly spread with the rapid
development of mobile technologies and growth of mobile industry. LBS (Location-
Based Services) [2], [3] is one of these services supplied by mobile service providers.
LBS gets real time locations of MUs (Mobile Users) and provides suitable service for
their location. In order to acquire locations of users, Location Server (LS) of LBS
needs a position reporting of users. This is position reporting frequency [3] which is
the location update process of LBS. In ideal LBS system, mobile station transmits
information of MUs' movement when they move to another location. However, due to
the limitation of Base Station (BS) processing and bandwidth of communication channel, reduction of location update is an important issue in mobile services like LBS.

---

* This research was supported the IITPA (Incheon Information Technology Industry Promotion
Agency), Korea, under the Complex terminal test & service technique development for air
distribution RFID equipment.

P. Thulasiraman et al. (Eds.): ISPA 2007 Workshops, LNCS 4743, pp. 69–76, 2007.

In this paper, we propose the QLP-LBS (Quantization and Location Prediction-based LBS) which effectively reduces location update cost. This LBS system uses a quantization theory [4] and statistical prediction mechanism for location estimation. To reduce location update cost, quantization-based LBS compares moving distance of MU with quantization range and it reduces location update from the compared result. However, quantization-based LBS generates location error according to the quantization. Thus, LBS can revise location error for providing services suitable for location of MU. QLP-LBS uses location prediction mechanism which analyzes historical path of MU and it also predicts MU's location when the location update reduces. In order to evaluate performance, we conducted two experiments. These experiments considered various mobility patterns of LBS users and the experiments were conducted in real university campus. First experiment was measuring reduction of location update cost in accordance with variation of quantization range. This experiment was to prove the effectiveness of reduction in location updates using quantization and to find the suitable threshold size for LBS system. Second experiment was to measure location accuracy of QLP-LBS. In this experiment, we used statistical prediction mechanism and this mechanism was to solve the problem of location error by using quantization.

2   LBS Based on Quantization with Location Prediction

2.1   Mobile User Modeling

To reduce the location updates, we need to observe mobility patterns of MU of LBS. We observe real movements of MUs in university campus. We used a satellite image of a university campus and this image was obtained from Google Earth™ [5]. And, for modeling of MU's movement, we simplified this image shown in Fig. 1 and it includes buildings, roads, parks, and parking lots.

$<R_1, R_2, \cdots, R_7>$ of Fig. 1 are roads. MUs on road are cars and people which move toward their destination. MUs, which use roads, walk or move using cars. Generally, they have their own destinations, but they changes roads or turn left or right through the pathway in order to go to their destination. Thus, pathway mobility model such as Manhattan mobility model [6] is suitable for modeling of MUs on roads. $<B_1, B_2, \cdots, B_8>$ are buildings. MUs in building (e.g. student) have various mobility patterns. Students in the class are in stop state. Some students could be talking to their friends and moving in random pattern. And, some students might be heading to classroom through the pathway. Thus, we must consider various mobility models and use stop state, random walk model [7], and Manhattan model with slow velocity for modeling of MUs in building. $<P_1, P_2, \cdots, P_4>$ are parking lots of the university campus. Most of MUs in parking lots are parked cars and their mobility states are stop state. $<P^*_1, P^*_2, \cdots, P^*_5>$ indicate parks. Random walk model is suitable for MUs in the park, because MUs moves randomly. And, PG is playground and has MUs of human type who are playing soccer or basketball. MUs in playground move within limited area with having their own path of direction. For an example, if people are playing soccer, they will be moving towards the ball. Their movement pattern is similar to GMM (Gaussian-Markov Model) [8]. GMM is mobility model for moving objects which move within a limited area with directions.

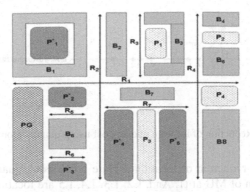

Fig. 1. Simplified map of University campus

As we described in above paragraph, MUs in LBS have various mobility patterns based on their whereabouts. Thus, consideration and usage of various mobility models are required to conduct practical experiment and proposing practical LBS system.

2.2 Quantization-Based Reduction of Location Update Cost

In the existing LBS system, the mobile state of MU transmits its location to BS according to its frequency rate. LS of LBS acquires location of MU from real time updates of location and provides services that are suitable for its location. However, if the number of MU is increased, then communication and computation overhead of both BS and LS will be increased. In this paper, we introduce quantization theory [4] to LBS system to reduce the location update cost.

Quantization theory [4] uses a discrete value that is divided by threshold (quantum range). If a value of real world is existed in an interval of particular threshold, threshold is considered as a quantized real value. Therefore, the quantized system transforms a continuous value/state into a discrete value/state. There is a component called quantizer [4] that trajectory of continuous real value/state converts into discrete value/state in computerized systems. Quantized system needs the threshold and it can change the output trajectory through the adjustment of threshold. In the case of large threshold, the variation of output trajectory after quantization is reduced. On the other hand, in the case of small threshold, output trajectory of quantizer is similar to variation of input trajectory. Therefore, if threshold is zero, both trajectory of input and output will be same.

This method applies quantum range called threshold to MU. If MU moves more than threshold, BS of LBS recognizes it as "movement." On the other hand, if MU moves within threshold, then BS regards MU as "stop" and does not transmit location update to LS. This quantization scheme effectively reduces location update costs in LBS. But, in this case, LBS system cannot pinpoint the exact location of MU therefore the location error will be generated.

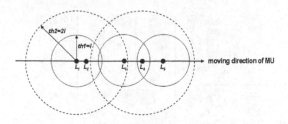

Fig. 2. Reduction of location update cost using quantization theory

Fig. 2 shows the reduction of location update costs using quantization theory. In Fig. 2, L1 is location of MU at t1. And, L2, L3, L4, L5 are location sequence of MU at t2, t3, t4, and t5. L1 is the start point of MU and L5 is the end point. Solid circle inside is th1 threshold and its size is l. Dotted circle is th2 and its size is 2l. If the threshold of LBS is set to th1, L2, location of MU at t2, is located within threshold of L1 and BS does not update location. If MU moves to point L3 at t3, it will be out of the threshold of L1. BS will report its location to LS and applies threshold to L3. If MU is moved to L4, it will be inside of threshold of L3 then L4 will not be updated. Now, if MU is moved to L5, it will go over the threshold of L3 and L5 will be updated. In the case when LBS set threshold to th2, which is greater than th1, locations of L1 and L4 will be updated and locations of L2, L3, and L5 will be ignored. Real moving path of MU is L1 → L2 → L3 → L4 → L5 and location update operation must be executed 5 times. When quantization-based LBS system set threshold th1, moving path of MU is L1 → L3 → L5 from at t1 to t5 and location update operation will be executed 3 times. If quantization-based LBS system set its threshold to th2, moving path of MU will be L1 → L4 and location update operation will be executed twice. As this example shows, threshold plays an important role to reduce the location update costs in LBS system. But, if quantization-based LBS set threshold th1, this LBS system cannot acquire locations of MU which are L2 and L4. And, if this LBS system set threshold to th2, the system cannot get the locations of MU located at L2, L3, and L5. Quantization-based LBS system generates location errors from quantization when location update operations are not executed. Location errors of quantized system are influenced by threshold size. When quantization-based LBS system uses small threshold size, number of location errors will be reduced since location of MU is frequently updated. If the threshold size is relatively large, location of MU will be less frequently updated and large number of location errors will be generated. Therefore, when LBS system uses quantization theory, LBS system must estimate the locations of MU that are not reported.

2.3 Location Prediction Mechanism

LS receives update signals which are filtered by quantizer. This quantization method is an effective way to reduce communication costs of LBS, but LBS cannot acquire exact location of MU. Thus, LS can estimate location of MU by using location predictor when location updates are filtered. In this paper, we predict location of MU using Brown's double exponential smoothing model [9].

$$P^{[1]}_{t+\Delta t} = (2+\alpha \cdot \Delta t/(1-\alpha))S^{[1]}_t - (1+\alpha \cdot \Delta t/(1-\alpha))S^{[2]}_t \qquad (1)$$

This double exponential smoothing is expressed in (1). $P^{[1]}$ is predicted result by double exponential smoothing and t is the current time and Δt is the time interval. If t_e is a prediction time, $\Delta t = t_e - t$. α is smoothing constant and generally has the value of $0 < \alpha < 1$. $S^{[1]}_t$ is the prediction result by single exponential smoothing model and P is the present data (e.g. direction of MU, x and y coordinate of MU). $S^{[1]}_t$ can be obtained by

$$S^{[1]}_t = \alpha \cdot P + (1-\alpha) \cdot S^{[1]}_{t-1} \qquad (2)$$

$S^{[2]}_t$ indicates double-smoothed statistic. And, $S^{[2]}_t$ can be obtained by

$$S^{[2]}_t = \alpha \cdot S^{[1]}_t + (1-\alpha) \cdot S^{[2]}_{t-1} \qquad (3)$$

The prediction accuracy is affected by smoothing constant (α) [9]. Therefore, revising prediction model is necessary through adjusting the value of smoothing constant (α) by constantly acquiring location data of MU and analyzing.

This double exponential smoothing model predicts location and to use this model, both moving velocity (v) and direction (θ) must be predicted. Estimated velocity (v_e) and predicted direction (θ_e) value can be calculated using (1), by inserting calculated data into (4), we can get the next coordinates of x and y. In (4), (x, y) represents MU's current coordinates at present time (t) and (x_p', y_p') is the MU's predicted coordinates at t_p.

$$x_p' = x + v_e \cdot (t_p - t) \cdot cos\theta_e, \; y_p' = y + v_e \cdot (t_p - t) \cdot sin\theta_e \qquad (4)$$

The difference between MU's predicted location (x_p', y_p') at t_p and real location (x_p, y_p) at t_p is prediction error.

2.4 Design and Workflow of the QLP-LBS

In order to implement the reduction of location update cost, we have designed and developed QLP-LBS. This LBS system consists of three main components which are MUs, BS with quantizer, and LS.

- *MU (Mobile User)* – the mobile users in the LBS.
- *BS (Base Station) with quantizer* – BS acquires MUs' location and transmits location information of MUs to LS. And, this BS has quantizer which applies threshold to each MU and is being used to reduce the location update cost.
- *LS (Location Server)* – LS is composed of LDB (Location DB) and LP (Location Predictor). LDB stores the location information of MU and LP predicts location of MU when location update is quantized. LS receives quantized location information from BS. If location update of MU is received, then LS stores this information to LDB. In the other hand, if location update is filtered, LS uses LP to estimate the location of MU and LS stores an estimated location of MU to LDB.

The process of QLP-LBS is composed of two processes; BS process and LS process. The BS side process consists of three steps which are location acquisition, quantization, and location update step. In location acquisition step, BS acquires location of MUs. In quantization step, quantizer in BS compares moving distance of MU with threshold. If MU moves more than the limit of threshold, BS updates its location to LS in LBS. On the other hand, if MU moves less than threshold, then BS filters location updates and number of the updates will be reduced. At this time, LS cannot acquire precise location of MU. Quantization step reduces location updates of MUs by using threshold of quantizer. And, last step is location update step. In this step, LBS system updates location information to LS when MU moves outside of threshold.

In the LS side, LS waits location updates from BS. If LS receives location update from BS, this location update is stored in LDB in LS. On the other hand, if LS does not receive location update, then LS will predict location of MU by using LP and stores estimated location of MU in LDB.

3 Experiments and Results

In order to evaluate the performance of QLP-LBS, we used 250 MUs and measured reduction of location update costs and location accuracy according to movement of MU in university campus. As shown in Fig.1, we have divided university campus into 25 regions. These regions consist of 7 roads, 8 buildings, 4 parking lots, 5 parks, and a playground. QLP-LBS compares distance of MU has traveled with threshold and then reduces location updates using compared result. However, most of MUs in parking lots are stop state. In parking lots, location updates of MUs will unlikely occurred. We figured that including parking lots as the part of the experiment was meaninglessness and decided to remove from the experiment. Thus, in this experiment, we used 21 regions by removing 4 parking lots. We assigned 10 MUs to each region and each MU was given suitable velocity and mobility pattern depends on its region as shown in table 1.

Table 1. Specification of MU used in experiments. (R: Region, VR: Velocity Range, MM: Mobility Model).

R	# of R	Type of MU	# of MUs	VR	MM
Road	7	Car	35	2.7~8.3m/s	Pathway
		Human	35	0.5~2m/s	Pathway
Building	8	Human	40	0.5~2m/s	Pathway
			40	0~0.5m/s	Random Walk
Park	5	Human	50	0~2m/s	Random walk
Playground	1	Human	10	0.5~2m/s	Gaussian-Markov

In this experiment, QLP-LBS system monitored the locations of 270 MUs for 1800 seconds (30 min.). We have conducted two experiments which were to measure the reduction rate of location update costs and the location accuracy of LBS according to reduction of location updates.

Reduction Rate of Location Update. This experiment measures location updates of all MUs in each second and reduction rate of location updates of all MUs using various threshold sizes. We used three sizes of threshold which are *av* (average velocity),

0.75•*av*, 0.5•*av*, and 0.25•*av*. Table 2 represents the reduction rate of location updates of QLP-LBS. Reduction rate of location updates of QLP-LBS are increasing according as the threshold size increases. Results are 20.51%, 35.05%, 56.00% and 76.30% when threshold sizes were 0.25•*av*, 0.5•*av*, 0.75•*av*, and 1•*av*, respectively. This experiment shows that quantization theory effectively reduces location update costs of LBS system. However, LBS system based on quantization generates location error from the quantization. Even with the effective reduction rate, LBS cannot provide suitable location-based services to MUs due to the inaccurate location information. Thus, location accuracy is important factor of LBS. we will measure the location accuracy of QLP-LBS in following experiment.

Table 2. Reduction rate of location update signal

Size of Threshold	0.25•*av*	0.5•*av*	0.75•*av*	1•*av*
Reduction Rate of Location Updates (%)	20.51%	35.05%	56.00%	76.30%

Location Accuracy of QLP-LBS. If LS of LBS does not receive location of MU from BS, LS must predict the location of MUs using prediction mechanism described in section 3.2. In this experiment we measure two location accuracies of QLP-LBS. First one is the accuracy from the calculation using entire updates from both reported and unreported. The other one is the accuracy from the calculation using location updates that were unreported and it is also showing the accuracy of predication mechanism in QLP-LBS. We have used four different sizes of threshold as we used in previous experiment. The results of this experiment are shown in table 3. In location accuracy of both cases, they were 77.74%, 82.19%, 83.03% and 91.79% when threshold sizes were set as 1•*av*, 0.25•*av*, 0.5•*av*, and 0.75•*av*, respectively.

Table 3. Location accuracy of QLP-LBS

Size of Threshold	1•*av*	0.75•*av*	0.5•*av*	0.25•*av*
Accuracy of both cases (reported & unreported) (%)	77.74%	82.19%	83.03%	91.79%
Accuracy of unreported cases (%)	70.82%	68.18%	69.21%	67.55%

Accuracies of unreported cases are between 67 and 71%. These results mean that prediction accuracy of location prediction model. The results did not meet our expected prediction accuracy (e.g. higher than 85%). In spite of low accuracy of prediction model in LBS, location accuracies of both cases were reasonable. When threshold size of QLP-LBS uses 1•*av*, location accuracy was 77.74% with 76.30% reduction rate for location updates. Location accuracies of both cases improve as the threshold size decreases. Location accuracies of both cases were better than 90% with 20.51% reduction rate for location updates when threshold size was 0.25•*av*.

4 Conclusion

This paper proposes QLP-LBS which effectively reduces location updates of MUs. However, quantized system accompanies errors from the quantization. Thus, QLP-LBS system generates location errors according to reduction of location updates. For reducing location error, LS in QLP-LBS uses statistical prediction which uses historical path of MU and reduces location error of QLP-LBS. We have set up experiments to consider various mobility patterns of MUs and evaluate performance of QLP-LBS. QLP-LBS reduces 76.30% of location updates with location accuracy of 77.74% when QLP-LBS set threshold av (average velocity). If QLP-LPB uses small threshold, then reduction of location update will be decreased, but location accuracy of LBS will be increased. QLP-LBS had 35.05% of reduction rate with 82.19% location accuracy, 56.00% reduction rate with 83.03% location accuracy, 91.79% reduction rate with 20.51% location accuracy when the threshold size was $0.75 \cdot av$, $0.5 \cdot av$, and $0.25 \cdot av$, respectively. In QLP-LBS system, threshold size was set to $0.25 \cdot av$ if the main priority was the location accuracy or if the location accuracy was required to be higher than 90%. If required location accuracy was around 80%, QLP-LBS can set threshold size between $0.75 \cdot av$ and $1 \cdot av$.

References

1. Karimi, H., Hammad, A.: Telegeoinfomatics: Location-based Computing and Services. CRC Press, Boca Raton, USA (2004)
2. Schiller, J., Voisard, A.: Location-based Services. Morgan Kaufmann, San Francisco (2004)
3. Busic, L.: Position Reporting Frequency for Location-Based Services. The 18th International Conference on Applied Electromagnetics, 1-4 (2005)
4. Lee, J.S., Zeigler, B.P.: Space-based Communication Data Management in Scalable Distributed Simulation. Journal of Parallel and Distributed Computing 32, 336–365 (2002)
5. Google EarthTM, http://earth.google.com/
6. Bai, F., Narayanan, S., Helmy, A.: IMPORTANT: a framework to systematically analyze the Impact of Mobility on Performance of Routing Protocols for Adhoc Networks. INFOCOM '03 , 825–835 (2003)
7. Akyildiz, I.F., Yi-Bing, L.: A new random walk model for PCS networks. IEEE Journal on Selected Areas in Communications 18(7), 1254–1260 (2000)
8. Liang, B., Haas, Z.J.: Predictive distance-based mobility management for PCS networks. INFOCOM '99 , 1377–1384 (1999)
9. McClave, J., Benson, P., Sincich, T.: Statistics for Business and Economics, 9th edn. Prentice-Hall, Englewood Cliffs (2004)

Positioning System in Taipei Children's Museum of Transportation and Communication

Tzu-Hsiang Chou[1], Ming-Hui Jin[2], Chi-Chung Chen[3], and Cheng-Yan Kao[4]

[1,4] Department of Computer Science and Information Engineering, National Taiwan University,
Taipei, Taiwan
[2,3] Institute for Information Industry, Taipei, Taiwan
r94922109@ntu.edu.tw, jinmh@iii.org.tw, astely@iii.org.tw,
cykao@csie.ntu.edu.tw

Abstract. This paper presents a 802.11-based positioning system developed and demonstrated in the Taipei Children's Museum of Transportation and Communication. Our positioning system partitions the service area into several regions and signal strength information which contains a sequence of access point IDs with the average power strength measured in the region will be collect. Our positioning system locates mobile users via collecting power strengths of the mobile users and then applies our algorithm to determine the regions in which the mobile users stay. A location database is applied to maintain the signal strength information. The experimental results validate that the location information provided by our positioning system assures high correctness of region classification.

1 Introduction

When we visit some building or spots, for example, museum, department, amusement region, the area of these places probably is very huge and maybe contains many exhibitions. Each exhibition has its own items on display, and we want to know the information about these exhibitions and items on display. Imagine that when we visit these places, we take some mobile devices that can display a map of the immediate surroundings, and guiding a user inside a building or spot in the screen or other object that can display the vision to mobile users or visitors. Or these mobile devices can show information about these places or regions we visit at that time. The goal of this study is proposing an automatic method used positioning or locating method for learning the mobile users' or visitors' positions correctly so that we can display the information data that are exhibited or surroundings information of the region which mobile users or visitors are in at that time on mobile computing devices.

The emerging field of pervasive computing introduces intelligent spaces that interact with users in a natural and graceful way [1]. Positioning offering the locations of the users has been a key component for mobile computing and context-aware computing technologies. With the help of the position information, mobile users could enjoy useful geographical information nearby in a natural and flexible manner. Several commercial applications such as vehicle fleet management, intelligent

P. Thulasiraman et al. (Eds.): ISPA 2007 Workshops, LNCS 4743, pp. 77–86, 2007.

transport systems, and location-based applications [2, 3] have recently driven the research and standardization activities in the field of mobile object positioning [4].

The global positioning system (GPS) is a well known positioning approach. It requires mobile users to be equipped with GPS receivers for learning their positions. Although GPS provides convenient locating services for mobile applications, the GPS approach carries several disadvantages. First of all, the size and cost of mobile transmitters would be considerably increased because of the incorporated GPS receiver. Moreover, a unblocked transmission path is required to receive usable GPS data of at least three satellites, which makes the system useless in buildings or roads surrounded by high buildings or mountains [5].

In the literatures, several positioning techniques have been proposed for mobile computing environment. They could be classified into three categories. The first category applies the Time of Arrival (TOA) or Time Difference of Arrival (TDOA) schemes to locate mobile users [4, 7]. The principle of TOA and TDOA is estimating the distance between the receiver and each sender according to the traveling time from the senders to the receivers and then calculating the position of the receiver with the help of the known positions of at least three senders [4]. The second category applies the Angle of Arrival (AOA) scheme to locate mobile users. The principle of AOA is estimating the angle of arrival signal and then calculating the position of the sender by the known positions of the receivers and the angles of arrival signals detected by each receiver [7]. The last category utilizes the attenuation of signal power strength of the senders nearby to locate mobile users. The principle of most methods is applying the propagation law to estimate the distance from the receiver and each sender [5, 7].

Although TOA and TDOA are simple and concrete, however, the derived technologies are difficult in practice. The main difficulty arises from time synchronization among the senders and time-delay (or arrival time difference) detection in the receivers. Without perfect time synchronization and time-delay detection technologies, the positioning results would be inaccurate. To ensure perfect synchronization, these locating technologies often require the senders to be equipped with an extremely accurate synchronized timer. Besides, the distance between the senders should be large enough to ensure the difference of the positioning signal arrival time distinguishable. The above constrains induce TOA and TDOA approaches not appropriate for positioning most users in the indoor environment. On the other hand, the AOA approach also requires the sender to be able to detect the direction of arrival signals. This also requires the access point to equip extra components such as the smart antennas [8]. Besides, the reflection problem due to the indoor natures such as walls and pillars often causes inaccurate positioning results.

Driven by the above regards, we adopt the power strength approach of the third category since it requires no extra equipment for both the access points and mobile users. Although the numerous huge obstructions such as the walls and the pillars make the propagation law invalid, however, they make the power strengths of each access point vary significantly in adjacent locations. This phenomenon implies that we can apply the sensed power strengths to determine the position of each mobile user. If the areas of most locations are small enough and the proposed classification mechanism is accurate enough, then we can apply the proposed classification mechanism to locate mobile users accurately.

Based on this notion, a novel positioning method is proposed by us in the paper. Our positioning method is a variety of the Best Signature Match (BSM) positioning method we proposed in [9]. Our positioning method requires the mobile users to equip with a mobile device which can sense the received signal strength of the nearby access points which are pre-installed inside the interesting area. A location database is adopted to maintain the signal strengths information of all the reference points in the positioning environment. As a mobile user estimates the signal strengths information of its position according to the power strength of the access points nearby, the mobile user will submit the signal strengths information to the system and then the system will apply the our positioning method to assign each region a matching score. With the max score of the regions, it will be probably our positioning result.

This paper is organized as follows. In Section 2, our system environment is presented. In Section 3 we propose our positioning method. Experiment design and results are described in Section 4 and the conclusion is drawn in Section 5.

2 System Environment

2.1 Region Naming

Region naming is an important issue for our positioning system. Our system is primarily used by buildings for in-door exhibition (ex. Taipei World Trade Center or the location of our constructed system, Taipei Children's Museum of Transportation and Communication), Fig. 1. shows the region hierarchy of our positioning environment. Areas are at the top of our hierarchy, it could be different floors or different halls (such as Taipei World Trade Center). Each area hosts several exhibitions for various objects and booths. These booths and objects in exhibition are our regions. Our system aims to identify the positions of mobile users or visitors among various regions.

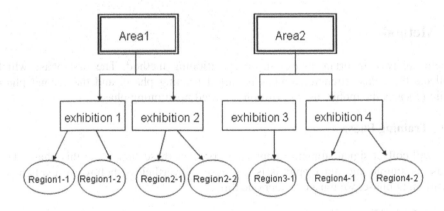

Fig. 1. The region hierarchy of our positioning environment

2.2 System Environment

The experiments were carried Transportation and Communication. Fig. 2 shows the layout of the second floor of our department building. The second floor of this building has dimension of 90 m by 80 m, an area of 7200 sq. m (about 75000 sq. ft.). There are totally four different types of exhibitions such as airplanes, trains, cars, and motors in the second floor of this building, and we partitioned each exhibition into three regions. In addition to these places there are the corridors and the Lobby in the second floor of our building. Hence, there are totally seventeen regions in our positioning environment. In the second floor of this building, we totally place nine 802.11b access points (APs). The gray circle of Fig. 2 shows the positions of our access points in the second floor of Taipei Children's Museum of Transportation and Communication.

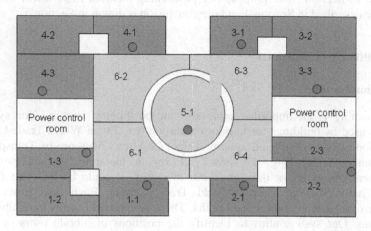

Fig. 2. The layout of the second floor of Taipei Children's Museum of Transportation and Communication

3 Method

There are two important phases in our positioning method. The first phase which collects the signal strength samples is called training phase, and the second phase which locates the mobile user's position is called positioning phase.

3.1 Training Phase

We will collect signal strength samples and process these samples at this phase. This phase is simple and our emphasis is not here. Nevertheless, before we explain our positioning phase, we must consider one thing:

The Effect of User's Presence

As the number of people in the building varies, the propagation characteristics of RF signals change as well. This is because the resonance frequency of water is at 2.4 GHz and the human's body consists of 70% water, the received signal strength (RSS) is absorbed when the user obstructs the signal path and causes an extra attenuation [10]. In experiments we performed, a single human body may on an average change the signal strength by as much as 5dBm. In more extreme cases, the change will be as high as 10 dBm. In other words, when we face APs to collect signal strength samples, there are not any obstructs between APs and the mobile user. While we collect signal strength opposing to AP, the change in signal strength may go as high as 10 dBm. Even if we don't face the opposite of AP, and collect signal strength in 90° direction, the signal strength collected will also have significant difference. So, the user's orientation has a significant impact on the signal strength measured at the APs. So, in the training phase, we collect signal strength samples in four directions of the reference point, such as north, east, west, and south.

3.2 Positioning Phase

Algorithm

1. We will calculate the Eucidean distance between the signal strength information (AP1,AP2,AP3,…,SS1,SS2,SS3…..) measured by the mobile user and the signal strength information stored in database (rpid, regionID, di, AP1,AP2,AP3,…,μ'1, μ'2, μ'3…..) to be the score of direction d_i at reference point rpid in the regionID, i.e., we will calculate $sqrt((SS1-\mu'1)^2+(SS2-\mu'2)^2+(SS3-\mu'3)^2)$. The smaller the Eucidean distance is, the higher the score is.
2. We assume there are m regions in our positioning environment, and we assume there are about n reference points in each region. According to step 1, there are one score in each direction of the reference points, and therefore there are totally four scores in each reference point, and therefore there are totally n*4 scores in each region. Then we choose X scores which are highest from the scores of n*4 scores, in our testing environment, Taipei Children's Museum of Transportation and Communication, after many experiments, we conclude that we choose ten instead of X that the accuracy will be higher. Therefore we sum these ten scores to be the scores of that region.
3. Compare the scores of these m regions in our positioning environment and choose the highest one. That region is our result of positioning.

Mobile user in the boundary of adjacent region

However, when the mobile user is nearby the boundary of adjacent regions, our algorithm is still difficult to correctly locate which region the mobile user is in at that time, especially, the mobile user is just at the boundary of adjacent regions. However, after many experiments, we find when the mobile user is at the gray part of Fig. 3, the score of each region which we calculate from step 2 has some phenomenon. We find the scores of the two regions which the gray part is between are higher than other regions, and the difference of the scores of these two regions are smaller than some fixed value. Therefore, we make a conclusion and add it to our algorithm:

4. When the difference of the highest scores of the two regions are smaller than some fixed value such as 50, we assume the mobile terminal is nearby the center part of these two regions. Fig. 4 shows the situation.

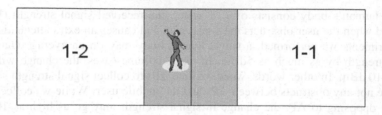

Fig. 3. mobile user in the boundary of adjacent region

Computing Reducing

From step 2, we will calculate the scores of m regions in each positioning. If m is very large, the calculation of our system will be very huge in each positioning. In order to lowering the calculation of our system and enhancing the efficiency of our system, we must slightly modify our method. How do we modify? Now if we are in the region 1-1, we can not move from region 1-1 to region 3-1 within a short enough time. If we want to reach the region 3-1, we must pass through the regions 6-1, 6-3 and 6-4. It is obvious, because physical constraints preclude a user from "jumping about" over large distances at randomly, the user's location at a given time instant is likely to be near that at the previous time instant. This shows that our method can only need to consider the region which it stay previously, or the adjacent regions which connect the region which it stay previously. It should be note that two regions are adjacent if all mobile objects in the regions in our building without pass through the regions nearby other regions. Fig. 4 below shows the adjacent relationship of the regions in Fig. 2. In Fig. 4, two circles i and j are connected by a solid line means the two regions are adjacent. Then we assume the distance of regions which are adjacent is one, and from region 3-2 to region 6-3, their distance is 2 and so on.

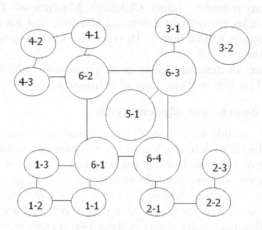

Fig. 4. The adjacent relationship of the regions

Now, the computing reducing procedure is proposed based on the assumption that the next position of each mobile object is still inside the region which it stay previously, or the adjacent regions which connect the region which it stay previously. Therefore, if the previous position of a mobile object is in the region R, we only need to consider calculating the grades of the region which it stay previously, or the grades the adjacent regions which connect the region which it stay previously. Therefore, our algorithm can continuously be added:

5. If the previous position of a mobile object is in the region R. In the next position, we will only calculate the grades of the region R which it stays previously or the grades of adjacent regions which connect the region R which it stay previously. Compare the scores of these regions and choose the highest one. That region is our result of positioning.

However, when the mobile user moves too fast so that the mobile user is not in the region which he stays previously, or the adjacent regions which connect the region which he stay previously. At this time, if we only consider the region which he stay previously, or the adjacent regions which connect the region which he stay previously, we will find mobile user is not in these regions. Therefore, it will make huge mistake. Therefore, our algorithm must continuously modify to:

6. Besides we calculate the grades of the region which mobile terminal stay previously and the adjacent regions which connect the region which mobile terminal stay previously, we will calculate the scores of the regions with the distance of two. Fig. 5 shows the regions we want to calculate, if region 5 is the region which mobile terminal stays previously. Compare the scores of these regions and choose the highest one. That region is our result of positioning.

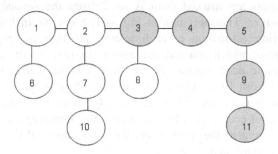

Fig. 5. the regions must be calculated

4 Accuracy Evaluation

In our method, the correctness of region classification is the most concern.

In the experiments, the client, carried by the user being tracked, is implemented on an HP PDA with a HP iPAQ Wi-Fi Adapter. The OS of the PDA is Windows Mobile 2003 Second Edition. The notebook is implemented on an Intel-processor with a Marvell Yukon Gigabit Ethernet 10/100/1000Base-T Adapter, Copper RJ-45. The OS of the notebook is Windows XP Professional SP2. Each AP belongs D-link Air Plus X TremeG. The Access Points(APs) provide overlapping coverage in portions of the floor, and together cover the entire floor.

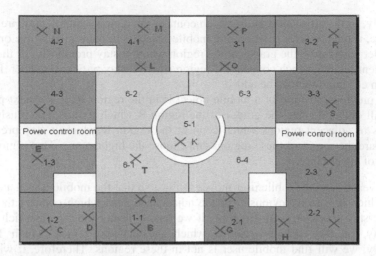

Fig. 6. The testing positions of our positioning environment

In each region, several positions called the reference points are selected. The layout of the reference points is like a matrix of positions and the distance between two adjacent reference points is about 2-3 meters. For each one of four directions in each reference point, the corresponding signal strength information contains the mean of at least 100 power strengths of each access point measured at the position. The testing positions are marked from A to T from the second floor of Taipei Children's Museum of Transportation in Fig. 6(The red Xs in Fig. 6). The signal strength information estimation at each testing position is calculated from 10 samples, each one of which contains the power strengths of the detectable access points and detectable access points ID or name and we calculate the mean and standard deviation from 10 samples as signal strength information which is send to our algorithm which is in our notebook. Our algorithm then queries the RDB to calculate the score of each region by our algorithm regarding the mobile user and then our algorithm returns the number and the information of the region regarding the best-match region to the mobile user.

4.1 Experiment Results

Fig. 7. show the accuracy of our positioning method presented in Section 3.2. The first column indicates the ID of the testing positions. The second column indicates the region which the testing positions are in. For example, B experiments are held in the region 1-1 in Fig. 7. The third column indicates the number of experiments held at the position. The fourth column indicates the testing position results of our positioning method. The fifth column indicates the hit rate of our experiments. Fig. 7. shows that in the 50 experiments individually held at A to T. We assure high correctness of our regions most of which are above 90% probability of region classification.

Testing position	The location of testing position	No. of Experiments	Positioning result and numbers	Hit rate
A	near 1-1 and 6-1 boundary	50	near 1-1 and 6-1 boundary:43	86%
B	1-1	50	1-1:47	94%
C	1-2	50	1-2:46	92%
D	near 1-1 and 1-2 boundary	50	near 1-1 and 1-2 boundary:45	90%
E	1-3	50	1-3:47	94%
F	near 2-1 and 6-4 boundary	50	near 2-1 and 6-4 boundary:45	90%
G	2-1	50	2-1:47	94%
H	near 2-1 and 2-2 boundary	50	near 2-1 and 2-2 boundary:46	92%
I	2-2	50	2-2:49	98%
J	2-3	50	2-3:46	92%
K	5-1	50	5-1:50	100%
L	near 4-1 and 6-2 boundary	50	near 2-1 and 6-4 boundary:44	88%
M	4-1	50	4-1:48	96%
N	4-2	50	4-1:46	92%
O	4-3	50	4-3:48	96%
P	3-1	50	3-1:47	94%
Q	near 3-1 and 6-3 boundary	50	near 3-1 and 6-3 boundary:44	88%
R	3-2	50	3-2:48	96%
S	3-3	50	3-3:47	94%
T	6-1	50	6-1:44	88%

Fig. 7. The accuracy of our positioning method

5 Conclusion and Future Work

The paper presented an 802.11 based positioning system. Our positioning system positions each mobile user according to the signal strength information estimated by the mobile user. The cost of this method is low without major modifications to the communication devices of both mobile users and service providers. The experimental results show that the location information estimated by our positioning system guarantees high hit rates of region positioning. However, the number of the samples collected by the confirmation mechanism may be insufficient, especially for larger regions. Therefore, the positioning service provider should design and implement more attractive services to increase the utility rate of our positioning system. Furthermore, although we can position the mobile user to nearby the boundary of the adjacent regions where the mobile user is nearby the boundary of these regions, we still have not answer that which region may mobile user is conclusively in at that time. We must unceasingly research and solve these questions. But our final goal is that when we walk to some display or exhibition, our algorithm can immediately position the mobile user that which booth or exhibition the mobile user is in and immediately shows the information of that booth or exhibition to the mobile user.

References

1. Satyanarayanan, M.: Pervasive Computing: Vision and Challenges. IEEE Personal Communications Magazine 8, 10–17 (2001)
2. Collier, W., Weiland, R.: Smart cars, smart highways. IEEE Spectrum 31, 27–33 (1994)

3. Jin, M.H., Wu, H.K., Horng, J.T.: An Intelligent Handoff Scheme Based On Location Prediction Technologies. IEEE European Wireless , 551–557 (2002)
4. Spirito, M.A.: On the Accuracy of Cellular Mobile Station Location Estimation. IEEE Transactions on Vehicular Technology 50(3), 674–685 (2001)
5. Hellebrandt, M., Mathar, R., Scheibenbogen, M.: Estimating Position and Velocity of Mobiles in a Cellular Radio Networks. IEEE Transactions on Vehicular Technology 46(1), 65–71 (1997)
6. Bahl, P., Padmanabhan, V.N.: RADAR: An In-Building RF-based User Location and Tracking System. IEEE INFOCOM, 775 – 784 (2000)
7. Rappaport, T.S., Reed, J.H., Woerner, D.: Position location using wireless communications on highways of the future. IEEE Communication Magazine 34, 33–41 (1996)
8. Mondin, M., Dovis, F., Mulassano, P.: On the use of HALE platforms as GSM base stations. IEEE Personal Communication Magazine, 8(2), 37–44 (2001)
9. Jin, M.H., Wu, E.H.K., Wang, Y.T., Hsu, C.H.: 802.11-based Positioning System for indoor Applications. In: Proceeding Communication Systems and Applications (2004)
10. Ladd, M., et al: Robotics-Based Location Sensing using Wireless Ethernet. Proc. MOBICOM (2002), 227–238 (2002)

Portable Patient Information Integration System for Patient Safety Improvement

Tu-Bin Chu[1], Ming-Hui Jin[2], Li-Xin Xu[3], Jong-Tsong Chiang[4], and Cheng-Yan Kao[5]

[1,4] Department and Graduate Institute of Business Administration, National Taiwan University,
Taipei, Taiwan
[1] Office of Continuing and Extension Education, Taipei Medical University, Taipei, Taiwan
[2] Networks and Multimedia Institute, Institute for Information Industry, Taipei, Taiwan
[3,5] Department of Computer Science and Information Engineering, National Taiwan
University, Taipei, Taiwan
benette@tmu.edu.tw, jinmh@iii.org.tw, r94922095@ntu.edu.tw,
jtchiang@mba.ntu.edu.tw, cykao@csie.ntu.edu.tw

Abstract. Nowadays, medical centers are working on setting a safe medicating environment by using information technology. This study tried to improve patients' safety environment, communications among medical workers and patients, medicating quality, and medical process efficiency through a wireless handheld RFID patient safety enhancement system for medical personnel. The proposed portable patient information integration system combines Radio Frequency Identification (RFID) technology, Wireless Network, Personal Digital Assistant (PDA) and Front-Monitoring System. Through the help of the proposed system, the medical workers can identify patients by non contact identification and get medical record immediately. Meanwhile the proposed system can record the history of the interaction between medical personnel and patients. It can also send alarm to the corresponding medical workers when reporting a high risk testing result and give medicine safety suggestion. The proposed system can improve the correctness and instantaneousness of patients' medical information and hence provide a safe environment for patients, and the Wan Fang Hospital is now verifying the performance of this system for improving the patients' safety.

1 Introduction

Currently, one particular phenomenon is observed in the health-care ecology of Taiwan: most unstable and critical patients are transferred to large hospitals or medical centers, causing the uproar loading of the personnel. The percentage of critical patients is getting higher, and the number of personnel is in shortage. According to statistics, each late shift nurse has to take care of 20 patients in average, and each pharmacist has to handle 400 to 600 prescriptions. Each social worker is responsible for 100 beds now; the number may increase to 150 in the future [1].

Early this year, lutein was given instead of antacids in National Taiwan University Hospital. This kind of medical treatment failure sometimes occurs in the hospitals and clinics. This event again reminds the hospitals that they are responsible to provide

P. Thulasiraman et al. (Eds.): ISPA 2007 Workshops, LNCS 4743, pp. 87–95, 2007.
© Springer-Verlag Berlin Heidelberg 2007

secure healthcare environment to guard patients' safety. To eliminate the medical treatment failures, the hospital administrators are devoted to improve the overall healthcare quality. Various studies have proposed factors and statistics influential to patient-safety.

In 2000, the annual report of Institute of Medicine (IOM), 'To Err is Human' and 'Crossing the Quality Chasm', have focused on patient safety, which aroused the awareness of the society. The U.S. healthcare evaluation organization Joint Commission on Accreditation of Healthcare Organization (JCAHO) proposed seven goals for all healthcare organization to improve patient safety, including accuracy of patient recognition, improving communications among healthcare service providers, elevate the safety in administration of high risk drugs, avoid mistakes in operation procedures and operation sites in patients, enhance the safety of liquid pump usage, reduce the risk of infection through healthcare [2]. In 2004, IOM proposed several tasks for improving the patient safety. One major task is to improve the healthcare procedures by enhancing the medical informatics techniques, especially the patient identification technology [3].

RFID has following characteristics: 1. non-contact data read/write; 2. miniature and variation of tags; 3. well adopted in various environments; 4. high data security; 5. reusable tags; 6. no restrictions on directionality; 7. large data contents. These characteristics make RFID suited to perform identification in hospitals.

Most studies on the applications of RFID are focused on improvement of procedures, e.g. tracking the movements of patients in emergency room (ER), record the time spend in ER, and use these information to improve patients' waiting time [4]. The nurse station applies identification technology to authenticate healthcare personnel and build real-time shift database, to provide information on patient clinical treatment and to queries on shift data. It also provides more basic patient information for later check and applications. These procedures which employ RFID technology not only replace paper works for confirmation and control in healthcare and shift procedures but also reduce manual operations and improve the accuracy of patient medical information promptly. During the outbreak of SARS, RFID was also applied in epidemic control tasks. The research team in the R&D program supported by MOEA, ITRI and Ton Yen Hospital developed "RFID tracking and control system" in collaboration. This system can track and segregate possible infected personnel rapidly. Later on, they developed a "RFID medical instruments management system". This system can manage the access personnel, quantity, and locations of instruments. It can also monitor the on shelf periods. Sun Yat-Sen cancer center applies RFID technology to pharmacy matching system, which could avoid controversies in misuse of drugs. For the improvement of patient safety, Taipei Medical University puts identification tags on patients in OR and provides related information, images, and audio to help medical personnel identify the patients.

The proposed portable patient information integration system differs from the above procedure-improving studies in that the proposed system not only applies RFID to improve patient safety, but also improves the entire healthcare process with information technologies and enhances the safety of the healthcare environment. Healthcare personnel can obtain all kinds of information for a patient, correctly identify the patients, give proper treatments, and improve the relationship between healthcare personnel and patients. To ensure that the proposed system does meet the requirements from the medical personnel, the system designers consist of medical personnel from the Wan Fang Hospital (including physicians and nurses) and the ICT development team from the National Taiwan University. Table 1 in the appendix shows the requirements from the medical personnel and the corresponding improving methods.

The rest of this paper is organized as follows. In Section 2.1, we present the system architecture of the proposed portable patient information integration system. The design, functionalities and implementation for the portable device is presented in Section 2.2 and Section 2.3. The conclusion and the future works are drawn in Section 3.

2   The Portable Patient Information Integration System

2.1   The System Architecture

Fig. 1 shows the system architecture for the proposed portable patient information integration system. This system has four major components, including "portable patient information integration interface", "Patient safety portal web service server", "clinical decision engine", and "hospital information system". In Fig. 1, the portable patient information integration interface is the PDA. Whenever the medical personnel applies the portable patient information integration interface to learn the identification of the interesting patient, the portable patient information integration interface uploads the patient's identification to the patient safety portal web service server through the 802.11 network. The patient safety portal web service server then

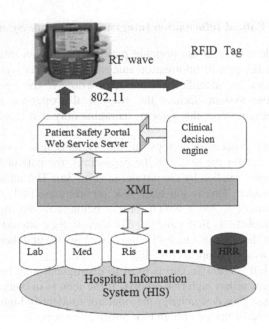

Fig. 1. Portable Patient Information Integration System Architecture

retrieves the patient's information from the hospital information system (HIS) by sending the identification of the interesting patient and the medical personnel who operates the portable patient information integration interface. The information exchanged between the HIS and the patient safety portal web server follows the XML specifications.

The HIS consists of all the medical databases such as the Lab, Med, Ris, etc and a special database called the HRR (High Risk Reminder). The HIS keeps track of all histological data regarding patients, and provide all information required by various services, including basic information, registration time, drug usage, diagnosis, treatment, examination results, and information from shifts. The HRR maintains the risk of each patient. The risks are estimated according to the patient's information maintained in other databases in the HIS and the rules designed by the domain experts.

The clinical decision engine is an expert system combine expertise of professional medical researchers. These professionals collect and build all sorts of clinical information to be used in the system. Possible mistakes in operations are included, so as the system can provide hints to medical personnel at any time, which in turn improve patient safety. Related decision information includes clinical directions, drug usage directions, and examination reports thresholds. Through clinical decision engine, the system can be expanded and lead in rapidly. For example, the decision engine can provide clinical directions to medical personnel. Also, clinical reports on patients can be compared with related knowledge stored in decision engine, and the information of patients exceed threshold will be passed to medical personnel immediately.

2.2   The Portable Patient Information Integration Interface System

Fig. 2 shows the flow chart of the portable patient information integration interface system. To operate the patient information integration interface system, the medical personnel first enters his identification and password. If the operator passes the password check, the system decides the role of the operator according to his identification. In current stage, this system maintains only two roles: The doctor and the nurse.

After the operator successfully logs in the system, this system retrieves the interesting patients list for the operator. To physicians, the patient list only includes information of patients handled by the physician (Fig. 3a). The information includes: 1. High Risk Reminder. This is the high risk reports classified by expert system, which help the operator to know which patient belongs to the high risk group. 2. Name. 3. Serial number. 4. Bed number. To nurses, they should select the room number (after select the floor in which the room is) (Fig. 3b) and then patients' list for the specified room will then appear (Fig. 3c).

The icon in the left (Figure 3a, 3c) is used to distinguish high risk patients. If the icon is in red, the patient has high risk reports; if the icon is in blue, the patient is not in the high risk group. This design helps the operator to identify high risk patients and hence improves the performance of high risk notification service.

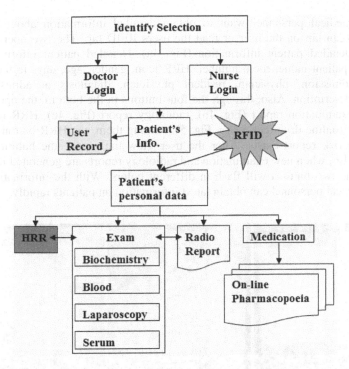

Fig. 2. The portable patient information integration interface system flow chart

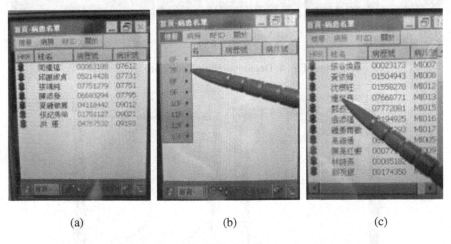

(a)   (b)   (c)

Fig. 3. Patient list

The system can also record the operator's actions. Operators can examine usage log, including all actions and their execution time after login. Medical personnel can rapidly lookup which rooms, patients, or RFID tags have been inspected. Also, analysis can be performed on these usage logs to improve system performance. Hospital can also track the contact between physicians and patients through these logs.

If the medical personnel want to obtain detailed information about a specific patient, he can tap on the user or read the users RFID tag. The two operations will bring up detailed patient information (Fig. 4a). Detailed patient information first shows the patient name, room number, HRR icon, gender, age, days in the hospital, date of admission, physician, resident physician, diagnosis at admission, and diagnosis description. Also, through the four buttons in the bottom, the operator may view the examination report (Fig. 4b), radiology report (Fig. 4c), HRR report, and drug usage (online drug dictionary, Fig. 5). Among them, the HRR button will flash when high risk report exists. After the user view the report, the button will stop flashing. Also, when new examination and radiology reports are generated in less than an hour, the two buttons will flash in different colors. With the information, heavy loaded medical personnel can obtain latest information on patients rapidly.

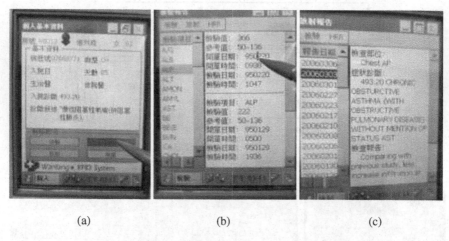

(a)   (b)   (c)

Fig. 4. Detail patient information

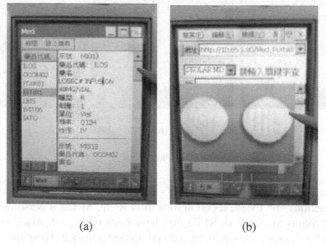

(a)   (b)

Fig. 5. Drug use and only drug dictionary

The use of drugs change frequently and more than 20,000 drugs are available in the Wan Fang Hospital. To avoid mistakes in drug use, the proposed system also provide query and display of patient drug usage. The system divides each day into 24 hours. When the operator selects one of the time slots, the statistics of drug use during the period will be presented, including drug code, drug name, dosage, advice type, pathway, frequency, and unit (Fig. 5a). The operator can query the drug in the online drug dictionary based on the selected drug number (Fig. 5b). More information can be obtained, including: image of the drug, indications, contraindications, pharmacology, etc. These information help medical personnel to explain these drugs to patients, also reduced mistakes in drug usage.

2.3 The System Implementation

The portable patient information integration system is based on Microsoft Visual Studio .NET 2003. Two types of projects are used: 1. Smart Device Application, this project is used for WinCE application development; 2. ASP.NET Web Service, Active Server Page (ASP) presents the interactions between Web Service and client. Server can pack services required by user into Web Services, and clients can access medical databases through these services. All data transfers follow XML standard.

Fig. 6. The Unitech PA960 PDA

Through a series of test and compares, we adopt Unitech PA960 as the hardware platform for the portable patient information integration interface system. Fig. 6 shows the hardware platform. This is an industrial PDA with built-in RFID reader, barcode reader, and 802.11 wireless network adapter. The strap in the PDA facilitates the medical personnel to carry around, especially in the highly mobile operation scenarios. The development environment of the interface is Microsoft Visual Studio .NET 2003. This makes the applications highly portable to other WinCE based hardware platforms.

3 Conclusions and Future Works

In this paper, we proposed a portable patient information integration system which integrates the RFID technology, wireless communication services and hospital information system to improve the patients' safety. The medical personnel can easily identify the patients and retrieve their information in highly mobile operating environment. The proposed system is now verifying in the Wan Fang Hospital and is accepted by most medical personnel. Although most medical personnel are satisfied with the system, they also proposed several expectations to this version as follow.

1. Simplify the operations. In this version, some information such as the examination report requires several steps operations. For heavy loaded medical personnel, simpler operation is expected. For the frequently accessed services, we are now trying to combine the necessary steps into one button click. Although this approach may simplify the operations, this approach reduces the extensibility since new services may be required to implement in this platform.
2. Minimize the response time. PDA accesses medical database through 802.11 wireless links. The transfer rate of wireless network is much slower than wired network. According to the experiment results, access to server and call a Web Service takes 3 to 5 seconds. If continuously access database in a single form, users have to wait a longer time and might misinterpret the system crashed. To solve this problem, we are now trying to download the information of the interesting patients previously. Since the memory size of the PDA system is not large enough to download the information of all the patients, the portable patient information integration system are expected to provide an intelligent pre-download service which can download the information of the interesting patients previously and accurately.
3. The screen of the PDA is small. Since the screen of the PDA is small, many information cannot be displayed in one page. Therefore, for large amount of data, finding the interesting information becomes difficult. Therefore, we are now trying to provide query service which accepts query by voice. Since the computing power of the hardware platform is inferior, we are now searching appropriate voice to text technologies which requires lower computing resource.

References

1. The Premier .NET Compact Framework Shared Source Site, http:// opennetcf.org/ CategoryView.aspx?category=Home
2. Joint Commission on Accreditation of Healthcare Organization, http://www.jcaho.org/
3. Institute of Medicine, http://www.iom.int/tsunami
4. Dey, A.K.: Understanding and Using Context. College of Computing & GVU Center, Georgia Institute of Technology, Atlanta, GA, USA

Appendix

Table 1. Strategy for Improvements

Requirements	Improvements
Identification	RFID, server-side authentication
Improve interactions between medical personnel and patients	Medical personnel use PDA to display patient information, including reports, diagnostic descriptions, drugs, etc. They can understand the status of patients rapidly and discuss with the patients.
Improve clinical notification system	Display high risk report (HRR) from expert system in high priority. Notify medical personnel to review HRR through interface and usage log.
High risk drug use safety	Queries on patient drug-usage, online drug dictionary
Reduce risks of infections from healthcare	Through usage log and RFID reading log, once the outbreak occurred, the system can help medical personnel understand the contact history between medical personnel and patients
Review of all kinds of reports on patients	Download all kinds of patient reports from HIS through hospital-wide wireless network and PDA
Inspection of basic information of patients	Download basic patient information from HIS through hospital-wide wireless network and PDA

Secure Session Management Mechanism in VoIP Service*

Insu Kim and Keecheon Kim**

Department of Computer Science & Engineering, Konkuk University
Seoul, Korea
{darkguy,kckim}@konkuk.ac.kr

Abstract. VoIP (Voice–over–IP) technology has come of age and is quickly gaining momentum on Broadband networks. VoIP packetizes phone calls through the same routes used by network and Internet traffic and is consequently prone to the same cyber threats that plague data networks today. These include denial - of service attacks, worms, viruses, and hacker exploitation. In addition to these traditional network security and availability concerns, there are also a plethora of new VoIP protocols that have yet to undergo detailed security analysis and scrutiny. The new challenges of VoIP security are session hijacking, abnormal termination, call flooding and spam. History has shown that many other advances and trends in information technology typically outpace the corresponding realistic security requirements that are often tackled only after these technologies have been widely adopted and deployed. In this paper, we describe the technology protects networks against the known VoIP threats, and propose security mechanism for VoIP session management.

1 Introduction

VoIP implementations are becoming more common. As a result, more networks and legacy systems are being connected to public networks, allowing organizations to reduce costs and improve their offerings while allowing users to enjoy a variety of new and advanced services. Various analyst firms project different growth percentages for the VoIP market, but they all agree that VoIP implementations are growing fast and are expected to grow even faster. One should remember that while the voice part of VoIP is more important for services and user experience (voice quality and latency), the IP part is important for data security. Security is an important consideration when implementing VoIP because each element in the infrastructure is accessible on the network like any computer and can be attacked or used as a launching point for deeper, inter network and inside-the-organization attacks.

VoIP calls are susceptible to Dos (denial-of-service) attacks[1], hacked gateways leading to unauthorized free calls, call eavesdropping and malicious call redirection[2]. VoIP also presents certain specific security challenges. Both parts of a VoIP call - the call setup messages and the actual call media stream - must be inspected.

---

* This research was supported by the Brain Korea 21 project.
** Corresponding author.

P. Thulasiraman et al. (Eds.): ISPA 2007 Workshops, LNCS 4743, pp. 96–104, 2007.
© Springer-Verlag Berlin Heidelberg 2007

There are several protocols that are entitled to carry the name "VoIP protocol." VoIP experts will advocate different protocols because they have different advantages, but when it comes to security, there are several considerations that are common to most VoIP protocols. Using security best practices will eliminate additional risk factors and attack vectors.

Each VoIP element contains a processor running software and a TCP/IP stack that can be attacked. Attacks on data communications can come through the IP voice infrastructure and vice versa. DoS attacks targeting weak VoIP elements could flood the network with bogus voice traffic, degrading network performance or shutting down both voice and data communications.

A gateway that has been hacked might be used to make unauthorized free telephone calls. Unprotected voice communications could be intercepted and stolen or corrupted. Unswitched voice packets can be sniffed out and listened to in real time. PC - based soft phones, phones that use software to convert a desktop PC into an IP - based phone, are vulnerable to eavesdropping if the PC is infected with a Trojan horse that snoops into LAN traffic. VoIP exploits can be used to launch bounce attacks against servers and hosts in the so - called DMZ or even worse, serve as a convenient launch site to attack more business - critical network components in the internal LAN. In short, VoIP opens voice communications to the same types of security threats that expose data communications to attacks.

2 Related Works

2.1 VoIP Protocols

There are a number of protocols that may be employed in order to provide the VoIP communication services. In this section, we focus on most common aspects for the majority of the devices already deployed or being deployed today.

Virtually every device in the world uses a standard called RTP (Real - Time Protocol) for transmitting audio and video packets between communicating computers. RTP is defined by the IETF (Internet Engineering Task Force) in the RFC 3550. The payload formats for a number of CODECs are defined in RFC 3551, though payload format specifications are defined in various ITU documents and in other IETF RFCs. The H.323 Protocol and SIP (Session Initiation Protocol)[3] both have their origins in 1995 as researchers looked to solve the problem of how two computers can initiate communication in order to exchange audio and video media streams. H.323 enjoyed the first commercial success, due to the fact that those working on the protocol in the ITU worked quickly to publish the first standard in early 1996.

SIP, on the other hand, progressed much more slowly in the IETF, with the first draft published in 1996, but the first recognized "standard" published later in 1999. SIP was revised over the years and republished in 2002 as RFC 3261, which is the currently recognized standard for SIP. These delays in the standards process resulted in delays in market adoption of the SIP protocol. SIP has, most recently, become more popular for use in instant messaging systems.

2.2 SIP (Session Initiation Protocol)

The SIP is a simple signaling protocol used for Internet conferencing and telephony. SIP was developed within the IETF MMUSIC working group. SIP specifies procedures for telephony and multimedia conferencing over the Internet. SIP has been modeled after the text - based SMTP (Simple Mail Transfer Protocol) and HTTP (Hypertext Transfer Protocol). It is based on a client - sever architecture in which the client initiates the calls and the server answers the calls. By conforming to these existing text - based Internet standards, troubleshooting and network debugging are facilitated.

SIP is an application - layer protocol independent of the underlying packet protocol (TCP, UDP, ATM, X.25) and requires only an unreliable datagram service. This protocol itself provides reliability using INVITE and ACK messages which define the process of opening a reliable channel. SIP addresses users by an email - like address and re - uses some of the infrastructure of electronic mail delivery such as DNS MX records or using SMTP EXPN for address expansion. SIP addresses can also be embedded in web pages. SIP is addressing - neutral, with addresses expressed as URLs of various types such as SIP, H.323 or telephone E.164. It depends on the SDP (Session Description protocol) for carrying out the negotiation for codec identification. It supports session descriptions that allow the participants to agree on a set of compatible media types. It also supports user mobility by proxying and redirecting requests to the user's current location. It provides the necessary protocol mechanisms so that end systems and proxy servers can provide services.

3 VoIP Security Consideration

3.1 VoIP Authentication

User registration is straightforward and well defined for SIP in RFC 3261. All SIP proxies and endpoints that authenticate users leverage the same challenge - response mechanism used by HTTP. However, it's still important to understand how authentication has been implemented in a given SIP solution[4]. Some only authenticate for specific services, such as access to the PSTN through a gateway, while others require authentication for all SIP transactions. Nevertheless, interoperability is high overall between different SIP vendors.

H.323 authentication[5] is defined in the H.235 series of standards and supports various types of challenge - response methods. Most recently, the H.235.5 standard relies on a Diffie - Hellman encrypted key exchange based on a gatekeeper password to set up encrypted signaling. H.235.5 addresses earlier concerns around initial authentication and dictionary attacks.

However, the algorithm employed and the type of authentication varies considerably among implementations, making it difficult to get H.323 authentication working between vendors. Though attractive to many enterprises for its simplicity, integrating VoIP user authentication with a central directory or AAA server is currently a challenge for both SIP and H.323. SIP is likely to solve the problem with proposed extensions to RADIUS that would enable an AAA server to provide user authentication for proxies or other SIP endpoints. Within H.323 the problem is less straightforward, although EAP (Extensible Authentication Protocol) could be used to address this issue.

3.2 VoIP Encryption

Encryption for VoIP takes on two forms: signaling and media. Signaling encryption protects the control channels for SIP or H.323 communications. Media encryption protects the RTP streams used for voice, video, or fax.

The idea behind signaling encryption is keeping sensitive control information from being exposed. Current SIP standards provide more than one way to protect signaling, starting with TLS (Transport Layer Security)[6]. TLS uses the same technique as secure Web connections and encrypts the SIP signaling from one SIP device to another, but does not ensure end - to - end encryption. TLS runs only over TCP and requires a certificate infrastructure to exist between communicating parties, thus adding significant provisioning and performance overhead to a SIP connection. As such, carrier - grade SIP deployments have not yet implemented secured TLS signaling, and to date, the authors are unaware of carriers offering secured signaling or media on SIP trunks to enterprises. Within enterprise equipment, TLS support is more common. For end to end SIP signaling encryption, a standard exists for encrypting the body and sensitive headers of a SIP message using S/MIME and certificate based cryptography. Yet despite having a SIP standard for S/MIME key exchange, it can be problematic to implement, and consequently SIP products rarely support this part of the standard. H.323 can use TLS for signaling encryption, but this is not widely supported.

Part of the H.235.5 standard supports efficient encryption of sensitive signaling elements, and provides efficient signaling encryption without the need for a PKI (Public Key Infrastructure). While many vendors are encrypting signaling between their own devices, it is very challenging to secure signaling between H.323 solutions from different vendors. So, we propose a more efficient key exchange mechanism for UAs in SIP environment.

4 Secure Session Management

In this paper, we propose a more efficient secure session management mechanism for nodes in a SIP domain. The movement of MN, which requires mobile IP services, is mostly local within the visited domain.

Registration is one of the most important function of SIP. Registration enables a user agent to use SIP services. It requires that registration needs authentication of user agent to protect VoIP user's URI. Registrar or AAA in a SIP domain can authenticate the user agent. And UAs that want to communicate each other, need their session key to protect their signal and media packets. However, UAs in SIP domain have not any security association. For end to end SIP signaling encryption, a standard exists for encrypting the body and sensitive headers of a SIP message using S/MIME and certificate based cryptography. Yet despite having a SIP standard for S/MIME key exchange, it can be problematic to implement, and consequently SIP products rarely support this part of the standard. So, we propose new authentication and key exchange mechanism.

4.1 SIP UA Registration

UA must register with sip:register when it start. SIP Proxy will extract sip:register message and forward them to AAA to authenticate UA. AAA decrypts an authenticator with UA-AAA shared secret to extract UA's SIP URI. If Authentication process is succeed, AAA forwards sip:register to Location Server to store UA's SIP URI. AAA constructs an answer message including a session key made by hashing function with AAA - UA shared secret and a nonce. AAA sends '200 OK' answer to SIP Proxy with session key encrypted by Proxy-AAA shared secret and nonce. SIP Proxy store the session key - URI fair into their storage, and forward '200 OK' answer to UA. UA calculate session key with nonce and AAA-UA shared secret.

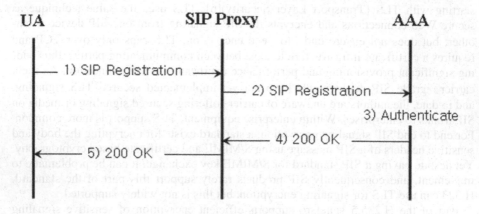

Fig. 1. SIP Registration

Session Key SK : H(Nonce, SSK$_{UA-AAA}$)

1) SIP Registration + H(URI, SSK$_{UA-AAA}$)
2) SIP Registration + H(URI, SSK$_{UA-AAA}$)
4) 200 OK + E(SK, SSK$_{AAA-Proxy}$) + Nonce
5) 200 OK + Nonce

H(x, y) : hashing x with y
E(x, y) : encrypting x with y
SSK$_{A-B}$: shared secret between node A and node B

4.2 Secure VoIP Signaling

In a SIP system, UAc sends a Invite message to the SIP Proxy to communicate with other UAs. In this message UA includes an message authenticator: this token is calculated based on a secret shared between the UA and SIP Proxy and it is used in order to authorize the transfer. This means that the UA and the SIP Proxy must share a secret.

As soon as the SIP Proxy receives a Invite message, it generates a key material, which includes the hashed session key between SIP Proxy and UAc, and the Invite message and media key to be transferred to UAs. This message is received by the UAs that verifies the message authenticator and sends a 200 OK message including the message authenticator. This authenticator is computed using the session key shared between the SIP Proxy and UAs.

For SIP communication, signaling and authentication must be executed in a IP telephony network. Authentication of UA is based on UA-AAA security association. A new signaling mechanism is required in SIP. In this paper, we propose a new signaling mechanism which can be obtained shown below.

INVITE and 200 OK must encrypted by session key. Because these messages are include media session information. SIP Proxy must generate media key use each session keys. SIP Proxy must send media key to UAc and UAs to protect media session. And these messages can include the message authenticator to avoid message spoofing. Each nodes authenticates the message with a message authenticator. And BYE message must protected by media key to prevent abnormal session teardown

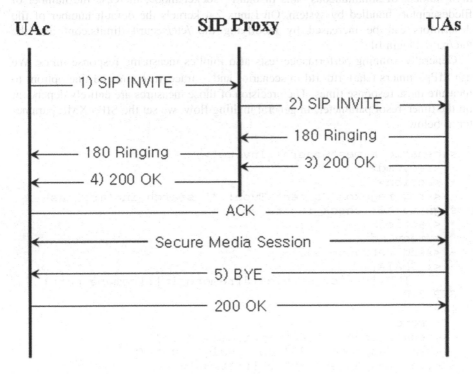

Fig. 2. SIP Signaling

Media Key MK : H(Call-ID, $SK_{UAc-Proxy}$ + $SK_{UAs-Proxy}$)

1) E(SIP INVITE, $SK_{UAc-Proxy}$) + H(SIP INVITE, $SK_{UAc-Proxy}$)
2) E(SIP INVITE + MK, $SK_{UAs-Proxy}$) + H(SIP INVITE, $SK_{UAs-Proxy}$)
3) E(200 OK, $SK_{UAs-Proxy}$) + H(200 OK, $SK_{UAs-Proxy}$)
4) E(200 OK + MK, $SK_{UAc-Proxy}$) + H(SIP INVITE, $SK_{UAc-Proxy}$)
5) E(BYE, MK) + H(BYE, MK)

H(x, y) : hashing x with y
E(x, y) : encrypting x with y
SK_{A-B} : session key between node A and node B

5 Performance Evaluation

In this section we analyze the performance of our proposal. We started our performance evaluation of the proposed method with SIPp testing tool. SIPp has been originally designed for SIP performance testing. Reaching high call rates and/or high number of simultaneous SIP calls is possible.

Use a Linux system to set up SIP Proxy. Limit the traces to a minimum. To reach a high number of simultaneous calls in multi - socket mode, increase the number of filedescriptors handled by system. On Linux 2.4 kernels the default number of file descriptors can be increased by modifying the /etc/security/limits.conf and the /etc/pam.d/login file.

Generally, running performance tests also implies measuring response times. We use SIPp's timers (start_rtd, rtd in scenarios and - trace_rtt command line option) to measure those response times. The precision of those measures are entirely dependent on the timer_resol parameter. In general inviting flow, we set the SIPp XML parameter as below:

```
<scenario name="General Invite">
- <recvCmd>
- <action>
  <ereg regexp="Content-Type:.*" search_in="msg" as-
sign_to="1" check_it="false" />
  </action>
  </recvCmd>
- <send retrans="500">
- <![CDATA[
      INVITE sip:[service]@[remote_ip]:[remote_port]
SIP/2.0
]]>
  </send>
  <recv response="100" optional="true" />
  <recv response="180" optional="true" />
- <recv response="200" crlf="true">
- <action>
  <ereg regexp="Content-Type:.*" search_in="msg" as-
sign_to="2" check_it="false" />
  </action>
  </recv>
- <send start_rtd="true">
- <![CDATA[
      ACK sip:[service]@[remote_ip]:[remote_port]
SIP/2.0
]]>
  </send>
  <recv response="200" crlf="true" />
  </scenario>
```

Illustrates the comparison results between basic SIP security model and proposed model, shown in Figure 3. The figure presents the UA's CPU utilization against 30

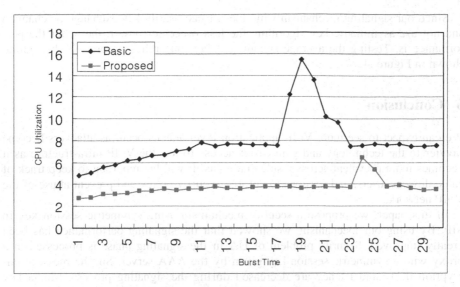

Fig. 3. Comparison of processor utilization

different bursts (calls/min), while total numbers of calls offered are 300 for every experiment. The blue dot in the figure indicates the basic operation and pink dot displays the proposed mechanism It can be seen from figure, the Increase in bursts from 1 to 30 (calls/min), the proposed algorithm is superior to basic algorithm. It's very important factor which have limited computing resource UAs, such as IP phone. Proposed mechanism decreases processor utilization. There are some investigation question tion arises, this is due to some running services on nodes affects the performance.

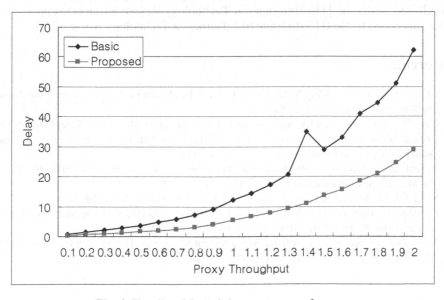

Fig. 4. Signaling delay relying on proxy performance

Since our signaling mechanism with doesn't necessarily key exchange mechanism and not use asymmetric key algorithm, the less processor power, the better the performance is. Testing the average signaling delay time relies on proxy's throughput shown in Figure .4.

6 Conclusion

We can expect to see more VoIP application level attacks occur as attackers become savvier to the technology and gain easier access to test the VoIP infrastructure as it becomes more prevalent across residential areas. It will be important to keep track of calls, devices, users, and sessions to enforce security policy and prevent abuse of the VoIP network.

In this paper, we propose a security mechanism using symmetric session key in SIP. By using our mechanism, we showed that the signaling performance has been greatly improved. Security problem of UA in the signaling phase is processed in a proxy with a symmetric session key given by the AAA server. So, the message encryption delay and latency are decreased during the signaling process. Media key exchange mechanism in signaling phase can protect the media stream and session termination signal. Our mechanism requires minimum processing power. The proposed mechanism is very useful, when the real VoIP systems are deployed. UAs maybe consist of IP Phone. IP phone can't have enough processing power to handle asymmetric key algorithm.

Acknowledgement

This research was supported by the MIC(Ministry of Information and Communication),Korea, under the ITRC(Information Technology Research Center) support program supervised by the IITA(Institute of Information Technology Assessment).

References

1. Larson, J., et al.: Defending VoIP Networks from DdoS attacks. In: Globecom VoIP Security Workshop, Houston, USA (2004)
2. Cao, F., Malik, S.: Security Analysis and Solutions for Deploying IP Telephony in the Critical Infrastructure. In: Proceedings of IEEE/Create?Net Workshop on Security and Quality of Service in Communication Networks (2005)
3. Rosenberg, J., Schulzrinne, H., Camarillo, G., Johnston, A., Peterson, J., Sparks, R., Handley, M.: SIP: Session Initiation Protocol. RFC 3261 (2002)
4. NIST SP 800?58, Security Considerations for Voice Over IP Systems (2005)
5. Jennings, C., Peterson, J.: Enhancements for Authenticated Identity Management in the Session Initiation Protocol (SIP). draft-ietf-sip-identity-05 (2005)
6. Jennings, C., Peterson, J.: Certificate Management Service for The Session Initiation Protocol (SIP). draftietf-sipping-certs-01 (2005)

An Effective Local Repair Scheme Using Candidate Node and Hello Message in AODV[*]

Sangmin Lee and Keecheon Kim[**]

Dept, of Computer Science & engineering, Konkuk University,
Gwang-jin Gu, Seoul, Korea
{leesm,kckim}@konkuk.ac.kr

Abstract. We propose an effective Local Repair scheme for AODV in mobile ad-hoc network environment. Even though the existing Local Repair scheme for AODV routing protocol can recover the disconnected path in some ways, however, they can not utilize the pre-connected routing nodes when we handle the nodes in Ad-hoc environment. In order to utilize the pre-connected routing nodes in recovering the path more effectively, we use a designated candidate nodes and changed Hello messages. The candidate nodes are used to recover the disconnected path using the pre-connected routing information. The Hello messages provides multipath for candidate nodes. This scheme produces better results with less control packets with faster path recovery time.

1 Introduction

The Mobile Ad-hoc Networks is a mobile network composed of more than two mobile terminals without fixed infrastructure. The Mobile ad-hoc networks are envisioned to have dynamic, sometimes rapidly changing, random, multi-hop topologies which are likely composed of relatively bandwidth-constrained wireless links. Legacy table driven routing protocol such as OSPF and RIP can not be applied to MANET because of its mobility supporting lack of capability. Therefore, several reactive routing approaches have been researched.[3][4]

The AODV Routing algorithm is reactive routing algorithm in Ad-hoc. The AODV provide high performance for Ad-hoc. But, The AODV has problem of local repair. The local repair is very important method in large network. The existing local repair scheme in AODV routing protocol can recover path disconnection in some ways. However, they can not utilize pre-connected routing nodes. It is serious probrem. If the network size is very large, the existing method increases the path recovery time and control messages. In order to utilize pre-connected routing nodes to recover the path more effectively. So, we propose new local repair scheme in AODV[1]. The scheme provides effective local repair using candidate nodes and hello messages.

---

[*] This research was supported by the Brain Korea 21 project.
[**] Corresponding author.

P. Thulasiraman et al. (Eds.): ISPA 2007 Workshops, LNCS 4743, pp. 105–114, 2007.
© Springer-Verlag Berlin Heidelberg 2007

The candidate node is need for candidate path. The candidae path is repair path to the destination node. When a link break in an active route occurs, the node can repair by its candidate node and candidate path. Our scheme needs to change Hello message format. The original hello message has a 1-hop TTL(time-to-live). But we need 2-hops TTL.

This paper is organized as follows. In section 2, related works are presented. Our local repair scheme is described in section 3. Performance analysis is presented in section 4. Finally, conclusions with future research works are presented in section 5.

2 Related Work

Recent performance advancements in computer and wireless communications technologies, advanced mobile wireless computing are expected to see increasingly widespread use and application. The vision of mobile ad hoc networking is to support robust and efficient operation in mobile wireless networks by incorporating routing functionality into mobile nodes. Such networks are envisioned to have dynamic, sometimes rapidly-changing, random, multihop topologies which are likely composed of relatively bandwidth-constrained wireless links. [3]

2.1 Ad Hoc On-Demand Distance Vector Routing Protocol

The Ad hoc On-Demand Distance Vector (AODV) algorithm enables dynamic, self-starting, multihop routing between participating mobile nodes wishing to establish and maintain an ad hoc network. The AODV allows mobile nodes to obtain routes quickly for new destinations, and does not require nodes to maintain routes to destinations that are not in active communication. [1]

The operation of AODV is loop-free, and by avoiding the Bellman-Ford "counting to infinity" problem offers quick convergence when the ad hoc network topology changes (typically, when a node moves in the network). When links break, AODV causes the affected set of nodes to be notified so that they are able to invalidate the routes using the lost link.

One distinguishing feature of AODV is its use of a destination sequence number for each route entry. It explains next section 2.2.

2.2 The Problem of Local Repair in AODV

Every route table entry at every node must include the latest information available about the sequence number for the IP address of the destination node. This sequence number is called the "destination sequence number." DSN is updated whenever a node receives new information from RREQ, RREP, or RERR messages. Be received related to that destination. The AODV depends on each node in the network to own and maintain its destination sequence number to guarantee the loop-freedom of all routes towards that node.

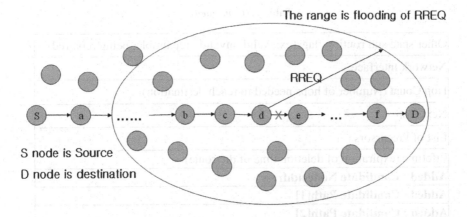

Fig. 1. The existing Local Repair Scheme

The AODV Using the DSN (Destination Sequence Number) ensures loop freedom. However, the DSN cause the problem. The local repair using DSN can not utilize pre-connected routing nodes.

3 An Effective Local Repair in AODV

We propose more effective path recovery scheme that uses the Candidate nodes and Hello messages. This scheme provides the solution that utilizes the pre-connected routing nodes. The proposed scheme needs to change the routing table and change the message formats.

3.1 Changed Routing Table

The existing Routing table can not support the candidate node and the candidate path. Therefore, we need to change the routing table. The candidate node address is added in the routing table to support the candidate node and the candidate path.

Table 1. Routing Table[1]

Table Name
Destination IP Address
Destination Sequence Number
Valid Destination Sequence Number flag

Table 1. *(Continued)*

Other state and routing flags(ex., valid, invalid, repairable, being repaired)
Network Interface
Hop Count (Number of hops needed to reach destination)
Next Hop
List of Precursors
Lifetime (expiration of deletion time of the route)
Added : Candidate Node address
Added : Candidate Path[1]
Added : Candidate Path[2]
Added : Candidate Path[3]
....
Added : Candidate Path[n-1]
Added : Candidate Path[n]

3.2 Changed Message Formats

The message formats needs to be changed to be used as candidate node. We explain the changed message formats in this section.

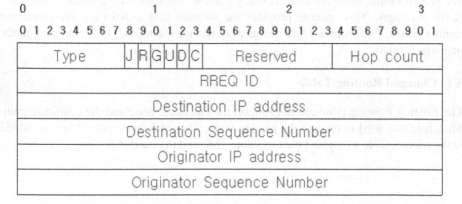

Fig. 2. New RREQ Message format

The RREQ (Route Request) Message format is changed. We added the flag C. If the flag C is set, .the nodes uses candidate node and candidate path. The flag C and R is set, the nodes executes proposed local repair scheme.

The RREP (Route Reply) Message format is changed. We added a candidate node IP address, and flag C. The candidate node IP address supports candidate path. If the flag C is set, the RREP message is local repair message for proposed scheme.

The Hello message changed only one field-TTL=2.

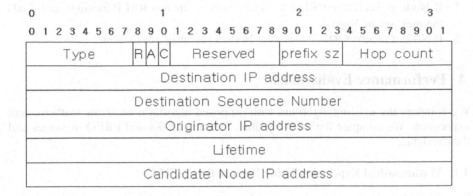

Fig. 3. New RREP Message format

3.3 The Scenario for New Local Repair

In figure 4, it explains the link repair scenario when it detects a broken link for the next hop of an active route in its routing table.

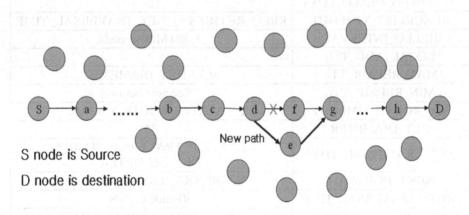

S node is Source

D node is destination

Fig. 4. The Link Repair using the proposed Scheme

1. Node d detects a broken link to Node f.
2. Node d chooses to execute the Local repair or reconfiguring the Link by Source Node.
3. If it selects to do a Local repair, Node d searches candidate path in its routing table.
4. If Node d has candidate path. Node d unicasts RREQ Message to Node g to repair the link If Node d does not have candidate path. Node d executes existing local repair scheme.

5. If Node g receives a RREQ message, Node g creates RREP message and sends the message to Node d.
6. If Node d receives RREP message, Node d reconfigures the link.

4 Performance Evaluations

We compare the existing algorithm with proposed algorithm using the mathematical expression. We compare the recovery time, the area of flooded RREQ messages and the overhead.

4.1 Mathematical Expression Using Parameters in RFC

The RFC3561 defines the parameters [1]. This paper uses these parameters. The Table 2 presented the parameters.

Table 2. Parameters in RFC [1]

Parameter Name	Value
ACTIVE_ROUTE_TIMEOUT	3,000 Milliseconds
ALLOWED_HELLO_LOSS	2
BLACKLIST_TIMEOUT	RREQ_RETRIES * NET_TRAVERSAL_TIME
HELLO_INTERVAL	1,000 Milliseconds
LOCAL_ADD_TTL	2
MAX_REPAIR_TTL	0.3 * NET_DIAMETER
MIN_REPAIR_TTL	See note below
MY_ROUTE_TIMEOUT	2 * ACTIVE_ROUTE_TIMEOUT
NET_DIAMETER	35
NET_TRAVERSAL_TIME	2 * NODE_TRAVERSAL_TIME * NET_DIAMETER
NEXT_HOP_WAIT	NODE_TRAVERSAL_TIME + 10
NODE_TRAVERSAL_TIME	40 milliseconds
PATH_DISCOVERY_TIME	2 * NET_TRAVERSAL_TIME
RERR_RATELIMIT	10
RING_TRAVERSAL_TIME	2 * NODE_TRAVERSAL_TIME * (TTL_VALUE + TIMEOUT_BUFFER)
RREQ_RETRIES	2
RREQ_RATELIMIT	10
TTL_START	1
TTL_INCREMENT	2
TTL_THRESHOLD	7

*The MIN_REPAIR_TTL should be the last known hop count to the destination.

4.2 Delay Time

Delay time of the exiting local repair can be calculated as below. LOCAL_REPAIR_TIME means the time required to finish the local repair

LOCAL_REPAIR_TIME <=
2 × NODE_TRAVERSAL_TIME × 2 × LR_RREQ_TTL

LR_RREQ_TTL =
MAX (MIN_REPAIR_TTL, 0.5 × #hop) + LOCAL_ADD_TTL

Since the minimum LR_RREQ_TTL is bigger then 4, the maximum LR_RREQ_TTL is 0.3 × NET_DIAMETER + 2.

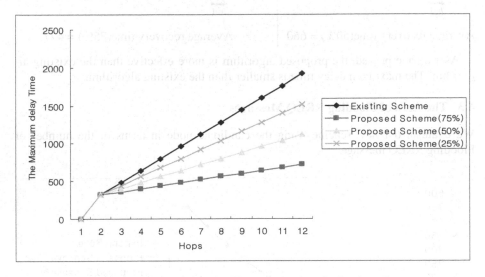

Fig. 5. The Maximum delay Time comparison for local repair

Delay time of propose scheme is calculated as below, in which NEW_LOCAL_REPAIR_TIME is the time required to finish the repair with our scheme.
  NEW_LOCAL_REPAIR_TIME =
(2 × NODE_TRAVERSAL_TIME × 2 × LR_RREQ_TTL × Pe) + {2 × NODE_TRAVERSAL_TIME × 2 × 2(hops) × (1 − Pe)}
* Pe = the probability of existence.
The path discovery time influences the range of a broadcast message. However, the proposed scheme provides faster local repair time. We check the maximum delay time of ad hoc network. As the size of the network increased, maximum delay time increases.
The sum of delay time in the Existing Scheme = ODT (OLD_DELAY_TIME)

The sum of delay time in the Proposed Scheme(Pe) =
NDT(Pe) (NEW_DELAY_TIME_Pe)

ODT = $$\sum_{h=1}^{h\rightarrow12} = ODT = 12320$$ Average recovery time = 1027	NDT(25%) = $$\sum_{h=1}^{h\rightarrow12} = NDT(25\%) = 10120$$ Average recovery time(25%) = 843
NDT(50%) = $$\sum_{h=1}^{h\rightarrow12} = NDT(50\%) = 7920$$ Average recovery time(50%) = 660	NDT(75%) = $$\sum_{h=1}^{h\rightarrow12} = NDT(75\%) = 5720$$ Average recovery time(75%) = 477

As we have proved, the proposed algorithm is more effective than the existing algorithm. The maximum delay time is smaller than the existing algorithm.

4.3 The Area of Flooding RREQ Messages

We evaluate our new scheme using the candidate node in terms of the number of Flooding RREQ message

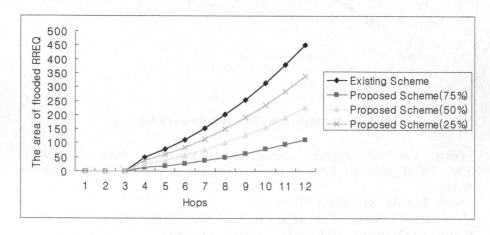

Fig. 6. The area of flooded RREQ

For the existing Scheme,
AREA_DELIVERY_LR_RREQ=∏ * (LR_RREQ_TTL)2

For the propose Scheme,
NEW_AREA_DELIVERY_LR_RREQ=∏ * (LR_RREQ_TTL)2 * Pe
* Pe = The probability of existence.

The area of flooded RREQ messages in the Existing Scheme = OAD (OLD_AREA_DELIVERY)

The area of flooded RREQ messages in the Existing Scheme(Pe) = NAD(pe) (NEW_AREA_DELIVERY_Pe)

$$\sum_{h\rightarrow1}^{h\rightarrow12} = OAD = 2098$$

The average Area = 175

$$\sum_{h\rightarrow1}^{h\rightarrow12} = NAD(25\%) = 1573$$

The average Area(25%) = 131

$$\sum_{h\rightarrow1}^{h\rightarrow12} = NAD(50\%) = 1049$$

The average Area(50%) = 87

$$\sum_{h\rightarrow1}^{h\rightarrow12} = NAD(75\%) = 524$$

The average Area(75%) = 44

As the size of the network increases, the area of flooded RREQ messages in the existing algorithm. But, the proposed algorithm uses candidate path. The candidate path does not need to flood RREQ. It reduces the number of flooded RREQ messages.

5 Conclusions and Future Works

In this paper, we propose an effective local repair scheme for AODV. The existing local repair scheme can not utilize the pre-connected routing nodes. But we propose scheme improves performance using the candidate node and hello message. The candidate nodes are used to recover the disconnected path using the pre-connected routing information : The candidate path. The proposed scheme provides a good result with less control packets and faster path recovery time. The ad hoc network is organized with mobile nodes. Ad hoc network needs more effective Algorithm. Our next goal is to make an effective routing protocol for ad hoc sensor network.

Acknowledgement

This research was supported by the MIC(Ministry of Information and Communication), Korea, under the ITRC (Information Technology Research Center) support program supervised by the IITA (Institute of Information Technology Assessment).

References

1. Perkins, R.C., Belding-Royer, E., Das, S.: Ad hoc On-Demand Distance Vector (AODV). RFC 3561 (2003).
2. Clausen, T., Jacquet, P. (eds.): Optimized Link State Routing Protocol (OLSR). In: RFC 3626 (2003)

3. Corson, S., Macker, J.: Mobile Ad hoc Networking (MANET): Routing Protocol Performance Issues and Evaluation Considerations. RFC 2501 (1999)
4. Johnson, D.B., Maltz, D.A., Hu, Y.-c., Jetcheva, J.G.: The Dynamic Source Routing Protocol for Mobile Ad Hoc Networks(DSR). Internet Draft, IETF MANET Working Group, draft-ietf-manet-dsr-07.txt (2002)
5. IETF MANET working Group, http://ietf.org/html.charters/manet-charter.html
6. Haas, Z.J., Perlman, M.R.: The Zone Routing Protocol(ZRP) for Ad Hoc Networks, Internet Draft. IETF MANET Working Group, draft-ietf-manet-zone-3.txt (2000)
7. http://www.netmeister.org/misc/zrp/zrp.html
8. Ko, Y.-B., Vaidya, N.H.: Location-Aided Routing(LAR) in mobile Ad-hoc network. Wireless Networks 6(4), 307–321 (2000)
9. Basagni, S., Chlamtac, I., Syrotiuk, V.R., Woodward, B.A.: A distance routing affect algorithm for mobility(DREAM). In: Proc. of the ACM/IEEE International Conf. on Mobile computing and Networking, pp. 76–84 (1998)
10. Karp, B., Kung, H.T.: GPSR: greedy perimeter stateless routing for wireless networks. In: Proc. of the international conf. on Mobile computing and networking, pp. 243–254 (2000)
11. Clausen, T., Dearlove, C.: Representing multi-value time in MANETs. Internet Draft, IETF MANET Working Group, draft-ietf-manet-timetlv-00 (2007)
12. Liao, W., Sheu, J., Tseng, Y.: GRID: A Fully Location-Aware Routing Protocol for Mobile Ad Hoc Networks. Telecom. Systems, 18, 37–60 (2001)
13. Clausen, T., Dearlove, C., Dean, J., Adjih, C.: Generalized MANET Packet/Message Format, Internet Draft. IETF MANET Working Group, draft-ietf-manet-packetbb-04 (2007)
14. IETF autoconf working Group, http://ietf.org/html.charters/autoconf-charter.html
15. Baccelli, E., Mase, K., Ruffino, S., Singh, S.: Address Autoconfiguration for MANET: Terminology and Problem Statement. Internet Draft, IETF autoconf Working Group, draft-baccelli-autoconf-statement-03 (2007)

A Frame-Based Selective Encryption Method for Real Time Video Transmission on VoIP*

Kwangmo Yang and Keecheon Kim**

Dept. of Computer Science & Engineering, Konkuk University,
Gwang-Jin Gu, Seoul, Korea
{eagle,kckim}@konkuk.ac.kr

Abstract. In the past, the main purpose of telephony network is to transfer the voice. But Since 1990, there have been many changes about it. First of all, wireless mobile communication network has enjoyed tremendous growth at the popularity. And the purpose of communication has been changed to data communication from voice one. Furthermore, people have started to require both data communication and voice communication. Because of these issues, VoIP (Voice over IP) is getting to be a matter of concern. And According to development of network and computer devices, people want to communicate by not only voice telecommunication but also video telecommunication. However because it uses public IP network, security issues are getting to be an important thing in VoIP. Actually, there are many solutions to protect data from attackers in VoIP System. But to serve video transmission needs more special care. To display real time video streaming on telephones need more bandwidth and computing power. This is a handicap for video streaming on the mobile device. Therefore we concentrate on the solution how to protect the video data from attackers with well quality of service. This is discussed in this paper.

1 Introduction

VoIP, voice over IP, converts the voice signal from telephone into a digital signal that transmitted over the Internet. It can allow you to make a call from a computer, a special VoIP phone, or a traditional phone. It requires real-time communication over IP that can transfer multimedia streaming. And VoIP service needs the position of UA to be registered. In SIP [5] based VoIP, SIP [5] server allow UA to establish session by providing position information if it is available.

VoIP packetizes phone calls through the same routes with public network that is Internet and is consequently it exposed by cyber threats. These include denial of service attacks, worm, viruses, and hacker exploitation. Of course, in addition to these traditional network security issues, there are also new issues for VoIP, such as spam and man in the Middle (eavesdropping and altering). So in VoIP, the security has the most important concern. In particular, to protect user's private information is very

---

* This research was supported by the Brain Korea 21 Project.
** Corresponding author.

P. Thulasiraman et al. (Eds.): ISPA 2007 Workshops, LNCS 4743, pp. 115–122, 2007.
© Springer-Verlag Berlin Heidelberg 2007

important. A call must cannot be intercepted or modified by a malicious third party. It should be impossible for a hacker to steal data between the end parties.

The challenge of VoIP security is not new. History has shown that many other advanced security solutions in information technology that typically satisfy the corresponding realistic security requirements. And these technologies have been widely adopted and deployed. However, in aspect about quality of service, to keep up reliable security is accompanied with less QoS. Quality of Service refers to the speed and clarity expected of a VoIP telecommunication. It makes attacks easier and defense harder. But to solve these problems, implementing proper security measures such as firewalls and encryption causes latency and jitter. To make matters more miserable, it carry serious QoS problem for video communication in VoIP.

In this paper, we concentrate on the solution for encryption of data. In order to improve QoS with security for video communication, we propose a frame-based selective encryption method. By considering reduced encryption delay using by the relationship between intra-coded frame and inter-coded frame, our method can support security and performance. For the purposes of our study, we use H.263 compression algorithm, because of its low encoding delay that well applied with the characteristic of VoIP. VoIP video transmission requires real time encoding, streaming and decoding because it used for telecommunication.

This paper is organized as fallows. In section 2, we describe the requirements and approaches with analyzing the relationship between intra-frame and inter-frame in H.263. And deduce that we don't have to encrypt all frames. In section 3, we propose a frame-based selective encryption method for VoIP video transmission. Simulation results to measure the method's performance are given in section 4. Finally, we conclude this paper in section 5.

2   Analysis of Requirements and Approaches

To supply QoS for video transmission in VoIP, it needs following requirements

- Encoding delay needs short latency
- In order to apply to wireless VoIP, it has to can transmit data with low bandwidth environment

Because of these factors, we choose H.263 [3] even if H.264 (AVC) [9] and MPEG 4 Visual [10] have double quality at same bandwidth compare with H.263. For the high compression rate and high quality, H.264 [9] and MPEG 4 Visual [10] have more encoding delay than H.263.

H.263 is an improved video coding standard for video conferencing and other audiovisual services transmitted in PSTN. It aims low bit-rate communications at bit-rates of less than 64 kbps. And H.263 [3] is a lossy compression technique. It uses predictive coding for inter-frames to reduce temporal redundancy and transform coding for the remaining signal to reduce spatial redundancy (for both Intra-frame and Inter-frame prediction).

3   Frame-Based Selective Encryption Method

Intra-frames are treated as independent images. Transform coding method similar to JPEG is applied within Intra-frame. And Inter-frames are not independent. Inter-coded frame composed by P-frame and B-frame. They are coded by referencing other Intra-frame or Inter-frame (P-frame). H.263 is organized by these three frames (B-frame is optional). Of course, to avoid propagation of coding errors, an I-frame is usually sent periodically.

(a)   (b)

Fig. 1. Displaying comparison between only Intra-coded frames and only inter-coded frames

At first, to analyze how displayed each frames we have an experiment by make a simple application using standard H.263 codec and RTP [1]. Fig. 1 (a) shows only Intra-coded frames and (b) shows only Intra-coded frames. Intra-frames have all information of picture but Inter-frames don't have. As this result we find it hard to recognize inter-coded frame pictures. So we suggest that inter-coded frames inherit their required security from the security of the Intra-frames. Of course, although this approach would reduce the encryption processing delay, in the displayed view of (b) that the achieved security level of this approached method is not robust. This is because the inter-coded frames (P- and B-frames) include many Intra-coded macro-blocks. But like the approach of Agi and Gong [12], if increase the frequency of Intra-frames in the video sequence in order to improve the security level, this reduces the efficiency of the compression algorithm and the achieved savings on the processing delays by selective encryption method. And as the result in Fig. 1 we consider that to encrypt only Intra-coded frames is enough to protect private information.

3.1   How to Discover Intra-Coded Frames

It is described by RFC 2190, "RTP Payload Format for H.263 Video Streams" [7] how to discover Intra-coded frames. Fig. 2 is RTP structure for H.263 [7] and Fig. 3 is H.263 payload header for RTP [7].

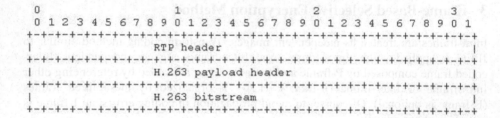

Fig. 2. RTP structure for H.263

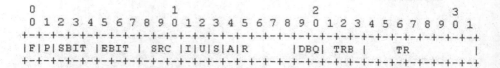

Fig. 3. H.263 payload header for RTP

Fig. 2 shows RTP structure for each RTP packet, the RTP fixed header is followed by the H.263 payload header, which is followed by the standard H.263 compressed bit-stream [3]. Fig. 3 is mode A of H.263 payload header for RTP. In this mode, an H.263 bit-stream will be packetized on a GOB boundary or a picture boundary. Packets of mode A always start with the H.263 picture start code [3] or a GOB.

In Fig. 3 we can see I-flag that is picture coding type. I flag is on the bit 9 in PTYPE defined by H.263 [3], "0" is intra-coded, "1" is inter-coded. RTP sender can assign flag I and send the packet to RTP receiver. And RTP receiver can judge which packet has encrypted frame by just seeing I flag.

3.2 Security Key Exchange

To protect key from brute force attack, the security key has to be changed periodically and transmitted to the receiver with encrypted form. Moreover to operate key exchange, key have to be transmitted over public network in VoIP. A public-key crypto system such as RSA standard algorithm is used for this purpose. This means that two keys are used in the encryption and decryption process. RSA has the advantage that the attacker can not apply the same method to attack the two keys. But the RSA standard requires long processing time. This makes it hard to apply on Mobile VoIP. We make an assumption that fundamental VoIP system provides robust key exchange algorithm with low cost.

3.3 Use Reserved Flag

We propose to use R flag on Fig. 3 that is reserved and must be set to zero. Using a bit we set the flag as "E." If E flag set to 1, a receiver receiving RTP streaming can know that packet is encrypted, otherwise 0. We didn't treat how to tell the information what kind of encryption algorithm is used.

4 Experiment and Results

In this section we have analyzed the performances of the proposed Selective Encryption Method. In order to simulate our proposal, a simple application is utilized including simulation module. In this implement, because we didn't care of the latency by exchange of key, there is no key exchange operation. Both sender and receiver have same security key in their memory. Used Encryption algorithm is DES 128 bit.

4.1 Test-Bed Architecture

Test-bed is organized by sender and receiver. Sender is divided by two modules. First one is Video Transmitter and second one is RTP Proxy. Sender's system structure is shown as Fig. 4. As Fig. 4, Video Transmitter module captures each picture formatted RGB at first. Then pictures captured by video capture device are sent to H.263 video

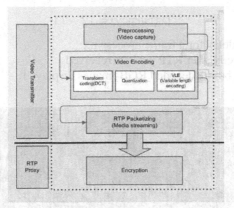

Fig. 4. System model of Sender

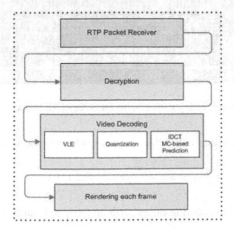

Fig. 5. System model of Receiver

encoder. Encoded frames are packetized by RTP packetizing module and sent to encryption module. In order to make it easy to realize two methods both selective frame encryption and all frames encryption, we encrypt RTP payload after frames are packetized. Encrypted RTP packet is sent by public IP network. We divided sender by two modules physically but actually these two modules would be in a device.

Receiver's system structure is shown as Fig. 5. Received each RTP packet is sent to decryption module. Then decrypted frames are decoded by H263 decoder. And display by GDI renderer.

4.2 Simulation Result

Both Fig.6 and Fig. 7 show that the processing delays by the time. In Fig. 1 experiment, all of frames are encrypted. And in Fig. 7, selected frames are encrypted. In Both graph, X axis means time and Y means latency by decryption. To measure the delay we use following expression

$$D \text{ (latency)} = T2 - T1$$

- D (latency): The delay for a frame processing
- T1: The time directly after RTP packets received
- T2: The time just before decoded RGB images displayed

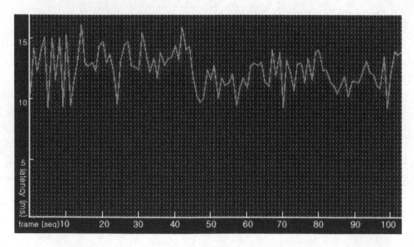

Fig. 6. Encryption Latency with 128 bit DES Key (All frames are encrypted)

To measure of processing time delay, we use following expression

$$T_n = \sum_{i=1}^{n} (T2_i - T1_i)$$

Tn: Total processing delay with an assigned number of times

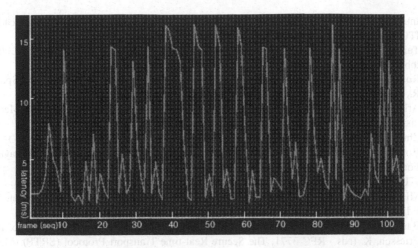

Fig. 7. Encryption Latency with 128 bit DES Key (Selected frames are encrypted)

In Fig. 6 the average of processing delay is 72 milli-seconds. On the other hand, in Fig. 7 the average of processing delay is 46 milli-seconds. According to these two simulation results, our approach reduces the decryption processing time by about 60~65%.

5 Conclusion

Video transmission is one of the most important emerging trends in telecommunications. VoIP has two advantages that have an important role to implement video telephony. The first one is cost saving factor and the second one is flexibility factor that allow new service and new application to be added to standard telephony services. But with all its advantages, VoIP is known it is difficult to supply reliable services due to security risks. There are many advanced security solutions for VoIP. However because of the characteristic of security, to support robust security carry high latency. That is deadly factor for video transmission because it needs more computing power and the next VoIP phone would be a mobile phone. Thus, frame-based selective encryption method for H.263-based RTP is proposed. It is designed for support security with high performance. Compared with typical SRTP [11], this proposal can improve the working performance. Moreover, experimental results show that this proposal has lower latency for cryptographic processing than related works.

References

1. Schulzrinne, H., Casner, S., Frederick, R., Jacobson, V.: RTP: A Transport Protocol for Real-Time Applications. RFC 1889 (January 1996)
2. Schulzrinne, H.: RTP Profile for Audio and Video Conference with Minimal Control. RFC 1890 (January 1996)

 3. International Telecommunication Union. Video Coding for Low Bit-rate Communication, ITU-T Recommendation H.263 (1996)
 4. Turletti, T., Huitema, C.: RTP Payload Format for H.261 Video Streams. RFC 2032 (October 1996)
 5. Rosenberg, J., Schulzrinne, H., Camarillo Ericsson, G., Johnston, A., Peterson, J., Sparks, R., Handley, M.: ICIR. In: SIP: Session Initiation Protocol (June 2002)
 6. Arkko, J., Torvinen, V., Camarillo Ericsson, G., Niemi, A., Haukka, T.: Security Mechanism Agreement for the Session Initiation Protocol (SIP). RFC 3329 (January 2003)
 7. Zhu, C.: RTP Payload Format for H.263 Video Streams, RFC 2190 (September 1997)
 8. Bormann, C., Sullivan, G., Wenger, S., Even, R(ed.): Polycom, RFC 4629, RTP Payload Format for ITU-T Rec. H.263 Video (January 2007)
 9. ITU-T H.264 Advanced video coding for generic audiovisual Services Mars (2005)
10. MPEG4 ISO/IEC 14496-2:2001, Coding of Audio-Visual Objects - Part 2: Visual, 2nd Edition (2001)
11. Baugher, M., McGrew, D.: Cisco Systems, Inc. In: Naslund, M., Carrara, E., Norrman Ericsson, K. (eds.) RFC 3771, The Secure Real-time Transport Protocol (SRTP) (March 2004)
12. Agi, I., Gong, L.: An Empirical Study of Secure MPEG-I Video Transmissions, Proceedings of SNDSS, 137–143 (1996)

ECG Anomaly Detection via Time Series Analysis

Mooi Choo Chuah and Fen Fu

Department of Computer Science & Engineering
Lehigh University
chuah@cse.lehigh.edu, fef205@lehigh.edu

Abstract. Recently, wireless sensor networks have been proposed for assisted living and residential monitoring. In such networks, physiological sensors are used to monitor vital signs e.g. heartbeats, pulse rates, oxygen saturation of senior citizens. Sensor data is sent periodically via wireless links to a personal computer that analyzes the data. In this paper, we propose an anomaly detection scheme based on time series analysis that will allow the computer to determine whether a stream of real-time sensor data contains any abnormal heartbeats. If anomaly exists, that time series segment will be transmitted via the network to a physician so that he/she can further diagnose the problem and take appropriate actions. When tested against the heartbeat data readings stored at the MIT database, our ECG anomaly scheme is shown to have better performance than another scheme that has been recently proposed. Our scheme enjoys an accuracy rate that varies from 70-90% while the other scheme has an accuracy that varies from 40-70%.

1 Introduction

Recent report [1] has indicated that an aging baby-boom generation is stressing the US healthcare system. Hospital administrators and other medical care-givers are looking for ways to maintain quality of care at reduced costs. Thus, some researchers [1] have proposed to shift from the familiar centralized, expert-driven, crisis-care model to one that allows senior citizens to live with informal caregivers e.g. family, friends, and community. They propose using wireless sensor networks that can provide capabilities that are valuable for continuous, remote monitoring [1]. In such sensor networks [1],[2],[9], wireless devices are integrated with a wide variety of environmental and medical sensors. Vital sign data can be collected automatically, thus enabling remote medical monitoring and diagnosis. It is envisioned that such a system needs to be designed efficiently since some of these monitoring devices run on battery and thus have limited power constraints. Usually sensor data is collected by some intermediate storage nodes which have higher wireless bandwidth. For better energy efficiency, the intermediate storage nodes can process these real-time streams to identify any abnormality. Once identified, only the abnormal data needs to be sent to the physician for further diagnosis while the rest of the normal data can be archived at the local storage nodes. The local storage nodes can further transfer such normal data to longer term storage units at a slower time scale (e.g. daily). The system can also provide a feature for the physician to request for more detailed immediate data from the local storage nodes or change the frequency of monitoring of the sensor nodes.

P. Thulasiraman et al. (Eds.): ISPA 2007 Workshops, LNCS 4743, pp. 123–135, 2007.
© Springer-Verlag Berlin Heidelberg 2007

Three important vital signs that are usually collected in such a medical sensor monitoring system are heartbeats, pulse rates and oxygen saturation. As described earlier, it is more energy efficient to transmit only abnormal data via wireless links. To decide if a real time sensor data stream contains abnormal data, one needs to use an anomaly detection scheme. In this paper, we propose an adaptive window-based discord discovery (AWDD) scheme to detect abnormal heartbeats within a series of heartbeat readings. Our scheme is an enhancement of the Brute Force Discord Discovery (BFDD) scheme proposed in [4]. Using the heartbeat records from the MIT-BIH arrhythmia database [3], we demonstrate that our AWDD scheme provides higher accuracy in distinguishing between normal/abnormal heartbeats within a 40 seconds excerpts of heartbeat readings when compared to the BFDD.

The rest of the paper is organized as follows: In Section II, we summarized related work. In Section 3, we describe both the BFDD and the AWDD schemes. In Section 4, we present the training and test results when the two schemes are applied to the records selected from the MIT-BIH arrhythmia database. We conclude in Section 5.

2 Related Work

Heart arrhythmias result from any disturbance in the regularity, rate, site of origin or conduction of the cardiac electric impulse [1],[2]. There are two groups of arrhythmias [2]: (i) the first group is life threatening and includes ventricular fibrillation and tachycardia, and (ii) the second group is not life threatening but may require medical attention to prevent bigger problems. There are well researched and successful detectors for detection of the first group of arrhythmias. Such detectors have high sensitivity and specificity [3],[4],[5],[6],[7]. However, these detectors have been tested using data collected from expensive medical sensors. In our work, we hope to use cheaper medical sensor nodes which may generate more noisy data. Thus, we are focusing more on the detection of the second group events.

Due to the limited power resources in a sensor-based medical information system, we need to use an anomaly detection scheme that is not computationally expensive. In a seminal paper [4], the authors introduce the new problem of finding time series discords. Time series discords are subsequences of a longer time series that are maximally different to all the rest of the time series subsequences. Time series discords have many uses for data mining including data cleaning, improving quality of clustering and anomaly detection. The authors in [4] propose two discord discovery algorithms, namely the Brute Force Discord Discovery (BFDD) and the Heuristic Discord Discovery (HDD) schemes. The BFDD scheme has a $O(m^2)$ time complexity while the HDD can have an $O(m)$ time complexity where m is the number of samples in the time series. The authors show that their schemes can be used to detect discords that exist within Electrocardiograms (ECGs) (which are a time series of the electrical potential between two points on the surface of the body caused by a beating heart). For example in Figure 1, the identified discord coincides with the location annotated by a cardiologist as containing an anomalous heartbeat. The Adaptive Window Based Discord Discovery (AWDD) scheme that we design in this paper is motivated by the two schemes in [4], and will be described in more details in Section 3.

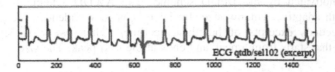

Fig. 1. The time series discord in an excerpt of electrocardiogram qtdb/sel102 (marked in bold) which coincides with a premature ventricular contraction [4]

3 Overview of the BFDD and AWDD Schemes

3.1 Notations Used

Before describing both the BFDD and the AWDD schemes that find discords in a time series, we first list the notations we use (which is the same as [4]):

Times Series: *A time series $T = t1, ..., tm$ is an ordered set of m real-valued variables. In this project, the real-valued variables are the heartbeat sensor readings.*

Subsequence: Given a time series T of length m, a subsequence C of T is a sampling of length $n{\leq}m$ of contiguous position from T, that is, $C = tp, ..., tp+n-1$ for $1 \leq p \leq m-n+1$.

Sliding Window: Given a time series T of length m, and a user-defined subsequence length of n, all possible subsequences can be extracted by sliding a window of size n across T and considering each subsequence Cp.

Distance: *Dist* is a function that has C and M as inputs and returns a nonnegative value R, which is said to be the distance from M to C. For subsequent definitions to work we require that the function D be symmetric, that is, $Dist(C,M) = Dist(M,C)$.

Euclidean Distance: Given two time series Q and C of length n, the Euclidean distance between them is defined as: $Dist(Q,C) = $ sqrt $[\sum (qi - ci)^2]$.

Non-Self Match: Given a time series T, containing a subsequence C of length n beginning at position p and a matching subsequence M beginning at q, we say that M is a non-self match to C at distance of $Dist(M,C)$ if $| p - q| \geq n$.

Time Series Discord: Given a time series T, the subsequence D of length n beginning at position l is said to be the discord of T if D has the largest distance to its nearest non-self match. That is, $\forall$ subsequence C of T, non-self match MD of D, and non-self match Mc of C, $\min(Dist(D, MD)) > \min(Dist(C, Mc))$.

3.2 Adaptive Window Based Discord Discovery (AWDD) Scheme

The original BFDD algorithm proposed in [4] is a one-pass algorithm which uses a fixed window size and hence a user needs to specify the window size. This algorithm compares a fixed length subsequence with another subsequence of the same length that is obtained by sliding down a given time series one sample at a time. Hence, the original BFDD scheme is very computational expensive. Our AWDD scheme is motivated by the BFDD scheme. The AWDD scheme is a two-pass approach with adaptive window size. In the first pass, we identify the peak points in the 40-seconds excerpts of heartbeat readings. Then, we consider only the subsequence that starts from a peak and ends at the next peak. The size of the sliding

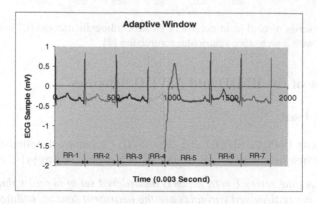

Fig. 2. Adaptive Window

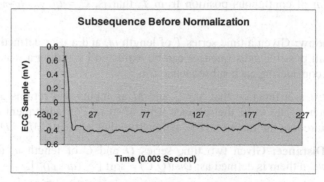

(a) Time-Series Subsequence: Before Normalization

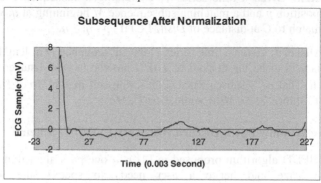

(b) Time-Series Subsequence: After Normalization

Fig. 3. Normalization of Time Series Subsequence

```
Function [dist, loc] = Brute_Force ( T, n )
best_so_far = 0
best_so_far = NaN
outer_cnt = 0

for  p = 1 to | T | - n + 1          // begin outer loop
        nearest_neighbor_dist = infinity
        for  q = 1 to | T | - n + 1    // begin inner loop
                if |p − q| ≥ n    // non-self match?
                        if Dist ( tp … tp+n-1,  tq … tq+n-1 ) < nearest_neighbor_dist
                                nearest_neighbor_dist = Dist ( tp … tp+n-1,  tq … tq+n-1 )
                        end
                end
        end
        if nearest_neighbor_dist > best_so_far_dist
                best_so_far_dist = nearest_neighbor_dist
                best_so_far_dist = p
        end
end
return [ best_so_far_dist , best_so_far_loc ]
```

(a) Pseudo Code for BFDD scheme

```
Function [dist, loc] = Brute_Force ( T )
best_so_far = 0
best_so_far = NaN
num_of_peaks = 0
p = 1
while  p < |T|                                          // locate each peak
        if tp is locally the biggest sample
                peak_loc [ num_of_peaks ++ ] = p
        end
end
outer_cnt = 0
p = peak_loc [0]
while  p < peak_loc [ num_of_peaks − 2 ] + 1            // begin outer loop
        nearest_neighbor_dist = infinity
        outer_len = peak_pos [ outer_cnt + 1 ] − peak_pos [ outer_cnt ]
        inner_cnt = 0
        q = peak_loc [0]
        while  q < peak_loc [ num_of_peaks − 2 ] + 1    // begin inner loop
                inner_len = peak_pos [ inner_cnt + 1 ] − peak_pos [inner_cnt ]
                if outer_len > inner_len
                        compress tp … tp+ outer_len  to have a length of inner_len
                end
                if outer_len < inner_len
                        compress tq … tq+ inner_len to have a length of outer_len
                end
                if |p − q| ≥ min ( outer_len, inner_cnt )
                        if Dist ( tp … tp+ outer_len,  tq … tq+ inner_len ) < nearest_neighbor_dist
                                nearest_neighbor_dist = Dist ( tp … tp+ outer_len,  tq … tq+ inner_len )
                        end
                end
                q = peak_loc [ ++ inner_cnt ]
        end
        if nearest_neighbor_dist > best_so_far_dist
                best_so_far_dist = nearest_neighbor_dist
                best_so_far_dist = p
        end
        p = peak_loc [ ++ outer_cnt ]
end
return [ best_so_far_dist , best_so_far_loc ]
```

(b) Pseudo-Code for the AWDD scheme

Fig. 4. Discord Discovery Schemes

window is of one heartbeat's length, as illustrated in Figure 2. In Figure 2, RR-i denotes the heartbeat to heartbeat (denoted as RR) interval between heartbeats i and $(i+1)$. As in the original BFDD scheme, each subsequence is normalized to have a mean of zero and a standard deviation of one before calling the euclidean distance function, since it is meaningless to compare time series with different offsets and amplitudes [8]. Note that we use only euclidean distance in this work. Figure 3 shows the effect of normalization on a subsequence of time series obtained from the patient record 205.

In the second pass, we consider each possible subsequence, and find the distance between this and its nearest non-self match. The subsequence that has the largest distance is the discord. The location of the discord is accomplished with nested loops, where the outer loop considers each possible candidate subsequence, and the inner loop is a linear scan to identify the candidate's nearest non-self match.

The time complexity of the AWDD scheme will be $O(h^2)$ where h is the number of heartbeats but the technique that is used in HDD to reduce the time complexity to $O(m)$ can be equally applied to the AWDD scheme to produce a scheme with a time complexity of $O(h)$. As far as space is concerned, AWDD only requires an additional array to keep location of peaks.

For clarity, the pseudo code of the BFDD algorithm is shown in Figure 4(a), and our enhanced algorithm is shown in Figure 4(b). Since we are using adaptive windows, we make two more changes to determine and compare the discords. The first change is to ensure that we can compare subsequences of different lengths. To do this, we compress the longer subsequence to match the shorter one. The subsequences are normalized before any potential compression takes place. Figure 5 illustrates the effect of the compression on a subsequence of record 205.

The next change is to deal with the fact that one subsequence-pair may have more samples than the other subsequence-pair and hence we cannot compare the computed distances directly. We overcome this by scaling all distances such that they correspond to the distance computed using the same number of samples.

Figure 6 shows a 40-second ECG excerpt of the patient record 205 with samples from 290th second to 330th second. In this excerpt, abnormal heartbeats start from the 296.875^{th} second and end at the 305.900^{th} second. When feeding this 40-second ECG excerpt to the discord discovery algorithm, our enhanced algorithm locates the discord at the 302.531^{th} second. Its nearest non-self match is at the 296.875^{th} second. Their distance is 7.483. By checking the ECG record annotated by the cardiologists, we can tell that there is indeed an anomaly sitting at the location of the discord found by our algorithm. Figure 7 illustrates the two subsequences, where the discord and the nearest non-self match reside.

However, the discord found by the algorithm may or may not be an anomaly of the ECG excerpt. Thus, we use a configurable threshold to decide whether or not a discord is an anomaly. If the distance between the discord and its nearest non-self match exceeds the threshold, we determine that the discord found by our algorithm is an anomaly. Otherwise, our program will not flag this as an anomaly. This threshold is different for each patient and is found by training.

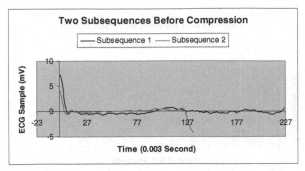

(a) Normalized Time-Series Subsequence: Before Compression

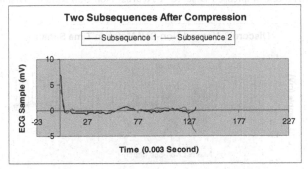

(b) Normalized Time-Series Subsequence: After Compression

Fig. 5. Compression of Normalized Time Series Subsequence

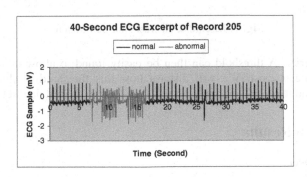

Fig. 6. A Sample 40-Second ECG Excerpt from MIT-BIH Record 205

We select some subsets of data from each patient's records as the training data. Each set of training data consists of 5 non-overlapping 40-second excerpts from the same patient, with at least one abnormal heartbeat (an abnormal ECG time series), and another 5 non-overlapping 40-second excerpts from the same patient, which do not contain any abnormal heartbeats (normal ECG time series). Then, we apply the algorithm to each set of training data. Our conjecture is that the distance for the discord in an abnormal ECG time series should be larger than the one in a normal

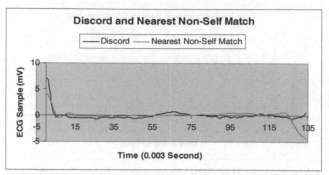

(a) Normalized & Compressed Discord & Nearest Non-Self Match: Distance = 7.843

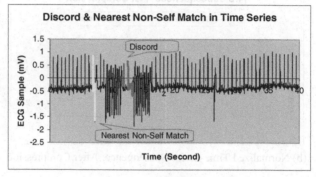

(b) Discord & Nearest Non-Self Match in the 40-Second ECG Excerpt (the same one as in Figure 6)

Fig. 7. Discord & Nearest Non-Self Match

ECG time series. A threshold can then be easily found to allow us to conclude if abnormal heartbeats exist. We will discuss how this threshold is chosen for each patient record and the results of applying this threshold to the test data set in Section 4.

4   Evaluation Results

4.1   ECG Datasets

Since our medical sensor boards are not ready yet, we use the ECG data from the MIT-BIH Arrhythmia Database [3]. The database contains 48 half-hour excerpts of two-channel ambulatory ECG recordings, obtained from 47 patients studied by the BIH Arrhythmia Laboratory. According to [3],[10], twenty-three of these recordings were chosen at random from a set of 4000 24-hour ambulatory ECG recordings collected from a mixed population of inpatients (about 60%) and outpatients (about 40%) at Boston's Beth Israel Hospital; the other 25 recordings were selected from the same set to include less common but clinically significant arrhythmias that would not be well-represented in a small random sample.

According to [3],[10], the recordings were digitized at 360 samples per second per channel with 11-bit resolution over a 10 mV range. Two or more cardiologists independently annotated each record; disagreements were resolved to obtain the computer-readable reference annotations for each beat (approximately 110,000 annotations in all) included with the database. Out of the 48 half-hour excerpts of two-channel ambulatory ECG recordings, we randomly select 6 half-hour excerpts, which are numbered as records 106, 108, 114, 205, 210, and 219 in the database. In each of the 6 half-hour ECG excerpts, we select 10 40-second excerpts, with 5 of them having abnormal heartbeats inside, and the other 5 having no abnormal heartbeats inside as the training set. We use the first channel ECG recordings, rather than use both channels' ECG recordings. Later, we select another 10 40-second excerpts from the same patient records as the test dataset.

4.2 Training and Testing Using Record 106

The 10 40-second ECG excerpts chosen from record 106 for training purposes are listed in Table 1. The first 5 40-second excerpts contain at least one abnormal heartbeat, and the remaining 5 excerpts do not contain any anomaly. The 3rd column indicates the location where the 1st abnormal heartbeat starts. For example, the 1st 40-second ECG excerpt from record 106 starts from the 80th second and ends at the 120th second, with the 1st abnormal heartbeat starting from 90.741^{th} second.

Using the BFDD scheme, the window is shifted by one ECG sample each time in both the inner and outer loops. The discord found in each of the 10 40-second ECG excerpts from record 106 is listed in Table 2(a). The last column tells if the heartbeat that the discord belongs to is an abnormal heartbeat. The distance column, which is next to that last column, tells the distance between a discord and its nearest non-self match. We can see that for excerpts 1-5, which do contain abnormal heartbeats, the reported distance between the located discord and its non-self match exceeds 6.5, and for excerpts 6-10, which do not contain abnormal heartbeats, the reported distance never exceeds 6.5, except excerpt 6. So we could set a distance threshold of 6.5, knowing that excerpt 6 will be misclassified as having an anomaly if similar data appear in the test set.

Table 1. 40-Second ECG Excerpts from MIT-BIH Record 106

Index of excerpts	start point - end point (second)	1st anomaly's location (second)
1	80-120	90.74
2	430-470	445.78
3	700-740	710.89
4	960-1000	965.98
5	1040-1080	1048.75
6	0-40	na
7	200-240	na
8	600-640	na
9	1320-1360	na
10	1380-1420	na

Table 2(b) show the results of applying this threshold to the ten test datasets using the BFDD scheme. We see that with a threshold of 6.5, excerpts 1,3 and 5 will not be classified as abnormal and except 10 will be classified as abnormal. So, our accuracy is only 60% (with 30% false negative and 10% false positive) using the BFDD scheme.

Table 2(a). Discords from the training set of MIT-BIH Record 106 using BFDD scheme

index of excerpts	start point - end point (second)	1st anomaly's location (second)	discord's location (second)	nearest non-self match's location (second)	distance between discord & nearest non-self match	is the discord an anomaly in reality?
1	80-120	90.741	86.611	80.917	7.21	No
2	430-470	445.783	440.611	467.917	6.56	No
3	700-740	710.886	728.25	731.222	7.14	Yes
4	960-1000	965.98	985.361	968.528	6.71	Yes
5	1040-1080	1048.75	1051.944	1056.861	6.78	Yes
6	0-40	na	na	Na	6.93	Na
7	200-240	na	na	Na	3.32	Na
8	600-640	na	na	Na	6.16	Na
9	1320-1360	na	na	Na	3.32	Na
10	1380-1420	na	na	Na	5.00	Na

Table 2(b). Discords from the test set of MIT-BIH Record 106 using BFDD scheme

index of excerpts	start point - end point (second)	1st anomaly's location (second)	discord's location (second)	nearest non-self match's location (second)	distance between discord & nearest non-self match	is the discord an anomaly in reality?
1	160-200	160.233	178.167	160.528	5.83	No
2	900-940	902.436	900.972	921.944	7.0	No
3	1200-1240	1203.213	1201.194	1207.25	5.92	Yes
4	1420-1460	1435.497	1421.639	1446.694	6.86	Yes
5	1600-1640	1614.7	1637.139	1627.222	5.0	Yes
6	270-310	na	na	Na	4.36	Na
7	320-360	na	na	Na	4.12	Na
8	380-420	na	na	Na	6.40	Na
9	500-540	na	na	Na	4.58	Na
10	560-600	na	na	Na	6.71	Na

Next, we train the AWDD scheme using the same training dataset. Table 3(a) shows the discord found in each of the 10 40-second ECG excerpts from the training set of patient record 106. We can see that for excerpts 1-5, which do contain abnormal heartbeats, their distance exceeds 2, and for excerpts 6-10, which do not contain abnormal heartbeats, their distance never exceeds 2. Thus, we could set a distance threshold of 2. If the distance between a discord and its nearest non-self match exceeds 2, we will declare the discovered discord as an anomaly and a cardiologist needs to examine the patient's time series.

In the test set shown in Table 3(b), all of the excerpts 1-5 have abnormal heartbeats. None of the excerpts 6-10 contain abnormal heartbeats. The results indicate that we can identify abnormality in excerpts 1-5 since the reported discord distance is greater than the threshold of 2 (which is chosen based on the training set). For excerpts 6-10 with normal heartbeats, only except 8, will report a discord distance which is slightly larger than the threshold of 2. Thus, we get an accuracy of 90% on this testing dataset using our adaptive window based discord discovery scheme. The false positive rate is 10%.

Table 3(a). Discords from the training set of MIT-BIH Record 106 using AWDD scheme

index of excerpts	start point - end point (second)	1st anomaly's location (second)	discord's location (second)	nearest non-self match's location (second)	distance between discord & nearest non-self match	is the discord an anomaly in reality?
1	80-120	90.741	116.675	96.828	3.17	Yes
2	430-470	445.783	452.653	446.261	2.13	Yes
3	700-740	710.886	725.464	729.858	20.85	Yes
4	960-1000	965.98	970.131	973.117	9.38	Yes
5	1040-1080	1048.75	1057.783	1043.897	7.41	Yes
6	0-40	na	na	na	1.36	na
7	200-240	na	na	na	0	na
8	600-640	na	na	na	1.49	na
9	1320-1360	na	na	na	1.38	na
10	1380-1420	na	na	na	0	na

Table 3(b). Discords from the test set of MIT-BIH Record 106 using AWDD scheme

index of excerpts	start point - end point (second)	1st anomaly's location (second)	discord's location (second)	nearest non-self match's location (second)	distance between discord & nearest non-self match	is the discord an anomaly in reality?
1	160-200	160.233	177.4	179.36	17.88	Yes
2	900-940	902.436	914.467	916.017	8.72	Yes
3	1200-1240	1203.213	1218.761	1220.578	9.9	Yes
4	1420-1460	1435.497	1446.622	1459.036	9.15	Yes
5	1600-1640	1614.7	1636.711	1625.739	2.9	Yes
6	270-310	na	na	na	0	na
7	320-360	na	na	na	0	na
8	380-420	na	na	na	2.08	na
9	500-540	na	na	na	0	na
10	560-600	na	na	na	1.06	na

4.3 Accuracy Comparison

We repeatedly performed the above operations on 20 40-second excerpts selected from patient records 108, 114, 205, 210 and 219. Ten excerpts are used for training purposes and ten excerpts are used for testing purposes. The accuracies of the reported anomalies using the BFDD and the AWDD schemes for the various patients are summarized in Table 4. In Table 4, the first number is the accuracy, the second number is the false negative rate, and the third number is the false positive rate. A higher false positive rate than the false negative rate is acceptable since it pays to check the patient slightly more frequently than to miss checking abnormal heartbeat events. The results indicate that our AWDD scheme can detect abnormality better than the BFDD scheme.

Table 4. Accuracy Using BFDD vs. AWDD Schemes

record	accuracy using fixed window (%)	accuracy using adaptive window (%)
106	60 (30,10)	90 (0, 10)
108	50 (10,40)	80 (10, 10)
114	70 (10,20)	80 (0, 20)
205	70 (30,0)	80 (10,10)
210	70 (0,30)	90 (0, 10)
219	40 (20, 40)	70 (30, 0)

5 Conclusion

In this paper, we have described an adaptive window-based discord discovery (AWDD) scheme for detecting abnormal patterns in the heartbeat related time series. Our scheme is motivated by the BFDD scheme proposed in [4] but we use adaptive rather than fixed windows. Our AWDD scheme uses a simple re-sampling method to compare two subsequences that are of different lengths. We apply both the BFDD and the ADWW schemes to ten 40-seconds excerpts of six patient records from the MIT-BH arrhythmia database. Our results show that the enhanced algorithm can achieve better accuracy in locating anomalies in the heartbeat time series of the patients.

We are currently building the Code-Blue mote-based medical sensors designed by Harvard [2]. Once we successfully test those Code-Blue sensors, we will collect heartbeat data from several volunteers. Then, we will apply the AWDD scheme to these more noisy heartbeat sensor data. We also hope to analyze the sensor data collected from pulse oximeters using the AWDD scheme to see if it is equally effective in detecting anomalies in time series of oxygen saturation readings. In addition, we intend to optimize this algorithm so that it can be run on a PDA. Software to display excerpts of medical sensor data with anomalies will also be developed.

Acknowledgment

This work is sponsored by PITA. Any opinions, findings, and conclusions or recommendations expressed in this material are those of the authors and do not necessarily reflect the views of PITA. We would like to thank Dr George Moody from MIT for patiently explaining the MIT-BIH database information and to Prof Keogh for making his code on HotSax available.

References

1. Wood, A., et al.: ALARM-NET: Wireless Sensor Networks for Assisted-Living Residential Monitoring, University of Virginia Computer Science Department Technical Report (2006)

2. Shnayer, V., et al.: Sensor Networks for Medical Care, Harvard University Division of Engineering and Applied Sciences Technical Report, TR-08-05 (2005)

3. MIT-BIH Arrhythmia Database: http://www.physionet.org/physiobank/database/mitdb/

4. Keogh, E., Lin, J., Fu, A.: HOT SAX: Efficiently Finding the Most Unusual Time Series Subsequence. In: The 5th IEEE International Conference on Data Mining (ICDM), IEEE Computer Society Press, Los Alamitos (2005)

5. Thaler, M.S.: The only EKG book you'll ever need, 3rd edn. Lippincott Williams & Wilkins, Philadelphia, PA (1999)

6. Chazal, P., O'Dwyer, M., Reilly, R.B.: Automatic Classification of Heartbeats Using ECG Morpholgy and Heartbeat Interval Features. IEEE transaction on biomedical engineering 51(7) (July 2004)

7. Evans, S., Hastings, H., Bodenheimer, M.: Differentiation of beats of ventricular and sinus origin using a self-training neural network. PACE 17, 611–626 (1994)
8. Clayton, R., Murray, A., Campbell, R.: Recognition of ventricular fibrillation using neural networks. Med. Biological Engineering and Computing 32, 217–220 (1994)
9. Lehigh's Sensor-Based Medical Information System (SBMIS)
10. http://www.cse.lehigh.edu/ chuah/research.html
11. Moody, G.B., Mark, R.G.: The impact of the MIT-BIH Arrhythmia Database. IEEE Eng. in Med. and Biol. 20(3), 45–50 (2001)

Semantics-Based Event-Driven
Web News Classification

Wei Hu and Huan-ye Sheng

Computer Science Dept, Shanghai Jiao Tong Univ,
200030 Shanghai, China
{no_bit, hysheng}@sjtu.edu.cn

Abstract. Web news classification is an unsupervised learning task, which is often accomplished by clustering methods. In traditional works, documents are first represented using the vector space model. Each vector generally consists of the keywords or phrases important to the document. Then vectors are clustered together according to some (dis)similarity measure. Such methods often take no or little semantic information into account. In this paper, we present a semantics-based event-driven approach. Event is represented by 3-tuple and document is associated with set of candidate events. These event sets are classified according to semantic dissimilarity. The preliminary experiment on Chinese web news classification shows that the proposed approach is promising.

1 Introduction

The number of news articles published on the Web had a dramatic increase over the last years. Readers often want to access all the news articles related to a particular topic from entire news collection. Some electronic publications already classify and chronologically organize their articles, but most of their methods are based on keywords matching, leading to a poor satisfaction of readers' information needs.

Document classification can often be accomplished by unsupervised, clustering methods, with little or no requirement of human labeled data [1-6]. In these works, documents are first represented using the vector space model (VSM). Each vector generally consists of the keywords or phrases important to the document [7,8]. Then vectors are clustered together according to some (dis)similarity measure [9].

Most VSM methods regard words or phrases as symbols and take little semantic information into account. In this paper, we propose a new methodology for computing dissimilarity between two documents by taking account of lexical semantics. And the new approach is event-driven not keyword-based.

An important force of event-driven document classification is Topic Detection and Tracking (TDT) [10]. The primary participants were Carnegie Mellon University, Dragon System, and the University of Massachusetts at Amherst. CMU takes an approach based on group average agglomerative clustering [11]. The UMass approach is similar to the extent that it uses a variant of single-link clustering and builds up (clusters) groups of related stories to represent events [12]. Dragon approach is based on observations over term frequencies, but using adaptive language models from speech recognition [10].

P. Thulasiraman et al. (Eds.): ISPA 2007 Workshops, LNCS 4743, pp. 136–143, 2007.
© Springer-Verlag Berlin Heidelberg 2007

In TDT, event is "something that happens at a particular time and place" [10]. Obviously, it is important for TDT to extract time and place from document and describe event precisely. But in our application of web news classification, action together with subject and object is sufficient to catch event information (We return to this topic in Section 2.1). Therefore an event is represented by a 3-tuple in this paper. And a document is associated with a set of candidate events, i.e. set of 3-tuples.

Our semantics-based event-driven approach can be depicted in two steps.

1. Compute candidate events for all documents in web news collection.
2. Classify sets of candidate events according to semantic dissimilarity.

The remaining sections of this paper would be organized as follow. In Section 2, we introduce 3-tuple-based representation of document; Section 3 and Section 4 discuss two steps of our approach in detail; In Section 5, experiments and results are shown and discussed; Section 6 gives a summary on our work.

2 Document Representation

In this section, we first illustrate why 3-tuple representation is sufficient to summarize event in our application. Then, we discuss how to associate document with (candidate) event set.

2.1 Event Representation

Consider, for example, we have three sentences:

Four-Star General may run Iraq transition. (Yahoo News)
Four-Star General will run Iraq transition next week.
Four-Star General will not run Iraq transition next week.

The first sentence is gathered from Yahoo News. The second and third sentences are potential reports form other media. The meanings of these sentences are different. Even the second sentence is opposite to the third one. But to the readers, whether Four-Star General will run Iraq transition is the event they concern and these three sentences just cover this event. They will not complain about poor consistency. On the contrary, reports from different media are welcome. In our application, 3-tuple *<run, Four-Star General, Iraq transition>* is capable of summarizing the event, regardless of modifiers in each sentence.

Consider another example:

The Spurs beat New Jersey 88-77. (NBA Official Site)
The Spurs 88-77 win over New Jersey. (NBA Official Site)
The Spurs lost to New Jersey.
The Spurs is beat by New Jersey.

The first and second sentences are gathered from NBA Official Site. It is clear the event mentioned in the first sentence is similar to that in the second sentence, and opponent to that in the third sentence. The fourth sentence is a passive voice, which express opponent meaning to the first sentence. Also readers will be interested in the gather of these four reports.

From the discussion above, we can conclude that ignoring modifiers and voice will not affect our news classification task. And 3-tuple representation is sufficient to catch event information. Also such representation will bring us some advantages. For example, parsing is a difficult task for natural language progressing. This is because human language generally has unstable structure. Flexible modifiers confuse the parser so that correct sentence structure can not be detected. And especially for Chinese, passive voice is much more complex than that in English. It is a hard job to determine the object and the subject of an action, due to few passive voice marks in Chinese. If we do not concern about the precise meaning of a sentence, modifier and voice can be ignored. Then parsing performance will be improved.

2.2 Candidate Events

Now we can associate document with set of 3-tuples (candidate events). There candidate events are organized hierarchically in the following recursive manner.

Suppose d is a document in web news collection. d_t is the title of d and d_f is the first paragraph of d. Set of candidate events at level i is denoted by CE_i.

$CE_1 = \{<a,s,o> \mid <a,s,o>$ is an event both mentioned in d_t and $d_f\}$
$CE_n = \{<a,s,o> \mid a$ is synonym or antonym of a' and $<a',s,o> \in CE_{n-1}\}$
$\qquad \cup \{<a,s,o> \mid <a,o,s> \in CE_{n-1}\} - \cup_{i=1:n-1} CE_i$

Here, synonym and antonym can be looked up from a lexical knowledge dictionary, WordNet for example. Such dictionary is also used in CE_1 extraction (discussed in Section 3).

We denote the union set of CE_i by CE.

3 Candidate Events Extraction

This section discusses how to extract candidate events from a given document. According to the recursive formula, CE_i $(i \geq 2)$ is easy to compute. So we focus on CE_1 extraction.

3.1 NLP Tools

Before discussing the approach in detail, several Natural Language Processing (NLP) modules are introduced first.

1. Part-Of-Speech Tagging
   Part-Of-Speech tagger assigns each word with a specific part-of-speech.
2. Named Entity Recognition
   Named entity includes person name, organization, date and time, location, nuber, etc.
3. Syntactical Parsing
   Syntactical parser identifies phrases and their attachments.

3.2 CE1 Extraction

CE1 extraction procedure is illustrated in Fig 1.

1. The title of given document is part-of-speech tagged and named entity recognized.
2. Document's first paragraph is parsed and a list of parser trees is generated. Every sentence in the first paragraph corresponds to one tree.
3. Candidate action a of an event is extracted. a should be a verb on a certain parser tree t and related to a word in the title. Here, "related" means synonymous or antonymous according a WordNet like lexical knowledge dictionary.
4. a's candidate subject s is extracted. s is a noun or named entity left to action a on the parser tree t OR s is a noun or named entity on t's previous parser tree if there is a pronoun left to a on t.
5. a's candidate object o is extracted. o is a noun or named entity right to action a on the parser tree t OR o is a noun or named entity on t's next parser tree if there is a pronoun right to a on t.

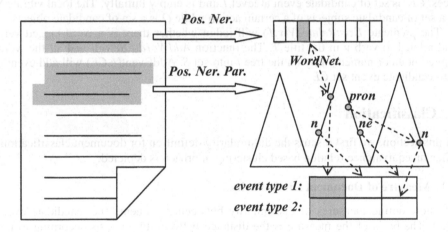

Fig. 1. CE1 Extraction Procedure

The extraction algorithm is described as follow:

```
Algorithm 1.  CE1E ( T, F, CE1 )
for all t such that t is a tree in F do
  for all v such that v is a word tagged verb on t do
    if ( ExistRelatedV ( v, T )) then
      S = O = ∅
      for all l such that l is a word left to v on t do
        if ( l's tag is noun or named entity ) then
          S = S ∪ {l}
        else if ( l's tag is pron ) then
          AddWord ( p, S )    p is a tree previous to t
        end if
      end for
      for all r such that r is a word right to v on t
```

```
            do
            if ( r's tag is noun or named entity ) then
                O = O ∪ {r}
            else if ( r's tag is pron ) then
                AddTree ( n, O )    n is a tree next to t
            end if
        end for
        for all s in S do
            for all o in O do
                AddEvent ( < v, s, o >, CE1 )
            end for
        end for
    end if
end for
end for
```

The formal parameter T is tagged and named entity recognized title. F is list of parser trees. CE_1 is set of candidate event at level 1 and is empty initially. The local vibrate S is a set of candidate subjects of a certain action while O is a set of candidate objects.

The predicate $ExistRelatedV(v,T)$ will judge whether there is a word tagged verb and related to verb v in the title T. The function $AddWord(t,S)$ will add all the word tagged noun or named entity on the tree t into set S. $AddEvent(e,CE)$ will add event e into candidate event set CE.

4   Classification

In this section, we first discuss the dissimilarity definition for document classification. Then an equivalence relation based clustering approach is depicted.

4.1 Measure of Document Dissimilarity

We now define measures of dissimilarity between documents (i.e. candidate event sets). The basis of the measure is the distance between two events according to the lexical dictionary. Dissimilarity measure dm is defined as

$$
dm\,(d_1, d_2) = \begin{cases} \infty, & \text{if } CE_1 \cap CE_2 = \varnothing \\ min\,\{l(e_1,CE_1) + l(e_2,CE_2) \mid e_1 = e_2 \text{ and } e_1 \in CE_1,\ e_2 \in CE_2\}, & \text{otherwise} \end{cases}
$$

where document d_1 is associated with candidate event set CE_1 while d_2 with CE_2 and $l(e,CE)$ is candidate event e's level in set CE.

4.2 Clustering Approach

Having defined the dissimilarity between documents, several clustering algorithms can be used [13-15]. In this paper, we cluster documents using an equivalence relation. Suppose that relation R_θ is defined as

$R_\theta\,(d_1, d_2) = \{<d_1, d_2> \mid dm(d_1, d_2) < \theta\}$

where θ is a threshold. R_θ's closure R_θ^* is an equivalence relation.

Our R_θ^*-based clustering approach is depicted as follow.

```
Algorithm 2.   WNC (   , WN, C )
for all d such that d is a document in WN do
   WN = WN - EquClass ( d,    )
   AddCluster ( EquClass ( d,    ), C )
end for
```

The formal parameter θ is the threshold associated with relation R_θ. WN is web news collection. C is a set of clusters.

The function $EquClass(d,\theta)$ will compute equivalence class of d according to the equivalence relation R_θ^*. $AddCluster(D,C)$ will add document set D into C.

5 Evaluation

To testify the validity of our approach, we have performed an experiment on Chinese web news classification.

5.1 Corpus

A corpus of sports news has been developed to support the evaluation. This corpus spans the period from Nov. 1, 2003 to Nov. 20, 2003 and includes nearly 16,073 news articles, with taken from 166 media [16].

The corpus is divided into four samples. Sample1 contains 3667 news articles. Sample2 contains 3969 articles. Sample3 contains 4343 articles. Sample4 contains 4094 articles.

5.2 Lexical Dictionary

HowNet, a WordNet like Chinese lexical knowledge dictionary and taxonomy is used to provide lexical knowledge.

It is a common-sense knowledge base unveiling inter-conceptual relations and inter-attribute relations of concepts in Chinese lexicons. About 1500 sememes are defined and organized into 7 basic taxonomies. More than 60,000 Chinese words are defined in about 110,000 entries. Each entry has an expression comprised of sememes and operators which express the semantic information of the word.

5.3 NLP Tools

Several NLP modules are used, some especially for Chinese.

1. Word Segmentation & Part-Of-Speech Tagging
Unlike English, Chinese words are written continuously without space between them. Word segmentor is used to segment the title and the sentences in the first paragraph into separated words. JSeg is a segmentation and part-of-speech tagging tool developed by ShanXi University.

2. Named Entity Recognition
A cluster-based approach is used to recognize the named entities [17].

3. Syntactical Parsing

The statistical parser we choose uses a grammar containing more than 20,000 probabilistic rules.

5.4 Experiments and Results

Experiments on sample sets are performed in the following manner. Assume that sample1 is to be processed.

1. Randomly draw 10% (377) documents from sample1.
2. Manually classify 377 documents.
3. Each of 377 documents is assigned a label to show which cluster it belongs to.
4. Classify sample1 using our approach. (θ=8) (sbed)
5. Classify sample1 using keyword-based k-means clustering algorithm. (kbk)
6. Randomly choose 10 documents from 377 documents and compare the learning result to manually clustering result.
7. Compute average performance.

In Table 1, experimental results are presented.

Table 1. Experimental Results

	Sample 1		Sample 2		Sample 3		Sample 4	
	kbk	sbed	kbk	sbed	kbk	sbed	kbk	sbed
Recall	80.2	93.7	83.7	96.3	77.0	91.2	80.2	93.9
Precision	82.8	84.2	84.6	86.5	83.3	81.9	81.9	84.6
Miss	19.8	6.3	16.3	3.8	23.0	8.8	19.8	6.1
F_1	81.5	88.7	84.1	91.1	80.0	86.3	81.0	89.0

6 Conclusion

We have presented our work on semantics-based event-driven classification approach. The preliminary experiment on Chinese web news classification shows that the proposed approach is promising.

Reference

1. Yang, Y., Lin, X.: A re-examination of text categorization methods. In: SIGIR, pp. 42–49 (1999)
2. Han, E., Karypis, G.: Centroid-Based Document Classification Analysis & Experimental Result. In: PKDD (2000)
3. Sebastiani, F.: Machine learning in automated text categorization. ACM Computing Surveys. 34(1), 1–47 (2002)
4. White, M., Cardie, C.: Selecting Sentences for Multidocument Summaries using Randomized Local Search. In: Proc. Of the Workshop on Automatic Summarization (including DUC 2002). Association for Computational Linguistics, Philadelphia, US, pp. 9–18 (2002)

5. Jing, H., Radev, D.R., Budzikowska, M.: Centroid-based summarization of multiple documents: sentence extaction, utility-based evaluation and user studies. In: Proceedings of ANLP/NAACL-2000 (2000)
6. Nomoto, T., Matsumoto, Y.: A New Approach to Unsupervised Text Summarization. In: Proc. Of the SIGIR'01, New Orleans, Louisiana, USA, pp. 26–34 (2001)
7. Mladenic, D.: Text learning and related intelligent agents. IEEE Expert (July 1999)
8. Korfhage, R.R.: Information Storage and Retrieval. Wiley, Chichester (1997)
9. Dagan, I., Lee, L., Pereira, F.: Similarity-based methods for word sense disambiguation. In: Proc. Of the 32nd Conference of the Association of Computational Linguistics, pp. 56–63 (1997)
10. Allan, J., Carbonell, J., Doddington, G., Yamron, J., Yang, Y.: Topic detection and tracking pilot study: Final report. In: Proceedings of the DARPA Broadcast News Transcription and Understanding Workshop (1998)
11. Yang, Y., Pierce, T., Carbonell, J.: A study on retrospective and on-line event detection. In: Proceedings of SIGIR'98 (1998)
12. Allan, J., Papka, R., Lavrenko, V.: On-line New Event Detection and Tracking. In: Proceedings of the 21th Ann. Int. ACM SIGIR Conference on Research and Development in Information Retrieval SIGIR'98, pp. 37-45 (1998)
13. Frigui, H., Krishnapuram, R.: A robust competitive clustering algorithm with applications in computer vision. IEEE Transactions on Pattern Analysis and Machine Intelligence 21(5), 450–465 (1999)
14. Kurita, T.: An Ecient Clustering Algorithm for Region Merging. IEICE Trans. of Information and Systems E78-D(12) (1995)
15. Gowda, K.C., Ravi, T.V.: Agglomerative clustering of symbolic objects using the concepts of both similarity and dissimilarity. Pattern Recognition Letters 16, 647–652 (1995)
16. Sina Sports News. From http://sports.sina.com.cn/normal/oldnews.shtml
17. Hu, W., Zhang, D.: Cluster-Based and Brute-Correcting Grammatical Rules Learning. In: International Conference on Natural Language Processing and Knowledge Engineering Proceedings (2003)

A Study on Application of Cyber Shopping Service with Utilization of Context Awareness in Smart Home Environment*

Jae-gu Song and Seoksoo Kim**

Hannam University, Department of Multimedia Engineering, Postfach, 306 791
133 Ojeong-Dong, Daedeok-Gu, Daejeon, Korea
bhas9@paran.com, sskim@hannam.ac.kr

Abstract. The study has proposed a method for implementing cyber shopping services within smart home environment to allow residents convenient shopping at home by using interoperable sensor technology. The proposed model uses RFID tag, USN sensor and TinyOS for transmitting information to mobile interfaces. Residents and products information get collected and categorized under proposed categorization module. Service providers supporting the cyber shopping are defined as brokers and more effective cyber shopping environment are serviced by sharing such information as well.

1 Introduction

Generally speaking, home is the most comfortable place people can be themselves. Presently, continuous efforts are exerted to maintain easy and comfortable living environment of people through application of diversified technologies. One of the leading technologies is the Smart Home, where the home itself recognizes certain changes in home environment and provides adequate services to residents. As complementary measures for implementing highly sophisticated technologies to home system, various research institutes, corporations and universities are conducting researches on context awareness, where home environment and resident information are collected through home network [1],[2]. Within such system, information get collected by various types of sensors installed. To provide adequate services by utilizing these information, researches on purge, neural network and artificial intelligence are being conducted actively by various researchers[3]. Specially, context awareness middleware for predicting behavioral pattern of people takes the central role in the system, as an intelligent helper for dynamically meeting demands of people in indoor environment[4]. Ultimately, such researches have made information sharing, among various devices composing the home network, possible within limited environments.

---

* "This work was supported by a grant from Security Engineering Research Center of Ministry of Commerce, Industry and Energy".

** Corresponding author.

P. Thulasiraman et al. (Eds.): ISPA 2007 Workshops, LNCS 4743, pp. 144–152, 2007.
© Springer-Verlag Berlin Heidelberg 2007

The study wants to propose a model for implementing cyber shopping services that utilize context awareness in smart home environment. The proposed model will be providing more convenient shopping experience to users by sharing user and environment information among devices composing the smart home. Moreover, the study wants to propose a method for implementing cyber shopping services within smart home, by analyzing purchasing pattern of users, in purchasing household products and personal products according to changes in device information and behavior of residents.

The study is structured as follows. In chapter 2, context information based smart home, context ontology and shopping pattern analysis will be dealt. In chapter 3, architecture of suggested system will be discussed. In chapter 4, scenario of suggested system will be defined and result of simulations will be explained. Lastly, the conclusion of the study is made in chapter 5.

2 Paper Preparation

In this chapter, the researcher will be investigating context aware based smart home and implementation of cyber shopping.

2.1 Context-Aware Based Smart Home

Generally speaking, smart home is an early stage model that integrates information technology devices, where individually operated devices are interconnected in a large network. That is, peripheral devices are coupled one at a time, creating a large network of devices, leading all home devices to be connected together. Like this, the smart home technology ultimately has to allow external devices to be easily connected to the network and it is most effective when external and internal connections maintain Always log on.

In the field of smart home, researches are being conducted for investigating information on resident and residential environment. This means that the smart home would recognize residents, location of residents and behavior of residents for providing suitable services while connecting residential environment information with information regarding residents for providing automated services suitable for that circumstance. Here, artificial intelligence technology is applied for collecting such information through utilization of various types of sensors for providing suitable services[5]. However, problems such as determining priority of information customized for a specific user and ready built (already designed) residential environment are faced by smart home technology. As complementary measures in solving these problems, various researches are being conducted actively to establish foundation for context acquisition and awareness to be adequately configured in Ubiquitous computing environment so that these measures can be introduced to smart home environment[6]. The MovHome Smart Home Project is a leading project that has realized Intelligent Home Environment. The project suggested resource optimization algorithm for architectural and behavior awareness, user position awareness and analysis on behavioral changes of users[7,8]. Like these, various researches are presenting progress in automation measures for analyzing interactions between residents and residential environment, investigation of behavioral patterns of residents by utilizing sensors, analyzing home and surrounding environment, human-like perception and communication between man and devices.

2.2 Context Ontology

Context ontology must be complete and should be configured to respond to the changing environment quickly. Generally speaking, context information is the most important data for supporting user centered customized prediction service. As shown in below table, context can be classified into two major categories, human factors and physical environment, with three types of subcategory respectively. Here, information pertaining to each category shall be continuously collected during the course of time[9].

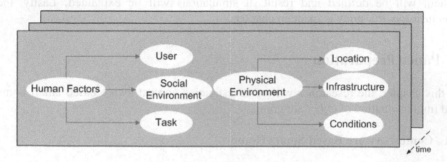

Fig. 1. Schmidt et al's Context Classification

As shown in Figure 1, Human Factor Category had been segmented into User Information, Social Environment Information and Task Information, and Physical Environment Category had been segmented into Positional Information, Basic Organizational Information and Physical Context Information. However, above mentioned three categories have difficulties in defining classification, thus, system applying context information hase to be configured to specific categorical classification. In the study, information required by home networking environment and cyber shopping are divided into specific categories.

2.3 Shopping Pattern Analysis

With commercialization of online shopping, purchasing patterns of people are changing. People are provided with environment where they could search the entire cyberspace to look for products that are cheaper, better and suitable for their requirements. That is, repeated purchasing pattern of people, purchasing the same item from the same store slowly disappeared and opportunity for them to visit variety of internet shopping malls for purchasing various types of products has been given. This phenomenon has broken locational barriers while providing substantial environment for shopping. One of a characteristic of online shopping is that sale is generated following method used in publication of product information and reception of these information.

The study will be analyzing purchasing pattern of consumer by categorizing purchase tendency of people in home network environment. Analyzed information will be used to acquire advertisement of products that are most interested by residents, resulting more convenience in product purchase to be provided.

3 System Architecture

3.1 Categorizing Context Information

The study has designed cyber shopping system in smart home network by considering necessity and requirements of context awareness computing. For collecting and providing context information on cyber shopping in smart home environment, the study has established following context information categories.

Table 1. Shopping Context Information Categorization Information

Classification	Information
Group Identification	Group ID, Group information
Product Identification	Product ID, Product information
Time	Time information
Weather	Weather information
Place	Location information
User Identification	User ID, User information
Advertisement Identification	Advertisement ID, information
Service Provider Identification	Service Providers Identification

These categories are classified into eight, namely, the group information including products, product information, time information, weather information, location information, user information, advertisement information and advertiser information. These categories are classified by the suggested system for providing more effective product information to users.

Table 2. Detailed Content of Context Information and Collection Method per Category

Classification	Context Information	Collection Method
Group Identification	Products Group ID (wardrobes, refrigerator, desks, beds…)	Sensor
Product Identification	Product ID (Clothes, drinks, foods…)	RFID
Time	Season, Day, Time	Official information
Weather	Temperature, Weather conditions	Official information
Place	Products location	Sensor
User Identification	User ID	Sensor(ID card)
Advertisement Identification	Advertisements ID	Data information
Provider Identification	Providers ID	Data information

Context information contained in eight categories and acquisition of this information is shown in Table 2.

Defined categorical context information had been designed with consideration of scalability following object (product) increase and diversification.

All information are categorized by User ID. Collection methods and tools used to collect these information will vary depending on the group and trait of information required by the group. Public information such as date, time, weather, etc., will be processed in background while information depending on the circumstances will be collected through sensors and tags.

3.2 System Framework

Overall framework of the system providing effective information on cyber shopping to consumers by collecting and managing categorized context information is as follows in Figure 2.

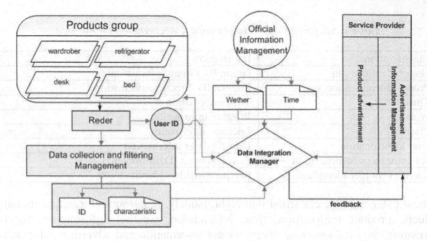

Fig. 2. System framework structure

Product Group that collects and manages information of products provided within the smart home environment; Data Acquisition and Filtering Management that collects and filters information acquired from the Product group through the reader for determining product ID, use-by date and properties; Official Information Management that collects user ID and external information analyzed by the reader then manages information on weather and time; Service Provider that manages product advertisement by collecting product advertisement information and information provided to home network users; Data Integration Manager that integrates context information collected from Data Collection and Filtering Manager, General Information Manager, Service Provider and User ID, for analyzing cyber shopping information that satisfies user and product features, generating context information on cyber shopping and integrating product link information for transmitting product group data, to be checked by users.

The study has adopted product group structure that is generally implemented in Smart Home environment. Meaning to say product group is the child group that manages all types of information such as wake up time, work, dining, etc., of residents for determining products used and behavior of residents. By collecting data generated from product group, User ID, resident related data, base information and newly introduced information will be compared for categorization. Newly introduced information will be integrated with existing information of the user and various other information provided by the service provider, so that service provider can provide information that is suitable for need and tendency of users.

Information provided by the framework can be classified into two stages, information collection and processing and information distribution system.

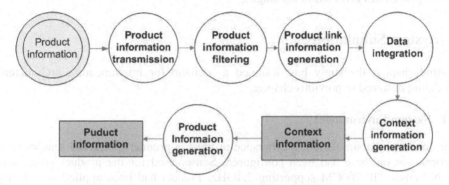

Fig. 3. Information Acquisition and Processing Stage

The first stage is the Information Acquisition and Processing stage. As shown in Figure 3, the stage is composed of product information, product information transmission, product information filtering, product link information generation, data integration, context information generation, context information, information of goods generation and information of goods Basing on the information of goods existing in the Smart Home, product related information will be transmitted. Such information will be filtered and compared with product information acquired from service provider. Through these procedures, link information linking goods existing in the Smart Home and advertisement generated by Service Provider gets generated. By basing on the link information, data will be integrated to generate context information. Then the information of product to be finally advertised to users gets selected.

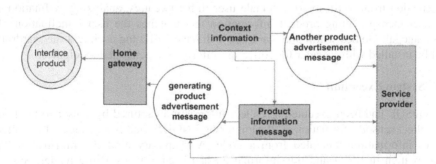

Fig. 4. Information Provision Stage

In the second stage, Information Distribution System stage, final product information generated in the previous stage is used for generating product advertisement message. Then, product information that matches inclination of users are transmitted to be viewed by users through home gateway system. In addition, the context information and product information get transmitted to service provider to be used as a basis for providing a product that matches requirements of users. Figure 4 shows procedures involved in the stage 2.

4   System Simulation

In this chapter, the study has designed a scenario for implementing architecture modeling designed in previous chapter.

4.1   System Environment

For conducting a simulation, a cyberspce product, a product group and sensors with information on these had been configured. Sensor used for the product group was USN Sensor TIP 700CM supporting 2.4GHz. Product had been applied with RFID tag and a commercialized product, INT-900H Model, that can accomodate all types of RFID information had been adopted by the study as the reader. In addition, Sensor Information Collection and Filtering Manager, Data Integration Manager and Service Provider had been run under respective servers and developed as PC compatible application softwares. NesC had been used to develop programs controlling sensors and C# language had been used for developing application softwares. Open source based DB program, PostgreSQL, had been used as DB.

4.2   System Scenario

The system suggested by the study utilizes sensors, devices that can safely read and collect data and smart home with reliable network connections for devices. Therefore, a hypothetical scenario had been set for conducting simulation of the system suggested by the study.

The simulation had been conducted by applying procedure of collecting information from wardrobe of a female user in her twenties, analyzing inclination of the user then providing product information that matches the user's inclination. At this stage, all clothes within the wardrobe will have RFID tag each and the wardrobe will be installed with a reader for collecting information generated by clothes.

4.3   System Execution

PostgreSQL had been executed to collect information captured by sensor to the host. To collect sensor information, TIP Monitering ENGINE had been executed to collect sensor information generated from a node. A temporary clothing information had been written in RFID and this information had been read by RFID reader. System configuration is shown in the following figure.

Hypotehtical clothing information gets captured from RFID tag and this information gets transmitted to the DB. Data generated from sensors are also collected and managed as data. After execitomg application software for generating type of cloth and context information, all collected information had been integrated to provide product information to home network users. Here, cloth related information provided by service providers had been applied during the data integratino. The simulation result had showns that information of clothes owned by users had been collected to determine favorite color, season, number of clothes owned, etc., and these information had been linked with information of products being offered, for displaying clothing information on devices used by users for viewing these information. All these information are important for determining preference of user on clothes, will be saved and provided to random service provider, for providing information of products owned by the service provider suiting style, color, seasonal variations, etc., prefered by the user.

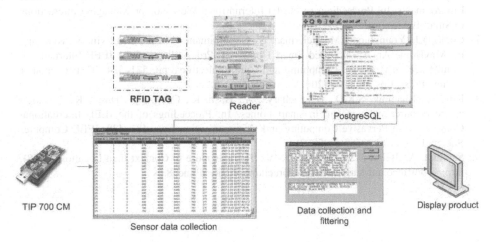

RFID TAG

Reader

PostgreSQL

TIP 700 CM

Sensor data collection

Data collection and fittering

Display product

Fig. 5. System execution environment

5 Conclusion

The study had suggested a method for providing cyber shopping services in smart home environment by applying technology of context awareness computing and designed the system through the use of hypothetical scenario. The system designed by the study has been designed to provide product information to user in smart home environment even before the user searches for these information else where. However, a large scale system development is required to categorize and search the most feasible information among diversified types of products and wide varieties of information on products generated by manufacturers.

The smart home environment in ubiquitous era will demand more customized information service to be provided. Lastly, the researcher expects more diversified applications to be generated by utilizing the system developed by the study on introduction of cyber shopping services in smart home environment with application of context awareness.

References

1. Kidd, C.D., Orr, R., Abowd, G.D., Atkeson, C.G., Essa, I.A.: The Aware Home: A Living Laboratory for Ubiquitous Computing Research (2000)
2. Meyer, S., Rakotonirainy, A.: A survey of Research on Context-Aware Homes. In: Proc. of the Australasian information security workshop conference, 159–168 (2003)
3. Mozer, M.C: The Neural network house: An environment that adapts to its inhabitants. In: Proceedings of International Symposium on Handheld and Ubiquitous Computing (2000)
4. Abowd, G.D., Day, A.K., Brown, P.J., et al.: Towards a better understanding of Context and context-awareness. In: Gellersen, H.-W. (ed.) HUC 1999. LNCS, vol. 1707, Springer, Heidelberg (1999)
5. Intille, S.S: Designing a Home of the Future. Pervasive Computing, 80–86 (2002)
6. Dey, A.K., Salber, D., Abowd, G.D.: A Context -based Infrastructure for Smart Environments. In: Proceedings of the 1st International Workshop on Managing Interactions in Smart Environments (1999)
7. Cook, D.J., Youngblood, M., Heierman, E., Gopalratnam, K., Rao, S., Litvin, A., Khawaja, F.: MavHome An Agent Based Smart Home. In: Processdings of the IEEE International Conference on Pervasive Computing and Communications, pp. 521–524. IEEE Computer Society Press, Los Alamitos (2003)
8. Roy, A., Bhaumik, S.K.D., Bhattacharya, A., Basu, K., Cook, D.J., Das, S.K.: Location aware resource management in smart homes. In: Proceedings of the IEEE International Conference on Pervasive Computing and Communications, pp. 481–488. IEEE Computer Society Press, Los Alamitos (2003)
9. Schmidt, A., Beigl, M., Gellersen, H.-W.: There is more to Context than Location (1998), http://www.teco.uni-karlsruhe.de/~albrecht/publication/imc98.ps

A Transparent Protocol Scheme
Based on UPnP AV for Ubiquitous Home

Jiyun Park, Hyunju Lee, and Sangwook Kim

Dept. of Computer Science, Kyungpook National University, Korea
{jypark,hyunju,swkim}@woorisol.knu.ac.kr

Abstract. There are a variety of AV devices and multimedia content in the
ubiquitous home and the sharing of content needs to have high quality of
transfer by using optimized transport protocol for the each content. This paper
presents the design and implementation of our proposed scheme that is based on
UPnP AV framework which can support various transport protocol
transparently. We validated and evaluated our proposed scheme and
experimental results show that it can stream content effectively.

1 Introduction

These days, there are various multimedia services in the ubiquitous home as much as
the users of home network are increasing[1]. There are also many kinds of AV
devices in the ubiquitous home and these devices perform high quality services and
have various multimedia content. Today's ubiquitous home provides technology to
share and use these services and content with AV devices, regardless of where the
contents are stored[2-3].

The Universal Plug and Play (UPnP) forum defined UPnP AV architecture as the
standard of the interoperability of the home network for sharing multimedia content
and controlling AV devices[4]. The UPnP AV architecture supports zero-
configuration networking and automatically discovers devices that dynamically join a
home network. It leverages TCP/IP and the Web to enable seamless proximity
networking so, it communicates via HTTP. However this means UPnP AV
architecture can not fully provide time-based multimedia services for audio and video
content because the best feature of HTTP is reliable and in-order delivery of data. We
propose enhanced UPnP AV architecture which can support various transport
protocols for multimedia content such as audio and video.

In this paper, we describe the design and implementation of UPnP AV System that
has transparent protocol scheme. This system can select transport protocol
transparently regardless of file type of content. We adopt the UPnP AV architecture
for interoperability of multimedia networking among home network devices and
HTTP and RTSP for transport protocol of the multimedia content. By implementing
the UPnP AV architecture with proposed module, our system provides not only the
real-time streaming from the media server to the media renderer but also the
guarantee of QoS for transfer of audio and video.

P. Thulasiraman et al. (Eds.): ISPA 2007 Workshops, LNCS 4743, pp. 153–162, 2007.

The rest of this paper organized in the following way: it starts with overview of the transparent protocol for audio and video on the application layer. Section 3 introduces UPnP AV architecture and section 4 presents a system design and an implementation of the proposed scheme. Section 5 will show the development and the evaluation of our UPnP AV System. Finally section 6 concludes with future works.

2   Real-Time Streaming Protocol

UPnP architecture is based on TCP and UDP and it uses HTTP to communicate and transfer data between devices. HTTP is a suitable protocol for data-sharing or communication but it is not suitable protocol for multimedia content such as audio and video. This section gives the knowledge about Real-time Streaming Protocol (RTSP) and the relationship with HTTP.

RTSP is a client-server application protocol for controlling the delivery of data with real-time properties[5]. It is developed by the IETF and published in 1998 as RFC 2326 and is used in streaming media systems for audio and video which allow client to control remotely a streaming media server, issuing VCR-line commands and allowing time-based access to files on a server[6]. RTSP uses UDP as default but it can also use TCP to deliver data if necessary. It uses TCP for player control messages and UDP for audio and video data.

RTSP is similar to HTTP in syntax and operation but it differs from HTTP in using protocol on the transport layer. HTTP is entirely based on TCP for web pages and TCP guarantees reliable and in-order delivery of data from sender to receiver. HTTP has rudimentary mechanisms for random access to files therefore it is not suitable for time-based seeking.

While HTTP is a stateless protocol, RTSP is a stateful. RTSP is designed to work with time-based media over UDP. UDP does not guarantee reliability and ordering that TCP does. UDP also does not have overhead of checking whether every packet arrived, it is faster and more efficient for time-sensitive purposes. RTSP has mechanisms for time-based seeks into media clips, with compatibility with many timestamp formats. In addition, RTSP is designed to control multicast deliver of stream and therefore, it could be a framework for multicast-unicast hybrid solutions for heterogeneous network like the Internet. The differences between two protocols result from their under layer protocols which are TCP and UDP.

3   UPnP AV Architecture

UPnP is a middleware solution proposed by Microsoft. The purpose is control and operating among network devices in home using IP network and HTTP. A device can dynamically join a network, obtain IP address, convey its capabilities, and learn about the presence and capabilities of other devices. Furthermore UPnP enabled device can control remote devices and transfer data to and from remote devices. In addition, device can leave a network smoothly and automatically without leaving any unwanted state behind.

UPnP AV framework defines three components that are Media Server, Media Renderer and Control Point, as depicted in Figure 1. Media Server functionality provides access to multimedia content and transfers them to other devices that are located in the network. It has Contents Directory, Connection Manager and AV Transport services. Media Renderer allows playback of a variety of rich media formats on devices. It has Rendering Control, Connection Manager and AV Transport services. Control Point allows user to discover and control devices in the network and multimedia content to flow between devices.

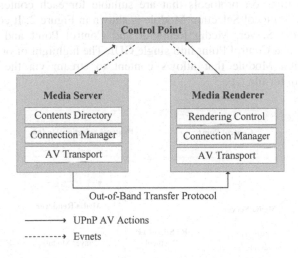

Fig. 1. UPnP AV Architecture

UPnP uses FIFO to transfer the messages among the components of UPnP AV framework. Control Point sends the requests of users to Media Server and Media Renderer and receives the event messages from them. And then Media Server streams multimedia content via HTTP to Media Renderer. Media Renderer requests the streaming to Media Server to playback multimedia content that is streaming from URL of contents that are known by Control Point. Media Server and Media Renderer send events which occur from each component to Control Point, and then users get information of multimedia content or messages from Control Point.

4   A Transparent Protocol Scheme

The main objectives of our implementation work are the validation of our proposed scheme and streaming contents between the media server and the media renderer via various transport protocols. This section describes the design, implementation and evaluation of our proposed scheme.

4.1 Our Proposed System Architecture

In the general AV system, which is based on UPnP AV framework, streams content only using HTTP-GET method. Standard UPnP AV framework defined by UPnP forum also communicates via HTTP. But it is not suitable transport protocol for time-based data such as audio and video that are used frequently in the home. For example, HTTP can not stream some kind of content such as mp4.

   To overcome this problem, we proposed transparent protocol scheme and added Protocol Selection Module in the control point of our system. This module can support various transport protocols that are suitable for each content format. The architecture with Protocol Selection Module is shown in Figure 2. It consists of three components-Media Server, Media Renderer and Control Point and we integrated Media Renderer and Control Point into single GUI. The highlight of our system is the Protocol Selection Module that allows content to stream via the most suitable transport protocol for file type.

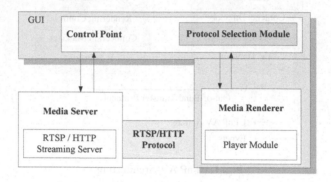

Fig. 2. Architecture of our UPnP AV System

   Figure 3 helps to understand relationship between content and available transport protocols in the media servers. Media Server 1 has Content A and Content B, and Contents A can use Protocol a or Protocol b for streaming to the media renderer. Thus if Content A want to stream, then Protocol Selection Module selects transport protocol between available ones (Protocol a, Protocol b) considering the best suited for data transport.

	Content A	Protocol a
		Protocol b
Media Server 1		Protocol a
	Content B	Protocol c
		Protocol d
Media Server 2	Content C	Protocol b
	Content D	Protocol a

Fig. 3. Composition of content in the media server

Figure 4 is a flow diagram which shows how to work Protocol Selection Module according to transparent protocol scheme. At first, the control point discovers the media servers and the media renderers in the home network using UPnP standard functions (GetDivice(), GetDirectory(), GetContents().etc.). And then, the media servers and the media renderers reply to the control point with their information, which is the descriptions is written in XML, such as content directories and the specification of renderers (device type, supporting content formats. etc.). Protocol Selection Module in the control point prepares to stream the content via selecting the transport protocol which is suitable for content format and can be supported by renderering module. This module is out of the UPnP AV framework and it makes UPnP AV system serves adaptive AV service. The media renderer requests the content to the media server using URI which received from the control point. Finally the media server starts to stream the content to the media renderer via transport protocol which is selected by Protocol Selection Module.

Step 1, 2 perform when each UPnP device connects or disconnects into home network and step 3, 4, 5 perform at each service request. If the media renderer can not support the content format, the AV service is denied at step 3. If content can not use optimized transport protocol to stream, then it uses default protocol at step 5.

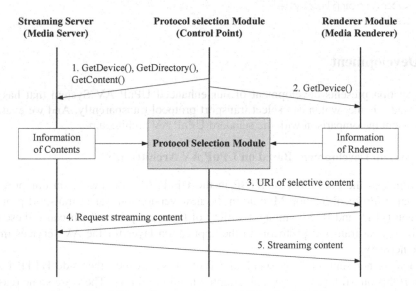

Fig. 4. Flow diagram of Protocol Selection Module

4.2 Operation of the Transparent Protocol Scheme

Our UPnP AV System consists of the media server, the media renderer and the control point like UPnP AV architecture does. We are implemented system except the media server so we used Intel AV Media Server. The media renderer used MPlayer for audio and video and ImageViewer for image as the player modules[7]. And our UPnP AV System used Freevo GUI module for the control point that is written in python. All modules of our system were relied on the UPnP API provided by the open source UPnP SDK for Linux and were formed of the C libraries.

Implementing Protocol Selection Module is key point of this paper. It extracts URI of the multimedia content from parsed DIDL (Digital Item Declaration Language) description. In most cases, only URI is enough to decide its transport protocol. But for reliability, our system further checks the file type of content. After the phase of checking it, Protocol Selection Module gives the URI of content to the media renderer, and then the media renderer requests media server to stream content via selective protocol. The following piece of XML code is the description of multimedia content.

```xml
<xsd:element name="CurrentURI">
    <xsd:complexType>
        <xsd:simpleContent>
            <xsd:extension base="upnp:string">
                <xsd:anyAttribute namespace="##other"
                    processContents="lax"/>
            </xsd:extension>
        </xsd:simpleContent>
    </xsd:complexType>
</xsd:element>
```

5 Development

This section presents development of our enhanced UPnP AV System that has our proposed scheme, which can select transport protocol transparently. And we evaluate our system in comparison with the standard UPnP AV architecture.

5.1 System Development Based on UPnP AV Architecture

We validated the possibility of RTSP in the UPnP AV framework on our previous version[8]. Protocol Section Module in the new version can select transport protocol between HTTP and RTSP among a variety of transport protocols, because these two are the typical transport protocols in the application layer for the AV services in the home network.

RTSP is not supported by standard UPnP SDK, on the other side HTTP is. To support this on MPlayer, our system adopted live555 Library. There are some reasons for choosing of this library. First, it can be complied for various OS (UNIX, Window, QNX) can be used to build streaming applications[9]. The live555 Library can be used to stream, receive and process MPEG, H.263 or JPEG video, and several audio codec. Another reason is that it can be easily extended to support additional codec, and can also be used to build basic RTSP client and servers. And this library has been used to add streaming support to existing media player applications, such as MPlayer. This is the main reason that we adapted.

Figure 5 illustrates the demonstration. We ran Intel AV Media server on PC running Window and our UPnP AV System on PC running Linux. As shown, the user can choose content on the friendly GUI of the control point that integrated media renderer, as mentioned. The content are classified into categories that are stored in the media server. As the content plays, it is immediately delivered to the player module for rendering.

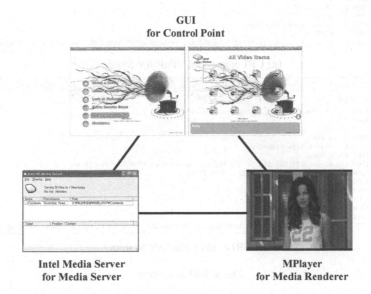

Fig. 5. Scenes of demonstration

5.2 System Evaluation

In this section, we present the evaluation of transparent protocol scheme that can choose transport protocol by file type of contents and support various file types.

5.2.1 Validation of Scheme

Our implementation of the proposed scheme was tested against a number of functional trials. For test, we set up two PCs hosting the media server and the media renderer. The media renderer was integrated into the control point that has our Protocol Selection Module.

Figure 6 shows the URI of content that is stored in the media server which is detected by the control point. Figure 6(a) shows the URI list which is detected by standard UPnP AV architecture, Figure 6(b) shows it which is detected by our implementation system. As figures demonstrate, even if content is the same, the URI is not. Because our Protocol Selection Module select the most suitable transport protocol for content and makes URI of content. In result, the media server sends it to the control point and then the media renderer receives the content using that URI.

160   J. Park, H. Lee, and S. Kim

(a) URI of standard UPnP AV System

(b) URI of our UPnP AV System

Fig. 6. URI of content

5.2.2 Analysis

Data communication between AV devices in the home network should be done and controlled via UPnP protocol on the IP layer. On this condition, HTTP works well via TCP and RTSP works well via UDP generally. We measured packet rates and byte rates on our UPnP AV System and standard UPnP AV architecture with mp4 video data using Ethereal[10]. The size of video data is 2.33M and we play it for 60sec.

Figure 7(a) shows the packet flow on standard UPnP AV System and Figure 7(b) does ours. The horizontal line is time and the vertical line is number of packets. The following table summaries this experiment, our UPnP AV System that used RTSP achieves more packet rate and bit rate comparison with standard UPnP AV

Table 1. Comparison between systems

	Ours	Standard
Avg. packets/sec	56.017	43.353
Avg. bytes/sec	35574	34249
Avg. MBit/sec	0.285	0.274

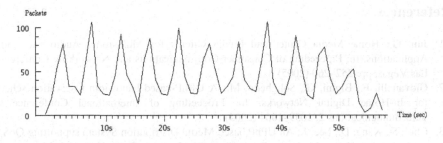

(a) Packet flow on standard UPnP AV System

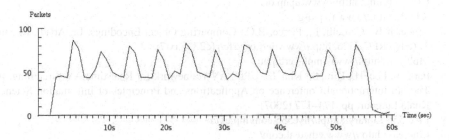

(b) Packet flow on our UPnP AV System

Fig. 7. Comparison of packet flow

architecture. This experiment validated RTSP is likely that the alternative application layer protocol for home network will support real-time streaming.

6 Conclusions

Transparent protocol scheme has been proposed in this paper. Based on UPnP AV architecture, this scheme enables a transport protocol selection service transparently and it provides a suitable protocol for the each content. This scheme that is described in this paper has already implemented. Our UPnP AV System is implemented on Linux, so it can be easily embedded in most AV devices. In other word, this system can be used widely in ubiquitous home network.

The implementation of the enhanced UPnP AV System for mobile devices is ongoing. Control Point for PDA is already implemented. So, a short-term perspective is to apply our framework to the various mobile devices. This makes real universal play in ubiquitous environment.

Acknowledgements

This research was supported by the MIC of Korea, under the ITRC support program supervised by the IITA(IITA-2006-C1090-0603-0026).

References

1. Jun, G.: Home Media Center and Media Clients for Multi-room Audio and Video Applications. In: Proceeding of Consumer Communications and Networking Conference, Las Vegas, pp. 257–260 (2005)
2. Giovanelli, F., Bigini, G., Solighetto, M.: A UPnP-based bandwidth reservation scheme for In-Home Digital Networks. In: Proceeding of International Conference on Telecommunications 2, 1059–1064 (2003)
3. Choi, S., Kang, D., Lee, J.: An UPnP based Media Distribution System supporting QoS in a Converged Home Network. Proceeding of Network Operations and Management Symposium, Vancouver, 1-4 (2006)
4. UPnP Forum.: http://www.upnp.org
5. RTSP.: http://www.rtsp.org
6. Bruce, K.B., Cardelli, L., Pierce, B.C.: Comparing Object Encodings. In: Abadi, M., Ito, T. (eds.) RFC 2326, http://www.ietf.org/rfc/rfc2326.txt7
7. Mplayer.: http://www.mplayerhq.hu
8. Park, J., Lee, H., Kim, S., Kim, S.: UPnP AV framework for Real-time AV Streaming. In: The 6th International Conference on Applications and Principles of Information Science, Kuala Lumpur, pp. 174–177 (2007)
9. Live 555 Library.: http://live555.com/mplayer
10. Ethereal.: http://www.ethereal.com/

Learning Fuzzy Concept Hierarchy and Measurement with Node Labeling

Been-Chian Chien[1], Chih-Hung Hu[2], and Ming-Yi Ju[1]

[1] Department of Computer Science and Information Engineering,
National University of Tainan
33, Sec. 2, Su-Lin St., Tainan 70005, Taiwan, R.O.C.
{bcchien,myju}@mail.nutn.edu.tw
[2] Department of Information Engineering, I-Shou University
Kaohsiung 840, Taiwan, R.O.C.

Abstract. A concept hierarchy is a kind of general form of knowledge representations. Since concept description is generally vague for human knowledge, crisp description for a concept usually cannot represent human knowledge completely and practically. In this paper, we discuss fuzzy characteristics of concept description and relationship. An agglomerative clustering scheme is proposed to learn hierarchical fuzzy concepts from databases automatically. We also propose the architecture of concept measurement and develop two node-labeling methods for measuring the effectiveness of fuzzy concept. Experimental results show that the proposed clustering method demonstrates the capability of accurate conceptualization in comparison with previous researches.

1 Introduction

Learning useful knowledge from databases is an important issue in the research area of knowledge discovery of late years. The objective of knowledge discovery is to examine how to extract knowledge automatically from databases or training data. The discovered knowledge from practical databases can be applied to many applications, such as business decision, marketing, medical diagnoses, and so on. For different applications, the different types of knowledge lead to lots of methodologies in the development of machine learning and data mining techniques. For example, the Apriori algorithm for mining association rules [6], classification learning algorithms for decision trees construction and unsupervised learning algorithms for clusters generation. Regardless of the mining approaches involved, we can imagine the various types of discovered knowledge as the concepts from different viewpoints.

Representing knowledge to users is also an important research topic. The discovered knowledge can be represented as various types of form such as association rules, decision trees, and so on. Concept hierarchy is a kind of general form of rule or concept description for representing knowledge. A concept hierarchy is a tree-like structure that each level of the hierarchy is a sequence of mapping from a set of low-level specific concepts to a set of high-level general concepts. The most general concept in the root is a universal concept, whereas the most specific concepts correspond to the specific values of attributes in the database. Each internal node in the tree of concept

P. Thulasiraman et al. (Eds.): ISPA 2007 Workshops, LNCS 4743, pp. 163–172, 2007.

hierarchy represents a concept which helps to express knowledge and data relationships. Formally, suppose that a taxonomy H is defined on a set of domains $D_i, \ldots, D_k$, we have $H_l : \{D_i \times \ldots \times D_k\} \Rightarrow H_{l-1} \Rightarrow \ldots \Rightarrow H_0$, where H_l denotes the set of concepts at the primitive level, H_{l-1} denotes the concepts at one level higher than those at H_l, and H_0 represents the most general concept on the top level denoted as "*ANY*".

However, concept description is generally vague for human knowledge. Traditional crisp description of concept usually cannot represent human knowledge completely and practically. In this paper, we study the characteristics of fuzzy concepts including their fuzzy description and fuzzy relationship. At first, fuzzy concept hierarchy is defined in Section 3. Then, we propose a unsupervised learning method to generate fuzzy concept in Section 4 and design a measurement procedure to evaluate the effectiveness of fuzzy concept in Section 5. Section 6 describes the experimental results and makes comparisons. Conclusion and future work are given in Section 7.

2 Related Works

The methods of concept generation are generally divides into three classes. The first approach is to specify concept hierarchies by users, experts or data analysts according to a partial or total ordering semantics of attributes explicitly at the schema level. The second approach is that given a set of attributes, the system then tries to generate the partial ordering of attributes automatically so as to construct a meaningful concept hierarchy. The third approach is to define a portion of taxonomy by clustering explicit data in databases. However, it is essentially unrealistic to define an entire concept structure by explicit values enumeration manually in a large database. Thus, most of methods of the third class focus on automatic generation of concepts by grouping data using clustering techniques.

The related researches for automatic hierarchical concept learning can be divided into two main methodologies. The first method is hierarchical clustering that is the most popular and efficient method to build a concept hierarchy. The related works include COBWEB [4], ClassIT [5], GCF [11] and the Liao's [2] methods. The other method is Formal Concept Analysis (FCA) method [3]. The main objective of FCA is to visualize the data in the form of concept lattice to make them more transparent and more easily discussed.

3 Definitions of the Fuzzy Concept Hierarchy

The hierarchical concept proposed here is described as a fuzzy hierarchical structure with a subordinate relation used to describe vague information. The definition of a fuzzy concept hierarchy is described as follows.

Definition 1: A fuzzy concept is defined as $C = (\mu_1, \ldots, \mu_i, \ldots, \mu_m)$ that μ_i denotes a fuzzy set defined on domain D_i with m linguistic terms $\{t_{i1}, \ldots, t_{ij}, \ldots, t_{im}\}$. Moreover, μ_{ij} is the membership values in μ_i corresponding to the fuzzy term t_{ij}. The fuzzy set μ_i can be represented as

$$\mu_i = \sum \mu_{ij} / t_{ij} = \mu_{i1}/t_{i1} + \mu_{i2}/t_{i2} + \ldots + \mu_{im}/t_{im}.$$

The sets of fuzzy terms with strong membership grades in the fuzzy sets can be used to represent the fuzzy concept of C, called the *representative concept, RC*.

Definition 2: The representative concept RC is defined as $RC = (r_1, \ldots, r_j, \ldots, r_m)$ where r_j is the linguistic term with the maximum membership value $\max\{\mu_{ij}(C)\}$ of the fuzzy set μ_i on the fuzzy concept C.

A subordinate relationship is defined as $R(C_k, C_{k'})$ to describe the degree of subsuming the concept C_k under the concept of $C_{k'}$.

Definition 3: Let H be a set of fuzzy concepts defined on the domain D_i. For C_k and $C_{k'}$ in H, $R(C_k, C_{k'})$ is a fuzzy relation that C_k is subordinate to $C_{k'}$, if $t_j \in \mu_i$, and $\mu_{ij}(C_k) \le \mu_{ij}(C_{k'})$. The degree of subsuming the concept C_k under the concept of $C_{k'}$ can be defined as

$$R(C_k, C_{k'}) = \frac{\sum\limits_{A_i \in H} \prod\limits_{t_{ij} \in \mu_i} \left(1 - \left(\mu_{ij}(C_k) - \mu_{ij}(C_{k'})\right)\right)}{|B|},$$

such that $\mu_{ij}(C_k)$ is the membership value of the fuzzy concept C_k on t_{ij}, which is the j-th linguistic term of i-th attribute A_i. B denotes the attribute set. $|B|$ is the number of attributes in B.

According to the definition of fuzzy partial ordering [8], a fuzzy binary relation is a fuzzy partial ordering if and only if it is reflexive, anti-symmetric, and transitive. $R(C_k, C_k)$ is reflexive *iff* $R(C_k, C_k)=1$, for all $C_k \in H$. $R(C_k, C_{k'})$ is anti-symmetric when $R(C_{k1}, C_{k2}) > 0$ and $R(C_{k2}, C_{k1}) > 0$, implies that $C_{k1} = C_{k2}$ for C_{k1}, C_{k2} in H. $R(C_k, C_{k'})$ is transitive (or more specifically, max-min transitive) if the following condition is satisfied for each pair of $< C_{k1}, C_{k3}>$ in H:

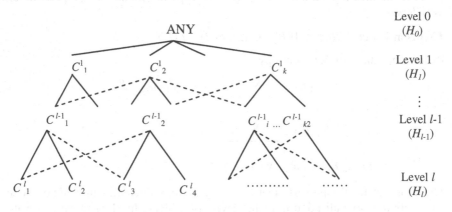

Fig. 1. Representation of a hierarchical fuzzy concept

$$R(C_{k1}, C_{k3}) \geq \max_{C_{k2} \in H} \min [R(C_{k1}, C_{k2}), R(C_{k2}, C_{k3})].$$

The set of concepts conforming to Definition 1, Definition 2, and Definition 3 builds fuzzy taxonomy if fuzzy partial ordering exists for all concepts. A fuzzy concept hierarchy H is defined on a set of domains $\{D_1, \ldots, D_m\}$, as shown in Fig. 1, and the set of concepts at the primitive level $H_l = \{ C_1^l, C_2^l, \ldots, C_n^l \}$ with m attributes in domains $\{D_1 \times \ldots \times D_m\}$. $H_{l-1} = \{ C_1^{l-1}, C_2^{l-1}, \ldots, C_{n'}^{l-1} \}$ denotes the set of concepts at one level higher than those at H_l. H_0 represents the most general concept on the top level denoted as "ANY".

4   Unsupervised Learning of Hierarchical Fuzzy Concept

For evaluating the importance of attributes on the given dataset X, we design a function of fuzzy entropy based on fuzzy set theory and fuzzy entropy measure. Let $X = \{x_1, x_2, \ldots, x_n\}$ be a non-empty finite set of objects with a non-empty finite set of attribute $A = \{A_1, \ldots, A_m\}$. μ_i denotes a fuzzy set of A_i containing a set of m linguistic terms $\{t_{i1}, t_{i2}, \ldots, t_{im}\}$. We define the fuzzy entropy $E(A)$ as follows.

Definition 4: Let $x \in X$, the fuzzy entropy of information based on a set of attributes A is

$$E(A) = \sum_{x \in X} \sum_{A_i \in A} \sum_{t_{ij} \in \mu_i} \frac{v_{ij}}{n} \times \mu_{ij}(x) \times \log_2 \frac{n}{v_{ij}},$$

where $\mu_{ij}(x)$ is the membership value of the object x on the j-th linguistic term of i-th attribute t_{ij} and v_{ij} is equal to the summation of $\mu_{ij}(x)$ for all $x \in X$, that is

$$v_{ij} = \sum_{x \in X} \mu_{ij}(x).$$

As we defined in Definition 4, the fuzzy entropy has monotonic property described as follows.

Theorem 1: Let $B, B' \subseteq A$. If $B' \subseteq B$, then $E(B) \leq E(B')$.

Proof. The values of fuzzy entropy

$$E(B) = \sum_{x \in X} \sum_{A_i \in B} \sum_{t_{ij} \in \mu_i} \frac{v_{ij}}{n} \times \mu_{ij}(x) \times \log_2 \frac{n}{v_{ij}},$$

$$E(B') = \sum_{x \in X} \sum_{A_i \in B'} \sum_{t_{ij} \in \mu_i} \frac{v_{ij}}{n} \times \mu_{ij}(x) \times \log_2 \frac{n}{v_{ij}}.$$

Since $B' \subseteq B$, trivially, we have $E(B') < E(B)$.

Theorem 1 states the property that the fuzzy entropy decreases monotonously in accord with the generalization in higher levels of a hierarchy. It is to say, the value of fuzzy entropy is smaller, the concept is more general.

The algorithm for clustering fuzzy concept with respect to a given database is described in eight main steps, as follows:

Algorithm 1: Fuzzy Concept Hierarchy Clustering Algorithm
Input: A database X with the set of attributes A.
Output: A fuzzy hierarchy H of concepts.

Step 1: Transform the objects $x \in X$ with quantitative attributes into linguistic terms using the defined fuzzy sets μ_i and fuzzy membership functions.

Step 2: Initialize the value $m' = |A|$.

Step 3: Generate the lowest level of hierarchy H_m with the set of attributes A. That is, $H_m = \{C_1^m, C_2^m, ..., C_n^m\}$, where $C_k^m = (\mu_1, \mu_2, ..., \mu_m)$ and μ_i is the i-th fuzzy set of attribute A_i. The representative concepts of H_m are $RC_k^m = (r_{k1}^m, ..., r_{kj}^m, ..., r_{km}^m)$ for $1 \le k \le n$. The set of reduced attributes $B = A$, initially.

Step 4: Let $|B|$ be the number of attributes in the set of reduced attributes B, we set $m' = |B| - 1$. Find $P_{m'}(B)$, which is the set of all possible subsets with m' attributes in the set of reduced attributes B.

Step 5: Compute the fuzzy entropy $E(B_j)$ for all $B_j \in P_{m'}(B)$.

Step 6: Generate a higher level of hierarchy $H_{m'}$ by the following sub-steps:

6.1) Find $B' = B_{j'}$ where

$$j' = \arg_{j}\{\min\{E(B_j)\}\},$$

for $B_j \in P_{m'}(B)$; then generate new representative concepts $RC_k^{m'}$ in $H_{m'}$. The $RC_k^{m'}$ is obtained by merging the same representative concepts in the lower level $H_{m'+1}$.

6.2) The corresponding fuzzy concept $C_k^{m'} = (\mu_1, \mu_2, ... \mu_i, ..., \mu_m)$ is generated from the representative concepts $RC_k^{m'}$, where μ_i is the minimum of membership grade for the merged fuzzy concepts with the same representative concepts in Step 6.1.

6.3) The remainder unchanged fuzzy concept in $H_{m'+1}$ is added into $H_{m'}$, directly.

Step 7: Calculate the degree of subordinate relationships $R(C_{k1}^{m'}, C_{k2}^{m'+1})$ between each pair of concepts in $H_{m'}$ and $H_{m'+1}$.

Step 8: Let the set of reduced attributes $B = B'$. If $B \ne \emptyset$, then go to Step 4; otherwise, output all levels of the fuzzy concept hierarchy $H_0, ..., H_m$.

5 Measurement of Fuzzy Concept

The induced fuzzy concept reflects the hierarchical structure of the given database should be evaluated. However, there are no target outputs associated with the inputs in unsupervised learning. The method used to evaluate unsupervised learning system is to compute predictive accuracy as that is done for supervised classifiers. The resulting accuracy serves as a measure of how well the system has discovered. As Fig. 2 illustrates, an evaluation is designed to test the fuzzy concept.

1. Preprocess: At first, the input dataset will be partitioned into test data and training data. Fuzzy process will generate membership functions from training data and transform the training and testing data into fuzzy sets.
2. Concept Learning: The proposed hierarchical clustering algorithm then cluster strong concepts from training data and construct a meaningful fuzzy concept hierarchy.
3. Evaluation: A node labeling algorithm used for labeling proper class to each node in constructed hierarchy. Then, a similarity measure is given to decide the best node in fuzzy concept hierarchy for each test datum.

In unsupervised learning, there is no class information for each cluster. Therefore, class information is required for concepts (or clusters) in constructed hierarchy to compute predictive accuracy. The labeling algorithm based on fuzzy confidence is described as follows.

Assume database $X = \{x_1, x_2, ..., x_n\}$, a class v_d and attribute set B, the confidence value C_k^l with the k-th concept of level l is calculated as the following formula:

$$FC^{v_d}(C_k^l) = \frac{\sum_{x \in X}\left(\min\left(\min_{r_i \in RC_k^l}\left(\mu_{r_i}(x)\right), \mu_{v_d}(x)\right)\right)}{\sum_{x \in X}\left(\min_{r_i \in RC_k^l}\left(\mu_{r_i}(x)\right)\right)},$$

where $\mu_{r_i}(C_k^l)$ is the membership value of the object x on the linguistic term r_i. r_i is the representative linguistic term of i-th attribute in the representative concept of C_k^l, RC_k^l.

Assume that the hierarchical concepts H is built from training data of database X with attribute set A. A contains a decision attribute $A_d \in A$. Let the set of possible values in A_d be $V = \{v_1, ..., v_i\}$. The node labeling algorithm for H is described in five main steps, as follows.

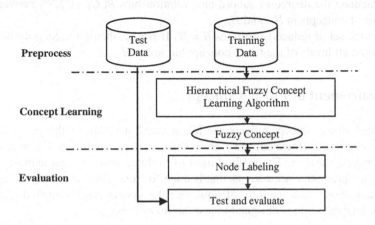

Fig. 2. The architecture of evaluation process

Algorithm 2: Node labeling based on fuzzy confidence
Input: A fuzzy taxonomy H with attribute set A including decision attribute A_d. The threshold α of fuzzy confidence.
Output: A taxonomy of labeled concepts H'.

Step 1: Initially, $l = 1$.
Step 2: Let $C = \{ C^l_k \mid C^l_k \in H_l \}$. The fuzzy confidences $FC^{v_i}(C^l_k)$ for all $C^l_k \in C$ are computed.
Step 3: Let v_i denote the i-th possible value of decision attribute A_d, $v_i \in A_d$. For v_{max} satisfying $FC^{v_{max}}(C^l_k) = \max_{v_i \in A_d} \{FC^{v_i}(C^l_k)\}$ for C^l_k, if the $FC^{v_{max}}(C^l_k) > \alpha$, the node with class v_{max} is labeled.
Step 4: If $l < |A| - 2$ then go to Step 4; otherwise, the results are outputted and the algorithm halts.
Step 5: Set $l = l + 1$, go to Step 2.

In order to find a suitable location for an unknown object in the built hierarchy, a similarity measure to evaluate the similarity of two concepts C_k and $C_{k'}$ is defined as follows,

$$ f(C_k, C_{k'}) = \frac{\sum\limits_{A_i \in A} \prod\limits_{t_{ij} \in \mu_i} \left(1 - |\mu_{ij}(C_k) - \mu_{ij}(C_{k'})|\right)}{|A|} . $$

The proposed similarity measure node labeling algorithm is used to predict suitable position for unknown objects in constructed hierarchy. The similarity between test data and concepts is measured by scanning the hierarchy from the highest level to the lowest level. Furthermore, two scoring methods are used to decide the best position of unknown objects. The first method is scored by the similarity between unknown objects and each concept,

$$ S(x, C^l_k) = f(x, C^l_k) , $$

where x denote an unknown object, C^l_k denotes the k-th concept of level l. The second method considers more about if the concept is good enough for representing all child concepts. Therefore, we consider both similarity and fuzzy confidence of each concept C^l_k as the scoring method:

$$ S_{sc}(x, C^l_k) = f(x, C^l_k) \times \max_{v_i \in V}(FC^{v_i}_B(C^l_k)) . $$

The most suitable concept having the highest score based on these two score methods is chosen. The detailed algorithm for evaluating fuzzy concept by classification is shown as follows.

Algorithm 3: Classification by similarity measure
Input: An unknown class data x and taxonomy of labeled concepts H'.
Output: The assigned class V_d for x

Step 1: Initially, $l = 1$, $C = \{ C^l_k \mid C^l_k \in H_l \}$, and $m = 0$.
Step 2: Compute $S(x, C^l_k)$ for all $C^l_k \in H_l$.

Step 3: Select C^l_{max} that

$$S(x, C^l_{max}) = \max_{C^l_k \in C}(S(x, C^l_k)).$$

If $S(x, C^l_{max}) > m$, assign V_d to be class of C^l_{max}; otherwise the algorithm stops.
Step 4: If $l \neq |B|$ go to Step 4; otherwise the algorithm stops.
Step 5: Set $l = l + 1$, $C' = \{C^l_{k'} | C^l_{k'} \in H_l$ and $C^l_{k'} \subseteq C^l_{max}\}$.
Step 6: If $C' = \varnothing$, the algorithm stops; otherwise go to Step 2.

Algorithm 4: Classification by similarity measure and fuzzy confidence
Input: An unknown class data x and a hierarchy of node labeled concepts H'.
Output: The assigned class V_d for x
Step 1: Initially, $l = 1$, $C = \{C^l_k | C^l_k \in H_l\}$, and $m = 0$.
Step 2: Compute $S_{sc}(x, C^l_k)$ for all $C^l_k \in H_l$.
Step 3: Select C^l_{max} such that

$$S_{sc}(x_k, C^l_{max}) = \max_{C^l_k \in C}(S_{sc}(x, C^l_k)).$$

If $S_{sc}(x_k, C^l_{max}) > m$, assign V_d to be class of C^l_{max}.
Step 4: If $l \neq |B|$, then go to Step 5; otherwise the algorithm stops.
Step 5: Set $l = l + 1$, $C' = \{C^l_{k'} | C^l_{k'} \in H_l$ and $C^l_{k'} \subseteq C^l_{max}\}$.
Step 6: If $C' = \varnothing$, the algorithm stops; otherwise go to Step 2.

Table 1. The selected datasets

Datasets	Number of attributes	Number of instances	Number of Classes
BCW	9	683	2
CLEVE	13	296	2
CRX	15	653	2
GLASS	9	214	7
HORSE	12	326	2
PIMA	8	768	2

6   Experiments and Evaluation Results

For illustrating the performance of the proposed method, several datasets are selected. The test datasets including the Breast Cancer dataset of Wisconsin, the Credit Approval dataset, the Glass Identification dataset, the Horse Colic dataset and the PIMA Indian Diabetes dataset that are selected from UCI Machine Learning Repository [1]. All selected datasets are summarized in Table 1.

In order to evaluate the efficiency of the learning and prediction processes, decision attribute is used only for testing, but hidden during training. The experimental results were obtained by performing 10-fold cross validation. From the experimental results, we observed the two scoring methods achieve good results in accuracy of different dataset. The threshold of fuzzy confidence α also affects the accuracy greatly. As Table 2 illustrates, we evaluate the constructed hierarchy from α is 0.5 to

0.65. In the selected six datasets, the concept will be too general when the threshold α is higher than 0.7 and the accuracy will decrease significantly.

We perform the experiments with the two scoring methods and compare the results with GCF, COBWEB and Liao's approach methods. The comparison of the scoring methods is shown as Table 3 with the average accuracy and the threshold of fuzzy confidence. Results show that the proposed method is better than other systems in most of datasets.

Table 2. Predictive accuracies by similarity measure examined in prediction

Datasets	稽	Similarity (%)	Similarity+fuzzy confidence (%)
BCW	0.50	96.50	94.88
	0.55	98.10	97.66
	0.60	96.77	96.77
	0.65	66.33	66.33
CLEVE	0.50	75.42	75.42
	0.55	76.51	76.51
	0.60	79.52	78.66
	0.65	78.44	78.66
CRX	0.50	75.33	75.33
	0.55	75.33	75.33
	0.60	76.55	77.24
	0.65	76.55	78.43
GLASS	0.50	46.20	39.17
	0.55	43.80	48.69
	0.60	43.81	60.71
	0.65	43.93	55.95
HORSE	0.50	75.26	75.15
	0.55	77.92	78.44
	0.60	80.62	80.13
	0.65	81.22	77.23
PIMA	0.50	67.42	65.18
	0.55	67.41	64.80
	0.60	70.38	69.46
	0.65	61.22	66.49

Table 3. The experimental results

Datasets	GCF	Cobweb	Liao's	Sim	Sim+FC
BCW	92.36	94.76	92.97	98.10	97.66
CLEVE	82.46	81.21	76.69	79.52	78.66
CRX	82.42	82.48	81.32	76.55	78.43
GLASS	59.08	57.73	56.07	46.19	60.71
HORSE	72.56	75.99	77.91	81.22	80.13
PIMA	68.58	67.64	67.84	70.38	69.46

7 Conclusion

The concept hierarchy is an explicit representation of knowledge and can be widely used in many applications. Fuzzy concept description is more suitable than crisp concept description in representing human knowledge. In this paper, we present the fuzzy concept hierarchy and propose an algorithm to generate fuzzy concept hierarchy based on fuzzy entropy. The algorithm can construct a meaningful fuzzy concept hierarchy automatically and represent fuzzy concepts with representative concepts and different grades of subsuming relationships among subordinate fuzzy concepts. Our experiments also show that the fuzzy concept can be labeled well and depict important concept effectively. This work can be extended to apply to find useful concept and knowledge structures in semantic web. The further work on related application is to help constructing ontology from database automatically.

Acknowledgments. This work was supported in part by the National Science Council under Grant NSC95-2221-E-024-014

References

1. Blake, C., Keogh, E., Merz, C.J.: UCI repository of machine learning database, Department of Information and Computer Science, University of California, Irvine (1998), http://www.ics.uci.edu/ mlearn/MLRepository.html
2. Chien, B.C., Liao, S.Y.: Mining Categorical Concept Hierarchies in Large Databases. Proceedings of 7th World Multiconference on Systemics, Cybernetics and Informatics, 2, 244–249 (2003)
3. Burmeister, P.: Formal Concept analysis with ConImp: Introduction to Basic Features. TU Darmstdt, Germany, Technical Report, http://www.mathematik.tudarmstadt.de/
4. Fisher, D.H.: Knowledge Acquisition via Incremental Conceptual Clustering. Machine Learning 2(2), 139–172 (1987)
5. Gennari, J.H., Langley, P., Fisher, D.: Models of incremental concept formation. Artificial Intelligence 40(1), 11–61 (1989)
6. Han, J., Kamber, M.: Data Mining: Concept and Techniques. Morgan Kaufmann, San Francisco (2001)
7. Jiang, J., Conrath, D.: Semantic similarity based on corpus statistics and lexical taxonomy. In: Proceedings of International Conference on Research in Computational Linguistics (1997)
8. Klir, G.J., Yuan, B.: Fuzzy sets and fuzzy logic: theory and applications. Prentice-Hall, Englewood Cliffs (1995)
9. Mangasarian, L., Wolberg, W.H.: Cancer Diagnosis via Linear Programming. SIAM News 23(5), 1–18 (1990)
10. Quinlan, J.R.: Induction of Decision Trees. Machine Learning 1(1), 81–106 (1986)
11. Talavera, L., Bejar, J.: Generality-Based Conceptual Clustering with Probabilistic Concepts. IEEE Transactions on Pattern Analysis and Machine Intelligence 23(2), 196–206 (2001)
12. Wu, Z., Palmer, M.: Verb Semantics and Lexical Selection. In: Proceedings of the 32nd Annual Meeting of the Association for Computational Linguistics (1994)

Prepositions and Conjunctions in a Natural Language Interfaces to Databases*

J. Javier González B.[1], Rodolfo A. Pazos R.[2], Alexander Gelbukh[3],
Grigori Sidorov[3], Hector Fraire H.[1], and I. Cristina Cruz C.[1]

[1] Instituto Tecnológico de Ciudad Madero, México
jjgonzalezbarbosa@hotmail.com,
hfraire@prodigy.net.mx, ircriscc@hotmail.com
[2] Centro Nacional de Investigación y Desarrollo Tecnológico (CENIDET), México
pazos@sd-cenidet.com.mx
[3] Centro de Investigación en Computación
{gelbukh,sidorov}@cic.ipn.mx

Abstract. This paper present the treatment of prepositions and conjunctions in natural language interfaces to databases (NLIDB) that allows better translation of queries expressed in natural language into formal languages. Prepositions and conjunctions weren't sufficiently studied for their usage in NLIDBs, because most of the NLIDBs just look for keywords in the sentences and focus their analysis on nouns and verbs getting rid of auxiliary words in the query. This paper shows that prepositions and conjunctions can be represented as operations using formal set theory. Additionally, since prepositions and conjunctions keep their meaning in any context, their treatment is domain independent. In our experiments we used Spanish language. We validate our approach using two databases; Northwind and Pubs of SQL Server, with a corpus of 198 different queries for the first one and 70 queries for the second one. The 84% of queries were translated correctly for the database Northwind and 80% for Pubs.

1 Introduction

The present situation with natural language interfaces to databases (NLIDBs) is such that they do not guarantee in general satisfactory translation of natural language queries into formal language representation [1]. Additionally, most NLIDBs are limited to certain database domains and they are usually configured manually by the DB administrators.

A survey of existing NLIDB architectures shows that most of them have the following characteristics [2]: a) Each NLIDB carries out a transformation from natural language into an intermediate representation language, from which a query is generated for obtaining results from the repository, b) they have an inherent dependency on the domain of the database information, c) NLIDBs implementations are modular and robust, but the queries that they can answer are

---

* This research was supported in part by CONACYT and DGEST.

P. Thulasiraman et al. (Eds.): ISPA 2007 Workshops, LNCS 4743, pp. 173–182, 2007.
© Springer-Verlag Berlin Heidelberg 2007

limited by the vocabulary and grammar defined for the NLIDB and d) NLIDBs were designed for obtaining answers for specific domains instead of trying to make them domain independent.

Additionally, most NLIDBs focus on the analysis of the sentence structure and only few concentrate on the meaning of the constituent elements or use discourse handling techniques. Still, practically all of them use some limited grammar for detection of syntactic relations between words.

Each phase of analysis supplies important information for the query translation process, but the largest effort has been focused on the morphological and syntactic analyses; however, exact understanding of users queries is far from being achieved by NLIDBs.

2   Related Work

In some NLIDBs, the semantic analyzer extracts the meaning of the sentence and generates a logical structure from the syntactic structure obtained using a syntactic parser [3]. One of the key tasks of the semantic processing consists in determining, which combinations of individual word meanings are possible while generating a coherent meaning of the sentence. This approach can be used for reducing the number of possible meanings for each word of the given sentence [4].

The semantic analysis of sentences is still a very complex task [5], just the determination of the meaning of words is a difficult task due to their polysemy; for example, file is a tool and also a place for keeping documents, etc.

In many NLIDBs, the semantic analysis of a natural language query involves searching of keywords in the input sentence, which are evaluated according to a predefined pattern through multiple database mappings. In some research works, the semantic analysis uses probabilistic models [6, 7], which need a corpus labeled with semantic information. This is a subjective approach and it requires a considerable manual effort, besides, these models were applied to specific tasks within a restricted semantic domain and use a semantic representation that usually consists of case-frames [8].

For carrying out the semantic analysis of a sentence, the computer needs mainly a structure for storing the meanings and relationships of each word, a dictionary that holds the general language knowledge (words, meanings, relationships, synonyms, antonyms, etc.), and algorithms and techniques for obtaining the relevant information for carrying out the translation into a formal language regardless of domain.

Prepositions and conjunctions were not sufficiently studied for tasks of processing natural language queries, because most of the NLIDBs just look for keywords in the sentence [13] and focus their analysis on nouns and verbs getting rid of auxiliary words in the query [14, 15].

3   Proposed Approach

The solution of the problem of obtaining an exact understanding of a users query can benefit from information regarding invariant parts of the sentence, like prepositions and conjunctions, which can be exploited for facilitating the query translation process.

In this project will be utilized the preposition de and the conjunction y, by having a very high frequency of use in the Spanish language[17].

The purpose of the proposed approach is designing a technique that permits better translation of a natural language query into Structured Query Language (SQL) and that requires minimum configuration effort for operating with different domains.

The proposed general architecture of the system is shown in Figure 1, and a short description of the constituent modules and their contribution to the translation module is given below.

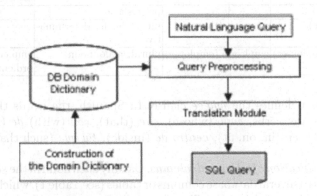

Fig. 1. General architecture of the system

Query Preprocessing: The preprocessor analyzes each word of the sentence in order to obtain its lexical, syntactic, and semantic information. The built-in parser extracts the lexical and syntactic information, whereas the semantic information can be extracted only by interacting with the domain dictionary.

The output of this module consists of the query labeled as shown in Table 1. The query is divided into words that are the minimal meaningful units of the sentence, and for each word information of the following types is included: **lexical** (word stems, synonyms and antonyms), **morphosyntactic** (grammatical category according to its function in the sentence) and **semantic** (meaning of the word with respect to the database). Table 1 shows an example of this information for a query.

Translation Module: This module receives the labeled sentence and processes it in three phases.

Phase 1: Identification of the select and where phrases. The query phrases that define the SQL select and where clauses are identified in order to pinpoint the columns (and tables) referred to by these phrases. Since these clauses always involve table columns, then, we assume that the phrases are query subphrases that include at least one noun (and possibly prepositions, conjunction, articles, adjectives, etc.) and that the phrase that defines the *select* clause always precedes

Table 1. Query Information

Word	Stem	Morphosyntactic information	Columns	Table
QUERY: Muestra los nombres de los empleados. (Show the names of the employees)				
muestra (show)	mostrar (show)	verb, imperative		
los (the)	el (the)	plural, male, determinative		
nombres (names)	nombre (name)	plural, male, noun	cat.catN, cust.comN, emp.fNom, ord.shNom	
de (of)	de (of)	preposition		
los (the)	el (the)	plural, male, determinative		
empleados (employees)	empleado (employee)	plural, male, noun	emp.empID ord.empID	Emp

the phrase that defines the *where* clause. In Spanish, the words that separate these phrases are: verbs, *cuyo* (whose), *que* (that), *con* (with) *de* (from, with), *donde* (where), *en* (in, on, at), *dentro de* (inside), *tal que* (such that), etc.

Phase 2: Identification of tables and columns. Usually each noun in the *select/where* phrases refers to several database columns or tables (see Table 1), which would yield several translations of the query. Therefore, in order to pinpoint the columns and tables referred to, it is usually necessary to analyze the preposition *de* (of) and conjunction *y* (and), since they almost always appear in *select/where* phrases expressed in Spanish [17]. Examination of prepositions and conjunctions permits, besides considering the meaning of individual nouns, to determine the precise meaning of a *select/where* phrase that involves nouns related by prepositions and conjunctions. For this, preposition *de* (of) and conjunction *y* (and) are represented by operations using set theory, because of the role they play in queries.

Preposition de (of) establishes a close relationship between a word and its complement, such that, if there exists a select/where phrase that includes two nouns p and q related by preposition de (of), then the phrase refers to the common elements (columns or tables) referred to by p and q. Formally, $S(p \text{ prep\_de } q) = S(p) \cap S(q)$, where $S(x)$ is the set of columns or tables referred to by phrase x. Conjunction y (and) expresses the notion of addition or accumulation, such that if there is a select phrase that involves two nouns p and q related by conjunction y (and), then the phrase refers to all the elements referred to by p and$q$. Formally, $S(p \text{ conj\_y } q) = S(p) \cup (q)$. Conjunction y (and) in a where phrase is treated as a Boolean operation.

For example, consider the query: *cuáles son los nombres y direcciones de los empleados* (which are the names and addresses of the employees). Consider the *select* phrase *nombres y direcciones de los empleados* (names and addresses of the employees). According to the above explanation, to extract the meaning of the *select* phrase it is necessary to apply two set operations: a union, corresponding to the conjunction *y* (and), and an intersection, corresponding to the preposition *de* (of). A heuristics is applied to determine the order of the two operations. In this case the preposition *de* (of) applies to the two nouns (*names and addresses of the employees = names of the employees and addresses of the employees*), therefore, the intersection operation has precedence above the union. The output of Phase 2 is the semantic interpretation of the *select* and *where* phrases (i.e. the columns and tables referred to by these phrases), which will be used in Phase 3 to translate them into the *select* and *where* clauses of the SQL statement.

The translation module has a tree structure that represents the database information, and additionally the relationships among database columns are included. The columns, tables and search conditions obtained in this phase are marked in the tree, and from this structure a graph is constructed that represents the user's query.

Phase 3: Construction of the relational graph. Once the graph has been constructed, an equivalent SQL expression is generated.

4   Invariant Parts of Sentences: Prepositions and Conjunctions

A sentence is a word or set of words that bears a complete meaning. Some of these words may remain unchanged in all situations; i.e., they do not change, for example, according to gender or number independently of the rest of the sentence (invariant sentence parts); while other words may change according to, say, gender and number (variable sentence parts) [9].

Usually, the invariant sentence parts are auxiliary words like prepositions and conjunctions. These categories are known also as relational elements because they are used for relating some elements to the other. A preposition links a main word with its complement, it links and subordinates simultaneously, while a conjunction links words or syntagms of the same category.

A careful examination of the labeled query reveals that each noun is related to one or more columns or tables (Table 1), to which it may refer, while prepositions and conjunctions express relationships among them. The rest of this section is devoted to demonstrating how prepositions and conjunctions can be represented as operations using set theory. This can be used for facilitating the query translation process.

4.1   Prepositions

Preposition, as mentioned previously, is an invariant that is used for linking a main word (syntactic core) with its complement (glass *of* wine, I am going *to* Rome). This complement is called *preposition term* because the relationship established by the preposition stops and is consummated at this point [10, 11].

Preposition *de* (*of*) establishes a close link between a word and its complement in such a way that the expression constituted by any word or noun *p* and its complement q linked by preposition *de* refers to the common elements represented by p and q.

$$p \ prep\_de \ q = R \ R = p \cap q.$$

For example, let us consider the following expression: *fecha de nacimiento* (*date of birth*).

Let p and q denote the set of columns and tables that are referred to by the nouns *fecha* (*date*) and *nacimiento* (*birth*). If we want to obtain the set represented by *fecha de nacimiento (date of birth)*, or equivalently, $p \ prep\_de \ q$, then the common elements of p and q must be obtained.

fecha=$\{c_{fecha}, t_{fecha}\}$
c_{fecha}=\{employees.birthDate, employees.hireDate,
     orders.orderDate, orders.requiredDate, orders.shipDate\}
t_{fecha}=$\{\emptyset\}$
nacimiento=$\{c_{nacimiento}, t_{nacimiento}\}$
$c_{nacimiento}$=\{employees.birthDate\}
$t_{nacimiento}$=$\{\emptyset\}$

where the t's stay for database tables and the c's denote table columns. Therefore, the information referred to by *fecha de nacimiento* is represented by

$$fecha \cap nacimiento = \{employees.birthDate\}$$

In the previous example none of the nouns (*fecha, nacimiento*) refers to a table, and consequently the intersection operates only on the columns. Now let us consider an example that illustrates a different situation: *direcciones de empleados* (*addresses of employees*)

$direcciones = \{c_{direcciones}, t_{direcciones}\}$
$c_{direcciones} = \{customers.address, employees.address, orders.shipAddress,$
     $suppliers.address\}$
$t_{direcciones} = \{\emptyset\}$
$empleados = \{c_{empleados}, t_{empleados}\}$
$c_{empleados} = \{employees.employeeID, employeesTerritories.employeeID,$
     $orders.empID\}$
$t_{empleados} = \{employees\}$

then

$$direcciones \cap empleados = \{c_{direcciones} \cap c_{empleados}\} \cup \{c_{direcciones} \cap t_{empleados}\}$$
$$\cup \{t_{direcciones} \cap c_{empleados}\}$$
$$= \{\emptyset\} \cup \{employees.address\} \cup \{\emptyset\}$$
$$= \{employees.address\}$$

Preposition *de* generally implies the intersection between the columns referred to by the two words, the columns referred to by one word and the tables referred to by the other word, and vice versa.

$$p \cap q = \{\{c_p \cap c_q\} \cup \{c_p \cap t_q\} \cup \{t_p \cap c_q\} \cup \{t_p \cap t_q\}\}$$

This type of operation is valid only for nouns that represent DB columns or tables. When the preposition establishes a link between a set of columns and a value, this case is treated differently. If preposition *de* operates on a column and a value, it will be considered as a comparison operator; for example: *salario de 20,000* (salary equal to 20,000).

Prepositions *con* (*with*) and *sin* (*without*) establish search conditions, and preposition *entre* (between) permits to establish a value range for a column; for example: *salario entre 15,000 y 25,000* (*salary between 15,000 and 25,000*).

4.2 Conjunctions

Conjunction has been traditionally defined as the sentence part that is used for linking two or more elements in an equality relationship [12].

Copulative conjunctions express the notion of addition or accumulation, such that the set of any two nouns p_1 and p_2 that are linked through a conjunction y (*and*) represents the set of all the elements represented by p_1 and p_2

$$p_1 \; conj\_y \; p_2 = R \quad R = p_1 \cup p_2.$$

When a query requires two or more operations of union or intersection (for example, *Muéstrame la fecha de nacimiento y el nombre del empleado*), it is nedeed to determinate which would be the priority of the operations. Thus, in order to evaluate prepositions and conjunctions, numeric values are asigned as follows:

Nomenclature: [n1 prep/conj n2]

- n1: a numeric value of the noun before to the preposition or conjunction (1 for a column, 2 for tables)
- prep/conj: a preposition de, conjunction y.
- n2: a numeric value of the noun after the preposition or conjunction (1 for a column, 2 for tables)

Cases

1. If a pattern [2 prep 2] is identified, it is changed to [1 prep 2] in the case that the first noun is a column that belongs to the table of the second noun.
2. A numeric value of 1 is given to the prepositions in the patterns [1 prep 1] and [2 prep 2].
3. A numeric value of 2 is given to the conjunctions in the patterns [1 conj 1] and [2 conj 2].
4. A numeric value of 3 is given to the prepositions in the pattern [1 prep 2].
5. A numeric value of 4 is in other case.

Now, the prepositions and conjunctions are processed in the order of their numeric value. Those prepositions or conjunctions with a numeric value of 1 are processed first, then those with a numeric value of 2 and so on.

In the example *Muéstrame la fecha de nacimiento y el nombre del empleado (Show me the birthday and name of the employees)*, a set of columns and tables are determined whit the treatment of prepositions and conjunctions. This query includes the cases 2 [1 prep 1], 3 [1 conj 1] y 4 [1 prep 2].

Query	fecha	de	nacimiento	y	nombre	de	empleado
Values	1	1	1	2	1	3	2
Priority		1		2		3	

The union between the nouns *fecha* and *nacimiento* are performed first. The last preposition *de* affects the elements: *fecha de nacimiento y nombre de empleados = fecha de nacimiento de empleados y nombre de empleados* (*birth day and name of employees = birthday of employees and names of employees*), and therefore the union must be performed before this intersection.

5   Experimental Results

For the experiment, the Northwind and Pubs databases of SQL Server 7.0 were used, and a group of 50 users was gathered in order to formulate queries in Spanish, collecting a corpus consisting of 198 different queries for the Northwind database and 70 queries for the Pubs database. For formulating their queries the users only were allowed to see the databases schemas (definitions).

The queries were classified in the following types according to the kind of information the users express: a) Queries with explicit attributes and relationships, b) Queries with implicit attributes and explicit relationships, c) Queries with explicit attributes and implicit relationships, d) Queries with implicit attributes and relationships, e) Queries that require special functions (average, sum, etc.) and f) Queries that need to be reformulated due to insufficient information to answer them. As far as translated queries are concerned, the following results were obtained: 84% of queries were translated correctly to Northwind Database (See Table 2) and 80% of queries were translated correctly to Pubs database (Table 3). The other percent had errors in translation. There exist two basic reasons that caused these errors: special functions or deduction processes are needed, and lack of explicit information for processing.

Additional experiments were conducted in order to assess the impact of the analysis of prepositions and conjunctions on the translation success. When this analysis was excluded from the translation process, most of the queries were answered with correct information; however, extra columns were obtained. This

Table 2. Results obtained for the Northwind database

Query Results	Query Type						Total	%	%
	1	**2**	**3**	**4**	**5**	**6**			
Answered correctly	31	57	19	49	0	0	156	79	84
Answered with additional information	0	0	5	5	0	0	10	5	
Incorrect answer	0	0	0	1	23	5	29	15	16
Unanswered	0	0	0	3	0	0	3	1	
Total	31	57	24	58	23	5	198	100	100

Table 3. Results obtained for the Pubs database

Query Results	Query Type						Total	%	%
	1	2	3	4	5	6			
Answered correctly	7	29	8	12	0	0	56	80	80
Answered with additional information	0	0	0	0	0	0	0	0	
Incorrect answer	0	0	0	1	10	1	12	17	20
Unanswered	0	0	0	0	1	1	2	3	
Total	7	29	8	13	11	2	70	100	100

show that the treatment of prepositions and conjunctions helps to the semantic analysis of the translation process to get correct results.

6   Conclusions

The elements that express syntactic relations like prepositions and conjunctions are invariant parts of sentences and provide information that is important for the query translation process. These relational elements link or subordinate word categories refining their meaning, thus enhancing the information discrimination. Additionally, since prepositions and conjunctions keep their meaning in all situations, their treatment favors domain independence.

Preposition *de* (*of*) and conjunction *y* (*and*) were studied, as well as their relationship to nouns. We are currently working on the analysis of the meaning of other invariant sentence parts and their relationship to the different syntactic categories aiming at using them in the semantic analysis during query processing.

The experiments conducted include simple and compound sentences that have a similar sentence structure. The experimental results show that it is possible to treat invariant parts of a user's query through the usage of set theory.

References

1. Popescu, A.M., Etzioni, O., Kautz, H.: Towards a Theory of Natural Language Interfaces to Databases. In: Proceedings of the 2003 International Conference on Intelligent User Interfaces, ACM Press, New York (2003)
2. Orea, M.Q.: Interfaz en Espanol para Recuperacion de Informacion en una Base de Datos Geografica. B.S. thesis. Universidad de las Americas. Puebla (2001)
3. AVENTINUS - Advanced Information System for Multinational Drug Enforcement, http://www.dcs.shef.ac.uk/nlp/funded/aventinus.html
4. Areas de Investigacion; Procesamiento de Lenguaje Natural. (1998), http://gplsi.dlsi.ua.es/gplsi/areas.htm
5. Sidorov, G.: Problemas actuales de Lingüistica Computacional. Revista Digital Universitaria 2(1) (2001), http://www.revista.unam.mx/vol.2/num1/art1/
6. Stallard, M.S., Bobrow, D., Schwartz, R.: A Fully Statistical Approach to Natural Language Interfaces. In: Proc. 34th Annual Meeting of the Association for Computational Linguistics (1996)

7. Minker, W.: Stochastically-Based Natural Language Understanding Across Task and Languages. In: Proc. of EuroSpeech97, Rodas, Greece (1997), http://citeseer.nj.nec.com/
8. Moreno, L., Molina, A.: Preliminares y Tendencias en el Procesamiento del Lenguaje Natural, Departamento de Sistemas Informaticos y Computacion. Universidad Politecnica de Valencia.
9. Profesor en Linea. Gramatica y Ortografia: http://www.profesorenlinea.cl/castellano/oracionpartesdela.htm
10. Enciclopedia Libre. Enciclopedia Libre Universal en Espanol (2004), http://enciclopedia.us.es/wiki.phtml
11. Prytz, O.: Notas sobre las Preposiciones Simples en Espanol Moderno (1994), http://www.digbib.uio.no/roman/Art/Rf1-94-1/Prytzb.pdf
12. Martin, V.G.: Curso de Redaccion. In: Martin, V. (ed.) Teoria y Practica de la Composicion del Estilo. Editorial Thomson. 33ª edicion, Madrid, España (2002)
13. Martin, A.: Una Propuesta de Codificacion Morfosintactica para Corpus de Referencia en Lengua Espanola. In: Martin, A. (ed.) Estudios de Lingüistica Espanola (ELiEs). Publicacion periodica de monografias sobre lingüistica espanola (1999), http://elies.rediris.es/elies3/cap31a.htm
14. Bridge, G., Harlow, S.: An Introduction to Computational Linguistics, Intelligent System Group. Department of Computer Science. University of York.
15. Meng, F., Chu, W.W.: Database Query Formation from Natural Language Using Semantic Modeling and Statistical Keyword Meaning Disambiguation. Computer Science Department. University of California
16. InBase-Online. English queries to personnel DB. Russian Research Institute of Artificial Intelligence (2001), http://www.inbase.artint.ru/nl/kadry-eng.asp
17. Montero, J.M.: Sistemas de conversion texto voz. B.S.thesis. Universidad Politecnica de Madrid. http://lorien.die.upm.es/~juancho

Zigbee Positioning System for Smart Home Application

Ming-Hui Jin, Chih-Hao Yu, Hung-Ren Lai, and Ming-Whei Feng

Networks and Multimedia Institute, Institute for Information Industry
6FL., 218, Tun-Hwa S. Rd., Sec. 2, Taipei, 106, Taiwan, R.O.C.
{jinmh,howei,hrlai,mfeng}@nmi.iii.org.tw

Abstract. This paper presents a smart home system prototype which employs an indoor positioning system called the Best Beacon Match (BBM) positioning method to intelligently trigger the appropriately services for the home members. To overcome the ninja problem in the BBM method, the signal filtering, adjustment and smooth procedures are proposed. We employ the Zigbee module to implement the prototypes of the components for the BBM positioning method, and the prototypes were pass the ZigBee Compliant Platform (ZCP) certification test. The proposed system prototype which intelligently controls the air condition and light system for smart home applications is also verifying in our demo room and in the smart house in National Taiwan University.

1 Introduction

Home automation is the primitive function of smart home. In Wikipedia, the contributors make the following descriptions to the building automation: Building automation is a programmed, computerized, "intelligent" network of electronic devices that monitor and control the mechanical and lighting systems in a building. The intent is to create an intelligent building and reduce energy and maintenance costs. [1] The goal of this study is proposing an automatic method for reducing the energy consumption for smart home.

In most buildings, lighting and air condition systems consume most energy usages. Some intelligent buildings attempt to reduce the power consumption of lighting and air conditions through the help of sensors. One typical example is to turn the lights in a space on for a half hour since the last motion was sensed.[1] This approach seems works in reducing the power consumption of the lighting system, however, it may bring uncomfortable scenarios. On typical example is the motion detector senses no mobile object in a room where some people sit there without move. Since the priority of providing comfortable environment is generally higher than reducing the power consumption, most users do not accept the motion detection solution.

This study attempts to employ the indoor positioning mechanisms to reduce the power consumption of the lighting and air condition system. If the positions of the building members are detectable, then the proposed system can turn on the corresponding systems such as lighting and air condition whenever the building members are approaching. And the system can turn off the corresponding systems after no building members stay there for a period of time.

P. Thulasiraman et al. (Eds.): ISPA 2007 Workshops, LNCS 4743, pp. 183–192, 2007.

Developing a power-efficient accurate positioning service has been critical for indoor context aware applications which construct a smart space to interact with users. The challenge to receive applicable GPS signals in the indoor environment has driven the position sensing capabilities for the advanced wireless networks. In the literatures, several positioning techniques have been proposed for mobile computing environment. They could be classified into three categories. The first category applies the Time of Arrival (TOA) or Time Difference of Arrival (TDOA) schemes to estimate the position of mobile users [2, 3]. The principle of TOA and TDOA is estimating the distance between the receiver and each sender according to the traveling time from the senders to the receivers and then calculating the position of the receiver with the help of the known positions of at least three senders [2]. The second category applies the Angle of Arrival (AOA) scheme to estimate the position of mobile users. The principle of AOA is estimating the angle of arrival signal and then calculating the position of the sender by the known positions of the receivers and the angles of arrival signals detected by each receiver [3]. The last category utilizes the attenuation of signal strength of the senders nearby to estimate the position of mobile users. The principle of the methods in this category is applying the propagation law to estimate the distance from the receiver and each sender [3, 4].

Although TOA and TDOA are simple and concrete, however, the derived technologies are difficult in practice. The main difficulty arises from time synchronization among the senders and time-delay (or arrival time difference) detection in the receivers. Without perfect time synchronization and time-delay detection technologies, the positioning results would be inaccurate. Besides, the distance between the senders should be large enough to ensure the difference of the positioning signal arrival time distinguishable. The above constrains make TOA and TDOA approaches not appropriate for positioning most users in the indoor environment. On the other hand, the AOA approach also requires the sender to be able to detect the direction of arrival signals. This also requires the access point to equip extra components such as the smart antennas [5]. Besides, the reflection problem due to the indoor natures such as walls and pillars often causes inaccurate positioning results.

Driven by the above regards, this study adopts the signal strength approach of the third category since it requires no cheap equipments for both the access points and mobile users. Although the numerous huge obstructions such as the walls and the pillars make the propagation law invalid, however, they make the signal strengths of each access point vary significantly in adjacent regions. This phenomenon implies that we can apply the sensed signal strengths to determine the region of each mobile user. For the functions of reducing the power consumption of the lighting and air condition systems, the ability of estimating the region of mobile users is sufficient.

This study proposed a novel positioning method called the Best Beacon Match (BBM) method by improving the best access point ID sequence match positioning method [6]. The BBM requires the mobile users to equip with a mobile device which can sense the Received Signal Strength Indicator (RSSI) of the nearby beacon which are pre-installed inside the interesting area. Since the power consumption of the mobile device decides the maintenance cost of the mobile device, therefore, power-saving is a crucial issue for the mobile device.

The Zigbee technology [7] provides short-range, low-cost and low power consumption wireless solutions in various applications, for instance, industrial automation, sensor network, home networking, replacement for wired computer peripherals, personal healthcare, remote control, monitoring etc. [8]. Based on those features, the proposed system employs the Zigbee technology to reduce the power consumption of the mobile device.

The rest of this paper is organized as follows. In Section 2, we present the architecture of the proposed system. The BBM positioning algorithm is presented in Section 3. Section 4 presents the application prototypes for smart home application. We make some discussions in Section 5. The conclusions and the future works are drawn in Section 7.

2 System Architecture

Fig. 1 shows the proposed smart home system architecture. In this system, several devices called the beacons were pre-installed in the interesting area. The mobile users are required to equip with a mobile device called the badge which periodically broadcasts echo requests to collect the positioning signals from the beacons and then forward the positioning signals to a nearby router. The positioning signal of a beacon contains the ID and the signal strength of the beacon.

Whenever a router received the positioning signals from a badge, it forwards the positioning signals to its coordinator directly or through the help of other routers. In Zigbee network, the coordinator is used to coordinate the operation of all the routers in the same network and collect packets from the routers. The packets are then forwarded to the home control server through the gateway which equips with the Zigbee communication module and the Ethernet communication module.

The positioning module in the home control server is used to estimate the positions of the badges according to the positioning signals from the badges. The estimate positions of the badges are then forwarded to the event trigger module. The event trigger module maintains numerous rules which control the household appliances. If the estimate position of a badge satisfies certain rules, the corresponding events will be triggered and some commands will be sent to corresponding household appliances to change their states.

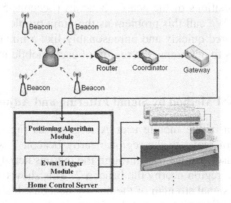

Fig. 1. The smart home system architecture

3   The BBM Positioning Algorithm

3.1   The Principle of the BBM Positioning Method and Its Challenges

The principle of the BBM method is simple and concrete. If a badge detects the signal strength of the beacons B_1, B_2, ..., B_n and the signal strength of B_i is S_i, then the position of the badge estimated by the BBM method is the position of B_j where $S_j = max \{S_1, ..., S_n\}$. Although the distance between a badge and a beacon is not in proportion to the signal strength of the beacon received by the badge, however, this method is simple and sometimes brings better effects. In Fig. 2, the signal strengths of the beacons 6 measured by the badge of the mobile user A are often stronger than that of the beacon 7 since there is a wall between them. In this scenario, the BBM method often estimates the position of A as the position of beacon 6. Although the nearest beacon of mobile user A is the beacon 7, set the position of A as the position of beacon 6 is much appropriate for most indoor applications.

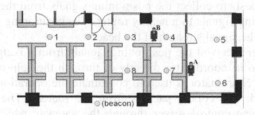

Fig. 2. The Best Beacon Match Method Scenarios

The BBM method conceals numerous problems. Those problems arise from the fact that the signal strengths of any beacon measured at any fixed position varies with time. According to our observations, the signal strengths of the beacon 7 measured by the badge of A are sometimes stronger than that of other beacons especially when the mobile user A closes and faces to the wall. Therefore, applying the BBM method directly without any improvement will bring a poor result: The position of the mobile user A is set to the positions of the nearby beacons (beacons 5, 6, and 7) randomly, and changed quickly. We call this problem as the ninja problem since the position of the mobile users changed quickly and unreasonably like a ninja. The main challenge of the BBM method is to determine the region of each mobile user while overcoming the ninja problem.

3.2   Improve the BBM Method by Signal Filtering and Adjustment

If the current position of the mobile user A is given as Fig. 2, it is clear that the mobile user A will not move to the region nearby beacon 7 within a short enough time, and the mobile user A must pass through the regions nearby by the beacon 4 and 5 before it reached the region nearby the beacon 7. This shows that the BBM method can only consider the signal strength of the nearby beacons. It should be note that two beacons B_i and B_j are adjacent if all mobile objects in the region nearby the beacon B_i can reach to the region nearby the beacon B_j without pass through the regions nearby

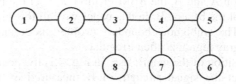

Fig. 3. The adjacent relationship of the beacons

other beacons. Fig. 3 below shows the adjacent relationship of the beacons in Fig. 2. In Fig. 3, two circles i and j are connected by a solid line means the two beacons B_i and B_j are adjacent.

Signal Filtering

The signal filtering procedure is proposed based on the assumption that the next position of each mobile object is still inside the region of the beacon it connects, or the regions of the adjacent beacons. Therefore, if the previous position of a mobile object is in the area of beacon B_i, then the signal filtering procedure ignores the signal strength of B_j if $B_i \neq B_j$ and B_i is not adjacent to B_j. This procedure ensures that the mobile objects will not pass through the wall like ninja.

Although the signal filtering procedure ensures that the mobile objects will move reasonably, however, it brings another problem called the straying problem. The straying problem occurred when the mobile object receives only the signal from the ignored beacons. It may happen in the fast-moving object. If a mobile object detects no signals for a period of time, it should be conscious that it suffers the straying problem. In this situation, it has to re-initialize it position by sensing the signal strength of all the beacons. The position re-initialization procedure chooses the beacon with the strongest signals as the position of the mobile object.

Signal Adjustment

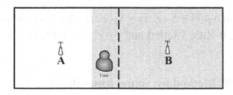

Fig. 4. The boundary identification problem

The recognition of the boundary of the adjacent regions is also a problem. Since the BBM method applies the signal strength to identify the position of mobile objects, the boundary of two adjacent regions recognized by the BBM method is not often identical to that recognized by human begins. Fig. 4 shows the boundary identification problem.

In Fig. 4, there are two adjacent beacons A and B. In the gray region the signal strength of B is stronger than A. The dotted line is the perpendicular bisector of the two beacons A and B, or a wall with a door. Although the dotted line should be the boundary of the region A and B, the BBM method still set the position of the mobile user as the position of the beacon B. In this paper we call this problem the ambiguous boundary problem. The ambiguous boundary problem is common and in real cases the boundary of the gray region is often irregular.

If the previous position of the mobile user in Fig. 4 is the position of the beacon A, appropriately subtract the signal strength of B measured by the mobile user is a strategy in reducing the errors caused by the ambiguous boundary problem. This shows that the signal strength collected by the badge of the mobile users should be adjusted before applying them to make position estimation.

After the beacons were installed in the interesting area, the proposed system suggests the system manager to collect the mean value of the signal strength of each two adjacent regions in their boundary. Let BS_A is that the mean value of the signal strength of the beacon A measured in the boundary of A and B, and BS_B is the mean value of the signal strength of the beacon B. If the previous position of the mobile user is in the region of the beacon A, the signal adjustment procedure adjusts the signal strength of B measured by the mobile user (denoted as S_B) as $S_B + BS_A - BS_B$.

The signal filtering and adjustment procedure can be performed simultaneously. To formally state the combination procedure, we make the following assumptions and definitions.

1. Assume that the previous position of a mobile user X is in the region of the beacon Y, and $Z_1, Z_2, ..., Z_k$ are all adjacent beacons of Y.
2. For each $1 \leq j \leq k$, $S_B(Y, j)$ is the mean value of the signal strength of the beacon Y measured in the boundary of Y and Z_j and $S_B(Z, j)$ is the mean value of the signal strength of the beacon Z_j.
3. For each $1 \leq j \leq k$, $S_X(Z, j)$ is the signal strength of Z_j measured by X and $S_X(Y)$ is the signal strength of Y measured by X.
4. The current position of X is denoted as CL_X, where $CL_X \in \{Y, Z_1, Z_2, ..., Z_k\}$

Based on the above assumptions and definitions, the signal filtering and adjustment procedure in the BBM algorithm applies the following rules to determine the value of CL_X.

Rule 1. $CL_X = Y$ if $S_X(Y) \geq S_X(Z, i) + S_B(Y, i) - S_B(Z, i)$ for all $1 \leq i \leq k$.

Rule 2. $CL_X = Z_j$ if Rule 1 failed and $S_X(Z, j) - S_B(Z, j) \geq S_X(Z, i) - S_B(Z, i)$ for all $1 \leq i \leq k$.

3.3 Improve the BBM Method by Signal Smooth

Given a beacon B and a position P, the signal strength of B measured at the position P is a random variable. In most cases the values generated by the random variable are close their mean but sometimes abnormal signal strength whose strengths are far from their mean appears. Since the signals with abnormal power strengths often misguide the BBM method, eliminates the signals with abnormal power strengths would be helpful in improving the ninja problem. In this paper, the procedure which eliminates the signals with abnormal power strength is called the signal smooth procedure. To formally state the signal smooth procedure, we make the following assumptions and definitions.

5. Assume that the badge applies m time slots to learn the signal strengths of all the beacons. For each beacon B, the communication module of the badge either senses no signal from B or returns a value as the signal strength of the signals form B.

6. For each beacon B, $S(B, i)$ is defined to be the signal strength of the signals from the beacon B measured by the badge in the ith time slot. $S(B, i) = NULL$ if the communication module of the badge sense no signal from B in the ith time interval.

7. $$\mu_B = \frac{\sum_{i=1, S(B,i) \neq NULL}^{m} S(B,i)}{\sum_{i=1, S(B,i) \neq NULL}^{m} 1}$$

Based on the above assumptions and definitions, the signal smooth procedure in the BBM algorithm can be stated as follow.

Step 1. Let $SB_1 = \{ S(B, i) \mid 1 \leq i \leq m$ and $S(B, i) \neq NULL \}$, $SB_2 = \phi$ and $j = 0$.
Step 2. Find s in SB_1 satisfying $\| s - \mu_B \| \leq \| t - \mu_B \|$ for all $t \in SB_1$
Step 3. Let $SB_1 = SB_1 - \{s\}$, $SB_2 = SB_2 \cup \{s\}$ and $j = j + 1$
Step 4. If $j \leq u$, go to Step 2. Otherwise terminates this procedure.

It should be noted that the values of m and u are system parameters satisfying $u < m$. The greater values of m and u usually improve the correctness of the positioning results but also enlarge the positioning response time.

4 The Zigbee-Based Smart Home System Prototypes

4.1 The Zigbee-Based Positioning System Prototypes

The positioning module in Fig. 1 has been detailed presented in Section 3. This subsection presents the prototypes of other components of the Zigbee positioning system.

Fig. 5. The III badge prototype and its layout

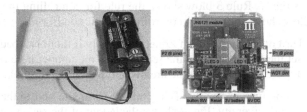

Fig. 6. The Zigbee hardware platform

Fig. 5 shows the badge prototype and its layout, and Fig. 6 shows the Zigbee hardware platform for performing the beacon, router and coordinator functions. With one AAA Alkaline battery, the life time of a badge is about 6 weeks (continuous use without sleeping). We design the badge and Zigbee hardware platform and we cooperate with the Jennic to implement those prototypes.

In May 2005, our prototypes successful passed the ZigBee Compliant Platform (ZCP) certification test using the TI/Chipcon platform. We therefore became the first organization in Asia to receive the certification proof. In July 2006, we passed the ZCP test using both the Jennic platform and the UBEC platform. Our institute and Freescale are both considered in obtaining the largest number of ZigBee certified platform in the world. Those remarkable records show that the proposed components are reliable for smart home applications.

The event trigger module contains a set of rules. Whenever it received an event, it sends the event to all the rules. The rules perform the corresponding procedure after they accept this event. Section 4.2 briefly presents the rules for controlling the lighting system and the air condition.

4.2 The Zigbee-Based Positioning System for Controlling the Air Condition and Lighting System

In current stage, the system prototype employs the RS816WP monitoring and control platform to monitor and control the air condition and lighting system. Remotely turn on/off the light through the help of this platform is trivial. To control the air condition, the system prototype applies this platform to control the thermometers of the air condition which detect the temperature of the return and outside air.

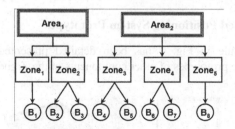

Fig. 7. The area hierarchy for the event trigger rules

The event trigger module partitioned all the beacons into several zones according to the natural of the interesting area, and the zones are furthered partitioned into several areas as Fig. 7. Rule 3 blow shows the rule for controlling the lighting system and Rule 4 below shows the rule for controlling the air condition.

Rule 3. Turn on all the lights in $Zone_i$ if and only if there is a badge in this zone.
Rule 4. Set the temperature of the return air as the temperature of the outside air if there is no badge in the area where the air condition is.

This system prototype is now verifying in our demo site and in the smart house of the Nation Taiwan University. Fig. 8 shows the layout of the second demo site. In the smart house of the National Taiwan University, the beacons in each room form a zone

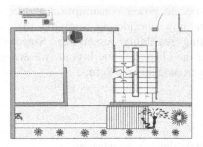

Fig. 8. The Smart House in Nation Taiwan University

and the beacons in the yard is a zone. Each floor is an area and the yard is also an area. There is no air condition for the yard.

5   Discussions

In this study, there are many theoretical strategies which are difficult in practices. Performance and accuracy are the main theoretical issues for this topic, but the cost and system reliability are the main practical issues. Although the proposed positioning method is not accurate enough, it is stable and reliable.

In Section 3.2, the signal adjustment procedure samples the signal strengths in the boundary of the adjacent beacons and then applies them to adjust the signal strength to overcome the ambiguous boundary problem. Although we realize that boundaries are irregular and sampling the signal strength in only one or two positions is not accurate enough, we state this in the SOP of constructing this system because the construction cost is limited.

In Section 3.3, the signal smooth procedure seems rough with no theoretical foundation. Some previous studies such as [6] employed some statistical methods to define the abnormal signals. Those methods seem reasonable, but they require larger values of m and u in the signal smooth procedure. This approach not only increase the system response time but also increase the system and maintenance cost.

6   Conclusions and Future Works

This paper presented an intelligent system prototype for smart home applications. The system prototype employs the position of the home members to trigger appropriate services for the home members. The design and implementation of the Zigbee positioning system were presented detailed presented. The prototypes of the badge and the Zigbee hardware platform for the beacons, routers and coordinators were implemented and are passed the ZigBee Compliant Platform (ZCP) certification test. Two smart home system prototypes were built and are verifying their performance and reliability.

Testing the performance in larger demo site with Zigbee embedded home appliances is desired. We are now contacting some home appliances manufacturers. Since Z-Wave is another wireless sensor network proposal which focus on the home applications, and the expected power consumption and cost are both less than the Zigbee standard, we are now considering applying the Z-Wave module and are process the corresponding feasibility researches. Since the ambiguity boundary problem may arise from the change of the layout, we are now designing automatic maintaining system to overcome this problem.

References

1. http://en.wikipedia.org/wiki/Building_automation
2. Spirito, M.A.: On the Accuracy of Cellular Mobile Station Location Estimation. IEEE Transactions on Vehicular Technology 50(3), 674–685 (2001)
3. Rappaport, T.S., Reed, J.H., Woerner, D.: Position location using wireless communications on highways of the future. IEEE Communication Magazine 34, 33–41 (1996)
4. Hellebrandt, M., Mathar, R., Scheibenbogen, M.: Estimating Position and Velocity of Mobiles in a Cellular Radio Networks. IEEE Transactions on Vehicular Technology 46(1), 65–71 (1997)
5. Mondin, M., Dovis, F., Mulassano, P.: On the use of HALE platforms as GSM base stations. IEEE Personal Communication Magazine 8(2), 37–44 (2001)
6. Jin, M.H., Wu, E.H.K., Wang, Y.T., Hsu, C.H.: An 802.11-Based Positioning System for Indoor Applications. In: Proceeding of the 4th IASTED International Multi-Conference on Wireless and Optical Communications, pp. 235–240 (2004)
7. http://www.zigbee.org/
8. Culler, D., Estrin, D., Srivastava, M.: Overview of Sensor Networks. Computer (2004)
9. IEEE 802.15.4: IEEE 802.15 WPANTM Task Group 4 (TG4), http://www.ieee802.org

Solving Unbounded Knapsack Problem Using an Adaptive Genetic Algorithm with Elitism Strategy

Rung-Ching Chen and Cheng-Huei Jian

Department of Information Management, Chaoyang University of Technology
168, Jifong E. Rd., Wufong Township, Taichung County 41349.
Taiwan, Republic of China
crching@mail.cyut.edu.tw

Abstract. The Knapsack problem is an NP-Complete problem. Unbounded Knapsack problems are more complex and harder to solve than the general Knapsack problem. In this paper, we apply the genetic algorithm to solve the unbounded Knapsack problem. We use an elitism strategy to overcome the defect of the slow convergence rate of the general genetic algorithm. The elitism strategy retains good chromosomes and ensures that they are not eliminated through the mechanism of crossover and mutation, while ensuring that the features of the offspring chromosomes are at least as good as their parents. The system automatically adapts the number of the initial population of chromosomes and the number of runs of the genetic algorithm. In addition, we use the strategy of greedy method to auto adaptive the sequence of chromosomes to enhance the effect of executing. Experimental results showed that our method could fast find the best solution of the problem.

1 Introduction

The general Knapsack problem is a well-known problem in the field of optimal operations research. It concerns the choice of items to be placed in a mountaineer's Knapsack: though each item benefits the climber, capacity is limited. The Knapsack problem consists of finding the best trade-off of benefit against capacity. The unbounded Knapsack problem is formally defined as follows: There are different types of items that have different values and weights. The number of each item is unbounded. There are no restrictions on choice. The problem lies in determining what combination of items yields the greatest benefit for the mountaineer under the capacity constraint? The equation is shown in (1.1) the condition of x_i is different from the Knapsack problem. The value of x_i is a positive integer including zero.

$$Maximize \sum_{i=1}^{n} x_i p_i \tag{1.1}$$

$$S.t. \sum_{i=1}^{n} x_i w_i \leq C$$

P. Thulasiraman et al. (Eds.): ISPA 2007 Workshops, LNCS 4743, pp. 193–202, 2007.
© Springer-Verlag Berlin Heidelberg 2007

$$0 \le x_i, x_i \in \text{integer}, i=1.....n$$

The unbounded Knapsack problem is defined as follows. We have n kinds of items, x_1 through x_n. Each item x has a profit value p and a weight w. The maximum weight that we can carry in the bag is C, and each item has many copies. Formulated this way, the unbounded Knapsack problem is an NP-hard combinatorial optimization problem.

The unbounded Knapsack problem is a kind of NP-hard problem in which the optimal solution cannot be found in short time when the number of selection items is large. Many papers have suggested different kinds of heuristic evaluation solutions, including genetic algorithms [4,6] and simulated annealing. More computing time is required to find solutions for heuristic evaluations, but the most feasible solution can usually be located. The method of randomly researching the optimal solution has been widely applied to different kinds of problems as well. In this research we describe the character of the unbounded Knapsack problem and search for an optimal solution by an adaptive genetic algorithms (GAs.).

Pisinger [2] gave an overview of all recent exact solution approaches for the Knapsack problem. But Pisinger's book does not offer any GAs to solve the Knapsack problem. GAs, originally proposed by Holland, has been applied to many different areas. Li [4] used GAs to solve unbounded knapsack, utilized problem-specific knowledge and incorporated a preprocessing procedure, but it was affected by knowledge.

One stumbling block to wider application of GAs is that general GAs cannot obtain get good results for many problems with large search spaces. To improve GAs, Haupt [7] showed that a small population size and relatively large mutation rate is superior to the large population sizes and low mutation rates. Zhiming [10] proposed an improved adaptive GAs. They used the selection probability based on the ranking of fitness values and used the probabilities of crossover and mutation adaptively varied to improve the search capacity. Zhou [5] developed a self-adaptive genetic algorithm (SAGA) that makes certain key parameters changeable with variable policy over the evolution. Yun [8,9] used a hybrid GAs with an adaptive local scheme to enhance efficiency.

In this paper we will propose a novel method for finding the optimal solution for the unbounded Knapsack problem based on an adaptive GAs with an elite selection strategy. The adaptive method can dynamically adjust the scale of population sizes and the number of runs, so for small-scale problems it is able to rapidly locate optimal solutions. It can also find solutions for large scale problems. The elitism selection strategy results in rapid convergence, saving time. The results indicate that our method is not only better than the greedy method or the general GAs, but it is capable of finding the optimal solution in our search space.

The remainder of the paper is organized as follows. We give a system overview in section 2. Section 3 introduces the adaptive genetic setting. In Section 4, we propose a genetic algorithm using the elitism strategy. Experimental results are given in section 5. Conclusions are presented in Section 6.

2   The System Overview

An example makes the following assumptions: The constraint of the knapsack's weight is C kg. The number of the items is i. In addition, the weight of each item is equal to $W_1, W_2,\ldots, W_i$. Each item has a different profits given by $P_1, P_2,\ldots, P_i$. The total capacity of the knapsack restriction be C. We use a genetic algorithm to find the optimal solution given a set profits and weight for each item. Figure 1 shows the workflow of the novel method. First, each initial possible combination has to be encoded into a chromosome. Next, the system automatically adapts the composition of chromosome by greedy method. Then, the system generates N number of chromosomes. Next, it checks each chromosome's weight and then keeps the

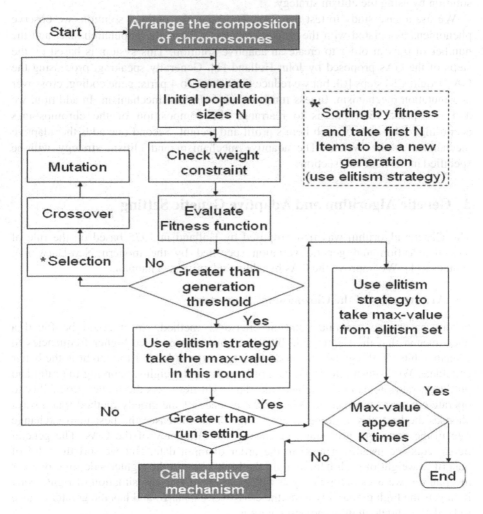

Fig. 1. The workflow of the genetic algorithm with Elitism Strategy

chromosomes under the weight constraint. In addition, it evaluates the fitness value of each chromosome. It then checks the number of generations against a threshold. If the number of generations is less than the threshold, the system will process the selection operation using the elitism strategy, performing conventional genetic operations: crossover and mutation. After the genetic algorithm is finished, the system takes up the chromosome with the maximum fitness value into the elite set. We take the chromosome with maximum fitness value from elite set to be the optimal solution after many runs of the GAs have been executed. Furthermore, we set an adaptive mechanism that guarantees an optimal value must appear K times at least. If the times of optimal value appearances are less than K times, we increase the number of runs until reaching the thresholds. Thus, the system gradually approaches the optimal solution by using the elitism strategy.

We use a case study to test the GAs. To obtain the optimal solution, we observe phenomena associated with the elitism strategy, such as the population size, and the number of runs in order to create an adaptive solution. This system is based on the steps of the GAs proposed by John Holland [1]. Generally speaking, processing the GAs requires 10 steps [6], but we reduce these steps to 4 parts: gene coding, crossover and mutation mechanism, fitness function, and selection mechanism. In addition, we add two parts. First one is to rearrange the composition of the chromosomes according to the ratio of each item's profit and weight. Second one adds the adaptive mechanism to the system. The adaptive mechanism and elitism strategy will be specified in the next two sections.

3   Genetic Algorithm and Adaptive Genetic Setting

The Genetic algorithm was first proposed by Holland in 1975 based on the rule of natural selection and genetic variation specified by the modern Neo-Darwinian synthesis [1]. We improve the GAs by adding adaptive mechanism.

3.1 Arrangement of the Chromosome Sequences

In this paper, we use one point of crossover method. So it could be found a phenomenon that the righter side bits of a chromosome have higher frequencies to exchange bits. In the greedy method, the large ratio of benefit to weight is the better candidate. We evaluate the input data of benefits and weights, counting the ratio and put larger ratio items in the righter side. The right item gets the higher probability to operate crossover mechanism. We use the essence of the greedy method that always chooses the best chromosome in each stage. That increases the best item exchange rate in the crossover procedure, enhancing the efficiency of the GAs. The general items sequence usually arrange in the order of input data. But we sort the ratio of benefit to weight of each item and put the high value in the righter side. In crossover mechanism, we uses one point type which we could find the situation of righter side item gets the high probability to do the crossover exchange and has the greater chance to be the candidate item of the best solution.

3.2 Adaptive Genetic Setting

In this paper, we consider the mechanisms of adaptive GAs are two parameters: runs, and population size but not mutation rate. Due to a smaller mutation rate results in shorter running times, but reduces the search space. When the mutation rate is higher, the convergence speed will be slow, meaning that the generations have to be settled higher in order to find better results. In our test, the best mutation is between 30% and 50%. We observed the results but did not find the best automatically adaptive trend for the mutation rate.

The number of runs was selected to ensure that the final value is the best. The system attempts it to make the best solution appear at least K times. If it does not reach the threshold, the number of runs is increased automatically. The system also attempts to avoid running too many runs, while still ensuring that the value obtained is optimum.

The other parameter is population size[3]. The system automatically increases group runs to R, and then it adds the parameter of population size, adjusting it in order to accelerate the procedure. It increases the population size twofold when the runs increase to R groups. If the runs do not reach R groups in the initial run, then the population size remains the same as the initial state. For example, if the population size is 20 and run is set to 5, R is set to 6, and K is set to 5 , that triggers at least 5 runs until the best solution appears 5 times. If the runs are greater than 30, the population size would be 60. The reruns would continue until the threshold is reached. We use this adaptive method to find the best solution.

4 Genetic Algorithm Using Elitism Strategy

The purpose of this paper is to find the solution to the unbounded Knapsack problem that yields the maximum benefit. In this section we offer a step by step description of the algorithm. First, the algorithm encodes the unbounded Knapsack problem into a suitable representation chromosome. Next, it measures the domain quantity of problem to set the size of the initial population and number of runs. The system then solves the problem based on GAs using the elitism strategy.

(1)Gene coding with reducing bits

The system will represent the unbounded Knapsack problem genetically. We begin with the weight of each item, consider the capacity constraint, and restrict the quantity of each item under the basic limitation of maximum weight that is less than or equal to C kg.

(a) Individual definition: Assume the weight of first item is W_1 kg and the combination is l_1 (the low bound integer of (C/W_1)). The number of options ranges from 0 to l_1, giving l_1+1 objects. The remaining options numbers for the other items are (l_2+1), (l_3+1), …,(l_k+1) . The mathematical model is depicted in equation (4.1).

$$S_i = \{x \mid x \in Integer; 0 \leq x \leq l_i+1\} \qquad (4.1)$$

$$S = \prod_{i=1}^{k} (l_i + 1)$$

S_i is the set of the number of item i selection options. x is the number of selections.

Assume the maximum capacity is 100kg and the selection is as given Table 1. There are a total of 94,594,500 options.

Table 1. Unbounded Knapsack problem with ten items

Item#	1	2	3	4	5	6	7	8	9	10
weight	22	50	20	10	15	16	17	21	8	25
cost	1078	2350	920	440	645	656	816	903	400	1125

Table 2. The representation of each item in binary form

item	possible combinations in binary form											
1	000	001	010	011	100							
2	00	01	10									
3	000	001	010	011	100							
4	0000	0001	0010	0011	0100	0101	0110	0111	1000	1001	1010	
5	000	001	010	011	100	101	110					
6	000	001	010	011	100	101	110					
7	000	001	010	011	100	101						
8	000	001	010	011	100							
9	0000	0001	0010	0011	0100	0101	0110	0111	1000	1001	1010	1011
10	000	001	010	011	100							

(b) Transfer the definition to binary codes: The system transfers the combination of candidates to binary code.

(c) Reduce the bits of binary code: With the exceptions of items 4 and 9, the item representations do not require 4 bits. Item 2 has 0, 1, or 2, a total of three options, so only 2 bits are required to represent it. Three bits are necessary for items 1, 3, 5, 6, 7, 8, 10, based on the number of possible combinations of each item. Each item is represented by the fewest possible bits, to promote the performance of the algorithm (Table 2).

(d) Chromosome representation: We combine each item for representation as a chromosome. For example: the code of a chromosome is 010,00,000,0000, 000,000,010,000,0011,000. The string means the first item has 2 pieces, the seventh item has 2 pieces and ninth item has 3 pieces.

(e) Arrangement the chromosome sequences: In this paper, we use one point of crossover method. So it can be found a phenomenon that the righter side bits have higher frequency to exchange bits. In greedy method, the large ratio of benefit to weight is the better candidate. We evaluate the input data of benefits and weights, counting the ratio and put the larger ratio items in the righter side. The right item gets the higher chance to do crossover. This involves using the essence of the greedy method, which always chooses the best chromosome in each stage. That increases the best item exchange rate in the crossover procedure, enhancing the efficiency of the GAs.

(2) Crossover and mutation mechanism

Generally speaking, there are three crossover methods: one-point crossover, two-point crossover and uniform crossover. One-point crossover: One crossover point between the two strings is taken, and all bits from that point to the end of the two strings are changed.

The one-point crossover method is used in this research. In our system, it generates a random number between 0 and J and is mated by a crossover rate. The value of J is the length of the chromosome. The random number adds 1 to count out the exchange location, and we change bits from the right side to the exchange location between the two chromosomes.

The mutation method follows the options of each item. For example, the sixth item has the combination 0, 1, 2, 3, 4, 5 and 6. It has 3 bits and should have the combination 111. It does not have the probability of 111 in this example, and the number 111 cannot be the option of the mutation choices.

(3)The definition of the fitness function:

The definition of fitness function for each individual chromosome is listed in equation (4.2). The constraint definition is shown in equation (4.3). There are n kinds of item i. Each item i has the benefit P_i and the weight W_i.

$$Maximize \sum_{i=1}^{n} x_i p_i \tag{4.2}$$

$$f(s) = \sum_{i=1}^{n} w_i x_i \leq c = 100 \tag{4.3}$$

$$0 \leq x_i, x_i \in \text{integer, i=1...n}$$

(4) The Elitism Selection Strategy:

The selection mechanism of this system is the "elite method" (or "tournament selection method"). If the new offspring cannot fit the capacity constraint, it is eliminated. New offspring can become the new population if their weight is less than the constraint. The goal is to obtain the maximum benefit. Based on the complexity of the search space, the system will choose a different number of initial chromosome population scale N. A small N maps to fewer options of a given problem, while a larger N maps to a larger number of options of a given problem. The system will then sort the chromosomes by benefit and select the top 70% of chromosomes to perform the process of selection, crossover and mutation to produce new populations. Fitness and objective functions are then evaluated again. The system keeps recycling until the first generation threshold is met. Then the system picks the best chromosome and puts it in the elitism pool. When all the runs have been executed, the optimal chromosome from the elitism pool is chosen as the solution.

5 Experimental Results and Analysis

The system was implemented using VB language on PC with Intel Pentium(R) processor 1.6GHZ. The system is capable of altering the benefit, weight, and maximum capacity, depending on the problem. The parameters of the GAs, including the population number, generations, crossover rate, and mutation rate, may also be controlled.

In general, the GAs modifies the crossover rate and mutation rate to search for optimal solutions. However, in this research we focus on the initial population size and runs, different from previous research [3,4]. In the first part of experiment, we focus on static parameter settings and observe the result. As discussed in the previous section, the population size and runs is updated depending on the number of options of the problem. The more options the problem has, the greater the population sizes and runs. We spread the net widely in the search space at each random initial population, and use the local convergence of the GAs to find the maximum value through the elitism strategy. There is a very high probability of finding the real solution under such conditions.

Assume the maximum capacity is 55 kg, 82 kg and 100 kg. The options are 435456, 11404800, 94594500, and the optimal results can be found. We previously calculated the options of the constraint of maximum capacity; set mutation rate to 3% and 90%; and population sizes to 20, 50 and 100. Thirty runs were executed. The larger the maximum capacity, the more options we obtain and the lower the possibility of obtaining the optimal solution. If the optimal solution with highest possibility is desired, we should increase the population size and the number of runs. The method enumerated above is capable of obtaining the optimal solution within acceptable time limits with fewer options, though the GAs are superior if the number of options is great. A feature of the genetic algorithm is that it converges to local optimum. When the number of options is large, we increase the size of the population and the number of runs.

The mutation rate represents a change in the chromosome. Its role is to provide a guarantee that the genetic algorithm is not trap on a local optimal. Mutations provide more variability than the parent genes, resulting in a greater search space. That is to say; search space and mutation are in direct proportion. Traditional GAs suffers from the problem of loss of the pioneer's best chromosomes under high mutation rates. This system uses the elitism strategy to overcome this problem and retain the useful genes in subsequent generations. With a large number of options, high mutation rates would become trapped in a random search and converge only with difficultly, or perhaps not at all. The process of search optimization takes place in a situation of oscillation. Though elitist selection and high mutation rates are used, fewer optimal values than low mutation rates are obtained.

We use elitism selection to enlarge the field of the search space when mutation rates increase. By contrast, if we reduce the mutation rate too much, the search spaces will be decrease. To optimize searches, a balance between convergences and enlarged search space should be found. The number of options depends on the size of the capacity constraint. The more weight the knapsack can take, the more options there are. The search space has a strong cubic of weight. When the search space becomes too large, it becomes too great for the enumeration method to calculate. In addition, our experiments also show that the method is better than the greedy method solution (Figure 2).

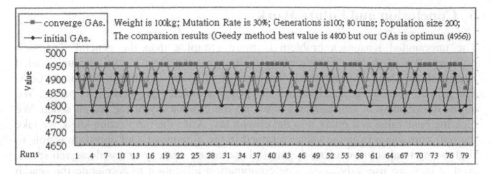

Fig. 2. The comparison of Greedy method and our genetic algorithm

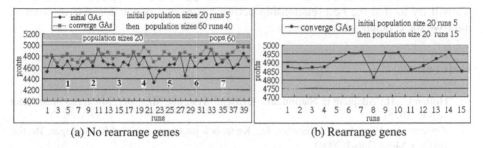

(a) No rearrange genes   (b) Rearrange genes

Fig. 3. The 100kg automatically adaptive mechanism

What population sizes should be set, and how many runs would be, are important issues that we looked at in light of the portfolio investments, a variant of the Knapsack problem. After observing those static parameters in experiments, we updated the program to let the system automatic self-adapt the parameters of runs and population size. The trend diagram is shown in Figure 3, where the capacity constraint is 100kg, initial population size is 20, and the number of initial runs is set to 5. The self-adaptive mechanism finds the optimal value five times in 40 runs, and the final population size adjusts to 60 automatically. After 30 runs the population size is 20 and only one optimal value appears. Between 31-40 runs, the population size increases to 60 and four optimal values are obtained. The real optimal value can be found by the method.

Using this approach, when the search space has less than 10^9 options, to find the real optimal solution is ensured in our experiments. We also tested the large search space with 10^{16} options. Our system can find the answer better than greedy method does within 100 seconds. We use a dynamic gene combination allocation to accelerate the search efficiency. In other words, we use the strategy of rearrange chromosome and find the great efficient in search process. It is different from Figure 3, because it reduces the runs of the adaptive processing. In Figure 3, it takes 40 runs and population size increases to 60. However, using rearrangement the sequence of chromosomes, it just takes 15 runs and population size keeps in 20. It just does 1/3 efforts.

6 Conclusion and Future Work

The unbounded Knapsack problem is more complex than the general Knapsack problem. We used the elitism strategy to improve the GAs for solving unbounded Knapsack problem, overcoming the problem of slow convergence in traditional GAs. The elitism strategy guarantees each offspring is at least as good as its parent. We adjust the population size and runs based on the complexity of the search space. We pick the best value and retain it in the elitism set. After the run is completed, we take the optimum value from the values retained in the elitism set. Our approach is able to find the optimal solution using the multiple selection strategy in a wide search space. And at last, we use a dynamic gene combination allocation to accelerate the search efficiency. Experiments have shown that this method is capable of finding the optimal solution of a problem under our test of searching spaces are 10^{16} options. In the future we will try to find the best relationship between runs and population size in order to improve the efficiency of our system.

References

1. Holland, J.H.: Adaptive in Natural and Artificial Systems. MI: Univ. Michigan Press, Ann Arbor (1975)
2. Kellerer, H., Pferschy, U., Pisinger, D.: Knapsack problems, pp. 3–540. Springer, Berlin, ISBN 3-540-40286-1(2004)
3. Costa, J., Tavares, R., Rosa, A.C.: An experimental study on dynamic random variation of population size. In: Proc. of the1999 IEEE Internet. Conf. on Systems, Man, and Cybernetics, pp. 607–612 (1999)
4. Li, K.-L., Guang-Mingdai, Li1, Q.-H.: A genetic algorithm for the unbounded Knapsack problem. Computer School, Huazhong University of Science and Technology, Wuhan, 430074, China, Departtnent of Computer, China University of Geo Science (2003)
5. Zhou, L., Shi-Xin, S.: A Self-Adaptive Genetic Algorithm for Tasks Scheduling in Multiprocessor System. In: Communications, Circuits and Systems Proceedings, International Conference (2006)
6. Negnevitsky, M.: Artificial Intelligence: A Guide to Intelligent Systems, 2nd edn. Addison-Wesley, Reading (2004)
7. Haupt, R.L.: Optimum Population Size and Mutation Rate for a Simple Real Genetic Algorithm that Optimizes Array Factors. In: Antennas and Propagation Society International Symposium, IEEE, Los Alamitos (2000)
8. Yun, Y.S., Mukuda, M., Gen, M.: Reliability Optimization Problems Using Adaptive Hybrid Genetic Algorithms. Advanced Computational Intelligence and Intelligent Informatics 8(4), 437–441 (2004)
9. Yun, Y.S.: Hybrid genetic algorithm with adaptive local search scheme. Computers & Industrial Engineering 51, 128–141 (2006)
10. Liu, Z.: New adaptive genetic algorithm based on ranking. In: Proceedings of the Second International Conference on Machine Learning and Cybernetics, X.'an (2-5 November, 2003)

Automatic Lexico-Semantic Frames Acquisition from Syntactic Parsed Tree by Using Clustering and Combining Techniques

Chaloemphon Sirikayon and Asanee Kawtrakul

Department of Computer Engineering, Kasetsart University, Bangkok, Thailand
g4685029@ku.ac.th, asanee.kawtrakul@nectec.or.th

Abstract. This article describes an unsupervised strategy to acquire lexico-semantic frames (LSFs) of verbs from sentential parsed corpora (in syntactic level). LSF is a crucial linguistic resource presents a set of semantic elements for exhibiting a meaning of lexeme. The problems of acquiring LSFs consist of verb senses ambiguity, diversity of linguistic usages, and lack of completed elements in a sentence. We propose an specific clustering and combining technique to acquire frame for each verb sense and specify constraints to each frame's slots. Our proposed clustering technique is based on the Minimum Description Length (MDL) principle and using information encoded in features of element instead of its frequency from the corpora.

1 Introduction

One of the most necessary resources to enhance the performance of the intelligent systems (e.g. Machine Translation (MT), Information Extraction (IE), Question Answering (QA), etc.) is linguistic knowledge, especially in semantic level. Among the numerous linguistic knowledge, semantic frame of lexicon, especially *verb*, is an essential one. For example, semantic frames can be used to map words that have the same meaning in different languages for MT [1]. IE can use semantic frames to create extraction patterns of relevant information [2]. And in QA [3], semantic frames can be used as a filter for slecting the answer of question.

This paper proposes the method to acquisite semantic frame of verb automatically, called Lexico-Semantic Frame (LSF). LSF will contain a set of semantic elements (SemEs). Each semantic element will be described with syntactic subcategorization, i.e. syntactic category (*cat*) and syntactic position (*syp*), and selectional constraint or semantic concept (*sem*), as shown in Fig. 1.

From Fig. 1(a), for example, word *"cut"* in sense cut#1[1] has the corresponding LSF which contains three slots of semantic element: *(1)*, *(2)*, and *(3)* to describe its meaning. The syntactic categories of *(1)*, *(2)*, and *(3)* are a noun or

---

[1] A LSF must correspond to only one sense of word. Remark: word#*n* stand for word in sense *n* from WordNet (http://wordnet.princeton.edu/).

P. Thulasiraman et al. (Eds.): ISPA 2007 Workshops, LNCS 4743, pp. 203–213, 2007.

(a)[(1) John] cut [(2) the rope] with [(3) his knife]. (b)[(1) The company] cut [(2) ticket prices] to [(3) 70%].

$$
\text{LSF(cut\#1)} = \begin{bmatrix}
(1): & \begin{bmatrix} cat & : & \text{NP} \\ syp & : & \text{A-L1} \\ sem & : & \text{person\#1} \end{bmatrix} \\
(2): & \begin{bmatrix} cat & : & \text{NP} \\ syp & : & \text{A-R1} \\ sem & : & \text{physical entity\#1} \end{bmatrix} \\
(3): & \begin{bmatrix} cat & : & \text{NP} \\ syp & : & \text{A-with} \\ sem & : & \text{instrumentality\#3} \end{bmatrix}
\end{bmatrix}
\qquad
\text{LFS(cut\#2)} = \begin{bmatrix}
(1): & \begin{bmatrix} cat & : & \text{NP} \\ syp & : & \text{A-L1} \\ sem & : & \text{organization\#1} \end{bmatrix} \\
(2): & \begin{bmatrix} cat & : & \text{NP} \\ syp & : & \text{A-R1} \\ sem & : & \text{possession\#2} \end{bmatrix} \\
(3): & \begin{bmatrix} cat & : & \text{NP} \\ syp & : & \text{A-to} \\ sem & : & \text{quantity\#1} \end{bmatrix}
\end{bmatrix}
$$

Fig. 1. Example sentences of "cut" and its corresponding LSFs: (a) cut#1 (in sense of "separate with or as if with an instrument") has *(1)*-Cutter, *(2)*-Cut_thing, and *(3)*-Instrument and (b) cut#2 (in sense of "cut down on; make a reduction in") has *(1)*-Reducer, *(2)*-Reduced_thing, and *(3)*-Quantity

noun phrase (NP), while the semantic concepts are person#1: a human being, physical entity#1: an entity that has physical existence, and instrumentality#3: an artifact (or system of artifacts) that is instrumental in accomplishing some end, respectively. Moreover, in active form of the sentence in the example, *(1)* is the closest element on left hand side of verb (A-L1[2].), *(2)* is the closest element on the right hand side (A-R1), and *(3)* can appear with preposition "with" in any position (A-with).

The attempt to manually create LSF like resources has been proposed in many languages, especially in English, where the most well-known resources are FrameNet [4] and PropBank [5]. Both resources were manually created by specialists (linguists, psychologists) with supported evidences (the annotated sentences). Hence, their projects are very costly in time and human effort and they may have a problem about disagreement of frame designers. Moreover, the lexicon growth is the nature of natural languages so it is necessary to continuously expand the LSFs to cover all lexicons. But expansion of the LSFs by human is not a trivial task because it have to check the consistency with the previously defined frames and their annotated sentences. Thus, it is better to have the automatic method for acquiring the LSFs from the corpus of really used sentences.

The remainder of this article begins by giving the problems that should be solved in acquiring lexico-semantic frames from text corpora (section 2) and related works in this field (section 3). Then, in section 4, we depict a general overview of our methodology and describe in detail with examples.

2   Major Problems of LSFs Acquisition from Syntactic Parsed Tree

Automatically acquiring lexico-semantic frames from syntactic parsed tree is not a trivial task. These are three major problems: verb senses ambiguity, diversity of linguistic usage, and lack of completed elements in a sentence.

---

[2] A: active voice; L1: the closest element on left hand side of verb.

2.1 Verb Senses Ambiguity

Since a single word can have more than one meaning in different contexts (i.e. polysemy), it can have two or more corresponding LSFs, each describes a different sense. For instance of *"cut"* in sense of cut#2, it has the LSF with different set of elements to describe its meaning as shown in Fig. 1(b).

2.2 Diversity of Linguistic Usage

One verb sense could have variety of usage. For example, cut#1, in Fig. 2, has two forms: "The knife" is subject while it acts as Instrument and "John" is also subject but acts as Cutter.

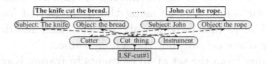

Fig. 2. This ambiguous of mapping between syntactic and semantic elements ("The knife": Subject⇔Instrument vs. "John": Subject⇔Cutter)

2.3 Lack of Completed Elements in a Sentence

The completed semantic elements might not be provided by single sentence. For example, the sentence "John cut the rope.", in Fig. 2, shows only two semantic elements: Cutter and Cut_thing, since the Instrument can be omitted in this sentence.

In this paper, we propose an **A**utomatic lexico-semantic **F**rame **A**cquisition from **S**yntactic parsed **T**ree (AFAST). It consists of two main processes: clustering all syntactic elements which belonging to the same semantic element and combining the associated semantic elements to be the LSFs, as shown in Fig. 3.

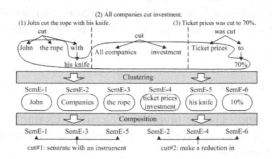

Fig. 3. Outline of AFAST with two main processes: Clustering and Combining

In clustering process, we propose the clustering technique to cluster syntactic elements into semantic elements (SemEs). Each SemE must have the generalized semantic concept (*sem*) with all possible syntactic position (*syp*) of its members.

Then, the heuristic rules, based on frame semantic theory [6], are used to compose semantic elements together to be the set of LSFs which one LSF correspond to one sense of verb. These rules restrict each LSF to be unique, one word's sense must has only one corresponding frame, and in each form of linguistic usage, one syntactic position must contain only one semantic element (SemE).

3   Related Work

There are several studies related to LSFs acquisition, either learning from a set of single element or learning from set of all elements in a frame. For considering on single element, Li and Abe [7] proposed a methodology to generalize values of a case frame slot for a verb. From an existing thesaurus, it obtains the optimal Tree Cut Model for a case slot by using the frequency of instances, based on MDL principle. The results provide only the selection restriction in semantic feature for one by one case slot, not the whole frame.

In case of learning from the set of all elements in frame, Kawahara and Kurohashi [8] presented a methodology to construct a case frame dictionary automatically from parsed results of a raw corpus. Based on statistical technique, they clustered predicate-argument examples which have the same usages and merged them to be case frames by considering the closest case components. Since there are millions of combinations between verb and its closest case component, it needs an enormous corpus (4,600,000 sentences) to make a wide-coverage case frame dictionary.

Another work, Gamallo et al. [9], described an unsupervised system to acquire syntactico-semantic requirements of nouns, verbs, and adjectives from partially parsed corpora. The system learned the syntactic positions in which the word appears and the semantic requirements associated with each syntactic positions. The result are lexicon with both syntactic subcategorization and selectional restrictions. Any way, the system could not solve the problem of word sense ambiguity and diversity of linguistic usage.

In this work, we proposed an unsupervised strategy to acquire LSFs of verbs from sentential parsed corpora without enormous corpus needed (see the next section).

4   AFAST System

AFAST system composes of one preprocessing called Example Construction and two main processes (Fig. 4), which are represented as rectangles and rounded rectangles are subprocesses.

4.1   Example Construction

From each syntactic parsed sentence, the system will collect main verb and its syntactic dependencies (*dep*) to create a *Dependency Set*. Each Dependency Set contains verb and its dependencies with three features: syntactic category

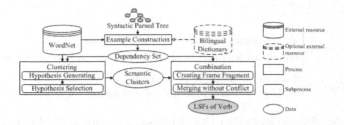

Fig. 4. System architecture of AFAST

(*dcat*), syntactic position (*dsyp*), and semantic concept (*dsem*). The collection of Dependency Sets that have identical verb and distinct set of dependencies is the input of clustering process.

Syntactic Category Feature (*dcat*). There are three types of verb dependencies: NP (noun or noun phrase), PP (preposition phrase), and CL (clause), that can have roles in the LSF, so the system discards the dependencies in other types. The syntactic category feature of those selected dependencies is assigned as the following:

$$dcat(dep) = \begin{cases} \text{NP} & \text{if } dep \text{ is NP or PP,} \\ \text{CL} & \text{if } dep \text{ is CL .} \end{cases}$$

Syntactic Position Feature (*dsyp*). This feature represents the voice of verb and relative position or case marker of dependency; such as A-L1, A-R1, and A-with in Fig. 1, as the following.

$dsyp(dep) = \text{Voice-Marker}$

$$\text{Voice} = \begin{cases} \text{A} & \text{if verb is active voice,} \\ \text{P} & \text{if verb is passive voice .} \end{cases}$$

$$\text{Marker} = \begin{cases} \text{preposition} & \text{if } dep \text{ is PP}(preposition\ e.g.\ with, from, to, etc.), \\ \text{case marker} & \text{if } dep \text{ has case marker (e.g. ga, wa, no, etc. in Japanese),} \\ \text{L}n & \text{if } dep \text{ has no case marker and appear before verb;} \\ & n = \text{distance between verb and } dep, \\ \text{R}n & \text{if } dep \text{ has no case marker and appear after verb .} \end{cases}$$

Semantic Concept Feature (*dsem*). The value of this feature is a set of semantic concepts from the hierarchy of WordNet[3] (*semc*), as the following.

$$dsem(dep) = \begin{cases} semc(dep) & \text{if } dep \text{ is NP,} \\ semc(np) & \text{if } dep \text{ is PP; } np = \text{NP following preposition,} \\ drf(v) & \text{if } dep \text{ is CL; } v = \text{main verb of } dep . \end{cases}$$

---

[3] http://wordnet.princeton.edu/

where

$$semc(x) = \begin{cases} \text{all semantic concepts of } x & \text{if } x \text{ is noun,} \\ \text{all semantic concepts of } n & \text{if } x \text{ is NP; } n = \text{head noun of } x \text{ .} \end{cases}$$

$$drf(v) = \dfrac{\text{all semantic concepts of nouns in}}{\text{WordNet's "Derivationally related forms" of } v \text{ .}}$$

In the case of languages other than English, they can apply English WordNet by using bilingual dictionary for translating words to English.

Fig. 5 shows the example construction of the verb "cut" which has 6 distinct Dependency Sets. These distinct Dependency Sets are the input of clustering process.

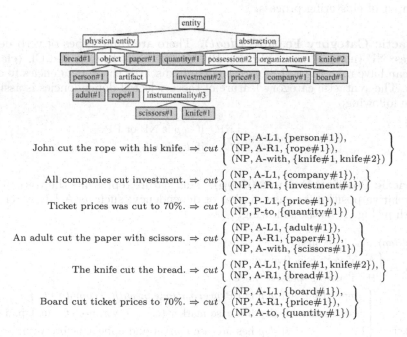

Fig. 5. Fragment of WordNet and Dependency Sets of "cut" derived from example sentences

4.2 Semantic Element Clustering

In this process, the input comes from the example construction process. The output is a set of SemE. SemE is the cluster of verb dependencies which will be described with syntactic category (cat), syntactic position (syp), and semantic concept (sem) where:

Syntactic Category feature (cat): All dependencies in cluster must have the same syntactic category which will be used as the value of this feature.

Syntactic Position feature (*syp*): All dependencies in cluster can have any syntactic position and the union of them is the value of this feature.

Semantic Concept feature (*sem*): All dependencies in cluster must have semantic concept in same family and the closest ancestor of them is the value of this feature.

Our proposed clustering technique is based on MDL principle [10] which states that the best probability model for given data is the one which requires the minimum code length in bits for the encoding of the model itself (i.e. model description length) and the given data observed through it (i.e. data description length). The minimum code length is computed by:

$$L_{\text{MDL}} = \min_{\mathcal{M} \in M} \left(L(\mathcal{M}) + L(D \mid \mathcal{M}) \right) \tag{1}$$

where $L(\mathcal{M})$ represents model description length, and $L(D \mid \mathcal{M})$ represents data description length.

In our system, we defined a proper model to describe data that is the same semantic element. This model has constraints for generating hypothesis which was described later. From the set of generated hypotheses, the system tried to find the one that gives the best compressed observed data (L_{MDL}). This is the problem of hypothesis selection based on (1).

$$\widehat{\mathcal{H}} = \underset{\mathcal{H} \in H \mid M}{\text{argmin}} \left(L(\mathcal{H}) + L(D \mid \mathcal{H}) \right) \tag{2}$$

where $\widehat{\mathcal{H}}$ is the selected hypothesis which describes the best clustering of data set according to the MDL principle and H is the set of generated hypotheses described in next section.

Hypothesis Generating. Our system can generate the set of hypothesis from the combination of cluster features under the model constraints. There are three constraints that are used to generate the hypotheses.

1. The hypothesis is a set of disjoint clusters. Each cluster (i.e. SemE) is the combination of all cluster features; that it must have a syntactic category and a semantic concept with a set of dependent syntactic positions.
2. The hypothesis must cover all dependencies in Dependency Sets of identical verb.
3. All members in a single cluster must come from the different Dependency Sets.

From this model, the system can generate the set of hypotheses, and then assigns each dependency to the proper cluster in order to compute the description length. From all clusters (C) in the selected hypothesis ($\mathcal{H}$), we compute the model description length according to (2) by the following mean:

$$L(\mathcal{H}) = \sum_{C \in \mathcal{H}} L(C) \tag{3}$$

$$L(C) = -\log \left(P(sem(C)) \cdot \sum_{s \in syp(C)} \frac{F(s \mid sem(C))}{F(sem(C))} \right) \tag{4}$$

where $F\big(sem(C)\big)$ and $F\big(s \mid sem(C)\big)$ represents the number of clusters that have semantic concept $sem(C)$ and the number of clusters that have semantic concept $sem(C)$ with syntactic position s, respectively. $P\big(sem(C)\big)$ is the distribution probability of concept in hierarchical structure (i.e. WordNet) and is defined as the following mean:

$$P(n) = \frac{P\big(parent(n)\big)}{F\big(relative(n)\big)}; \ P(root) = 1 \tag{5}$$

where $F\big(relative(n)\big)$ is the number of sibling of n plus one (for n).

Hypothesis Selection. Given the set of generated hypotheses, the system will select the most proper hypothesis that has the minimum description length (L_{MDL}), according to (2).

This process will assign every dependencies to each cluster in the hypothesis for selecting the hypothesis that has the minimum description length. The system computes the data description length, $L(D \mid \mathcal{H})$, by considering the difference between each dependency and the cluster in two features: semantic concept (i.e. *dsem* vs. *sem*) and syntactic position (i.e. *dsyp* vs. *syp*). Moreover, there is another probabily that has an effect on $L(D \mid \mathcal{H})$, the unity of cluster. It is the probalility of members in cluster that have alliance (i.e. others dependencies in Dependency Set) in the same group of clusters in hypothesis.

So, we can compute $L(D \mid \mathcal{H})$ by the following means.

$$L(D \mid \mathcal{H}) = \sum_{C \in \mathcal{H}} \left(-\log \prod_{d \in C} \left(\frac{P\big(dsem(d)\big)}{P\big(sem(C)\big)} \cdot \frac{F\big(dsyp(d) \mid C\big)}{size(C)} \right) \prod_{a \in alc(C)} \frac{F(a)}{size(C)} \right) \tag{6}$$

where $F\big(dsyp(d) \mid C\big)$ is the number of dependency in the cluster that has syntactic position $dsyp(d)$ and $size(C)$ represents the number of member in cluster. The aliance cluster $\big(Alc(C)\big)$ is a set of clusters in $\mathcal{H}$ excepted C, and $F(a)$ is the number of member in C that has other dependencies from the same dependency set in cluster a.

From section 4.1, the dependency can have many values of semantic concept and it also effect to the value of alliance cluster too. In order to select the most proper hypothesis, the system has to select the concept of dependency which yields the minimum data description length as the following mean:

$$\widehat{L}(D \mid \mathcal{H}) = \min_{dsem(d)} L(D \mid \mathcal{H}) \tag{7}$$

Table 1 shows some examples of generated hypotheses from hierarchical concepts and Dependency Sets in Fig. 5 with their description lengths. From all generated hypotheses, the system selects hypothesis C that has minimum value of L_{MDL}.

4.3   Combining

Each clusters in the selected hypothesis from clustering process represents a semantic element (SemE) that must be composed together to be the set of LSFs

Table 1. An excerpt of generated hypotheses and their description lengths which the best one is hypothesis C (* means the best)

Hypothesis	$L(\mathcal{H})$	$L(D \mid \mathcal{H})$	L_{MDL}
A. (NP, entity, {A-L1, P-L1}), (NP, entity, {A-R1, P-to}), (NP, entity, {A-with, A-to})	4.9658	69.5552	74.5210
B. (NP, physical entity, {A-L1, P-L1}), (NP, abstraction, {A-L1, P-L1}), (NP, entity, {A-R1}), (NP, entity, {A-with, A-to, P-to})	8.1293	66.7207	74.8500
*C. (NP, organization, {A-L1}), (NP, person#1, {A-L1}), (NP, physical entity, {A-R1}), (NP, possession, {A-R1, P-L1}), (NP, instrumentallity, {A-L1, A-with}), (NP, quantity#1, {A-to, P-to})	18.4150	26.8496	45.2646

correspond to senses of verb. This process is done in the following two steps: creating frame fragment and merging without conflict.

Creating Frame Fragment. In this subprocess, the system joins the associated semantic elements together, according to their based Dependency Sets by replacing each dependency with its covering cluster (i.e. SemE). These combinations are frame fragments (frag[n]) and may have some redundancy.

Merging without Conflict. In this subprocess, the system merges the associated frame fragments to be the completed LSFs which each LSF correspond to each sense of verb. By considering on LSF, the senses of verb are different if the LSFs have different number of elements and they are not subset of the others or the LSFs have the number of elements equally but at least one element differs from the others.

Therefore, the system removes frame fragments that are subset of the others. The rest frame fragments represent either different senses or same sense that one has semantic elements (SemEs) that was omitted in the other. Then the system merges all frame fragments which have no element conflict. It means that there is no more than one element that correspond to one syntactic position. The algorithm of merging frame fragments is shown in Fig. 6. The final result is the set of LSFs that each one corresponds to a sense of verb as shown in Fig. 7.

5 Experiment and Discussion

We used 44 sentences that have "cut" as main verb in two senses (34 sentences in sense of "make a reduction" and 10 sentences in sense of "separate"). They were parsed by Stanford Parser[4] and provide 112 syntactic elements. With our proposed clustering technique, the system grouped them into 10 clusters. After the system creates the fragment frames and combines them together, we got 2 LSFs. The first LSF describe "cut" in sense of "separate" with five semEs:

---

[4] http://nlp.stanford.edu/downloads/lex-parser.shtml

```
Input    Set of distinct frame fragments created from selected hypothesis and Dependency Sets (frag)
Output   Set of LSFs corresponding to each sense of verb
         1: For i = 1 to size of frag step 1
         2:    CanMerge = FALSE
         3:    For j = i + 1 to size of frag step 1
         4:       For each cluster x in frag[i]
         5:          If (x ∉ frag[j] AND syp(x) ⊄ ∪_{y∈frag[j]} syp(y)) Continue 3:
         6:       Next x
         7:       frag[j] = frag[i] ∪ frag[j]
         8:       CanMerge = TRUE
         9:    Next j
        10:    If (CanMerge = TRUE) remove frag[i]
        11: Next i
        12: Return frag
```

Fig. 6. Algorithm of merging with out conflict

$$
LSF(cut\#1) = \begin{cases} (1): \begin{bmatrix} cat & : NP \\ syp & : A\text{-}L1 \\ sem & : person\#1 \end{bmatrix} \\ (2): \begin{bmatrix} cat & : NP \\ syp & : A\text{-}R1 \\ sem & : physical\ entity\#1 \end{bmatrix} \\ (3): \begin{bmatrix} cat & : NP \\ syp & : A\text{-}L1, A\text{-}with \\ sem & : instrumentality\#1 \end{bmatrix} \end{cases}
\quad
LFS(cut\#2) = \begin{cases} (1): \begin{bmatrix} cat & : NP \\ syp & : A\text{-}L1 \\ sem & : organization\#1 \end{bmatrix} \\ (2): \begin{bmatrix} cat & : NP \\ syp & : A\text{-}R1, P\text{-}L1 \\ sem & : possession\#1 \end{bmatrix} \\ (3): \begin{bmatrix} cat & : NP \\ syp & : A\text{-}to, P\text{-}to \\ sem & : quantity\#1 \end{bmatrix} \end{cases}
$$

$[_{(1)}$ John] cut $[_{(2)}$ the rope] with $[_{(3)}$ his knife].
$[_{(1)}$ An adult] cut $[_{(2)}$ the paper] with $[_{(3)}$ scissors].
$[_{(3)}$ This knife] can cut $[_{(2)}$ the rope].

$[_{(1)}$ All companies] cut $[_{(2)}$ investment].
$[_{(2)}$ Ticket prices] was cut to $[_{(3)}$ 70%].
$[_{(1)}$ Board] cut $[_{(2)}$ ticket prices] to $[_{(3)}$ 70%].

Fig. 7. Final LSFs of "cut" with supported sentences

Cutter, Cut thing, Instrument, Purpose, and Time. The other LSF describe "cut" in sense of "make a reduction" with six semEs: Reducer, Reduced Thing, Source Quantity, Target Quantity, Purose, and Place. The result of clustering and final LSFs are comparable with FrameNet and PropBank which are manually created by linguists. However, our approach relies on hierarchical semantic concepts. If we want to acquire LSF in more specific domain (e.g. agriculture), we need more rich semantic cencepts.

6   Conclusion and Future Work

This article has presented a particular unsupervised strategy to automatically acquire LSFs of verb from syntactic parsed tree. Our proposed methodology consists of two main processes: clustering and combining. We also propose the novel cluster technique for this specific purpose based on MDL. It can partition the syntactic elements to be the clusters of semantic elements without using the frequency of elements. Then, with merging without conflict policy, we can compose the clusters of semantic elements to be the LSF according to verb sense that it describes.

In future work, we will do our experiment on various domains. Moreover, we plan to integrate automatic syntactic parser in our system in order to acquire LSFs from raw corpora. We also plan to extend the strategy to acquire LSF of any kind of word, especially noun.

References

1. Boas, H.C.: Bilingual FrameNet Dictionaries for Machine Translation. In: Proceedings of the Third International Conference on Language Resources and Evaluation, vol. 4, pp. 1364–1371 (2002)
2. Moschitti, A., Morarescu, P., Harabagiu, S.M.: Open Domain Information Extraction via Automatic Semantic Labeling. In: Proceedings of the 2003 Special Track on Recent Advances in Natural Language at the 16th International FLAIRS Conference (2003)
3. Narayanan, S., Harabagiu, S.: Question Answering Based on Semantic Structures. In: Proceedings of the 20th international conference on Computational Linguistics, Association for Computational Linguistics Morristown, NJ, USA (2004)
4. Johnson, C.R., Fillmore, C.J., Petruck, M.R.L., Baker, C.F., Ellsworth, M., Ruppenhofer, J., Wood, E.J.: FrameNet Theory and Practice. Technical report, International Computer Science Institute (2002)
5. Palmer, M., Gildea, D., Kingsbury, P.: The Proposition Bank: An Annotated Corpus of Semantic Roles. Computational Linguistics 31(1), 71–106 (2005)
6. Fillmore, C.J.: Frames and the semantics of understanding. Quaderni di Semantica 6(2), 222–254 (1985)
7. Li, H., Abe, N.: Generalizing case frames using a thesaurus and the MDL principle. Comput. Linguist. 24(2), 217–244 (1998)
8. Kawahara, D., Kurohashi, S.: Japanese case frame construction by coupling the verb and its closest case component. In: Proceedings of the first international conference on Human language technology research, San Diego, pp. 1–7. Association for Computational Linguistics (2001)
9. Gamallo, P., Agustini, A., Lopes, G.: Clustering Syntactic Positions with Similar Semantic Requirements. Computational Linguistics 31(1), 107–146 (2005)
10. Grünwald, P.D., Myung, I.J., Pitt, M.A.: Advances In Minimum Description Length: Theory and Applications. MIT Press, Cambridge (2005)

Intelligent Home Network Authentication: S/Key-Based Home Device Authentication

Deok-Gyu Lee[1], Ilsun You[2], Sang-Choon Kim[3], Yun-kyung Lee[1], Jong-wook Han[1], and Kyo-il Chung[1]

[1] Electronics and Telecommunications Research Institute,
161 Gajeong-dong, Yuseoung-gu, Daejeon, Korea
{deokgyulee,neohappy,hanjw,kyoil}@etri.re.kr
http://www.etri.re.kr
[2] Department of Infomation Science, Korean Bible University,
205 Sanggye-7 Dong, Nowon-ku, Seoul, 139-791, South Korea
isyou@bible.ac.kr
[3] Information & Communication Engineering, Kangwon National University,
1 Joongang-ro, Samcheok, Gangwon-do, South Korea
kimsc@kangwon.ac.kr

Abstract. The intelligent home network environment is thing which invisible computer that is not shown linked mutually through network so that user may use computer always is been pervasive. As home network service is popularized, the interest in home network security is going up. Many people interested in home network security usually consider user authentication and authorization. But the consideration about home device authentication almost doesn't exist. In this paper, we describes home device authentication which is the basic and essential element in the home network security. We proposed S/Key based authentication, scheme for secure remote access in smart home networks. And our device authentication concept can offer home network service users convenience and security.

1 Introduction

The intelligent home network computing aims at an environment in which invisible computers interconnected via the network exist. In this way, computers are smart enough to provide a user with context awareness, thus allowing the user to use the computers in the desired way. Intelligent home computing has the following features: Firstly, a variety of distributed computing devices exist for specific users. Secondly, computing devices that are uninterruptedly connected via the network exist. Thirdly, a user sees only the personalized interface because the environment is invisible to him/her. Lastly, the environment exists in a real world space and not in a virtual one. As the home devices have various functions and have improved computing power and networking ability, the importance of home device authentication is increasing for improving of home network users' security. In using home network service, user authentication and authorization technology are applied to home network services only for authorized persons to use the home network services. But It has some

P. Thulasiraman et al. (Eds.): ISPA 2007 Workshops, LNCS 4743, pp. 214–223, 2007.
© Springer-Verlag Berlin Heidelberg 2007

problems : the leakage of user authentication information by user's mistake, usage of guessable authentication information, and finding of new vulnerability about existing authentication method. So it is necessary that home network service user can be served the secure home network service by only using credible device. This means that home device authentication besides user authentication and authorization is essential to the secure home network service. Also, the unauthorized accessing possibility for our home network is very high by the device included in neighbor home network because of the home network characteristic; various wired/wireless network devices is used in the home network. This is an additional reason about the necessity of device authentication.

Finally, we think that the secure relationship among home network devices is very important factor because home network service evolves into more convenient one; user's role in receiving home network service is minimized and the service served by cooperation among home devices is maximized. Device authentication ensures that only specific authorized devices by specific authorized credential is compromised, the security between two parties is still protected as long as the authorized device is not used. Besides this, the authentication is a mandatory technology that enables emerging context-aware services and remote access services providing service automatically through device cooperation without user intervention, and DRM systems also need the device authentication [1, 2]. This paper describes device authentication. Sections 2 briefly discuss previous related researches and home device authentication framework. In section 3, we propose the S/Key based Lightweight authentication protocol. Finally, our paper concludes with section 4.

2   Related Work and Home Device Authentication

So far, several mechanisms have been proposed for this purpose. Some industries suggest hardware fingerprint based approach [3,4] that extract the secret information from the unique hardware fingerprint and trust the device by verifying the secret. Bluetooth [5] and Zigbee [6] provide device authentication mechanism based on shared symmetric key, and CableLab [7] also provides PKI based one. Personal CA [8, 9] provides localized PKI model. However, to the best of our knowledge none of them are applicable for multi-domain environment for several reasons [10].

2.1   S/Key Based One-Time Password

Since user mobile devices tend to be resource constrained, we consider the S/Key scheme and its variants, which uses lightweight cryptographic operations such as exclusive-OR and Hash function. This section briefly describes the S/Key based authentication schemes.

The S/KEY one-time password scheme is designed to protect a system against replay or eavesdropping attacks [2,3]. With S/Key, the user's secret pass-phrase never needs to cross the network at any time such as during the authentication or passphrase changes. Moreover, no secret information needs to be stored on any system, including the server being protected. Although the S/KEY scheme protects a system against passive attacks based on replaying captured reusable passwords, it is vulnerable to server spoofing, preplay, and off-line dictionary attacks [7,9]. Several researches have been conducted to solve these drawbacks of the S/KEY scheme [4-9]. Mitchell and Chen propose two possible solutions to resist against server spoofing and preplay attacks. One is to locally store the predictable challenge in a client so that a server has no need to send the challenge in every login. The other is to digitally sign the predictable challenge. Yen and Liao propose a scheme that uses a shared tamper resistant cryptographic token, which includes a SEED, to prevent offline dictionary attacks. Yeh, Shen and Hwang propose an one-time password authentication scheme which enhances the S/KEY scheme to resist against the above attacks. The scheme uses smart cards to securely preserve a pre-shared secret, SEED, and simplify the user login process. Also, it provides a session key to enable confidential communication over the network. However, since the scheme uses user's weak pass-phrase and utilizes SEED as a pre-shared secret, the exposure of the SEED causes the scheme to retain the flaws of the S/KEY scheme [11]. Consequently, the scheme cannot achieve the strength of the S/KEY scheme that no secret information needs to be stored on the server. In addition, it cannot defend against server compromises and is vulnerable to several attacks such as stolen-verifier attacks, denial of service attacks and Denning-Sacco attacks [11-13]. Lee and Chen propose an improvement on Yeh-Shen-Whang's scheme to prevent its vulnerability from stolen verifier attacks [8,9]. With such improved security, their scheme still provides the same efficiency as Yeh-Shen-Whang's scheme. However, it is vulnerable to denial of service (DoS) attacks and also allows a compromise of past session keys [5].

2.2 Requirements for Intelligent Home Network

With the advent of user-oriented home network computing, which is described as pervasive, or invisible computing, a user can concentrate on tasks without being aware that he is using computers. Despite the many benefits of the digital technology that home network computing utilizes, home network computing has unseen problems. Without addressing these problems, home network computing cannot be applied. Since a user uses many devices, user information can be copied in large volume and can be transmitted to unauthorized devices. This illegitimately collected user information can be used maliciously after changes on the network. These features and the environment of ubiquitous computing have allowed for a wide range of malicious attacks and uses, which are likely to become huge obstacles to the development of home network computing. Thus, to overcome these problems, the following requirements must be met when designing the home network computing system.

- Mobility: A user's home device that contains the authentication information must be mobile and be used for all services.
- Entity Authentication: Even when a user with home device moves away from single-domain, the user must be authenticated using the information of home device in other single-domain.
- Corresponding Entity Authentication: When home device is located in single-domain, the corresponding entity authentication verifies that home device and identity are identical entities. This method implements the authentication for

devices through the previous user's entity when several devices are connected to one domain. This method can provide a wide range of protection functions.

• Connection/Non-connection Confidentiality: Home device in single-domain must provide connection confidentiality for the user data. Single-domain receives home device's information to obtain the final authentication from the higher-level device. Non-connection confidentiality means that device B must provide confidentiality for the user data prior to the connection to a specific domain.

2.3 Home Device Authentication Framework

This paper proposes home device authentication mechanism using PKI. It covers intra-home device authentication and inter-home device authentication. We consider not personal CA [8, 9] but public CA. The use of personal CA [8, 9] may be proper solution if only device authentication in the intra-PAN (Personal Area Network) is considered. But if we consider inter-home network, public CA is more proper. Figure 1 shows our home device authentication framework.

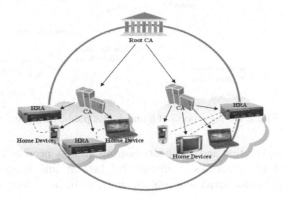

Fig. 1. Home device authentication framework

In figure 1, our home device authentication framework has hierarchical PKI (Public Key Infrastructure) structure. That is, root CA (Certificate Authority) manages it's subordinate CAs and CAs manage home devices and HRA(Home Registration Authority). HRA is a home device which has enough computing power for public key operation, communication ability with other home devices and user interface equipment (for example, monitor, keypad, etc.). And it functions as RA (Registration Authority) and has more authority and requirement.

The devices in the figure 1 means home devices included in the home network. They can communicate with each other and have basic computing ability. That is, internet-microwave, internet-refrigerator, digital TV such as IPTV, internet-washing machine, PDA, notebook computer, wall-pad, PC, cellular phone, etc. are included in our home device. Many home devices are used in everyday life. And more and more home devices will be developed.

Device certification path will be root CA -> CA1 -> CA2-> ... -> HRA/device. And it will be different if the devices are included different CAs. In this case, home devices are authenticated by using CA's trust list which is made by agreement between the CAs.

2.4 Home Device Registration and Certificate Issuing

This section describes home device registration and device certificate issuing process. Figure 2 shows home device registration and certificate issuing process.

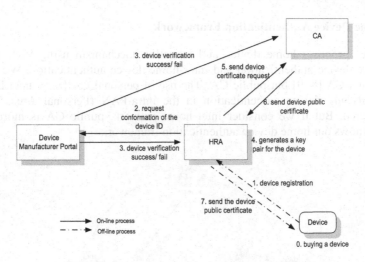

Fig. 2. Issuing process of home device public certificate

Home device registration and certificate issuing process need user intervention. In figure 2, (1) and (7) processes expressed by broken line specially are off-line processes by user. Home device registration and certificate issuing processes are as follows;

(0) Buy home device with home networking ability and bring it home.
(1) Register the home device through HRA at home. In this time, user must input device identity information and other information which is necessary for certificate issuing.

$$Device \rightarrow HRA : [ID_D, AP]$$

(2) TLS channel is established between HRA and device manufacturer portal. HRA requests device manufacturer portal to verify the validity of that device by forwarding the device identity through the TLS channel.

$$HRA \rightarrow Manufacturer : [ID_D, ID_{HRA}, AP]$$

(3) Device manufacturer portal checks whether the device is his product or not through the received device identity.
(4) If HRA receives 'verification success' message from device manufacturer portal, then HRA generates a key pair: public key and private key for the device.
(5) HRA sends the request of the device certificate issuing to CA.

$$HRA \rightarrow CA : [ID_D, ID_{HRA}, AP]$$

(6) If CA receives 'verification success' message from device manufacturer portal and 'certificate request' message from HRA, then CA issues a certificate of the home device. If CA doesn't receive 'verification success' message from device manufacturer portal, then CA rejects the certificate request. And CA can reject the certificate request if the device is already registered and is included in a report of the lost devices.

$$CA \rightarrow HRA : Cert_{CA}[ID_D, ID_{HRA}, AP]$$

(7) HRA sends the received certificate of the home device and generated key pair to the device. This process needs user intervention. Maybe it is processed by off-line method for security.

$$HRA \rightarrow Device : HRAC = Cert_{HRA}[ID_D, h(Cert_{CA} \| r)] \| AP$$

Home device identity referred before is a factor which can identify a device. It can be a new device identity system or existing information such as device serial number, barcode, or MAC address, etc.

Our HRA verifies the certificate contents and the identity of the device like RA (Registration Authority) in general PKI. Two RA models exist in general PKI. In the first model, the RA collects and verifies the necessary information for the requesting entity before a request for a certificate is submitted to the CA. the CA trusts the information in the request because the RA already verified it. In the second model, the CA provides the RA with information regarding a certificate request it has already received. The RA reviews the contents and determines if the information accurately describes the user. The RA provides the CA with a "yes" or "no" answer [12]. Our HRA is similar to the first model of general RA, but it is not CA had public trust but a home device of the kind. It is a device that has the same or more computing power, memory, and data protection module. So, HRA generates key pair and requests and receives certificates for other home devices.

2.5 Home Device Certificate Profile

Home device certificate follows the basic form of internet X.509 certificate [13]. That is, it is the same with X.509 version 1 certificate, but it adds some other extensions about home device authentication. Whatever they has different target: our home device certificate authenticates home devices, but internet X.509 certificate

Table 1. Basic device certificate profile

version
serialNumber
signature
issuer
validity
* subject
subjectPublicKeyInfo
* extensions
signatureAlgorithm
signature

authenticates human, enterprise, server, router, and so on. It is more efficient that home device certificate is implemented based on X.509 certificate because of popularity of the X.509 certificate. It means that implementation of our home device authentication frame work can be easier and spread of our mechanism can be faster.

Table 1 and 2 show our home device certificate profile.

In Table 1, subject and extensions fields signed with '*' are different with those of X.509 certificate. In table 2, four extensions signed with '*' are newly added in our home device certificate.

Table 2. Extensions of home device certificate

Extensions	Explain
*Device information	Home device manufacturer and device identity
*HRA information	The location of HRA(Home Registration Authority)
*Device ownership	The information of home device owner and whether the device is HRA or not
*Device description	Description about the basic function of home device
Authority key Identifier	Provides a means for identifying certificates signed by a particular CA private key
Subject key identifier	Provides a means for identifying certificates containing a particular public key
Subject alternative name	Additional information about home device
Issuer alternative name	Additional information about CA
Basic constraints	Maximum number of subsequent CA certificates in a certification path Where it is end device or not
CRL distribution points	Acquisition method of CRL information
Authority information access	The method of accessing CA information and services (LDAP location)

Now, we describe home device certificate fields which are different with X.509 certificate fields.

3 Lightweight Authorization Protocol (LAP)

LAP is divided into the out-home network and in-home network protocols.

Out-Home Network Protocol: This protocol allows Device in external networks to access the home network through HRA. It is composed of HDC(Home Device Certificate) issue phase, HRA authentication phase and HS(Home Service) authentication phase as shown in Figure 3. In HDC issue phase, the login stage of LWAS(Lightweight Authentication Scheme) or PKAS(Public Key Authentication Scheme) is performed during the steps (1)-(3). If the login is successful, HRA issues a HDC to Device in the step (4). Then, HRA allows Device to access in-home network through itself, while starting a new session between Device and itself. Device can prove itself as the owner of the issued HDC through the session key K established during the login stage. During the valid period of the issued HDC, if the session finishes, Device needs not to perform this phase. Instead, Device performs HRA authentication phase to authenticate itself to HRA. If this authentication is positive, Device establishes a session, over which the home network can be accessed through

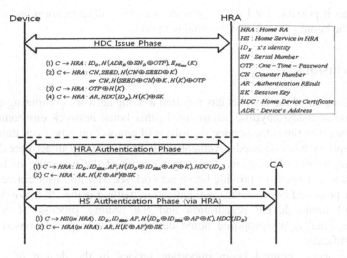

Fig. 3. Out-Home Authentication Protocol

HRA. Especially, because this phase includes only lightweight cryptographic operations. To access a home network service over the established session, Device performs HS authentication phase. During HS authentication phase, HS verifies Device's HDC and H(id⊕hs⊕ts⊕K). If the verification is positive, it can be sure that Device is valid. Then, it authorizes Device according to the attributes included in Device's HDC.

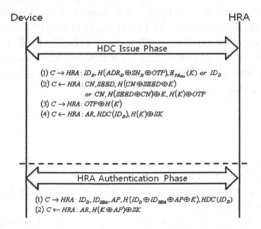

Fig. 4. In-Home Authentication Protocol

In-Home Network Protocol: This protocol is designed for the case that Device is in the home network. As illustrated in Figure. 4, if Device is successfully authenticated through HDC issue phase, it can directly access home network services without HRA. Except for HRA authentication, this protocol is same as out-home network protocol.

That makes it possible for LAP to provide seamless authentication and authorization between the home network and external networks.

4 Conclusions

Rapid expansion of the Internet has required a home network computing environment that can be accessed anytime anywhere. In this home network environment, a user ought to be given the same service regardless of connection type even though the user may not specify what he needs. Authenticated devices that connect user devices must be used regardless of location. This paper described the necessity of home device authentication. It needs to provide home network security and user convenience. And this paper proposed home device authentication method using PKI. We described the process of home device registration and the issuing process of home device certificate. Finally, we proposed home device certificate profile based on internet X.509 certificate.

Remote access control is an important service in the design of digital home networks. The service allows residential users to remotely access and control home appliances such as TVs, lights, washing machines, and refrigerators. However, in spite of such conveniences, the remote control service causes digital home networks to have various security threats. Therefore, it is necessary to provide strong security services in digital home networks. In particular, user authentication is a key service required for remote access control. Recently, we have proposed two S/Key based authentication schemes for secure remote access in digital home networks. However, because they, like other S/Key based schemes, focus on only authentication, they don't provide authorization, which is one of the important security services at home network. In this paper, we analyze and extend the schemes to support the authorization service. For this goal, we propose a lightweight attribute certificate LAC and an authorization protocol LAP. Through the LAC, LAP allows clients to be seamlessly authenticated and authorized regardless of their location. Especially, this protocol where the involved parties need only lightweight cryptographic operations can reduce computational cost with single sign-on.

References

[1] Lee, J., et al.: A DRM Framework for Distributing Digital Contents through the Internet. ETRI Journal, 25(6), 423–436 (2003)
[2] Jeong, Y., Yoon, K., Ryou, J.: A Trusted Key Management Scheme for Digital Right Management. ETRI Journal 27(1), 114–117 (2005)
[3] Gehrmann, C., Nyberg, K., Mitchell, C.J.: The personal CA-PKI for a personal area network. In: IST Mobile and Wireless Telecommunications, pp. 31–35 (Summit 2002)
[4] Intermediate specification of PKI for heterogeneous roaming and distributed terminals, IST-2000-25350-SHAMAN (March 2003)
[5] Hwang, J.-b., Lee, H.-k., Han, J.-w.: Efficient and User Friendly Inter-domain Device Authentication/Access control in Home Networks. In: Sha, E., Han, S.-K., Xu, C.-Z., Kim, M.H., Yang, L.T., Xiao, B. (eds.) EUC 2006. LNCS, vol. 4096, Springer, Heidelberg (2006)

[6] O'Gorman, L.: Comparing Passwords, Tokens, and Biometrics for User Authentication. Proceedings of the IEEE, 91(12) (December 2003)

[7] Al-Muhtadi, J., Ranganathan, A., Campbell, R., Mickunas, M.D.: A Flexible, Privacy-Preserving Authentication Framework for Ubiquitous Computing Environments. ICDCSW '02 , 771–776 (2002)

[8] Roman, M., Campbell, R.: GAIA: Enabling Active Spaces. 9th ACM SIGOPS European Workshop, Kolding, Denmark, September 17th-20th (2000)

[9] Lee, G.-H.: Information Security for Ubiquitous Computing Environment. In: Symposium on Information Security 2003, KOREA, pp. 629–651 (2003)

[10] Lee, S.-Y., Jung, H.-S.: Ubiquitous Research Trend & Future Works, Wolrdwide IT 3(7), 1–12 (2002)

[11] Lee, Y.-C.: Home Networks Technology & Market Trend. ITFIND Weeks Technology Trend(TIS-03-20) 1098, 22–33 (2003)

[12] Lee, D.G., Kang, S.-I., Seo, D.-H., Lee, I.-Y.: Authentication for Single/Multi Domain in Ubiquitous Computing Using Attribute Certification. In: Gavrilova, M., Gervasi, O., Kumar, V., Tan, C.J.K., Taniar, D., Laganà, A., Mun, Y., Choo, H. (eds.) ICCSA 2006. LNCS, vol. 3983, pp. 326–335. Springer, Heidelberg (2006)

[13] Lee, Y.-k., Lee, D.-G., Han, J.-w., Chung, K.-i.: Home Network Device Authentication: Device Authentication Framework and Device Certificate Profile. The international workshop on Application and Security Service in Web and pervAsive eNvironments (ASWAN 07) (2007)

[14] Sun, H.: Home Networking. Mitsubishi Electric Research Laboratories (2004), http://www.merl.com/projects/hmnt/

[15] Haller, N.: The S/KEY One-time Password. RFC 1760 (1995)

[16] Haller, N., Metz, C., Nesser, P., Straw, M.: A One-time Password System (1998)

[17] You, I., Cho, K.: A S/KEY Based Secure Authentication Protocol Using Public Key Cryptography. The KIPS Transactions: Part C 10-C(6) (2003)

[18] Mitchell, C.J., Chen, L.: Comments on the S/KEY User Authentication Scheme. ACM Operating Systems Review 30(4), 12–16 (1996)

[19] Yeh, T.C., Shen, H.Y., Hwang, J.J.: A Secure One-Time Password Authentication Scheme Using Smart Cards. IEICE Transaction on Communication E85-B(11), 2515–2518 (2002)

[20] Lee, N.Y., Chen, J.C.: Improvement of One-Time Password Authentication Scheme Using Smart Cards. IEICE Transaction on Communication E88-B(9), 3765–3767 (2005)

[21] Yen, S.M., Liao, K.H.: Shared Authentication Token Secure against Replay and Weak Key Attacks. Information Processing Letters 62, 77–80 (1997)

[22] You, I., Cho, K.: Comments on YEH-SHEN-HWANG's One-Time Password Authentication Scheme. IEICE Transaction on Communication E88-B(2), 751–753 (2005)

[23] Denning, D., Sacco, G.: Timestamps in Key Distribution Systems. Communications of the ACM 24(8), 533–536 (1981)

[24] Kim, S., Kim, B., Park, S., Yen, S.: Comments on Password-Based Private Key Download Protocol of NDSS'99. Electronics Letters 35(22), 1937–1938 (1999)

GA Based Optimal Keyword Extraction in an Automatic Chinese Web Document Classification System

Chih-Hsun Chou[1], Chin-Chuan Han[2], and Ya-Hui Chen[1]

[1] Department of Computer Science and Information Engineering,
Chung Hua University, No.707, Sec.2, WuFu Rd.,
Hsinchu, 300 Taiwan, R.O.C.
chc@chu.edu.tw
[2] Department of Computer Science and Information Engineering,
National United University, Miaoli, Taiwan, R.O.C.

Abstract. The main steps for designing an automatic document classification system include feature extraction and classification. In this paper a method to improve feature extraction is proposed. In this method, genetic algorithm (GA) was applied to determine the threshold values of four criteria for extracting the representative keywords for each class. The purpose of these four threshold values is to extract as few representative keywords as possible. This keyword extraction method was combined with two classification algorithms, vector space model (VSM) and support vector machine (SVM), for examining the performance of the proposed classification system under various extracting conditions.

1 Introduction

There are two major approaches for web documents search, the keyword search method and the directory structure service. The keyword search method usually facilitates keywords to automatically search the Internet, providing a great quantity from a wide spectrum of web documents containing a lot of undesired information. The directory service, provided by portal websites and managed by the website managers who laboriously classify the web document once it is registered, provides precise search results but wastes manpower. Both services have their shortcomings. Therefore, an automatic search strategy that saves manpower and achieves satisfactory search results would be a great improvement.

In general, document classification consists of two major steps: feature extraction and automatic classification. The feature extraction selects keywords for representing a specific class of document. Automatic classification classifies every document into a suitable class according to keyword distribution. For feature extraction, the statistical indices include term frequency [1-3], inverse document frequency [1-3], mutual information, Chi-square statistics and information gain, while novel approaches such as the strong class information words method, the mean and variance of term frequency, html tags and length, the discriminative learning rule and the conformity and uniformity [4, 5] have also been applied. For automatic classification, many methods, including linear classifiers, the vector space model (VSM) [6, 7], the

P. Thulasiraman et al. (Eds.): ISPA 2007 Workshops, LNCS 4743, pp. 224–234, 2007.

probabilistic model, fuzzy clustering, neural networks, support vector machines (SVM) [8, 9], boosting algorithms, a generalized instance set algorithm, the k-NN classifier and Bayesian inference have been applied.

In this study, four statistic criteria were used for keyword selection. The first two, term frequency and document frequency, are the most popular criteria used for keyword selection. The last two, conformity and uniformity, based on the concept of entropy, were used for improving the efficiency of the first two. These criteria, used for keyword extraction, require the setting of threshold values, which was achieved by the genetic algorithm (GA). This feature extraction policy integrated with two classifiers, VSM and SVM, forms two automatic web document classification systems for examining the proposed feature extraction methods.

The remaining of this paper is organized as follows: Section 2 demonstrates the structure of the proposed document classification system, in which the GA for optimal criteria threshold settings is described in Section 3, experimental results are presented in Section 4, Section 5 gives a conclusion.

2 The Structure of the Proposed Classification System

The structure of the proposed web document classification system contains two major parts: feature extraction and automatic classification. The feature extraction consists of three steps namely preprocessing, word segmentation, and keyword selection. After discarding the figures, tables, and frames appearing in the web document in the preprocessing, word segmentation is performed. Some popular and effective methods for word segmentation include long word priority rule, maximum matching rule, PAT tree-based rule, probabilistic learning rule and the n-gram rule [4]. In this study, the n-gram rule was employed. As indicated in [10, 11], about 63.6% of the words in the Chinese dictionary are of length 2, and the 3-gram rule is practical for segmentation. A conservative 4-gram rule was used here and is described as follows:

Step 1   Delete the punctuation marks.
Step 2   Delete function words such as particles, prepositions, pronouns, and so on. These function words, often widely appearing in documents, are usually meaningless.
Step 3   Delete the characters appearing just once and then delete the 1-letter words.
Step 4   Construct 2 to 4-gram words by the n-gram rule and delete the n-gram words appearing just once.
Step 5   Keep the 2-gram words and extract the 3 and 4-gram words by using the word database [12] constructed by IIS, Academia Sinica, Taiwan. The word database contains 43,028 commonly used 3 and 4-gram words.

Example 1:

Given the following paragraph:

"防火牆"是電腦網路安全防護體系中最基礎的組成部分，每年在全球網絡安全防護產品市場占有最大銷售份額。2002年，我國國內的防火牆市場銷售增長勢頭良好，根據市場調查數據顯示，2003年的大型行業、企業用戶採購仍有傾向選用國外高端防火牆產品的趨勢。國家機關、金融、稅務、工商與電信等部門也仍然會優選國內領先的防火牆產品。

The candidate keywords after the rule are as follows:

N-Gram words	Times	N-Gram words	Times	N-Gram words	Times	N-Gram words	Times	N-Gram words	Times
防火	4	火牆	4	防火牆	4	網路	2	路安	2
安全	2	全防	2	防護	2	網路安	2	路安全	2
安全防	2	全防護	2	網路安全	2	路安全防	2	安全防護	2
產品	3	市場	2	銷售	2	國內	2	牆產	2
牆產品	2	防火牆產	2	火牆產品	2				

By applying the 4-gram rule to all the documents of the same class as well as the sentences in their hyperlinks, many candidate keywords were obtained for that class. In this study, statistical criteria including term frequency, document frequency, conformity and uniformity were used for selecting keywords from the candidates. These four criteria are the following:

1) Term frequency

The probability of keyword k_i appearing in C_j is defined by

$$T\hat{F}_{ij} = \frac{t_{ij}}{\sum_{i=1}^{m} t_{ij}} \qquad (1)$$

where t_{ij} denotes the times of k_i appearing in C_j, and m is the total number of candidate keywords. The term frequency is derived by normalizing $T\hat{F}_{ij}$ as

$$TF_{ij} = \frac{T\hat{F}_{ij}}{\sum_{j=1}^{n} T\hat{F}_{ij}} \qquad (2)$$

where n is the number of classes. If the keyword k_i occurs frequently in class C_j and rarely in other classes, $T\hat{F}_{ij}$ will have a large value. Therefore, the greater value of $T\hat{F}_{ij}$, the more representative of k_i for class C_j.

2) Document frequency

This measure defines the number of documents in a class that a candidate keyword appears in. The probability that keyword k_i appears in class C_j is defined as

$$D\hat{F}_{ij} = \frac{l_{ij}}{l_j} \qquad (3)$$

where l_{ij} denotes the number of documents in class C_j containing candidate keyword k_i; l_j is the number of documents in class C_j. The document frequency is then defined as follows:

$$DF_{ij} = \frac{D\hat{F}_{ij}}{\sum_{j=1}^{n} D\hat{F}_{ij}} \qquad (4)$$

3) Uniformity

In general, a keyword of a specific class will occur in the documents of this class as uniformly as possible. To reflect this property, the measure "Uniformity" is defined as

$$q_{ik} = \frac{\frac{tf_{ik}}{l_j}}{\sum_{k=1}^{l_j} tf_{ik}} \tag{5}$$

$$U_{ij} = -\sum_{k=1}^{l_j} q_{ik} \log q_{ik} \tag{6}$$

where l_j is the number of documents in C_j, tf_{ik} denotes the times a candidate keyword k_i appears in document d_k of class C_j, q_{ik} is a normalization of tf_{ik} and defines the conditional probability of k_i appearing in d_k of C_j given that k_i occurs in C_j. The greater value of U_{ij}, the more representative of k_i for C_j.

4) Conformity

Uniformity measures the occurrence degree of a keyword within a class. Conformity, on the other hand, measures the concentrative degree of a keyword in all classes. Usually, a keyword would appear only in some and not in a lot of classes. The conformity, CF_i, of a keyword k_i is defined as

$$d_{ij} = \frac{l_{ij}}{\sum_{j=1}^{n} l_{ij}} \tag{7}$$

$$CF_i = -\sum_{j=1}^{n} d_{ij} \log d_{ij} \tag{8}$$

A typical keyword k_i should have as small a conformity value as possible.

A candidate keyword, to be a representative keyword for a class, requires the satisfaction of its statistical information to the extraction criteria thresholds, so that the suitable setting of these thresholds plays an important job in keyword extraction. In section 3, the GA is employed to resolve this.

There are many classification methods of which VSM and SVM have been widely applied in document classification [3, 6-9]. In this study, both of them were used for the automatic classification process and are described in the following.

A. VSM-based classification

A simplified keyword-class matrix $K\hat{C} = \left[k\hat{c}_{ij} \right]$, $i = 1,2, ..., \overline{m}; j = 1,2, ..., n$, describing the relationship between each keyword and each document class where $\overline{m}$ is the number of keywords, n is the number of classes and

$$k\hat{c}_{ij} = \frac{t_{ij}/l_j}{\sum_{j=1}^{n} t_{ij}/l_j}, \tag{9}$$

in which l_j is the number of documents in class C_j , t_{ij} denotes the times of the keywords k_i appearing in C_j. After the normalization process, $K\hat{C}$ becomes $KC = \lfloor kc_{ij} \rfloor$, where

$$kc_{ij} = \frac{k\hat{c}_{ij}}{\sqrt{\sum_{s=1}^{\bar{m}} k\hat{c}_{sj}^2}}, \ i = 1, 2, ..., \bar{m}, \ j = 1, 2, ..., n.$$

(10)

The jth column of KC, referred to as the keyword vector $\mathbf{kc}_j = [kc_{1j} \ kc_{2j} \ \cdots \ kc_{\bar{m}j}]^T$, represents the feature vector of class C_j. During the classification process, the number of times each keyword appears in the examining document are computed and normalized as a feature vector $\mathbf{kd}$

$$\mathbf{kd} = [kd_1 \ kd_2 \ \cdots \ kd_{\bar{m}}]^T.$$

(11)

The identified class of the examining document can be determined by

$$\arg\max_j \frac{\mathbf{kd} \cdot \mathbf{kc}_j}{\|\mathbf{kd}\| \|\mathbf{kc}_j\|}.$$

(12)

B. SVM-based classification

In this study, the software LIBSVM [13] was used for SVM-based classification. To train the SVM using a set of training documents, a normalized document-keyword matrix $D\overline{K} = [dk_{ki}]$ based on the selected keywords was constructed as training data, where

$$dk_{ki} = \frac{d\widetilde{k}_{ki}}{\max_{j=1,2,...,\bar{m}} \{d\widetilde{k}_{kj}\}}, \ k = 1, 2, ..., l, \ i = 1, 2, ..., \bar{m},$$

(13)

l is the number of documents and $d\widetilde{k}_{ki}$ denotes the number of times keyword k_i appears in document d_k. The LIBSVM searches the best parameters for the kernel function in the SVM. In this study, a radial basis function was utilized as kernel function.

3   GA for Optimal Setting of the Criteria Threshold

When applying binary GA to the document classification, most research uses gene positions in the chromosome to represent candidate keywords. The gene values of a chromosome represent a keyword selection from the candidate keywords, so that the GA can determine the most probable chromosome that reflects the optimal keywords [14-17]. In this study, instead of directly encoding the candidate keywords into evolving a chromosome, the GA was applied to determine the optimal thresholds of the four classification criteria, so that a candidate keyword satisfying these four thresholds was regarded as a keyword of some class(es). To examine the performance of the proposed extraction method, only the simple GA was applied in this study. The process for threshold setting is described in the following:

Step 1. For each candidate keyword k_i and each document d_k, compute $d\tilde{k}_{ki}$

Step 2. Normalize $d\tilde{k}_{ki}$ with the following equation

$$dk_{ki} = \frac{d\tilde{k}_{ki}}{\max_{j=1,2,\dots,m}\{d\tilde{k}_{kj}\}}, \ k = 1, 2, \dots, l, \ i = 1, 2, 3, \dots, m \cdot \tag{14}$$

where l and m are the number of documents and number of candidate keywords, respectively. Construct the document-keyword matrix $DK = [dk_{ki}]$

Step 3. According to Yahoo's classification result, construct document-class matrix

$$DC = [dc_{kj}], \ k = 1, 2, 3, \dots, l, \ j = 1, 2, 3, \dots, n \cdot \tag{15}$$

where n is the number of classes and dc_{kj} is defined as follows:

$$dc_{kj} = \begin{cases} 1, & \text{if document } d_k \text{ is classified into class } C_j \\ 0, & \text{otherwise} \end{cases} \tag{16}$$

Step 4. Encode the binary chromosome for the four classification criteria parameters with 8 bits for each criterion, and initialize the population with size 20.

Step 5. Compute the fitness value of each chromosome with the following steps:

1) Decode the chromosome into four threshold values
2) Construct keyword-class matrix $K\tilde{C}$ for the threshold values

$$K\tilde{C} = [k\tilde{c}_{ij}], \ i = 1, 2, 3, \dots, m, \ j = 1, 2, 3, \dots, n \tag{17}$$

in which $k\tilde{c}_{ij} = 1$ if keyword k_i satisfies all four thresholds in class C_j, and $k\tilde{c}_{ij} = 0$ otherwise.

3) Calculate document-class matrix

$$D\hat{C} = DK \cdot K\tilde{C} = [d\hat{c}_{kj}], \ k = 1, 2, \dots, l, j = 1, 2, \dots, n \tag{18}$$

This matrix exhibits the degree a document belonging to a class.

4) Compute the binary form of $D\hat{C}$, $D\tilde{C} = [d\tilde{c}_{kj}]$,

$$d\tilde{c}_{kj} = \begin{cases} 1 & \text{if } d\hat{c}_{kj} = \max_{r=1\dots n}(d\hat{c}_{kr}) \\ 0 & \text{otherwise} \end{cases}, \tag{19}$$

$d\tilde{c}_{kj} = 1$ indicates document d_k is classified into class C_j

5) Compute the fitness value

$$fitness = \frac{\sum_{k,j} dc_{kj} \cdot d\tilde{c}_{kj}}{l} \qquad (20)$$

Table 1. Three classified catalogues

Code(Ci)	First level	Second level	Third level	Code(Ci)	First level	Second level	Third level
C1	電腦通訊	電腦遊戲	線上遊戲	C12	醫療保健	疾病資訊	精神科
C2	電腦通訊	電腦遊戲	模擬器	C13	醫療保健	疾病資訊	癌症
C3	電腦通訊	網際網路	搜尋引擎	C14	醫療保健	疾病資訊	心臟科
C4	電腦通訊	網際網路	網路賺錢術	C15	醫療保健	傳統醫學	氣功
C5	電腦通訊	系統安全	電腦病毒	C16	醫療保健	醫療院所	虛擬醫院
C6	電腦通訊	系統安全	防火牆	C17	醫療保健	醫療藥品	維他命
C7	電腦通訊	電腦多媒體	數位藝術	C18	生活資訊	交通運輸	飛機
C8	醫療保健	SARS		C19	生活資訊	交通運輸	火車
C9	醫療保健	保健常識	減肥	C20	生活資訊	交通運輸	機車
C10	醫療保健	疾病資訊	腸病毒	C21	生活資訊	公益彩券	
C11	醫療保健	疾病資訊	漢他病毒	C22	生活資訊	電話服務	

Step 6. Perform the genetic operators. The roulette wheel rule was employed for the reproduction process in which the best chromosome was reserved. A two point crossover with crossover probability equal to 0.4 was used. The mutation probability for each bit was set as 0.01.

Step 7. Stop the evolution if the best chromosome is fixed by 100 generations, else go to step 5.

4   Experimental Results

The experiments dealt with web documents containing the original complex form of Chinese characters without considering figures and synonyms. The experimental data were gathered from three of the major classified catalogues (電腦通訊, 醫療保健, 生活資訊) on Yahoo's Chinese website. Each of these catalogues contains three levels as shown in Table 1 resulting in a total of 22 sub-catalogues. Table 2 gives the details of the experimental data in Table 1. There are in total 1,203 documents for the 22 sub-catalogues after ignoring useless documents. These 1,203 documents, after the word segmentation process, generated 12,594 candidate keywords. About 75% of the documents of each class were randomly selected for training, and the remaining for testing as shown in Table 2. The classification efficiency was evaluated in terms of the recall rate ($R_i = |A_i|/(|A_i| + |B_i|)$) and precision rate ($P_i = |A_i|/(|A_i| + |E_i|)$) for each class, and correctness ($H = S/N$) for the overall system, where $|A_i|$ denotes the number of documents classified to class i that actually belong to class i, $|B_i|$ denotes the number of documents belonging to class i that are misclassified, $|E_i|$ denotes the number of documents that are misclassified to class i, S denotes the number of documents actually classified to their corresponding classes, and N is the number of documents.

4.1 The Optimal Thresholds Obtained by Applying the GA

After the GA evolution, the obtained optimal thresholds were 0.0510, 0.7725, 0.5294 and 0.0314. That is, a candidate keyword of a class with term frequency $\geq$ 0.0510, document frequency $\geq$ 0.0314, uniformity $\geq$ 0.5294 and conformity $\leq$ 0.7725 was verified as a keyword of that class. The keyword selection process extracted 1,179 keywords from the 12,594 candidate keywords reducing the feature dimension by about 90.64%. Meanwhile, the class-keyword pairs were reduced from 58,712 to 7,232, a total of 87.68%. The top 10 representative keywords for each of the 22 sub-catalogues are shown in Table 3.

Table 2. Experimental data collected from Yahoo's Chinese web-site

First level category	Second level	Third level category	Number of documents	Useless Documents	Training documents	Testing Documents
電腦通訊						
	電腦遊戲					
		線上遊戲	78	14	48	16
		模擬器	96	23	55	18
	網際網路					
		搜尋引擎	85	17	51	17
		網路賺錢術	75	14	46	15
	系統安全					
		電腦病毒	95	29	50	16
		防火牆	84	18	50	16
	電腦多媒體					
		數位藝術	34	8	20	6
醫療保健						
	SARS		62	9	40	13
	保健常識					
		減肥	94	28	50	16
	疾病資訊					
		腸病毒	85	19	50	16
		漢他病毒	73	13	45	15
		精神科	53	7	35	11
		癌症	84	18	50	16
		心臟科	62	9	40	13
	傳統醫學					
		氣功	57	17	30	10
	醫療院所					
		虛擬醫院	53	13	30	10
	醫療藥品					
		維他命	49	7	32	10
生活資訊						
	交通運輸					
		飛機	66	14	39	13
		火車	61	8	40	13
		機車	57	9	36	12
	公益彩券		78	12	50	17
	電話服務		32	4	21	7
	Summary		1513	310	908	295

4.2 Experimental Results

In the following, two experimental studies are given including A) the combinations of the criteria, and B) A comparison of VSM and SVM.

A Combinations of the criteria

Part A discusses the exploitation of the optimal threshold for a single classification criterion. In this experiment, more than one criterion was used. The performances when using two, three and all of the criteria with both classification methods are shown in Tables 4. It can be seen that using more criteria achieves a better performance.

Table 3. Top 10 representative keywords

class ranking	公益彩券	線上遊戲	氣功	癌症	精神科	漢他病毒	腸病毒	心臟科	減肥	維他命	SARS
1	樂透彩	遊戲	氣功	癌症	精神	病毒	腸病毒	心臟	減肥	維他命	肺炎
2	號碼	線上	人體	細胞	精神科	症候群	病毒	心臟病	體重	健康	sars
3	彩券	虛擬	身體	檢查	醫療	出血熱	感染	動脈	健康	保健	非典
4	公益	時間	自然	治療	醫學	感染	流行	血管	控制	醫藥	典型
5	電腦	活動	中國	死亡率	醫師	老鼠	毒感	疾病	飲食	蛋白	衛生
6	遊戲	問題	保健	腫瘤	醫院	血熱	預防	死亡率	營養	醫學	病毒
7	查詢	功能	呼吸	早期	門診	症狀	衛生	氧化	運動	建議	感染
8	線上	專業	健康	人體	治療	傳染	發燒	醫藥	食物	疾病	呼吸
9	特別	專區	活動	症狀	臨床	疾病	衛生署	臨床	身體	避免	預防
10	時間	資源	醫學	預防	症狀	呼吸	傳染	保健	藥物	專業	嚴重
class ranking	機車	火車	飛機	模擬器	數位藝術	電腦病毒	防火牆	電話服務	網路賺錢術	虛擬醫院	搜尋引擎
1	機車	火車	飛機	模擬器	數位	病毒	防火牆	商業金融	賺錢	醫院	搜尋引擎
2	交通	鐵路	航空	模擬	藝術	電腦病毒	安全	電話	網路賺錢	網路醫院	搜尋
3	技術	歷史	飛行	遊戲	教育	電腦	保護	公司行號	廣告	醫療	新聞
4	專業	交通	國際	討論區	大學	防治	系統	電信	上網	醫師	引擎
5	引擎	照片	旅遊	軟體	科技	程式	技術	通訊	資訊網	虛擬醫院	電腦
6	控制	資訊網	全球	日本	設計	軟體	企業	行動	連結	問題	娛樂
7	商品	活動	時間	工具	媒體	感染	網際	電子	電話	醫學	社會
8	設計	民眾	世界	研究	檔案	企業	手機	娛樂	娛樂	健康	科學
9	休閒	業務	交通	娛樂	活動	執行	問題	國際	樂透	諮詢	軟體
10	運動	旅遊	引擎	連結	執行	系統	電腦	電訊	組織	治療	電子

Table 4. Performances when using various criteria

Term frequency: Tf; Document frequency: Df; Uniformity: U; Conformity: C

index	VSM			SVM		
	Recall rate	Precision rate	Correctness	Recall rate	Precision	Correctness
None	81.88%	84.21%	82.71%	69.84%	77.88%	71.86%
Tf	84.12%	85.98%	84.41%	81.75%	88.40%	83.05%
Df	84.47%	85.18%	84.07%	83.70%	89.42%	85.08%
U	84.08%	86.88%	85.08%	84.32%	84.73%	84.07%
C	84.97%	85.90%	84.41%	85.41%	89.32%	85.42%
Tf+Df	84.66%	86.50%	84.75%	82.34%	86.19%	83.05%
Tf+U	84.41%	86.49%	85.08%	83.76%	86.69%	84.41%
Tf+C	85.21%	85.98%	84.41%	85.77%	87.34%	85.42%
Df+U	84.88%	87.18%	85.42%	84.18%	87.49%	84.07%
Df+C	85.92%	86.86%	85.08%	85.81%	87.00%	84.75%
U+C	86.71%	87.51%	86.10%	86.43%	90.47%	86.44%
Tf+Df+U	85.72%	86.94%	85.76%	85.84%	85.68%	85.08%
Tf+Df+C	86.26%	86.84%	86.78%	86.78%	87.19%	86.10%
Tf+U+C	87.84%	87.98%	87.12%	87.88%	87.69%	86.78%
Df+U+C	88.41%	90.22%	88.81%	88.02%	89.10%	87.46%
All	90.32%	90.94%	89.83%	90.84%	90.43%	90.17%

B. A comparison of VSM and SVM.

To compare the application of VSM and SVM classifiers in the proposed system, all four criteria were used in this experiment, and the classification results are shown in Table 5. This Table shows that VSM outperforms SVM in terms of precision rate, and is inferior in the other. This result agrees with the trade-off between recall rate and precision rate. In addition, the SVM achieved a higher correctness.

Table 5. Comparison of VSM and SVM

index method	Recall rate	Precision rate	Correctness
VSM	90.32%	90.94%	89.83%
SVM	90.84%	90.43%	90.17%

5 Conclusion

Automatic document classification of an Internet website can save manpower and quickly update website catalogues. To design such a system, it is necessary to extract the representative keywords for each document class. In this study, four statistical criteria including term frequency, document frequency, uniformity and conformity were used for keyword extraction. Each criterion was verified by a threshold value, and a candidate keyword of a class satisfying the four criteria was regarded as a keyword for that class. In this study, the GA was used to obtain the optimal thresholds for keyword extraction, which, integrated with two classifiers, VSM and SVM, formed the proposed automatic web document classification systems. Comparisons of the experimental results show the performances of the proposed systems.

References

[1] Liao, S.H., Jiang, M.H.: A Combined Weight method in Automatic Classification of Chinese Text. Proc. ICNN&B '05 2, 625–630 (2005)
[2] Lam, W., Han, Y.Q.: Automatic textual document categorization based on generalized instance sets and a metamodel. IEEE Trans. Patt. Analysis Mach. Intell. 25, 628–633 (2003)
[3] Liang, J.Z.: SVM based Chinese Web page automatic classification. Proc. 2003 Intern. Conf. Mach. Learn. Cybern. 4, 2265–2268 (2003)
[4] Yang, Y.Y.: Document Automatic Classification and Ranking. Master Thesis, Dept. Comp. Sci., National Tsing Hua University, Taiwan R.O.C (1992)
[5] Maron, M.E.: Automatic indexing: an experimental inquiry. Journ. ACM. 8, 417–440 (1961)
[6] Tai, X.Y., Ren, F.J., Kita, K.J.: An information retrieval model based on vector space method by supervised learning. Inform. Proc. Manag. 38, 749–764 (2002)
[7] Tan, S.B.: Neighbor-weighted K-nearest neighbor for unbalanced text corpus. Exp. Syst. Appl. 28, 667–671 (2005)
[8] Tong, S., Koller, D.: Support vector machine active learning with applications to text classification. In: Proc. 17th Intern. Conf. Machine Learning, pp. 999–1006 (2001)

[9] Liu, C.H., Lu, C.C., Lee, W.P.: Document categorisation by genetic algorithms. In: Proc. 2000 IEEE Intern. Conf. Systems, Man, Cybern. 5, 3868–3872 (2000)

[10] Nie, J.Y., Ren, F.J.: Chinese information retrieval- using characters or words. Inform. Proc. Manag. 35, 443–462 (1999)

[11] Zhou, G.D., Lua, K.T.: Interpolation of n-gram and mutual-information based trigger pair language models for Mandarin speech recognition. Comp. Speech Lang. 13, 125–141 (1999)

[12] Academic Sinica Balanced Corpus of Modern Chinese. Institute of Information Science and CKIP group in Academia Sinica: http://www.sinica.edu.tw/SinicaCorpus/

[13] Chang, C.C., Lin, C.J.: LIBSVM: A Library for Support Vector Machines. (2001), http://www.csie.ntu.edu.tw/cjlin/libsvm

[14] Zhang, W.F., Xu, B.W., Cui, Z.F.: A document classification approach by GA feature extraction based corner classification neural network. In: Proc. Intern. Conf. Cyberworlds (2005)

[15] Martin-Bautista, M.J., Vila, M.-A., Larsen, H.L.: Building adaptive user profiles by a genetic fuzzy classifier with feature selection. Proc. FUZZ IEEE. 1, 308–312 (2000)

[16] Cheatham, M., Rizki, M.: Feature and Prototype Evolution for Nearest Neighbor Classification of Web Documents. In: Proc. ITNG, pp. 364–369 (2006)

[17] Martin-Bautista, M.J., et al.: Fuzzy genes- improving the effectiveness of information retrieval. Proc. 2000 Congr. Evolut. Comput. 1, 471–478 (2000)

Design and Implementation of Context-Aware Security Management System for Ubiquitous Computing Environment*

Seon-Ho Park, Joon-Sic Cho, Young-Ju Han, and Tai-Myoung Chung

Internet Management Technology Laboratory,
School of Information and Communication Engineering,
Sungkyunkwan University,
300 Cheoncheon-dong, Jangan-gu,
Suwon-si, Gyeonggi-do 440-746, Republic of Korea
{shpark,jscho,yjhan}@imtl.skku.ac.kr, tmchung@ece.skku.ac.kr

Abstract. This paper discusses security considerations of a ubiquitous computing environment and presents the context-aware security management system. The system supports the management and enforcement of context-aware security policies, and manages the context of users and resources in the ubiquitous computing environment. The system provides partial credential based user authentication and context aware access control service. This paper presents a calculation algorithm of an authentication credential value using fuzzy if-then rule for partial credential based user authentication.

1 Introduction

Ubiquitous computing environment has new security challenges from a security perspective, since it has several features different from traditional computing environment, such as context-awareness and pervasive deployment of various computing devices [1,2]. Many applications in the ubiquitous computing environment are context-aware and their operation can be customized based on the context in which an access request is made[3].

Let us think about the smart home, as an example of the ubiquitous computing environment. The smart home is equipped with various networked sensor devices such as cameras, microphones, location-aware sensors. Given the sensitivity of context information that is generated in the smart home, authorization policies can potentially be quite complex. The authorization policy can restrict access to resources based on several factors, including user attributes, the specific resource or the context information. For example, users can be classified as "parent" or "child", "resident" or "guest", or even as "people" or "pet". Then, access

---

* This research was supported by the MIC(Ministry of Information and Communication), Korea, under the ITRC(Information Technology Research Center) support program supervised by the IITA(Institute of Information Technology Advancement) (IITA-2006-C1090-0603-0028).

P. Thulasiraman et al. (Eds.): ISPA 2007 Workshops, LNCS 4743, pp. 235–244, 2007.

rights can depend on the user's classification, as well as the associated identity. In addition, access control may be restricted based on the user's location, or based on environmental factors such as temporal information or location-related data. For example, parents may restrict their children's access to the television, allowing the watching of television between 6:00 p.m. and 9:00 p.m. and only while they are 1.5 meters away from the television. In this case, the access control policy depends on the context information composed of location and time information[1].

In addition to the authorization policy problem, the management of differentiated credential level of principals and authenticators is important issue, because various authentication methods can be used in the ubiquitous computing environment. In the ubiquitous computing environment, many authentication devices and protocols can be used. These various authentication methods have different credential levels. Unlike traditional computing system using one authentication mechanism, the ubiquitous computing system can use multi-authentication for secure, active service. Therefore, the mechanism to manage the different confidence of various authentication mechanisms must be required for the security of the ubiquitous computing environment.

We propose the CoASec(Context Aware Security Management system) that enables management of context-aware security policies and enforcement of context-aware security services including user authentication and access control. CoASec security services are based on context-role based access control model and partial-credential based authentication management using the authentication credential value. We have designed the architecture of the CoASec and implemented it. Also, we made a simulation program to test the CoASec in the virtual smart home environment.

The rest of this paper is organized as follows. Section 2 explores related works. Section 3 illustrates an overview of the CoASec. Section 4 illustrates security models of the CoASec. Section 5 illustrates the system architecture and functions of core components of the CoASec. Section 6 discusses implementation of the CoASec. Section 7 concludes the paper.

2 Related Works

The Cerberus [4] and the CASA project[5] are the representative studies on security framework of ubiquitous computing environment. The Cerberus which is a core service of the Gaia [6] project provides identification, authentication, context awareness, and reasoning. The Cerberus security service uses *Inference Engine*. The access control uses context for making access control decisions and configuring policy. However, access control policy of Cerberus uses access control lists defined centrally by a system administrator. These access control mechanism is easy to maintain, but lack flexibility. The authentication uses a multi-level authentication scheme which has associated confidence values describing the trustworthiness of the authentication achieved. However, it is insufficient that the method for calculating the credential value.

The CASA provides context aware access control based on GRBAC(generalized role based access control) [7] model for security of Aware Home. GRBAC is an extension of traditional RBAC. It enhances traditional RBAC by incorporating the notion of object roles and environment roles, with the traditional notion of subject roles. But GRBAC has some problems. First, GRBAC is not suitable for large and complex organizations, because of defining too many roles in the system. Second, RBAC loses its advantage of data abstractions by object role. RBAC abstract user-level information from system level information by notion of permission is relationship between objects and operations. In GRBAC, because object role violates this relationship, the data abstraction could not be achieved. In addition, this problem violates user-to-role and role-to-permission associations. Finally, GRBAC has an unnecessary overlapping that environment roles and object roles, because certain physical environmental things can be also objects[1].

3   CoASec Overview

The CoASec is context-aware security management system which provides context-aware based authorization service and user authentication service that applies the credential level of users based on the features of authentication material. The CoASec can be useful as an integrated security management module for ubiquitous computing environment. For example, home gateways or home servers of smart home systems can include the CoASec as a security module to securely control every entities such as user, control devices, and various appliances in the smart home environment. Also, the CoASec can be deployed as the security management framework in other ubiquitous computing systems.

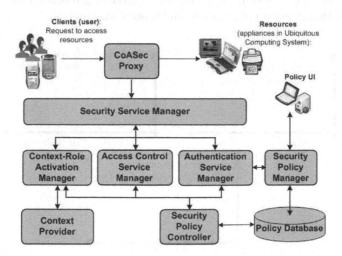

Fig. 1. The CoASec overview

Fig. 1 illustrates the high-level overview of the CoASec architecture. The CoASec *proxy* is an interface for the CoASec to intercommunicate respectively clients and resources. When clients attempt to access any resources, the CoASec *proxy* intercepts the request of the client. As soon as the CoASec *proxy* receives a message for a resource access, it formulates a request for a policy decision and sends it to the *security service manager*. Then, the *security service manager* initiates requests to the underlying modules, namely *authentication service manager* and *access control service manager*, in order to decide about allowing or denying access for the requested operation at the resources. Finally, the allow or deny message is sent to the resource through the CoASec *proxy*.

The access control of the CoASec is based on the Context-Role Based Access Control(CRBAC) model. The CRBAC model [1] completely includes advantages of traditional RBAC model and also enables the context-based access control. The authentication of the CoASec manages user authentication using the ACV. The ACV is used to manage differentiated credential level of authentication mechanisms and authenticated user. Also, the ACV can be used to activate user role in the access control process. The detailed explanation about CoASec security models is talked in the following section 4.

4   CoASec Security Model

4.1   ACV Calculation Algorithm

The CoASec provides partial credential user authentication using Authentication Credential Value(ACV). We used a fuzzy if-then rule as the ACV calculation method. Fuzzy logic is suitable to decide a level of authentication credential, since the authentication credential is ambiguous information.

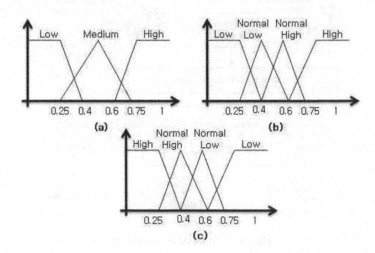

Fig. 2. (a) Loss risk (b) Copy risk (c) Partial credential

Table 1. ACV implication rules

1. IF LR is Low and CR is Low then PC is High
2. IF LR is Low and CR is S-Low then PC is S-High
3. IF LR is Low and CR is S-High then PC is S-High
4. IF LR is Low and CR is High then PC is Medium
5. IF LR is Medium and CR is Low then PC is S-High
6. IF LR is Medium and CR is S-Low then PC is S-High
7. IF LR is Medium and CR is S-High then PC is Medium
8. IF LR is Medium and CR is High then PC is Low
9. IF LR is High and CR is Low then PC is Medium
10. IF LR is High and CR is S-Low then PC is Medium
11. IF LR is High and CR is S-High then PC is Low
12. IF LR is High and CR is High then PC is Low

We define a loss risk and a copy risk as the *condition* and the partial credential value as the *conclusion* part. The fuzzy sets of the conditions and the conclusion are illustrated in the fig.2.

We can make 12 ACV implication rules based on the three loss risks and four copy risks. The rules are defined in the table 1. Finally, we used the middle-of-maxima method as the defuzzification method.

For example, we set up that the loss risk of smart cards is 0.35 and the copy risk of smart card is 0.31 then this case is included the *first, second,* and *sixth rules.* In each rule, we can get the fuzzy graph using two input values. After calculating the fuzzy graph of each rule, these values are combined into a fuzzy graph. Finally, we can get the result the ACV is "0.57" using middle-of-maxima defuzzification.

4.2 Context-Role Based Access Control

The CRBAC[1] model is extended RBAC model that adds a notion of context-role to a traditional RBAC[8] in order to apply security-sensitive context information to configuration and enforcement of the access control policy. The context-role represents environmental state of the system by a mapping context-roles and context information.

The role activation is very important and has to be carefully executed, since the principal of SoD may be violated because of many-to-many relationship of users and roles. We solve this problem by means of relationship between the strength of permission that a role has and ACV of authenticated user. Allowing a user that possesses higher ACV to have stronger permission is very natural, because ACV means the credential of authenticated user. The CoASec provides function to assign appropriate activation level to every user roles and only users that are assigned higher ACV value than activation level of certain role are able to activate the role.

*Example*1. Fig. 3 is an example of a user role hierarchy tree and relationship of assignment of users and user roles. A user U6 is assigned to role R3, R5, and

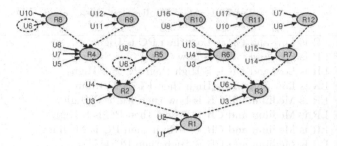

Fig. 3. An example of a user role hierarchy tree and assignment relationships of users and roles

R8. These roles have a different set of permissions and sensitive levels of each permission set are different respectively. We assume that U6 can be authenticated by an ID/password, a smart card, and a fingerprint, and the ACVs of them are "0.35", "0.57", and "0.89", respectively. We can assign appropriate ACV to each role to configure a condition for role activation. Let us assign respectively 0.3, 0.5, and 0.8 to R3, R5, and R8. To active these roles, users are authenticated with ACV that is higher than activation level of respective roles. If U6 is authenticated by ID/password, only R3 is activated and R5 and R8 are not activated for U6. Similarly, if U6 is authenticated using the smart card, R3 and R5 are activated but R8 is not activated for U6.

5   CoASec Architecture

This section describes detailed architecture and functions of core components of CoASec. The CoASec is composed of the security service manager(SSM), authentication service manager(ASM), access control service manager(ACSM), context-role activation manager(CRAM), security policy controller(SPC), context provider, and CoASec proxy. These are modules to support security service, while the security policy manager(SPM) is a module to manage security policy. The CoASec modules and their interaction appear in the class diagram of Fig.4.

The SSM controls main security service modules such as the ASM and the ACSM, and manages security sessions after enforcement of access control. The SSM receives security service requests through CoASec proxy and analyzes the request. Then, the SSM formulates a request for user authentication and sends it to the ASM. The SSM updates authentication status of the user after the user authentication process and formulates a request for authorization service and sends it to the ACSM. Finally, the SSM receives an allow or deny message, then it sends the result message of the security service request to the client and application through the CoASec proxy. Then the SSM updates the security session list and monitors the context condition changes. Security sessions are maintained only while context conditions that are related to the sessions are valid. Therefore the SSM must always listen to context conditions through the CRAM module.

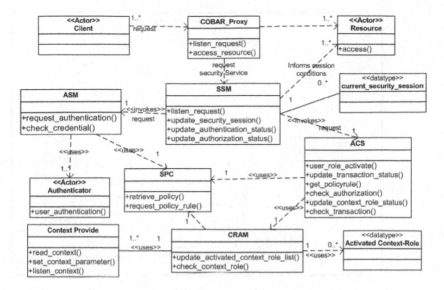

Fig. 4. The system architecture class diagram

The ASM enforces user authentication and manages authentication mechanisms. The ASM supports a dynamic method for adding new authentication devices and associating them with security policies. Because of the various authentication methods and their different strength, the ASM should assign different ACV to different authentication methods.

The ACSM enforces the access control of authenticated users based on CR-BAC mechanism. The ACSM receives a client id, client ACV, object, and operation from the SSM after the user authentication. Then the ACSM create the request message for policy transaction retrieve and sends it to the SPC. As soon as the ACSM receives transactions related to the access request, it checks current active context-roles and finds the valid security transaction. Finally, the ACSM retrieves the policy rules that is related to the transaction and checks the permission bit of the policy rule in order to decide about allowing or denying access for the requested operation at the object(applications). Finally, an allow or deny result is sent to the SSM.

The CRAM manages the activation of context-role based on role activation rules. The CRAM receives context information from the context provider and transforms low-level physical data from the high-level logical data, using the data abstraction rules. The context-role can be represent various type of context data. For example, the context-role can include the location-related data, temporal data, system resource data, and even the temperature or illumination data. The CRAM maintains the active context-role list and provides ACSM and SSM with active context-roles. The context provider gathers the context information including the system status information, the resource status information, and the environmental information and provides the context data to CRAM.

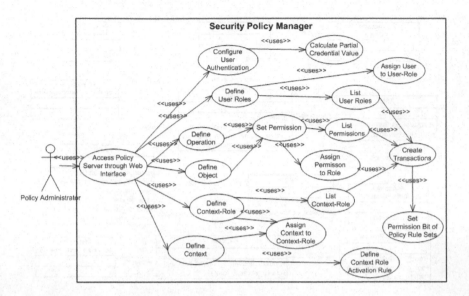

Fig. 5. The security policy configuration use case diagram

The above described modules gain the policies from the SPC. The SPC retrieves security policies from the policy database. Security policies are managed by the SPM. The SPM provides functions for configuration of system information of management domain as well as security policies to security administrator. The system functionalities about security policy configurations are illustrated in the UML use case diagram of Fig.5.

The sequence diagram that corresponds to the logical invocation path of the access request, through the modules of the CoASec, is illustrated in Fig.6.

6   Implementation

In this section we discuss our implementation, where we use CoASec to authenticate users, capture context, and control access decisions for applications of the smart home that is our testbed. The smart home is simple testbed that is composed several authentication devices, sensor devices that are connected through the wireless network, and a program that simulates the home network system based on a context-aware system. Our authentication devices include smart card, ID/password, and fingerprint scanners. Simulation program includes various appliances such as TV, audio, lamp, humidifier, etc. We decide to use simulation program to test operations of CoASec, because it is difficult to implement a real environment for testing of our system and the focus of our work is only security management system. Sensor devices can capture a temperature, humidity, an illumination, and a gas leakage. We also use time and location information

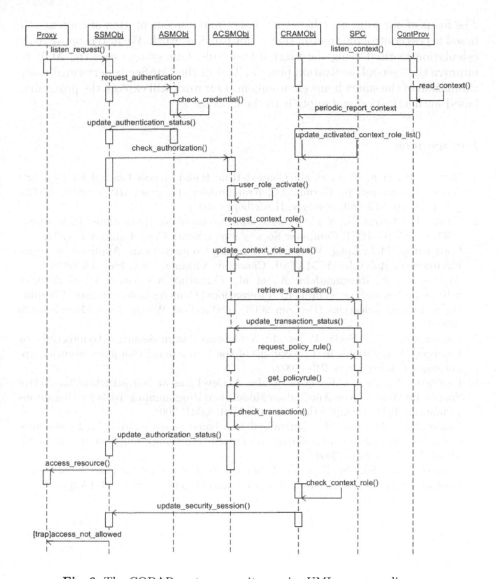

Fig. 6. The COBAR system security service UML sequence diagram

as well as context information that are captured sensor devices. The policy of CoASec is configured through web-based graphical UI, therefore policy manager can easily access and manage the policy.

7   Conclusion

The context-awareness of ubiquitous computing environment requires the new security paradigm. We introduce context aware security management system.

The focus of our work is architecture design and implementation of context-role based access control mechanism that is our previous work. We also propose ACV calculation method using the fuzzy if-then rule. Our system uses the ACV to improve the user-role activation process. Test of the CoASec is performed using simulation of the smart home environment. Our work will explore the proximity-based authentication and apply it to the CoASec.

References

1. Park, S.-H., Han, Y.-J., et al.: Context-Role Based Access Control for Context-Aware Application. In: Gerndt, M., Kranzlmüller, D. (eds.) HPCC 2006. LNCS, vol. 4208, pp. 572–580. Springer, Heidelberg (2006)
2. Schilit, B., Adams, N., et al.: Context-aware computing applications, In WMCSA 1994, pp. 85–90. IEEE Computer Society Press, Santa Cruz, California (1994)
3. Convington, M.J., Long, W., et al.: Securing Context-Aware Applications Using Environment Roles. In: ACMAT'01, Chantilly, Virginia, USA, May 3-4 (2001)
4. Al-Muhtadi, J., Ranganathan, A., et al.: Cerberus: A Context-Aware Security Scheme for Smart Spaces. In: IEEE International Conference on Pervasive Computing and Communications (PerCom 2003), Dallas-Fort Worth, Texas, March 23-26 (2003)
5. Convington, M.J., Fogla, P., et al.: A Context-Aware Security Architecture for Emerging Applications. In: Proceedings of the 18th Annual Computer Security Applications Conference, p. 249 (2002)
6. Cerqueira, R., Hess, C.K., et al.: Gaia: A Development Infrastructure for Active Spaces. In: Workshop on Application Models and Programming Tools for Ubiquitous Computing held in conjunction with the UBICOMP 2001
7. Moyer, M.J., Ahamad, M.: Generalized role based access control. In: Proceedings of the 2001 International Conference on Distributed Computing Systems (ICDCS), Mesa, AZ, April 2001 (2001)
8. Ferraiolo, D.F., Sandhu, R., et al.: Proposed NIST Standard for Role-Based Access Control. ACM Transactions on Information and System Security 4(3) (August 2001)

Forward Secure Privacy Protection Scheme for RFID System Using Advanced Encryption Standard

Sang-Soo Yeo[1], Kouichi Sakurai[1],
SungEon Cho[2], KiSung Yang[2], and Sung Kwon Kim[3]

[1] Dept. of Computer Science & Communication Engineering, Kyushu University,
Fukuoka, Japan
ssyeo@itslab.csce.kyushu-u.ac.jp, sakurai@csce.kyushu-u.ac.jp
[2] Dept. of Computer & Communication, Sunchon National University,
Suncheon, Jeonnam, Korea
chose@sunchon.ac.kr, ksyang@fumate.com
[3] School of Computer Science & Engineering, Chung-Ang University, Seoul, Korea
skkim@cau.ac.kr

Abstract. There are many researches related to privacy protection in RFID system. Among them, Ohkubo's hash-based scheme is provably secure and it can protect user's privacy, prevent location tracking, and guarantee forward security completely. Unfortunately, one-way hash functions, which play important roles in Ohkubo's schem, can't be implemented into the current RFID tag hardware. So we propose a new secure protocol for RFID privacy protection, and it is a modified version of Ohkubo's scheme using Feldhofer's AES module for RFID tag. Our new scheme has almost all of advantages of Ohkubo's scheme and moreover it can be embedded into RFID tag hardware easily.

1 Introduction

In the near future, we will live in more convenient world, which is commonly called 'ubiquitous world'. Ubiquitous environment will enable us to connect to networks at any time at any place and it will provide specific and appropriate services to each of us. And automatic identification technology plays an important role in this environment. Automatic identification technologies can be categorized into two broad categories. The first is automatic recognition technologies for humans such as fingerprinting, iris, speech, and face recognition. These recognition technologies uses unique biological information of each person. The second is automatic identification technologies for objects, such as OMR, OCR, bar-code system, and RFID(Radio Frequency IDentification).

The bar-code system is the most widely used automatic identification technology. A bar-code reader scans a bar-code data from an object's label with optical scanning. In this system, each objects should be contacted to an optical scanner, i.e. a bar-code reader. If the bar-code label of an object is contaminated, it is impossible to read the bar-code value by optical scanning. On the contrary, the

P. Thulasiraman et al. (Eds.): ISPA 2007 Workshops, LNCS 4743, pp. 245–254, 2007.

RFID system uses radio frequencies for communications between RFID readers and tags, so it is strong against surface contamination and moreover it guarantees fast identification with contactless radio frequency scanning.

These advantages have caused many researches for RFID and its applications. We're sure that RFID will be one of important technology in our ubiquitous world. However, we don't have to look on the bright side of RFID technology. It has some problems in the views of security and privacy fields. Especially, the invasion of user privacy in RFID system will be a big social problem.

In this paper, we address some privacy protection schemes and refer to Ohkubo's hash based scheme, which is a provably secure scheme for privacy protection in RFID system. And then we proposed a new scheme that preserves the almost advantages of Ohkubo's scheme and can be implemented into the RFID tag more easily than Ohkubo's.

2   Related Work

In this section, we introduce the two basic requirements for RFID privacy protection scheme, which are already introduced at other research papers [1,2,3,4,5,6]. And then we mention about two existing scheme for RFID privacy protection. The first is Ohkubo's hash-based scheme [1] and the second is Feldhofer's AES-based authentication scheme [7]. The former one guarantees user privacy effectively and offers forward security, which is an important property, but there is no scheme for supporting this property except Ohkubo's scheme and its variants. The latter one is strong against unauthenticated access to tags and it prevents to counterfeit tags. Unfortunately, both of them have some problems that make them difficult to be used for the current RFID systems.

2.1   Basic Requirements for RFID Privacy Protection Scheme

RFID Privacy problems can be categorized into two subproblems and there are two security requirements for solving them [1].

Privacy Problems

Information Leakage: RFID tag gives data to any readers. The privacy of the consumer, who has tag-embedded items, should not be guaranteed. If anyone have a RFID reader, he can acquire tag data easily and guess the owner's personality.

Traceability: If the tag always answers identical data such as unique ID, its owner's location can be traced continuously.

Security Requirements

Indistinguishability: This means that the output of the tag must be indistinguishable from truly random values and the output should be unlinkable

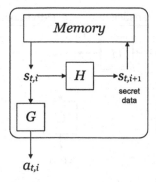

Fig. 1. Tag hardware in Ohkubo's scheme

to its own ID [1]. If the output of the tag is always indistinguishable, it guarantees the complete prevention of information leakage and the partial prevention of traceability.

Forward Security: This means that even if the adversary, who has a set of readings between tags and readers, acquires the secret data stored in the tag, he cannot find the relation to past events in which the tag was involved [1]. Because the tag can be tampered physically, this requirement is important in RFID privacy problem. This requirement guarantees the complete untraceability.

2.2 Ohkubo's Hash-Based Scheme

In Ohkubo's scheme, a tag has two one-way hash functions and these two hash functions make this scheme more secure in the view of user privacy. First one-way hash function, $h()$, refreshes tag's secret value, s_i, on every tag-reading transaction and it offers forward security to this scheme; $s_{i+1} = h(s_i)$. The other one-way hash function, $g()$, transforms tag's secret value, s_i, into tag's one-time output, a_i, on every tag-reading transaction and it offers indistinguishability to this scheme; $a_i = g(s_i)$. Eventually, a tag refreshes its secret data by itself on every transaction and the past secret values are in the same hash chain; $\{s_1, s_2, \ldots, s_i, \ldots\}$.

An attacker, who rubbed the tag, can get the current secret data, s_t, from the tag using the physical or mechanical attacking method, but he can't guess the past secret values, s_i ($i < t$), of the tag. Because the current secret value was computed by an one-way hash function, he can't computed previous values with the current values. So this scheme guarantees forward security.

Another attacker, who is listening to many tags' outputs in the restrict area, can try to distinguish one tag from the others. However, he can't do that, because all tags emit unlikable outputs made by another one-way hash functions. In other words, in order to guess a_{i+1}, he firstly have to compute s_i with output value, a_i, but one-way hash function, $g()$, makes it infeasible. Fig. 1 shows tag's hardware

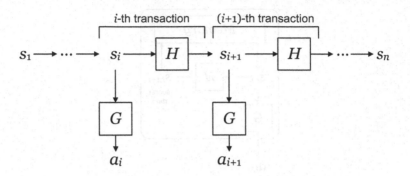

Fig. 2. Tag operation in Ohkubo's scheme

and fig. 2 shows its operation. Back-end server stores all tag's the first secret values, so it can identify a tag by comparing all tag's hash-chain values with the tag's output value.

Ohkubo's scheme are considered as the most secure scheme in the view of RFID privacy protection [3,4,5,6,8,9]. Unfortunately, this scheme has some critical problems related to its implementation. The first is that back-end server's computational complexity is very high in this scheme, so it doesn't offer server's scalability [3,4,5,6]. The second is that secure one-way hash functions, such as SHA-1, SHA-256, MD5, and MD4, can't be implemented into the current tag chip, which doesn't have enough gate logic area and doesn't have enough power for security modules [7,10].

The current tag hardware has less than 10,000 20,000 gates equivalents area and can afford less than 15 20 μA power consumption [7,10]. And it can offer only at most 5,000 gates equivalents in area and offer only a few μA in power consumption. However, SHA-256 needs at least 10,000 GEs and 15 μA to be operated on the tag [10]. It's a big problem with manufacturing tags.

2.3   Feldhofer's AES-Based Authentication Scheme

Feldhofer introduced an AES(Advanced Encryption Standard) module for RFID tag and a authentication scheme for RFID system using the AES module [7]. Originally AES was designed to be implemented in various internal architectures, such as 8-bit, 16-bit, and 32-bit architectures. Feldhofer used 8-bit internal architecture in the AES module 3, and this reduced the number of s-boxes, the die size, and mean current consumption. This module's size is about 3,400 GEs and its mean current consumption is only 8.15 μA, so it seems to be embedded into the current RFID tag such as EPC class1 generation2 tag.

Feldhofer's authentication protocol uses this AES module, so it is very secure in the view of authentication [7]. It strongly prevents information leakage, unauthorized access, and tag forgery. However, now we have to focus on invasion of

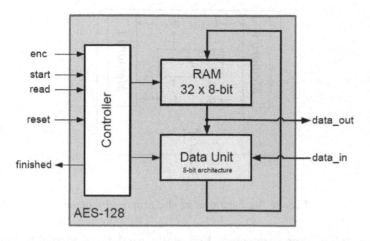

Fig. 3. The abstract diagram for Feldhofer's 8-bit architecture AES-128

user privacy. It doesn't guarantee indistinguishability and forward security, so it can't preserve customer's privacy. Because a tag in that scheme always emits unique value

3   The Proposed Scheme

In this section, we suggest a new scheme for privacy protection in RFID system. Our scheme is one of the modified version of Ohkubo's has-based scheme, but we use Feldhofer's AES module in the tag instead of one-way hash function of the original Ohkubo's scheme. Back-end server's process and reader-to-tag communication are very similar to the original Ohkubo's scheme.

3.1   RFID System and Parameters

In our scheme, RFID system consist of three main components; tag, reader, and back-end server. The RFID *tag* is embedded in an object to be identified. The tag, which has not own battery for reducing the manufacturing cost, receives a reader's query through radio signal and sends its answer to the reader using harvested energy from the electromagnetic field of the reader's radio signal. The RFID *reader* communicates several tags at the same time and identifies their identifiers or serial numbers through back-end server systems. The *back-end server* has a database and manages various types of information related to each tag. The answer of the tag is transmitted securely to the back-end server through authenticated reader and it is used to identify the tag. The back-end server must be trusted and must have the capability to process every query from a lot of readers concurrently. And we assume in our scheme that there is an authentication mechanism between the reader and the back-end server. So only legally authenticated readers can access to the back-end server.

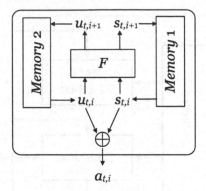

Fig. 4. Tag hardware in the proposed scheme

Now we define some parameters. Especially, we define a virtual hash function F, which is Feldhofer's AES module. It is difficult to implement one-way hash functions into the current tag hardware, so we adopted the AES module instead of one-way hash functions in Ohkubo's scheme. AES needs a key and an input data for encryption, but we provide the same value to a key and to a input data for AES encryption. Though someone knows the result cipher text, he can't guess neither the key or the input data for the result.

E : Feldhofer's AES module with 128-bit key and 128-bit block size.
F : our virtual hash function. $F(x) = E_x(x)$.
m : the number of tags.
n : the maximum length of the hash chain for each tag.
T_t : the t-th tag, which has two secret values and a virtual hash function F.
R : the reader, which communicates with B through a secure channel.
B : the back-end server, which manages a database of $(id_t, s_{t,1}, u_{t,1})$, in which $s_{t,1}$ and $u_{t,1}$ are created randomly for each tag.
id_t : the ID of tag t, where $t = 1, 2, \cdots, m$.
$s_{t,1}$: the first hash seed of tag t.
$u_{t,1}$: the second hash seed of tag t.
$s_{t,i}$: the i-th hash chain value of tag t, where $i = 1, 2, \cdots, n$.
$u_{t,i}$: the i-th hash chain value of tag t, where $i = 1, 2, \cdots, n$.

3.2   Scheme Outline

The main concerns of our scheme are in satisfying indistinguishability and forward security without one-way hash functions in the tag. We already defined a virtual function F as a substitute of a one-way hash functions, using 128-bit AES module. Fig. 4 shows the schematic diagram of our scheme's tag hardware. Our scheme's tag hardware can be implemented more easily than Ohkubo's, because we excluded one-way hash functions and we added only one more 128-bit memory for the additional secret value $u_{t,i}$.

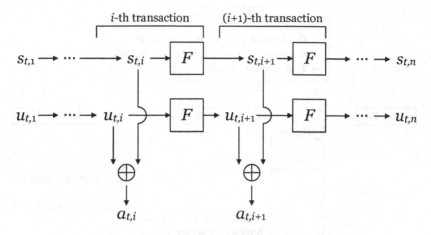

Fig. 5. Tag operation in the proposed scheme

Whenever a tag is queried by readers, the tag computes its one-time output data, $u_{t,i} \oplus u_{t,i}$ and answer to the readers. And then the tag changes its two secret data $s_{t,i}$ and $u_{t,i}$, using the virtual hash function F (fig. 5). Back-end server can find $(id_t, s_{t,1}, u_{t,1})$ by checking $a_{t,i} = F^{i-1}(s_{t,1}) \oplus F^{i-1}(u_{t,1})$, for all $1 \leq i \leq n$ and for all $1 \leq t \leq m$.

Detailed protocol:

1. Reader, R
   (a) sends a request to the tag.

2. Tag, T_t
   (a) computes $a_{t,i} = s_{t,i} \oplus u_{t,i}$.
   (b) sends $a_{t,i}$ to the reader.
   (c) refreshes its two secret data; $s_{t,i+1} = F(s_{t,i})$, $u_{t,i+1} = F(u_{t,i})$.

3. Reader, R
   (a) receives $a_{t,i}$ from T_t.
   (b) sends $a_{t,i}$ to B through a secure channel.

4. Back-end Server, B
   (a) receives $a_{t,i}$ from the authenticated R.
   (b) finds $(id_t, s_{t,1}, u_{t,1})$ by checking $a_{t,i} = F^{i-1}(s_{t,1}) \oplus F^{i-1}(u_{t,1})$,
       for all $1 \leq i \leq n$ and for all $1 \leq t \leq m$.
   (c) sends id_t to the authenticated R through a secure channel.

5. Reader, R
   (a) receives id_t of T_t from B.
   (b) offers R's specific service such as selling, check-out, and recycling.

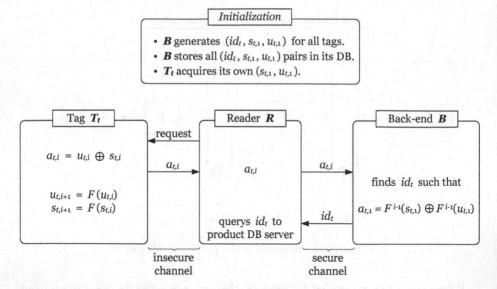

Fig. 6. The overview of the proposed scheme

4   Security Analysis

We can think two kind of attacks in our scheme. The first is eavesdropping on insecure channel between the reader and the tag. The second is physical attacking against the tag using laser-etching or so. In the case of eavesdropping, an attacker can listen $a_{t,i}$ from the tag. He will try to tracking the tag and its holder. He has to guess $a_{t,i+1}$ for tracking the tag, and he has to compute the proper $s_{t,i}$ and $u_{t,i}$ from $a_{t,i}$ for know the exact $a_{t,i+1}$. However, it is very difficult to compute the proper $s_{t,i}$ and $u_{t,i}$ from $a_{t,i}$ without any additional information. Though he has all $a_{t,j}$ ($j < i$) with other tags' outputs in his database, he can't distinguish the tag's outputs from other outputs.

In the case of physical attacking, an attacker can acquire the current secret values of the tag. He will try to know the location history of the tag and its holder. He has to compute $s_{t,i-1}$ and $u_{t,i-1}$ from $s_{t,i}$ and $u_{t,i}$ for knowing $a_{t,i-1}$. However, it is very difficult to compute the proper $s_{t,i-1}$ from $s_{t,i}$ because $s_{t,i}$ was created by AES encryption. He doesn't know this encryption's input data and key, but he just knows the fact that this encryption's input data and key have the same value. Maybe this fact will makes it easier to attack against AES cipher. However, we are sure that his cost must be much bigger than his benefits that comes from successful attacking.

5   Conclusion

Ohkubo's hash-based scheme is a good privacy protection scheme, which guarantees indistinguishability and forward security in RFID system, but it is still infeasible to embed its important module, one-way hash functions, into the current tag. On the contrary, Feldhofer designed a AES module for being embedded into the current tag and he suggested an authentication scheme that is based on his AES module. His scheme offers strong authentication mechanism, but it has privacy problems.

In this paper, we propose a new RFID privacy protection scheme that satisfies indistinguishability and forward security in the view of user privacy. The key point of our scheme is that we modified secure privacy protection scheme of Ohkubo, using Feldhofer's AES module. So our scheme can be implemented in the current tag hardware easier than Ohkubo's scheme. And our scheme satisfies the two important requirements for RFID privacy protection; indistinguishability and forward security.

Acknowledgement. This work was supported by the Korea Science & Engineering Foundation(KOSEF) grant funded by the Korea government(MOST) (No. R01-2005-000-10568-0).

References

1. Ohkubo, M., Suzuki, K., Kinoshita, S.: Cryptographic approach to "privacy-friendly" tags. In: RFID Privacy Workshop, MIT, MA, USA (November 2003)
2. Ohkubo, M., Suzuki, K., Kinoshita, S.: Efficient hash-chain based RFID privacy protection scheme. In: International Conference on Ubiquitous Computing – Ubicomp, Workshop Privacy: Current Status and Future Directions, Nottingham, England (September 2004)
3. Avoine, G., Oechslin, P.: A scalable and provably secure hash based RFID protocol. In: International Workshop on Pervasive Computing and Communication Security – PerSec 2005, Kauai Island, Hawaii, USA, pp. 110–114. IEEE Computer Society Press, Los Alamitos (2005)
4. Avoine, G.: Adversary model for radio frequency identification. Technical Report LASEC-REPORT-2005-001, Swiss Federal Institute of Technology (EPFL), Security and Cryptography Laboratory (LASEC), Lausanne, Switzerland (September 2005)
5. Avoine, G., Oechslin, P.: RFID traceability: A multilayer problem. In: Patrick, A.S., Yung, M. (eds.) FC 2005. LNCS, vol. 3570, pp. 125–140. Springer, Heidelberg (2005)
6. Yeo, S.S., Kim, S.K.: Scalable and flexible privacy protection scheme for RFID systems. In: Molva, R., Tsudik, G., Westhoff, D. (eds.) ESAS 2005. LNCS, vol. 3813, pp. 153–163. Springer, Heidelberg (2005)
7. Feldhofer, M., Dominikus, S., Wolkerstorfer, J.: Strong authentication for RFID systems using the AES algorithm. In: Joye, M., Quisquater, J.-J. (eds.) CHES 2004. LNCS, vol. 3156, pp. 357–370. Springer, Heidelberg (2004)
8. Kim, S.C., Yeo, S.S., Kim, S.K.: MARP: Mobile agent for rfid privacy protection. In: Domingo-Ferrer, J., Posegga, J., Schreckling, D. (eds.) CARDIS 2006. LNCS, vol. 3928, pp. 300–312. Springer, Heidelberg (2006)

9. Yeo, S.S., Kim, S.C., Kim, S.K.: eMARP: Enhanced mobile agent for RFID privacy protection and forgery detection. In: Nguyen, N., Grzech, A., Howlett, R., Jain, L. (eds.) First KES Symposium on Agent and Multi-Agent Systems – AMSTA 2007. LNCS, vol. 4496, pp. 318–327. Springer, Heidelberg (2007)

10. Feldhofer, M., Rechberger, C.: A case against currently used hash functions in RFID protocols. In: Printed handout of Workshop on RFID Security – RFIDSec 06 (July 2006)

Polygon-Based Similarity Aggregation for Ontology Matching

Feiyu Lin and Kurt Sandkuhl

School of Engineering, Jönköping Universiy, Gjuterigatan 5,
551 11 Jönköping, Sweden
{feiyu.lin,kurt.sandkuhl}@jth.hj.se

Abstract. Due to an increased awareness of potential ontology applications in industry, public administration and academia, a growing number of ontologies are created by different organizations and individuals. Although these ontologies are developed for various application purposes and areas, they often contain overlapping information. In this context, it is necessary to find ways to integrate various ontologies and enable use of multiple ontologies. In this paper, we extend previous work on ontology matching using polygon-based similarity aggregation. The main ideas we contribute to the research field are (1) an improved approach to aggregate the results of distance calculations between concepts in different ontologies by creating polygons for each ontology and (2) to compare the area of these polygons for deciding on similarity.

1 Introduction

Due to an increased awareness of potential ontology applications in industry, public administration and academia, a growing number of ontologies are created by different organizations and individuals. Although these ontologies are developed for various application purposes and areas, they often contain overlapping information. Furthermore, ontology users or engineers do not only use their own ontologies, but also want to integrate or adapt other ontologies, or even apply multiple ontologies. In this context, it is necessary to find ways to integrate various ontologies and enable cooperation. In this paper, we extend previous work [12] on ontology matching using polygon-based similarity aggregation.

Ontologies are considered as important contribution used to solve the data heterogeneity problem. However, ontologies themselves can also be heterogeneous [5], e.g. the ontology can be expressed in different languages, e.g. OWL [15], RDFS, OKBC, KIF, etc. Different languages use different syntax, different logical representation, different semantics of primitives and language expressivity. Even using the same ontology language does not solve heterogeneity problems. An ontology on motor-vehicles for example, may include the concept "motor-bike", whereas another ontology on the same subject may ignore it. Klein [10] categorized possible mismatches of the ontologies heterogeneity by two levels:

P. Thulasiraman et al. (Eds.): ISPA 2007 Workshops, LNCS 4743, pp. 255–264, 2007.
© Springer-Verlag Berlin Heidelberg 2007

- Language level mismatches, e.g. syntax, logical representation, semantics of primitives, language expressivity etc.
- Ontology level mismatches, e.g. conceptualization, terminological, style of modeling, encoding, etc.

As the translation between the ontologies languages can be considered as independent issue [4], it is recommendable to translate different ontologies into the same language before comparing them on ontology level. For this paper, we assume the compared ontologies are expressed in the same language, i.e. we focus on the ontology level problems.

We are proposing to use a polygon-based approach to aggregate the results of distance calculation for determining similarity on ontology level. The approach is work in progress, i.e. needs to be further evaluation in application cases.

The rest of this paper is organized as follows. In section 2, we introduce different methods that can be used to calculate distance between concepts and we discuss related work. In section 3, we describe our similarity aggregation method based on polygons. In the final section we discuss the future work about polygon similarity.

2 Similarity Computation and Related Work

There are many approaches that can be seen related to ontology matching. [4] presents a good state of the art in ontologies matching. This chapter will summarize different methods for distance calculation between subjects (2.1) and discuss selected systems for ontology marching (2.2).

2.1 Distance Calculation

Different methods can be used to calculated distance between concepts in ontologies:

- String Similarity: [2] has good survey of the different methods to calculate string distance from edit-distance like functions (e.g. Levenstein distance, Monger-Elkan distance, Jar-Winkler distance) to token-based distance functions (e.g. Jaccard similarity, TFIDF or cosine similarity, Jense-Shannon distance).
- Synonyms (with the help of dictionary or thesaurus): Synonyms can help to solve the problem of using different terms in the ontologies for the same concept. For example, an ontology might use "diagram", the other could use "graph" referring to the same meaning. The famous tool WordNet [20] can support improving the similarity measure.
- Structure Similarity: This usually is based on is-a or part-of hierarchy of the ontology in the graph. For example, if two classes' super classes and sub classes are same, we may say these two classes are same.
- Based on instances: Examples are GLUE [3] or FCA-Merge [19]. GULE uses multiple machine learners and is exploiting information in concept instances and taxonomic structure of ontologies. GULE uses a probabilistic model to combine results of different learners. FCA-Merge is a method for comparing ontologies that have a set of shared instances or a shared set of

documents annotated with concepts from source ontologies. Based on this information, FCA-Merge uses mathematical techniques from Formal Concept Analysis to produce a lattice of concepts which relates concepts from the source ontologies.

2.2 Ontologies Matching Systems

There are some ontology matching systems available using some or all above methods. Examples are

- PROMPT [14] s a semi-automatically tool and a plug-in for the open-source ontology editor PROTÉGÉ [17]. It determines string similarity and analyzes the structure of ontology. It provides guidance for the user for merging ontologies. It suggests the possible mapping and determines the conflicts in the ontology and proposes solutions for theses conflicts.
- Chimaera [1] is a tool for the Ontolingua editor. It supports merging multiple ontologies and diagnosing individual or multiple ontologies. If string matches are found, the merge is done automatically, otherwise the user is prompted for further action.
- FOAM [8] is a tool to fully or semi-automatically align two or more OWL ontologies. It is based on heuristics (similarity) of the individual entities (concepts, relations, and instances). These entities are compared using string similarity and SimSet for set comparisons.
- OLA [6] takes care of all the possible characteristics of ontologies (i.e., terminological, structural and extensional). String similarity is used to calculate the labels' similarity. The structures constraints are considered during the matching.
- ASCO [11] uses as much available information in ontology as possible (e.g. concepts, relations, structure). It applies string similarity. TF/IDF is used for calculating similarity value between descriptions of the concepts or relations. WordNet is integrated to find synonyms. Structure matching is used for modifying or asserting the similarity of two concepts or relations.
- S-MATCH [7] takes structures as input and gives semantic relationships like equivalence, more general, less general, mismatch and overlapping between the nodes of graphs as output.

3 Similarity Aggregation Based on Polygons

Based on the methods discussed in 2.1, it is possible to calculate similarity expressed by the distances between concepts of ontologies. But even if we get the concepts' distances, we need an algorithm to aggregate the results of distance calculation in order to determine similarity on ontology level. In most of the systems discussed in 2.2, aggregation of the distances is based on mean value or on weight (the sum of weights is 1). However, using mean values removes the high and low values' effect. When using weight it is difficult and decisive to set the weight value.

In [12], we present an initial approach for aggregating the results of distance calculation. The main idea of our approach is to compare similarity between objects by comparing the area of polygons corresponding to each object, i.e. if polygons have exactly the same area, similarity between the two objects represented by the polygons is maximal. An object in this context is a class within an OWL-ontology including subclasses, properties and individuals. If we want to calculate the similarity of different objects, we also need to take into account the similarity of properties, subclasses and individuals. The creation of the polygon is based on a coordinate system with one half-axis for each attribute (i.e. property or individual) of the object. The initial approach has known shortcomings, like skipping nodes with no similarity when creating the polygons. For example, if two ontologies have many attributes without any similarity but three or four attributes with 100% match, the similarity between these two ontologies will be 100% if we just skip attributes which have no similarity. To solve this problem, we modify the initial approach and introduce the use of a circle to create the polygons.

3.1 Example Ontologies

Two onotlogies Biblio.owl and BibTex.owl which are developed in Maponto [13] project are chosen as our examples. Biblio ontology is a bibliographic ontology based on FRBI [16]. It has 12 classes, 37 object properties and 64 data type properties in Biblio ontology. BibTex ontology is a bibliographic ontology based on the bibTeX record. It has 43 classes, 22 object properties and 24 data type properties. Both ontologies have no instances.

For example, both ontologies have the class "Agent" (see Figure 1 and Figure 2). The subclasses are connected directly in the figures (e.g. Person and Corporate_Body). The domain and range of the relationships (either object or datatype properties) are connected by arrows.

The "Agent" concepts' similarity is considered on two levels. The first level includes subclasses and relationships. The first level for the Biblio ontology includes 14 concepts: Person, Corporate_Body, Manifestation, manufacturer, publicsher, distributor, isProducedBy, responsibility, Work, isCreatedBy, Expression, isRealizedBy, Item, isOwnedBy. There are 7 concepts in BibTex on this first level: Person, Corporate_Body, Location, hasAddress, Work, hasCreator, publication.

The second level is the subclasses' subclasses and relationships. The second level for Biblio ontology has two parts. Person's part includes: string, firstName, designation, LastName, bop, dod, dob. Corporate_Body's part includes: Event, event, string, numberDesignation, uniformName. In the same way, we get two parts on second level for the BibTex ontology.

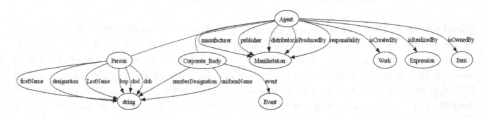

Fig. 1. Agent in Biblio Ontology

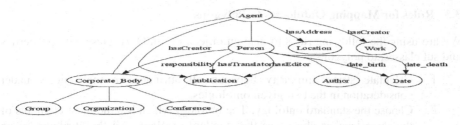

Fig. 2. Agent in BibTex Ontology

3.2 String Similarity Calculation

Comparison of strings is a much issued topic in the field of ontology research. Many ways of comparing strings can be used, and the efficiency and accurateness of the result depends on the situation and the parties involved.

SecondString [18] is an open-source package of string matching methods based on the java language. These methods follow a big range of approaches and have been designed according to different criteria and perspectives, such as statistics, artificial intelligence, information retrieval, and databases. Based on the string similarity methods comparison result in [9], Slim TFIDF string-distance method is the most appropriate method for our approach.

3.2.1 Example Ontologies String Similarity Result

After calculating Slim TFIDF string-distance using SecondString tool with threshold 0.72, we get the results shown in Table 2 for the example ontologies presented in section 3.1. Table 1 shows some strings similarities scores that are under 0.72, we can find that they are not accurate. The scores under 0.72 will not be used. In this example, the string similarity just can be found in the first level.

Table 1. String distance under 0.72

Similarity	Biblio	BibTex
0.70	isRealizedBy	hasAddress
0.67	uniformName	Conference
0.50	designation	date_death

Table 2. String distance in the ontologies

Similarity	Biblio	BibTex
1.0	Person	Person
1.0	Corporate_Body	Corporate_Body
1.0	Work	Work
0.73	publisher	publication
0.72	isCreatedBy	hasCreator
0.72	Manifestation	Location

3.3 Rules for Mapping Ontologies to Polygons

We are using the following rules to map an object, i.e. an OWL class with properties and subclasses, to polygons:

1. Calculate string similarity between all attributes of the objects under consideration in the two given ontologies.
2. Choose the standard ontology. The ontology which has the most elements of the same level is chosen as the standard ontology. All the attributes of an object of the standard ontology, i.e. class properties and individuals, are marked as 1 unit when creating the polygon. In the following, the string distances are mapped to polygons as unit. For example, since the first level of Biblio has 14 elements, it is chosen as the standard ontology.
3. Use circle's radiuses to present the similarities' objects' attributes. The circle is divided the number of similarity's elements. The points are added clockwise. For example, from the Table 2 we know that there are six elements similarity between Biblio and BibTex in the first level, every 60° has one radius. The polygon of Biblio is constructed as Figure 3. In the same way, 6 points are added clockwise every 60° with string distance unit (see Table 2 and Figure 4). The polygon is constructed by connecting the points created. When similarity is 0, this node is not taken into account when connecting the points.

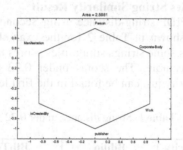

Fig. 3. Polygon for Similarity Elements in Biblio

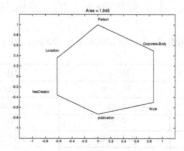

Fig. 4. Polygon for Similarity Elements in BibTex

4. Calculate similarity elements weight based on circle. The circle is divided in equal parts by the number of ontology's elements in the same level. For example, there are 14 elements in the first level of Biblio. Fourteen points are added every 25.71° (see Figure 5). Six points are connected as present 6 similarity elements (see Figure 5). In the same way, 7 points are added every 51.43° for BibTex. Six points with string distance unit are connected every 51.43° (see Table 2 and Figure 6).

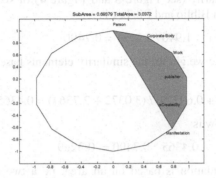

Fig. 5. Polygon of Agent in Biblio

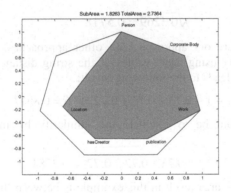

Fig. 6. Polygon of Agent in BibTex

5. If the objects' attribute has sub-attributes, introduce a new polygon based on current radius (current value divided by 2). Since there are no second level similarities in our examples, we will not illustrate here.

3.4 Calculation of Ontologies' Similarity

The area of polygon for Biblio is 2.5981 (see Figure 3). The area of polygon for BibTex is 1.946 (see Figure 4).

According to our definition of polygon similarity and the rules presented for creating the polygons, we now need to relate the areas of the polygons created for Biblio and BibTex to each other. We propose to calculate the area similarity by dividing the sum of the areas of all polygons related to standard ontologies by the sum of the areas of all polygons related to non-standard ontologies.

$$SimOnto(a,b) = \frac{\sum_{i=1}^{n} NonS\tan dardArea(i)}{\sum_{i=1}^{n} S\tan dardArea(i)} \qquad (1)$$

Thus, the area similarity (see Figure 3 and Figure 4) of six similarity elements of concept Agent between Biblio and BibTex is:

$$1.946 / 2.5981 = 0.7490 \qquad (2)$$

Now we calculate the weight for the similarity elements based on results of Figure 5 and Figure 6:

$$(1.8263 + 0.69379) / (3.0372 + 2.7364) = 0.4365 \qquad (3)$$

So, the similarity now is:

$$0.4365 * 0.7490 = 0.3269 \qquad (4)$$

Since the area calculation is based on an area, i.e a two dimensional geometric figure, we should transform it to an expression reflecting just one dimension. The similarity of Agent between Biblio and BibTex then would be:

$$\sqrt{0.3269} = 0.5718 \qquad (5)$$

In order to compare our approach with other approaches, we can for example calculate the similarity using mean values of the string distances or multiplying the string distances. This leads to the following result:

$$(1 + 1 + 1 + 0.73 + 0.72 + 0.72\ ) / 6 = 0.8617 \qquad (6)$$

Another way would be to calculate the similarity by multiplying the string distances:

$$1 * 1 * 1 * 0.73 * 0.72 * 0.72\ = 0.3784 \qquad (7)$$

We can see that the area result in this example is between the mean value and the multiplication value. Using mean value removes the high and low values' effect. Using multiplication zooms out the low values' effect.

4   Summary and Future Work

This paper presented an approach for calculating similarity between objects and their different attributes based on polygons. By using this approach for evaluating similarity between different concepts in an ontology including their properties, this approach can be considered as one element for performing ontology matching. It is not intended or expected to substitute other elements of ontology matching, like structural comparison, but to contribute to improving the accuracy of the matching.

The approach presented is still under development, i.e. the paper presents work in progress. Currently, a number of advantages and several shortcomings can be identified. Since objects can have many attributes, we consider polygons as suitable to represent these attributes.

- It is relatively easy to add or remove attributes in the polygon.
- It is a natural way to estimate object similarity by using shapes.
- It is easy to calculate similarity between polygons.

But there are still some problems which need to be solved in future work:

- How to add weights to the polygons reflecting the importance of attributes?
- How to combine our approach with other ontology matching methods, like synonyms, instance matching, structure matching, etc.
- Use of an alternative method to calculate polygon similarity instead of area. Currently, polygons with the same area have maximal similarity, even if they in reality are not identical.

The above problems will be investigated in future work. Furthermore, this approach is partly implemented and it will be evaluated in the applications.

Acknowledgment. Part of this work was financed by the Hamrin Foundation (Hamrin Stiftelsen), project Media Information Logistics.

References

1. Chimera: http://www.ksl.stanford.edu/software/chimaera/
2. Cohen, W.W., Ravikumar, P., Fienberg, S.E.: A Comparison of String Distance Metrics for Name-Matching Tasks IJCAI-2003 (2003)
3. Doan, A., Madhavan, J., Dhamankar, R., Domingos, P., Halevy, A.: Learning to match ontologies on the Semantic Web. The VLDB Journal 12(4), 303–319
4. Euzenat, J., Bach, T.L., Barrasa, J., Bouquet, P., Bo, J.D., Dieng, R., Ehrig, M., Hauswirth, M., Jarrar, M., Lara, R., Maynard, D., Napoli, A., Stamou, G., Stuckenschmidt, H., Shvaiko, P., Tessaris, S., Acker, S.V., Zaihrayeu, I.: State of the art on ontology alignment. NoE Knowledge Web project deliverable (2004)
5. Euzenat, J., Castro, R.G., Ehrig, M.: D2.2.2: Specification of a benchmarking methodology for alignment techniques. NoE Knowledge Web project deliverable (2004)
6. Euzenat Jr., Valtchev, P.: Similarity-based ontology alignment in OWL-lite. In: Proc. 15th ECAI, Valencia (ES) (2004)
7. Fausto, G., Pavel, S., Mikalai, Y.: S-Match: an algorithm and an implementation of semantic matching (2004)
8. Foam: http://www.aifb.uni-karlsruhe.de/WBS/meh/foam/
9. Güemes, A.H.: A Prototype System for Automatic Ontology Matching Using Polygons. In: Computer and Electrical Engineering, Jönköping University (2006)
10. Klein, M.: Combining and relating ontologies: an analysis of problems and solutions. In: Gomez-Perez, A., Heiner, M.G.a., StuckenschmidtandUschold, M. (eds.) Workshop on Ontologies and Information Sharing, IJCAI'01, Seattle, USA (2001)

11. Le, B.T., Dieng-Kuntz, R., Gandon, F.: Ontology Matching: A Machine Learning Approach for building a corporate semantic web in a multi-communities organization. In: ICEIS 2004, Porto, Portugal (2004)
12. Lin, F., Sandkuhl, K.: Towards Polygon-based Similarity Aggregation in Ontology Matching. In: 3rd International Conference on Web Information Systems and Technologies (WEBIST07), Barcelona, Spain (2007)
13. Maponto: http://www.cs.toronto.edu/semanticweb/maponto/
14. Noy, N.F., Musen, M.A.: The PROMPT Suite: Interactive Tools for Ontology Merging and Mapping. In: SMI (ed.) Stanford University, CA, USA (2003)
15. Owl: http://www.w3.org/TR/owl-features/
16. Plassard, M.-F.: Functional Requirements for Bibliographic Records (1998)
17. Protégé: http://protege.stanford.edu/
18. SecondString, http://secondstring.sourceforge.net/
19. Stumme, G., Maedche, A.: FCA-Merge: Bottom-up merging of ontologies. In: 7th Intl. Conf. on Artificial Intelligence (IJCAI '01), Seattle, WA (2001)
20. WordNet: http://wordnet.princeton.edu

A User-Controlled VoiceXML Application Based on Dynamic Voice Anchor and Node

Hyeong-Joon Kwon and Kwang-Seok Hong

School of Information and Communication Engineering, Sungkyunkwan University, 300,
Chunchun-dong, Jangan-gu, Suwon, Kyungki-do, 440-746, Korea
katsyuki@skku.edu, kshong@yurim.skku.ac.kr
http://hci.skku.ac.kr

Abstract. VoiceXML is new markup language which is designed for web resource navigation via voice based on XML. An application using VoiceXML is classified into computer-directed and mixed-initiative form dialog structure. Such dialog structures can't construct services which provide free navigation of web resource by user because a scenario is decided by application developer. In this paper, we propose VoiceXML application structure using user-controlled form dialog system which decides a service scenario according to user's intention. The proposed application automatically detects recognition candidates from requested information by user, and then system uses recognition candidate as voice-anchor. Also, system connects each voice-anchor with new voice-node. An example of proposed system, we implement news service with IT term dictionary, and we confirm detection and registration of voice-anchor and make an estimate of hit rate about measurement of a successive offer from information according to user's intention and response speed. As the experiment result, we confirmed possibility which is more freely navigation of web resource than existing VoiceXML form dialog systems.

1 Introduction

In 2000, the VoiceXML Forum released VoiceXML 1.0 to the public. Shortly thereafter, VoiceXML 1.0 was submitted to the World Wide Web Consortium (W3C) as the basis for the creation of a new international standard [1]. VoiceXML 2.0 is the result of this work based on input from W3C member companies, other W3C Working Groups, and the public [1].

VoiceXML restricts input from the user to a set of predefined phrases called the grammar. This grammar is usually a simple list of words specified in the VoiceXML document by the developer of the VoiceXML application. To provide navigation, the developer of the VoiceXML document divides the document into a number of forms, gives a name to each of the forms, and then prompts the user (through a set of menus) at the end of the document is always controlled by the page author. If the developer or writer of the VoiceXML document fails to anticipate the interaction scenario the user or listener desires, then this interaction pattern is left unspecified in the document, depriving the listener of that particular interaction. These problems are exacerbated by

P. Thulasiraman et al. (Eds.): ISPA 2007 Workshops, LNCS 4743, pp. 265–272, 2007.

the fact that, unlike visual navigation, aural navigation is necessarily linear in nature. Note that a grammar (really a list of words) in a VoiceXML document specifies all the words that the listener may possibly speak while giving input to the VoiceXML application. Any word spoken outside of this grammar will not be recognized. This is because current voice recognition technology cannot recognize an arbitrary utterance from an arbitrary user. In an existing paper, the authors articulated the shortcomings of VoiceXML that prevent listeners from having complete control over navigation of audio-based documents. They developed the concept of a voice-anchor, namely, audio labels that a user can associate with the forms of a VoiceXML document. The user can then access these labeled forms at will by simply recalling the anchor name [2]. In this paper, we propose a new and unique (or more intellectual) system for a user's resource navigation. It is a User-Controlled application for more free resource navigation and for making a scenario based on a user's intention. Current major services using VoiceXML are comparatively simple, such as an Automatic Response System (ARS) for a call center and a small-scale voice portal. This is because the structure of an application using only the form dialog of VoiceXML is a one-sided flow of a scenario. The system we propose which applies a voice-anchor and voice-node is similar to the anchor and node structure of hypertext and hypermedia. The proposed system is similar to the resource navigation method of a visual environment. It can offer to the user a new type of service via a user's voice. Some examples are an intellectual word dictionary, a user-oriented e-commerce ordering service, and voice news with an included constrained vocabulary dictionary.

The structure of this paper is as follows. In Section 2, we explain a Form Interpretation Algorithm and the existing primary structure of VoiceXML together they form the dialog architecture. Then, we also discuss related existing research and the limitations of the VoiceXML Form Dialog. In Section 3, we propose a new application structure that uses either the Common Gateway Interface (CGI) or a Server-Side Script for proposed application structure. We, then, discuss a proposed system and the results of an experiment using this system in Section 4. Finally, we conclude in Section 5.

2 Existing VoiceXML Form Dialog

A VoiceXML document consists of a set of dialogs that are reiterations of possible interactions between a user's answers and the questions provided by the system's application developers. In this section, we explain how the system decides on a sequence for processing of the application and then we will discuss those limitations.

2.1 Existing Form Dialogs

The structure of the VoiceXML application is classified into a Computer-Directed Form Dialog or a Mixed-Initiative Form Dialog that changes some flow of a scenario based on user input. When a user uses a service based on VoiceXML, the system running the VoiceXML application and user will talk via voice that is the most effective interaction among people. But, these forms are not like talking with another person as they request a user to speak in a particular order unilaterally or user inputs the order. Figure 1 shows different flows of a scenario for a Computer-Directed Form Dialog and a Mixed-Initiative Form Dialog [3], [4].

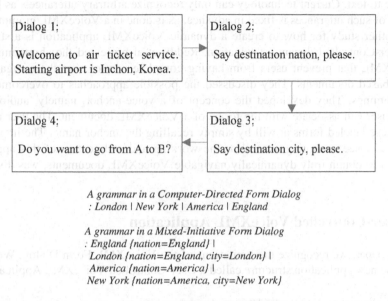

A grammar in a Computer-Directed Form Dialog
: London | New York | America | England

A grammar in a Mixed-Initiative Form Dialog
: England {nation=England} |
  London {nation=England, city=London} |
  America {nation=America} |
  New York {nation=America, city=New York}

Fig. 1. An example of existing VoiceXML application and grammar descriptions

Figure 1(a) may not apply in a complex application because applying this simple flow would always result in a tedious repeat of questions and answers. It can be only used in a simply application such as with a help desk. However, if the author of a VoiceXML document makes full use of the Form Dialog of Figure 1(b), the application can appear more intelligent and flexible. For example, in Figure 1(b), when users are speaking London or New York, (a certain city) the application would not then request a nation for the destination as the user already input a destination which implicitly specified the nation. Then the user can go on and reserve an air ticket. For development of a complex application, the Mixed-Initiative Form Dialog is more useful than the Computer-Directed Form Dialog. It is difficult to develop dynamic and intelligent appearing applications by creating only pure VoiceXML documents.

For this reason, VoiceXML is using for construction of a call-center or Automatic Response System (ARS). So, we propose user-controlled application using dynamic grammar. For dynamic applications, the developer of the application can get access to a database using CGI or a Server-Side Script. The developer can construct a proper grammar. A more detailed explanation of all of this is in Sections 2.2 and 3.

2.2 Related Research for Alleviating the Limits of VoiceXML

Current VoiceXML design does not support dynamic voice anchors or markers. Allowing a user defined voice-anchor requires supporting grammars in VoiceXML documents that are defined at runtime, i.e., at the time the document is served. It also requires modifications to VoiceXML browsers so that they support such dynamic grammars. As mentioned earlier, current voice recognition technology cannot recognize a seemingly arbitrary utterance spoken by an arbitrary user and convert this utterance to text. Current technology can only recognize arbitrary utterances, as long as the set of such utterances is fixed in advance, as is done in a VoiceXML grammar [2].

Another study for how to create a dynamic VoiceXML application is a study on Listener-Controlled dynamic navigation. Reddy et al presented the shortcomings of VoiceXML that prevent users from having complete control over the navigation of audio-based documents. They discussed the possible approaches to overcome these shortcomings. They developed the concept of a voice-anchor, namely, audio labels that a user can associate with the forms of a VoiceXML document. The user can access these labeled forms at will by simply recalling the anchor name. The implementation of voice anchoring as well as the working and architecture of this approach, adopted to obtain truly dynamically navigable VoiceXML documents, was discussed in [2].

3   User-Controlled VoiceXML Application

In this paper, we recognize the limitations of the VoiceXML Form Dialog. We, then, propose new application structure called a User-Controlled VoiceXML Application.

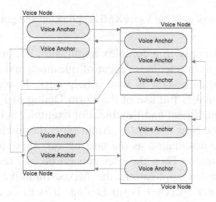

Fig. 2. The voice-anchor and voice-node structure

The proposed system can detect a recognition candidate automatically in contents that it will then provide to the user for the user's consideration and later use. Also, the system makes an entry for the detected recognition candidate in the grammar using CGI or a Server-Side Script. The structure of applications using this approach is similar to Figure 2. Figure 2 show a partial cross section of the proposed system. The voice-node is one of the contents that will be provided to a user. Also, this system includes voice-anchors that will be detected and registered by this particular processing. For detecting and registration of the recognition candidate, we use a dual method:

1) The Regular-Expression is used for detecting specific words, mostly nouns in this system. Figure 3 shows recognition from any string. Some of the detected words are voice-anchors that will link voice-nodes [6]. This method needs to be used in recognizing Korean or another language which has a similar construction as Korean. The biggest different thing between Korean and English is the word order. We normally put the verb in the end of the sentence. But for English is located in the middle or after subject. That is the example for the difference. In this paper, we use Regular-Expression with other feature of Korean. It is postposition. Korean postposition is equal to English preposition from meaning point of view. But, in Korean, the postposition is sticking to end of noun. We delete the postposition for detection of noun as voice-anchor after tokenizing an inputting sentence with space. A case of English, this process is not necessary.

Inputting Sentence :
진보의 크기는 그것이 요구하는 희생의 크기에 의하여 평가되는 것이다.
[jinboeui keugineun geugeoti yoguhaneun huisaengeui keukie euihayeo pyenggadoeneun geotida]

Deleted Pattern by Proposed System :
-는 [-neun], -에 [-e], -의 [-eui], -하는 [-haneun], -을 [-eul], -되는 [-doeneun]

Output Words :
진보, 크기, 그것이, 요구, 희생, 크기, 의하여, 평가, 것이다.
[jinbo], [keugi], [geugeoti], [yogu], [huisaeng], [keugi], [euihayeo], [pyengga], [geotida]

Fig. 3. An example of a Regular-Expression using an Active Server Pages (for Korean)

2) The Iterator Pattern of a Design Pattern was proposed by the four authors of often referred to as the gang of four (GoF) [7]. This method compares each detected word with a beforehand identified keyword that is in the database. Then, if the compared result is the same, the system adds the words to the grammar. The structure of this application structure is similar to the structure of hypertext and hypermedia. Namely, when a user navigates an application that uses this system, a user experiences similarity to a visual environment.

Taken altogether, the proposed system properly integrates two systems

1) It is a type of traditional system that an application developer has added a recognition candidate.
2) This system detects and adds recognition candidates from content which then can be provided to the user for the sake of being user-oriented. For effective control of the integrated system, we use a hook-up module.

The hook-up module is the effective integration of two systems in a dynamic grammar. The traditional system takes charge of the flow control of the system. The current proposed system serves, in fact, as a help for a user's navigation through the system. In other words, this module decides whether the recognition candidate is added by a developer or detected and added by the system. Subsequently, it decides a process sequence for the system.

4   Experiments and Performance Evaluation

For verification of the proposed system, we have developed a VoiceXML application using this system, a news service that includes an IT term dictionary. We, then, experimented using the application with 10 people in a general office. In this project, we used a VoiceXML server solution called the "Huvois Solution" from the KT Corporation and an IIS Web server from Microsoft. We, then, confirmed that the system, via Internet Explorer, detected and registered recognition candidates from contents automatically as shown in Figure 4.

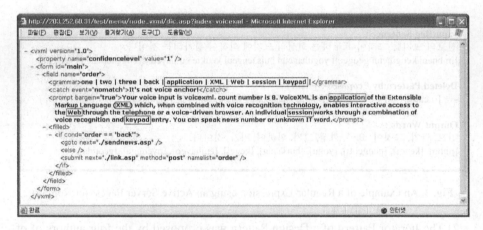

Fig. 4. Confirmation of the registered recognition candidates

As a result, the proposed system could detect and register a voice-anchor from contents that were requested from users. Also, we measured a hit rate for an estimate of whether a user got needed information successfully. This hit rate is indicated in Table 1. Improving the hit rate involves developing an application with effective Regular Expressions, much detection of voice-anchors, and based on sufficient construction of the database. In the next experiments, Testees designated as testee (A1, A2, ...) were people who were experienced using a voice-enabled service; testees designated as testee (B1, B2, ...) were not experienced using a voice-enabled service. If voice-enabled service continues to be popularized, related research is needed to resolve the deficiencies relating to people's lack of experience when using this kind of system.

When the proposed system processes and with provision of enterprise-class contents, we confirmed the response time and recognition rate as shown Table 2. In spite of the system's processing of several strings of data, by and large, there were some good results.

Table 1. Measurement results of the hit rate

Testee	Hit Count	Hit Rate (%)
A1	17 / 20	85
A2	16 / 20	80
A3	19 / 20	95
A4	18 / 20	90
A5	16 / 20	80
B1	17 / 20	85
B2	15 / 20	75
B3	16 / 20	80
B4	17 / 20	85
B5	18 / 20	90
Total 10 people	Total 169 / 200	Average 84.5

Table 2. Measurement result recognition rates and response times

Testee	Count	Recognition Rate (%)	Response Time (Maximum)
A1	18 / 20	90	1.3 sec
A2	19 / 20	95	1.0 sec
A3	18 / 20	90	1.2 sec
A4	20 / 20	100	1.2 sec
A5	18 / 20	90	1.0 sec
B1	16 / 20	80	1.0 sec
B2	13 / 20	65	1.2 sec
B3	14 / 20	70	1.1 sec
B4	13 / 20	65	1.2 sec
B5	12 / 20	60	1.1 sec
Total 10 people	Total 161 / 200	Average 80.5 %	Average 1.13 sec

5 Conclusions

In this paper, we proposed a new idea for implementing a user's resource navigation in voice recognition systems. It is called a User-Controlled application. It provides for more free resource navigation. It constructs a scenario for subsequent usage based on a user's intention. For a design and implementation of the system, we used a Regular-Expression (Korean). Also, we made use of the Iterator Pattern in the Gang of Four (GOF)'s design pattern. The proposed system may affect the future of studies dealing with the interaction between humans and computers. If any system can reflect a user's mind, users will call it more useful and feel that it is a more intelligent system than most of the existing systems that act very mechanically. We now could embody a series of applications using this paradigm via this study. However, the proposed system did not what match we want. Accordingly, we will continue our work on developing more effective intelligent systems.

Acknowledgment

This research was supported by MIC, Korea under ITRC IITA-2006-(C1090-0603-0046).

References

1. McGlashan, S., Burnett, D.C., Carter, J., Danielsen, P., Ferrans, J., Hunt, A., Lucas, B., Porter, B., Rehor, K., Tryphonas, S.: Voice Extensible Markup Language Version 2.0 Specification (2004), http://www.w3c.org/TR/voicexml20
2. Reddy, H., Annamalai, N., Gupta, G.: Listener-Controlled Dynamic Navigation of VoiceXML Documents. In: Miesenberger, K., Klaus, J., Zagler, W., Burger, D. (eds.) ICCHP 2004. LNCS, vol. 3118, pp. 347–354. Springer, Heidelberg (2004)
3. Miller, M.: VoiceXML. Wiley Publishing INC, Chichester (2002)
4. Park, S.: VoiceXML for Voice Web Application Construction. Hanbit Media (2001)
5. Vankayala, R.R., Shi, H.: Dynamic Voice User Interface Using VoiceXML and Active Server Pages. In: Zhou, X., Li, J., Shen, H.T., Kitsuregawa, M., Zhang, Y. (eds.) APWeb 2006. LNCS, vol. 3841, pp. 1181–1184. Springer, Heidelberg (2006)
6. Friedl, J.E.F.: Mastering Regular Expressions, 3rd edn., O'Reilly (2006)
7. Gamma, E., Helm, R., Jhonson, R., Vissides, J.: Design Patterns. Addison-Wesly Publishing Co, London, UK (1995)
8. Gonzalez-Ferreras, C., Cardenoso-Payo, V.: Building Voice Applications from Web Content. In: Sojka, P., Kopeček, I., Pala, K. (eds.) TSD 2004. LNCS (LNAI), vol. 3206, pp. 587–594. Springer, Heidelberg (2004)
9. Shin, J.-H., Hong, K.-S., Eom, S.-K.: Implementation of New CTI Service Platform Using Voice XML. In: Laganà, A., Gavrilova, M., Kumar, V., Mun, Y., Tan, C.J.K., Gervasi, O. (eds.) ICCSA 2004. LNCS, vol. 3046, pp. 754–762. Springer, Heidelberg (2004)
10. Chugh, J., Jagannathan, V.: Voice-Enabling Enterprise Applications. In: Proceeding of the Eleventh IEEE International Workshops on Enabling Technologies: WETICE'02, pp. 188–189. IEEE Computer Society Press, Los Alamitos (2002)

Grid Computing in New York State, USA

Jonathan J. Bednasz[1], Steven M. Gallo[1], Russ Miller[2,3], Catherine L. Ruby[2], and Charles M. Weeks[3]

[1] Center for Computational Research, SUNY-Buffalo, Buffalo, NY USA 14203
[2] Dept of Computer Science & Engineering, SUNY-Buffalo, Buffalo, NY USA 14260
[3] Hauptman-Woodward Medical Research Inst, 700 Ellicott Street, Buffalo, NY USA 14203

Abstract. We have designed and deployed the New York State Grid (NYS Grid), which consists of an integrated computational and data grid. NYS Grid is used in a ubiquitous fashion, where the users have virtual access to their data sets and applications, allowing the user to perform tasks without knowledge of the physical hosts for data storage or compute systems. A wide variety of applications have been ported to NYS Grid, including critical programs in a variety of fields that are ideally suited to a multiprocessor computing environment with distributed datasets. Two applications from structural biology are presented as exemplars, including our Grid portal version of the *SnB* program, which has been run simultaneously on all computational resources on NYS Grid, as well as on the majority of the tens of thousands of processors available through the Open Science Grid. This paper also discusses previous grids that we developed, including the Buffalo-based (ACDC) experimental grid and the Western New York Grid, as well as a wide variety of advances that we have made in terms of grid monitoring, predictive scheduling, grid portal design, and grid-enabling application templates, to name a few.

1 Introduction

The Grid is a rapidly emerging and expanding technology that allows geographically-distributed and independently-operated resources to be linked together in a transparent fashion [2, 4]. These resources include CPU cycles, data storage systems, sensors, visualization devices, and a wide variety of Internet-ready instruments. The power of both computational grids (*i.e.*, seamlessly connecting compute systems and their local storage) and data grids (*i.e.*, seamlessly connecting large storage systems) lie not only in the aggregate computing power and data storage, but also on its ease of use. Numerous government-sponsored reports state that grid computing is a key to 21st century discovery by providing seamless access to the high-end computational infrastructure required for revolutionary advances in contemporary science and engineering.

Numerous grid projects have been initiated, including GriPhyN, PPDG, EGEE, EU DataGrid, Open Science Grid, TeraGrid, NASA's Information Power Grid (IPG), and iVDGL, to name a few. However, the construction of a production-quality, heterogeneous, general-purpose grid is in its infancy since a grid requires coordinated resource sharing and problem solving in a dynamic, multi-institutional scenario using standard, open, general-purpose protocols and interfaces that deliver a high quality of service.

P. Thulasiraman et al. (Eds.): ISPA 2007 Workshops, LNCS 4743, pp. 273–284, 2007.
© Springer-Verlag Berlin Heidelberg 2007

The immediate focus of grid deployment continues to be on the difficult issue of developing high-quality middleware (www.nsf-middleware.org/).

As Grid computing initiatives move forward, issues of interoperability, security, performance, management, and privacy need to be carefully considered. In fact, security is concerned with various issues relating to authentication in order to insure application and data integrity. Grid initiatives are also generating best practice scheduling and resource management documents, protocols, and API specifications to enable interoperability. Several layers of security, data encryption, and certificate authorities already exist in grid-enabling toolkits such as Globus Toolkit.

2 New York State Grid: Overview, Middleware, Portal, Monitor

The *New York State Grid* (*NYS Grid*) was designed and deployed by the SUNY-Buffalo Cyberinfrastructure Laboratory (www.cse.buffalo.edu/faculty/miller/CI/), in collaboration with the SUNY-Buffalo Center for Computational Research, following extensive efforts in developing a Buffalo-based grid (ACDC-Grid) and a Western New York Grid (WNY Grid). NYS Grid includes resources from institutions throughout New York State[1] and is available in a simple and seamless fashion to users worldwide. NYS Grid contains a heterogeneous set of resources and utilizes general-purpose IP networks [8-11]. A major feature of this grid is that it integrates a computational grid (compute clusters that have the ability to cooperate in serving the user) with a data grid (storage devices that are similarly available to the user) so that the user may deploy computationally intensive applications that read or write large volumes of data files in a very simple fashion. In particular, NYS Grid was designed so that the user does not need to know where data files are physically stored or where the application is physically deployed, while providing the user with easy access to their files in terms of uploading, downloading, editing, viewing, and so on. Of course, a user who wishes to more closely manage where the data is stored and where the applications are run also has the option to retain such control.

The core infrastructure for NYS Grid includes the installation of standard grid middleware and the use of an active Web portal for deploying applications. Several key packages were used in the implementation of NYS Grid and other packages have been identified in order to allow for the anticipated expansion of the system. The Globus Toolkit provides APIs and tools using the Java SDK to simplify the development of OGSI-compliant services and clients. It supplies database services and Monitoring & Discovery System index services implemented in Java, GRAM service implemented in C with a Java wrapper, GridFTP services implemented in C, and a full set of Globus Toolkit components. The recently proposed Web Service-Resource Framework provides the concepts and interfaces developed by the OGSI specification exploiting the Web services architecture.

NYS Grid represents the current Grid in an evolution that included an experimental Buffalo-based grid involving a variety of independently run organizations at SUNY-Buffalo and other local institutions, as well as a persistent and hardened

---

[1] Current institutions on the NYS Grid include Columbia, the Hauptman-Woodward Institute, Marist College, NYU, SUNY-Binghamton, SUNY-Buffalo, SUNY-Geneseo, SUNY-Stony Brook, Niagara University, RIT, Syracuse University, and the University of Rochester.

heterogeneous[2] Western New York Grid that includes Niagara University, Geneseo State College, the Hauptman-Woodward Medical Research Institute, and SUNY-Buffalo. NYS Grid supports a variety of applications of interest to its user base. In addition, NYS Grid serves as a gateway for the user to the Open Science Grid, Tera-Grid, MCEER and NEES, to name a few.

In the early 2000's, Miller's Cyberinfrastructure Laboratory began to design an integrated computational and data grid that would provide disciplinary scientists with an easy to use extension of their desktops in order to enable breakthrough science and engineering. The Cyberinfrastructure Laboratory partnered with the Center for Computational Research, during Miller's tenure as founding Director, and other organizations in the Buffalo area to create a prototype grid. This prototype grid, which was referred to as the ACDC-Grid (Advanced Computational Data Center Grid), provided a platform for the Cyberinfrastructure Laboratory to experiment with critical packages, such as Globus and Condor, and to begin to work with critical worldwide organizations, such as the Open Science Grid.

However, the most important aspect of this prototype grid was that it provided a platform upon which members of the Cyberinfrastructure Laboratory could develop middleware that was deemed critical to the deployment of a transparent and integrated computational, data, and applications oriented grid.

A key project was the development of a Grid Portal [8,11,16]. While it is true that Globus and other packages provide a variety of avenues for command-line submission to a Grid, most require that the user be logged into a system upon which the appropriate package (e.g., Globus or Condor) has been installed. The approach of the Cyberinfrastructure Laboratory was to provide critical middleware that was accessible to users worldwide, regardless of whether or not they had easy access to machines upon which such packages were installed and supported. Note that in the early 2000s, trying to keep up with the rapidly changing versions of such packages was a nontrivial and fairly time-consuming task.

The New York State Grid Portal was derived from the ACDC-Grid Portal and can be found at http://grid.ccr.buffalo.edu/. This portal currently provides access to a dozen or so popular compute-intensive software packages, large data storage devices, and the ability to submit applications to a variety of grids containing tens of thousands of processors. Our Grid Portal integrates several software packages and toolkits in order to produce a robust system that can be used to host a wide variety of scientific and engineering applications. Specifically, as shown in Figure 1, our portal is constructed using dynamically generated HTML, JavaScript, and the PHP scripting language and is served by the Apache HTTP server with a MySQL database used for persistent data storage. Several other tools are also utilized including PHPMyAdmin, MDS/GRIS/GIIS from the Globus Toolkit, OpenLDAP, WSDL, and related open source software.

Our Grid Portal provides a single-point of access to NYS Grid for those users who want to concentrate on their disciplinary research and scholarship and do not want to be burdened with low-level details of utilizing a Grid. Applications are typically

---

[2] Equipment on the Western New York Grid includes one or more significant Sun Microsystems clusters, Apple Clusters, and Dell Clusters, in addition to a variety of storage systems.

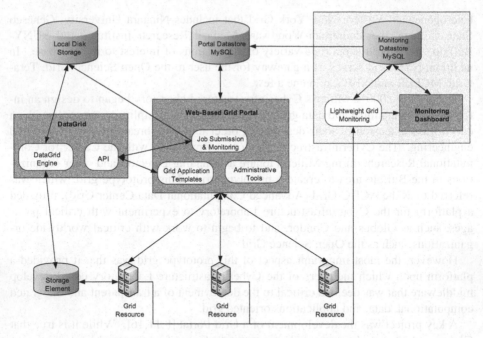

Fig. 1. Overview of the construction of our Grid Portal

ported to the Grid Portal through our Grid-Enabling Application Templates, which provide developers with a template for porting a fairly traditional science or engineering application to our Grid-based Web Portal. This approach provides the developer with access to various databases, APIs, PHP scripts, HTML files, shell scripts, and so on, in order to provide a common platform to port applications and for users to efficiently utilize such applications. The generic template for developing an application provides a well-defined standard scientific application workflow for a Grid application. This workflow includes a variety of functions that include data grid interactions, intermediate data processing, job specification, job submission, collection of results, dynamic run-time status, and so forth. The template provides a flexible methodology that promotes efficient porting and utilization of scientific routines. It also provides a systematic approach for allowing users to take advantage of sophisticated applications by storing critical application and user information in a MySQL database. Most applications have been ported to our Grid Portal within 1-2 weeks.

Our lightweight Grid Monitoring software [17] (http://osg.ccr.buffalo.edu/) is used to monitor resources from a variety of Grids, including the New York State Grid, Western New York Grid, Open Science Grid, Open Science Grid Testbed, and Tera-Grid, to name a few. With production Grids still in their infancy, the ability to efficiently and effectively monitor a grid is important for users and administrators. Our Grid Monitoring System runs a variety of scripts continually, stores information in a MySQL database, and displays the information in an easy to digest and navigate Grid Dashboard. The Dashboard is served by an Apache Server and is written in JavaScript and PHP. It provides a display that consists of a radial plot in the center of the main page that presents an overview of an available Grid, surrounded by histograms and other visual cues that present critical statistics. By clicking on any of these individual components, the user can drill down for more details on the information in question. These drilldown presentations include dynamic and interactive representations of current and historical information. For example, a user or administrator can easily determine the number of jobs running or queued on every system of any available Grid, the amount of data being added or removed from nodes on a grid, as well as a wealth of current and historical information pertaining to the individual nodes, Grids, or virtual organizations on an available Grid. Our work contributes to the widespread monitoring initiative in the distributed computing community that includes NetLogger [19], GridRM [1], Ganglia [25], and Network Weather Service [24], to name a few.

Our Grid Operations Dashboard (http://osg.ccr.buffalo.edu/operations-dashboard.php) was designed to provide discovery, diagnosis, and the opportunity for rapid publication and repair of critical issues to grid administrators. The operational status of a given resource is determined by its ability to support a wide variety of Grid services, which are typically referred to as *site functional tests* [15]. Tests are performed regularly and sequentially in order to verify an every more complex set of services on a resource. These results are reported in our Operations Dashboard in an easy to read color-coded matrix chart.

The development of data storage solutions for the Grid and the integration of such solutions into Grid Portals [18] is critical to the success of heterogeneous production-level Grids that incorporate high-end computing, storage, visualization, sensors, and instruments. Data grids typically house and serve data to grid users by providing virtualization services to effectively manage data in the storage network. The Storage Resource Broker is an example of such a system. Our Intelligent Migrator, currently being integrated into our Grid Portal, represents an effort to provide a scalable and robust data service to the New York State Grid users. The Intelligent Migrator examines and models user utilization patterns in an effort to make efficient use of limited storage so that the performance of our physical data grid and the services provided to our computational grid are significantly enhanced. Our integrated Data Grid provides New York State Grid users with seamless access to their files, which may be distributed across multiple storage devices. Our system implements data virtualization and a simple storage element installation procedure that provides a scalable and robust system to the users. In addition, our system provides a set of on-line tools for the users so that they may maintain and utilize their data while not having to be burdened with details of physical storage location.

An on-going project with very positive, yet preliminary, results is our intelligent scheduling system. This system uses optimization algorithms and profiles of users, their data, their applications, as well as network bandwidth and latency, to improve a grid meta-scheduling system.

3   NYS Grid Exemplar: Shake-and-Bake

Shake-and-Bake is a powerful algorithmic formulation of direct methods that, given accurate diffraction data to 1.2Å or better resolution, has made possible the *ab initio* phasing of complete crystal structures containing as many as ~2000 independent non-H atoms [5]. It has also been used to determine the anomalously scattering substructures of selenomethionyl-substituted proteins containing as many as 160 selenium sites using 3-4Å data [20]. *Shake-and-Bake* belongs to the class of phasing methods known as 'multisolution' procedures [7] in which multiple sets of trial phases are generated in the hope that one or more of the resultant combinations will lead to a solution. Solutions, if they occur, are identified on the basis of the value of a suitable figure of merit. Since each of the sets of trial phases can be processed independently, the *Shake-and-Bake* algorithm can be easily adapted to a coarse-grained parallel processing approach and implemented on a computational grid.

The distinctive feature of *Shake-and-Bake* is the repeated and unconditional cyclical alternation of reciprocal-space phase refinement with a complementary real-space process that seeks to improve phases by imposing constraints through a physically meaningful interpretation of the electron density [13, 22]. The *Shake-and-Bake* procedure has been implemented in a computer program, *SnB*, in a manner convenient for both protein substructures and complete structures [14, 16, 23]. In addition, the two-step process of substructure determination and protein phasing has been combined in the program *BnP* [21], which provides a common interface for *SnB* and components of the *PHASES* suite [6]. Thus, *BnP* provides an automated pathway from processed intensities to an unambiguous protein electron-density map. This pathway includes *SnB* substructure determination, heavy-atom site validation, enantiomorph determination, substructure and protein phase refinement, and solvent flattening.

The repetitive shuttling of trial structures between real and reciprocal space gives the *Shake-and-Bake* algorithm its power, but the need to perform two Fourier transformations in each cycle yields a computationally-intensive procedure. In fact, the running time for *SnB* or *BnP* varies widely, from just a few seconds to many hours for large structures or structures with diffraction data of marginal quality that typically require a large number of trial structures to be examined before a solution is found. In such cases, the ability to increase throughput by processing many trial structures simultaneously on a cluster or a computational grid is invaluable.

4   Using NYS Grid Through Its Grid Portal

Both the *SnB* and *BnP* program have been ported to the NYS Grid Portal via our Grid-enabling Application Templates [11]. *SnB* has been run on NYS Grid and Open Science Grid through the Portal, as well as through command-line submission, to compute hundreds of thousands of trial structures using nearly 100,000 CPUs.

BnP combines the *Shake-and-Bake* substructure determination step with protein phasing calculations that are applied to a successful *Shake-and-Bake* substructure trial. The processing of trial substructures is distributed to a large number of computational nodes. In most cases, *BnP* can determine when a substructure solution has occurred and then move to the next step. Since jobs on different machines are independent once they have been spawned, multiple solutions are possible, which is advantageous for a variety of reasons. In particular, this scenario increases the probability that at least one solution will be found in a modest amount of time.

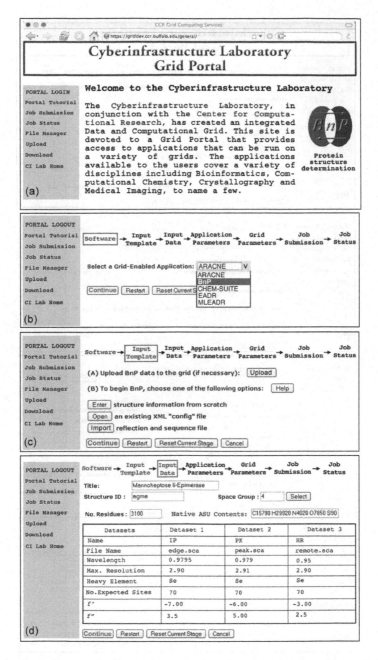

Fig. 2. Job submission, monitoring, and examination of results using the grid portal. (a) Login to the SUNY-Buffalo grid portal. (b) Select *BnP* as the software application to be used. (c) Select execution options and upload files from the home computer. (d) Input additional information about the structure.

Fig. 2 (cont'd). (e) Assign values to program parameters that will be varied in different jobs. Some additional parameters (constant for all jobs submitted simultaneously) are accessible from a pop-up window. (f) Supply information controlling job execution on the grid. (g) Review all parameters and start the jobs. (h) Check whether the jobs are still running.

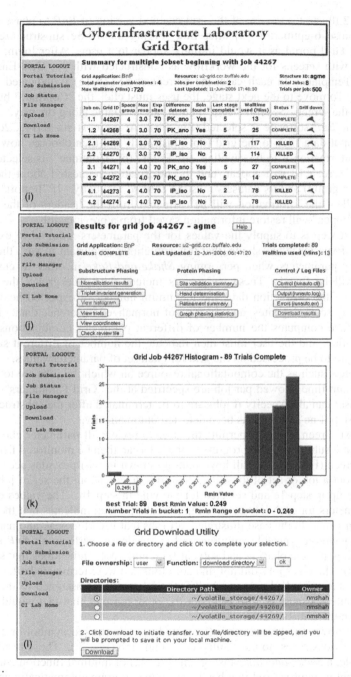

Fig. 2 (cont'd). (i) Drilldown to check the execution status of individual components of a multiple job set. (j) Drilldown to inspect the results of an individual job. (k) Figure-of-merit histogram for the selected job. (l) Download the output files to the home computer.

Figure 2 illustrates the use of the grid-enabled version of *BnP* to phase the protein mannoheptose 6-epimerase [3] after first solving the 70-Se substructure. Fig. 2a shows the Grid portal as it would initially appear to a user. After login, the user is presented with screens for the workflow as constructed with our Grid-Enabling Application Template. In each case, the current stage (1b-1g) is indicated by the red rectangle. To move to the next stage, the user must click the "Continue" button at the bottom of the screen. Several "Help" buttons are available along the way.

First, the *BnP* software is selected (Fig. 2b). At the next stage (Fig. 2c), the user uploads input data files to the grid (not illustrated) and then chooses how additional required information is to be supplied. If "Enter" (or "Continue") is selected, a blank version of screen 1d will appear, and the information requested about the structure (*e.g.*, space group) and its datasets must be entered manually. If "Import" is chosen, most or all of the information will be extracted from the headers of the input data files, and "Open" will restore information saved from a previous job.

The next step is to supply the values for the parameters required to execute *BnP* (Fig. 2e). Experience has shown that it is sometimes important to vary the values of certain key parameters when performing *Shake-and-Bake* in order to ensure that a solution will be found. These parameters include the space group, the maximum resolution of the diffraction data, the maximum number of expected heavy-atom or anomalously scattering sites, and the type of normalized difference data. The intelligent interface computes the number of different parameter combinations that have been specified, and the user must then indicate the number of different substructure trials that are to be processed on the grid for each set of parameter values.

Parameters such as the computational resource on which the jobs are to be run and the maximum time allowed per job are specified at the "Grid Parameters" stage (Fig. 2f). The user can also specify if jobs are to be terminated after the substructure determination step if no solution has been detected automatically.

The next screen (Fig. 2g) permits the user to review all parameter choices before the job(s) are submitted. The progress of the jobs can then be monitored from the "Job Status" screen (Fig 2h). A drilldown button (shown in red) provides access to information about a job or set of jobs. Fig. 2i shows details about the set of jobs (number 44267) set up in step 1e and selected for viewing in step 1h. The values of the variable parameters for each job are given in the table, which indicates that the jobs were grouped in pairs. In the case illustrated, all jobs that used the peak anomalous difference data gave recognizable solutions and proceeded to perform all *BnP* tasks up to and including protein phasing and solvent flattening (note indications that stage 5 was completed). The other jobs did not find solutions and were terminated after the *Shake-and-Bake* stage (#2) had processed all 500 trial structures assigned to them. If any jobs had failed because of *BnP* errors or for other reasons, that fact would have been indicated in the status column.

Drilling down one level further (indicated here by the red symbol on the line for job 1.1) provides access to the results for a single job (Fig. 2j). Those results include, for example, a *Shake-and-Bake* histogram (Fig. 2k) of minimal function values for the 89 trials that were processed in job 1.1 before the program automatically detected that a probable solution had been found. Finally, clicking the "Download results" button (on Fig. 2j) causes the screen shown in Fig. 2l to be displayed with options for downloading the files resulting from the *BnP* calculations to a local computer.

5 Conclusions

The New York State Grid (NYS Grid) is a state-of-the-art, integrated computational and data grid. Using Grid-enabling Application Templates, the *SnB* and *BnP* programs have been adapted to this grid in a straightforward fashion, as have applications that include Ostrich (groundwater modeling), EADR (earthquake engineering), POMGL (hydrodynamic circulation model), Titan (geophysical mass flows), Q-Chem (quantum chemistry), NWChem (computational chemistry), ARACNE (an Algorithm for the Reconstruction of Accurate Cellular Networks), and Split (a groundwater flow modeling), to name a few. The Web-based Grid Portal provides convenient access to these programs for users with access to a Web-enabled device. Users do not need to know details of where their files are maintained, nor where the computations are performed, although details are always available for those who wish to be informed.

Acknowledgments

The authors would like to thank Mark Green, Jason Rappleye, Tony Kew, Sam Guercio, Adam Koniak, Martins Innus, Dori Macchioni, Amin Ghadersohi, and Cynthia Cornelius for their contributions to the efforts described in this paper. This work has been funded by several grants from the National Science Foundation (MRI, ITR, and CRI), a grant from the National Institutes of Health, the State of New York, federal appropriations, as well as from institutions that are mentioned throughout the paper.

References

1. Baker, M.A., Smith, G.: Grid2002 (2002)
2. Berman, F., Hey, A.J.G, Fox, G.C. (eds.): Grid Computing: Making the Global Infrastructure a Reality. John Wiley, New York (2003)
3. Deacon, A.M., Ni, Y.S., Coleman, W.G., Ealick Jr. S.E.: Structure 8, 453–462 (2000)
4. Foster, I., Kesselmann, C. (eds.): The Grid: Blueprint for a New Computing Intrastructure. Morgan Kaufmann Publishers, San Francisco (1999)
5. Frazão, C., Sieker, L., Sheldrick, G. M., Lamzin, V., LeGall, J., Carrondo, M.A.: J. Biol. Inorg. Chem. 4, 162-165 (1999)
6. Furey, W., Swaminathan, S.: Meth. Enzymol. 277, 590-620 (1997)
7. Germain, G., Woolfson, M.M.: Acta Crystallogr. B24, 91-96 (1968)
8. Green, M.L., Miller, R.: Annals of the European Academy of Sciences, 191-218 (2003)
9. Green, M.L., Miller, R.: Parallel Computing 30, 1001-1017 (2004)
10. Green, M.L., Miller, R.: Parallel Computing 30, 1057-1071 (2004)
11. Green, M.L., Miller, R.: Parallel Processing Letters 14, 241-253 (2004)
12. Miller, R., DeTitta, G.T., Jones, R., Langs, D.A., Weeks, C.M., Hauptman, H.A.: Science 259, 1430-1433 (1993)
13. Miller, R., Gallo, S.M., Khalak, H.G., Weeks, C.M.: J. Appl. Cryst. 27, 613-621 (1994)
14. Prescott, C.: (2005),
    http://osg-docdb.opensciencegrid.org/cgi-bin/ShowDocument?docid=83
15. Rappleye, J., Innus, M., Weeks, C.M., Miller, R.: J. Appl. Cryst. 35, 374-376 (2002)
16. Roure, D.D.: Grid Computing: Making the Global Infrastructure a Reality, 65-100 (2003)

17. Ruby, C.L., Green, M.L., Miller, R.: Parallel Processing Letters 16, pp. 485–500 (2006)
18. Ruby, C.L., Miller, R.: Handbook of Parallel Computing: Models, Algorithms, and Applications (in press)
19. Tierney, B., et al.: IEEE High Performance Distributed Computing Conf. (1998)
20. Von Delft, F., Inoue, T., Saldanha, S.A., Ottenhof, H.H., Schmitzberger, F., Birch, L.M., Dhanaraj, V., Witty, M., Smith, A.G., Blundell, T.L., Abell, C.: Structure 11, pp. 985–996 (2003)
21. Weeks, C.M., Blessing, R.H., Miller, R., Mungee, R., Potter, S.A., Rappleye, J., Smith, G.D., Xu, H., Furey, W.: Z. Kristallogr. 217, 686-693 (2002)
22. Weeks, C.M., DeTitta, G.T., Hauptman, H.A., Thuman, P., Miller, R.: Acta Crystallogr. A50, 210–220 (1994)
23. Weeks, C.M., Miller, R.: J. Appl. Cryst. 32, 120-124 (1999)
24. Wolski, R., Spring, N., Hayes, J.: Journal of Future Generation Computing Systems 15, 757-768 (1999)
25. Massie, M.L., Chun, B.N., Culler, D.E.: Parallel Computing 30, 817-840 (2004)

A Data Allocation Method for Efficient Content-Based Retrieval in Parallel Multimedia Databases

Jorge Manjarrez-Sanchez, José Martinez, and Patrick Valduriez

INRIA and LINA, Université de Nantes
{Jorge.Manjarrez,Jose.Martinez}@univ-nantes.fr,
Patrick.Valduriez@inria.fr

Abstract. Scaling up to large multimedia databases with high dimensional metadata descriptions while providing fast content-based retrieval (CBR) is getting increasingly important for many applications. To address this objective, we strive to exploit the popular parallel shared-nothing architecture. In this context, a major problem is data allocation on the different nodes in order to yield efficient parallel content-based retrieval. In this paper, assuming a clustering process and based on a complexity analysis of CBR, we propose a data allocation method with an optimal number of clusters and nodes. We validated our method through experiments with different high dimensional synthetic databases and implemented a query processing algorithm for full k nearest neighbors.

1 Introduction

Modern digital technologies are producing, in different domains, vast quantities of multimedia data, thus making data storage and retrieval critical. Retrieval of multimedia data can be modeled in a space where both the queries and the database objects are mapped into a multidimensional abstract representation, using signal processing and analysis techniques. Each dimension is a describing feature of the content. For instance, an image can be represented as a 256 dimensional feature vector where each value corresponds to a bin in a color histogram.

Content Based Retrieval (CBR) of multimedia objects is performed in a query by example approach. With CBR, the user supplies an example of the desired object which is used to find a set of the most similar objects from the database. This winning set can be obtained by a range approach or a best match approach. In the range approach, a threshold value is used to indicate the permissible similarity (or dissimilarity) of any object in the database from the query object and all qualifying objects within this range are returned. The similarity between the multidimensional representation of the query and each database object is estimated by computing their distance, usually the Euclidean distance (L2). For the best match approach, the winning set is restricted to the *k-nearest neighbors (kNN)*[1]. kNN is the most useful kind of query in CBR. Conceptually, kNN query processing requires computing the distance from every feature vector in the database to the feature vector of the object example to determine the top best similarities. Obviously, performing a

P. Thulasiraman et al. (Eds.): ISPA 2007 Workshops, LNCS 4743, pp. 285–294, 2007.

sequential scan of the database for CBR can be very inefficient for large data sets. Two main approaches have been proposed to avoid sequential scan and speed up CBR: multimedia indexing and clustering.

Indexing of the feature vectors helps to speed up the search process. Using a data space or space partitioning approach [2], the feature vectors are indexed so that non interesting regions can be pruned. However, because of the properties of the multidimensional data representation (time complexity is exponential with the number of dimensions), the best recent results show that only queries up to 30 dimensions can be handled [3][4]. Above this limit, the search performance of indexing becomes comparable to sequential scan [5]. Other works propose to map the multidimensional data representation to another space with reduced dimensions. This allows dealing with a more manageable space at the expense of some loss of precision [6,7].

Clustering is a data partitioning approach. The aim is to form groups of similar objects, i.e. *clusters*. Most of the clustering schemes [8][9] construct a hierarchical structure of similar clusters or make use of an index structure to access rapidly some kind of cluster representative, such as the *centroid*, which in general is the mean vector of features for each cluster. In the searching process, this hierarchy or index is traversed by comparing the query object with the cluster representatives in order to find the clusters of interest. In both index and cluster-based strategies, the cost of computing the distances to determine similarity can be very high for large multimedia databases.

In this paper, we address the problem of CBR performance in large multimedia databases by exploiting parallelism, i.e. using a parallel database system. We assume a parallel (multiprocessor) system with the popular *shared-nothing (SN)* architecture [10], where each node has its own processor(s), local memory and own disk. Each node communicates with other nodes through messages over a fast interconnect. The main advantage of SN (e.g. over shared-disk) is excellent cost/performance and scalability. In this context, a major problem is data allocation on the different nodes in order to yield parallel content-based retrieval. The process of data allocation consists in data partitioning (producing a set of clusters) and data placement of the clusters onto the different SN nodes. The problem can be stated as follows: *given a database of n multimedia objects, find the optimal number of clusters and nodes to yield efficient CBR.*

Assuming a clustering process such as k-means and based on a complexity analysis of CBR using clusters, we propose a data allocation scheme which computes an optimal number of clusters and nodes. Furthermore, the high dimensional representation of the multimedia objects is general enough to apply to other kinds of data. Thus we could apply our allocation scheme to any data that can be represented as multidimensional data objects, e.g. geographical maps, DNA sequences...

The rest of the paper is organized as follows. In Section 2, we present our allocation scheme, with its data partitioning and placement methods. In Section 3, we validate our proposal through simulation. Section 4 discusses related work. Section 5 concludes.

2 Data Allocation Scheme

Our data allocation scheme proceeds in two steps: (1) data partitioning which produces a set of clusters, and (2) data placement which places the clusters on the nodes of the SN parallel system.

2.1 Data Partitioning

To overcome the problem introduced by the dimensionality of the data objects, which eventually deteriorates a search into a sequential scan or worst, one possibility is to rely on a clustering of the database. Tough this process is computationally expensive; it can be done off-line, in a preprocessing step before query execution. The goal is to minimize the number of objects distances to compute, by grouping them together based on their similarity. We do not suggest the use of any specific clustering process. This has been the focus of several works [11, 12, 13] which we can use to yield efficient CBR. Thus, we assume that a given database of size n, can be partitioned by using some clustering process, which produces a set C of clusters of similar data objects.

Based on this partitioning of the database, when executing a query, the set of clusters C can be pruned to a subset of candidate clusters C' containing the most similar objects. Our objective of this section is to propose an optimal number for $|C|$ based on the complexity analysis of the general searching process based on clustering.

For the case of searching via some data clustering, we can write the general complexity as:

$$O(f(C)) + O(g(C')) \tag{1}$$

In order to achieve optimal processing, an algorithm bounded by this complexity should satisfy the following constraints:

- to minimize $O(g(C'))$ as a function of the number of candidate clusters, i.e., $|C'| \ll |C|$;
- to ensure that $O(f(C)) \leq O(g(C'))$;
- to ensure that $|C| \ll n$.

Let us consider the worst case of a search algorithm with:

- a linear selection of the candidate clusters;
- a sequential scan within each selected cluster;
- a full sort based on the merging of the results issued from the selected clusters.

Under these constraints then the general complexity (1) becomes:

$$O(C) + O\left(C' \cdot \frac{n}{C} + C' \cdot \frac{n}{C} \cdot \log_2\left(C' \cdot \frac{n}{C} \right) \right) \tag{2}$$

Lemma 1. The search algorithm modeled by equation 2 is optimal in $O(\sqrt{n} \log_2 n)$ under the conditions:

$|C| = \sqrt{n} \log_2 n$; $|C'| \leq \log_2 n$. and classes of similar cardinalities.

Proof. (omitted for space considerations).   □

Our proposal for partitioning the database is then $|C| = \sqrt{n}\log_2 n$. Additionally, it can be derived some algorithmic variations, from optimal to suboptimal in $O\left(\sqrt{n}\log_2 n\right)$, under less restrictive conditions, $|C| \in \left\lfloor\sqrt{n}, \sqrt{n}\log_2 n\right\rfloor$ and $|C'| \le log_2 n$, the optimal case can be obtained with a near multiplicative factor λ, since C' is small and independent of n.

2.2 Data Placement

Once the database is partitioned into clusters according to our proposal (above), we need to place them onto the nodes of the parallel system. Our solution for the placement of the clusters is to determine the number of nodes which yields the best (asymptotically) achievable performance. Thus we state the following theorem,

Theorem. *Assume a shared nothing parallel system of at least $log_2 n$ nodes, then the average complexity of any query is in* $O\left(\sqrt{n}\right)$.

Proof. The proof can be achieved as a result of Lemma 1 and of a uniform placement of the clusters over the available nodes. That is, distributing $\sqrt{n}\cdot\log_2 n$ clusters over $log_2 n$ nodes, each node will have $\sqrt{n}$ clusters each one containing in average $n/\sqrt{n}\log_2 n$ objects. With $|C'| \le log_2 n$ clusters selected, in the worst case the average number of selected classes on each node is only one. Furthermore, the placement algorithm can take into consideration proximities between classes to distribute the nearest ones over different nodes. The local complexities, executed in parallel over all the participating nodes, are then (details are omitted by space reasons):

$$\approx \frac{\sqrt{n}}{\log_2 n}\cdot\frac{1}{2}\cdot\log_2 n = \frac{1}{2}\cdot\sqrt{n} \in O\left(\sqrt{n}\right)$$

Consolidation of results must be carried out by merging the local results, which are limited to the best k found data objects. In the worst case, each node returns as many results as there are objects in the treated class, that is $n/\sqrt{n}\log_2 n$, and all the nodes participate in the merging of the results, and the parallel complexity of the process is in :

$$\frac{n}{\sqrt{n}\log_2 n}\cdot\log_2 n \in O\left(\sqrt{n}\right).$$

The optimality is derived from the average size of the classes: increasing the number of nodes does not reduce the local complexities, they remain in $O\left(\sqrt{n}\right)$ ∎

The fact that the number of nodes obeys a logarithmic progression makes realistic its implementation, in particular because our proposal is conceived to deal with very large values of n.

3 Validation and Experimental Platform

To validate the efficiency of our proposal, we have developed an experimental platform. (It is written in Java 1.5 running on a Pentium processor at 3 GHz with 1 GB of main memory). In this section, we describe the datasets generated, the k nearest neighbor process and the performance results.

3.1 Data Sets

To validate our proposal we have crafted a synthetic cluster generator. The data generated simulate hyper-spherical clusters of feature vectors with supposed uncorrelated features. First, $|C|$ d-dimensional centers are uniformly generated with a fixed radius, providing the positioning of each cluster in the multidimensional space.

Therefore, each dataset is characterized by $\langle n, d, |C| \rangle$, the number of points, the size of the multidimensional space and the number of clusters respectively. Uniform and non uniform datasets were generated with the following range of values:

$$n \in \{10^6, 10^7\}, d \in \{10, 20, 50, 100, 150, 200, 256, 500, 1000\}, C \in \{\sqrt{n}, \sqrt{n} \log_2 n\}$$

Second, each cluster c is populated with n_c d-dimensional Gaussian points. Each cluster is characterized by $\langle r, \delta, \rho \rangle$. Radius r defines the space a cluster occupies; δ is the density, i.e. the number of points per unit of volume. The population ρ determines the number of d-points in the cluster. They have the following range of values: $r \in \{1, [1,3]\}$, the first value indicates uniform radius and whereas the second one means radius is non uniform and is generated randomly in the interval using these values as coefficients to the analytical cluster size. Similarly, the population is generated with $\rho \in \{1, [\frac{1}{3}, 3]\}$. For fairness of query processing, all generated datasets are normalized in $[0,1]^d$ by dividing all the vectors values by the highest dimension component value, irrespective of the dimension. We graphically "validate" the generated datasets by examining the distributions of the feature values along each dimension. The use of non uniform datasets allows to experiment with a near to real workload.

3.2 kNN Searching Process

We are going to describe our simple but effective algorithm to enable fast CBR in the parallel system. Keep in mind that the process follows the parameters given in section 2.2 and it is disk based.

Step 1. Data Distribution
We did not try yet to develop an algorithm for optimizing the placement of the clusters. They are distributed on the $\log_2 n$ machines in a round-robin way. Therefore, all the nodes are almost equally populated

Step 2. Cluster Selection
Query points are generated randomly under the same assumptions than the generated datasets. To find the set of kNN objects for a query $\mathbf{q}$, a sufficient number of classes

must be selected in order to ensure to return the best k d-points. Firstly, a sequential disk-based search is executed to compare **q** with all the centroids, using the common Euclidean distance, and using the radiuses to find the nearest clusters[1]. The first log_2n clusters are considered. For each selected cluster, we know the node it has been placed during step 1.

With this simply heuristic, we aim at retrieving all the kNN which is equivalent to a full search. Indeed, in several research works on kNN query processing [14, 15] it is proposed a threshold which guarantees the retrieval of all or a high percentage of the NN. Here, taking the first ranked log_2n clusters is a threshold large enough to achieve full precision.

Step 3. Sequential Scans of the Selected Clusters

Once known the node for each cluster of interest, a parallel search is executed on them to retrieve up to k objects. On each node, the scan of the locally selected class takes place in the form of a mere sequential search and the use of a bounded priority queue to keep the best k responses. Therefore, each node returns a set of k sorted elements to the master node.

Step 4. Merging

The master node merges the various results, prunes the list of the first k answers, and returns it to the user or the application.

3.3 Performance Evaluation

In order to obtain experimental evidence of the validity of our proposal, we processed 1000 kNN queries for the above mentioned datasets. We measure the average response time for disk based query processing, the number of distance comparisons and disk IO's. The results presented here are for databases of 10^7 data objects. The sizes of k for the queries are 50, 100 and 150.

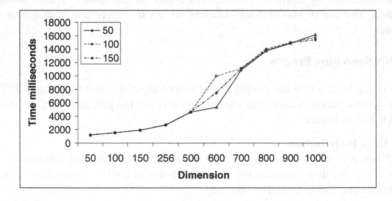

Fig. 1. Execution times for 1000 queries for 50, 100 and 150 kNN for $n=10^7$ non uniform databases of different data dimensionalities

---

[1] Let us note that even though the descriptions of the clusters could fit into main memory we test for worst case conditions, then the process is disk-based.

Figure 1 shows the behavior of the query algorithm for non uniform datasets. Even when the trend to increase processing time with the dimensionality is exhibited, in none of our experiments, it is exponential; it means no curse of dimensionality affectation happens. It has also a tendency to increase less rapidly as expected from our proposal.

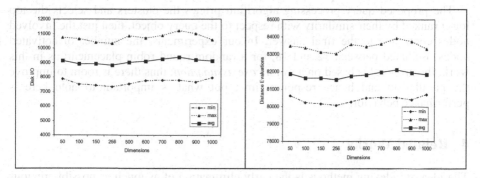

Fig. 2. Disk I/O count and distance computations for the 50 kNN query processing over databases of different dimensionalities

Figure 2 have almost steady curves. This is due to the query processing algorithm. In all cases, the parallel search is performed in the top log2n clusters of non uniform populations as would happen with real data, and each processor returns at most k results. Almost similar values are obtained for k = 100 and 150, thus making unnecessary to present the curves. Here the cluster size is the influence factor. This allows us to conclude that relatively small sizes for the clusters help to reduce searching time. The key is then the cluster pruning process. Thus, it is not required to be concerned on efficiency issues for the search at the interior of the selected clusters. Even in the case when the CBR process is used for browsing; i.e. when the user is not sure of her needs and needs a variety of results, we consider better to wait and let the user lead the retrieval process as it happens when relevance feedback is used.

3.4 Effect of the Size of k

For most related works the size of k is a factor of influence in the number of Disk I/O and distances computed, directly affecting the response time. Under our scheme this is not a main concern. The heuristic threshold allows selecting the most relevant clusters which are processed locally and only in the final merging result can have an effect; which is however small as the results are merged from sorted lists and finally pruned to k. For example, for 256 dimensional data sets from figure 1 the process time is 2,709, 2,697 and 2,698 milliseconds for k=50, 100 and 150 respectively.

3.5 Effect of Data Placement

To maximize parallelism, the selected clusters C^s by the searching algorithm must be equally distributed on the nodes and no more than $\left\lceil \dfrac{C^s}{nodes} \right\rceil$ clusters should be retrieved from each one. That is, all the nodes are activated simultaneously and contribute to speed up the processing of a query and as it is retrieved an equal number of clusters from each one, the workload is balanced. Theoretically, this should happen in an ideal situation, but given that one can not anticipate all the possible queries so that all the nearest clusters are distributed in different nodes, it is a NP-complete problem and it has been proved that the optimal can be achieved in a very few cases [17].

The proposed query processing algorithm prunes the clusters and selects the top $\log_2 n$ ranked by their similarity with respect to the query object, then just the involved nodes contribute to the final answer. In our experiments, the number of activated nodes oscillated between 12 and 18, for a random round robin placement; as in this work, the proposal is based on a *worst case assumption*, thus there is room to improve the parallelism and hence response time, but what is important to note here is performance behavior.

4 Related Works

The idea of indexing methods is the early elimination of as much as possible regions of the data space that are not of interest to the query, thus yielding a minimal subset to search in. However they are good in average for 30 dimensional data. Above 30, the problem known as curse of dimensionality arises and these methods are outperformed by simple linear search [5]. Some noticeable recent work is iDistance [3][4] which reports good performance up to 32 dimensions. Among the clustering methods, Clindex [8] and ClusterTree [9] aim to fight the so called curse of dimensionality which affects indexing methods. Even though they provide acceptable performance, there is no report of how these structures can be implemented or behave in parallel settings. In [17] it is presented an architecture of one processor-multiple disks to process range queries using an interesting concept called proximity index allocation which measures the similarity between nodes to later place them on the disks, avoiding to put similar nodes together, this allows a near optimal allocation process. A shared nothing based implementation is presented by [18], however they are based on the R-Tree which is used to spatial data. In [19] Berchthold et al proposed an allocation method for the X-Tree using a graph coloring algorithm. It has been reported that the Pyramid tree outperforms the X-Tree by a factor of 800 in response time in centralized settings [9]. In [20] it is presented a four disk architecture concerned mainly with the placement within each disk, i.e. a very low level placement scheme of wavelet coefficients. This architecture is used for browsing image thumbnails by exploiting parallelism but the final selected images must be reconstructed in the clients' side from the wavelet coefficients (kind of feature vector). The Parallel M-Tree [21] and one extension [22] address the problem of distributing the nodes of the M-Tree in the parallel system by computing the distance of each newly object placed in a node with all the objects already available, it is achieved by performing a range query with a radius equal to the distance from the object to its parent. In [23][24], the authors propose an hybrid architecture of redundant multidisk and shared nothing, to improve disk IO based in the Parallel R-Tree. However, they provide results for 100, 000 data of up to 80 dimensions which are outperformed by our proposal with much less resources.

5 Conclusions

We have presented a data allocation scheme for efficient retrieval of multimedia data in a shared nothing architecture. It is based on the partitioning of the database of size n into $|C|$ clusters of similar objects which are placed into $\log_2 n$ nodes. The number of clusters is based on the complexity analysis of the general search problem for CBR and the number of nodes in the parallel architecture is proposed on the same principle but taking into consideration that it must be a feasible to implement architecture. We have validated our method for different non uniform datasets under worst case considerations, any improvement such as a better placement scheme and putting into main memory the centroids must signify a performance improvement. Here we showed that our proposal stands for the derived algorithmic complexities.

Acknowledgements

The first author thanks the support of the CONACYT and IPN from Mexico, as well as INRIA France.

References

1. Roussopoulos, N., Kelley, S., Vincent, F.: Nearest Neighbor Queries. In: SIGMOD 95. Proceedings of the International Conference on Management of Data, San Jose, California, May 22-25, pp. 71-79 (1995)
2. Böhm, C., Berchtold, S., Keim, D.A.: Searching in high-dimensional spaces: Index structures for improving the performance of multimedia databases. ACM Comput. Surv. 33(3), 322–373 (2001)
3. Ooi, B.C., Tan, K.L., Yu, C., Zhang, R.: Indexing the Distance: An Efficient Method to KNN Processing. In: VLDB '01: Proceedings of the 27th International Conference on Very Large Data Bases, pp. 421-430 (2001)
4. Ooi, B.C., Tan, K.L., Yu, C., Zhang, R.: iDistance: An adaptive B+-tree based indexing method for nearest neighbor search. Journal of the ACM Transactions on Database Systems 30-2, 364–397 (2005)
5. Weber, R., Schek, H.J., Blott, S.: A Quantitative Analysis and Performance Study for Similarity-Search Methods in High-Dimensional Spaces. In: VLDB 98: Proceedings of the 24th International Conference Very Large Data Bases, pp. 194-205 (1998)
6. Aggarwal, C.C.: On the Effects of Dimensionality Reduction on High Dimensional Similarity Search. In: ACM PODS '01. Symposium on Principles of Database Systems Conference, pp. 256–266. ACM Press, New York (2001)
7. Aggarwal, C.C.: An efficient subspace sampling framework for high-dimensional data reduction, selectivity estimation, and nearest-neighbor search. IEEE Transactions on Knowledge and Data Engineering, October 2004, vol. 16(10), pp. 1247–1262
8. Li, C., Chang, E., Garcia-Molina, H., Wiederhold, G.: Clustering for approximate similarity search in high-dimensional spaces. IEEE Transactions on Knowledge and Data Engineering 14(4), 792–808 (2002)

9. Yu, D., Zhang, A.: ClusterTree: Integration of Cluster Representation and Nearest Neighbor Search for Large Datasets with High Dimensionality. IEEE Transactions on Knowledge and Data Engineering 15(5), 1316–1337 (2003)
10. Özsu, M.T., Valduriez, P.: Principles of Distributed Database Systems, 2nd edn. Prentice-Hall, Englewood Cliffs (1999)
11. Jain, A.K., Dubes, R.C.: Algorithms for Clustering Data. Prentice-Hall, Englewood Cliffs (1988)
12. Kanungo, T., Mount, D.M., Netanyahu, N., Piatko, C., Silverman, R., Wu, A.Y.: An efficient k-means clustering algorithm: Analysis and implementation. IEEE Trans. Pattern Analysis and Machine Intelligence 24, 881–892 (2002)
13. Attila Gürsoy, E.E.: Data Decomposition for Parallel K-means Clustering. In: Wyrzykowski, R., Dongarra, J.J., Paprzycki, M., Waśniewski, J. (eds.) Parallel Processing and Applied Mathematics. LNCS, vol. 3019, pp. 241–248. Springer, Heidelberg (2004)
14. Berrani, S.-A., Amsaleg, L., Gros, P.: Approximate Searches: k-Neighbors + Precision. In: CIKM '03. Proceedings of the 12th ACM International Conference on Information and Knowledge, pp. 24–31. ACM Press, New York (2003)
15. Chavez, E., Navarro, G.: Probabilistic proximity search: Fighting the curse of dimensionality in metric spaces. Information Processing Letters 85(1), 16, 39–46 (2003)
16. Abdel-Ghaffar, K.A.S., El Abbadi, A.: Optimal Allocation of Two-Dimensional Data. In: ICDT '97. Proceedings of the 6th International Conference on Database Theory, pp. 409–418 (1997)
17. Kamel, I., Faloutsos, C.: Parallel R-trees. In: SIGMOD '92. Proceedings of the ACM international Conference on Management of Data, pp. 195–204. ACM Press, New York (1992)
18. Schnitzer, B., Leutenegger, S.T.: Master-Client R-Trees: A New Parallel R-Tree Architecture. In: SSDBM '99. Proceedings of the 11th International Conference on Scientific and Statistical Database Management (1999)
19. Berchtold, S., Böhm, C., Braunmüller, B., Keim, D.A., Kriegel, H.: Fast parallel similarity search in multimedia databases. SIGMOD Rec. 26(2), 1–12 (1997)
20. Prabhakar, S., Agrawal, D., El Abbadi, A., Singh, A., Smith, T.: Browsing and placement of multi-resolution images on parallel disks. In: Multimedia Systems, vol. 8–6, pp. 459–469. Springer, Heidelberg (2003)
21. Zezula, P., Savino, P., Rabitti, F., Amato, G., Ciaccia, P.: Processing M-trees with parallel resources. In: Research Issues In Data Engineering. Eighth International Workshop on Continuous-Media Databases and Applications, pp. 147–154 (1998)
22. Alpkocak, A., Danisman, T., Ulker, T.: A Parallel Similarity Search in High Dimensional Metric Space Using M-Tree. In: Grigoras, D., Nicolau, A., Toursel, B., Folliot, B. (eds.) IWCC 2001. LNCS, vol. 2326, pp. 166–171. Springer, Heidelberg (2002)
23. Bok, K.S., Seo, D.M., Song, S.I., Kim, M.H., Yoo, J.S.: An Index Structure for Parallel Processing of Multidimensional Data. In: Fan, W., Wu, Z., Yang, J. (eds.) WAIM 2005. LNCS, vol. 3739, pp. 589–600. Springer, Heidelberg (2005)
24. Bok, K.S., Song, S.I., Yoo, J.S.: Efficient k-Nearest Neighbor Searches for Parallel Multidimensional Index Structures. In: Lee, M.L., Tan, K.-L., Wuwongse, V. (eds.) DASFAA 2006. LNCS, vol. 3882, pp. 870–879. Springer, Heidelberg (2006)

Optimization of VoD Streaming Scheduling for IPTV Multi-channel Support[*]

Lin-Huang Chang[1,2], Ming-Yi Liao[3], Yung-Fa Huang[2], and Yu-Lung Lo[4]

[1] Department of Computer and Information Science
National Taichung Univ., Taichung, Taiwan, R.O.C.
albertchang04@gmail.com
[2] Graduate Institute of Networking and Communication Engineering
[3] Department of Computer Science and Information Engineering
[4] Department of Information Management
Chaoyang Univ. of Technology, Taichung, Taiwan, R.O.C.

Abstract. It is important to develop the multicasting technology for video on demand (VoD) services in Internet Protocol Television (IPTV) system with multiple channels. In this paper, we proposed an architecture combining multicast and unicast batching channels without scheduled multicasting streams. To provide an acceptable service rate and waiting latency, the 80% multicast channel rate under the experimental scenario is believed to be the optimized allocation between unicast and multicast VoD channels. Depending on the time zone of the arrival and the popularity of the requested videos, the batching scheme with five different time zones was designed to increase the efficient usage of the transmission bandwidth, especially for the request on popular videos, and to reduce the unnecessary waiting latency, especially at cold time zone.

1 Introduction

Video on Demand (VoD) systems basically employ real-time transport protocol (RTP) and real time streaming protocol (RTSP) to deliver digital multimedia data from the streaming server. Typically, each VoD server is capable of supporting hundreds of stored digital videos and delivering more than hundreds of high quality streams simultaneously. Load balancing among multiple servers [5], network cards and processors is also provided for these VoD systems. However, the large scale deployment of commercial VoD services is not popular due to the complexity of such systems. On the other hand, the advances of digital video streaming and high speed networks during the last decade have made Internet Protocol Television (IPTV) service feasible [1-2]. According to [3], IPTV is predicted to surge among the technology winners. IPTV covers both live TV and stored video through multicasting/broadcasting or unicasting. The TV programs and videos are usually requested upon customers' demands. Therefore, through the cable TV or Internet, the

---

[*] This work was supported by National Science Council of ROC Grant NSC 95-2221-E- 324-020 and NSC 95-2622-E-324-013-CC3.

P. Thulasiraman et al. (Eds.): ISPA 2007 Workshops, LNCS 4743, pp. 295–304, 2007.

geographically distributed customers are allowed to request and view high quality videos from the multimedia server complexes. Although the potential of the two-way broadband connectivity used by IPTV may enable new capabilities which will dramatically improve the IPTV experience for consumers, it is needed to ensure that the customers have an overall video quality of experience at least as enjoyable for the IPTV system, especially for VoD services [4].

The scalability and reliability issues of VoD services in IPTV systems can be solved by using geographically distributed servers to reduce the loading of core network and original server. However due to the growing bandwidth requirements in the access network, even the installation of VoD servers at the edge of regional networks is not efficient or sufficient for a large scale deployment of video services in IPTV. Therefore, many studies have investigated multicast/broadcast delivery schemes to improve the utilization of bandwidth resource and scheduling efficiency [10]. Such strategies are defined to be Near VoD (NVoD) systems as compared to the True VoD (TVoD) systems which employ the unicast delivery for every request immediately.

On the other hand, the popularity of the videos will affect the requested probability of the videos which makes the scheduling strategies and delivery schemes complicated. Also, the requested rate at different time zones due to the different behaviors or leisure time of human being will be another issue needed to be taken into account for scheduling strategies. Therefore, the optimization of VoD scheduling considering the popularity of the videos, requested time zones and multicast/unicast batching will be the important issues for realizing large scale VoD services in IPTV system.

In this paper, we analyzed the influence of the batching scheduling on the video selection and requested time zones. By employing the proposed batching strategy combining multicast and unicast streams, we will provide the optimization of VoD scheduling for IPTV multi-channel support. The idea of dynamic batching time was especially designed to prevent the impatient logout and to fulfill the optimization of resource usage under dense requests.

The rest of this paper is organized as follows. Section 2 presents a brief review of the related works in IPTV system. Section 3 shows the architecture and system design of proposed VoD services in IPTV system. The simulation results and analyses are carried out in Section 4. Finally, we conclude this research in Section 5.

2 Related Works in Implementing VoD System

The implementations of the VoD services over high speed networks or cable TV networks have been discussed previously [7-9]. In [7], the authors reported their progress in supporting delivery of MPEG-2 audio/video streams over various types of high-speed networks, e.g. ATM, Ethernet and wireless. The research in this testbed included video transmission with heterogeneous Quality of Service (QoS) provision, variable bit rate (VBR) server scheduling and traffic modeling, as well as video transmission over the Internet and IP-ATM hybrid networks. In [8], the authors implemented the VoD system at National Tsing Hua University in Taiwan by buffering the incoming streams at the intermediate routing nodes. The VoD tried system over a cable TV infrastructure, was also implemented in the Science-Based Industrial Park, Hsinchu, Taiwan. More than two hundred household TVs connected to the network through the set-top-boxes (STB) were served over that system.

In addition to the commercialization and implementation of VoD systems discussed above, many researches continuously work on the design of high performance VoD systems capable of handling large numbers of services simultaneously over geographically large scaled internet. While the TVoD system provides a very short latency it might be inappropriate and impossible to provide each request a unicast channel for implementing large scaled VoD services. The major problems of the TVoD system are the dedicated transmission channel for every single customer and the large access loading to the VoD servers. These result in high cost to customers and a low service rate or a long waiting queue on the unicast channels for the TVoD systems. On the other hand, NVoD systems make the large scaled VoD implementation realistic by employing multicast streaming technology. Several researches [11-19] have worked on the various batching policy, channel allocation and admission control for VoD using multicasting and unicasting technologies. Improved performance in service rate and short latency were achieved by researches [15-17]. The double-rate batching policy [15] was proposed to reduce the start-up delay of VoD service. The tradeoff of these VoD systems was using scheduled multicasting for one single video all the time. This consequently resulted in the limited video selections and inefficient usage of the transmission bandwidth no matter how frequent the customers request for the same video.

The key issue in applying large scaled VoD services in IPTV system, however, is cost rather than technology. For VoD services in IPTV system, it is expected for the server to get as many isochronous requests as possible for the same streaming video. It is common for the popular videos, especially. The popular videos are defined to be the videos being requested simultaneously or at a short interval by various customers. Usually, the majority of people requests for a video at the same period such as evening time after work or weekends. The popular videos are not only because of their popularity but also because of the similar leisured schedule of human being. Therefore, it is important to apply a dynamic batching scheme when we implement the VoD services of IPTV system in a large scale.

3 System Design

In this paper, we assume that there are totally N channels of which N_M channels are used for multicasting and N_U are unicast channels in the architecture of the proposed VoD batching scheme in IPTV system. We assume the network bandwidth at the client side can accommodate two streaming videos simultaneously. Also, minimum local buffer size is required to access the proposed NVoD services in IPTV system. The allocated unicast and multicast channels for batching scheme is shown in Fig. 1. The values of variables N_M and N_U will affect the service rate and waiting latency of the VoD services. Theoretically, more N_M channels will promote the service rate but the waiting latency may increase which leads the system to be NVoD. On the other hand, more N_U channels will reduce the waiting latency to fulfill the TVoD service, however, the blocking rate may significantly increase when the number of requests is larger than the total available channels.

While (*the queue request R arrive*) then
   If(*usage of unicast queue* $\leq N_U$) then
      Vod server : Allocate a new unicast queue for the request R ;
   Else if (*usage of multicast queue* $\leq N_M$) then
      Vod server : Run the dynamic batching time scheme ;
   Else
      Vod server : Block the request ;
   End
End

Fig. 1. The allocated unicast and multicast channels for batching scheme

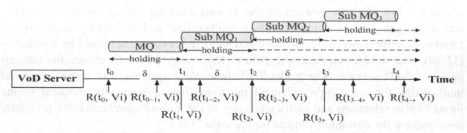

Fig. 2. The timing flow of the proposed batching scheme

The timing flow of the proposed batching scheme is shown in Fig.2. When a request arrives at time t, the system first checks the database in the server to see if there is any request with the same video on queue of multicasting. If there is no same request before, the system initiates a multicast queue (MQ) and sets $t=t_0$. The requested multicast stream will be started after seconds (i.e. at time t_1, where $\delta = t_1-t_0$), where δ is the admission threshold of waiting queue. If there is already an MQ being initiated and the arrival time t is in between t_0 and t_1, the request will be put into the MQ and starts the multicasting after (t_1-t) seconds. However, if a consumer requests for the same video arriving at time between t_k and t_{k+1} (k=1, 2, 3), where $t_{k+1}-t_k=\delta$, it will cache the on-playing multicast stream right away. In the mean while, it will be put into the kth sub-multicast queue (Sub-MQ$_k$). The system will start the sub-multicast stream at t_{k+1} for the Sub-MQ$_k$ consumers arriving at time between t_k and t_{k+1}. For instance, if the request arrives at time t between t_1 and t_2, the client will cache the multicast video data and join the Sub-MQ$_1$ right away. At time t_2, the client will start playing the requested video with the initiation of the sub-multicast stream. After $t-t_1$ second video play, it will release this sub-multicast steam and continue play the video from the local storage of the cached multicast stream thereafter which has missed the first $t-t_1$ second data of the video. So, the client needs to provide the cache buffer as large as $t-t_1$ second video data and will experience the playback latency for t_2-t seconds. After time t_4, no more sub-multicast stream will be initialized for the same batching. Instead, the VoD system will allocate a new multicast stream and restart the batching time scheme. The reason for this design is to keep the client from significant overload to the local buffer and long duration of occupied network bandwidth.

Taking the approximation as reference [22] with M/G/k/k queueing system, it is possible and fair to obtain the average latency of the VoD services in IPTV as $\delta/2$.

From our NVoD system and other researches [12-16], the average playback latency is on the order of minutes (e.g. 2 min.) or even less. This will be acceptable for non-time sensitive videos. For those with time-sensitive videos, the request can be allocated using unicast channel to provide TVoD. In this paper, however, we will focus on the non-time sensitive VoD services.

For the cached buffer issue, our batching scheme requires the local client to store up to 3δ seconds of video data. If the video is encoded as MPEG-1 with average rate of 1.5 Mbps, it is needed to batch video up to 360 seconds at a local client with 67.5 MB buffer which will not cause too much problem for current clients. The flexibility of selecting video will be the contribution from our NVoD system due to the free timetable of the multicast streams compared with other NVoD and TVoD systems [13-17]. Therefore, our proposed system is expected to provide a good serving rate with the acceptable playback latency. Furthermore, due to the similarity of the spare time of human being and the difference in the popularity of the requested video, it is not practical to model the VoD system simply with single approximation. Therefore, it is important to apply a dynamic batching time scheme when we implement the VoD system realistically.

The customer blocking is another important factor to the design of VoD services in IPTV system. The loading of the server and the usage of the transmission bandwidth, however, are the basic issues of the blocking probability. They are mostly contributed from the popular videos during the heavily requested time period, which is defined as hot time zone. Maximization of the multicast channels and acceptable waiting latency could be applied to this condition to increase the efficiency of the VoD services in IPTV systems. The cold time zone, on the other hand, is defined as low demands of server loading and less usage of the transmission bandwidth. Therefore, it is not necessary to put the requests in the normal waiting queue during the cold time zone.

From this point of view, our VoD system will dynamically adjust the admission threshold of waiting queue depending on the arriving period. We divided one day into five time zones, which are Hot time (HT), Sub hot time (SHT), Normal time (NT), Sub cold time (SCT), and Cold time (CT), and set different admission thresholds to these time zones which are between maximum threshold and minimum threshold. The idea of minimum threshold has been pointed out from the previous research, proposed by Almeroth [18] and impatient customer statistic results [21]. However, the complete implementation algorithm has not been reported yet. From the best knowledge of authors, there was no research on the maximum threshold, either. The minimum threshold in our system is expected to approach the TVoD nature. It is true especially for the less popular videos at cold time zone. The chance to gather two or more videos for the same video at the same batching period is low under such circumstance. Therefore, it should be a smart strategy to minimize the latency for the customers by providing unicast services or multicast channels with minimum admission threshold.

On the other hand, the maximum admission threshold will reduce the blocking probability of requested customers. This is especially true for the popular videos being requested at hot time zone. Under this situation, it is expected for the server to collect as many requests as possible within one batching time. The longer the admission threshold is, the more requests the same batching collects. Maximizing the admission threshold will benefit the system utilization a lot in this case and consequently reduce the blocking probability of the VoD services in IPTV system. However, it should not detract from the on-demand nature due to the maximization of the waiting latency. According to the leisured schedule of human being and the statistic results from requests, we dynamically adjust our batching system to five different time zones, which are sets of time intervals. The first one is hot time zone (HT), e.g. sever to ten o'clock in the daily evening. The second zone, called sub-hot time zone (SHT), could be distributed around one to two hours before or after the HT. Normal time zone (NT) with adjustment of the normal admission threshold usually is the time period with one hour before or after people's working hours. Sub-cold time zone (SCT) is defined as the forth time zone which is roughly around one to two hours before or after wake up. The last one is the cold time zone (CT) which covers most of the deep night period. We set the indicated threshold δ according to the different time zone, with conditions $\delta_{HT} > \delta_{SHT} > \delta_{NT} > \delta_{SCT} > \delta_{CT}$ (where $\delta_{HT}=\delta_{max}$ and $\delta_{CT}=\delta_{min}$). The algorithm of our dynamic adjustment of the batching time scheme is shown in Fig. 3. We assume the arrival time is t, and U_m is the utilization of multicast channels which is equal to [(Using multicast channel) / N_M].

As shown in Fig. 3, when a new request arrives, the VoD server will check the utilization of multicast channels. If most of the available multicast channels are free at the moment, the customer does not need to wait for a long time since the loading of server and the usage of transmission bandwidth is low in general for both popular and less popular videos. On the other hand, if the VoD server is very busy and the utilization of the available multicast channels is high, the requested consumer is expected to wait for a longer time.

During sub cold time zone, we keep the requests for the popular videos with δ_{SCT} latency to increase the efficient usage of the transmission bandwidth. The admission threshold is back to the average queueing latency δ_{SHT} at the normal time zone for all provided videos. At sub hot time zone, the admission threshold is increased to δ_{HT} to release the increasing usage of transmission bandwidth. Finally, during hot time zone,

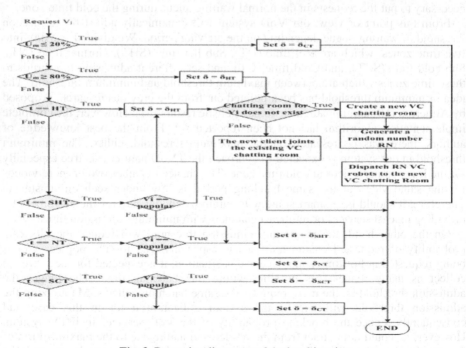

Fig. 3. Dynamic adjustment of the batching time

we keep the requests for the popular videos to δ_{HT} which is equal to δ_{max} and the less popular video is not provided at this moment. It is understood that the popular videos usually group more requests at one batching than the less frequent ones. It is also suggested from Zipf's research [20] and movie rental statistics [21] that a small percentage of the movie offerings at one time, especially the popular ones, will experience the largest requested volume. Obviously, in this case, every stream for the popular videos will gather more requests due to the maximized admission threshold and increasing chances for requesting popular videos. Therefore, compared to the action taken during SHT, the loading of VoD server is expected to be further reduced. It should be noted that at HT the service rate is increased dramatically by removing the service of less frequent videos and maximizing the admission threshold.

4 Simulation Results and Analyses

We have designed a simulator to simulate the proposed dynamic batching time scheme. The purpose of our experiment is to prove that the batching time scheme is a tradeoff between the waiting latency and blocking probability and then provides the optimization of the VoD streaming scheduling. We can make the channel more efficient in hot time zone by setting the tolerable threshold. And the dynamic batching time scheme could adjust the batching time flexibly to reduce the unnecessary waiting latency. We refer to the data in [23] which showed the TV rating of one day in Taiwan and divided a day into five time zones, which are HT, SHT, NT, SCT and CT zones, as listed in Table 1. In the simulation scenarios, we set the total usable channel number as 500 channels, and the total number of videos as 1000. The length of each video is 30 minutes and the popular videos occupy 20% of all videos in the simulation.

Table 1. The allocation of time zone in one day

Time (o'clock)	Time zone	Time	Time zone	Time	Time zone
00-01	SCT	08-09	SCT	16-17	NT
01-02	SCT	09-10	SCT	17-18	SHT
02-03	CT	10-11	NT	18-19	SHT
03-04	CT	11-12	NT	19-20	HT
04-05	CT	12-13	SHT	20-21	HT
05-06	CT	13-14	SHT	21-22	HT
06-07	CT	14-15	NT	22-23	SHT
07-08	SCT	15-16	NT	23-00	SHT

The simulation was run for the whole day which consists of 86400 seconds in simulation duration totally. The request arrives with Poission distribution and the arrival rate λ is decided according to the time zone. The arrival rate and batching time for different time zones are listed in Table 2.

The blocking rate is defined to be the ratio of requests with no available channel or queue to the total requests. The waiting time of each successful request is accumulated and divided by the number of served requests to come out with average waiting time. We did not consider the blocked requests in the waiting time issue. The unicast channel rate (R_U) is the ratio of allocated unicast channels (N_U) to the total channels. Similarly, the multicast channel rate (R_M) is defined to be the ratio of allocated multicast channels (N_M) to the total channels (N). The utilization of R_M (R_U)

Table 2. The arrival rate and the batching time for different time zones

Time Zone	Arrival rate λ (req./min)	Batching time δ (s)
Hot (H)	50	60
Sub Hot (SH)	15	20
Normal (N)	6	7
Sub Cold (SC)	2	2
Cold (C)	1	1

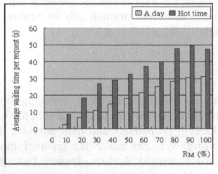

Fig. 4. Relationship of average waiting time and R_M in a day and at hot time period

Fig. 5. The dependence of blocking rate in a day and at hot time on different R_M

is set to be ratio of the allocated multicast (unicast) queues and channels at the time of request to the pre-assigned total multicast (unicast) channels.

In Fig. 4 we illustrated the relationship between the average waiting time in a day or at hot time period and R_M. From the results shown in Fig. 4 we can see that the average waiting time increases with the multicast channel rate R_M. This is because less unicast channels, which introduce no latency, are provided with higher multicast channel rate. However, the blocking rate increases significantly when the multicast channel rate is less than 70%, especially for the case of hot time requests, as shown in Fig. 5. The batching time scheme in the pre-arranged multicast channels makes the contribution in gathering more consumers using the same multicast channel. Consequently, the blocking rate is reduced significantly with more than 70% of multicast channel rate. The trade-off between average waiting time and blocking rate again was illustrated from these results.

To provide acceptable service rate and waiting latency, we will take the multicast channel rate as 80% for further experiments. This will provide the VoD service in IPTV system with less than 3% blocking rate and experience the latency about 47 seconds at hot time period or 28 seconds in average. From the practical point of view in streaming playback, several seconds to couple tens of buffering, which contributes to the waiting latency, is common and acceptable. In the mean while, with the designed dynamic batching time scheme, both parameters can be further improved simultaneously, as discussed next.

We further conducted the simulation to compare the performance of dynamic batching time with static batching time. The static batching time was kept fixed to be 2, 7, 20, 60 and 120 seconds each run. The dynamic batching time, however, varied

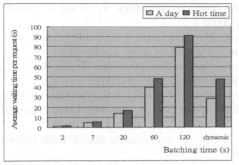
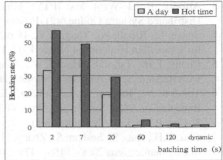

Fig. 6. The average waiting time with static and dynamic batching time

Fig. 7. The blocking rate with static and dynamic batching time

from 2 to 120 seconds according to the requested time period. The multicast channel rate R_M was set to be 80%, as explained previously. The simulation result is pictured in Fig. 6, where both HT case and whole day in-average cases were carried out. As shown in Fig. 6, the average waiting time with 2, 7 and 20-second batching time is relatively low compared to those with 60 or 120-second batching time. However, their corresponding blocking rates are much higher, as illustrated in Fig. 7. The designed dynamic batching time adjusts the batching time according to the utilization of N_M and time zones. This adjustment will keep the blocking rate at relatively low level while maintaining an acceptable average waiting time (about 28 seconds in average).

5 Conclusions

In this paper, the scheduling strategy proposed is believed to provide a very good batching scheme for the realistic implementation of the VoD services in IPTV system. The tradeoff between average waiting time and blocking rate for requesting VoD services was analyzed. To provide an acceptable service rate and waiting latency, the 80% multicast channel rate under the experimental scenario is believed to be the optimized allocation between unicast and multicast VoD channels. By employing the proposed dynamic batching time scheme, both waiting latency and blocking rate were further improved simultaneously. Depending on the time zone of the arrival and the popularity of the requested videos, the batching scheme with five different time zones was designed to increase the efficient usage of the transmission bandwidth, especially for the request on popular videos, and to reduce the unnecessary waiting latency, especially at cold time zone.

References

1. Kerpez, K., Waring, D., Lapiotis, G., Lyles, J.B., Vaidynathan, R.: IPTV service assurance. IEEE Journal in Communications Magazine 44(9), 166–172 (2006)
2. Park, W., Choi, C., Jeong, Y.K.: An Implementation of the Broadband Home Gateway supporting Multi-Channel IPTV. In: Proc. of IEEE ISCE, pp. 1–5. IEEE Computer Society Press, Los Alamitos (2006)

3. Alfonsi, B.: I Want My IPTV: Internet Protocol Television Predicted a Winner. Distributed Systems Online 6(2) (February 2005)
4. Souza, L., Ripoll, A., Yang, X.Y., Hernadez, P.: Designing a Video-on-Demand System for a Brazilian High Speed Network. In: Proc. of 26th ICDCS, pp. 43–50 (2006)
5. Chang, L.H., Tai, C.F., Hou, T.W.: Adaptive Arrival Rate Dependent Traffic Balancing with Redundancy. Computer Communications 30(6), 1220–1228 (2007)
6. Tokekar, V., Ramani, A.K., Tokekar, S.: Analysis of Batcing Policy in View of User Reneging in VOD System. In: Proc. of IEEE INDICON, pp. 399–403. IEEE Computer Society Press, Los Alamitos (2005)
7. Chu, Y.H., Rao, S., Seshan, S., Zhang, H.: A case for end system multicast. IEEE Journal in Communications 20(8), 1456–1471 (2002)
8. Chang, S.F., Eleftheriadis, A., Anastassiou, D., Jacobs, S., Kalva, H., Zamora, J.: Coolumbia's VoD and multimedia research testbed with heterogeneous network support. Journal on Multimedia Tools and Applications (1997)
9. Dynamic service aggregation for interactive information delivery over networks: http://hulk.bu.edu/projects/summary.html
10. Poon, W., Lo, K., Feng, J.: Provision of Continuous VCR Functions in Interactive Broadcast VoD Systems. IEEE Transactions Broadcasting 51(4), 460–472 (2005)
11. Bouras, C., Kapoulas, V., Konidaris, A., Sevasti, A.: A dynamic distributed video on demand service. In: Prof. of 20th ICDCS, pp. 496–503 (2000)
12. Dan, A., Sitaram, D., Shahabuddin, P.: Dynamic batching policies for an on-demand video server. Multimedia System, 112–121 (1996)
13. Han, K., Kim, J.H., Won, Y.H.: SRS: a viewer scheduling strategy using client's buffer in video-on-demand systems. In: Proc. of IEEE TENCON, pp. 317–320. IEEE Computer Society Press, Los Alamitos (1999)
14. Su, T.C., Wang, J.S.: Buffered multicast routing for video-on-demand systems. Proc. of IEEE ICC'99 , 1000–1004 (1999)
15. Poon, W.F., Lo, K.T., Feng, J.: Batching policy for video-on-demand in multicast environment. Electronics Letters, 1329–1330 (2000)
16. Poon, W.F., Lo, K.T., Feng, J.: Design and analysis of multicast delivery to provide VCR functionality in video-on-demand systems. In: Proc. of 2nd ICATM, pp. 132–139 (1999)
17. Lee, J.Y.: UVoD: an unified architecture for video-on-demand services. IEEE Communication Letters 3(9), 227–279 (1999)
18. Almeroth, K.C., Ammar, M.H.: The use of multicast delivery to provide a scalable and interactive video-on-demand service. IEEE Journal on Selected Areas in Communications 14, 1110–1122 (1996)
19. Chang, L.H., Liao, M.Y., Liaw, J.J.: A VoD System with Dynamic Batching Time to Support Multi-Channel IPTV. WSEAS Transactions on Communications 6(3), 478–485 (2007)
20. Zipf, G.: Human behavior and the principle of least effort. Addison-Wesley, Reading (1994)
21. Yoshida, J.: The video-on-demand demand: opportunities abound, as digital video becomes a reality. Electronics Eng. Times (1993)
22. Allen, A.O.: Probability, Statistics, and Queueing Theory with Computer Science Applications, 2nd edn. Academic, New York (1990)
23. Directorate-General of Budget, Accounting and Statistics, Execlutive Yuan, R.O.C (Taiwan), http://www129.tpg.gov.tw/society/

Continuous Kernel-Based Outlier Detection over Distributed Data Streams

Liang Su, Weihong Han, Peng Zou, and Yan Jia

School of Computer Science National University of Defense Technology Changsha
410073, China
liangsumail@gmail.com, 13808419839@hnmcc.com, zpeng@nudt.edu.cn,
jiayanjy@vip.sina.com

Abstract. Stream data are often transmitted over a distributed network, but in many cases, are too voluminous to be collected in a central location. Instead, we must perform distributed computations, guaranteeing high quality results in real-time even as new data arrive. In this paper, firstly, we formalize the problem of continuous outlier detection over distributed evolving data streams. Then, two novel outlier measures and algorithms are proposed which can identify outliers in a single pass. Furthermore, our experiments with synthetic and real data show that the proposed methods are both efficient and effective compared with existing outlier detection algorithms.

1   Introduction

Following with the fast improvement of hardware and communication technologies, many social and military applications are deployed in distributed settings and are producing stream data continuously. For example, networking applications (multiple web/blog crawlers, intrusion detection, network monitoring), financial services (distributed fraud detection, financial monitoring, click stream analysis), sensor networks (environmental or traffic sensors) and military application(soldier location streams), etc. In such environment, all stream data generally has these characters: continuous and unbounded, distributed and evolvable over time. So, distributed data stream model was provided, which matches with these applications very well.

Motivated by these abundant applications, in this paper we study a quintessential monitoring problem on continuously changing distributed data sources, namely, *outlier detection*, which is an important part of typical data mining. And the outliers may point out some surprising and suspicious activities, extreme or relatively extreme values or observations which appear to be inconsistent with the remainder data. Formally, we assume there are $m + 1$ distributed nodes (one coordinator node and m child nodes). Each child node i has a changing source of data S_t^i at time t, and individual data items in the sources may be high dimensional including numerical values, text, audio or video. We are more concerned about monitoring some desirable properties of the union $\bigcup_{i=1}^m S_i^t$ of

P. Thulasiraman et al. (Eds.): ISPA 2007 Workshops, LNCS 4743, pp. 305–314, 2007.

data distributed over all nodes in real time. Therefore, we develop efficient online outlier detection techniques. And our contributions are as follows:

1. We propose two novel outlier measures which are compatible with distance-based outlier and density-based outlier (see definitions 1, 2).

2. We provide the first algorithms for this problem, which use *kernel density estimators* to approximate the stream data distribution. Our algorithms can minimize the overall communication between nodes with accuracy guarantees.

3. We adopt the *fading strategy* to keep pace with the transient and evolving stream data, and mico-cluster technique (commonly used for data compression or summarization) to conquer the data partition.

4. Finally, extensive experiments including synthetic and real data sets, demonstrate that our proposed methods are both efficient and effective.

The rest of this paper is organized as follows. Section 2 discusses related research in the area of outlier detection. Section 3 presents the problem definitions and some Preliminaries used in the rest of the paper. Section 4 and section 5 provide two effective algorithms. Section 6 evaluates the effectiveness and efficiency of the two algorithms. Section 7 concludes the paper.

2   Related Work

Methods for outlier detection are drawing increasing attention. The salient approaches can be classified as either distribution-based, clustering, distance-based, or density-based.

Distribution-based approach [1, 2] assumes the data following a distribution model (e.g. Normal) and flags as outliers those objects which deviate from the model. Thus, such approaches do not work well in moderately high-dimensional (multivariate) spaces, and have difficult to find a right model to fit the evolving data stream. To overcome these limitations, researchers have turned to various non-parametric approaches (clustering, distance-based, and density-based). Most clustering algorithms (e.g. DBSCAN [3], BIRCH [4]), are to some extent capable of handling exceptions. However, they are developed to optimize clustering, and regard them as "by-products".

Distance based approaches [5, 6], first proposed by E.M. Knorr and R.T. Ng [5] detect outliers by computing distances among points. A point p in a data set T is a distance-based outlier $(DB(\rho, r)$-outlier) if at most a fraction ρ of the points in T lie within distance r from p. It has an intuitive explanation that an outlier is an observation that is sufficiently far from most other observations in the data set. However, it will be no effect when the data points have different densities, because this outlier definition is based on a single criterion determined by the parameters ρ and r, so more robust density-based techniques were provided.

Density-based approaches proposed originally by M. Breunig, et al. [7] which defines a local outlier factor (LOF) for each point depending on the local density of its neighborhood. In general, points with a high LOF are flagged as outliers.

It has attracted considerable attention [8,9], and a large number of algorithms have been developed, such as, LOCI [8] method.

In the distributed data stream environments, Amit Manjhi, et al. [10] thought of finding recently frequent items. Graham Cormode, et al. [11] considered continuous clustering. To the best of our knowledge, there is no similar work existing in the literature in the context of outlier detection over distributed data streams.

3 Preliminaries and Problem Statement

In this section, first, we introduce the two preliminaries: distributed data stream model and kernel density estimation. Then, we propose two novel outlier measures which are compatible with distance-based and density-based outlier.

Distributed Data Stream Model: A data stream consists of an unbounded sequence $D_1, D_2, \cdots$ of numeric values which $D_i = (D_i^1, D_i^2, \cdots, D_i^d)$ and $D_i^j \in \mathbb{R}$ for $i, j \in \mathbb{N}, j \in [1, d]$. Then, distributed data stream model composes of $m+1$ nodes: a central *coordinator node* N_c, and m remote stream monitor nodes $N_1, N_2, \cdots, N_m$. Each node just monitors one stream data. Except otherwise stated, we assume the stream data as *independent and identical distributed(**iid**)* observations of an unknown continuous random variable which is reasonable for most distributed data stream applications. We only care about the data in the *sliding window* (W) which contains the most recent N elements.

Kernel Density Estimation: Kernel density estimation is to reveal the unknown density of a distribution by selecting a suitable density estimator and has been successfully applied in diverse application scenarios [12]. Theoretically, kernel density function $\widetilde{f}_h(x)$ is sure to converge to the real density $f(x)$ function for arbitrary distribution. More formally, assume that we have a data set $\mathcal{D}$, containing n points whose values are $\overline{X_1}, \overline{X_2}, \cdots, \overline{X_n}$. We can approximate the underlying distribution $f(x)$ using the following kernel function ($\mathcal{K}(x)$, *kernel function*, is a function of random variable X. h, *kernel width*, determines the smoothing level of kernel function):

$$\widetilde{f}_h(x) = \frac{1}{nh} \sum_{i=1}^{n} \mathcal{K}\left(\frac{x - \overline{X_i}}{h}\right), \quad x, \overline{X_i} \in \mathbb{R}, \quad \int_{x \in \mathbb{R}} \mathcal{K}(x)dx = 1 . \quad (1)$$

Common used kernel functions are Epanechnikov, Gaussian, Quartic and Triweight kernel, etc. Since the Gaussian kernel is unbounded ($x \in (-\infty, +\infty)$), it exacerbates the cost of computing integral. Quartic and Triweight kernel are fourth and sixth function each other. So, we choose the Epanechnikov kernel which is a square function, more easy to integrate and has bound, as follows:

$$\mathcal{K}\left(\frac{x - \overline{X_i}}{h}\right) = \begin{cases} \frac{3}{4} \cdot \frac{1}{h}\left(1 - \left(\frac{x - \overline{X_i}}{h}\right)^2\right), & \left|\frac{x - \overline{X_i}}{h}\right| < 1 \\ 0 & otherwise \end{cases} \quad (2)$$

Novel Outlier Measures: There are several formal definitions of an outlier in Section 2. Naturally we can come to a conclusion — the probability of one point is more close to zero, the point is more likely to be an outlier. So, we can use the following formula (3) to measure the outlier degree for the kernel density estimation setting.

$$\Phi(p,r) = P[p-r, p+r] = \int_{p-r}^{p+r} \widehat{f_h}(\mathbf{x}) d\mathbf{x} \ . \tag{3}$$

Distance-based Kernel Estimation Outlier: It is a variation of *Distance-based Outlier* [5]. Naturally, we present the definition of *Distance-based Kernel Estimation Outlier* (DisKE-Outlier) (see definition 1). However, it also has the same limitations as distance-based methods. So we provide a more robust outlier measure: *DenKE-Outlier* in definition 2.

Definition 1 (DisKE-Outlier). *A point is a "DisKE-Outlier" if $\Phi(p,r) \leq \rho$.*

Density-based Kernel Estimation Outlier: It is a variation of *Density-based Outlier* [7]. Spiros Papadimitriou, et al. [8] provided an outlier metric — Multi-Granularity Deviation Factor(MDEF). For any given point, MDEF is a measure of how the neighborhood count of p (in its counting neighborhood) compares with that of the points in its sampling neighborhood. A point is flagged as an outlier, if its MDEF is significantly different from that of the local averages. r is the sampling neighborhood distance and αr ($\alpha \in (0,1)$) is the range over which the neighborhood counts are considered. Correspondingly, we can define a *Density-based Kernel Estimation Outlier*(DenKE-Outlier) as follows:

Definition 2 (DenKE-Outlier). *A point is defined as a "DenKE-Outlier" that $\frac{\Phi(p,\alpha r)}{\sum_{q\in\Omega_r}\Phi(q,\alpha r)/|\Omega_r|} < \xi$, ξ is a real value parameter to define how significant the point p is to the average of its neighbors. Ω_r is a point set that contains all points which distances are below r to point p. $|\Omega_r|$ is the count of Ω_r.*

4   Naïve Outlier Detection Algorithm

Selecting Kernel Width: The kernel density estimation indicate that the *kernel width* significantly affects the shape of a kernel function. A widely used rule for approximating the kernel width is the Scott's rule [12] below formula (4). However, these strategies depend on the complete sample, which is impracticable in data stream scenario. To overcome this problem, we adopt an approximate solution, only considering the data in sliding window. The number of sliding window (N) is more large, the approximate kernel width $\widehat{h}$ is more close to h. σ is the standard deviation of whole stream data and $\widetilde{\sigma}$ is the sample standard deviation of sliding window.

$$h \approx 2.345\sigma n^{-1/5} \approx \widehat{h} \triangleq 2.345\widetilde{\sigma}(N)^{-1/5} \ . \tag{4}$$

Capturing Evolution Over Data Stream: To capture the evolution, we are conscious of the problem in formula (1): each kernel entry is equally weighted with constant $\frac{1}{n}$. So we present a *fading strategy* that couple the kernel density estimation with exponential smoothing [13]. The basic idea of fading strategy is to give older data less weight and to gradually discount the history data, which is widely used in the area of time series analysis and forecasting. Then, formula (1) is adjusted to formula (5). Notice that the sum of weights in formula (5) is $\sum_{i=1}^{N} \frac{\omega^{N-i}}{\sum_{j=1}^{N} \omega^{j-1}} = 1$, which is equal to $\sum_{i=1}^{n} \frac{1}{n} = 1$ in formula (1). When $\omega = 1$, formula (5) comes back to formula (1).

$$\widehat{f_h}(x) = \frac{1}{h} \sum_{i=1}^{N} \left(\frac{\omega^{N-i}}{\sum_{j=1}^{N} \omega^{j-1}} \cdot \mathcal{K}\left(\frac{x - \overline{X_i}}{h}\right) \right), \quad x \in \mathbb{R}, \quad \omega \in (0,1] . \quad (5)$$

Comparison for Different Distributions: The difference of two distributions can seriously influence the traffic between the coordinator node and other child nodes. Intuitively, the less change of distribution in one node, the less traffic between this node and the coordinator. One widely used measure is f-divergences in formula (6) [14], which is more natural than distances based on ℓ_p norms. $p(x)$ and $q(x)$ are probability distribution functions over random variable x, Ω is the value set of x. The JS-divergence (in formula (7)), one of most common in all f-divergences, is symmetric, non-negative real number and unbounded. In practical, we can select a parameter λ (*divergence threshold*) as the upper-bound of $D_{JS}(p,q)$. If $D_{JS}(p,q) > \lambda$, there is a significant change and corresponding node transfer its kernel estimation function to the coordinator node. Otherwise, no transformation.

$$D_f(p,q) = \int_{x \in \Omega} \left(q(x) f\left(\frac{p(x)}{q(x)}\right) \right) dx, \quad f(1) = 0 \Longrightarrow p(x) = q(x) . \quad (6)$$

$$f(u) = \ln \frac{2}{1+u} + u \ln \frac{2u}{1+u}, \quad D_{JS}(p,q) = \sum_{i=1}^{n} \left(p_i \ln \frac{2p_i}{p_i + q_i} + q_i \ln \frac{2q_i}{p_i + q_i} \right) \quad (7)$$

Naïve Algorithm: The *Naïve Distributed Outlier Detection Algorithm* (NOD Algorithm) can deal with the two outlier categories (DisKE-Outlier and DesKE-Outlier). By observation of the definition of DisKE-Outlier, it is easy to find that the coordinate node need only to examine the values that have been marked as outliers by its child nodes. We want to identify outliers in the coordinate node. All the other data values can be safely ignored, since they cannot possibly be outliers. However, DesKE-Outliers (See definition 2) are non-decomposable because the neighbors of one point may be distributed in different child nodes. A feasible solution is that all child nodes have a copy of the kernel density function of coordinator node. The child node transfers its kernel estimation function to the coordinator node when its $D_{JS}(p,q) > \lambda$, and the coordinator node broadcasts its kernel estimation function to its child nodes when $D_{JS}(p,q) > \lambda$ in N_c. The NOD algorithm is described in algorithm (1).

Algorithm 1. Naïve Distributed Outlier Detection Algorithm

Input: m data streams $S_1, \cdots, S_m$ in $N_1, \cdots, N_m$, the divergence threshold λ, ρ is the outlier proportion in DisKE-Outlier, the distance r, α is the distance proportion in DesKE-Outlier.

Output: the outlier set O_c

Procedure OutlierDetection()

1 $BDisKE \Leftarrow$ **true**; // variable $BDisKE = true$ indicates using DisKE-Outlier detection method, otherwise using DesKE-Outlier detection method.
2 **CoordinatorProcess()**; // initiate the process for the coordinator node;
3 for($i = 1$ to m) do
4   **ChildProcess()**; // initiate the process for each child node;

Procedure CoordinatorProcess()

1 when receiving a new point data p from a child node;
2 if($p \notin O_c$) then isOutlier(p);
3 update $\widetilde{f}_h(x)$; // using formula (1) and Epanechnikov kernel in formula (2);
4 if($D_{JS}(\widetilde{f}_h^{new}, \widetilde{f}_h^{old}) > \lambda$) then broadcast $\widetilde{f}_h^{new}$ to its all child nodes;
5 if($p \in O_c$, or is marked as an outlier) then report point p as an outlier;

Procedure ChildProcess()

1 if($p \notin N_i$) then isOutlier(p);
2 update $\widetilde{f}_h(x)$; // using formula (1) and Epanechnikov kernel in formula (2);
3 if($D_{JS}(\widetilde{f}_h^{new}, \widetilde{f}_h^{old}) > \lambda$) then send the point p and to $\widetilde{f}_h^{new}$ coordinator node;

Procedure isOutlier(point p)

1 if($BDisKE =$ **true**) then
2   if($\Phi(p,r) < \rho$) then mark p as an outlier and add to O_c;
3 else compute the Ω_r;
4   if($\frac{\Phi(p,\alpha r)}{\sum_{q \in \Omega_r} \Phi(q,\alpha r)/|\Omega_r|} < \xi$) then mark p as an outlier and add to O_c;
5 update $\widetilde{f}_h(x)$; // using formula (1) and Epanechnikov kernel in formula (2);

---

5 Micro-Cluster Based Outlier Detection Algorithm

Although the NOD algorithm is effective and universal, it has two main problems: fist, the time complexity of NOD algorithm has space to improve, for example, computing the JS-divergence and selecting more efficient kernel width. And second, it can not scale very well for large data sets in distributed data stream, especially the coordinator node. To solve these problems, a general strategy is to apply data compression or summarization which can save the memory and run time. Then, we select the micro-cluster CF-tree [4] data structure to condense the stream data. The micro-clusters only save the smaller data set and the information of their close neighbors. We will describe the *Micro CF-Tree Based Distributed Outlier Detection Algorithm* (MOD Algorithm) in detail.

Approximate JS-divergence: The time complexity for computing JS-divergence,directly using Equation (7), is $O(dn)$. Theoretically, a new data incoming the sliding window or an old data being dropped out will change the kernel density for all data points in the whole sliding window. Obviously, it is too inefficient and unscalable to suit the evolving data stream. Intuitively, the incoming data and dropped data are a very small proportion to the capacity of sliding window. The points are more close to the changeable data, the influence is more serious. To balance the accuracy and complexity, we provide an approximate JS-divergence (see formula 8) which is only concerned about the changeable data (S_{in} and S_{out}) and their k-nearest neighbors set (see definition 3). S_{in} is a points set of coming to the sliding window, and S_{out} is a points set which dropped out by the sliding window. As the number $|\Delta_{S_{in} \cup S_{out}}|$ is much less than n, time complexity is reduced to $O\left(d\left(|\Delta_{S_{in} \cup S_{out}}| + \log n\right)\right)$ which $\log n$ is the time spending to search k-nearest neighbor set.

Definition 3 (k-nearest neighbor set). D_p^k *is the distance between point p and its k-nearest neighbor. Δ_p, named " k-nearest neighbor set of point p", is defined as a set that contains all points which distance is not larger than D_p^k. Δ_S, named " k-nearest neighbor set of set S", is defined as $\bigcup_{p \in S} \Delta_p$.*

$$\widehat{D}_{JS}(p,q) = \sum_{i \in \Delta_{S_{in} \cup S_{out}}} \left(p_i \ln \frac{2p_i}{p_i + q_i} + q_i \ln \frac{2q_i}{p_i + q_i} \right) . \tag{8}$$

Improved Kernel width: The "rule-of-thumb" width will increase very fast following by the $\widetilde{\sigma}$ and n in equation (4). To balance the quality and efficiency, we consider the distance between the point and its k-nearest neighbors. So an improved kernel width is listed in formula (9). D_x^k is the distance between point x and its k-nearest neighbor.

$$\widehat{h} = \min \left\{ 2.345 \widetilde{\sigma} n^{-1/5}, D_x^k \right\} . \tag{9}$$

Micro-Cluster Definition and MOD Algorithm: It stores a compact summarization for each cluster in a *CF-Tree* [4] which is a balanced tree structure similar to an R-tree. We define the concept of micro-cluster-based outlier more precisely, as follows:

Definition 4. *An extended micro CF-tree for a set of d-dimensional points $D_{i_1}, D_{i_2}, \cdots, D_{i_n}$ with time-stamp $T_{i_1}, T_{i_2}, \cdots, T_{i_n}$ and each point $D_j = (d_j^1, d_j^2, \cdots, d_j^d)$, is defined as the $(4d+1+|\Delta_C|+|O_C|)$-tuple $(\overline{ACF1(C)}, \overline{ACF2(C)}, \overline{MIN(C)}, \overline{MAX(C)}, \Delta_C, O_C, n(C))$. $(\overline{ACF1(C)}, \overline{ACF2(C)}, \overline{MIN(C)}, \overline{MAX(C)}$ are four vectors of d entries. The definition of each of these entries is as follows:*

- *The p-th entry of $\overline{ACF1(C)}$ is equal to $\sum_{j=1}^{n(C)} d_{i_j}^p$, The p-th entry of $\overline{ACF2(C)}$ is equal to $\sum_{j=1}^{n(C)} (d_{i_j}^p)^2$;*
- *The p-th entry of $\overline{MIN(C)}$ is equal to $\min_{j=1}^{n(C)} d_{i_j}^p$, The p-th entry of $\overline{MAX(C)}$ is equal to $\max_{j=1}^{n(C)} d_{i_j}^p$;*
- *The Δ_C is defined in definition (3), O_C holds the outliers in cluster C, $n(C)$ is the count number in Micro-Cluster C.*

The centroid G_C and radius R_C of micro cluster can be represented as: $G_C = \frac{\overline{ACF1(C)}}{n(C)}$ and $R_C = \left(\frac{\sum_{j=1}^{n(C)} (D_j - G_{Cj})}{n(C)} \right)^{\frac{1}{2}} = \left(\frac{\overline{ACF2(C)} + n(C)G_C - 2G_C \overline{ACF1(C)}}{n(C)} \right)^{\frac{1}{2}}$.

Algorithm 2. CF-Tree Based Distributed Outlier Detection Algorithm

---

Input: same as Naïve Algorithm 1
Output: the outlier set O_c
Procedure CoordinatorProcess()
1 find the closest micro-cluster from the CF-Tree to the point p which a new point
   from a child node, assumed the cluster as GC which is a leaf node in the CF-Tree;
2 **if**$(p \notin O_{GC})$ **then isOutlier**(p, GC);
3 update $\widetilde{f}_{\widehat{h}}(x)$; // using formula (1) and kernel width in formula (9);
4 **if**$(\widehat{D}_{JS}(\widehat{f}_{\widehat{h}}^{new}, \widehat{f}_{\widehat{h}}^{old}) > \lambda)$ **then** broadcast $\widehat{f}_{\widehat{h}}^{new}$ to the all child node;
5 **if**$(p \in O_{GC}$, or is marked as an outlier) **then** report point p as an outlier;
6 **else** insert p to micro-cluster GC;
Procedure ChildProcess()
1 find the closest micro-cluster from the CF-Tree to the new point p, assumed as LC
   which is a leaf node in the CF-Tree;
2 **if**$(p \notin O_{LC})$ **then isOutlier**(p, LC);
3 update $\widetilde{f}_{\widehat{h}}(x)$; // using formula (1) and kernel width in formula (9);
4 **if**$(\widehat{D}_{JS}(\widehat{f}_{\widehat{h}}^{new}, \widehat{f}_{\widehat{h}}^{old}) > \lambda)$ **then** send the point p and $\widehat{f}_{\widehat{h}}^{new}$ to the coordinator node;
5 **if**$(p \notin O_{GC}$, and is not marked as an outlier) **then** insert p to LC;
Procedure isOutlier(point p, micro cluster MC)
1 **if**$(BDisKE = \mathbf{true})$
2   **if**$(\Phi(p, r) < \rho)$ **then** mark p as an outlier and add to O_{MC};
3 **else** sum up to $\Omega_r = \bigcup_{q \in MC} \Delta_q$;
4 **if**$(\frac{\Phi(p, \alpha r)}{\sum_{q \in \Omega_r} \Phi(q, \alpha r)/|\Omega_r|} < \xi)$ **then** mark p as an outlier and add to O_{MC};
5 update $\widetilde{f}_{\widehat{h}}(x)$; // using formula (1) and kernel width in formula (9);

---

6 Experiments

We will present experimental results for our two algorithms comparing with two typical algorithms(NL algorithm [5] and LOCI algorithm [8]). There are three primary purposes: (1) Comparing the precision and recall ratio in four real data sets. (2) Verifying the algorithm scalability in high dimensions and large numbers of child nodes. (3) Checking the efficiency of two kernel widths ($\widetilde{h}$ and $\widehat{h}$).

All experiments were run on 3.2 GHz PentiumIV PCs with 1GB memory and Windows XP. To evaluate the efficiency and scalability of our two algorithms, real and synthetic data sets are used. Real data sets include adult, KDD cup 99, forest and stock price series. The last data set consists of the price for a single stock taken at frequent intervals over a six year period. Total count is $330K$ values. The other three data sets come from the UCI machine learning repository. All algorithms are implemented by Visual C++ 6.0.

Efficiency of NOD and MOD algorithms: The first experiment focused on the efficiency of four algorithms. We use two measures, namely *precision* and *recall*, defined as follows. *Precision* represents the fraction of the values reported by our algorithms as outliers that are true outliers. *Recall* represents the fraction of the true outliers that our algorithms identified correctly. We set the sliding

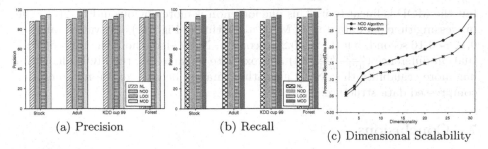

(a) Precision   (b) Recall   (c) Dimensional Scalability

Fig. 1. Precision and Recall in four real datasets, and dimensional scalability

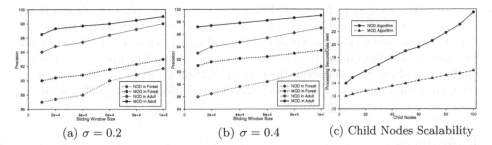

(a) $\sigma = 0.2$ (b) $\sigma = 0.4$ (c) Child Nodes Scalability

Fig. 2. Precision when varying the sliding window size, and nodes scalability

window size $N = 10000$. Unless particularly mentioned, the nearest neighbor $k = 8$, divergence threshold $\lambda = 0.1$ and fading factor $\omega = 0.2$. We selected five real value columns in the real data sets (The stock price series data set only has one column and we constructed five columns by simply duplicating the column). The experiment results in Fig. 1 (a) and (b) indicate that our NOD algorithm is better than the corresponding distance-based NL algorithm, the MOD algorithm also exceeds the LOCI, although only $0.2 \sim 3.1\%$ improvement.

Selecting the Kernel Width: Kernel width is a virtual parameter in kernel density estimation. In this experiment, we select two very large data sets (adult and forest cover). We consider the precision change with the sliding window size. The sliding window varied from 10000 to 100000. In Fig. 2 (a) the $\sigma = 0.2$ in the real data selected and Fig. 2 (b) is 0.4. The results show the MOD algorithm has more better precision than the NOD algorithm, especially in Fig. 2 (b). The precision in MOD algorithm is less sensitive than NOD algorithm following with the change of sliding window. This owes to the kernel width. In MOD algorithm, we considered the influence of k-nearest neighbors.

Algorithm Scalability: The scalability is an important criteria to judge whether an algorithm is suitable for distributed environment or not. Our synthetic data were random sample columns from adult data sets. We used ten PCs to simulate the 100 child nodes (each node simulate ten child nodes) and one PC as the coordinator node. each In Fig. 1(c) and Fig. 2(c), we change the dimension(d) and child nodes(N) to check the precision of NOD and MOD algorithms. The results show that: NOD algorithm is exponential proportional to the dimension, but the MOD is linear to it. This phenomenon is more obvious in Fig. 2(c). The processing time per data item of MOD algorithm in Fig. 2(c) only varied range of $0.12 \sim 0.16$ second, but $0.14 \sim 0.25$ second in NOD algorithm. The ratio of fluctuation difference ($\frac{0.25-0.14}{0.16-0.12} \approx 3$) approximate to three. So, the MOD algorithm has more scalability than NOD algorithm, mainly because of the micro-cluster compressed data structure.

7 Conclusions

In this paper, we study the problem of continuous outlier detection over distributed data streams. Outlier detection is very important in this context, since it enables the analyst to focus on the interesting events over vast stream data. We propose two novel outlier measures and algorithms which adopt the kernel density estimation technique. We adopt the fading strategy to conquer evolution and mico-cluster technique to scale for large distributed environments. Both a mathematical analysis and experimental evaluation on real and synthetic data show that the proposed methods are efficient and effective comparing with existing outlier detection algorithms.

References

1. Barnett, V., Lewis, T.: Outliers in statistical data, 3rd edn. Wiley, Chichester (2001)
2. Eskin, E.: Anomaly detection over noisy data using learned probability distributions. In: ICML (2000)
3. Ester, M., Kriegel, H.P., Xu, X.: A database interface for clustering in large spatial databases. In: KDD (1995)
4. Zhang, T., Ramakrishnan, R., Livny, M.: Birch: an efficient data clustering method for very large databases. In: SIGMOD (1996)
5. Knorr, E.M., Ng, R.T.: Algorithms for mining distance-based outliers in large datasets. In: VLDB (1998)
6. Tao, Y., Xiao, X., Zhou, S.: Mining distance-based outliers from large databases in any metric space. In: KDD (2006)
7. Breunig, M.M., Kriegel, H.P., Ng, R.T., Sander, J.: Lof: identifying density-based local outliers. In: SIGMOD (2000)
8. Papadimitriou, S., Kitagawa, H., Gibbons, P.B., Faloutsos, C.: Loci: Fast outlier detection using the local correlation integral. In: ICDE (2003)
9. Jin, W., Tung, A.K.H., Han, J., Wang, W.: Ranking outliers using symmetric neighborhood relationship. In: PAKDD (2006)
10. Manjhi, A., Shkapenyuk, V., Dhamdhere, K., Olston, C.: Finding (recently) frequent items in distributed data streams. In: ICDE (2005)
11. Cormode, G., Muthukrishnan, S., Zhuang, W.: Conquering the divide: Continuous clustering of distributed data streams. In: ICDE (2007)
12. Scott, D.W.: Multivariate Density Estimation: Theory, Practice, and Visualization. Wiley, Chichester (2001)
13. Gijbels, I., Pope, A., Wand, M.: Automatic forecasting via exponential smoothing: Asymptotic properties (1997)
14. Ali, S.M., Silvey, S.D.: A general class of coefficients of divergence of one distribution from another. J. Roy. Statist. Soc. Ser B 28, 131–142 (1966)

A Resource Discovery and Allocation Mechanism in Large Computational Grids for Media Applications

Chun-Fu Lin and Ruay-Shiung Chang

Department of Computer Science and Information Engineering
National Dong Hwa University, Hualien, Taiwan
d9321010@em93.ndhu.edu.tw, rschang@mail.ndhu.edu.tw

Abstract. There has been significant effort to build high throughput computing systems out of many distributed multimedia servers. These systems should accommodate a larger number of servers and should handle the ever-growing user demands. Recently, Grid computing has become one of the promising technologies that can deliver such a system. Among the many problems encountered in building Grid computing systems, resource discovery, overhead reduction, workload balancing and fault tolerance are the most challenging. In this paper, we present a resource discovery and allocation mechanism (RDAM) in a computational Grid system.

1 Introduction

The Grid technologies [1] have been widely adapted in science, engineering computing, biological computation and so on. A computational grid is a set of hardware and software resources that provide seamless, dependable, and pervasive access to high-end computational capabilities. Resource on the grid may be geographically distributed and belongs to different administrative domains.

A computational grid is an emerging computing infrastructure that enables effective access to high performance computing resources. The computational grid technology mainly consists of three parts [6]: computational broker for dividing a job to smaller tasks, resource manager for resource discovery, allocation and maintenance, and task scheduler for assigning tasks to resources. The computational broker's main capacity is to divide a user submitted job into smaller pieces suitable for individual computing resource such that it can be executed efficiently and job will be completed faster by the grid systems. The resource manager's main function is resource discovery and maintains resource table that records the states of resource providers for the grid system. The job scheduler's main function is to transmit tasks to resources that will execute this job.

In the grid environment, resource filter [9] and fault tolerance [7] are two key concerns when developing grid applications. Different types of computing need different resources in a grid computing system. Furthermore, effective allocation of resources is becoming very important. Monitoring the states of tasks and guaranteeing tasks are finished are equally important problems.

In this paper, we propose a mechanism for efficient resource discovery with the help of an agent. The agent accepts a task submission from users. Parameters such as CPU

P. Thulasiraman et al. (Eds.): ISPA 2007 Workshops, LNCS 4743, pp. 315–325, 2007.
© Springer-Verlag Berlin Heidelberg 2007

speed and memory size may accompany with the task submission to the agent. The agent will then have the scope of requirement and will deliver the request to a resource manager. The resource manager (RM) will discover the suitable resources in three steps. If suitable resources can be found, the RM will return a set of eligible resource providers to the agent. Agent allocates a suitable provider to a task by a utilization algorithm. In this paper, we analyze the factors that affect the performance of computational grid in our resource discovery and allocation method. The goal is to devise a new resource and allocation mechanism for computational grids. We hope the mechanism should be efficient, suitable and fault tolerant.

The rest of this paper is organized as follows. Section 2 presents the system architecture for resource discovery in a computational grid. Section 3 presents the resource discovery and allocation mechanism. Finally, conclusions are given in Section 4.

2 System Architecture

For small to medium scale Grids, solutions such as the approach used in Globus [11] will be fine. However, for large, up to global-scale Grids, approach used in Globus is not efficient and scale well. In this paper, we propose a new resource discovery and allocation mechanism (RDAM) in a large Grid system.

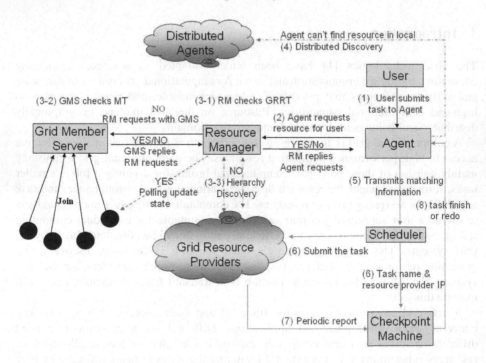

Fig. 1. The system architecture in a large computational Grid

The architecture consists of grid users, Grid Resource providers, Resource Manager (RM), Grid Member Server (GMS), Agent, Scheduler and Checkpoint machine. Fig. 1 illustrates the architecture of RDAM, the functions of RDAM are as follows.

- Task submitted:
  (1) Users submit tasks with minimum demands and resource weights to Agent.
- Resources restricted:
  (2) Agent accepts tasks from users. It restricts the scope of resource demands and then sends out *Agent_Query* to RM to ask for resources specified by user submitted tasks.
- Resource discovery in Local:
  RM will discover a set of eligible resource providers to Agent using three steps.
  (3-1) RM inquires about resources by Global Resource Record Table (GRRT). If they can be found in this stage, RM will forward those providers' resource information to Agent.
  (3-2) The function of Grid member Server (GMS) is mainly to record the IP address and the computing capacity of resource provider joining newly in member table (MT). If resource providers found by Grid Member Server (GMS), RM updates those providers' state, delete in MT and record in GRRT.
  (3-3) If resource providers can't be found in GRRT and MT, GRRT will upgrade partly by hierarchy discovery.
- Resource discovery in global:
  (4) If resource provider can't be found in local, Agent will send out *Agent_Query* to Distributed Agents to ask for resource.
- Resource allocation
  (5) In a set of eligible resource providers that offered by RM or distributed agents, Agent will extract out suitable provider according to the condition of resource utilization (RU) and transmit the matching information to Scheduler.
- Assign Task:
  (6) The Scheduler not only submits the task to resource provider but also forward the task name and resource provider IP to Checkpoint Machine.
- Task monitoring:
  The checkpoint machine [8] mainly capacity is monitor resource that have tasks executing for fault tolerance.
  (7) The resource provider periodic reports the progress of task to Checkpoint Machine during the task begins to finish.
  (8) The Agent will resend *Agent_Query* to look for replacer while checkpoint machine failing to receive periodic progress with deadline.

We adopt hierarchical type to resource discovery according to RU. The GRRT, GMS and resource discovery are three steps of resource providers in this paper, we will introduce in detail to follow.

3 Resource Allocation and Discovery

In [10], agent has capacity all in one, the capacity include resource discovery, resource table updating for self and updating table. Agent-based system will be effect heavy overhead. In [2, 4, 5], the mechanism of resource discovery is to find out resource that can assign to task but not consider about suitable match. It will cause low-demand task assign to high-performance provider and high-demand task bounded waits for resource. This is an important about workload balancing for grid system. It could be happen performance making down situation for integration grid system. These problems can be solved in our approach.

We propose a mechanism for efficient resource discovery in three steps for enhancing hit rate for task requirement and resource filter for task assign to suitable resource, in order to guarantee the workload balancing and make down overhead in integration grid system.

As the follow show, there are three types of table used in computational grid and our solution is based on a Distributed Hash Table (DHT) implementation as described in Chord [3]. A DHT is a distributed and often decentralized mechanism for associating hash values (keys) with some kind of content. Participants in the DHT each store a small section of the contents of the hash table. The main advantage of DHTs is their scalability: a typical search on a DHT requires only $O(log(n))$ network traffic where n is the number of participants in the DHT. This compares very favorably to gnutella-style search, which requires $O(n)$ traffic, and super peer style networks, which require about $O(sqrt(n))$ traffic to perform a complete search.

(i)   Global Resource Record Table (GRRT) in RM: it records resources that can be offered.
(ii) Local Resource Record Table (LRRT): it records resources of itself and its neighbors.
(iii) Member Table (MT) in GMS: it records the IP address and the computing capacity of resource node joining newly.

GRRT and LRRT have the same content that consists of seven entries as the follow:

(1) Provider IP: We used physical address to discern the resource provider.
(2) Usable Memory_MB: The quantity of memory that resource provider can be used.
(3) CPU_MHz: the grade of CPU that can execute the task.
(4) Storage_GB: the capacity of storage that can be used for task.
(5) Network_Kbps: The resource provider periodic ping RM and derive out the quality of network according to round trip time.
(6) Computing capacity: It records what kinds of computing capacity can be offered.
(7) Resource utilization (RU): each provider has the ability of calculate the resource utilization of its processor, storage and network connectivity as below:

$$i = \text{CPU utilization}$$
$$j = \text{Memory utilization}$$
$$k = \text{Storage utilization}$$
$$l = \text{Quality of network}$$

The users have an option of choosing the providers that best meet their requirements. An example of user option is given bellows:

Minimum demands	Resource Weight
CPU_MHz = a	CPU= α
Memory_MB=b	Memory= β
Storage_GB=c	Storage= γ
Network_Kbps=d	Network= ϑ

Computing capacity= Matrix

The limitations of α, β, γ and ϑ are coefficient values.

3.1 Agent

Most methods of resource discovery adopt the criterion of minimum requires and random select for the task. It may cause the powerful provider is used in task with small demand because the number of requirements are not limited and can be extended. If Agent temporarily unable to offer resources, it will cause the task waits to appoint seriously. In this paper we propose resource filter (RF) in order to solve the upper problems. The main function of RF is limiting the requirement resource scope for task by n time's constraint rule.

Agent will restricts the range of demands when receive task requirement with the minimum demands of task are CPU_MHz = a, Memory_MB=b, Storage_GB=c and Network_Kbps=d. The RF equation will as bellow:

$$F = \left\{ V_i = (A, B, C, D) \begin{vmatrix} a \leq A \leq \omega a \\ b \leq B \leq \xi b \\ c \leq C \leq \psi c \\ d \leq D \leq \zeta d \end{vmatrix} \right\}$$

Where ω, ξ, ψ, ζ are adjust coefficient

A simplified example of RF is shown in Fig. 2. The user minimum demands of CPU_MHz = 1000 and Memory_MB=512 for task. If we use 2 time constraint rule, it will be narrow the scope of resource providers. Adopt the criterion of minimum requires without constraint (blue cover area) is wider than RF (orange area). The aim of RF is looking for a set of eligible resource providers but not allocate the most powerful provider. Thus, RF can promote the efficiency of the whole.

The policy of resource selection and accept the request of user are the mainly function of agent. When agent receives the replies from RM, it will extract which provider is responsible for task by different RU.

For example, if resource weight $\alpha > \beta > \gamma > \vartheta$, agent will compare utilization in the set of eligible resource providers according to the order of i, j, k and l. Agent selects resource provider of low utilization to execute task. The advantage of resource selection by RU is reaching workload balancing.

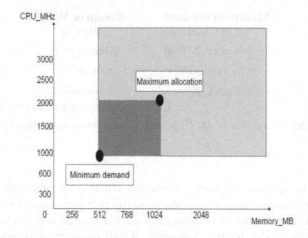

Fig. 2. Resource filtering with 2 rules

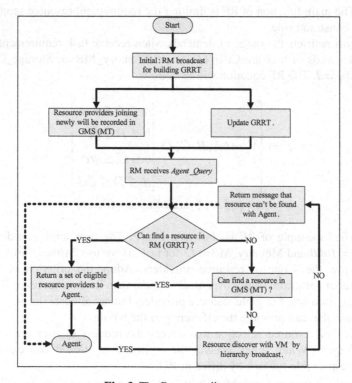

Fig. 3. The Resource discovery

3.2 Resource Manager

When RM receives *Agent_Query*, it will discover a set of eligible resource providers to agent with the mechanism of three steps. Resource discovery will take place in three kinds of situations as the follow shown:

(1) Initial: RM will broadcast to catch resources of all providers because GRRT and MT are empty.
(2) Resource in GRRT: RM replies to agent.
(3) Resource in GMS: RM forwards *Agent_Query* to GMS; it will check the MT accorded with the request. If resource provider in MT accord with the demand, RM will poll update the detailed resource state of provider, delete it in the content of MT and record in GRRT.
(4-1) local Agent sends out *Agent_Query* to Distributed Agents to ask for eligible resource providers. The global discovery rule of distributed agents is looking for resource in GRRTs and GMTs.
(4-2) by hierarchy discovery: If providers can't be found by GRRT and MT, GRRT will upgrade partly by hierarchy discovery.

By three steps of resource providers, the resource discovery of this paper possess lower overhead and high hit rate. The flowchart is shown in Fig. 3.

The opportunity of starting hierarchy discovery is not found resources in GRRT and MT. The mechanism of discovery is adopting hierarchy search by the constraint of RU. In this paper, we adopt linear equation to calculate the average RU. The operation type of RU as below:

$$ Provider\_RU \ = \ \frac{1}{3}(i \ + \ j \ + \ k \ + \ l) $$

Assume the constraint of RU is *N* percent; when the resource provider receives the query of RM, it will carry out the following procedure and the flowchart is shown in Fig. 4.

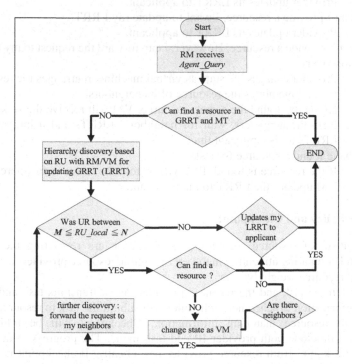

Fig. 4. The hierarchy discovery procedure

Procedure   //hierarchy discovery
// Compare the constraint of RU with its own RU
Input N
$M: = 0$ // M is the border RU
{For P=1, P=P+1
   $N:= PN$ && $N \leqq 100\%$ // N is the constraint of RU
   If $M \leqq RU\_local \leqq PN$
     { If resource is suitable for request
     then acknowledge RM the resource in where and updates its LRRT to the
          applicant
       else provider state=VM, forward request and
           wait for later generation to updates LRRTs to the applicant
}
  else updates the LRRT to the applicant
    $M:= PN$ // M is the border RU
    $N:= (P+1)N \square N \leqq 100\%$ // N is the constraint of RU
    }
    Exit

A provider can act on a resource in some of states, as below:

(1) Yes, I can provide a resource for task and discovery finish successfully.
- Provider updates its LRRT to applicant.

(2) No, I can't provide a resource. I want to update my LRRT.
- Provider updates its LRRT to applicant.

(3) No, I can't provide a resource. However, I can forward the request to my neighbors for further discovery.
- Provider changes the state as virtual machine, rearranges the resources of it's and maintains the resource of its neighbors.
- No matter found the correct resource, VM will receive the Acknowledge form the neighbors, wait for neighbors' LRRTs and it integrates those LRRTs to the applicant thus.

(3) Yes, I have found a resource for task.
- If the resource is found, RM will be told the resource in where First and VM updates the LRRT to the applicant.

3.3 Agent Policy and Checkpoint

The mechanism of resource selection and allocation are restricting the scope of demands and comparing utilization in the set of eligible resource providers according to the order of resource weight by user.

After match the task and the resource provider, agent transmits task and resource matching information to scheduler. Scheduler will submit the task to resource provider according to resource matching information. Checkpoint will be told relevant information to include both provider IP and task name. The progress of task will be report to Checkpoint from resource provider periodically. If checkpoint receives the information of task had finish, it will stop monitoring the state of task.

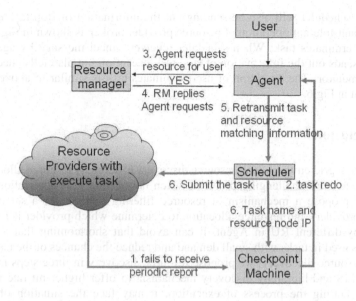

Fig. 5. The Agent, Scheduler and Checkpoint Machine cooperation architecture for task executions

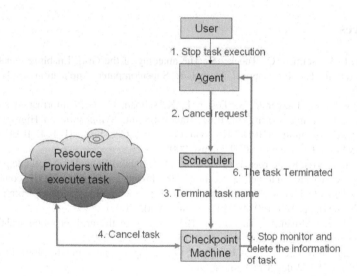

Fig. 6. Task termination

There are two kinds of station need to be emphasized:

(1) Resource provider broken: Agent will be told that task loses efficiency by checkpoint when it fails to receive periodic report from resource provider. Agent will retransmit the same task to other resource provider. Besides above-mentioned

work, scheduler will also be sending out the information of stop task execution. The fault-tolerant operation of resource provider broken is shown in Fig. 5.

(2) User terminates task: When scheduler receives cancel message by agent, it not only sends out the information of stop task execution but also tells checkpoint to stop monitor. The operation of user terminates task is similar to above which is shown in Fig.6.

4 Conclusions

In computing grid environment, resource discovery efficiency, resource allocation and fault tolerance are challenging problems when developing grid applications. In this paper, we propose a mechanism of resource filtering to look for a set of eligible resource providers and resource allocation to determine which provider is responsible for task by different RU in Agent. It can avoid that shortcoming that a powerful provider is used in tasks with small demand and reduce the chances of the task waiting time. In resource discovery, we propose resource discovery in three steps includes of GRRT, GMS and hierarchy discovery mechanism to offer higher hit rate and lower overhead. During the process of execution, it may face the situation of resource provider crash. We propose a checkpoint mechanism by monitor the state of executing tasks for fault tolerances.

References

[1] Foster, I., Kesselman, C., Tuecke, S.: The anatomy of the Grid: Enabling scalable virtual organization. The International Journal of Supercomputer Applications 15(3), 200–222 (2001)

[2] Czajkowski, K., Fitzgerald, S., Foster, I., Kesselman, C.: Grid information services for distributed resource sharing. In: Proc. 10th IEEE Int. Symposium on High-performance distributed computing (HPDC-10), San Francisco, CA, pp. 181–194. IEEE Computer Society Press, Los Alamitos (7-9 August, 2001)

[3] Stoica, I., Morris, R., Karger, D., Kaashoek, M.F., Balakrishnan, H.: A scalable peer-to-peer lookup service for internet applications. In: Proceedings of the 2001 conference on applications, technologies, architectures, and protocols for computer communications (SIGCOMM), pp. 149–160. ACM Press, New York (2001)

[4] Foster, I., Kesselman, C., Tuecke, S.: The anatomy of the grid: enabling scalable virtual organizations. Int. J. Supercomput. Appl. 15(3), 200–222 (2001)

[5] Berman, F., Fox, G.C., Hey, A.J.G. (eds.): Grid computing: making the global infrastructure a reality, p. 557. Wiley, Chichester (2003)

[6] Othman, A., Dew, P., Djemamem, K., Gourlay, I.: Adaptive Grid Resource Brokering,Cluster Computing. In: Proceedings. 2003 IEEE International Conference, pp. 172–179. IEEE Computer Society Press, Los Alamitos (2003)

[7] Lee, H.M., Chin, S.H., Lee, J.H., Lee, D.W., Chung, K.S., Jung, S.Y., Yu, H.C.: A resource manager for optimal resource selection and fault tolerance service in Grids, Cluster Computing and the Grid, CCGrid 2004. In: IEEE Conference on Cluster Computing and grid, pp. 572–579. IEEE Computer Society Press, Los Alamitos (2004)

 [8] Bonacorsi, D., Colling, D., Field, L., Fisher, S.M., Grandi, C., Hobson, P.R., Kyberd, P., MacEvoy, B., Nebrensky, J.J., Tallini, H., Traylen, S.: calability tests of R-GMA-based grid job monitoring system for CMS Monte Carlo data production. Journal of Nuclear Science 51(6)part 1, 3026–3029 (2004)
 [9] Chunlin, L., Layuan, L.: Pricing and resource allocation in computational grid with utility functions, Information Technology: Coding and Computing, 2005. ITCC 2005 International Conference 2, 175–180 (2005)
[10] Ding, S., Yuan, J., JiubinJu, H.L.: A heuristic algorithm for agent-based grid resource discovery. In: IEEE International Conference on e-Technology, e-Commerce and e-Service, pp. 222–225. IEEE Computer Society Press, Los Alamitos (2005)
[11] Globus, http://www.globus.org

Impact of Dynamic Growing on the Internet Degree Distribution

Rogelio Ortega Izaguirre[1], Eustorgio Meza Conde[1], Claudia Gómez Santillán[1,2], Laura Cruz Reyes[2], and Tania Turrubiates López[2]

[1] Centro de Investigación en Ciencia Aplicada y Tecnología Avanzada (CICATA). Carretera Tampico-Puerto Industrial Altamira, Km. 14.5. Altamira, Tamaulipas. Teléfono: 01 833 2600124

[2] Instituto Tecnológico de Ciudad Madero (ITCM). 1ro. de Mayo y Sor Juana I. de la Cruz s/n CP. 89440, Tamaulipas, México.Teléfono: 01 833 3574820 Ext. 3024

rortegai@ipn.mx, emezac@ipn.mx, cggs71@hotmail.com, lcruzreyes@prodigy.net.mx, tania_251179@hotmail.com

Abstract. A great amount of natural and artificial systems can be represented as a complex network, where the entities of the system are related of non-trivial form. Thus, the network topology is the pattern of the interactions between entities. The characterization of complex networks allows analyzing, classifying and modeling the topology of complex networks. The degree distribution is a characterization function used in the analysis of complex networks. In this work a comparative study of the degree distribution for three different instances of the Internet was carried out, with information about the interconnection of domains. The Internet has a degree distribution power-law, that is, it has a great amount of weakly connected domains while a few domains have a great number of connections. Our results show that Internet has a dynamic growing maintaining the degree distribution power-law through the time, independently of the growth in the number of domains and its connections.

1 Introduction

The science of networks includes several scientific disciplines as Mathematics, Physics, Biology, Sociology and Computer Sciences. A complex network denotes a graph with a non-trivial topological structure. The interest to know the topological properties of real networks is growing [1][2]. The Internet is an example of a complex network growing constantly, which allows us to analyze its structural changes in the time.

This research analyzes the changes in the degree distribution produced by the accelerated growth of Internet in the time. The topology of Internet at domain level is considered. A domain is a set of computers, routers and telecommunication devices. We consider the Internet topology as a complex network where physical links (edges) connect domains each other. Finally, the node degree is the number of its adjacent nodes.

The study of the topology is important since it allows to identify characteristics that can be used to develop search algorithms of distributed resources [4][5], and

P. Thulasiraman et al. (Eds.): ISPA 2007 Workshops, LNCS 4743, pp. 326–334, 2007.
© Springer-Verlag Berlin Heidelberg 2007

mathematical models that are useful to simulate networks of the real World [6]. In related works it was demonstrated that the Internet has a power-law degree distribution. In the Internet there are few nodes with very high degree while most of nodes have a small degree [3]. Our results show that Internet has a dynamic growth that maintains its degree distribution power-law independently of the number of domains and its connections.

2 Definitions

In this section, we formally define the degree distribution and explain several types of complex networks found in literature.

2.1 Degree Distribution

Consider $G = (N,E)$ as an undirected graph, where N is the set of nodes, E is the set of edges, $n = |N|$ is the number of nodes and $e = |E|$ is the number of edges in G. Let $i \in N$, a node in G. In the same way $k(i) = k_i$ is the degree for a node i. Hence, $\delta(G)$ is defined as the minimum degree and $\Delta(G)$ is the maximum degree in G. The average degree in G is defined as $\langle k \rangle >= 2e/n$. Based on all the above, $1 \leq k \leq \Delta(G)$, denote the set of possible degree values for any node $i \in N$. Finally, X_k^G is defined as the number of nodes in G with degree k. The probability that a node in G has degree k is expressed by,

$$P(k) = \frac{X_k^G}{n}.$$ (1)

If $P(k)$, $\forall k$ is calculated, the degree distribution for G is obtained [10]. In Fig. 1, the procedure to calculate the degree distribution is showed. In Fig. 1(a) the topology

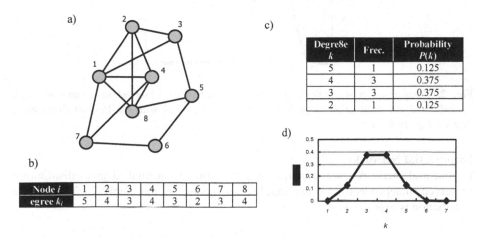

Fig. 1. Procedure to calculate the degree distribution for a graph

for a graph G is presented. In Fig. 1(b) the table shows the degree for each node, $i \in N$. In the same way Fig. 1(c) presents a table with the frequency and probability for each degree $1 \leq k \leq \Delta(G)$ found in G. Finally, Fig. 1(d) shows a plot with the probabilities $P(k)$.

2.2 Degree Distribution Characterization

The growth of the real networks is a complicated process that produces different types of degree distributions [6, 11-15]. Thus, the degree distribution allows us to classify natural and artificial complex networks as: random graphs, exponential networks and scale-free networks.

Random Graphs
Random graphs are characterized by a binomial distribution when the number of nodes in the network is small. If $n \to \infty$, the degree distribution follows a Poisson distribution,

$$P\left(k = k_i\right) = \frac{\langle k \rangle^k e^{-\langle k \rangle}}{k!}, \tag{2}$$

Equation (2) allows to obtain analytically the probability that a node i in the graph has degree k. Fig. 2 shows the degree distribution, $P_G(k=k_i)$, obtained from a random graph with 3072 nodes, 19778 edges, $\delta(G)=3$, $\Delta(G)=30$, $\langle k \rangle=12$ [19]. The solid line represents the degree distribution, $P(k=k_i)$, calculated with the equation (2).

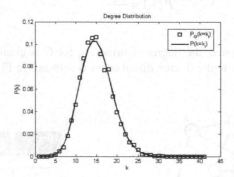

Fig. 2. Comparison between the distribution of probability observed in a random graph $P_G(k=k_i)$ and the distribution of probability that is calculated with the Poisson distribution $P(k=k_i)$, Equation (2)

Exponential Networks
Exponential networks are characterized by an exponential degree distribution preserved independently to the number of nodes in the network. The degree distribution is expressed as,

$$P\left(k = k_i\right) = \frac{1}{e^{k/m}},$$ (3)

where m represents the minimum degree in the network [6 ,11]. The equation (3) allows us to obtain analytically the probability that a node i in the graph has degree k.

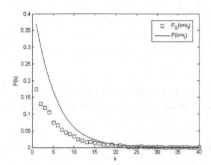

Fig. 3. Comparison between the distribution of probability observed in an exponential network $P_G(k=k_i)$ and the distribution of probability $P(k=k_i)$ that is calculated with Equation (3)

Fig. 3 shows the degree distribution, $P_G(k=k_i)$, that was obtained from an exponential network with 3072 nodes, 15338 edges, $\delta(G)=5$, $\Delta(G)=44$, $\langle k \rangle=9$ [20]. The solid line denotes the degree distribution, $P(k=k_i)$ calculated with Equation (3). The exponential degree distribution can be observed in the electrical power network of the South California [21] and in the National Railroad of India [22].

Scale-free Networks
Scale-free networks are characterized by a power-law degree distribution maintained independently of the number of nodes and edges in the network. The degree distribution power- law is expressed as,

$$P\!\left(k = k_i\right) = \frac{1}{k^\gamma},$$ (4)

where γ is obtained from the linear regression of the degree distribution in the logarithmic double space [3]. Equation (4) allows to obtain analytically the probability that a node i in the graph has degree k. Fig. 4 shows the degree distribution, $P_G(k=k_i)$, obtained from a scale-free network with 3072 nodes, 15339 edges, $\delta(G)=5$, $\Delta(G)=220$, $\langle k \rangle=9$ [6]. The solid line denotes the degree distribution, $P(k=k_i)$, calculated with Equation (4).

Although in this research work only the degree distribution of Internet is analyzed, there are other functions of characterization in literature that allow to obtain information from the network topology, for example, the shortest path length [17], the clustering coefficient [17], and the efficiency [4]. We use the degree distribution because it is widely used in the research area of complex networks [1, 3, 9].

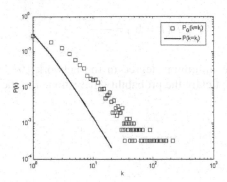

Fig. 4. Comparison between the distribution of probability observed in a scale free network $P_G(k=k_i)$ and the distribution of probability $P(k=k_i)$ that is calculated with Equation (4)

3 Experimentation

In order to carry out the experimentation, three real data sets of interconnections between the Internet domains have been analyzed. Data were recovered from the National Laboratory of Applied Network Research (NLANR) [7]. The NLANR uses routing equipment and tables BGP[1] to obtain data of other connected routers. Data sets correspond to observations made in 1997, 2000, and 2003. In Table 1, the number of nodes, the number of edges, the average degree, the minimum and the maximum degree are showed for each Internet instance.

Table 1. Information about Internet data sets for 1997, 2000 and 2003

Name	N	E	$\langle k \rangle$	$\delta(G)$	$\Delta(G)$
INT-1997	3,015	5,156	3.42	1	590
INT-2000	6,474	12,572	3.88	1	1,458
INT-2003	192,244	609,066	6.33	1	1,071

For each data set the degree distribution is calculated with Equation (1), and it is plotted in double logarithmic scale. In addition, using the procedure proposed by Faloutsos et. al [3], a small percentage of nodes with high degree and frequency X_k^G equal to 1 are removed. Specifically, $P(k)$ is plotted for degrees k, beginning in $k=1$ and until reaching the degree frequency 1. The value of frequency close to 1, shows that it is little probable that nodes with that degree k exist, thus, the analysis is made with nodes that have a frequency greater than 1. Finally, we found the value of the exponent γ of the power-law degree distribution, Equation (4), making a linear regression analysis in the double logarithmic space.

---

[1] The Border Gateway Protocol (BGP) is a routing inter-domain protocol using on Internet.

In Table 1, it is possible to observe that INT-2000 contains approximately two times the number of nodes and edges that we found in INT-1997. This increment in the number of nodes and edges motivates an increase in maximum degree, $\Delta(G)$, of INT-2000. However, although INT-2003 contains a number of nodes and edges much greater than INT-2000, exist a reduction in the maximum degree. This is a very important characteristic because in INT-2003, the increase in the number of nodes and edges aren't correlated with the increase of $\Delta(G)$. This behavior of $\Delta(G)$ indicates a better distribution of edges in the network and this distribution prevents the existence of nodes with a very high degree.

Fig. 5 shows the degree distribution in double logarithmic scale for data sets (a) INT-1997, (b) INT-2000, and (c) INT-2003. It is evident that independently of the number of nodes and the number of edges in each data set (Table 1), the degree distribution power-law is preserved. This is, the probability of finding nodes with small degree is high whereas if k is increased, the probability of finding nodes with high degree is reduced drastically

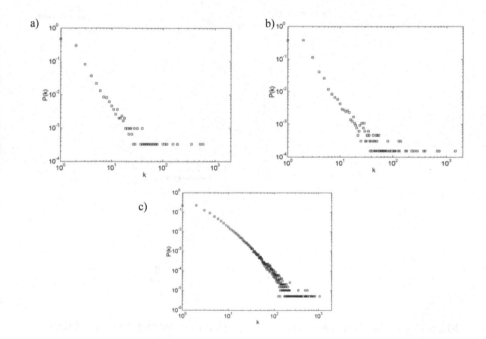

Fig. 5. Degree distribution $P(k)$ for data sets (a) INT-1997, (b) INT-2000, (c) INT-2003

On the other hand, Fig. 6, shows the degree distribution of data sets in double logarithmic scale, when the nodes of high degree have been eliminated. The solid line is the result of the linear regression. As a result of the linear regression analysis, we found γ with values 2.15, 2.12 and 2.23 for INT-1997, INT-2000, and INT-2003, respectively. The coefficients of correlation between data sets and the linear regression were 0.9915, 0.9790 and 0.9846 respectively.

In Fig. 6(a) the probability for $k=1$ is slightly below the curve, whereas, for $2 \leq k \leq 3$ the probability is over the regression curve. On high degrees a good adjustment of the probabilities is observed. Although Fig. 6(b) shows a similar behavior than Fig. 7(a), Fig. 6(b) presents a slight dispersion of the probabilities on high degrees. Unlike INT-1997 and INT-2000, in Fig. 6(c) the probability of $1 \leq k \leq 4$ is below the resulting curve of the linear regression. It shows that in the data set INT-2003, there is a reduction of the nodes with a small degree. In figure 6(b), a slight dispersion of the probabilities on high degrees is observed. Table 1 shows that INT-2003 has an exponential growth in the number of nodes, edges, and degree average, in contrast to the reduction in the maximum degree. Based on all the above we can deduct that there is a best distribution of the edges in the Internet, this is, these changes are related to communication channels and devices improvements that has been carried out in the time.

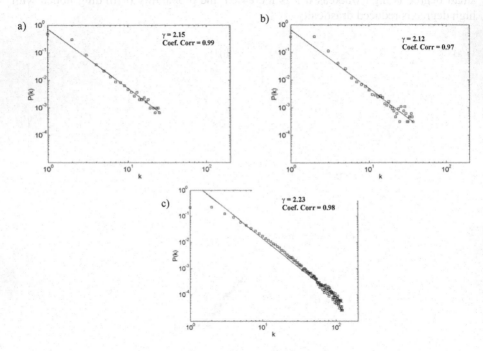

Fig. 6. Degree distribution $P(k)$ for data sets (a) INT-1997, (b) INT-2000, (c) INT-2003

4 Conclusions

The characterization of complex networks allows the analysis, classification, and the topology modeling of natural and artificial networks [18]. Our analysis confirms that Internet has a dynamic growing that in general terms has been maintaining the power-law degree distribution.

In INT-1997 and INT-2000 an increment in the number of nodes and edges motivates an increase in maximum degree, $\Delta(G)$. However, although INT-2003 contains an exponential number of nodes and edges there are a reduction in $\Delta(G)$. This observation is very important because we show that the addition of new nodes and edges to a scale-free network as the Internet does not increase its maximum degree and it preserves its degree distribution.

However, INT-2003 makes evident that the dynamic growing of the Internet is affected by technological factors that avoid the increase of the maximum degree and motivate the reduction of the number of nodes with small degrees. These features must be considered when new mathematical models are proposed to reproduce the Internet topological characteristics.

In future works it is contemplated to demonstrate that the edges in the Internet have changed and at the present time they are better distributed, however, an analysis detailed of these changes during the process of growth of the Internet is required. The preliminaries results with complementary metrics as clustering coefficient and network efficiency give us an indication of a better distribution in connections.

References

[1] Albert, R., Barabási, A.L.: Statistical Mechanics of Complex Networks. Reviews of Modern Physics. 74(1), 47–97 (2002)
[2] Maslov, S., Sneppen, K., Zaliznyak, A.: Detection of topological patterns in Complex Networks: Correlation profile of the Internet. Physica A 333, 529–540 (2004)
[3] Faloutsos, M., Faloutsos, P., Faloutsos, C.: On power-law relationship on the internet topology. ACM SIGCOMM Computer Communication Review. 29(4), 251–262 (1999)
[4] Latora, V., Marchiori, M.: Efficient Behavior of Small World Networks. Physical Review Letters 87(19) (2001)
[5] Adamic, L.A., Lukose, R.M., Puniyani, A.R., Huberman, B.A.: Search in power law network. Physical Review E 64, 046135-1– 046135-8 (2001)
[6] Barabási, A.L., Albert, R.: Emergence of Scaling in Random Networks. Science , 509–512 (1999)
[7] National Laboratory for Applied Network Research. Routing data. Supported by NSF (2005), http://moat.nlanr.net
[8] Albert, R., Barabási, A.L.: Statistical Mechanics of Complex Networks. Reviews of Modern Physics. 74(1), 47–97 (2002)
[9] Newman, M.E.J.: The structure and function of complex networks. SIAM Review. 45(2), 167–256 (2003)
[10] Bollobás, B., Riordan, O.M.: Mathematical results on scale-free random graphs. In: Handbook of Graphs and Networks, pp. 1–32. Wiley-VCH, Berlin (2002)
[11] Barabási, A.L., Albert, R., Jeong, H.: Mean-Field theory for scale-free random networks. Physica A. 272, 173–189 (1999)
[12] Bollobás, B., Riordan, O.M.: The diameter of Scale-free Random Graphs. Hungary 24, 5–34 (2004)
[13] Pierce, G.B., Deryk, O.: Popularity Based Random Graph Models Leading to a Scale-free Degree Distribution. Discrete Mathematics 282, 53–68 (2004)
[14] Kumar, R., Raghavan, P., Rajagopalan, S., Sivakumar, D., Andrew, T., Upfal, E.: Stochastic models for the web graph. In: Symposium on Foundations of Computer Science, pp. 57–65 (2000)
[15] Cooper, C., Frieze, A.: A General Model of Web Graphs. Random Structures & Algorithms 22, 311–335 (2003)

[16] Quian, C., Hyunseok, C., Ramesh, G., Sugih, J., Scott, J.S., Walter, W.: The Origin of Power Laws in Internet Topologies Revisited. In: Infocom 2002, Twenty-First Annual Joint Conference of the IEEE Computer and Communications Societies. Proceedings IEEE., pp. 608–617. IEEE Computer Society Press, Los Alamitos (2002)

[17] Watts, D.J., Strogatz, S.H.: Collective dynamics of small-world network. Nature. 393, 440–442 (1998)

[18] Costa, L., Rodrigues, F.A., Travieso, G., Villas, P.R.: Characterization of Complex Networks: A survey of measurements (2006), http://arxiv.org/abs/cond-mat/0505185

[19] Bélla, B.: Random Graphs, p. 34. Cambridge University Press, Cambridge (2001)

[20] Liu, Z., Lai, Y., Ye, N., Dasgupta, P.: Connectivity distribution and attack tolerance of general networks with both preferential and random attachments. Physics Letters A. 303, 337–344 (2003)

[21] Amaral, L.A.N., Scala, A., Barthelemy, M., Stanley, H.E.: Classes of small world networks. Proceedings of the National Academy of Sciences. 97(21), 11149–11152 (2000)

[22] Sen, P., Dasgupta, S., Chatterjee, A., Sreeram, P.A., Mukherjee, G., Manna, S.S.: Small-world properties of the Indian Railway network. Physical Review E 67 (2003)

Simulation-Based Evaluation of Distributed Mesh Allocation Algorithms

Leszek Koszalka

Chair of Systems and Computer Networks, Faculty of Electronics,
Wroclaw University of Technology, 50-370 Wroclaw, Poland
leszek.koszalka@pwr.wroc.pl

Abstract. In recent years, grid and mesh structures have received increasing attention. The mesh based multicomputers are the future of processing. As we slowly reach natural limits of semi-conductor spatial density supercomputer design depends more heavily on parallel and distributed processing. This paper concerns mesh allocation algorithms effectiveness assessment and the experimentation system that was developed to provide testing environment. Most focus was put on creation of such a system that would represent the highest scope of real supercomputers inner working routines and at the same time supply a way to input measured processing data as a base of allocation algorithm load computation. In investigations reported different allocation algorithms, including own WSBA, and various task parameters are considered.

1 Introduction

It is a fact that electronics technology slowly reaches its limits. Transistor based computing is naturally limited by the size of elementary particle, by material resistance and capacitance, by material power vulnerability to damage. That is why leading processor producers tend to parallel processing.

In recent years, grid and mesh structures have received increasing attention. Recently, multicomputers and computer networks with nodes connected through high-speed links have become a common computing platform. The mesh structure for such networks is very reasonable because of its simplicity, regularity and scalability [11]. Mesh-connected supercomputers vary in number of executional units from a thousands like Cray Inc. Cray X1E with 1024 CPUs to hundreds of thousands IBM eServer Blue Gene Solution with 131072 CPUs [14]. They are also designed to handle different kinds of tasks like live video compression and analyzing research data (NASA - Goodyear MPP). As the appliances differ there is a substantial need for a simulation system that would give a way for testing efficiency of algorithms.

A good task allocation algorithm should achieve such objectives as finding free resources for executing incoming tasks in a short time and with productive utilization of available supplies. In mesh-connected systems, the allocation is concerned with assigning the required number of executors to incoming tasks [10]. An allocation algorithm is responsible for finding a free submesh. If such a submesh does not exist, the task remains in the queue until an allocated job finishes its executions and releases

P. Thulasiraman et al. (Eds.): ISPA 2007 Workshops, LNCS 4743, pp. 335–344, 2007.
© Springer-Verlag Berlin Heidelberg 2007

a proper submesh (*dynamic mode*) or, it is simply dropped (*static mode*). In literature, there are presented many processor allocation algorithms for mesh-structured systems. They based on e.g. buddy strategy [3], frame sliding technique [7], and quick allocation scheme [8]. In [5], the stack-based concept of allocation is described, including the proof of recognition-completeness of SBA algorithm. The modifications of SBA, called BFSBA and SSBA are described in [4]. The new stack-based WSBA for static mode was presented in [1] and [2]. In this paper, the extended, corrected version of this algorithm for dynamic mode is shown.

The kernel of the paper is the experimentation system for evaluating properties of allocation algorithms in dynamic case. The system allows for observing relations between *inputs* like mesh-size, the total number of jobs, the time characteristics of tasks, including features of probability distributions, and first of all the kind of algorithm used and *outputs* which are the introduced measures to efficiency. The initial concept of such a system was presented in [6]. The designed and implemented system gives opportunities for (i) designing experiment along with multistage approach [4], (ii) on-line observing the process of allocation, and (iii) presenting results of series of experiments on properly informative charts.

The paper is organized as follows: Section 2 contains problem statement and an initial discussion concerning properties of algorithms, in particular the proposed WSBA. Section 3 presents the experimentation system: its logical structure and the way of implementation. It the same section you may find the system benefits. Section 4 presents some results of investigations made using the system. In Section 5 appear conclusions and some ideas of future work.

2 Mesh Allocation Algorithms

Problem. Main objective of the mesh algorithms in MPP (Massive Parallel Processing [13]) system is to allocate a rectangular task defined as $T(w_T, h_T)$ onto the free submesh of a processor mesh defined as $M(w_M, h_M)$. Fig. 1 shows an example of 2D rectangular mesh structure with allocated tasks.

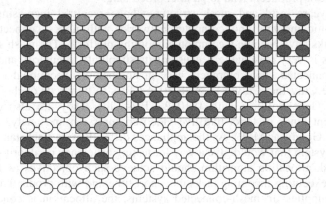

Fig. 1. A state of $M(16,12)$ mesh - nine allocated tasks is being executed

When a task is allocated it occupies a number of processing elements completely until it is finished and then mesh space it was taking can be allocated again. Algorithm should deal with reallocation as efficiently as with allocation to provide most efficient mesh utilization. We concentrate on the dynamic case stated as follows:

- *given*: the 2D rectangular or shaped mesh, dynamically coming tasks (along with one of the considered probability distribution) with known sizes and known times of executions (in fact, determined at random along with one of the considered probability distributions) ,
- *to find*: allocation of tasks within the mesh and reallocation of submeshes freed after execution of tasks,
- *such that*: to ensure the shortest possible allocation time and the shortest length of queue of tasks to be allocated.

In the paper, there are considered four known allocation algorithms for solving the above problem, including **FS** (*Full Search*), **SBA** (*Stack Based Algorithm*), **SSBA** (*Sorted Stack Based Algorithm*), **BFSBA** (*Best Fit Stack Based Algorithm*) and fifth algorithm called **WSBA** (*Window Stack Based Algorithm*) implemented by author.

Measures of Algorithm Efficiency. There are few factors that can be used to determine algorithm efficiency, e.g. [3], [4]. Ones used here are:

- The total number of operations needed to allocate and reallocate a set (queue) of tasks. This index of performance is corresponded to the total allocation time for a given set of tasks.
- The queue size throughout the allocation process,
- The fragmentation which may be regarded as the percentage count of holes within mesh active area throughout the allocation process.

Moreover, we introduced the measure called *Expected Task Fill Ratio* defined by the formula (1).

$$\text{ETFR} = \frac{\text{E}w_T \cdot \text{E}h_T}{w_M \cdot h_M} \tag{1}$$

This factor may help to clarify algorithms dependency on the possible number of task which can be active on the mesh. It takes into consideration mean values for particular conditions (chosen parameter distribution and total task number) and fixed mesh size.

Properties of Algorithms. An initial analysis conducted here involves on known algorithms operating routines.

Full Search algorithm finds a place on the mesh by browsing through all mesh nodes until it finds empty submesh big enough to hold incoming task. This involves checking task size number of processing elements for every free node found while searching for an empty submesh [12]. This operating routine is assumed to be least effective but it is important to note that its single task allocation complexity does not really depend on amount of task currently operating neither on the mesh nor on their parameters. The main drawback of this algorithm is that is highly afflicted by fragmentation which can be defined as number of holes within already active area.

Stack Based Algorithm [6] finds a place on mesh by cross-checking every *Candidate Block* (a free submesh) with every *Coverage* (a set of nodes which if taken then makes a given task to be overlapped with busy submesh) listed within the algorithm. By using spatial subtraction on a *Candidate Block* algorithm produces new *Candidate Blocks* and cross checks them with *Coverage* they have not been cross-checked before. This algorithm is widely documented in [2], [4], and [6]. Its complexity (a value describing the time needed for carrying out all computations required) of allocating a single task heavily depends on number of the tasks on the mesh in the moment new task comes in. The worst operating case for this algorithm is when high fragmentation occurs with high number of task on the mesh. It is worth to be noticed that big number of tasks can be inflicted by low *ETFR*.

Sorted Stack Based Algorithm [4] is a modification of *SBA*. It uses the sorted *busy submeshes* queue [9] for *Coverage* generation which enables it to cut off cross-checking with *Candidate Blocks* earlier. It has two drawbacks which are suspected to increase its complexity even further in conditions which are unfavorable to generic *SBA* (i) *busy submeshes* queue sorting by insertion on every task allocation, and (ii) an additional checking incorporated in the cut off condition.

Best Fit Stack Based Algorithm [4] chooses the order of the *Coverage* on the stack so the fragmentation would be minimized. This algorithm has no visible drawbacks against *SBA*. As the only load it brings is choosing the appropriate *Candidate Blocks* order. Its advantages are created mainly by Best Fit idea [7]. Disadvantages are expected to be similar to SBA but mesh capacity with its usage increases.

Window Stack-Based Algorithm. The basic idea of the algorithm [1] consists in presenting knowledge of accessible allocation space (i.e. all free nodes available within mesh) in the form of the set of maximum submeshes (*maximum windows*). Maximum windows should have the least as possible common nodes. These windows are placed on the inner stack of the algorithm (window stack) and they are sorted according to left-upper corner, at first along columns, next along rows. After successful allocation, the windows on the stack are updated. The algorithm operates in a loop as a two-step procedure: (i) *comparing the size of task being allocated with maximum windows on the stack*. Incoming task is always located in the first window on the stack that is big enough to contain it. After successful allocation of a given task go to the next step, (ii) *Up-dating all windows on the stack*. It requires following such rules as "none of windows would contain the nodes taken by that allocated task", "a window which is contained in the other window has to be popped from the stack", "windows are being cut into maximum windows that do not contain the busy nodes", "the correctly prepared windows are pushed onto the stack in an orderly manner".

In Fig. 2, an example of the actualization of the set of maximum windows in the dynamic mode is visualized (in the figures, the blackened nodes are busy). The updating was made at the moment in which one of the tasks (grey color) was ended and freed the occupied submesh of the size 7x4 in the middle of the mesh. It may be observed (Fig. 2a - Fig. 2d), how maximum windows are created.

The important feature of the algorithm is that it uses an inner description of free space available on the mesh by keeping a stack holding maximum possible rectangular windows. The algorithm is capable for choosing the right place on the mesh instantly but it has to update the free space description after. Update is based mainly on cutting and sorting free space description. Its main drawback is reallocation process which involves updating all the windows within the required maximum description condition.

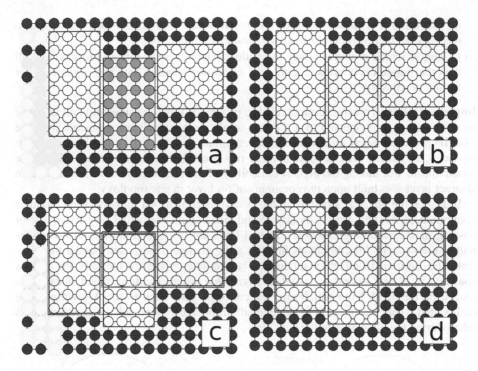

Fig. 2. The WSBA in action

3 Experimentation System

In order to check the properties of algorithms an experimental investigations should be done. An experimentation system should allow testing the algorithms in various conditions what could give opportunities for deeper analysis of their properties. By dynamical task generation and providing a way to simulate execution of tasks, algorithm complexity can be obtained as a result of performing allocation and reallocation processes in distributed experimental system.

Logical Design. The proposed experimentation system was designed with an intention to separate as far as it is possible particular modules representing those available in real working system. The system is composed of the following modules:

(i) *Task Generator* which provides reliable and scalable generation of load according to chosen parameter distributions. It is supplied with a way to input real data into it and approximate distributions that exist in real supercomputers,

(ii) *Mesh* which simulates task execution by receiving the task with coordinates and returning space when its execution cases,

(iii) *Algorithm* which here is the investigated module. It receives tasks from *Task Dispatcher* generated with certain parameters and according to specific stochastic process which elementary distribution may be chosen or estimated. As a result of its execution it returns a point on the mesh where task should be placed. It also receives all data considering freed submeshes on the mesh.

(iv) *Captain* which provides a way to conduct batch experiments and to navigate all the other modules. It helps to gather the execution specific data and organize it for further processing.

Implementation. To achieve most reliable processor time measurements all of those modules where implemented as a separate applications which communicate over the TCP/IP protocol. Such a distributed implementation done within the Linux system provides us with a way to obtain from the process header the exact CPU time consumption. For having the highest scalability of the architecture described above an abstract layer was built upon the communication layer in star topology.

In Fig. 3, the physical structure of the system is shown. All four specified modules communicate through *Server* module. Solid lines stand for actual physical ways of passing messages through modules. Dotted lines are visualization of control routines within the system. All commands involving the change of state are passed that way from the *Captain* to all other modules. Dashed lines visualize the way the task is spawned in *Task Generator* passed to *Algorithm* where (with assigned place) it is placed on the *Mesh* from which after execution it goes back to the *Algorithm* to be reallocated. After the process is completed *Algorithm* reports all the measurements taken during the allocation to the *Captain*.

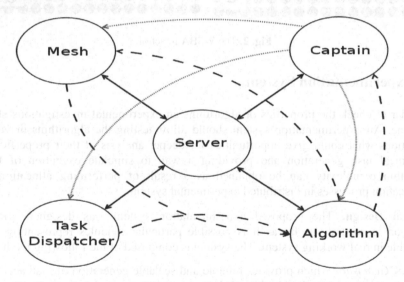

Fig. 3. Logical system architecture confronted with its physical dependencies

As all modules are separate processes we already have eliminated the interference inflicted by running tests within one process. Still the Heisenberg rule applies here as well and we must eliminate from results the weight of the tool thus the communication layer. To unify the way algorithms are to be tested special precautions were taken whilst the design of the *Algorithm* module. The idea was to separate the sole algorithm from all communication dependant interferences and thus to estimate the influence of the tool and remove it from the actual results. Load of the tool can be determined by implementation of a *Null Algorithm* which does not return any real results and places tasks always in one place. Information from such a run can help in determining the load of the system itself.

System Interface. Two modules of the system are supplied with graphical interfaces and those are *Mesh* and *Captain* as they provide user with *Algorithm* process diagnostics and the way of controlling the whole system. *Algorithm* process displays its operating statistics by outputting to the console task flow.

Fig. 4. Interface screen of *Captai*

In Fig. 4, the *Captain* GTK interface is shown, where its elements denote: 1-Mesh size entry field, 2-Task parameter distribution generator adjustments, 3-Tasks amount field, 4-Algorithms checkboxes, 5-Number of batch tests to be performed to obtain mean results, 6-Experiment start button, 7-Status bar, 8-Experiment start button displays single run progress. The system gives opportunities for visualization of allocation processes using *OpenGL* library.

4 Investigations

In this section some results of two complex experiments for two cases of allocation: with low *ETFR* and with high *ETFR* are presented. In experiments the different probability distributions were taken into consideration, including :

$B(n, p)$ - Bernoulli distribution (n - sample size, p - probability),

$U[a,b]$ - Uniform distribution, note its range (a, b) of values $\in N$,

$G(\lambda)$ - Geometric distribution.

These distributions are described in details in e.g. [15]. More on tasks queue modeling may be found in [7]-[9]. The parameters describing tasks are denoted as follows: t – task width, y – task height, t – task duration (execution time), d – task generation delay (time instant when task will come to the queue). Each single simulation was always repeated 100 times for each of the five examined algorithms.

Experiment # 1. The case with high *ETFR* factor.

- Design of experiment:
    - $x \sim 5 + B(30;0.5)$
    - $y \sim 5 + B(30;0.5)$
    - $t \sim [300 + 100 \cdot G(0,5)]ms$
    - $d \sim 100 \cdot U[20,50]ms$
    - Mesh size: 128x128,
    - Total number of tasks: 80
    - Estimated: $ETFR = 0,0122070313125$

- Results

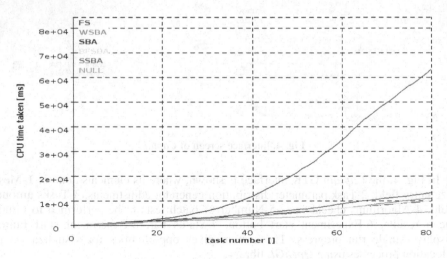

Fig. 5. CPU time consumption – high *ETFR* factor

- Comment

As we try to analyze the preliminary results obtained by the applications we see that destined areas of application for algorithms vary. In case of relatively high *ETFR*, *SBA* family algorithms (*SBA, BFSBA, and SSBA*) are approximately as complex as *WSBA* and a lot less complex than *FS* (Fig. 5).

Experiment #2. The case with low *ETFR* factor.

- Design of experiment:
  - $x \sim 5 + B(20;0.5)$,
  - $y \sim 5 + B(20;0.5)$,
  - $t \sim [1000 + 100 \cdot G(0,5)]ms$,
  - $d \sim 100 \cdot U[20,40]ms$,
  - Mesh size: 128x128,
  - Total number of tasks: 100.
  - Estimated: $ETFR = 0,006866455078125$

- Result:

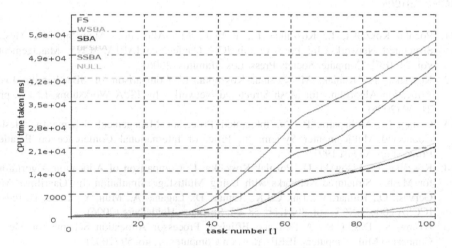

Fig. 6. CPU time consumption – low *ETFR* factor

- Comment:

In this case the preliminary thesis was confirmed really more than in Experiment # 1. One may observe that complexity of *WSBA* algorithm is even smaller. *SSBA* algorithm has the problems as predicted (Fig. 6).

Acknowledgment. I would like to give an appreciation to Mr. M. Kubiak, graduate students at Computer Science and Engineering, Wroclaw University of Technology, for help in implementation of experimentation system.

5   Final Remarks

We justified that corrected *WSBA* algorithm used to perform the tests has an area of appliance of is own and presumably it would be for low *ETFR*. Commonly used *SBA* has its weaknesses which may come forth into the light in future as more stupendous supercomputers with more and more *CPUs* will be developed.

The experimentation system presented here gives opportunities for providing very informative results which can be used to make general allocation algorithm assessment with pointing out precise area of appliance for a certain algorithm. Complex simulation experiments should be conducted to gather information about the scope of appliance of a particular task placing routine.

Real data samples should be used to estimate parameters of probability distributions utilized in generating queues of tasks to simulate certain supercomputers. It is possible that with using estimated sample data in simulation we may achieve precise algorithm assessment tool in scope of a certain machine. And that would be an idea for future research in the subject.

References

1. Pozniak-Koszalka, I., Koszalka, L., Kubiak, M.: Allocation Algorithm for Mesh-Structured Networks. In: Proc. of 5th ICN Conference IARIA, ICN5: Management, vol. 24, IEEE Computer Society Press, Los Alamitos (2006)
2. Koszalka, L., Kubiak, M., Pozniak-Koszalka, I.: Comparison of SBA-Family Task Allocation Algorithms for Mesh Structured Networks. In: ISPA Workshops, LNCS, pp. 21–30 (2006)
3. Chang, C., Mohapatra, P.: An Integrated Processor Management Scheme for Mesh-Connected Multicomputer System. In: Proc. of International Conference on Parallel Processing (August 1997)
4. Koszalka, L., Lisowski, D., Pozniak-Koszalka, I.: Comparison of Allocation Algorithms for Mesh - Structured Networks with Using Multistage Simulation, In: Gavrilova, M., Gervasi, O., Kumar, V., Tan, C.J.K., Taniar, D., Laganà, A., Mun, Y., Choo, H. (eds.) ICCSA 2006. LNCS, vol. 3984, pp. 58–67. Springer, Heidelberg (2006)
5. Byung, S., Das, C.R.: A Fast and Efficient Processor Allocation Scheme for Mesh-Connected Multicomputers. IEEE Trans. on Computers 1, 46–59 (2002)
6. Koszalka, L.: Static and Dynamic Allocation Algorithms in Mesh Structured Networks, ICDCIT, LNCS, pp. 89–101 (2006)
7. Sharma, D.D., Pradhan, D.K.: Submesh Allocation in Mesh Multicomputers Using Busy-List: A Best-Fit Approach with Complete Recognition Capability. Journal of Parallel and Distributed Computing 1, 106–118 (1996)
8. Chu, Y-K., Yen, I-L., Rover, D.T.: Guiding Processor Allocation with Estimated Execution Time for mesh Connected Multiple Processor Systems. In: Proc. of 28-th Annual HICSS, pp. 163–172 (1995)
9. De, M., Das, D., Ghosh, M.: An Efficient Sorting Algorithm on the Multi-Mesh Network. IEEE Trans. on Computers 10, 1132–1136 (1997)
10. Yang, Y., Wang, J.: Pipelined All-to-All Broadcast in All-Port Meshes and Tori. IEEE Trans. on Computers 10, 1020–1031 (2001)
11. Kasprzak, A.: Packet Switching Wide Area Networks, WPWR, Wroclaw, /in Polish/ (1997)
12. Liu, T., Huang, W., Lombardi, F., Bhutan, L.N.: A Submesh Allocation for Mesh-Connected Multiprocessor Systems. In: Parallel Processing, pp. 159–163 (1995)
13. Batcher, K.E.: Architecture of a massively parallel processor. In: Proc. of International Conference on Computer Architecture, pp. 174-179 (1998)
14. (2006), http://www.top500.org/
15. Jakubowsk, J., Stencel, R.: Introduction to Probability Theory, SCRIPT, /in Polish/ (2001)

A New Method for Describing the Syntax and Semantics of VIEWCHARTS

Ayaz Isazadeh[1], Jaber Karimpour[1], and Hosein Isazadeh[2]

[1] Faculty of Mathematical Sciences, Tabriz University, Tabriz, Iran
{Isazadeh,Karimpour}@Tabrizu.ac.ir
[2] Savalon Information Technology Inc. 79 Queensway, Ontario Canada
hi@savalon.com

Abstract. In this paper, we present a method for describing the syntax and semantics of Viewcharts. Viewcharts is a visual formalism for describing the dynamic behavior of system components. We define the syntax of Viewcharts as attributed graphs and, based on this graph, describe dynamic semantics of Viewcharts by Object Mapping Automata. This approach covers many important constructs of Viewcharts, including hierarchy of views, ownership of elements, scope, and composition of Views in SEPARATE, OR and AND ways. It also covers completion and interlevel transitions without violating the independence of views. Viewcharts was originally based on Statecharts; in this paper we also change the basis of Viewcharts to an extended version of Finite State Machine(EFSM).

1 Introduction

A complete and precise requirements specification is an important part of the software engineering process. The Precise specification of the requirements, in turn, requires a formal method. For large-scale software systems, however, using current formal methods can be complex and difficult. Visual formalisms are introduced as an attempt to simplify the presentations of formal specification. Visual formalisms are generally FSM-based techniques, the most popular of which is Statecharts.

1.1 Complexity of Scale

In conventional finite state machines, the number of states grows exponentially as the scale of the system grows linearly. Drusinsky and Harel [1,2] prove that Statecharts is exponentially more succinct than finite state machines. If we assume that an increase in the scale of a system results in additional orthogonal components in the corresponding statechart, then the number of states in the statechart has a linear relationship with the scale of the system. Orthogonality is, infact, a powerful feature in Statecharts. However, it is not clear that any increase in the scale of a system does result in additional orthogonal components.

Another problem with Statecharts is the *global name space*. There is no "visibility" control mechanism in Statecharts. (The term *visibility* is defined in terms

P. Thulasiraman et al. (Eds.): ISPA 2007 Workshops, LNCS 4743, pp. 345–354, 2007.

of *declaration*, *scope*, and *binding*; a visibility control mechanism, essentially, refers to a mechanism that controls scope [3].) When an event occurs, it is sensed throughout the system, so it must have a unique name. Managing the name space in the global environment of Statecharts, for large scale software systems, can be difficult.

These problems, specially the *complexity of scale*, are inevitable problems as log as we try to specify the system as a whole. How practical is it to accurately and fully describe a system while we can only work with our limited "views" of the system? One can only describe one's "view" of the world. A user's attempt to specify a system, at best, can only result in the specification of his or her "view" of the system. The Viewcharts formalism [4] accepts this reality and specifies the behavior of a system, formally and visually, as a composition of "views". And, that is the formalism which we will work with.

1.2   Problem

The overall and general problem is to discover whether there can be a practical and useful formal method for behavioral requirements specification of large and complex systems. A solution to this problem is to pick (and if necessary modify) an existing formalism, or introduce a new one, with the following desirable characteristics:

1. Must be visual and thereby simple to use.
2. Must solve the problem of *complexity of scale* in the best possible way.
3. Must solve the problem of *global name space* in the best possible way.
4. Must have precise and sound syntax and semantics.
5. Must allow the possibility of system modeling, simulation and verification.
6. Must allow the possibility of formally reasoning about the system behavior.

The problem addressed by this paper is to present the solution, satisfying the items 1-4 above, and setting the stage ready for a future work on the next two items.

1.3   Paper Outline

The paper is organized in four sections. In this section, we have stated the problem and have provided the desirable characteristics of the proposed solution. Section 2 provides a brief overview of Viewcharts, which is the notation of our choice, and the related work on this notation. Section 3 describes our solution by presenting the sound syntactic and semantic foundation for Viewcharts. Finally, In Section four we will conclude the paper with a summary of the results and future direction.

2   Previous Work

In this section, we provide a brief overview of the Viewcharts formalism from[4].

The Origin of Viewcharts. Introduced by Ayaz Isazadeh in his Ph.D. thesis [5], the Viewcharts notation was defined based on Statecharts [6,7]. Statecharts, however, has no concept of behavioral views. Viewcharts extends Statecharts to include views and their hierarchical compositions. The leaves of the hierarchy, described originally by independent statecharts, represent the behavioral views of the system or its components. The higher levels of the hierarchy are composed of the lower level views.

The first thing we do in this paper is to use classic Finite State Machines, with some extensions (EFSM), to represent the leaves of the Viewcharts hierarchy. This would provide us with a firm foundation for our syntax and semantics.

Ownership of Elements. Viewcharts normally limits the scope of an element (event, action, or variable) to a given view. However, composition of views may require communication between the composed views; the scope of an event in one view, for example, may be extended to cover other views. In a given view, therefore, Viewcharts must distinguish two different types of events:

- Events that *belong* to (or are *owned* by) the view: These are the events that the view *can trigger*. They must be declared by the view.
- Events that *do not belong* to the view: The view cannot trigger these events. An event of this type can occur only if it is triggered elsewhere and if the view is covered by the scope of the event.

An action belongs to the view (or views) that generates (or generate) the action. Similarly, a variable belongs to the view that declares it. The scope of a variable declared by a view is the view and all its subviews. An event or action may have multiple owners.

Syntactically, elements owned by a view can be declared by listing them following the name of the view either in the viewchart, as in Figure 1, or out of it as a separate text. It may be necessary to identify a view by its fully or partially *qualified name*, which consists of the *base name* prefixed by the names of its ancestors in the hierarchy separated by dots.

Composing Behavioral Views. Views can be composed in three ways: SEPA-RATE, OR, and AND compositions. Except for the effect of ownership and scoping restrictions, the OR and AND compositions of views, in Viewcharts, are similar to the OR and AND compositions of states, in Statecharts. The SEPARATE composition of views, however, is specific to Viewcharts. In a composition of views, similar to the notion of depth in Statecharts, the composed views form a superview which is an *encapsulation mechanism*, inherent to the composition.

In a SEPARATE composition of views, all the views are active if any one of them is active;[1] no transition between the views is allowed; the scopes of all the elements are unaffected; and any subview or state in one view is hidden from (i.e., cannot be referenced by) the other views. Visually, the SEPARATEed views are drawn on the top of each other, giving the impression that they are located

---

[1] A view is *active* whenever the system is in a state of the view.

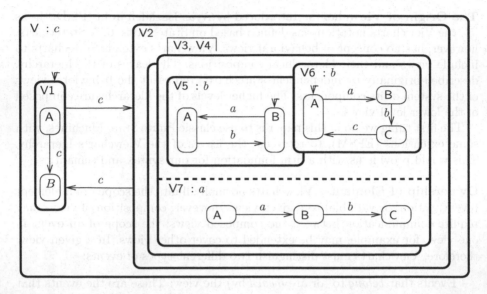

Fig. 1. Composition of views in a viewchart (From [5])

on different planes and, consequently, are hidden from each other. As shown in Figure 1, these views are either identical, like V3 and V4, or different, like V5 and V6. The OR and SEPARATE compositions are similar, except that in an OR composition, only one view can be active and there can be transitions between the views. Like the SEPARATE composition, any subview or state in one view is hidden from (i.e., cannot be referenced by) the other views. In Figure 1, for example, the view V consists of an OR composition of V1 and V2.

In an AND composition of views, all the views are active; the scopes of all the elements owned by each view are extended to the other views. All the subviews and states in one view are visible to (i.e., can be referenced by) the other views. The viewchart of Figure 1, for example, is composed of a SEPARATE composition of V5 and V6, which in turn is ANDed with V7 forming V3. A SEPARATE composition of two identical views V3 and V4 forms V2. The full view V is an OR composition of V1 and V2.

2.1   Related Work

Work on the formal syntax and semantics of Viewcharts is limited to the following two major cases:

1. *a set theoretic-based semantics of Viewecharts* [5] and,
2. *an algorithmic semantics of Viewcharts via translattion to Statecharts* [8].

In the first case, Isazadeh establishes a sound foundation for the formalism by providing a set theoretic-based semantics. The resulting semantics, however, does not have any tool support and is not suitable to interface with modeling tools, violating the characteristics 5 and 6 of our solution. The second case is an attempt to establish the semantics of Viewcharts via translating it to Statecharts. This attempt, at its best, would loose any advantages that Viewcharts has compared to Statecharts, violating the characteristics 2 and 3 of our solution. Consequently, a formal semantics, providing an unambiguous interpretation of Viewcharts diagrams, independent of Statecharts is needed.

3   Syntax and Semantics of Viewcharts

Our method for describing the syntax and semantics of Viewcharts is inspired by Jin Yan and others [9], where the syntax of UML statechart represented by the Graph Type Definition Language(GTDL), which is a small domain-specific language and part of the Moses tool suite[10].

3.1   Syntax Definition

This section briefly outlines the description of the syntax of Viewcharts. Given a Viewcharts, its abstract syntax(kinds of elements and their connectedness), is defined as an *attributed graph*. Formally, an *attributed graph* is a tuple:

$$(Ver, Edg, src, dst, cntr, \alpha)$$

where

- Ver and Edg are disjoint sets of vertices and edges,
- $src, dst : Edg \rightarrow Ver$ are total functions, mapping each edge to its source and target vertices.
- $cntr : Ver \rightarrow Ver$ is a partial *container function* mapping a vertex $v \in Ver$ to its *container*.
- $\alpha : (Ver \cup Edg) \times A \rightarrow U$ is a partial *attribute function* mapping a graph object $o \in Ver \cup Edg$ and an *attribute name* in A to an *attribute value* in U. Here, we assume A and U are universal sets of attribute names and values respectively.

The *attribution function* α contains all information except for the connection structure of the graph. It is important to choose U to contain a relevant set of different kinds of attribute values, e.g., attributes may contain subgraphs. Figure 2 illustrates a part of the GTDL syntax specification for Viewcharts. After attribute definition, types of graph objects are defined in specification. These include three kinds of vertices(composite view, basic view and history pseudostates) and one kind of edge(transations). In defining each vertex or edge, the semantic attributes of this type are listed. For example, in CompositeView vertex, an attribute hold the graph type of that graph for describing hierarchy of views. In addition to semantic attributes, each type of graph object also can have attributes representing their graphical appearance(e. g. shape, color

---

graph type Viewcharts{
1.   **attribute set** *Events, Actions, Variables.*
2. **vertex type** CompositeView(**String** Name, **graph**(Viewcharts, Subview),
    bool isSEPARATE, **bool** isConcurrent)
    graphics(**string** shape= "RoundRect", ...)
3. **vertex type** BasicView(**String** Name, **graph**(FSM))
    graphics(**string** shape= "RoundRect", ...)
4. **vertex type** History(**bool** isDeep)
    graphics(**string** shape= "Ellipse", Lable= if **Deep** then "H*" else "H", ...)
5. **edge type** Transition (**expr** trigger, **expr** guard, **expr** action)
    graphics(...).
6. **predicate** P_1 : $\forall t \in$ **Transition**:
    $src(t)$ and $dst(t) \in$ BasicView+History+CompositeView
7. **predicate** P_2 : $\forall v \in$ **Vertex**:
    $\alpha(v, LocallyElements) = Events + Actions + Variables$
8. **predicate** P_3 : $\forall v \in$ **Vertex**:
    $\alpha(v, VisibleElements) = LocallyElements+$
    $\alpha(cntr(v), VisibleElements)$
9. **predicate** P_4 : $\forall t \in$ **Transition**:
    $t(trigger) \in \alpha(v, VisibleElements)$
... }

Fig. 2. Syntax definition of Viewcharts(abridged)

and default size). Apart from these, a composite view have additional boolean attributes(attribute isSEPARATE indicate if it is a SEPARATE view and attribute *isCuncurrent* show if it is a AND view). Predicates describe the well-formedness rules of Viewcharts(Number 6-9). Each predicate defines a boolean formula which must be true for every well-formed Viewcharts diagram. A predicate my be declared to declare attributes of a vertex. For instance, predicate P_2 declares local elements(events, actions and variables) of a vertex and predicate P_3 shows that the visible elements of a given view are elements either declared by it or declared by its superview. Predicate P_4 shows that each view can only trigger its visible events.

As mentioned in Section 2, In Viewcharts a basic view is defined as an statechart. In our definition Viewcharts, however, we use an Extended version of Finite State Machine(EFSM) to represent a basic view. It is easy to describe the syntax specification of the EFSM.

3.2 Semantics Definition

In this section, we use Object Mapping Automata(OMA) as a formal language to define the semantics of Viewcharts.

OMA algebraic structure formalization. Given the attributed graph of a Viewcharts diagram $(Ver, Edg, src, dst, cntr, \alpha)$, we first compile it into OMA algebraic structures.

First of all, we classify the View and state vertices in Fig. 3. Views and mutually disjoint sets are identified according to attribute "type" of the vertices including composite views V_c, basic views V_b, simple states S_s, final states S_f and initial states S_i. Depending on attribute "isConcurrent" and "isSEPARATE", V_c is further divided into three disjoint views: AND views V_{cc}, SEPARATE views V_{se} and OR views V_{sc}. We define three kinds of pseudostates: initial P_i, shallow history P_{sh} and deep history P_{dh}. Each pseudostate include set of views and states. We let $P_h = P_{sh} \cup P_{dh}$ and $P = P_i \cup P_h$. Also on the basis of the edges Edg, we let $T := Edg$ for set of transitions in Viewcharts.

---

1. $V_c \equiv \{v \in Ver | \alpha(v, \text{"type"}) = \text{"CompositeView"}\}$
2. $V_b \equiv \{v \in Ver | \alpha(v, \text{"type"}) = \text{"BasicView"}\}$
3. $V_{cc} \equiv \{v \in V_c | \alpha(v, \text{"isConcurrent"}), \alpha(v, \text{"VisibleElement"}) := \bigcup_{\forall v \in V_{cc}} \alpha(v, \text{"VisibleElement"})\}$
4. $V_{se} \equiv \{v \in V_c | \alpha(v, \text{"isseparate"})\}$ $V_{sc} \equiv V_c \backslash (V_{cc} \cup V_{se})$ $V \equiv V_b \cup V_c$
5. $S_s \equiv \{v \in V_b | \alpha(v, , \text{"type"}) = \text{"Simple"}\}$ $S_f \equiv \{v \in V_b | \alpha(v, \text{"type"}) = \text{"Finale"}\}$
6. $S_i \equiv \cup \{v \in V_b | \alpha(v, \text{"type"}) = \text{"Initial"}\}$ $S \equiv S_s \cup S_f \cup S_i$

Fig. 3. Views and states classification

We next model the view hierarchy, graphically represented in the diagram, using the OMA in Fig. 4. First of all, *cntr* is a containment function mapping a ver-

---

1. $cntr \equiv \{v \to t | v \in V \cup S \cup P, t \in V_c, cntr(v) = t\} \cup \{v \to \text{TOP} | v \in V, cntr(v) = \bot\}$,
2. $subs \equiv \{(cntr(v), v) | v \in V, v \neq \text{TOP}\} \cup \{\emptyset | cntr(v) \in V_b\}$,
3. $default \equiv \{cntr(src(e)) \to dst(e) | e \in T, src(e) \in P_i\}$,
4. $cover \equiv \{(v, u) | v \in V, u \in V \cup S, v \in cntr^+(u)\}$, $\acute{cover} \equiv cover \cup \{(v, v) | v \in V\}$.

Fig. 4. View hierarchy decoding

tex into the composite vertices directly enclosing it. A vertex v with $cntr(v) = \bot$ is at the top level. Also, for a given composite view $v \in V_c$, $subs(v)$ refers to the set of (direct) subviews of v. We let $subs(v)$ return an empty set for a simple states in Basic view. For example we have $subs(V) = \{V1, V2\}$, $subs(V3) = \{V5, V6, V7\}$, $subs(V7) = \{A, B, C\}$ and $subs(A) = \emptyset$ in Fig. 1. Additionally, given two views u and v, the boolean function "*cover*" determines whether v transitively contains u, in other words, whether there exists a sequence of composite views $v_1, ..., v_k \in V_c$ for $k < |V_c|$ such that $cntr(u) = v_1, ..., cntr(v_k) = v$. In the figure, $cntr^+$ denotes the transitive closure of $cntr$. For instance in Fig. 1, $(V, V2), (V, V5), (V7, A) \in cover$ and $(V1, V2) \notin cover$.

1. Set $\triangle = \emptyset$; TOP:=Full VIEW; Set $\varphi := \{\text{TOP}\}$.
2. $\forall \mathsf{v} \in \varphi$:
   $\quad \triangle := \triangle + \{\mathsf{v}\}, \varphi := \varphi - \{\mathsf{v}\}$,
   $\quad$ if $\mathsf{v} \in V_{cc}$ then $\varphi := \varphi + subs(\mathsf{v})$; if $\mathsf{v} \in V_{sc}$ then $\varphi := \varphi + \{default(\mathsf{v})\}$;
   $\quad$ if $\mathsf{v} \in V_{se}$ then $\varphi := \varphi + subs(\mathsf{v})\}$;   if $\mathsf{v} \in V_b$ then $\varphi := \varphi + \{default(\mathsf{v})\}$;
3. $genCmplevt$

Fig. 5. Initialization rules

Initialization. If we represent the system by Viewcharts(where the system can be in many states of these machines at any instance in time), we will refer to the state of a system as the *configuration* of the system; We let $\triangle$ denote the current configuration of a Viewcharts in Fig. 5.

1. **set** $Q_{evt} = \emptyset$; **bool** $cmplevt = false$; **function** hc **arity** 1;
2. **rule** *exequte*:
3. $Q_{evt} = \{e \in \alpha(\mathsf{v}, VisibleElements) | \mathsf{v} \in \triangle\}$
4. $\quad$ **if** $cmplevt$ **then** $handleCmplevt$
5. $\quad$ **elseif** $Q_{evt} \neq 0$ **then**
6. $\quad\quad$ **choose** $ce \in Q_{evt}$:
7. $\quad\quad Q_{evt} := Q_{evt} - \{ce\}$,
8. $\quad\quad enabled = \{t \in T | trg(t) = ce \wedge src(t) \subseteq \triangle \wedge \mathbf{eval}(grd(t), \triangle)\}$
9. $\quad\quad$ **firing**$(enabled)$

Fig. 6. Execute rule

Specifying executable steps. In Fig, 6, Q_{evt} represents the event queue of a view. $cmplevt$ is a boolean variable indicating the existence of a pending completion event. The *exequte* rule firstly set events e triggered by active views in Q_{evt}, then this rule checks for a pending completion event and, if it succeeds, handles it using a macro *handleCmplevt*. If no such an event exists, it randomly dequeues an event ce in the event queue (if any) of an active view. This event is called the current event. Next, a set of transitions enabled by ce is computed. This set consists of transitions whose source views or states are all currently active, whose triggers match the current event, and whose guards are evaluated to TRUE. The guards are evaluated by **eval**(), which we have assumed is an external function provided by the runtime environment. When enabled transitions are present, a macro **firing**$(enabled)$ (Fig, 7) is used.

The main job of **firing** is to compute and fire a maximal subset of the enabled transitions which are not in conflict with each other. The execution of a

```
1. firing(enabled) ≡ begin
2. set firable = ∅;
3. loop
4.     choose t ∈ enable − firing
5.     with (conflict_transitions(t) ∩ firable = ∅ ∧ priority(t)
                   ∩enabled = ∅ ∧ conflict_views = ∅)
6.         firable := firable + t
7. endloop
8. do forall t ∈ firable: exit(ms(t)); exec(eff(t)); enter(mt(t), dst(t));
9. genCmplevt()
```

Fig. 7. Firing enabled transitions

```
1. exit(ms) ≡ begin
2. set φ = △ ∩ cover′(ms) : 'setHistory(ms)
3.     do forall s ∈ φ with subs(s) ∩ △ = ∅ :
         △ := △ − {s}, φ = φ − {s}; if s ≠ ms then φ = φ + {cntr(s)}
```

Fig. 8. Exiting the main source

```
1. enter(mt, TS) ≡ begin
2. set φ := {mt}, AT := TS :
3. loop
4.     do forall v ∈ φ
5.         φ = φ − {v}
6.         if v ∈ P_{sh} then φ = φ + hc(v), AT := AT + hc(v)}
7.         elseif v ∈ P_{dh} then
8.             φ := {q ∈ hc(v)|∀q′ ∈ (v), cover′(q, q′)}, AT := AT + hc(v)
9.         else
             △ := △ + {v},
             if v ∈ V_{cc} then φ = φ + subs(v);   if v ∈ V_{sc} then φ := φ + {default(v)};
             if v ∈ V_{se} then φ := φ + subs(v)};  if v ∈ V_b then φ := φ + {default(v)};.
```

Fig. 9. Entering the main target

single transition consists of a sequence of steps (Line 6): exiting the main source, executing the transition effect, and entering the main target.

Exit(*ms*) macro in Fig. 8 involves exiting all views or states in given *main source(ms)*. Entering the *main target* results in views and states including the main target and some views or states covered by it to be entered in Fig. 9.

4   Conclusion

We have presented a method for describing the syntax and semantics of Viewcharts. We have picked Viewcharts, changed its basis from Statecharts to an Extended Finite State Machine (EFSM), and presented as our solution to the overall and general problem discussed in Section 1.2.

Using an independent graph definition language GTDL, not only we have defined the syntax of Viewcharts, but also we have described its static semantics. Furthermore, our choice of the formal Object Mapping Automata language has enabled us to describe the operational semantics of Viewcharts, covering many important constructs of Viewcharts. More importantly, this method for describing the syntax and semantics of Viewcharts makes it suitable for a variety of tool support and, thereby, setting the stage ready for our future work on the last two characteristics of the solution.

References

1. Drusinsky, D., Harel, D.: On the power of cooperative concurrency. In: Vogt, F.H. (ed.) Concurrency 88. LNCS, vol. 335, pp. 74–103. Springer, Heidelberg (1988)
2. Drusinsky, D., Harel, D.: On the power of bounded concurrency I: Finite automata. Journal of the Association for Computing Machine (ACM) 41, 517–539 (1994)
3. Wolf, A.L., Clarke, L.A., Wileden, J.C.: A model of visibility control. IEEE Transactions on Software Engineering 14, 512–520 (1988)
4. Isazadeh, A., Lamb, D.A., Shepard, T.: Behavioural views for software requirements engineering. Requirements Engineering Journal 4, 19–37 (1999)
5. Isazadeh, A.: Behavioral Views for Software Requirements Engineering. PhD thesis, Department of Computing and Information Science, Queen's University, Kingston, Canada (1996)
6. Harel, D.: Statecharts: A visual formalism for complex systems. Science of Computer Programming 8, 231–274 (1987)
7. Harel, D., Naamad, A.: The STATEMATE semantics of Statecharts. Technical report, i-Logix, Inc., 22 Third Avenue, Burlington, Mass (1995)
8. Isazadeh, A., Lamb, D.A.: An algorithmic semantics for Viewcharts. In: Proceedings of IEEE International Conference on Engineering of Complex Computer Systems (ICECCS'96), Montreal, Canada, pp. 293–296. IEEE Computer Society Press, Los Alamitos (1996)
9. Jin, Y., Esser, R., Janneck, J.W.: A method for describing the syntax and semantics of uml statecharts. Software and Systems Modeling (SoSyM) 3, 150–163 (2004)
10. Janneck, J.W.: Moses project. Computer Engineering and Communications Laboratory, ETH Zurich (1997), http://www.tik.ee.ethz.ch/moses

A New Formalism for Describing Concurrent Systems

Ayaz Isazadeh[1], Jaber Karimpour[1], and Hosein Isazadeh[2]

[1] Faculty of Mathematical Sciences, Tabriz University, Tabriz, Iran
{Isazadeh,Karimpour}@Tabrizu.ac.ir
[2] Savalon Information Technology Inc. 79 Queensway, Ontario Canada
hi@savalon.com

Abstract. In this paper we will present a formal technique for describing complex systems consisting a number of interacting components. To meet this, we will consider a mathematical model for a single component and specify abstract communication protocols of components by using a lightweight formal language *Interface Automata*. To model hierarchal design for hierarchal systems, beside the basic component's model, we will present other components, called *Nodes*. A *Node* consists of a set of components interacting under the supervision of a *Controller*. A *Controller* is a set of interface automata that specify interaction protocol of components inside a *Node*. In addition, we will prove that each *Node* is equal to a component. Therefore, a *Node* can be composed of components which are in turn *Nods*. To address state space explosion problem in system verification, a *Node* will not be directly analyzed, Instead, we will analyze the *Controller* and prove its conformance.

1 Introduction

It is widely known that mathematically-based formal specification and verification methods can present useful help in displaying ambiguity and inconsistency of informal system descriptions, and increase confidence in the correctness of system[1]. In recent years, Component-based Software Engineering has become more popular for the development of large-scale software applications. By building systems from independently developed components, software reuse, reduced cost, rapid development and complexity management is provided. In component-based systems, a component provides its services through interactions with the other components. The independence of components is achieved by separating their interfaces from implementations. The components use communication protocols for interactions. This protocol describes the way it reacts to its inputs and what is expects from its environment. However, there is not a general formal technique for describing components interactions.

The need for precise description of component interaction protocols has been widely recognized by the research community. Many formal language based approaches have been proposed in the literature to overcome the ambiguity of

P. Thulasiraman et al. (Eds.): ISPA 2007 Workshops, LNCS 4743, pp. 355–364, 2007.

informal documentation used in the industry. For example, [2] uses process algebra, [3,4] interface automata, [5] finite state machines (FSMs), [6] regular expressions. Automat based models like[3,4,5] are usually supported by automated verification tools. However, these models are designed for modeling of component interaction only and therefor are unable to describe the interaction structure of hierarchical component architecture which also influence the behavior and sometime they are limited to one-to-one communication or synchronization. A major weakness for Algebra and logical based approaches is that applying such approaches require the user to have a sound knowledge of the underlying formalisms and experts in mathematics.

Interface Automata(IA) is a formal lightweight language for describing protocols[3,4]. The authors established a simple and well-defined semantics for them and defined their composition by two-party synchronization. Also, alternating simulation was proposed to determine a refinement relationship between *Interface Automata*. This relationship takes an optimistic view of the environment by assuming that it is always helpful, only providing inputs expected by an automaton. This view allows more possible implementations than a pessimistic approach where the environment can behave as it pleases.

To apply IA in practical works, Y. Jin and et al[7] have defined mathematical formula for discrete event components and used *Interface Automata* as notion for describing components protocols. They have checked the conformance of components to a given IA by calculating the local state space of the component respect to IA and checking the state space for the absence of error states. Additionally, they allow *interface automata* to be composed in terms of synchronization vectors, a more general composition mechanism introduced by Arnold [8]. In [9], This approach has been used for compositional verification of component based heterogeneous systems.

In this paper, we will extend Jin's work in the following four directions:

1. In Component-based Software Systems it is important to define hierarchical description of systems. To achieve this, beside the basic component's model, we will present other components, called *Nodes* consisting of a set of components(sub-nods) interacting under the supervision of a *Controller*. A *Controller* is a set of conformance interface automata that specify interaction protocols of components inside the *Node*.

2. To model hierarchal design for hierarchal systems and revenue advantages of architecture description languages (ADLs) like SOFA 2.0[10], COSA[11,12] and Darwin[13], we will prove that each *Node* is equal to a component. Therefore, a *Node* can be composed of components which are in turn *Nodes*.

3. The synchronized product of transition system is too abstract to be practical use for software engineers. In order to express broadcast communications, we allow *Interface Automata* to be composed in term of extended synchronization vectors model.

4. We will assign priorities to synchronization vectors and use priorities in composition of components.

The rest of this article is structured as follows. In Section 2, discrete-event components and interface automata are defined and followed by the conformance relation between them. In Section 3, we introduce the hierarchical components, called *Node* and its interfaces called *Controller*. In section 4, we verify he consistency of *Node* with its associated *Controller*. Finally, conclusions are drawn in Section 5.

2   Independent Components

In this section we consider general definition for *Discreet Event Components (DECs)* and *Interface Automata(IAs)*. In [7], Jin et al. have specified general definitions for discreet event components by specializing Reactive Transaction Systems(RTSs) in [8]. They have described providing services of a component by protocols and considered input and environment assumptions. They have used *IAs*, a formal light wight language, as the notion for describing protocols and by this language, they have presented a formal technique which focuses on communication protocols while abstracting away from the data value being communicated.

2.1   Component Model

Discrete-event component model is specialized reactive transition systems(RTSs) in two ways.

1. Considering two parts including kind and value for an event such that, kinds were used to classify events while values were represented communicated data;
2. Presenting ports for each component to communicate with others that is, a component always receives data (or messages) fed to its input ports and produces data (or messages) via its output ports.

Therefore, event values are important to component computation but less relevant to component composition, while ports play important roles in component composition but have little impact on the computation of individual components. This approach results following benefits.

- The ports can form a components behavior view of the rest of the system and decouple the outside world from the component.
- Reduces the interdependency between components.
- Allows the designer to compose components by simply connecting ports, and takes them over from the labor of relating individual events.

Definition 1. *A Discrete Event component(DEC) is defined as a 6-tuple*

$$DEC = (\rho, \mu, s^0, S, , \Sigma, T)$$

where

- ρ *is a finite set of ports,* $\rho = \rho^I \cup \rho^O$, *in which* ρ^I *is a set of input ports and* ρ^O *is a set of output ports;*
- $\mu : \rho \longrightarrow 2^V$ *is a total function, mapping each port to a subset of values from the universe;*
- S *is a set of states and* s^0 *is the the initial state;*
- $\Sigma = \Sigma^I \cup \Sigma^O \cup \Sigma^H$ *is a set of input, output and hidden events, where* $\Sigma^I = \{(e, v)|e \in \rho^I, v \in \mu(e)\}$, $\Sigma^O = \{(e, v)|e \in \rho^O, v \in \mu(e)\}$ *and* $\Sigma^H \cap \rho = \emptyset$;
- $T \subseteq S \times \Sigma \times S$ *is a set of transitions, that contains at least* $\langle c, \epsilon, c \rangle$ *for any* $s \in S$;

In some configurations, one may want to specify that an event is allowed to occur only if there are no other events with higher priority than the first. Let $\Sigma = \Sigma^+ \cup \{\epsilon\}$ be a set of events. A priority relation on Σ is a partial ordering $<_\Sigma$ of Σ such that $\forall a \in \Sigma^+$, $a <_\Sigma \epsilon$ and $\epsilon <_\Sigma a$. This means that the invisible event cannot be related by any priority relation to any other event. By considering event priority constraints, in this paper we extend definition of *DEC* as follows.

Definition 2

$$C = (\rho, \mu, s^0, S, , \Sigma, <_\Sigma, T)$$

Where T is the set of all transitions $\langle s, e, s' \rangle$ *such that* $\forall s'' \in S, \forall e' \in \Sigma, \langle s, e', s'' \rangle \in T \Rightarrow e <_\Sigma e'$. *It is clear that if* $<_\Sigma$ *is the empty ordering (i.e, there is no priority between the events), then* $DEC \equiv C$.

Interface Automata. Industrial and academics study in component based systems show that the ports of component are very useful for guiding the development or selection of individual components and for further study of a system design, and thus should be formally specified. The *IAs* have been employed to serve this purpose.

Definition 3. *An Interface automaton(IA) is defined as a finite transection system* $IA = (s^0, S, \Sigma, <_\Sigma, T)$ *where:*

- S *is a set of states and* $s^0 \in S$ *is the initial state.*
- $\Sigma = \Sigma^I \cup \Sigma^O$ *is a set of input and output events.* $<_\Sigma$ *is a priority relation on* Σ
- $T \subseteq S \times \Sigma \times S$ *is a set of steps.*

Let the events of *IAs* correspond to the ports of *Cs*. Then the information conveyed by an *IAs* is twofold. On the one hand, it restricts the kinds of output events that a component under consideration can produce. On the other hand, it states the component's assumption that the environment never provides input events of an unspecified kind.

The conformance of component with a given Interface automata is defined by alternating simulation method. This approach takes an optimistic view of the environment by assuming that it is always helpful, only providing inputs expected by an interface automaton.

Definition 4. *We say component* C *conforms to an interface automaton* A, *written* $C \prec A$, *if there exists an alternating simulation relation* $\prec \subseteq S_C \times S_A$ *such that* $s_C^0 \prec s_A^0$ *and a component state* q *simulates an* IA *state* s ($q \prec s$), *the following conditions hold.*

- *First of all, the resultant component state must simulate the previous IA state* s *after the component takes an internal step from* q, $\forall e \in \Sigma_C^H, \exists (q, e, q') \in T_C$ *implies* $q' \prec s$.
- *The component must not produce an output event that the IA cannot produce it,* $\forall f.v \in \Sigma_C^O, \exists (q, f.v, q') \in T_C$ *implies that* $\exists (s, e, s') \in T_A$ *such that* $q' \prec s'$.
- $\forall f \in \Sigma_A^I, \exists (s, f, s') \in T_A$ *implies that* $\forall v \in \theta_C(f), (q, f.v, q') \in T_C$ *such that* $q' \prec s'$.

We can result the conformance of a C with a given IA by using following theorem[9,7].

Theorem 1. *Let* $L_\oplus = \{s_\oplus^0, S_\oplus, \Sigma_\oplus, \triangle_\oplus\}$ *be the local state space of component* C *with respect to Interface Automata* A. *Then* C *conforms to* A *if and only if* $\forall s \in S_\oplus, \pi_J \neq \bot$. *In which* J *is the most abstract implementation of* A *and* $\pi_J(s)$ *is an event sequence consisting of the events that* J *takes from state* s.

In about theorem, for check the conformance of a C with a given IA, instead of building the cartesian product of their states as proposed by de Alfaro and Henzinger[3], we can do like [9,7]. First of all, we can calculate the local state space of the C utilizing the context assumptions of the IA, and then determine the conformance by checking the state space for the absence of error states.

3 *Nodes* of Components

One of the important featurees that is really important in practical systems is the possibility to define hierarchical systems. Architecture Description Languages(ADLs), like SOFA 2.0[10], COSA[11,12] and Darwin[13] are very suitable for specification of hierarchical component architecture with define interconnection among components and behavior constraints put on component communication and interaction. The weaknesses of ADLs are less formal and usually didn't supported by automated verification tools. In particular, we develop an automata-based formalism which allows for the specification of components interactions according to the interconnection structure described in ADLs. The novel feature of our formal approach in this paper is ability to describe hierarchical systems. To access this, instead of composing components as networks and interact them by means of synchronization vectors, we define *Nodes*.

A *Node* consisting of a set of components interacting under the supervision a *Controller*. A *Controller* of a *Node* is a set of *IAs* such that each *IA* conforms with a one sub-node. In this way, The *Controller* capturers interconnection protocols expected by designer of a *Node* and has a very important role.

A typical component-based design process combines top-down and bottom-up design. *IAs* are obtained during system decomposition, together with the synchronization patterns and event priority between them. By using these *IAs* we can find conformable components or develop new ones. These obtained components are next composed to form a concrete component-based design, viz. a closed *Node*, where the synchronization of *IAs* as a *Controller* are reused as the interactions between sub nods of the *Node*. Hence the *Controller* captures the interaction protocols expected by the designer of the *Nods*.

In this paper, we lay the foundation for this approach by formal defining *Node* and its *Controller*.

Definition 5. *A Node is a tuple*

$$N = (\rho, \mu, Controller, C_1, C_2, ..., C_n)$$

where:

- ρ *is a finite set of external ports of the the node, consisting of tow disjoint sets of input ports ρ^I and output ports ρ^O we let $\rho^\sharp = \rho \cup \{\epsilon\}$;*
- $\mu : \alpha \longrightarrow 2^V$ *is a total function, mapping each port to a subset of values from the universe;*
- *Controller* $= (W, \gamma)$ *is called the Controller of the node N, where, W is finite set of IAs and γ is extended synchronization vector. Each IA is conform with a sub-node. This Controller captures the interaction protocols expected by designer of the Node. $\gamma \subseteq \rho^\sharp \times \prod_{i=1}^n \rho^\sharp_{C_i} \times 2^{[1,n+1]}$ is a relation indexed by $\rho^I \cup \bigcup_{i=1}^n \rho^O_{C_i}$. We call γ a set of interconnection that formed set of broadcast synchronization vectors. Furthermore, we assume that γ always contains the vector $\overrightarrow{\epsilon} = \langle \epsilon, ..., \epsilon, \{0\} \rangle$;*
- *for $i = 1..n$, $C_i = (\rho_i, \mu_i, s_i^0, S_i, , \Sigma_i, T_i)$ is a component, called a sub-node;*

We call the *Node* closed if $\rho = \emptyset$, or open otherwise. In a *Node*, an event occurring in one component may be synchronous with some other events occurring in some other components. Synchronization vector were introduced in Arnold-Nivate model[8] and used in [9,7] is a general mathematical model to express all kinds of such synchronization of events. However, in several models, these synchronization vectors are not expressive enough. For instance, let us consider an electric circuit with several lamps. In case of an event "power failure", all the lamps simultaneously be put out. But some of them are already off and can not execute "light off". Although it is possible to model this circuit with synchronization vectors in such a way that in case of power failure only lighted lamps turn off, bot this model increase the size of the model.

In our model we consider a way that if a component is not able to react by the specified event to another event, it is not obliged to do so. we do this by tagging this events by a question mark in the synchronization vector. for example in synchronization vector $\langle a, b?, c? \rangle$ the possible events will be $\langle a, b, c \rangle$, $\langle a, \epsilon, c \rangle$, $\langle a, b, \epsilon \rangle$ and $\langle a, \epsilon, \epsilon \rangle$.

In addition, we use an additional constraint to such vectors that to count the number of reacting components. For example in vector $\langle a, b?, c? \rangle$ with the constraint $\{2\}$ mean that two and only two components have to react. In mathematical model let $v = \langle e'_1, e'_2, ..., e'_n, D \rangle \in \rho_1 \times \rho_1 \times ...\rho_n \times 2^{[0,n]}$. we select the vector $u = \langle e_1, e_2, ..., e_n, \rangle \in \rho_1 \times \rho_2 \times ...\rho_n$ is an instance of v if

- for any $i = 1, 2, ..., n$
  1. if $e_i' \in \rho_i$ then $e_i = e_i'$;
  2. if $e_i' = b?$ with $b \in \rho_i - \{\epsilon\}$ then $e_i = b$ or $e_i = \epsilon$;
- The cardinal of the set $\{i| 1 \le i \le n, e_i \ne \epsilon\}$ is in D;

Definition 6. *Consider a Controller* $= (W, \gamma)$, *the synchronized product of a Controller is an interface automaton* $IA = (s^0, S, \Sigma^I, \Sigma^O, T)$ *where:*

- $s^0 = \prod_{l \in W} s_l^0$ *and* $S \subseteq \prod_{l \in W} S_l$ *is the smallest set such that* $s^0 \in S$ *and* $\forall s \in S, (s, e, s') \in T$ *implies* $s' \in S$.
- $\Sigma_{IA}^I = \bigcup_{l \in W} \Sigma_l^I$ *and* $\Sigma_{IA}^O = \bigcup_{l \in W} \Sigma_l^O$
- *T consists of input steps*

$$\{(s, e, s')| \exists e \in \Sigma_{IA}^I, \exists r \in \gamma, \alpha_r = env \wedge e = \pi_{env}(r)$$
$$\wedge \forall l' \in \eta_l, (s_{l'}, \pi_{l'}(r), s_{l'}') \in T_{l'} \wedge \forall h \in \varphi_r, s_h = s_h'$$
$$(s, e, s)| e \in \Sigma_{IA}^I, r \in \gamma, \alpha_r = env \wedge e = \pi_{env}(r)\}$$

Where $\alpha_r \in W$ *is producer of synchronization vector* $r \in \gamma$, $\pi_{\alpha_r}(r)$ *is called produced event of* r *and* $\eta_r \subseteq W$ *is a set of consumers of* r. *The input step of IA is take off by event occurs from synchronization vector produced by environment. This step also synchronizes the corresponding input steps of the consumer.* $\varphi_r \in W$ *is a set of idlers of* r. *If there is not exist such synchronization vector, the Controller remains in the same state after consuming the input event.*

- *T consists of output steps*

$$\{(s, e, s')| \exists e \in \Sigma_{IA}^O, \exists r \in \gamma, l \in W, l = \alpha_r \wedge e = \pi_{env}(r) \wedge \forall(s_l, \pi_l(r), s_l') \in T_l$$
$$\wedge \forall l' \in \eta_r, (s_{l'}, \pi_{l'}(r), s_{l'}') \in T_{l'} \wedge \forall h \in \varphi_r, s_h = s_h'$$

The IA will perform an output step when the produce r *of a synchronous vector generates the produced event, provided that environment is a consumer of the vector.*

We consider the situation that a component of a *Node* can be another *Node*.

Proposition 1. *Foe each Node* $N = (\rho, \mu, C_1, C_2, ..., C_n, \gamma)$ *There exist an equivalent Component* $C = (\rho, \mu, s^0, S, , \Sigma, \prec_\Sigma, T)$.

Proof. By consider a given *NodeN* we can make an equivalent component C, where

- $s^0 = \prod_{i=1}^n s_{C_i}^0$ *and* $S \subseteq \prod_{i=1}^n S_{C_i}$ *is the smallest set such that* $s^0 \in S$ *and* $\forall s \in S, (s, e, s') \in T$ *implies* $s' \in S$. We assume a projection between S and each sub-node states in Node as $\pi_C : S \rightarrow S_C$, where $C \in \bigcup_{i=1}^n C_i$.
- $\Sigma_C^I = \{(e, v)| e \in \rho^I, v \in \mu(e)\}$, $\Sigma_C^O = \{(e, v)| e \in \rho^O, v \in \mu(e)\}$ *and* $\Sigma_C^H \subseteq \bigcup_{i=1}^n \Sigma_{C_i}^{ctrl}$ *where* $\Sigma_C^{ctrl} = \Sigma_C^O \cup \Sigma_C^H$

- A transition of the node consists of a vector of simultaneous transitions of the *Controller* and all the sub-nodes. T consists of input steps, output steps and internal steps. The input and output steps are like input and output steps of *Controller* synchronized product in definition 6. An internal step taken by any sub-nods is an internal step of component. This step clearly has no impact on other sub-nodes or the *Controller*.

$$\{(s, e, s') | \exists c \in \bigcup_{i=1}^{n} C_i, e \in \Sigma_c^H \land (s_c, e, s_c') \in T_c \land \forall c' \neq c, s_{c'}' = s_{c'}\}$$

Also, an output step taken by a sub-node becomes internal to the component, when the corresponding synchronization vector involves no network events.

$$\{(s, e, s') | \exists r \in \gamma, \exists c \in \bigcup_{i=1}^{n} C_i, \pi_{env}(r) = \epsilon \land c = \alpha_r \land e \in \Sigma_c^O$$
$$\land (s_c, \pi_c(r), s_c') \in T_c \land \forall c' \in \eta_r, (s_{c'}, \pi_{c'}(r), s_{c'}') \in T_{c'} \land \forall h \in \varphi_r, s_h = s_h'\}$$

- For each $T \subseteq S \times \Sigma \times S$, such that $(s, e, s') \in T$ satisfies $\forall s'' \in S$, $C \in \bigcup_{i=1}^{n} C_i$, $\forall r \in \gamma, \langle C, \pi_C(r), C'' \rangle \in T \Rightarrow e \leq \pi_C(r)$, means that when two transitions are friable in a configuration of a Node, the *Controller* has the possibility of selecting on of them according to the priority relation.

The interpretation on a Node in terms of components in proposition 1 enables us to model hierarchal design for hierarchal systems. In other word, a Node can be composed of components which are in turn Nods.

4 Verification of Consistency for Nodes

As noted in section 3, *IAs* and *Controllers* capture the abstract interaction protocols of components and *Nods*. In this section we will prove the consistency of a *Node* by means of it's *Controller*.

4.1 Consistency of a Closed Node

Consistency of a closed *Node* is that each event sequence of a sub-node in the *Node* is correspond to a trace of its associated *IA* in the *Controller*. In other words, a closed *Node* is consistent if the environment of each component never provides input events that force the component to enter error state or execute some error report.

Definition 7. *We let association and trace projection between a component of a Node $C \in N$ and interface automaton $A \in$ Controller as a total function $\beta : C \rightarrow U^{ia}$ $|\forall (C, A) \in \beta, \rho_C^I \subseteq \Sigma_a^I, \rho_C^O \subseteq \Sigma_a^O$ and C conforms to A, where ρ_C is the connected port of C in the Node. Let σ is a trace of node N from S_N^0 and it is free from unexpected reception with respect to function β and $q \in S_N$ be a state reachable via σ, $(C, A) \in \beta$, and $s_a \in S_{Controller}$ be a state reachable via $\pi_C(\sigma) \uparrow \Sigma_a$ (sequence of ports of C) from s_a^0. Then s_a is a unique state reachable in a via $\pi_C(\sigma) \uparrow \Sigma_a$ and $\pi_C(q) \prec s_a$ because $\Sigma_A^H = 0$ and A is deterministic.*

The following proposition shows that, to verify the consistency of a closed Node, it is sufficient to prove both the conformance of every component with its corresponding IA and the consistency of the derived Controller.

Proposition 2. *Consider a closed Node $N = (Controller, C_1, C_2, ..., C_n, \gamma)$ sketched by function β. Let Controller be the derived controller of N, then N is consistent with respect to β if Controller is consistent.*

Proof. We prove that for each event sequence of *Node* is correspond to a trace of its derived *Controller*. We do by induction on the length of a trace σ of N from $S^0 \in N$. Let $q \in S_N$ be a state reachable via σ and $\xi_A = \pi_C(\sigma) \uparrow A$ be the trace projection of σ on IA A for $(C, A) \in \beta$. Then at each step of the induction, we prove that σ is correspond to a trace of the Controller. Firstly, when $\sigma = \lambda$, we know $q = s_N^0$. Clearly clime holds. Next, suppose clime holds on an arbitrary trace σ of N from s_N^0. For any step $q \rightarrow_N^e q'$, let a trace $\sigma' = \sigma.e$, then we should prove the clime hold on σ'. then from definition 7 we can get $\forall (p, a) \in \beta, \pi_C(q) \prec \pi_A(s)$.

- if $\exists C \in N$ such that $e \in \Sigma_C^H$, then $\xi'_A = \xi_A$ for all $A \in Controller$ and thus the clime holds.
- if $\exists C \in N$ such that $e \in \Sigma_C^O$, we know $\pi_C(q) \rightarrow_C^e \pi_C(q')$. Let $e = f.v$, then $\exists s'_A \in S_A, \pi_A(s) \rightarrow_A^f s'_A \wedge \pi_C(q') \prec s'_A$. Thus $\xi'_A = \xi_A.f$ is a trace of A.
- For any component $g \in N\backslash C$ such that $\exists f \in \gamma, \pi_g(f) \in \alpha_g^I$, let $f' = \pi_g(f)$, then we have $\exists \pi_g(q) \rightarrow_g^{f'.v} \pi_g(q')$. Let $b = \beta(g)$, then since $f' \in \alpha_g^I \wedge \alpha_g^I \subseteq \Sigma_b^I$, we know $f' \in \Sigma_b^I$. Because the *Controller* is consistent, no error state exists in $L_{Controller}$ and thus $f' \in en_b^I(\pi_b(s))$. Since $\pi_g(q) \prec \pi_b(s)$, we know $\exists s'_b \in S_b$ such that $\pi_b(s) \rightarrow_b^{f'} s'_b \wedge \pi_g(q') \prec s'_b$. Hence $\xi'_b = \xi_b.f'$ is a trace of A.
- For any other component $g \neq C$, let $b = \beta(g)$ and $s'_b = \pi_b(s)$, then $\xi'_b = \xi_b$ is a trace of b.

Consequently, σ' is free from unexpected reception and s'_A is reachable via σ' in A for all $A \in Controller$

5   Conclusion

In this paper, we did following works:

1. We presented a mathematical model called *Node* for composing of components (sub-nods) interacting under supervision of a *Controller*.
2. We proved that each *Node* is equal to a component. Therefore, a *Node* can be composed of components which are in turn *Nods*.
3. In order to express broadcast communications, we allowed *Interface Automata* to be composed in term of extended synchronization vectors model and we assigned priorities to synchronization vectors.
4. We verified consistency of a *Node* by means of consistency of it's *Controller*.

In the future, we will concentrate on basic property such as consistency and deadlock freedom. We will present Modular approaches to verifying these *Nodes*, which utilize the more abstract *Controller* to alleviate the state space explosion.

References

1. Parnas, D.L.: Requirements documentation: Why a formal basis is essential. In: Fourth IEEE International Conference On Requirements Engineering (ICRE2000), IEEE Computer Society Press, Los Alamitos (2000), available online at, http://web.cps.msu.edu/sens/temp/ICRE2000/parnas.pdf
2. Bernardo, M., Ciancarini, P., Donatiello, L.: Families of software systems with process algebras. ACM TOSEM 11, 386–426 (2002)
3. de Alfaro, L., Henzinger, T.: Interface automata. Foundation of Software Engineering, Softw. Eng. Notes 26, 109–120 (2001)
4. de Alfaro, L., Henzinger, T.: Interface-based design. In: Marktoberdorf Summer School, pp. 50–65. Kluwer, Dordrecht (2004)
5. DePrince, W., Hofmeister, C.: Enforcing a lips usage policy for corba components. In: New Waves in System Architecture, In EUROMICRO Conf., pp. 53–60 (2003)
6. Plasil, F., Visnovsky, W.: Behaviour protocols for software components. IEEE TSE 28, 1056–1076 (2002)
7. Jin, Y., Lakos, C., Esser, R.: Modular consistency analysis of component-based designs. Journal of Research and Practice in Information Technology 36, 186–208 (2004)
8. Arnold, A.: Finite Transition Systems: Semantics of Communicating Processes. Prentice-Hall, Englewood Cliffs (1994)
9. Jin, Y.: Compositional Verification of Component-based Heterogeneous Systems. PhD thesis. In: The School of Computer Science University of Adelaide (2004)
10. Bures, T., Hnetynka, F.P.P.: Balancing advanced features in a hierarchical component model. In: Proceedings of SERA, Seattle, USA, IEEE CS, pp. 40–48. IEEE CS, Los Alamitos (2006)
11. Khammaci, T., Smeda, A., Oussalah, M.: Mapping cosa software architecture concepts into uml 2.0. icis-comsar 0, 109–114 (2006)
12. Smeda, A., Khammaci, T., Oussalah, M.: Operational mechanisms for component-object based software architecture. In: Proceeding of Information and Communication Technologies: From Theory to Applications, vol. 19, pp. 591–592 (2004)
13. Magee, J., Dulay, N., Kramer, J.: A constructive development environment for parallel and distributed programs. In IEE/IOP/BCS Distributed Systems Engineering Journal 1 (1994)

Distributed Multi-source Regular Path Queries

Maryam Shoaran and Alex Thomo

University of Victoria, Canada
{maryam,thomo}@cs.uvic.ca

Abstract. Regular path queries are the building block of almost any mechanism for querying semistructured data. Despite the fact that the main applications of such data are distributed, there are only few works dealing with distributed evaluation of regular path queries. In this paper we present a message-efficient and truly distributed algorithm for computing the answer to regular path queries in a multi-source semistructured database setting. Our algorithm is general as it works for the larger class of weighted regular path queries on weighted (as well) semistructured databases.

1 Introduction

Semistructured data is the foundation for a multitude of applications in many important areas such as information integration, Web and communication networks, biological data management, etc. The data in these applications is conceptualized as edge-labeled graphs, and there is an inherent need to navigate these graphs by means of a recursive query language. As pointed out by seminal works in the field (cf. [8,13,5,6,7]), regular path queries (RPQ's) are the "winner" when it comes expressing navigational recursion over semistructured data. These queries are in essence regular expressions over the database edge symbols, and in general, one is interested in finding query-matching database paths, which spell words in the (regular) query language.

Taking an example from spatial network databases (such as [19]), suppose that the user wants to find database paths consisting mainly of highway segments and tolerating up to k provincial roads or city streets. Clearly, such paths can easily be captured by the regular path query

$$Q = highway^* \parallel (road + street + \epsilon)^k,$$

where $\parallel$ is the shuffle operator.

In this paper, we consider generalized RPQ's with preference weights as introduced in [11]. For example, the user can write

$$Q = (highway : 1)^* \parallel (road : 2 + street : 3 + \epsilon)^k,$$

to express that she ideally prefers highways, then roads, which she prefers less, and finally she can tolerate streets, but with an even lesser preference.

P. Thulasiraman et al. (Eds.): ISPA 2007 Workshops, LNCS 4743, pp. 365–374, 2007.

Moreover, inherent database edge weights (or importance) can be naturally incorporated to scale up or down query preferences. Thus, in our spatial example, the edge importance could simply be the edge-length, and so, traversing a 100 kms highway would be less preferable than traversing a 49 kms provincial road, even though in general provincial roads are less preferable than highways.

Based on query-matching paths, there are two ways of defining the answer to an RPQ. The first is the single-source variant [1,3], where the answer is defined to be the set of objects reachable from a given source by following some query-matching path. The second is the multi-source variant [13,5,6,7,11], where the answer is defined to be the set of *pairs* of objects that are connected by some query-matching path.

For generalized RPQ's, in the single-source variant, the answer is the set of (b, w) pairs, where w is the weight of the cheapest query-matching path connecting the database source object with object b.

On the other hand, in the multi-source variant, the answer is the set of (a, b, w) triples, where w is the weight of the cheapest query-matching path connecting database objects a and b.

In this paper, we focus on the second variant of generalized RPQ's. As the main applications based on semistructured data are distributed, we look at RPQ's from a distributed strategy angle.

Computing the answer to a generalized RPQ in the multi-source variant amounts to computing the "all-pairs shortest paths" in the subgraph of database paths spelling words in the query language. However, for each user query, there would be a new subgraph on which to compute all-pairs shortest paths, and such a subgraph cannot be known in advance, but rather only after the query evaluation finishes. This is "too late" for applying algorithms, which need global knowledge of the whole graph. With such algorithms, the user cannot see partial answers while waiting for the query to finish, and there is extra computation and communication overhead incurring after the subgraph [relevant to the query] is determined. Thus, the Flloyd-Warshall algorithm and its distributed variants are not approriate to our database setting.

Regarding work on distributed shortest path computation, we remark here Haldar's algorithm in [12], which computes all-pairs shortest paths with the best known number of messages. Our algorithm is in part inspired by this work. We consider our algorithm a generalization of Haldar's algorithm. However, Haldar's algorithm makes two simplifying (global knowledge) assumptions, which are: (1) each node knows the graph size and (2) each node knows the identities of all other nodes. Clearly, as we explained above they are not true in our setting, and our generalization is essential. Also, due to the fact that the subgraph [relevant to a query] is computed on the fly, we have challenging subtleties that need to be carefully addressed.

Our algorithm works under the assumption that the nodes of the relevant graph are computed on demand and they have local [neighbor] knowledge only. The central idea of our algorithm is to overlap computations starting from different database objects. We achieve this overlap in a careful way in order to guarantee the expansion of the best path first, in a similar spirit with the Dijk-stra's methodology. However, at the same time we allow multiple expansions at different processes, which is what makes the algorithm truly distributed.

To the best of our knowledge, only very few works present a distributed evaluation of regular path queries. In [17], a distributed algorithm is presented, which works based on local knowledge only. However, it has a message complexity which is quadratically worse than our complexity in this paper.

Besides [17], other works that have delt with distributed RPQ's are [3,18,16,14]. All four consider the single-source variant of RPQ's.

Finally, regarding the usefulness of weighted RPQ's, we refer the reader to [9,10,17,11], which study such queries in a multitude of important applications.

The rest of the paper is organized as follows. In Section 2 we give the definitions we are based on. In Section 3, we present our distributed algorithm. In Section 4, we discuss the message complexity.

2 Databases and Weighted RPQ's

We consider a database to be an edge-labeled graph with positive real values assigned to the edges. Intuitively, the nodes of the database graph represent objects and the edges represent relationships (and their importance) between the objects.

Formally, let Δ be an alphabet. Elements of Δ will be denoted $R, S, \ldots$. As usual, Δ^* denotes the set of all finite words over Δ. We also assume that we have a universe of objects, and objects will be denoted $a, b, c, \ldots$. A *database* DB is then a weighted graph (V, E), where V is a finite set of objects and $E \subseteq V \times \Delta \times \mathbb{R}^+ \times V$ is a set of directed edges labeled with symbols from Δ and weighted with numbers from $\mathbb{R}^+$.

Before talking about weighted preference path queries, it will help to first review the classical path queries.

A *regular path query* (RPQ) is a regular language over Δ. Computationally, an RPQ is a finite state automaton (FSA) $\mathcal{A} = (P, \Delta, \tau, p_0, F)$, where P is the set of states, Δ is the alphabet, $\tau \subseteq P \times \Delta \times P$ is the transition relation, p_0 is the initial state, and F is the set of final states. For the ease of notation, we will blur the distinction between RPQ's and FSA's that represent them.

Let $\mathcal{A}$ be a query FSA and $DB = (V, E)$ a database. Then, the *answer* to $\mathcal{A}$ on DB is defined as

$$Ans(\mathcal{A}, DB) = \{(a, b) \in V : a \xrightarrow{w} b \text{ in } DB \text{ and } w \text{ is accepted by } \mathcal{A}\},$$

where $\longrightarrow$ denotes a path in the database.

Now, let $\mathbb{N} = \{1, 2, \ldots\}$. A *weighted finite state automaton* (WFSA) $\mathcal{A}$ is a quintuple $(P, \Delta, \tau, p_0, F)$, where P, p_0, and F are similarly defined as for a classical FSA, while the transition relation τ is now a subset of $P \times \Delta \times \mathbb{N} \times P$. Query WFSA's are given by means of weighted regular expressions (WRE's). The reader is referred to [2] for efficient algorithms translating WRE's into WFSA's.

Given a weighted database $DB = (V, E)$, and a query WFSA $\mathcal{A} = (P, \Delta, \tau,$ $p_0, F)$, the preferentially *scaled weighted answer* (SWAns) of $\mathcal{A}$ on DB is

$$SWAns(\mathcal{A}, DB) = \{(a, b, r) \in V \times V \times \mathbb{R}^+ :$$

$$r = \inf\left\{ \sum_{i=1}^{n} k_i r_i : (p_{i-1}, R_i, k_i, p_i) \in \tau, (c_{i-1}, R_i, r_i, c_i) \in E \right\} \right\},$$

where $p_n \in F$, $c_0 = a$, and $c_n = b$.

As an example, consider the database DB and query automaton $\mathcal{A}$ in Fig. 1. There are three paths going from object a to object c. The shortest path consisting of a single edge T of weight 1, is not the cheapest path according to the query. Rather, the cheapest path is the one spelling RS. The other path, spelling RT, does not match any query automaton path, so it is not considered at all. Hence, we have that $(a, c, 3)$ is the answer with respect to a and c.

Similarly, we find the other query answers and finally have $SWAns(\mathcal{A}, DB) = \{(a, b, 1), (a, c, 3), (a, d, 6), (a, a, 7), (b, c, 5), (b, d, 8), (b, a, 9)\}$.

In order to help understanding of our distributed algorithm, we will first review the well-known method for the evaluation of classical RPQ's (cf. [1]). The evaluation proceeds by creating state-object pairs from the query automaton and the database. For this, let $\mathcal{A}$ be a query FSA. Starting from an object a of a database DB, we first create the pair (p_0, a), where p_0 is the initial state in $\mathcal{A}$. Then, we create all the pairs (p, b) such that there exists a transition from p_0 to p in $\mathcal{A}$, and an edge from a to b in DB, and furthermore the labels of the transition and the edge match. In the same way, we continue to create new pairs from existing ones, until we are not anymore able to do so. In essence, what is happening is a lazy construction of a Cartesian product graph of the query automaton with the database graph. Of course, only a small (hopefully) part of the Cartesian product is really contructed. This ultimately depends on the selectivity of the query.

After obtaining the above Cartesian product graph, producing query answers becomes a question of computing reachability of nodes (p, b), where p is a final state, from (p_0, a), where p_0 is the intial state. Namely, if (p, b) is reachable from (p_0, a), then (a, b) is a tuple in the query answer.

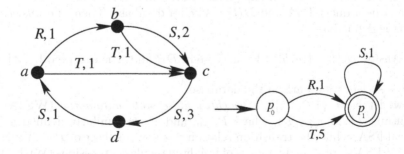

Fig. 1. A database DB and a query automaton $\mathcal{A}$

Now, when having instead a weighted query automaton and database, one can build a weighted Cartesian product graph. It is not difficult to see that, in order to compute weighted answers, we have to find, in the Cartesian product graph, the cheapest paths from all (p_0, a) to all (p, b), where p is a final state in the query automaton $\mathcal{A}$.

As we mentioned in the Introduction, in general there is a different Cartesian product graph for each query. Thus, a useful distributed algorithm must not rely on having global knowledge about the topology of this graph, since it will only be known after the completion of the query evaluation.

3   Distributed Algorithm

The key feature of our algorithm is the overlapping of computations starting from different database objects. We assume that each database object has only local knowledge about the database graph, that is, it only knows the identities of its neighbors and the labels and weights of its outgoing edges. Further, we assume that each object a, is being serviced by a dedicated process for that object P_a. Our algorithm can be easily modified for the case when subgraphs of the database (as opposed to single objects) are being serviced by the processes. In such a case, many of the basic computation messages are sent and received locally by the processes from and to themselves.

First, the query automaton is sent to each process. Such a service is commonly achieved by distributively creating a minimum spanning tree (MST) of the processes before any query starts to be evaluated (cf. [4] for a message optimal MST algorithm).

We can note here that such an MST can be used by the processes to transmit their id's and get so to know each other. However, we do not require this coordination step. Even if such a step is undertaken, the real challenge [which remains] is that the relevant subgraph of the [query–database] Cartesian product cannot be known in advance for a new query. In other words, a shortest path algorithm has to work with a target graph not known beforehand.

Continuing the description of our algorithm, each process starts by creating an initial task for itself. The tasks are "keyed" (uniquely identified) by the automaton states, with the initial tasks being keyed by the initial state p_0. Each task has three components:

1. an automaton state,
2. a status flag that can switch between *active*, *passive*, and *completed* values, and
3. a table (or set) of tuples representing knowledge about "objects reached so far" along with additional information (to be precisely described soon).

A typical task will be written as $\langle p_x, status, \{\dots\} \rangle$. We will refer to the table $\{\dots\}$ as $P_a.p_x.T$ or $p_x.T$ when P_a is clear from the context. The tuples in this table have four components, and will be written as $[(c, p_z), (b, p_y), weight, status]$, where

1. (c, p_z) states that the algorithm, starting from object a and state p_x, has reached (possibly through multiple hops) object c and state p_z,
2. (b, p_y) states that the best path (known so far) to reach (c, p_z) is by passing via object b and state p_y, where b and p_y are neighbors of a and p_x in the database and query automaton respectively,
3. *weight* is the weight of this best path (determined as in Section 2), and
4. *status* is a flag switching from *prov* to *opt* values telling whether *weight* is provisional and would possibly be improved or optimal and permanently stay as is.

Initially, when a p_x-task is created, process P_a tries to find all the outgoing edges from a, which match (w.r.t. the symbol label) outgoing transitions from p_x. Let (a, R, r, b) be such an edge which matches transition (p_x, R, k, p_y). Then, P_a inserts tuple $[(b, p_y), (b, p_y), k \cdot r, prov]$ in table $P_a.p_x.T$. If there are multiple $(a, \_, \_, b)$ - $(p_x, \_, \_, p_y)$ edge-transition matches, then only the match with the cheapest weight product is considered.

Each process P_a starts by creating and initializing a *passive* p_0-task, which is possibly selected next for processing. We say "possibly" because a process might receive new tasks from neighboring processes.

When a task is selected for processing, its *provisional*-status tuples (or *provisional* tuples in short) will be "expanded" in a best-first order with respect to their weights. If there are no more *provisional* tuples in the table of the p_0-task, then the task attains a *completed* status, and the process reports its *local termination*.

All (working) processes run in parallel exactly the same algorithm, which consists of four concurrent threads. These threads are as follows:

Expansion: A process P_a selects a *passive* task, say p_x–task, which still has provisional tuples in its table.

Then, P_a makes the p_x–task *active*, and selects for expansion the cheapest *provisional* tuple in its table $P_a.p_x.T$.

The *active* status for the p_x–task prevents the expansion of other *provisional* tuples in $P_a.p_x.T$.

Next, P_a sends a request message to its neighbor P_b asking it to: (1) create a task p_y, and (2) send its "knowledge" regarding the $[(c, p_z), \_, \_, \_]$ tuple.

Task Creation: When a process P_b receives a request message from P_a (w.r.t p_x) for the creation of a task, say p_y, it creates a p_y-keyed task (if such does not exist) and properly initializes it. Next, P_b establishes a virtual communication channel between its p_y-task and the p_x-task of P_a. This communication channel is specialized for the relevant tuple (keyed by (c, p_z)), whose expansion caused the request message. The weight of the channel will be equal to the cost of going from (a, p_x) to (b, p_y), which is in fact the weight of the (b, p_y)–keyed tuple in $P_a.p_x.T$.

Notably, overlapping of computations happens when process P_b receives another request message for the same task from a different neighboring process. In such a case, the receiving process P_b only establishes a communication channel with the sending process.

Reply: After creating the communication channel, process P_b will send table $P_b.p_y.T$ backward to task $P_a.p_x$. This backward message will be sent only when the (c, p_z)-keyed tuple in $P_b.p_y.T$ attains an *optimal* status. The weight of the communication channel is added to the weights of the tuples as they are bundled together to be sent. We refer to this modified (message) table as $P_b.p_y.T^*$.

Update: When a process P_a receives from some process P_b a backward reply message, which is related to a tuple $[(c, p_z), \_, \_, prov]$ of task $P_a.p_x$, and contains the table $P_b.p_y.T^*$, it will: (1) update (relax) the *provisional* tuples in $P_a.p_x.T$ as appropriate (if there are tuples with the same keys in $P_b.p_y.T^*$), (2) add to table $P_a.p_x.T$ all tuples of $P_b.p_y.T^*$, which do not have any "peer" (tuple with the same key) in $P_a.p_x.T$, and (3) change the status of the p_x-task to *passive*.

Formally our algorithm is as follows.

Algorithm 1

Input:
1. A database DB. For simplicity we assume that each database object, say a, is being serviced by a dedicated process for that object P_a.
2. A query WFSA $\mathcal{A} = (P, \Delta, \tau, p_0, F)$.

Output: The answers to query $\mathcal{A}$ evaluated on database DB.

Method:
1. **Initialization:** Each process P_a creates a task $\langle p_0, passive, \{\ldots\} \rangle$ for itself. The table $\{\ldots\}$ (referred to as $P_a.p_0.T$) is initialized as follows:
   (a) insert tuple $[(a, p_0), (a, p_0), 0, opt]$, and
   (b) For each edge-transition match,
       (a, R, r, b) in DB and
       (p_0, R, k, p) in $\mathcal{A}$,
       insert tuple $[(b, p), (b, p), k \cdot r, prov]$
       (if there are multiple $(a, \_, \_, b) - (p_0, \_, \_, p)$ edge-transition matches, then the cheapest weight product is considered.)
   If at point (b) there is no edge-transition match, then make the status of the p_0-task *completed*.

2. Concurrently execute all the four following threads at each process in parallel until termination is detected. [For clarity, we describe the threads at two processes, P_a and P_b.]

3. **Expansion:** [At process P_a]
   (a) Select a passive p_x-task for processing. Make the status of the task *active*.
   (b) Select the cheapest *provisional*-status tuple, say $[(c, p_z), (b, p_y), w, prov]$ from table $P_a.p_x.T$.
   (c) Request P_b, with respect to state p_y, to provide information about (c, p_z).

For this, send a message $\langle p_y, [p_x, (c, p_z), w_{ab}]\rangle$ to P_b, where w_{ab} is the cost of going from (a, p_x) to (b, p_y), which is equal to the weight of the (b, p_y)–keyed tuple in $P_a.p_x.T$.

(d) Sleep, with regard to p_x-task, until the reply message for (c, p_z) comes from P_b.

4. **Task Creation:** [At process P_b]
Upon receiving a message $\langle p_y, [p_x, (c, p_z), w]\rangle$ from P_a:
if there is not yet a p_y-task
then create a task $\langle p_y, passive, \{\ldots\}\rangle$ and initialize its table similarly as in the first phase.
That is,
(a) insert tuple $[(b, p_y), (b, p_y), 0, opt]$, and
(b) For each edge-transition match,
   (b, R, r, d) in DB and
   (p_y, R, k, p_u) in $\mathcal{A}$,
   insert tuple $[(d, p_u), (d, p_u), k \cdot r, prov]$
   (if there are multiple $(b, \_, \_, d)$–$(p_y, \_, \_, p_u)$ edge-transition matches, then the cheapest weight product is considered.)
Also, establish a virtual communication channel with P_a. This channel relates the p_y-task of P_b with the p_x-task of P_a. Further, it is indexed by (c, p_z) and is weighted by w_{ab} (the weight included in the received message).
else [P_b has already a p_y-task.] Do not create a new task, but only establish a communication channel with P_a as described above.

5. **Reply:** [At process P_b]
When in the p_y-task, the tuple $[(c, p_z), (\_, \_), \_, \_]$ is or becomes optimally weighted, *reply back* to all the neighbor processes, which had sent a task requesting message $\langle p_y, [\_, (c, p_z), \_]\rangle$ to P_b.
For example, P_b sends to such a neighbor, say P_a, through the corresponding communication channel, the message $\langle P_b.p_y.T^*\rangle$, which is table $P_b.p_y.T$ after adding the channel weight to the weight of each tuple.

6. **Update:** [At process P_a]
Upon receiving a reply message $\langle P_b.p_y.T^*\rangle$ from a neighbor P_b w.r.t. the expansion of a (c, p_z)-keyed tuple in table $P_a.p_x.T$ do:
(a) Change the status of (c, p_z)-keyed tuple to *optimal*.
(b) For each tuple $[(d, p_u), (\_, \_), v, s]$[1] in $P_b.p_y.T^*$, which has a smaller weight (v) than a same-key tuple $[(d, p_u), (\_, \_), \_, prov]$ in $P_a.p_x.T$, replace the latter by $[(d, p_u), (b, p_y), v, s]$.
(c) Add to $P_a.p_x.T$ all the rest of the $P_b.p_y.T^*$ tuples, i.e., those which do not have corresponding same-key tuples in $P_a.p_x.T$.
Also, change the via component of these tuples to be (b, p_y).
(d) **if** the p_x-task does not have anymore *provisional* tuples,

---

[1] s is the status which can be *prov* or *opt*.

then make its status *completed*.
  If $p_x = p_0$, then report that all query answers from P_a have been computed.
  else make the status of the p_x-task *passive*.

Finally upon termination, which happens when all the tasks in every process have attained *completed* status, set

$$eval(\mathcal{A}, DB) = \{(a, b, r) : [(b, p_y), (\_, \_), r, opt)] \in P_a.p_0.T \text{ and } p_y \in F\}.$$

In the full paper[2], we show the soundness and completeness of our algorithm. Based on them, the following theorem can be stated.

Theorem 1. *Upon termination of the above algorithm, we have that*

$$eval(\mathcal{A}, DB) = SWAns(\mathcal{A}, DB).$$

It is worth mentioning here that any snapshot of $eval(\mathcal{A}, DB)$ at any time during the execution of the above algorithm is a partial answer to the query. Hence, an answer can be immediately reported as soon as the corresponding tuple attains an optimal status. Upon termination, all the answers would have been reported. Also, in the full paper we show that

Theorem 2. *Algorithm 1 (positively) terminates.*

4   Complexity

In this paper, we restrict our discussion to message complexity only. We show that the upper bound of the message complexity for Algorithm 1 is quadratic in the number of database objects. In fact, we can further qualify this as the number of database objects involved in the Cartesian product explained in Section 2. This number ultimately depends on the query selectivity, and in practice one hopes that the (lazy) Cartesian product size is much smaller than the size of the database (cf. [1]).

Theorem 3. *The maximum number of messages required for a query evaluation is* $2 \cdot n^2 \cdot s^2$, *where* n *is the number of objects in* DB, *and* s *is the number of states in* $\mathcal{A}$.

Proof. We base our claim on the following facts:

1. The number of tasks in each process is bounded by s.
2. Between two tasks in different processes, there can be up to $n \cdot s$ communication channels, which are indexed by an object-state pair.
3. Only one forward message is needed to cause the creation of a communication channel.
4. Each communication channel is traversed only once, which happens when the tuple keyed by the object-state of the channel becomes optimally weighted.

Since we have n processes, the upper bound for the total number of messages is $n \cdot s \cdot (n \cdot s) \cdot (1 + 1) = 2 \cdot n^2 \cdot s^2$.   □

---

[2] http://www.cs.uvic.ca/~thomo/all_to_all.pdf

References

1. Abiteboul, S., Buneman, P., Suciu, D.: Data on the Web: From Relations to Semistructured Data and XML. Morgan Kaufmann, San Francisco CA (1999)
2. Allauzen, C., Mohri, M.: A Unified Construction of the Glushkov, Follow, and Antimirov Automata. In: Královič, R., Urzyczyn, P. (eds.) MFCS 2006. LNCS, vol. 4162, pp. 110–121. Springer, Heidelberg (2006)
3. Abiteboul, S., Vianu, V.: Regular Path Queries with Constraints. J. of Computing and System Sciences 58(3), 428–452 (1999)
4. Awerbuch, B.: Optimal Distributed Algorithms for Minimum-Weight Spanning tree, Counting, Leader Election and Related Problems. In: Proc. of STOC'87, pp. 230–240. ACM Press, New York (1987)
5. Calvanese, D., Giacomo, G., Lenzerini, M., Vardi, M.Y.: Answering Regular Path Queries Using Views. In: Proc. of ICDE'00, pp. 389–398. IEEE Computer Society Press, Los Alamitos (2000)
6. Calvanese, D., Giacomo, G., Lenzerini, M., Vardi, M.Y.: Reasoning on Regular Path Queries. SIGMOD Record 32(4), 83–92 (2003)
7. Calvanese, D., Giacomo, G., Lenzerini, M., Vardi, M.Y.: View-based Query Processing: On the Relationship between Rewriting, Answering and Losslessness. In: Eiter, T., Libkin, L. (eds.) ICDT 2005. LNCS, vol. 3363, pp. 321–336. Springer, Heidelberg (2004)
8. Consens, M.P., Mendelzon, A.O.: GraphLog: A Visual Formalism for Real Life Recursion. In: Proc of PODS'90, pp. 404–416. ACM Press, New York (1990)
9. Flesca, S., Furfaro, F., Greco, S.: Weighted Path Queries on Semistructured Databases. Inf. Comput. 204(5), 679–696 (2006)
10. Grahne, G., Thomo, A.: Regular Path Queries Under Approximate Semantics. Ann. Math. Artif. Intell. 46(1–2), 165–190 (2006)
11. Grahne, G., Thomo, A., Wadge, W.: Preferentially Annotated Regular Path Queries. In: Schwentick, T., Suciu, D. (eds.) ICDT 2007. LNCS, vol. 4353, pp. 314–328. Springer, Heidelberg (2006)
12. Haldar, S.: An "All Pairs Shortest Paths" Distributed Algorithm Using $2n^2$ Messages. J. of Algorithms, 24(1), 20–36 (1997)
13. Mendelzon, A.O., Wood, P.T.: Finding Regular Simple Paths in Graph Databases. SIAM J. Comp. 24(6), 1235–1258 (1995)
14. Miao, Z., Stefanescu, D., Thomo, A.: Grid-Aware Evaluation of Regular Path Queries on Spatial Networks. In: Proc. of AINA'07, pp. 158–165. IEEE Computer Society Press, Los Alamitos (2007)
15. Planet-Lab: http://www.planet-lab.org
16. Stefanescu, D., Thomo, A., Thomo, L.: Distributed Evaluation of Generalized Path Queries. In: Preneel, B., Tavares, S. (eds.) SAC 2005. LNCS, vol. 3897, pp. 610–616. Springer, Heidelberg (2006)
17. Stefanescu, D., Thomo, A.: Enhanced Regular Path Queries on Semistructured Databases. In: Grust, T., Höpfner, H., Illarramendi, A., Jablonski, S., Mesiti, M., Müller, S., Patranjan, P.-L., Sattler, K.-U., Spiliopoulou, M., Wijsen, J. (eds.) EDBT 2006. LNCS, vol. 4254, pp. 700–711. Springer, Heidelberg (2006)
18. Suciu, D.: Distributed Query Evaluation on Semistructured Data. ACM Trans. on Database Systems, 27(1), 1–62 (2002)
19. TIGER: Topologically Integrated Geographic Encoding and Referencing system, US Census Bureau: http://www.census.gov/geo/www/tiger
20. Vardi, M.Y.: A Call to Regularity. In: Proc. PCK50-Principles of Computing & Knowledge, Paris C. Kanellakis Memorial Workshop '03, ACM Press, New York (2003)

Parallel Matrix Multiplication Based on Dynamic SMP Clusters in SoC Technology

Marek Tudruj[1,2] and Łukasz Masko[1]

[1] Institute of Computer Science, Polish Academy of Sciences
21 Ordona Str., 01-237 Warsaw, Poland
[2] Polish-Japanese Institute of Information Technology,
86 Koszykowa Str., 02-008 Warsaw, Poland
{tudruj, masko}@ipipan.waw.pl

Abstract. The paper concerns a special architecture of dynamic shared memory processor (SMP) clusters organized at program run-time. In this architecture, designed for implementation in System on Chip technology, a new mechanism of the communication on the fly is provided. It is a combination of dynamic processor switching between SMP clusters and parallel data reads on the fly. This mechanism enables direct communication between processor data caches and eliminates many data transactions on memory busses. The paper presents the principles of the new architecture and evaluates its efficiency for execution of matrix multiplication with recursive matrix decomposition into quarters. The evaluation is done by simulation experiments with symbolic execution of parallel program graphs with different parallelization grain.

1 Introduction

This paper presents a new cluster-based shared memory system architecture applied to parallel numerical computations. The system structure assumes dynamically reconfigurable shared memory processor (SMP) clusters whose composition can adjust to requirements of application programs. Dynamic SMP clusters correspond to data exchange sub-networks which connect processors with shared memory modules. Processors can be switched between clusters for program defined time, preferably longer than for a single memory transaction. It provides features of dynamically reconfigurable embedded systems whose structure meets program needs accordingly to a pre-compiled strategy based on program analysis.

Cluster-based systems, supported by efficient communication solutions such as discussed in this paper, can strongly increase execution efficiency of parallel programs. Data communication between processors from different clusters, assumed in this paper, is implemented using a new method. It is based on dynamic switching of processors from one SMP cluster to another with relevant data ported in processors data caches [9, 10, 11]. While a processor writes data from its cache to the target cluster memory other processors in this cluster can do parallel reads of data (reads on the fly, similar to cache injection [8]) to their data caches. Such synergy of reads on the fly with processor switching, is called "communication on the fly". It enables inter-cluster data exchange, without transactions through shared memory modules.

P. Thulasiraman et al. (Eds.): ISPA 2007 Workshops, LNCS 4743, pp. 375–385, 2007.

The proposed cluster-based shared memory system architecture perfectly matches current possibilities and development trends of the System on Chip (SoC) technology [1-3]. This architecture assumes that many SoC modules composed of processors and shared memory modules with dynamic processor clustering and communication on the fly are connected by a central global network. Another important feature of the proposed architecture is the data cache-driven macro-data flow program execution paradigm. Tasks in programs are organized in a similar way as in macro data flow graphs. A task execution can be started only after all data required for a task have been transferred to the processor's data cache. By these means all data thrashing in processor data caches can be eliminated. In this respect, the proposed strategy provides significant improvements as compared to other new caching strategies like cache pre-fetching [6], data-forwarding [7] and cache injection [8]. The processors data caches are multi-ported at the side of memory module busses. It enables performing several data cache – memory transactions in a processor in parallel. This extends the design space of efficient solutions for data caching in parallel numerical applications [4, 5]. The paper presents simulation experiments with execution of graphs of square matrix parallel multiplication with recursive data decomposition. They show that in the discussed parallel multiplication algorithms, different to those known for distributed memory systems [13, 14], the proposed shared memory system architectural solutions give very good results for fine and coarse grain parallelization.

The paper is composed of three parts. In the first part, the new system architecture is described. In the second part, program structuring methods for communication on the fly are discussed based on a new program graph representation. In the third part, simulation experiment results with symbolic graph execution for parallel matrix multiplication for different size of parallel computation grain are presented.

2   System of Dynamic Shared Memory Clusters for SoC Technology

The proposed system structure is based on highly modular approach based on SoC technology, Fig. 1 (left). Processors (P) and memory modules (M) with local networks (memory busses) are embedded in SoC modules. SoC modules are interconnected by a global network (a crossbar switch), which is implemented as a network on chip NoC circuit. A SoC module general internal structure is presented in Fig. 1 (right). Each processor (Pi) has a separate data and instruction caches. A set of local cluster networks (memory busses) enables connecting processors (i.e. their data caches) with memory modules dynamically at program run-time. A set of processors attached to a memory module bus is considered a processor cluster. Each processor data cache is built of many data cache banks which can work in parallel and can be connected to many memory modules at a time. Due to this multi-ported cache design, a processor can belong to many clusters at the same time. Thus, a processor can load data cache banks in parallel from many memory modules and, at the same time, it can write to many memory modules from its data cache banks. The address sub-spaces of all data memory modules are shared by all the processors. Memory modules inside a SoC module are also connected to an Inter-Cluster Network, which has a connection with the Global Network. The Global Network enables data reads from memory modules performed by non-local processors to memory modules they are locally connected to. Data availability bits (with Ready/Empty values) exist in data words in memory. They synchronize reads and writes to the shared memory locations. Data communication in programs can be organized using reads on the fly, communication on the fly and standard write/read/transactions through memory modules.

A read on the fly consists in capturing by many processors the data, which are being written by one processor through a memory bus in a cluster. It is done by snooping the address lines on the memory bus. All the reading processors are synchronized with the writing processor. A special inter-processor synchronization path is included in the system to enable parallel synchronization for many reads on the fly. On requests coming from application programs, processors can be disconnected from clusters (memory module busses) and connected to other clusters under control of respective bus arbiters. A processor switched to a new cluster can bring some data in its data cache, which are required for computations in the target cluster. Processors already present in the target cluster can read on the fly the data the switched processor writes over the cluster bus to the cluster memory module. This inter-cluster data transfer mechanism is called communication on the fly.

Programs are composed of computational tasks according to their macro data flow graphs. Before a task can start execution all its data have to be prefetched to the processor data cache by special cache pre-fetch instructions (block transfers from memory modules). Pre-fetch instructions can use old or new target addresses. New addresses are used when data will be modified by parallel tasks. These single assignment rule avoids the memory and cache consistency problem. Current computation results are written to the data cache. Space must be reserved for them. Data can be written to the cluster memory module only after task execution is over. Due to such data cache behavior thrashing is eliminated. In write instructions old or new target addresses can be used. Data transfers concerning data caches and memory modules are performed in response to requests coming from application programs.

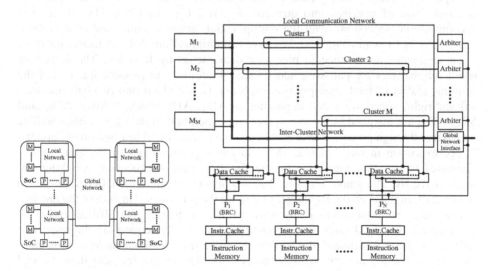

Fig. 1. General system structure (left), the internal structure of a SoC module (right)

A program can generate write requests and 2 types of read requests: standard and on the fly. Processors are supplied with Bus Request Controllers (BRCs) which have separate queues for different types of requests. The requests are stored in the queues in the order of their priorities. Writes have higher priority than reads and smaller data transfers have higher priorities. Memory module busses have arbiters, which co-ordinate memory read and write accesses from the side of processors. All processor BRCs send to the arbiters requests from the top of their respective queue(s). Each arbiter selects the highest priority request and sends to the corresponding processor BRC an access permission. When the transmission is over the arbiter is notified and a new request is selected. For read on the fly requests each BRC has a separate memory address snooping table which controls the memory bus snooping unit. The requests deposed in these tables contain initial data block transfer addresses and the transmission lengths. Additionally, for each read on the fly request the target addresses for captured blocks of data are stored in the BRCs. These requests are fulfilled without arbiter control. When the bus snooping unit discovers a match of the source address of a read on the fly request stored in the address snooping table, data from the memory bus are directed to the processor data cache.

3   Extended Macro-Data-Flow Graph Representation

For parallel program structural design and simulation experiments, we use a special extended macro data flow graph (EMDFG) representation. There are new kinds of nodes in the EMDFG graphs: data read nodes (R) from memory modules to processor's data caches, data write nodes (W) from data caches to memory modules, processor switch nodes (crossed boxes), memory module bus arbiter nodes (CA), the global data network arbiter node (GA), and barriers (Bi).

We will discuss programs execution in the proposed system architecture using an example of square matrix parallel multiplication $\mathbf{A} \times \mathbf{B} = \mathbf{C}$. It is based on decomposition of matrices into quarters ($A_{i,j}$, $B_{i,j}$, $C_{i,j}$, $i,j \in \{0, 1\}$). At the 1-st decomposition (recursion) level the multiplication graph is composed of 4 isolated sub-graphs as shown in Fig. 2 a). We have 8 multiplications MLi of matrix quarters. Their arguments are fetched to processor data caches by R nodes. The respective result sub-matrices are pair-wise added using 4 additions to produce quarters of the resulting matrix C. Each multiply result sub-matrix is divided into two half-matrices, left and right, which are added in parallel, in AD_{iL}, AD_{iR} nodes. If ML_1 , AD_{1L} ,and ML_2, AD_{1R} are assigned to the same processors, then half of data for addition will be transferred through processor data caches and the addition will last two times shorter.

For execution in our dynamic SMP clusters a program has to be appropriately structured to use communication on the fly composed of processor switching and reads on the fly. The graph from Fig. 2 a) is transformed into a EMDFG graph shown in Fig. 2 b). In reads on the fly (larger ovals), all the processors (including the one that writes data) are synchronized by barriers Bi. A barrier is fulfilled when all participating reading threads have deposed read on the fly requests in the respective BRC units. After fulfillment of a barrier, the write from the data cache to a memory module takes place and all involved processors can capture the sent data. Special

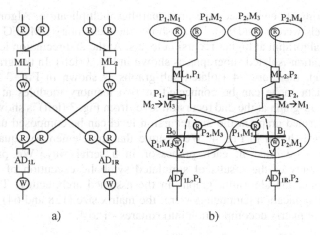

a)   b)

Fig. 2. Elementary EMDFG of matrix multiplication at 1-st recursion level a), the EMDFG with communication on the fly b)

nodes (crossed rectangles) represent switching of processors (their data cache banks) from the cluster identified by the memory module M_i to the new cluster (M_j). When a switched processor writes data to the memory, the data are copied to the data cache accordingly to the read target address. The sub-graph in Fig. 2 b) has been structured to the use of 2 processors (P_1, P_2) and 4 memory modules (M_1, M_2, M_3, M_4). First, two clusters (ovals) are created for each processor P_1, P_2 to fetch in parallel data for multiplications ML_i. After multiplications have been completed, the processors (P_1, P_2) are switched to other clusters to pre-fetch data for additions by reads on the fly.

4   Simulation Experiments

The simulation experiments aimed in examining efficiency of the square matrix parallel multiplication for matrices decomposed into quarters. We used a graph execution simulator in the proposed architecture written in C/C++ language. The simulator is cycle accurate if the data communication control is concerned.

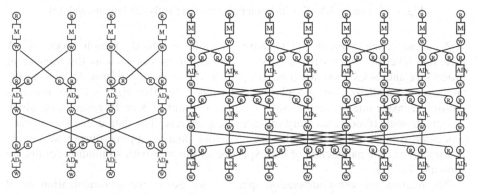

Fig. 3. Elementary EMDFG: 2nd recursion level (left) and 3rd recursion level (right)

First experiments concerned fine grain parallel multiplication. Algorithms with 4 recursion levels were considered. Fig. 3 shows the elementary EMDFG subgraphs of the analyzed algorithm at higher recursion levels. At the 2nd recursion level, there are 16 communication-isolated subgraphs as shown in Fig. 3 (left). In the graph at the 3rd recursion level, there are 64 isolated sub-graphs as shown in Fig. 3 (right). Each processor's data cache can be connected to two memory modules at a time. The transformed sub-graph at the 2nd recursion level from Fig. 3 (left) is shown in Fig. 4.

The transformed graph at the 3rd recursion level can be composed using methods similar to those shown in Fig. 4. We assume that the elementary square submatrix multiplications are done in each processor in a serial way. We present below comparative study of the results of simulated symbolic execution of the proposed matrix multiplication algorithm graphs in the assumed architecture. The basic fine grain parallel application parameters were: the matrix size (128 and 64) and the level of the recursive matrix decomposition into squares - 1 to 4.

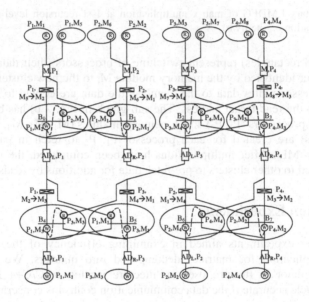

Fig. 4. Elementary EMDF with communication on the fly- 2nd recursion level

A single computation thread is assumed to be executed in each processor. A recursion level determines the necessary system parameters such as the number of processors and SoCs modules used for the execution of algorithms as well as the application parallelization granularity determined by the sizes of the matrices multiplied inside one processor. SoC modules are built of 8 or 16 processors, which co-operate with 16 or 32 memory modules, respectively. The data cache size in each processor is assumed sufficiently big to avoid data swapping during sequential computations. The parameters of the experiments together with simulation results are shown in Table 1.

The relation between computation speed of processors and communication speed i.e. the frequency of the memory bus was assumed 2:1. This is equivalent to 1.6

GFLOPS processors (their data caches) co-operating with data memory modules via 800 MHz busses. The assumed operation execution times were as follows: 1 unit for floating point 8-byte scalar addition and multiplication on data taken out of the data cache with results written also there, 2 units for transmission of such a 8-byte scalar between data cache and memory. The costs of barrier execution, processor switching between clusters and bus arbitration are 1 unit as executed in a totally hardware way.

Simulation results for different recursion levels as a function of the number of processors (8- and 16-processor SoCs) are shown in Fig. 6. The parallel speedup was computed against the best sequential execution, which used recursive matrix decomposition into quarters and Strassen method [14] or standard multiplication of quarters, depending on which method was supplying better results. In the same way, using the Strassen method or standard multiplication of quarters, the elementary serial multiplications in parallel algorithms were executed. For the 128x128 matrix multiplication, the parallel implementation based on 64x64 elementary serial multiplication (1 SoC module with 8 processors) gives speedup of 7 with the parallelization efficiency of 0.88. 32x32 multiplication (2nd recursion level) gives speedup of 49 out of 64 processors (4 SoCs) with the efficiency 0.77. 16x16 elementary multiplication gives speedup of 348 out of 512 processors with the efficiency 0.68. 8x8 elementary multiplications are still good with the efficiency of 0.60. For the 64x64 matrix multiplication, the implementation based on 32x32 elementary multiplication gives speedup of 7 with the efficiency of 0.88. 16x16 elementary multiplication gives in this case much improved speedup of 50 out of 64 processors with efficiency 0.78. 8x8 elementary multiplications are still good with the speedup of 348 out of 512 processors and the parallellization efficiency of 0.68. 4x4 elementary multiplications give low efficiency of 0.43. These results show that the parallellization efficiency of fine grain matrix multiplication with the elementary parallel computation grain decreasing down to that of sequential 8x8 matrix multiplication, is very good.

Table 1. Fine grain computations

recursion level	0	1	2	3	4
no. of SoCs	1	1	4	32	256
total no. of proc.	1	8	64	512	4096
Total matrix size 128 x 128					
matrix size/proc.	128	64	32	16	8
speedup	1	7	49	348	2371
parallelization efficiency	1	0.88	0.77	0.68	0.60
Total matrix size 64 x 64					
matrix size/proc.	64	32	16	8	4
speedup	1	7	50	341	1728
parallelization efficiency	1	0.88	0.78	0.68	0.43

Graphical representation of the experiment results is shown in Fig. 5, where the results are additionally compared to execution in the proposed SoC architecture without application of the Strassen method to the elementary serial multiplication.

These results are the lower bounds of improvement, since the serial multiplication algorithms were constructed in the possibly best way, using dual ported data caches, recursive Strassen method and the fairly large data cache sizes, which have eliminated any data swapping from the data cache during multiplication computations.

We will now present the efficiency of the proposed matrix multiplication method in the assumed architecture for coarser parallel grain matrix multiplication algorithms

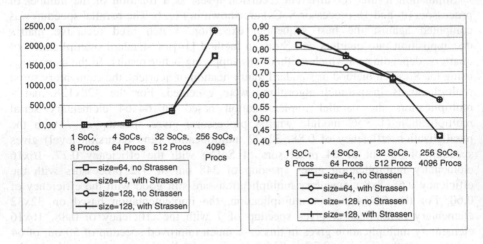

Fig. 5. Fine-grain matrix multiplication parallel speedup (left), parallelization efficiency (right); with/without serial Strassen method and for matrix sizes 64 and 128

based on matrix recursive decomposition into quarters. The assumed A, B matrix size is 2048 x 2048. The relation between computation speed of processors and communication speed as well as the operation execution times were assumed the same as in the previous fine grain experiments. The experiment parameters with large matrix size and the simulation results are shown in Table 2. For large matrices, an important parameter is the assumed data cache size which was 32 MB at the first recursion level (very difficult to be matched at the current technology level, therefore the 1-st recursion level results are given only as theoretical assessments), 8MB at the 2nd recursion level, 2 MB at the 3rd recursion levels and 0.5 MB at the 4th recursion level. With such data cache sizes, the computation nodes in the algorithm graphs could be executed with data cache pre-fetching and so, entirely without swapping in data caches. The same data cache sizes were assumed for the sequential matrix multiplication algorithms, which were performed using the sequential recursive Strassen method. The obtained speedups for different system sizes against sequential execution are similar to those obtained for 128 x 128 matrix size. It means that the assumed system architecture behaves in a similar way providing that the parallel computation grain is larger than 4 x 4. With such restrictions, the parallelization efficiency changes from 0.88 to 0.59, the latter is for the highest recursion level and the finest parallel computations. Depending on the number of SoC modules and processors, we can select the appropriate recursion level, which will provide satisfactory parallelization efficiency - not lower than 0.59.

Table 2. Coarse grain computations

recursion level	0	1	2	3	4
no. of SoCs	1	1	4	32	256
total no. of proc.	1	8	64	512	4096
Total matrix size 2048 x 2048					
matrix size/proc.	2048	1024	512	256	128
speedup	1	7	49	344	2411
parallelization efficiency	1	0.88	0.77	0.67	0.59

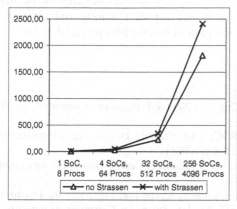 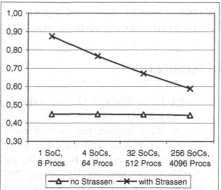

Fig. 6. Coarse grain matrix multiplication speedup (left), parallelization efficiency (right), with/without serial Strassen method

Fig. 6 shows the graphical representation of simulation results for the coarse grain multiplication. This figure also shows the comparison of the parallel speedup and parallelization efficiency with and without application of the serial Strassen multiplication method. Comparing the very fine grain computations (small matrix sizes), here the situation is different, since for multiplications of larger matrices, the Strassen method brings much stronger multiplication speedup. The presented simulation results show that the proposed matrix multiplication method in the assumed architecture provides good speedup and parallelization efficiency also for coarser parallel computation grain.

5 Conclusions

The paper has presented a new system architecture with dynamic SMP clusters and communication on the fly applied in simulation experiments on matrix multiplication with recursive data decomposition. A program graphs execution simulator was used with cycle accurate simulation of data communication control.

In the studied example of matrix multiplication, all communication through standard data exchange network involving multiple reads of shared data could be transformed into processor switching between dynamic clusters with data reads on the fly inside SoC modules. It enables overlapping of all data reads with writes and reduces overall traffic on system data networks. The presented experiments have shown that the proposed system architecture gives very good results equally for fine grain computations and higher parallelization grains. It confirms the potential of the proposed architecture for typical numerical computations on regular data sets.

Current works on the proposed architecture and program execution paradigms concern automatic program graph structuring and scheduling for execution in the proposed architecture, based on heuristic approach [12]. Another direction of further research concerns numerical algorithms, with stronger data sharing and intensive communication for which the proposed architecture offers the best potential.

References

1. Benini, L., de Michelli, G.: Networks on Chips: A New SoC Paradigm. Computer , 70–78 (January 2002)
2. Rowen, Ch.: Engineering the Complex SOC; Fast, Flexible Design with Configurable Processors. Prentice Hall PTR, Englewood Cliffs (2004)
3. Nurmi, J., Tenhunen, H., Isoah, J., Jantsch, A.: Interconnect-Centric Design for Advanced SoC and NoC. Springer, Heidelberg (2004)
4. Wilson, K., Olukotun, K., Rosenblum, M.: Increasing Cache Port Efficiency for Dynamic Super-scalar Microprocessors. In: 23-rd ISCA - Int. Symp. on Computer Architecture, Philadephia (May 1996)
5. Nayfeh, B.A., Olukotun, K.: Exploring the Design Space for a Shared-Cache Multiprocessor, 21-st ISCA - Int. Symp. on Computer Architecture (February 1994)
6. Tullsen, D.M., Eggers, S.J.: Effective Cache Pre-fetching on Bus Based Multi-processors. ACM Trans. on Comp. Systems 13(1), 57–88 (1995)
7. Koufaty, D.A., et al.: Data Forwarding in Scaleable Shared Memory Multi-Processors. IEEE Trans. on Parallel and Distr. Technology 7(12), 1250–1264 (1996)
8. Milenkovic, A., Milutinovic, V., Cache Injection, A.: Novel Technique for Tolerating Memory Latency in Bus-Based SMPs, In: Bode, A., Ludwig, T., Karl, W.C., Wismüller, R. (eds.) Euro-Par 2000. LNCS, vol. 1900, pp. 558–566. Springer, Heidelberg (2000)
9. Tudruj, M., Masko, L.: Dynamic SMP Clusters with Communication on the Fly in NoC Technology for Very Fine Grain Computations. In: The 3rd Intl. Symp. on Parallel and Distributed Computing - ISPDC 2004, Cork, Ireland, pp. 97–104. IEEE CS Press, Los Alamitos (2004)
10. Tudruj, M., Masko, L.: Dynamic SMP Clusters in SoC Technology - Towards Massively Parallel Fine Grain Numerics. In: Wyrzykowski, R., Dongarra, J.J., Meyer, N., Waśniewski, J. (eds.) PPAM 2005. LNCS, vol. 3911, pp. 34–42. Springer, Heidelberg (2006)
11. Tudruj, M., Masko, L.: Towards Massively Parallel Computations Based on Dynamic SMP Clusters wih Communication on the Fly. In: Proceedings of the 4th International Symposium on Parallel and Distributed Computing, ISPDC 2005. Lille, pp. 155–162. IEEE CS Press, Los Alamitos (2005)

12. Masko, L.: Scheduling Task Graphs for Execution in Dynamic SMP Clusters with Bounded Number of Resources. In: Wyrzykowski, R., Dongarra, J.J., Meyer, N., Waśniewski, J. (eds.) PPAM 2005. LNCS, vol. 3911, pp. 871–878. Springer, Heidelberg (2006)
13. Choi, J., Dongarra, J., Walker, D.: PUMMA: Parallel Universal Matrix Multiplication Algorithms on Distributed Memory Concurrent Computers, Technical Report TM-12252, Oak Ridge National Laboratory (August 1993)
14. Luo, Q., Drake, J.B.: A Scalable Parallel Strassen's Matrix Multiplication Algorithm for Distributed-Memory Computers. In: 1995 ACM Symposium on Applied Computing, pp. 221–226 (1995)

Multi-Agent Design of Urban Oriented Traffic Integration Control System

Feizhou Zhang[1], Dongkai Yang[2], Xuejun Cao[1], and Jia Chen[1]

[1] Institute of Remote Sensing and GIS, Peking University, Beijing 100871, PRC
[2] School of Electronic Information Engineering, Beihang University, Beijing 100083, PRC

Abstract. In order to solve the key technologies of urban traffic in China, the intelligent means and approach, combined artificial intelligent with tradition control ones, are adopted in the paper. Some hypotheses are elicited on the basis of the characteristics of Chinese urban traffic control system structure and function requirement, a kind of frame structure of urban traffic intelligent control system is stated based on multi-agents cooperation. A kind of better design ways and means for urban traffic real-time, rational and reasonable control system is established according to the frame structure, the system design of urban cross control and area control based on multi-agents is implemented. In this way, successful realization of goal for urban traffic intelligent control is insured so as to increase the capacity of urban road network and to improve our urban traffic control and management modes. Therefore urban surroundings quality will be enhanced. And the comfortable and delightful traffic surroundings will be built.

Keywords. Multi-Agent; Urban Traffic; Integrated Control; Intelligent Transport System (ITS).

1 Introduction

Urban traffic system has complex control problem from the point of theory and application. Its main characteristics are that a large of cross roads is in the road network. To avoid the vehicle conflict from different directions, the traffic flow needs to be guided with high accuracy control information to the drivers and the passengers. The traditional control strategy is timing control with open loop, and it has bad adaptive capability. The inductive control is a kind of close loop control method with adaptive capability according to the vehicle information. Some literature introduces the combination of fuzzy theory, neural network theory and hierarchical control to be used for the urban traffic trunk line control and overcome the difficulty without the high accurate math model. However, the urban area traffic control has not been solved with successful result at home and abroad [1, 2]. In this paper, the artificial intelligence and traditional method are combined and applied in the urban area traffic control system in accordance with Chinese urban traffic system framework and function requirements. The urban traffic intelligent control system framework based on the Multi-Agent is mainly studied and its four levels, i.e. decision level, strategic level, tactics level and executive level are discussed. The system design is given based on some system presumption for the urban area traffic control system in this paper.

P. Thulasiraman et al. (Eds.): ISPA 2007 Workshops, LNCS 4743, pp. 386–393, 2007.

2   Agent and Its System Modeling

A   Agent

One valid resolution different from the traditional traffic control is distributed control by some intelligent entities which can get the task automatically and finish them. It does not integrate or partly integrate the subsystems, and it supplies a kind of coordination mechanism between the loosely coupled subsystems. The self-governing capability of subsystems is improved to improve the control capability of control system [3]. In the artificial intelligence field, agent is defined as the entity with sensing, problem resolving and information exchanging capability. From the software programming, it is a computer program exchanged the information with outside entities through the pre-defined protocol. The process management via the loosely coupled distributed control has the performance as fast response, good flexibility and adaptive. Furthermore, the obstacle resulted from the time, space, software and hardware environment difference can be overcome during the product development. Some system control model can be established using agent, which will unify the human behavior and the control unit behavior to get a generalized description method. Agents are connected through the computer network and each agent is intelligent node in the network to compose a distributed Multi-Agent (MA) system.

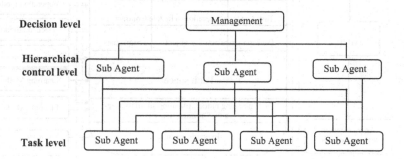

Fig. 1. Hierarchical Control Architecture of MA

Hierarchical control architecture of MA is shown as in Fig. 1[3, 4]. The whole task can be divided into some sub-tasks which are finished by each agent independently, so the entire task is divided into each agent through hierarchical architecture. After that, the each result is combined to the management agent to get the complete result. The data of control subsystem is generally classified into two classes, the first one is operated only inside the subsystem and they have fully local characteristics to be called local data. The second one is that transmitted and operated between the other subsystems. This data needs a common format and it is the basis for the communication among all the subsystems to be called global data with unified description format. During the task execution, the subsystems with dependent relationship must be coordinated [4]. Generally these subsystems have no coordination capability so that the coordination is maintained by the central controller and the subsystem is being self-governing unit. On the one hand, the problem resolving capability must be abundant and improved for the subsystem. On the other hand, the coordination capability for the subsystem and the outside environment needs to be enhanced. One valid method is increasing some functions for the subsystems such as independent decision making, communication, local data storage, global data storage to make the subsystem to be independent, and also coordinated with other subsystem. Through this way, the original hierarchical control, tightly coupled way becomes into loosely coupled way to improve the robust performance.

B System Modeling

The first task for the MA system modeling establishment is convert the functional module of traffic control system into independent self-governing agent. And the functional architecture is established individually for each agent in accordance with the agent's functions.

Fig. 2 shows one general functional model for the agent [5]. In Fig. 2, the content for each module can be changed according to the different functions.

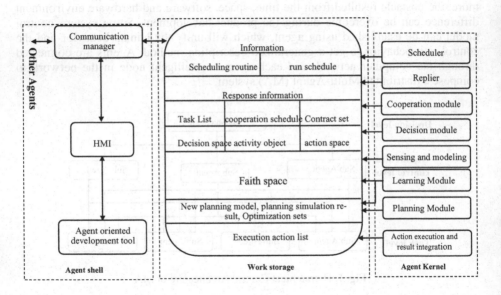

Fig. 2. Function Model of Agent

One agent is defined as a set with two elements, i.e. agent kernel and agent shell. Agent kernel is mainly for the calculation task, process and execution detailed action, storage and maintenance system knowledge base. It is composed of problem calculator and action processing, knowledge base and its manager. Agent shell is mainly for the agent behavior control and coordination with users, other agents and the environment. It includes some function modules and the corresponding structure local information and data field. Agent shell is looked as the bridge between the agent and the environment with good exchanging capability. It is composed of a group of knowledge system, expert system and problem resolving program.

3   MA Based Urban Traffic Control System Architecture

Urban traffic control system is to increase the traffic flow and improve the transportation environment by using the road status detector, monitor and analyzer. And the road cross signal optimal control, dynamic route guidance is also applied to coordinate various traffic conditions.

In the urban traffic control system, intelligent integration and information sharing makes the whole system have coordination and flexible adjustment capability, thus the correct control policy and organization system will be selected at any time and any place to guarantee the whole benefit for the traffic system.

Urban traffic signal control system is the focus for the studying because traffic signal control is the direct control way and main management step during all the traffic process.

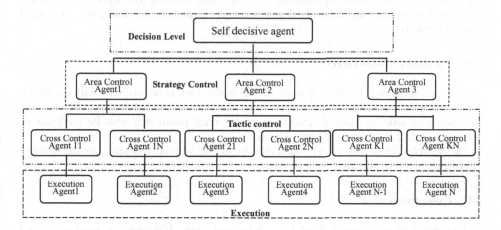

Fig. 3. Urban Traffic Control System Architecture Based on MA

Especially the hierarchical structure and self similarity are applied, and the modeling, development method and the techniques in urban traffic signal control system are used to implement other control system.

The urban traffic control system should have the following functions:

➢ Data collection: Real time traffic information is collected by various detection and information processing techniques.
➢ Data analysis: road status are analyzed to make macro control decision and improve the traffic flow, also the incident conditions are processed.
➢ Execution: the signal scheme is designed and executed according to all the level control strategies come from the control decision.
➢ Communication: The control system will communicate and exchange information with traffic information display, dynamic route guidance etc.

The traffic control system can be divided into four levels, i.e. decision level, strategy control level, tactic control level and execution level which is shown as in Fig. 3 [1,5,6].

(1) Decision Level

It is composed of urban traffic control decision making system. It makes evaluation for the running status of whole road network in accordance with the road network structure, traffic demand prediction and traffic jam, so as to get the optimal control effect. It looks like the human cerebra which make decision according to the various information and it has self-organization capability and similar as the management agent in MA system.

(2) Strategy Control Level

It is composed of many area coordination control system. It makes its own decision on the basis of comprehensive evaluation of decision level with local road status information and signal scheme limitations. At the same time, it transmits the traffic requirement prediction and control effect to decision level as its reference with the target optimal control.

(3) Tactical Control Level

It includes many cross control system. It makes decision in accordance with the traffic monitoring data and the analysis result from the execution level and the coordination control from strategy control level. Its own control result will also be feedback to strategy control level as the decision basis.

In the MA system framework, the hierarchical control level can simulate the strategy and tactic levels as the area control.

(4) Execution Level

It includes detectors, signal controllers and signal light. It detects the road status and send the data to tactic control level for the analysis and control. In the MA, this level is task level for the hardware control to get the function implementation.

4 System Design

A Assumptions

As the major city traffic management, traffic signal control plays an irreplaceable role in the city traffic control system. We expatiate on the design and implementation of traffic signal control based on the traffic signal timing control of the crossroad. The following assumptions are made:

(1). Crossroad is the basic control unit. The traffic control system of a city is composed of total n crossroads and the road amongst them.

(2). The basic traffic lights periods of any directions is the same, the periods starting time is marked with symbol $t = 0,1,2,\cdots$

(3). $L_i(t)$ is the vector to describe the number of vehicle waiting in the crossroad i at the moment t. And $L_i(t) = (X_i(t), Y_i(t), \cdots,)$, the mark $X_i(t), Y_i(t), \cdots$ denote the length of the waiting vehicle queue of different direction of crossroad i at the moment t, $L_i(t)$ is state variable.

(4). The mark $X', Y', \cdots$ denotes the threshold of the length of the waiting vehicle queue for the different directions, and the threshold is set by the system. Once the length of a waiting queue exceeds the threshold of that direction, the Agent begins to consultation and collaboration to make it close to or below this threshold. The thresholds should be dynamic modified according to the specific circumstances.

(5). The mark $g(t)$, denotes the proportion of green light in a periods which is started at the moment t. $g(t)$ is a control variable. The intelligent traffic management system based on multi-agent is not used to deal with this simple assumption; it is designed to solve the problem caused by the traditional traffic control who over simplify the traffic model. The variables involved in the assumptions are precisely modeled and calculated. The content of the knowledge database and the complexity of sensor can be increased to deal with the complex reality situation and the more function need.

B Architecture

The system structure is shown in figure 4[3,7]. The system includes two kinds of agent. One is area control agent (ACA) the other is cross control agent (CCA). Each CCA can communicate with other adjacent CCAs, and connected to the only ACA. CCA and ACA are introduced below.

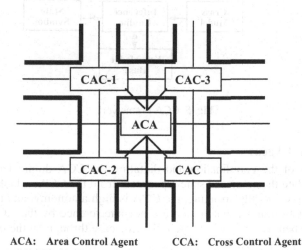

ACA: Area Control Agent   CCA: Cross Control Agent

Fig. 4. System Framework

1) Cross Control Agent

CCA is a classic collaborative agent. That is all the CCA have a goal: to make the traffic flow of the area expedite. And each CCA has a local goal which is the same as global goal: to make traffic flow of the crossroad expedite. Each crossroad of a city has and only has a CCA. The basic function of CCA is that adjust the traffic light timing scheme $g(t)$ to minimums the length of waiting vehicle queue of the crossroad, and keep the every component of L_i less than the threshold. CAA sends the crossroad information of that time to the adjacent CCAs and the ACA belonged. When a certain component of L_i (ie. X_i) is bigger than the given threshold X', this CCA sends cooperation request according to the 4 adjacent CCAs and the state of the crossroad. For example, request the CCA of upstream crossroad i to reduce $g_i(t_1)$) at the moment t_1 or request the CCA of downstream crossroad j to increase $g_j(t_2)$ at the moment t_2, in order to keep the traffic flow of the crossroad expedite. When a CCA receive a cooperation request from the adjacent CCA, it can accept, reject or consultation according to the current situation of the crossroad. Furthermore, CCA can also accept the control and strategy adjacent instruction sent from ACA. The structure of CCA is shown in figure 5[3,7]. All CCA have the same structure, including the control module, illation engine, sensor, execute module, state bar, knowledge database, crossroad model and other components.

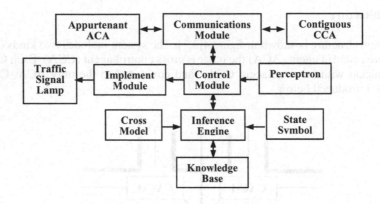

Fig. 5. CCA Framework

2) Area Control Agent

ACA in charge of the coordination and dictation the CCA dominated, and collect, analyze and collate the crossroad state report sent from the CCAs which are under the jurisdiction of it. Generally speaking, the CCA is high autonomy, and the traffic control, the consultation and collaboration are not interference by the ACA. ACA only interference the behavior of CCA in the following case throughout the instructions:

(1). Unexpected incidents: for example, if there were a fire engine wants to pass a road, ACA can force all crossroads in this road direction to be green light in a given time.

(2). Find a serious imbalance in area networks load, ACA should rationalization it in the overall perspective. In addition, after collecting, collating, summarizing and analyzing the information sent from CCAs dominated, ACC can dynamic adjacent the control strategy of each CCA such as the basic traffic light periods $\triangle t$, the basic threshold, and so on. And ACA can also weighted the different requirements of a traffic expedite, according to the reality situation. Like CCA, ACA can cooperate with the adjacent ACAs, only to treat the entire area as a big crossroad. Similarly, there can be more senior management upon ACA. The model described here has only one ACA.

The structure of ACA is similar with CCA, it is composed of communication module, control module, illation engine, I/O module, knowledge database, crossroad model, state bar and other parts.

5 Conclusion

In this paper, the traditional method and artificial intelligence are combined together for the urban traffic control system. The integration control system design framework is described based on the MA. This intelligent control method can be used to improve Chinese urban traffic control method and the management mode. And it can guarantee the vehicle and passengers' safety and it is also expandable.

References

1. Zhai, G., Zha, J., Cheng, E.M.: The propose of Integrated Intelligent Urban Traffic Control System Architecture. System Engineering-theory and Applications 20(7), 80–84 (2000)
2. Huang, L.: Integrated Intelligent Urban Traffic Control System Architecture. System Engineering-theory and Applications 21(1), 120–124 (2001)
3. Yu, Z., Li, J.: The Application of Multi-Agent in Traffic Control System. The Journal of Traffic Engineering 1(1), 55–57 (2001)
4. Ou, H., Zhang, W., Zhang, W., Xu, X.: The urban intelligent traffic Control System based on Multi-Agent. Journal of Electronics 28(12), 52–55 (2000)
5. Yu, D., Yang, Z., Wang, Y., Sun, J.: The urban road traffic control system and its coordination optimization based on multi-agent. Journal of Jilin University 36(1), 113–118 (2006)
6. Li, Z., Chen, D.: A Game Theoretical Model of Multi-Agents in Area Coordination and Optimization of Traffic Signal. Journal of Highway and Transportation Research and Development 21(1), 85–89 (2004)
7. Yang, Z., Sun, J.P., Yu, D., Cao, L.: Optimization of Area Wide Traffic Control in the Condition of Mixed Traffic and Simulation. In: 8th In2ternational Conference on Application of Advanced Technologies on Transportation Engineering (2004)

Register File Management and Compiler Optimization on EDSMT

Qingying Deng, Minxuan Zhang, and Jiang Jiang

PDL, College Of Computer, National University Of Defense
Technology, Changsha 410073, Hunan, P.R. China
freesunnybird@gmail.com
{mxzhang,jiang_jiang}@nudt.edu.cn

Abstract. Register file design is very important in high performance processor design. Register Stack and Register Rotation are effective ways to improve performance. Compiler optimizations are often driven by specific assumptions about the underlying architecture and implementation of the target machine. SMT(simultaneous multithreading) processors execute instructions from different threads in the same cycle, which has the unique ability to exploit ILP(instruction-level parallelism) and TLP(thread-level parallelism) simultaneously. EPIC(explicitly parallel instruction computing) emphasizes importance of the synergy between compiler and hardware. In this paper, we present our efforts to design and implement register file management mechanism on a parallel environment, which includes an optimizing, portable parallel compiler OpenUH and SMT architecture EDSMT based on IA-64. Meanwhile, its compile optimization is also considered to improve the performance.[1]

1 Introduction

SMT [1] and CMP(chip multiprocessing) [2] are two architectural approaches to exploit thread-level parallelism using available on-chip resources. SMT allows instructions from multiple threads to share several critical processor resources, thus increasing their utilization. The advantage of SMT is area-efficient throughput [3]. CMPs, on the other hand, improve system throughput by replicating processor cores on a single die. As both these paradigms are targeted toward multi-threaded workloads, comparing their efficiency in terms of performance, power, and thermal metrics has drawn the attention of several researchers [4][5][6].

DSMT (Dynamic SMT) integrates dynamic threads extracting and threads switching mechanism into SMT architecture, which further improves the ability to exploit TLP parallelism. Based on the software-hardware cooperation, EPIC can effectively exploit ILP with relatively low hardware complexity. A new microarchitecture called EDSMT was proposed to expand EPIC with simultaneous multithreading execution.

[1] This work was supported by "863" project No. 2002AA110020, Chinese NSF No. 60376018, No. 60273069 and No. 90207011.

P. Thulasiraman et al. (Eds.): ISPA 2007 Workshops, LNCS 4743, pp. 394–403, 2007.
© Springer-Verlag Berlin Heidelberg 2007

SMT processors require large register files to hold multiple thread contexts. By supporting better inter-thread sharing and management of physical registers, an SMT processor can reduce the required registers and improve performance for a given register file size.While processors with register renaming are effective at knowing when a new physical register must be allocated, they are limited in knowing when physical registers can be deallocated. This may cause performance degrading.

We studied EDSMT Microarchitecture and developed its simulator EDSMT-SIM. OpenUH(based on Pro64 and OpenMP) developed by University of Houston was used to construct our parallel compiler with some modifications. We carefully designed EDSMT's register file structure and register rename mechanism, compiler is helped to deallocate registers.

We introduce Register Stack and Register Rotation in section 2. In section 3 we present MTRM (Mapping Table-based Register Management) mechanism in EDSMT. In section 4 shows some compiler optimizations for MTRM. We introduce our Parallel Infrastructure in section 5. In section 6, some experiment results are given. Conclusions and future work are given in section 7.

2   Register Stack and Register Rotation

The general register file in IA-64 is divided into static and stacked subsets[7]. The static subset is visible to all procedures and consists of the 32 registers from GR0 through GR31.The stacked subset is local to each procedure and may vary in size from zero to 96 registers beginning at GR32. The static subset must be saved and restored at procedure boundaries according to software convention. The stacked subset is automatically saved and restored by the Register Stack Engine (RSE) without explicit software intervention.

IA-64 avoids the unnecessary spilling and filling of registers at procedure call and return interfaces through compiler-controlled renaming. At a call site, a new frame of registers is available to the called procedure without the need for register spill and fill (either by the caller or by the callee). Register access occurs by renaming the virtual register identifiers in the instructions through a base register into the physical registers. The callee can freely use available registers without having to spill and eventually restore the caller's registers. The callee executes an alloc instruction specifying the number of registers it expects to use in order to ensure that enough register are available. If sufficient registers are not available (attack overflow), the alloc stalls the processor and spills the caller's registers until the requested number of registers are available.

At the return site, the base register is restored to the value that the caller was using to access registers prior to the call. Some of the caller's registers may have been spilled by the hardware and not yet restored. In this case (stack underflow), the return stalls the processor until the processor has restored an appropriate number of the caller's registers. The hardware can exploit the explicit register stack frame information to spill and fill registers from the register stack to memory at the best opportunity (independent of the calling and called procedures).

Modulo scheduling of a loop is analogous to hardware pipelining of a functional unit since the next iteration of the loop starts before the previous iteration has finished. Modulo scheduling allows the compiler to execute loop iterations in parallel rather than sequentially. The concurrent execution of multiple iterations traditionally requires unrolling of the loop and software renaming of registers. IA-64 allows the renaming of registers which provide every iteration with its own set of registers, avoiding the need for unrolling. This kind of register renaming is called register rotation. The result is that software pipelining can be applied to a much wider variety of loops-both small as well as large with significantly reduced overhead.

The register resources in processor are very precious. In order to support software pipelining and register rotation, sequential logic registers are allocated for procedure's logic stack frame, the physical registers in physical stack frame after renaming are also sequential. These physical registers can only be released after their executions.

3   MTRM in EDSMT

In order to support software pipelining and register rotation, we propose MTRM (Mapping Table-based Register Management)for EDSMT register file design. Sequential logic registers can be mapped to discontinuous physical registers by the Mapping Table. MTRM focuses on the effective sharing of registers in an EDSMT processor, using register renaming to permit multiple threads to share a single global register file. Fig.1 shows its logic structure.

MTRM assigns a Mapping Table for each thread to mapping their logic registers to physic registers. The physical register number is acquired from Idle Physic Register Number Queue.By adopting this mechanism, the thread's physical register numbers could be discontinuous, while each thread uses its own physic registers to avoid interference by each other. If a thread's Mapping Table entries are full, a part of register numbers in the Mapping Table should be spilled to the Backing Store with special format, then, restored when needed. When all the physic registers are used up (Idle Physic Register Number Queue is empty), a part of physic registers should be spilled to the Backing Store for releasing a number of physic registers.

Mapping Table adds a middle level into Itanium's original rename mechanism. Register Stack based on physic register in Itanium, while in MTRM based on Mapping Table (idle register numbers organized as a queue used by Mapping Table); the logic register number was renamed to Mapping Table's entry address instead of Itanium's physical register. The specific design consideration is described as follows:

– The Mapping Table's entry addresses are form 32 to 127(96 addresses in total). Sequential Logic registers in logic frame are renamed to the Mapping Table frame's sequential addresses (virtual sequential physic register numbers)(in Itanium are mapped to sequential physical register numbers directly). Actual physic register numbers are filled into Mapping Table from Idle Physic Register Number Queue (register numbers may be discontinuous). Physic register number is filled when needed and deleted after its last use. By adopting Mapping Table, the register resource can be effectively used, meanwhile, the procedure's Mapping Table frame's entries are kept sequential, thus, software pipelining and register rotation are also supported.

– In Itanium, logic register number in a frame begins at 32, while the physic register frame starts by Rse.bof. By using Mapping Table, the frist logic register number in a frame still renamed to Rse.bof, but the Rse.bof also acts as one of the Mapping Table's entry addresses. Fill and delete physic register number are invisible to software. The RSE mechanism also suits MTRM, only needs to change the operation form physic register number to Mapping Table's entry number.

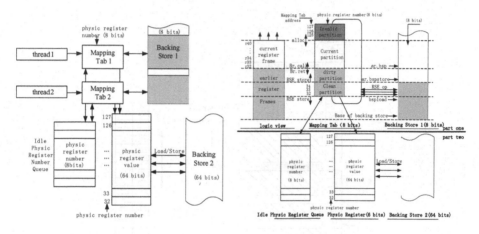

Fig. 1. EDSMT's Register Management Structure

Fig. 2. MTRM Mechanism

Fig.2 depicts the MTRM's basic structure. It includes two parts: one is register rename implemented by Mapping Table, the other is physical register's Backing Store (only needed when the physic registers are used up). Mapping Table is in the place of the original Itanium's physical register frame, the basic operations are the same except for the physic register's stack (numbers from 32 to 127) becoming to Mapping Table(address numbers from 32 to 127), and the content changing from 65 bits data to 8 bits data(physic register number), thus the Backing Store Region 1 is 8 bits wide. Physic register number is acquired from the Idle Physic Register Number Queue. If the queue is empty, that means the 96 registers are taken, a number of physic registers' values should be removed to the Backing Store Region2 , then these registers can be used again. Some physic registers' values stored to the Backing Store Region2 at procedure call or thread switching; when procedure returns, these values should be restored back to the physic registers.

Procedures' parameters are passing through the overlap region of the frames like the RSE operations in Itanium. Mapping Table also has 4 partitions: Clean, Dirty, Current and Invalid. When procedure calls, if the Mapping Table's frame is crossing the boundary of Clean partition and Dirty partition, the physic register number stored in Dirty partition of the Mapping Table will be spilled to the Back Store 1. At the return site, if the Mapping Table's frame is passing though Dirty partition to the bottom of Clean partition, the physic register number will be filled back from the Back Store 1 to the Mapping Table. As Mapping Table is invisible to software, the rename logic, related parameters and RSE instructions needn't to be changed.

The physic registers (96 in total) are still small for many applications. When registers provided by Idol Physic Register Number Queue can't fulfill the new frame's size, a number of physical registers will be spilled to the Backing Store 2, as we can see in Fig. 3.

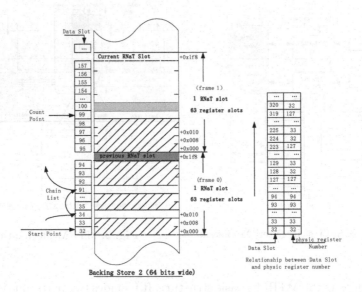

Fig. 3. MTRM's Backing Store

The detailed procedure is described as follows: item Data Slot is the label of Backing Store which connects physic register with Backing store 2. It begins at 32, and adds 1 to the next register except for the RNat Slot. As we can see in the Fig.3, the Backing Store 2 starts at the 32th Data Slot, and a RNat Slot exists between the 94th Data Slot and 95th Data Slot. There are 63 Data Slots in a frame. Count Point points at the first Data Slot which physic register's data can be stored into. As we can see in the Fig.3, Count Point is pointing at the 99th Data Slot, while physic registers' values are stored under the 99th Data Slot(from 32 to 98). A chained list is used to link the unused Data Slot under the Count Point. Fig.3 's right part depicts the relation between Data

Slot and physic register number of the physic register stored into the Backing Store 2. These stored physic registers' numbers can be released to the Idle Physic Register Number Queue.

4   Compiler Optimizations for MTRM

MTRM focused on supporting the effective sharing of registers in an EDSMT processor, using register renaming to permit multiple threads to share a single global register file. In this way, one thread with high register pressure can benefit when other threads have low register demands. Unfortunately, existing register renaming techniques cannot fully exploit the potential of a shared register file. In particular, while existing hardware is effective at allocating physical registers, it has only limited ability to identify register deallocation points; therefore hardware must free registers conservatively, possibly wasting registers that could be better utilized.

There are two types of dead registers can be deallocated: (1)registers allocated to idle hardware contexts, and (2) registers in active contexts whose last use has already retired. We propose compiler support to the later.

To address the second type of dead registers, those in active threads, we investigate two mechanisms that allow the compiler to communicate last-use information to the processor, so that the renaming hardware can deallocate registers more aggressively. Without this information, the hardware must conservatively deallocate registers only after they are redefined.

1)Special Bit communicates last-use information to the hardware via dedicated instruction bits (using some reserved bits in IA-64 ISA), with the dual benefits of immediately identifying last uses and requiring no instruction overhead. It can serve as an upper bound on performance improvements that can be attained with the compiler's static last-use information.

2)Special Instruction is a more realistic implementation of Special Bit. Rather than specifying last uses in the instruction itself, it uses a separate instruction to specify one or two registers to be freed. Our compiler generates a Free Register instruction (an unused opcode in the IA-64 ISA) immediately after any instruction containing a last register use (if the register is not also redefined by the same instruction). Like Special Bit, it frees registers as soon as possible, but with an additional cost in dynamic instruction overhead.

Current renaming hardware provides mechanisms for register deallocation (i.e., returning physical registers to the Idle Physic Register Number Queue) and can perform many deallocations each cycle.

5   Parallel Infrastructure

Multi-source Multi-target, Multilevel, and Multigrid became the trend of parallel compilation[8], OpenUH is one of that kind. It is based on SGI's open source Pro64 compiler, which targets the IA-64 Linux platform. OpenUH merges work from the two major branches of Open64 (ORC and Pathscale) to exploit all upgrades and bug fixes. It is a portable OpenMP compiler, which translates OpenMP 2.5 directives in conjunction with C, C++, and FORTRAN 77/90 (and some FORTRAN 95). It has a full set of optimization modules, including an interprocedural analysis (IPA) module, a loop nest optimizer (LNO), and global optimizer. A variety of state-of-the-art analyses and transformations are available, sometimes at multiple levels[9].

The OpenUH consists of the frontends, optimization modules, OpenMP transformation module, a portable OpenMP runtime library, a code generator and IR-to-source tools. Fig. 4 shows the structure. It is a complete compiler for Itanium platforms, for which object code is produced, and may be used as a source-to-source compiler for non-Itanium machines using the IR-to-source tools.

Simultaneous Multithreading (SMT) processors improve performance by allowing running instructions from several threads simultaneously at a single cycle. Co-scheduled threads share some resources, such as issue queues, physical registers, and functional units. Explicitly Parallel Instruction Computing(EPIC) architectures developed by HP and Intel allow the compiler to express program instruction level parallelism directly to the hardware to deal with increasing memory latencies and penalties. Specifically, the Itanium architecture deploys a number of EPIC techniques which enable the compiler to represent control speculation, data dependence speculation, and predication to enhance performance. These techniques have individually been shown to be very effective in dealing with memory penalties. In addition to these techniques, the Itanium architecture provides a virtual register stack to reduce the penalty of memory accesses associated with procedure calls and to leverage the performance advantages of a large register file.

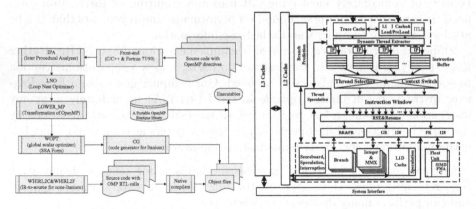

Fig. 4. OpenUH Infrastructure   **Fig. 5.** Microarchitecture of EDSMT

DSMT(Dynamic SMT) [10]and EPIC[11] design philosophy became the two basic points of our EDSMT research. Based on DSMT and EPIC, EDSMT should fully use the resources in Itanium. Fig.5 shows the Microarchitecture of EDSMT. It is carefully designed to improve the performance.

Simulator is important in architecture design. As EDSMT is a new Microarchitecture, We developed a simulator–EDSMTSIM for our research. EDSMTSIM is a trace-driven microprocessor simulator which adopts some technologies in the Multithreading simulator-SMTSIM.

6   Experiment Results

Our experiments were designed to evaluate the deallocation schemes on SPECint 2000 programs for EDSMT. EDSMTSIM is used as simulator and configuration details are provided in Table 1. For a compiler we use the OpenUH which affords a greater degree of flexibility and more aggressive utilization of EPIC features than would be available in commercial production compilers or GCC.

For the initialization phases of the applications, we used a fast simulation mode that warmed the caches, and then turned on the detailed simulation mode once the main computation phases were reached.

Table 1. Baseline Configuration of Simulator

Parameter	EDSMTSIM
Fetch Width	2 bundles,6 instructions per cycle
Basic Fetch Policy	ICOUNT2.2
Instruction Queues	16 for each separated Queues
Functional Units	2 IU, 4 MU, 2 FU, 3 BU
Physical Registers	128 GR, 128 FR, 64 PR, 8 BR per thread
L1I cache, L1D cache	16KB, 4-way, 64-bytes lines, 1 cycle access
L2 cache	256KB, 8-way, 64-bytes lines, 10 cycles latency
L3 cache	3MB, 12-way, 64-bytes lines, 50 cycles latency
Main Memory Latency	100 cycles

The two register deallocation schemes are compared in Fig. 6 and Fig.7, which charts their speedup versus no explicit register deallocation under different thread configurations. The Special Bit bars show that register deallocation can (potentially) improve performance significantly for small register files (80% on average, but ranging as high as 120%). The Special Bit results highlight the most attractive outcome of register deallocation: by improving register utilization, an EDSMT processor with small register files can achieve large register file performance. With multiple register contexts, an EDSMT processor need not double its architectural registers if they are effectively shared. Our results show that an 4-context EDSMT with the effective RSE and compiler assistant can alleviate physical register pressure.

Special Bit is more effective at reducing the number of dead registers, because it deallocates them more promptly, at their last uses. When registers are a severe bottleneck with small register files, Special Instruction has a good result; while

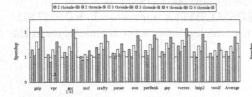
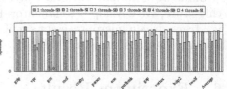

Fig. 6. Special Bit and Special Instruction schemes speedup over no explicit register deallocation with 128 full shared registers

Fig. 7. Special Bit and Special Instruction schemes speedup over no explicit register deallocation with 256 full shared registers

instruction overhead will cause a low performance with larger register files and applications with low register usage.

We also examined a variety of register file sizes, ranging between 128 and 256, to gauge the sensitivity of the register file management techniques to register size. With more than 256 registers, other processor resources, such as the instruction queues, become performance bottlenecks. At the low end, at least 128 registers are required to hold the architectural registers for all four contexts. Smaller register files are attractive for several reasons. First, they have a shorter access time; this advantage could be used either to decrease the cycle time (if register file access is on the critical path) or to eliminate the extra stages we allow for register reading and writing. Second, they take up less area. Third, smaller register files consume less power.

In this section, we describe and evaluate two mechanisms that allow the compiler to convey register last-use information to the hardware, and show that they improve register utilization on EDSMT processors with MTRM register file organization. The proposed mechanisms are either new instructions or fields in existing instructions that direct the renaming hardware to free physical registers. Simulation results indicate that these mechanisms can reduce register deallocation inefficiencies; in particular, on small register files, the best of the schemes attains speedups of up to 2.2 for some applications, and 1.8 on average. These mechanisms also followed EPIC design philosophy.

7   Conclusions and Future Work

Because typical server workloads have very low amounts of instruction-level parallelism and many memory stalls, most of the hardware associated with superscalar instruction issue is essentially wasted for these applications. SMT and chip multiprocessors are making significant inroads into the marketplace.

We proposed a parallel infrastructure, including an optimizing, portable parallel compiler OpenUH and SMT architecture EDSMT based on IA-64. We studied some techniques that increase register utilization, permitting a smaller, faster register file, while still satisfying the processor's need to support multiple threads. Our techniques involve coordination between the compiler, and the MTRM hardware to provide more effective register use for both single-threaded and multithreaded programs. The result is improved performance for a given number of hardware contexts and the ability to handle more contexts with a given number of registers.

In the future, we will focus on other optimizations such as fetch policy, resource organization and allocation, cache structure, thread scheduling and so on. Meanwhile, we are considering a compact EDSMT to construct homogeneous and heterogeneous CMP systems.

References

1. Tullsen, D., Eggers, S., Levy, H.: Simultaneous Multithreading: Maximizing On-Chip Parallelism. In: The 22rd Annual International Symposium on Computer Architecture (ISCA), pp. 392–403 (1995)
2. Olukotun, K., Nayfeh, B.A., Hammond, L., Wilson, K., Chang, K.: The Case for a Single-Chip Multiprocessor. SIGOPS Oper. Syst. Rev. 30(5), 2–11 (1996)
3. Li, Y., Brooks, D., Hu, Z., Skadron, K., Bose, P.: Understanding the Energy Efficiency of Simultaneous Multithreading. In: The 2004 International Symposium on Low Power Electronics and Design, pp. 44–49 (2004)
4. Sasanka, R., Adve, S.V., Chen, Y.-K., Debes, E.: The Energy Efficiency of CMP vs. SMT for Multimedia Workloads. In: The 18th Annual International Conference on Supercomputing, pp. 196–206 (2004)
5. Kaxiras, S., Narlikar, G., Berenbaum, A.D., Hu, Z.: Comparing Power Consumption of an SMT and a CMP DSP for Mobile Phone Workloads. In: The 2001 International Conference on Compilers, Architecture,and Synthesis for Embedded Systems, pp. 211–220 (2001)
6. Li, Y., Skadron, K., Hu, Z., Brooks, D.: Performance, Energy, and Thermal Considerations for SMT and CMP Architectures. In: The Eleventh IEEE International Symposium on High Performance Computer Architecture (HPCA), pp. 71–82. IEEE Computer Society Press, Los Alamitos (2005)
7. Itanium Processor Microarchitecture Reference: for Software Optimization 05, http://www.developer.intel.com/design/ia64/itanium.htm (2002)
8. Jianhua,Y.,Hongmei,W.: Actuality and Trend of Parallel Language and Compilation. Computer Engineering 97-98 (December 2004)
9. OpenUH: An Optimizing, Portable OpenMP Compiler. (2006), http://www2.cs.uh.edu/copper/pubs.html
10. Akkary, H., Driscoll, M.A.: A dynamic multithreading processor. In: The 31st annual ACM/IEEE international symposium on Microarchitecture (1998) 226-236
11. Schlansker, M.S., Rau, B.R.: EPIC: Explicitly Parallel Instruction Computing[J]. IEEEComputer 32(2), 37–45 (2000)

Services, Standards, and Technologies for High Performance Computational Proteomics

Mario Cannataro and Pierangelo Veltri

Laboratory of Bioinformatics, University Magna Græcia of Catanzaro, 88100 Catanzaro, Italy
{cannataro, veltri}@unicz.it

Abstract. Proteomics is about the study of the proteins expressed in an organism or a cell. Computational Proteomics regards the computational methods, algorithms, databases, and methodologies used to manage, analyze and interpret the data produced in proteomics experiments. The broad application of proteomics and the increasing resolution offered by technological platforms, especially in Mass Spectrometry-based high-throughput proteomics, make the analysis of proteomics experiments difficult and error prone without efficient algorithms and easy-to-use tools. The paper discusses the requirements of Mass Spectrometry-based Computational Proteomics applications and surveys important services, standards, and technologies useful to build modular, scalable and reusable applications in this field.

1 Introduction

Proteomics [1] is about the study of the proteins expressed in an organism or a cell. It is a fundamental discipline to understand mechanisms at the basis of life and diseases and is a main technique in the discovery of biomarkers, e.g. markers that indicate a particular disease, as well as in controlling effects and effectiveness of drug treatments.

Computational Proteomics [2,3] is about the computational methods, algorithms, databases, and methodologies used to manage, analyze and interpret the data produced in proteomics experiments. The broad application of proteomics in different biological and medical fields, as well as the increasing resolution and precision offered by technological platforms, make the analysis of proteomics experiments difficult and error prone without efficient algorithms and easy-to-use tools. This is especially true in Mass Spectrometry-based high-throughput proteomics, where the production of huge datasets is coupled with the need of on-the-fly data analysis.

Mass Spectrometry-based proteomics [4] requires computational methods for analyzing data in qualitative (e.g. peptide/protein identification in tandem mass spectrometry) and in quantitative proteomics (e.g. protein expression in samples). Other important issues regard the way how spectra are cleaned, pre-processed, organized, and stored in an efficient way. The data heterogeneity introduced by several available platforms, as well as the need to conduct repeatable biomedical experiments on large populations (e.g. for outcome research), demand for suitable standards for the representation, storage, transmission, and sharing of proteomics data among different research centers.

The realization of the concept of "genomic medicine", where genomics and proteomics are used to improve healthcare, requires the integration of knowledge from

P. Thulasiraman et al. (Eds.): ISPA 2007 Workshops, LNCS 4743, pp. 404–413, 2007.

biology and medicine [5]. The semantic integration and further analysis of genomic, proteomics, and clinical data is a first step towards the deployment of novel biomedical applications involving research-oriented competence centers, specialized proteomics facilities, and health centers where clinical guidelines are applied.

In summary, Computational Proteomics requires a combination of (i) recognized standards for data representation and exchange, (ii) efficient algorithms and tools constituting the building blocks of proteomics studies, (iii) computer science technologies enabling an easy composition of tools, sharing of data, and repeatability of experiments.

After presenting requirements of Computational Proteomics applications, with a special focus on Mass Spectrometry-based Proteomics, the paper describes main standards, tools, and technologies for building scalable, reusable, and portable applications in this field.

Section 2 introduces Mass Spectrometry data and recalls main phases of Computational Proteomics applications. Section 3 discusses services and standards needed to realize Computational Proteomics analysis pipelines. Section 4 discusses some relevant computer science technologies useful for building such applications. Finally, Section 5 concludes the paper.

2 Requirements for Mass Spectrometry-Based Computational Proteomics

Mass Spectrometry (MS) is a technique allowing to identify the masses of macromolecules in a compound. The mass spectrometer separates gas phase ions according to their m/z (mass to charge ratio) values [6]. The sample can be inserted directly into the ionization source or can be separated into different components which enter the spectrometer sequentially, e.g. by using Liquid Chromatography (LC). Common ionization techniques are Electrospray Ionization (ESI), Surface Enhanced Laser Desorption/Ionization (SELDI), and Matrix-Assisted Laser Desorption/Ionization (MALDI), coupled with different kind of mass analyzers such as Time Of Flight (TOF).

Mass Spectrometry output can be represented as a (large) sequence of value pairs (spectrum). Each pair contains a measured *intensity*, which depends on the quantity of the detected biomolecule, and a mass to charge ratio (m/z), which depends on the molecular mass of the detected biomolecule. As an example, Figure 1 shows a set of LC-MS spectra generated from a real biological sample.

Mass Spectrometry-based proteomics [4] requires computational methods for analyzing data in qualitative and in quantitative proteomics studies. Thus, the availability of such computational methods makes Mass spectrometry-based proteomics an important tool for biomarker discovery. Body fluids as well as tissues can be routinely used to generate protein profiles, containing potential disease markers whether individual proteins or sets of interacting proteins [7]. Data Mining is commonly used to discover biomarker patterns in spectra data [8], but a number of technical challenges need to be faced, among which is the extremely high-dimensionality of mass spectra and the possible high noise. A typical mass spectrum has several thousands of attributes that exhibit a high degree of spatial redundancy. The exact number depends on the type of mass spectrometry instrument that is used, its resolution, and the mass range it covers.

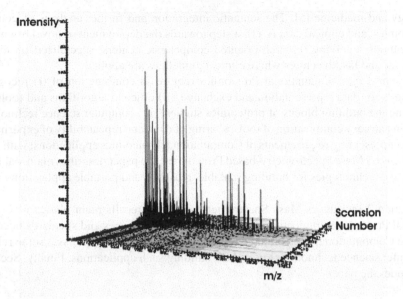

Fig. 1. Example of a LC-MS spectrum

In the following we discuss the main steps of a typical Computational Proteomics application, e.g. used for biomarker discovery:

1. **Spectra acquisition.** Spectra data need to be acquired from the mass spectrometry instrument. The data heterogeneity introduced by several available technological platforms demands for suitable standards for representation, storage, and sharing of proteomics data. Moreover, data conversion tools converting proprietary formats in standard ones need to be provided.

2. **Dataset selection.** MS raw files need to be adorned by metadata to link spectra subsets with clinical conditions, e.g. healthy or diseased classes. Moreover, spectra produced in different experiments may be analyzed in combination, so raw spectra datasets may be combined to form logical datasets for in silico experiments.

3. **Data preprocessing.** Spectra are usually preprocessed to reduce noise (e.g. to eliminate false peaks) and data dimension, so that statistical or data mining analysis is more efficient and accurate.

4. **Data preparation.** Before conducting data analysis (e.g. data mining) data need to be reorganized to fit requirements of software tools. For instance, some continuous data may be transformed in discrete one, outliers may be identified and eliminated to reduce bias, and so on. Finally, a very common activity is a transposition and a collation of data in a unique file, such as the ARFF file in the WEKA data mining platform [9]).

5. **Data analysis.** Common techniques are data mining (e.g. classification, clustering, association rules), statistical analysis, pattern extraction, or direct spectra comparison.

6. **Data visualization.** Although spectra data can contain thousands of peaks, graphical visualization of set of spectra may be very useful to show graphically tendency

in the data, or to focus on identified biomarkers (e.g. a set of peaks/peptide up- or down-expressed in a disease).

7. **Knowledge models sharing.** Discovered knowledge may be shared among laboratories or, more simply, analyzed datasets annotated with the discovered knowledge models may be made available to the scientific community. Often, raw datasets are made available on the Internet, but the discovered models are only found in the literature describing those datasets and experiments. Annotating datasets with the used data preprocessing and analysis pipeline (e.g. expressed through workflows) and with the discovered knowledge models (e.g. expressed in a language like PMML or CRISP-DM), would make the sharing and use of the whole experiment more easy. The Predictive Model Markup Language (PMML) [10] is an XML-based language which allows to define statistical and data mining models and to share them between PMML compliant applications. CRISP-DM [11] is an industry standard methodology for data mining and predictive analysis.

3 Services and Standards

This section describes main services and standards useful in Computational Proteomics.

3.1 Spectra Preprocessing Services

Spectra may be affected by errors and noise so they are usually preprocessed before conducting any further data mining or pattern extraction analysis, e.g. classification of diseased vs healthy patients. Spectra preprocessing aims to correct intensity and m/z values in order to reduce noise, reduce the amount of data, and make spectra comparable [12,13,14,15]. *Binning* performs data dimensionality reduction by aggregating measured data into *bins*: a set of peaks from a spectrum is substituted with a unique peak $(I, m/z)$, whose intensity I is an aggregate function of the original intensities (e.g. their sum), and the mass m/z is usually chosen among the original mass values (e.g. the median value). *Peaks alignment* corrects errors on m/z measurements finding a common set of peak locations in a set of spectra, in such a way that all aligned spectra will have common m/z values for the same biological entities .

3.2 Spectra Analysis Services

Common techniques are data mining (e.g. classification, clustering, association rules), statistical analysis, pattern extraction, or direct spectra comparison. Usually spectra are preprocessed and prepared to take full advantage of existing, off-the-shelf, algorithms and tools. Nevertheless, some problems may remain that reduce quality of analysis, among those: (i) in clinical studies often very few samples are available, and each one can yet exhibit hundreds or thousands of peaks after preprocessing; (ii) due to instrument approximation, some outliers may yet exist after pre-processing and they need to be found before analysis; (iii) using off-the-shelf tools may require a manual reorganization and transfer of files between platforms, that may become a bottleneck in high-throughput proteomics. Moreover, often only a small number of individuals are chosen to be included in clinical study, so data analysis has to deal with the problem of high dimensionality small sample size.

For these reasons, different data analysis techniques should be considered and made available to the scientists, in such a way that the same data can be analyzed, possibly in parallel, with different approaches.

3.3   Protein Sequencing and Identification

Protein identification is the task of identifying the sequence of a protein contained in a biological sample. It is an important task of proteomics that is currently performed by tandem mass spectrometry. When sequencing and identifying proteins by tandem mass spectrometry, the proteins are first enzymically digested (i.e. separated in a number of short peptides) by enzymes such as trypsin, and than the MS-MS spectrum of each peptide is measured. Enzymatic digestion is used since it is difficult to measure intact proteins using tandem mass spectrometry.

In LC/MS/MS, the peptides are separated by liquid chromatography (LC) and then analyzed by the mass spectrometer. The peptides are ionized and the mass-to-charge (m/z) ratios are measured. A peculiar characteristic of tandem mass spectrometry regards the criterium used to select the peptides to be analyzed: only ions within a given range of intensity are selected and fragmented, yielding to further m/z measurements. The resulting tandem mass spectra, comprising m/z ratios and corresponding intensities, are then used for the identification of the original protein or peptide.

Identification can be performed either by correlating the spectra with existing nucleic acid sequences by database searching, or by deriving the peptide sequence directly, without the help of any sequence database (de novo peptide sequencing). More specifically, peptide identification algorithms can be classified into four categories [16]: (i) database searching; (ii) de novo sequencing; (iii) sequence tagging; and (iv) consensus of multiple engines.

Database searching is the most widely used approach for identification when the peptide of interest is known to be in a protein database. The measured spectrum is used to search a sequence database (e.g. SwissProt) for sequences which, when digested by the given enzyme, will match the given set of masses. Thus, in such software the proteins in the database are digested virtually into peptides and each resulting peptide is compared with the input spectrum. For a given input spectrum, different peptides in the database can match it, thus such algorithms use various criteria to determine the likelihood that the peptide found in the database is that contained in the spectrum, and then they give as result the most likely peptide according to such criteria. Common criteria consider the peptide mass and the number and intensity of the matches between the real peaks and the theoretically-computed ones. The most used database search algorithms are SEQUEST [17] and MASCOT [18].

De novo sequencing [19] can be used when the peptides are not contained into a protein database. It can be considered as the identification of the peptide corresponding to a generic combination of amino acids, thus it is more difficult than searching a database with a limited number of known peptides.

Sequence-tagging approaches find the sequence of a peptide by searching a database with partial sequence information inferred from the MS/MS spectrum. In sequence tagging, characteristic partial sequences are individuated from the ions of the spectrum. Such partial sequences, referred to as sequence tags, are then used in database searching, to filter the search itself.

3.4 Spectra Visualization Services

Although spectra data can contain thousands of peaks, graphical visualization of set of spectra may be very useful, to show tendency in the data or to focus on identified biomarkers (e.g. a set of peaks/peptide up- or down-expressed in a disease). Moreover, spectra visualization may be very useful in experiments where data are collected with respect to time. For instance, in liquid chromatography tandem mass spectrometry (LC/MS/MS) different spectra are taken at regular intervals, and the comparison between different samples has to consider that.

SpectraViewer [20] is a Java-based tool for the three-dimensional (3D) and two - dimensional (2D) visualization of spectra and their conversion into the mzData format [21]. The user may zoom, move and rotate the graphic representing a spectrum or a collection of spectra. SpectraViewer supports the visualization of LC-MS and MALDI-TOF spectra, and allows the interactive visualization of ion properties. Pep3D [22] supports LC-MS and LC-MS/MS spectra but does not provide 3D visualization nor mzData conversion. In Pep3D data are represented as a two dimensional density plot. For MS/MS experiments using collision-induced dissociation, links are embedded in the image to the daughter spectra and the corresponding peptide sequences.

3.5 Standards for Spectra Representation and Sharing

The Human Proteome Organization-Proteomic Standard Initiative (HUPO-PSI) is defining novel standards for proteomics data and experiments such as *mzData* (i.e. spectra data and metadata about proteomics experiments), *analysisXML* (for capturing parameters and results of search engines for peptide identification), and a controlled vocabulary that will provide classifiers for both mzData and analysisXML [21].

Having standards for spectra is very important not only for sharing experimental data, but also to unify some commons activities like preprocessing and to enable remote querying and thus data aggregation. mzData allows to represent spectra data in a compressed form, enriched with metadata information simplifying spectra sharing and distribution. In this case, the spectrum is treated as an encoded string and it is simply shareable among scientists, but [intensity, m/z] couples cannot directly be accessed.

Standards about spectra need to be implemented in software tools (e.g. tools to convert a proprietary spectrum in mzData) and spectra repositories (how spectra should be stored, accessed and retrieved). While format conversion tools are easy to understand, important design issues arise when considering spectra repositories. Two main functions are required when accessing spectra data: (i) specific portions of spectra may be requested (e.g. set of peaks during pre-processing); (ii) entire spectra having certain characteristics may be requested (e.g. find all spectra belonging to diseased patients affected by breast cancer). In the former, a data organization that explicitly represents peaks ([intensity, m/z] couples) is necessary, while in the latter metadata about experiments and eventually annotation about discovered knowledge models are important.

While mzData is useful to share spectra and to store metadata, it is less suitable to support direct peaks inspection.

SpecDB [23] is a specialized spectra database implemented on the Grid. In SpecDB data is stored into three different formats: (i) original files (i.e. produced by spectrometers), managed on the file system; (ii) mzData format, stored into an XML database, obtained either by spectrometers supporting such a format or generated locally by a conversion routine; (iii) relational format, i.e. spectra are stored with their values and meta information describing them, into relation tables. Information retrieval can be conducted either locally, by considering portions of spectra data, or in a distributed scenario, exploiting metadata and annotations about spectra datasets stored on the Grid. mzViewer [24] is a simple lightweight viewer that allows 2D visualization of mzData. CCWiffer [25] is a system that converts spectra from the proprietary WIFF format into mzData.

4   Technologies

We consider some well known or emerging technologies that may have an important role for simplifying and enabling the building of Computational Proteomics software platforms: (web/grid) services, ontologies, workflows, Grids.

Services. The Service Oriented Architecture (SOA) allows to integrate different software tools made available as Web services. The W3C defines a Web service as a software system designed to support interoperable machine-to-machine interaction over a network. Basic cornerstones of web services are SOAP (Simple Object Access Protocol), WSDL (Web Services Description Language) and UDDI (Universal Description, Discovery, and Integration). SOAP is an XML-based, extensible message envelope format, with may be transported by different underlying protocols (e.g., HTTP, SMTP and XMPP). WSDL is an XML format that allows to describe service interfaces, their bindings to specific protocols, and are typically used to generate server and client code, and for configuration. UDDI is a protocol for publishing and discovering metadata about Web services, to enable applications to find Web services, either at design time or run-time. Only recently some bioinformatics tools start to be wrapped as web services and in the next future also biological databases will be made available as web services.

Service Discovery. Discovering a service that fits the requirements of the user or of others services can be a challenge. Currently, existing directory services, such as those based on UDDI or those used in Grids (e.g. MDS [26]), support a simple key-based discovery based on a matchmaking of a set of attribute types describing the service itself. Due to the richness of properties of objects and actors of Computational Proteomics, a need for a standard service description and a semantic-based service discovery arises [27]. Interesting approaches in semantic-rich service discovery systems use ontologies to find semantic properties of services and basic middleware information systems such as UDDI or MDS to find more specific details about services and resources [28].

Ontologies. Designing the data analysis side of a proteomics experiment involves different experts and requires the contemporary use of different knowledge, among those:

(i) basic concepts of MS, related to the content and the format of spectra generated by different MS techniques; (ii) concepts of data management, related to the efficient organization, retrieval, and preprocessing of spectra; (iii) concepts of knowledge discovery, related to the different available data mining algorithms and discovered knowledge models, and to the data reorganization requirements of data mining algorithms; (iv) bio-medical knowledge, that directly guides first the choice of biological analysis and then of data analysis task. The ontologies constitute a well established tool to model different domains, thus they can play an important role for modelling the different steps of a Computational Proteomics application. An ontology [29] consists of (i) a set of concepts, (ii) a set of relations describing concept hierarchy or taxonomy, (iii) a set of relations linking concepts non taxonomically, and (iv) a set of axioms, usually expressed in a formal language.

Grids. The Grid offers the storage and computational power to store huge spectra data and perform spectra preprocessing and analysis algorithms. Recently, the Open Grid Services Architecture (OGSA) introduced service orientation in Grids, leveraging the results of Web Services. A Grid Service is a Web Service that conforms to a set of conventions for the controlled, fault resilient and secure management of stateful services and exposes capabilities via standard interfaces. The Life Science Grid Research Group [30] of the Global Grid Forum [31] aims to investigate how bioinformatics requirements can be fitted and satisfied by Grid services and standards. Emerging BioGrids leverages bioinformatics tools wrapped as Grid Services.

Workflows. A workflow is a partial or total automation of a business process, in which a collection of activities must be executed by some entities (humans or machines), according to certain procedural rules. In this context, Workflow Management Systems are well established technological infrastructures, aiming at facilitating the design of a workflow, and supporting its enactments, by scheduling different activities on available entities. A comprehensive taxonomy of workflow management systems for Grids can be found in [32].

High-throughput application execution can be supported by workflows of Web/Grid services and in fact many workflow-based bioinformatics platforms do exist, such as *Pegasys* [33] and *myGrid* [34]. Nevertheless, few of them are related to mass spectrometry-based computational proteomics and they do not completely support the analysis pipeline of computational proteomics. MS-Analyzer [35] is a Grid-based Problem Solving Environment specifically designed for the management and processing of mass spectrometry-based proteomics data. It uses ontologies to model software tools and spectra data and workflow techniques to design applications. MS-Analyzer provides a collection of specialized spectra management services, including data movement, spectra preprocessing for noise cleaning and data reduction, spectra preparation for data mining or statistical analysis, spectra mining (e.g. classification or clustering), spectra and knowledge models visualization. An ontology-based workflow editor supports application development, while experimental datasets are managed by a specialized spectra database.

5 Conclusions

Computational Proteomics is an emerging field where data coming from heterogeneous technological platforms are analyzed for investigating mechanisms of life and disease. The paper described requirements and basic services, standards, and technologies of Mass Spectrometry-based Computational Proteomics. The use of the Service Oriented Architecture to build reusable services, the compliance to emerging proteomics standards for data representation and sharing, the use of consolidated data analysis methodologies, as those provided by data mining, and the deployment on the Grid, allow to build modular, scalable and reusable Computational Proteomics applications.

Acknowledgments

This work has been partially supported by project PRIN 2006 under Grant 2006063220.

References

1. Tyers, M., Mann, M.: From genomics to proteomics. Nature 422, 193–197 (2003)
2. Bafna, V., Reinert, K.: Mass spectrometry and computational proteomics. In: Jorde, L., Little, P., Dunn, M., Subramaniam, S. (eds.) Encyclopedia of Genetics, Genomics, Proteomics and Bioinformatics, John Wiley and Sons Ltd., Chichester (2006)
3. Boguski, M., McIntosh, M.: Biomedical informatics for proteomics. Nature 422, 233–237 (2003)
4. Aebersold, R., Mann, M.: Mass spectrometry-based proteomics. Nature 422, 198–207 (2003)
5. Breton, V., Dean, K., Solomonides, T.: The healthgrid white paper. In: Solomonides, T., McClatchey, R., Breton, V., Legrè, Y., Norager, S. (eds.) From Grid to Healthgrid, IOS Press, Amsterdam (2005)
6. Glish, G.L., Vachet, R.W.: The basic of mass spectrometry in the twenty-first century. Nature Reviews 2, 140–150 (2003)
7. Wu, B., Abbott, T., Fishman, D., McMurray, W., Mor, G., Stone, K., Ward, D., Williams, K., Zhao, H.: Comparison of statistical methods for classification of ovarian cancer using mass spectrometry data. Bioinformatics 1, 1636–1643 (2003)
8. Gopalakrishnan, V., William, E., Ranganathan, S., Bowser, R., Cudkowic, M.E., Novelli, M., Lattazi, W., Gambotto, A., Day, B.W.: Proteomic data mining challenges in identification of disease-specific biomarkers from variable resolution mass spectra. In: Proceedings of SIAM Bioinformatics Workshop 2004, Lake Buena Vista, FL, pp. 1–10 (2004)
9. Witten, I.H., Frank, E.: Data Mining: Practical machine learning tools and techniques, 2nd edn. Morgan Kaufmann, San Francisco (2005)
10. (PMML) Predictive Model Markup Language: http://www.dmg.org/
11. (CRISP-DM): http://www.crisp-dm.org/
12. Cannataro, M., Guzzi, P.H., Mazza, T., Tradigo, G., Veltri, P.: Preprocessing of mass spectrometry proteomics data on the grid. In: CBMS, pp. 549–554. IEEE Computer Society Press, Los Alamitos (2005)
13. Jeffries, N.: Algorithms for alignment of mass spectrometry proteomic data. Bioinformatics 21, 3066–3073 (2005)
14. Wong, J.W.H., Cagney, G., Cartwright, H.M.: Specalign - processing and alignment of mass spectra datasets. Bioinformatics 21, 2088–2090 (2005)

15. Yasui, Y., McLerran, D., Adam, B., Winget, M., Thornquist, M., Feng, Z.: An automated peak identification/calibration procedure for high-dimensional protein measures from mass spectrometers. Journal of Biomedicine and Biotechnology 1, 242–248 (2003)

16. Xu, C., Ma, B.: Software for computational peptide identification from MS-MS data. Drug Discovery Today 11, 595–600 (2006)

17. Eng, J.K., McCormack, A.L., Yates, J.R.: An approach to correlate tandem mass spectral data of peptides with amino acid sequences in a protein database. J. Am. Soc. Mass Spectrom 5, 976–989 (1994)

18. Perkins, D.N., Pappin, D.J., Creasy, D.M., Cottrell, J.S.: Probability-based protein identification by searching sequence databases using mass spectrometry data. Electrophoresis 20, 3551–3567 (1999)

19. Lu, B., Chen, T.: Algorithms for de novo peptide sequencing via tandem mass spectrometry. Drug Discovery Today:Biosilico 2, 85–90 (2004)

20. Cannataro, M., Cuda, G., Gaspari, M., Veltri, P.: An interactive tool for the management and visualization of mass-spectrometry proteomics data. In: Masulli, F., Mitra, S., Pasi, G. (eds.) WILF. LNCS (LNAI), vol. 4578, pp. 635–642. Springer, Heidelberg (2007)

21. Orchard, S., Hermjakob, H., Binz, P., Hoogland, C., Taylor, C.F., Zhu, W., Julian Jr., R., Apweiler, R.: Further steps towards data standardisation: The proteomic standards initiative hupo 3rd annual congress, beijing 25-27th october, 2004. Proteomics 5, 337–339 (2005)

22. Li, X., Pedrioli, P., Eng, J., Martin, D., Yi, E., Lee, H., Aebersold, R.: A tool to visualize and evaluate data obtained by liquid chromatography-electrospray ionization-mass spectrometry. Anal. Chem. 76, 3856–3860 (2004)

23. Veltri, P., Cannataro, M., Tradigo, G.: Sharing mass spectrometry data in a grid-based distributed proteomics laboratory. Information Processing and Management 43, 577–591 (2007)

24. (mzViewer),
    http://www.bioinformatics.bbsrc.ac.uk/projects/mzviewer/

25. (CCWiffer),
    http://www.charlestoncore.org/docs/ccwiffer/usermanual.html

26. Foster, I.T.: Globus toolkit version 4: Software for service-oriented systems. In: Jin, H., Reed, D., Jiang, W. (eds.) NPC 2005. LNCS, vol. 3779, pp. 2–13. Springer, Heidelberg (2005)

27. Sivashanmugam, K., Verma, K., Sheth, A.P., Miller, J.A.: Adding semantics to web services standards. In: Zhang, L.J. (ed.) ICWS, pp. 395–401. CSREA Press (2003)

28. Cannataro, M., Guzzi, P., Mazza, T., Tradigo, G., Veltri, P.: Managing ontologies for grid computing. Multiagent and Grid Systems 2, 29–44 (2006)

29. Maedche, A.: Ontology Learning for the Semantic Web. Kluwer Academic Publishers, Dordrecht (2002)

30. (LifeScienceGrid), http://forge.gridforum.org/projects/lsg-rg

31. (GlobalGridForum), http://www.gridforum.org

32. Yu, J., Buyya, R.: A taxonomy of scientific workflow systems for grid computing. SIGMOD Rec. 34, 44–49 (2005)

33. Shah, S.P., He, D.Y., Sawkins, J.N., Druce, J.C., Quon, G., Lett, D., Zheng, G.X., Xu, T., Ouellette, B.F.: Pegasys: software for executing and integrating analyses of biological sequences. BMC Bioinformatics 5 (2004)

34. Stevens, R., Robinson, A., Goble, C.: mygrid: Personalised bioinformatics on the information grid. Bioinformatics 19, 302–302 (2004)

35. Cannataro, M., Veltri, P.: MS-Analyzer: Composing and Executing Preprocessing and Data Mining Services for Proteomics Applications on the Grid. In: Concurrency and Computation: Practice and Experience, 19 Dec 2006, Wiley Published, Chichester (in press, 2006)

High Throughput Protein Similarity Searches in the LIBI Grid Problem Solving Environment

Maria Mirto[1], Ivan Rossi[2,3], Italo Epicoco[1], Sandro Fiore[1], Piero Fariselli[2], Rita Casadio[2], and Giovanni Aloisio[1]

[1] SPACI Consortium & ISUFI University of Salento, Lecce & CACT of NNL/CNR-INFM
{maria.mirto,italo.epicoco,sandro.fiore,
giovanni.aloisio}@unile.it
[2] Biocomputing Group, University of Bologna, Italy
piero@biocomp.unibo.it, casadio@alma.unibo.it
[3] BioDec Srl, Casalecchio di Reno, Bologna, Italy
ivan@biodec.com

Abstract. Bioinformatics applications are naturally distributed, due to distribution of involved data sets, experimental data and biological databases. They require high computing power, owing to the large size of data sets and the complexity of basic computations, may access heterogeneous data, where heterogeneity is in data format, access policy, distribution, etc., and require a secure infrastructure, because they could access private data owned by different organizations. The Problem Solving Environment (PSE) is an approach and a technology that can fulfil such bioinformatics requirements. The PSE can be used for the definition and composition of complex applications, hiding programming and configuration details to the user that can concentrate only on the specific problem. Moreover, Grids can be used for building geographically distributed collaborative problem solving environments and Grid aware PSEs can search and use dispersed high performance computing, networking, and data resources. In this work, the PSE solution has been chosen as the integration platform of bioinformatics tools and data sources. In particular an experiment of multiple sequence alignment on large scale, supported by the LIBI PSE, is presented.

1 Introduction

Biological data needs to be reusable, shareable and suitable for "in silico" experiments. In bioinformatics, an experiment is generally characterized by a search in huge biological databases and by the execution of tools that need to access such data intensively. A complete and integrated software environment to execute biological applications is needed, in order to assist scientists and researchers during management and coordination of all of the tasks of an "in silico" experiment, requiring large computational power. Grid Problem Solving Environments (GPSEs) can offer a solution for handling and analyzing so much disparate data connecting many computers within and among institutions through middleware software.

Indeed, according to the definition given by Gallopoulos, Houstis, and Rice: "A PSE is a computer system that provides all the computational features necessary to solve a

P. Thulasiraman et al. (Eds.): ISPA 2007 Workshops, LNCS 4743, pp. 414–423, 2007.

target class of problems.... PSEs use the language of the target class of problems." [5]. Moreover, Grid computing [6] represents an opportunity for PSE designers and users. It can provide an high-performance infrastructure for running PSEs and, at the same time, a valuable source of resources that can be integrated in PSEs. Grids can be used for building geographically distributed collaborative problem solving environments, and Grid aware PSEs (G-PSE) [12] can search and use dispersed high performance computing, networking and data resources.

An user can compose her experiment by using a graphical user interface, accessible via Web, through a Grid Portal, that is an access point to the Grid Problem Solving Environment, based on heterogeneous grid resources exploiting several Grid Middleware such as Globus [14] and gLite [13]. The Grid Portal provides several bioinformatics tools, both sequential and parallel, allowing transparent usage of the underlying grid resources.

This work presents an experiment of multiple sequence alignment (MSA) of human proteins on large scale, by using Workflow technology [16] in a Grid environment. In particular, we have used the Position Specific Iterative (PSI)-BLAST [18], a sensitive sequence similarity search tool, that uses an iterative searching method and a unique scoring scheme to detect weakly related homologues.

Our goal has been the multiple alignment of a large number of human proteins, stored in the UniProt [1] and TRemBL data banks, against those present in the Uniref90 data bank. Taking into account that the number of proteins is very huge, about 70.000, Grid resources are needed in order to reduce the computational time as well as to automate several steps needed for performing the experiment and obtaining the result. In order to run this experiment, a Grid PSE has been developed. It is based on efficient mechanisms for extracting the data and solutions for running several applications composed in a given order, i.e. a workflow. In particular a Workflow engine and a workflow editor have been developed.

The workflow is a component developed inside the Italian LIBI (International Laboratory of BioInformatics) Project [17], supported by the MIUR (Ministry for Education, University and Research) which aims at the creation of a virtual laboratory where e-scientists can share data and bioinformatics tools.

The remainder of the paper is organized as follows. Section 2 introduces the LIBI project whereas Section 3 describes the experiment with the implementation details. Section 4 describes the LIBI Grid Problem Solving Environment with the experimental results and finally, Section 5 draws the conclusions and highlights future work.

2   The LIBI Project

The Italian FIRB 2003 LIBI project, International Laboratory of BioInformatics, funded by the MIUR (Italian Ministry for Education, University and Research) is active since 2005 until 2009.

Main goal of this project is the setting up of an advanced Bioinformatics and Computational Biology Laboratory, focusing on the central activities of basic and applied research in modern Biology and Biotechnologies.

Project activities involve:

- the construction and the maintenance of genomic, proteomic and transcriptomic databases (such as MitoRes, UTRdb, UTRefdb, UTRSite, ENSEMBL, etc.);
- the development of new databases of pathogens relevant for humans, animals and plants;
- the design, development and maintenance of a cell cycle database;
- the design and implementation of new algorithms and software for the analysis of genomes and their expression products.

Two kind of actors have equal responsibility in the LIBI: technological and bioinformaticians partners.

Technological Research Units (URs) are CINECA in Bologna, INFN of the Padova, Bari and Bologna Sections, SPACI & ISUFI University of Salento, Lecce & CACT-NNL, IBM Semea Sud, that is the industrial partner, whereas bioinformaticians RUs are CNRBA, Biomedical Technologies Institute, CNR, Section of Bari, UNIBO of the University of Bologna, UNIMI of the University of Milan, CBMTS of the Center of Molecular Biomedicine, Trieste in Italy.

3 Workflow Experiment

The biggest step in the prediction of protein structures (secondary or tertiary) was obtained by adopting evolutionary information, usually in the form of protein profiles [2]. This is achieved by aligning to a query sequence all the retrieved similar chains detected using a similarity search algorithm. Routinely the most widely used program is PSI-BLAST, because of its speed and its accuracy [18]. In practice, any modern state of the art tool used to predict protein structures and features (such as secondary structures, membrane protein topology, protein solvent accessibility, protein-protein interactions protein stability changes etc.) takes in input some form of evolutionary information to achieve an accuracy compatible with real-world applications. However, the similarity search and the compilation of the sequence profiles is the most time consuming step for the prediction, but it is a necessary constituent of the majority of the prediction tools. For this reason, a system that can speed up the similarity search step can be profitable both for accelerating the prediction phase and for testing more ideas to improve the current state of the art methods.

In this optic an experiment related to the MSA of about seventy thousand human proteins against the data bank of UniProt NREF Uniref90 has been supported.

The data flow (see Fig. 1) consists in the extraction of the sequences by several files, for each sequence a run of a MSA tool is carried out and then an optimization of the results is made.

Involved tools are:

- a library for the sequence extraction;
- PSI-Blast of the NCBI for the multiple sequence alignment;
- a tool for the result adjustment.

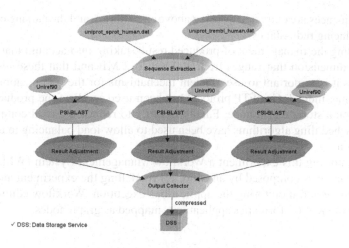

Fig. 1. Experiment Data Flow

A library has been developed for extracting the sequences by annotated input files, i.e. that contains both sequences and other information about the specie, organism, bibliographic references, etc., in EMBL format.

Indeed, dynamic libraries for accessing biological flat files are available inside the library in order to simplify the access to flat files and to provide seamless access. Some features of this library are: i) connection to flat files; ii) data manipulation; iii) information extraction; iv) printing the result in various formats such as Fasta and XML; v) creation of an XML dump of flat files. Moreover, other functions support previous APIs.

PSI-BLAST is a sensitive sequence similarity search tool that uses an iterative searching method and unique scoring scheme to detect weakly related homologues [18].

Finally, in order to reduce the redundancy of the results, taking into account that each result file contains several iterations and last is the most important, a module for reducing the dimension of output files has been developed. It parses output files and deletes the intermediate iterations.

In order to support this experiment, several requirements have been met:

- Access to flat file data bank (UniProt NREF Uniref90) with dimension about 800MB;
- Extraction of 70.845 sequences by annotated input files (human protein - UniProtKB database);
- For each run, the application produces the result of several iterations, specified by the user (three iterations in this experiment). Last iteration is the most important so output files must be updated;
- Management of produced results;
- Need to reduce the total computing time.

In order to satisfy the access to the data bank, it has been installed on grid nodes, where the application is run, and hence indexed. Indeed PSI-Blast runs just on indexed data banks.

The sequences are extracted by using above cited library and the parsing of the results allows reducing redundancy.

Regarding the management of produced result, taking into account that each result file has a dimension that ranges from 200 KB to 2 MB and that these results are on grid nodes it is important to use efficient mechanisms for the optimization of the file transfer time. Indeed, GridFTP protocol has been used so all of the produced files are retrieved on a storage grid node. Finally in order to reduce the total computing time, dynamic scheduling algorithms have been used to allow load balancing in a distributed environment.

For supporting this experiment a Workflow Management System (WMS) has been implemented. It is composed by an editor for modelling the experiment and an engine for scheduling and monitoring the applications execution. Workflow editor allows the discovery of the bioinformatics applications, mapped as graph nodes.

4   The LIBI Grid Problem Solving Environment

PSEs are typically designed for a specific application domain: this simplifies the designer task and generally produces an environment that is particularly tailored for a particular application class. Moreover, PSE users must have transparent access to dispersed and de-coupled components and resources. Thus, managing distributed environments is another main issue in PSEs design and use. Distributed and parallel computing systems are used for running PSEs both to get high performance and for facing distribution of data, machines, and software components.

The Grid is an high-performance distributed infrastructure that combines parallel and distributed computing systems: it is a distributed computing infrastructure whose main goal is resource sharing and coordinated problem solving in "dynamic, multi-institutional virtual organizations".

Thus, the role of the Grid is fundamental to build PSEs, since it provides an enormous number of hardware and software resources that can be transparently accessed by a PSE.

The designed G-PSE has a layered architecture built on a network infrastructure for information exchange (see Fig. 2).

Starting from the top, the first layer includes the services that can be used by the final user (*Application Services*). A graphical user interface allows the user defining a problem and contains the logic to guide the user in the choice of the applications needed for solving a given problem. While a single component of an application is a service, a more complex application is obtained by composing more services using workflows.

At the second level (*Programming Tools and Environment*) are the design tools to support the applications such as digital libraries, software components, etc. These contain the description of each single application and mechanisms for searching the programs and validating their composition. Moreover, the Grid Portal contains the application logic in order to access distributed systems through simple interfaces.

At the third and fourth level (*Grid Middleware Services*) are Grid services that constitute the middleware and, in particular, Data Management, Resource Management and Information Services represent their high-level services.

The Data Management (*Data Mng*) incorporates the grid logic of advanced data management, allowing a dynamic data management, a resource reuse and optimization mechanisms on computational grids such as to improve performances. This service also includes data transfer mechanisms on Grid offered through advanced protocols also able to assure high performances without neglecting security. An information service allows discovering the resources and to know their availability.

Resource Management (*Resource Mng*) functionalities are thought to receive user requirements, planning the operations to be run in the Grid, contacting monitoring and scheduling services for optimal resource allocation in a distributed environment.

Finally, the Security service (*Security*) is transversal to the previous indicated services and its invocation is the first step to be followed in a distributed environment, in order to access services and resources. Finally, at the bottom layer there are local services, containing physical Grid resources and infrastructures (e.g. computers, clusters, networks, instruments, etc.).

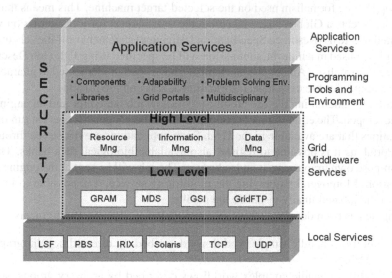

Fig. 2. Grid PSE Architecture

LIBI G-PSE reflects this architecture and several services have been built. Regarding the Application Services layer, today are available the following applications:

- PSI-Blast, used in the experiment;
- MrBayes [7] for the Bayesian estimation of phylogeny;
- Gromacs [3] for performing molecular dynamics, i.e. simulate the Newtonian equations of motion for systems with hundreds to millions of particles;
- PatSearch [11] for pattern matching in order to find a well defined pattern against a given sequence(s) or database (primary or specialized) divisions.

Regarding the Data Management, the LIBI exploits the federated database approach, accessible through the DB2 Integrator system. Several data banks have been already federated such as MitoRes, Mitonuc, GenBank and other. In order to allow the access in Grid, a driver for DB2 Integrator has been developed inside the GRelC (Grid Relational Catalog) toolkit [10]. This toolkit allows the access to distributed resources by using Web Services technology and allowing dynamically and transparently access to the relational and not relational databases.

Regarding the Resource Management, the LIBI exploits an extension of the GRB (Grid Resource Broker) [9] Meta Scheduler in order to schedule the jobs in a Grid environment. Indeed, GRB has been extended for submitting and checking jobs on Globus-based as well as gLite-based machines. Today, the extension at the Unicore-based machines is previous [4].

These services are built on top of basic services offered by Globus and gLite middleware. GRB takes the burden to guarantee the interoperability among heterogeneous middleware by means of different drivers each one in charge to translate the user request in the opportune formalism used on the selected target machine. This means that if the scheduler selects a Globus-based machine, the user request for job submission will be translated in a RSL (Resource Specification Language) statement or if the scheduler selects a gLite based machine the submission will be specified using JDL (Job Description Language) formalism. Analogous mechanisms have been implemented to guarantee the interoperability for file exchange, information access and job tracking.

Finally, for guaranting the execution of workflow job, an editor and an engine have been developed. The editor, implemented in the Java language, discovers at run time the applications that are available in the Grid. Such applications are registered through the LIBI Portal, as it is possible to register also available biological data banks. The user can compose own graph, save it and submit it. The job will be sent at the engine for the submission. Moreover, by querying the monitoring service, it is possible to know the status of the job and finally visualize the results.

The engine has been designed taking into account the following requirements:

1. ability to handle simple workflows described dy directed acyclic graphs (DAGs);
2. ability to handle complex workflows described by arbitrary graphs, supporting cycles and conditions;
3. support for recursive composition i.e., the possibility to define a workflow vertex;
4. scheduling and monitoring of jobs on different grid middleware: Globus, gLite and Unicore.

Major details about this service are in [15].

4.1   Implementation

As cited above, a Grid Portal for accessing to the G-PSE has been built.

The implementation is based on CGI written in C using g-SOAP with GSI-plugin [8] in order to contact the GRB scheduler service. Moreover the portal uses a MySQL

DBMS in order to store configuration data as well as user specific environment data. In particular for simulating the experiment, it is possible to use two graphical interface: a web page that contains all of the parameters in input at the algorithm and the workflow editor (Fig. 3(a)) for composing the graph (Fig. 3(b)). Moreover it is possible to monitor the status of the execution of a job and visualize/download the results by using a simple interface.

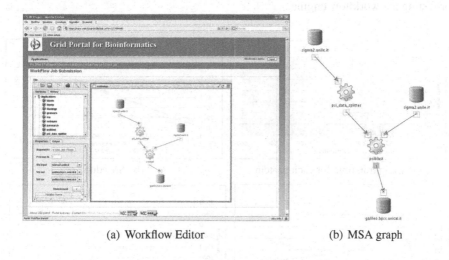

(a) Workflow Editor   (b) MSA graph

Fig. 3. LIBI Grid Portal

4.2   Results

The experiment has been run on the SPACI Grid (Italian Southern Partnership for Advanced Computational Infrastructures), a partnership among University of Salento, University of Calabria and University of Naples "Federico II". The SPACI Grid is based on three geographically spread High Performance Computing centers located in southern Italy, namely, the MIUR/HPC Center of Excellence of University of Calabria, the CACT/NNL (Center for Advanced Computational Technologies) of University of Salento, and the Naples/DMA (Dept. of Mathematics and Applications) of University of Naples "Federico II".

The parallel application is characterized by a not uniform distribution of tasks to be distributed among the available processes, this implies that the best choice is a dynamic scheduling policy based on a on-demand distribution of tasks. The performance has been evaluated on 500 proteins ranging the number of processes from 1 to 128. This experiment highlighted that the algorithm achieves the best efficiency up to 32 processors. Beyond this limit the execution time can not be reduced due to the existence of a task that takes 130 minutes (Fig. 4(a)). Running the algorithm with 70845 proteins we improved the scalability of the application maintaining an high efficiency. MSA result has been obtained taking a time of about 65 hours, using 128 processors against an estimated 96 days of computing on a single CPU. Moreover, taking into account that each result file is 1,7 MB, the disk storage occupancy is about 120 Gigabytes; with the adjustment of the results, the storage has been reduced at 20 GB.

The preliminary analysis of the application performance shows that the scalability (Fig. 4(b)) and efficiency (Fig. 4(c)) are pretty good. This is due to the fact that the application is embarrassing parallel with no communication among the parallel tasks. Indeed the Fig. 4(d) shows a great decrease of the execution time when the number of processors grows. This experiment has been an interesting testbed for our platform also for testing the workflow engine.

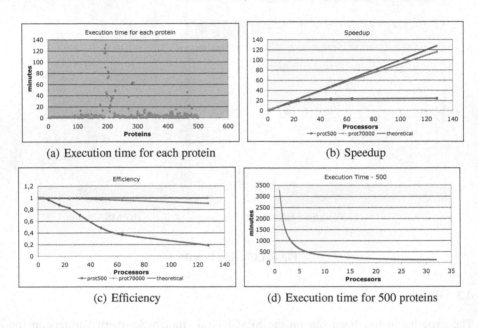

(a) Execution time for each protein   (b) Speedup

(c) Efficiency   (d) Execution time for 500 proteins

Fig. 4. Computational Time

5 Conclusions

This paper presented an experiment of multiple sequence alignment of human proteins, simulated into a Grid Problem Solving Environment. By using this system has been possible to compose several applications, obtaining a reduction of the computational time. The simulation has been carried by using a workflow, both for designing the graph and for scheduling it into a Computational Grid. Used Middleware are Globus and gLite and this allows using a large amount of resource involved into the SPACI and Egee Projects. Future work involves the design of other experiments to cover the integration in this system of several bioinformatics applications and the full integration of the Unicore middleware into the environment. This work was supported by the MIUR (Italian Ministry for Education, University and Research) in the LIBI (International Laboratory of BioInformatics) project, F.I.R.B. 2003, under grant RBLA039M7M.

References

1. Bairoch, A., Apweiler, R., Wu, C.H., Barker, W.C., Boeckmann, B., Ferro, S., et al.: The Universal Protein Resource (UniProt). Nucleic Acids Res. 33, 154–159 (2005), http://www.uniprot.org
2. Rost, B., Sander, C.: Progress of 1D protein structure prediction at last. Proteins 23, 295–300 (1995)
3. Van der Spoel, D., Lindahl, E., Hess, B., Groenhof, G., Mark, A.E., Berendsen, H.J.C.: GRO-MACS: Fast, flexible, and free. J. Comput. Chem. 26, 1701–1718 (2005)
4. Erwin, D.W., Snelling, D.: UNICORE: A Grid Computing Environment. In: Sakellariou, R., Keane, J.A., Gurd, J.R., Freeman, L. (eds.) Euro-Par 2001. LNCS, vol. 2150, Springer, Heidelberg (2001)
5. Houstis, E., Gallopoulos, E., Bramley, R., Rice, J.: Problem-Solving Environments for Computational Science. IEEE Comput. Sci. Eng. 4(3), 18–21 (1997)
6. Berman, F., Hey, A.J.G., Fox, G.: Grid Computing: Making The Global Infrastructure a Reality. Wiley & Sons, Chichester (2003)
7. Ronquist, F., Huelsenbeck, J.: MrBayes 3: Bayesian phylogenetic inference under mixed models. Bioinformatics 19, 1572–1574 (2003)
8. Aloisio, G., Cafaro, M., Lezzi, D., Van Engelen, R.: The GSI plug-in for gSOAP: Enhanced Security, Performance, and Reliability. In: Proceedings of Information Technology Coding and Computing (ITCC 2005), vol. I, pp. 304–309. IEEE Computer Society Press, Los Alamitos (2005)
9. Aloisio, G., Cafaro, M., Carteni, G., Epicoco, I., Fiore, S., Lezzi, D., Mirto, M., Mocavero, S.: The Grid Resource Broker Portal. In: Concurrency and Computation: Practice and Experience, Special Issue on Grid Computing Environments. (to appear, 2006)
10. Aloisio, G., Cafaro, M., Fiore, S., Mirto, M.: The Grid Relational Catalog Project. In: Grandinetti, L. (ed.) Advances in Parallel Computing, Grid Computing: The New Frontiers of High Performance Computing, pp. 129–155 (2005)
11. Grillo, G., Licciulli, F., Liuni, S., Sbisà, E., Pesole, G.: PatSearch: A program for the detection of patterns and structural motifs in nucleotide sequences. Nucleic Acids Res. 31, 3608–3612 (2003)
12. Von Laszewski, G., Foster, I., Gawor, J., Lane, P., Rehn, N., Russell, M.: Designing Grid-based Problem Solving Environments and Portals. In: Proceedings of International Conference on System Sciences (HICSS-34) (2001)
13. gLite Project: http://glite.web.cern.ch/glite/documentation/
14. Foster, I., Kesselman, C.: Globus Toolkit Version 4: Software for Service-Oriented Systems. In: Jin, H., Reed, D., Jiang, W. (eds.) NPC 2005. LNCS, vol. 3779, Springer, Heidelberg (2005)
15. Cafaro, M., Epicoco, I., Mirto, M., Lezzi, D., Aloisio, G.: The Grid Resource Broker Workflow Engine. In: IEEE Proceedings of The 6th International Conference on Grid and Cooperative Computing, Urumchi, Xinjiang, China, August 16-18, IEEE Computer Society Press, Los Alamitos (to appear, 2007)
16. Workflow management coalition reference model: http://www.wfmc.org/
17. The LIBI Project: http://www.libi.it
18. Altschul, S.F., Madden, T.L., Schäffer, A.A., Zhang, J., Zhang, Z., Miller, W., Lipman, D.J.: Gapped BLAST and PSI-BLAST: a new generation of protein database search programs. Nucleic Acids Res. 17(25), 3389–3402 (1997), http://www.ncbi.nlm.nih.gov/cgi-bin/BLAST/nph-psi

Grid and Distributed Public Computing Schemes for Structural Proteomics: A Short Overview

Azhar Ali Shah, Daniel Barthel, and Natalio Krasnogor

Automated Scheduling optimization And Planning (ASAP) Group,
School of Computer Science and Information Technology,
University of Nottingham, NG8 1BB, UK
(aas,dxb, nxk)@cs.nott.ac.uk
www.cs.nott.ac.uk/~{aas,dxb,nxk}

Abstract. Grid and distributed public computing schemes has become an essential tool for many scientific fields including bioinformatics, computational biology and systems biology. The adoption of these technologies has given rise to a wide range of projects and contributions that provide various ways of setting up these environments and exploiting their potential resources and services for different domains of applications. This paper aims to provide a distilled overview of some of the major projects, technologies and resources employed in the area of structural proteomics. The major emphasis would be to briefly comment on various approaches related to the gridification and parallelization of some flagship legacy applications, tools and data resources related to key structural proteomics problems such as protein structure prediction, folding and comparison. The comments are based on theoretical analysis of some interesting parameters such as performance gain after gridification, user level interaction environments, workload distribution and the choice of deployment infrastructure and technologies. The study of these parameters would provide a basis for some motivating justification needed for further research and development in this domain.

1 Introduction

A thorough overview of recent scientific literature related to life sciences provides evidence that the Grid and distributed public computing schemes have become essential tools for disciplines such as bioinformatics, computational biology and systems biology. This may be perhaps due to the interdisciplinary, problem-rich and resource-hungry nature of these disciplines coupled with the ever growing number and size/complexity of biological databases and analytical tools. For example, there are about one thousand biological databases dispersed around the world [1] and several thousands of analytical tools packed as different suites and libraries (e.g. European Molecular Biology Open Software Suite (EMBOSS) [2]). These are made available by different institutes and organizations as web services to be added to custom programs and applications. The availability of these large-scale databases and analytical tools has given rise to a number of institutional, national and international grid-related projects and applications that explore the exploitation of proper grid infrastructures and enabling technologies for life sciences (e.g. myGrid [3], EGEE [4],

P. Thulasiraman et al. (Eds.): ISPA 2007 Workshops, LNCS 4743, pp. 424–434, 2007.

Swiss BioGrid [5]). These dedicated grid projects build their infrastructure setup through the federation of different *institutionally-owned* resources and allow their respective research communities for the authenticated and authorized exploitation of shared resources. There are also some other projects that build their infrastructure setup around *publicly-owned* unused computing resources which are voluntarily provided throughout the world (aka distributed *public computing schemes*) such as the World Community Grid [6] that supports the Human Proteome Folding Project, Folding@Home [7], Predictor@Home [8] and Rosetta@Home [9] etc. All these projects attempt to provide an integrated environment for e-Science through appropriate layers of service infrastructure as shown in Figure 1.

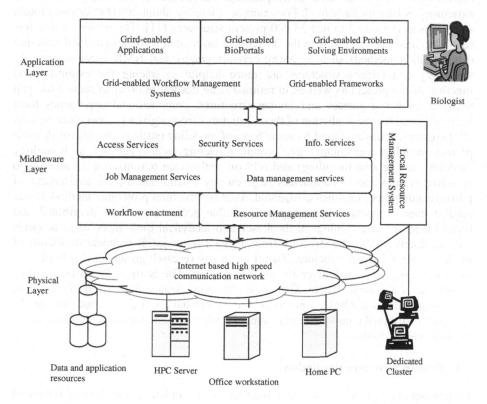

Fig. 1. Components and Services of a Generic BioGird Infrastructure (reproduced from [10])

This paper focuses on the exploration of some of these flagship projects in terms of their use in key research areas of structural proteomics that deals with the high-throughput determination of protein 3D-structures, their comparison and functional annotation. A particular focus is to find out and compare various approaches related to the gridification/parallelization of some flagship legacy applications, tools and data resources by analyzing key parameters such as job/data distribution and management, user level interaction environments, deployment technologies and infrastructures, and the effect of gridification on overall performance of the system. The output of these findings is summarized in section **2**, whereas Section **3** provides further information on middleware tools/approaches for grid-based management of structural proteomics data. Finally section 4 concludes with some comments on the indication and description of potential future trends related to the further exploitation of the Grid and its enabling technologies for structural proteomics.

2 Major Projects and Applications

Even though a very large number of protein primary structures (sequences) are known, the number of their corresponding 3D-strcutures (secondary or tertiary structures) is lagging far behind. For example, there are about 200,000 known protein sequences as compared to just 33,000 protein structures [11]. The reason behind this sequence-structure gap is due to the difficulties associated with experimental structure determination methods such as X-ray crystallography and NMR spectroscopy. As secondary and tertiary structures are more helpful in tracing the evolution and function of the protein as well as in rational drug design, in order to reduce the gap between known sequences and known structures, computational approaches have been proposed for the prediction of these structures from a given protein sequence. As all these approaches are based on some form of modeling (such as *ab initio* or *de novo* protein modeling and comparative protein modeling techniques such as homology modeling and protein threading) and rely on multi-scale optimization techniques to optimize various model parameters (e.g. energy minimization), the availability of powerful computing facilities is essential. That is, structural proteomic methodologies require huge computational power and reliable access to various distributed and (often) heterogeneous biological databases and analytical tools in order to properly and accurately predict the structure from a given sequence or compare thousands of models against a target structure. Therefore, many research groups in this field such as Baker Laboratory at University of Washington, The Scripps Research Institute (TSRI) at California, Pande Group at Stanford University, High Throughput Computing Group at Osaka University and others have started to make use of the Grid and distributed computing environments. We discuss some of these initiatives in the following sections.

2.1 Protein Structure Prediction

Protein structure prediction has remained an open problem in the field of structural proteomics [12]. New methods are being explored and investigated at various research institutes and groups throughout the world. Evaluation of the quality and performance of these methods is carried out every two years through the *Critical Assessment of Techniques for Protein Structure Prediction* (CASP) competition. In order to provide best predicted results for a target protein, the use of grid and distributed computing public schemes has been successfully demonstrated through various projects. For example, researchers at TSRI (*The Scripps Research Institute*) have developed a distributed public computing based protein structure prediction super computer (*Predictor@Home*)[8] using *Berkley Open Infrastructure for Network Computing* (BOINC) software. The BOINC software provides a set of different daemons that can be used for job submission, distribution and management as well as for data access, integration and storage in a distributed global grid environment consisting of publicly devoted heterogeneous PCs interconnected through the internet (aka *CPU-scavenging or cycle-scavenging*). The predictor itself consists of a set of complex protocols with increasingly sophisticated models that rely on standard software tools such as BLAST, SAM-T02, PSIPRED, MFOLD simulation (for conformational sampling) and CHARMM (for molecular simulations). It is reported that during the 6th *Critical Assessment of Protein Structure Prediction Methods* (CASP) competition 6786 users participated in the Predictor@Home project and contributed a total compute time of about 12 billion seconds, the equivalent of about 380 years of computation on a single desktop machine, within just 3 months time. This computation power had been exploited for appropriate conformational sampling and refinement of the predicted structures of 58 CASP6 targets. The quality of the predicted structures utilizing the public computing infrastructure was compared with results using a dedicated local cluster (64 nodes, 2.4 GHz Pentium Xeon processors, 1GB RAM, 1GB Ethernet network). The results of the comparison indicate that the vastly larger distributed computing power afforded by the BOINC implementation resulted in far better predictions than using the dedicated cluster.

Another grid based approach that enhances the quality and performance of structure prediction has been demonstrated in [13]. It builds on the standalone web server named ROKKY (designed at Kobe University) that was ranked 2nd best prediction web server in the fold recognition category of CASP6 experiment. ROKKY uses a combination of standard analysis tools (PSI-PLAST and 3D-Jurry) and the *Fragment Assembly Simulated Annealing* (FASA) technique using the SimFold [14] software package. In order to further enhance the quality of prediction and performance, a grid-based workflow design and control tool was added that allows the end-user to create/design a structure prediction experiment and submit it for execution on the Grid. As compared to *Predictor@Home*, the addition of a GUI-enabled workflow in ROKKY facilitates the dynamical interaction between the user and the prediction experiment during its execution. That is, the user can modify input parameters and/or methods based on the real-time inspection/monitoring of the current predicted results. It has been reported [13] that for target T0198, the workflow-based prediction gave a faster result that was closer to to the target structure compared to employing a non-workflow based prediction, which uses simple batch files for job submission. This illustrates the importance of allowing the user to dynamically interact with the "production pipeline" even when the software is being distributed across the grid.

Likewise, another ambitious project, *Encyclopedia of Life* (EoL), attempts to predict structural information for all the proteins in all known organisms. The estimated computation time required for annotation of about 1.5 million sequences (as of 2003) using a pipeline of computational tools (such as TMHMM, PSORT, SignalP, WU-BLAST, PSI-BLAST and 123D) has been approximated to be 1.8 Million CPU hours (more than 300 years!) on a single 1.8 GHz CPU. In order to facilitate this task, a grid-based workflow management systems has been proposed and demonstrated [15], which builds on the *AppLeS Parameter Sweep Template* (APST) technology providing an appropriate application deployment logistic and an adaptive scheduling and execution environment. The workflow was tested by running more than 54,000 proteome annotation jobs requiring 13670.5 CPU hours during the four days of the Super Computing Conference (SC'03) on a grid testbed. This consisted of 215 CPU nodes managed at ten different sites having different operating systems and local resource management software. Further details of some grid-based protein structure prediction applications are presented in Table 1.

Table 1. Grid-based applications for *protein structure prediction*

Project/ Application	Grid technologies and tools	Job/data distribution	Effect of gridification
ProtFinder [16,17] Prediction of thermodynamic properties of orthologous proteins	– Globus based *GridWay Framework* that uses adaptive scheduling for dynamic grids – Condor/G based GRAM – GIIS Server for resource discovery, GASS and GridFTP for data handling – User interaction with job submission agent through API or command line.	– Prediction of 88 sequences of the Triose Phosfate Isomerase enzyme was carried out in parallel by submitting an array job with 88 parallel tasks specified in a *Job Template* File.	– Jobs were run on 64 heterogeneous nodes located at different sites of IRISGrid and EGEE project. – It took an average of about 43 minutes for the entire experiment
PSA/GAc [18]: Parallel Simulated Annealing using Genetic crossover	– *NetSolve* based client-server application model through GridRPC API – NetSolve agent keeps the service registry and monitoring information – Client queries the agent and then communicates with the introduced server through GridRPC – API for user interaction	– Several iterated *simulated annealing* calculations were distributed in parallel for execution on NetSolve servers, whereas *genetic algorithm crossover* was performed at the client side in order to reduce the communication delays	– It took about 16 minutes for the prediction job with population of 16 and crossover interval of 100 MCsweep

2.2 Protein Folding

Unlike the problem of protein structure *prediction,* where the goal is to obtain the final configuration of a given protein sequence, the problem of protein *folding* is to determine the dynamical aspects of the process involved. Folding is a thermodynamically driven process taking a few micro seconds, in which a protein adopts its native state. A proper understanding of this process would shed light into many issues at the core of biotechnology, such as the design of new proteins with a desired functionality, the understanding of some incurable diseases such as cancer or neurodegenerative diseases (e.g. Alzheimer's, Creutzfeldt-Jakob disease(CJD), Cystic fibrosis (CF), Huntington's disease (HD) and many other practical implementations of nanotechnology. The computational technique that helps in understanding the folding process uses simulations that require extremely high computational power far beyond the limits of any single traditional super computer or local cluster. It has been demonstrated in the *Folding@Home* project [7] that this requirement can be met with a world wide distributed public-resource computing network that interconnects thousands of loosely coupled heterogeneous publicly-owned and voluntarily devoted PCs. *Folding@Home* uses an *'ensemble dynamics'* algorithm that performs *M* independent simulations with the same amino acids coordinates but with different velocities on *M* distributed processors such that each simulation starts with a slightly different initial condition and pushes the system through a free energy minimization process. This algorithm gives an *M* times speedup for the simulation of folding dynamics and thus avoids the overall waiting in free energy minima. Similarly, the process can be repeated in order to effectively handle multiple free energy barriers (multiple translations for complex folding dynamics). Using a modified version of the Tinker [12] molecular dynamics code, *β-hairpin* and *villin* were simulated and their folds successfully determined. Based on the diversity of the simulation results for a variety of molecules (*'from the nonbiological PPA helices to the 36-residue villin headpiece'* [7]) it has been observed that there is no single universal folding process and even sequences which fold to the same structure may have different folding processes. Further details on a selection of grid-enabled protein folding applications are presented in Table **2**.

Table 2. Grid-enabled applications for *Protein Folding*

Project/ Application	Grid technologies and tools	Job/data distribution	Effect of gridification
CHARMM [19] Chemistry at HARvard Molecular Mechanics	– *Legion* grid operating system that provides process, files system, security services and resource management – Simple command line interface with basic commands for job submission, monitoring and result visualization	– Overall task: to study the energy and entropy of folded and unfolded states of a protein – About 400 CHARMM jobs were run in parallel with different initial conditions	– Grid test-bed :1020 nodes at 6 institutional sites – 15% speedup in computational time.
CHARMM [20]	– United Devices (UD) MetaProcessor (MP) platform for DesktopGrid – Master/worker model – Master (MP Server) controls and manages all the tasks and uses IBM DB2 for data storage – Each worker runs a *UD Agent* with task API to run the task module and communicate with the server. – API based user interaction	– The overall job was to obtain efficient protein folding of 56 residue protein src-SH3 domain with different algorithmic approaches such as best-first, depth-first and breadth-first. – The job is distributed into set of 50 work units (*work pool*) each having the same protein conformation but different random seed number. – Each work-unit consists of 100,000 simulation steps	– A work-pool consisting of 50 work-units was shot every 5 minutes on the heterogeneous platform of 45 desktop machines. – Analysis of the results indicates that DesktopGrids are suitable for protein folding.

2.3 Protein Structure Comparison

The comparison of protein three-dimensional structures based on a variety of similarity measures is a key component of the most challenging structural proteomic tasks, such as understanding the evolution of protein networks, protein function determination and, of course, protein folding and protein structure prediction.

As the number of known protein structures goes on increasing the size of their corresponding databases (such as PDB) also increases and hence, the process of structure comparison requires more efficient algorithms, which could exploit the power of web and grid computing technologies to provide accurate and optimal results with enhanced reliability and fault tolerance. One such approach has been demonstrated in [21], which employs a distributed grid-aware algorithm with indexing techniques based on geometric properties. Hash tables are used in order to partition the PDB database into sub-tables that can be dynamically updated with new entries in the PDB and provide fast and accurate comparison results. It used a Globus and MPICH based Grid testbed consisting of four nodes (each with 300 MHz CPU). Experiments were performed comparing a target against 19,500 PDB structures in about 19 seconds.

Table 3. Grid-based protein *structure comparison*

Project/application	Grid technologies and tools	Job/data distribution	Effect of gridification
FROG [23,24] Fitted Rotation and Orientation of protein structure by means of real-coded Genetic algorithm	– Ninf Grid RPC – Master-slave model – Asynchronous parallel programming in C language – Web-based interactive user interface through NinfCalc tool.	– The initial population is generated on the master node, which then copies three non-redundant parents to each node in the grid repeatedly.	– With a generation size of 2000, population size of 100 and a crossover rate of 50, the comparison of 1j7n_d4 and 4tli took about 97 minutes on a single machine where as it takes only 17 minutes on a grid testbed of 16 nodes.
PROuST [25] Ontology and workflow based grid-enablement of PROuST application for protein structure comparison.	– PROTEUS problem solving environment with Globus-based grid infrastructure. – Unified Modeling Language (UML) activity diagram workflow language specification – Graphical user interfaces for workflow composition, browsing, selection and result visualization.	– The PROuST application is divided into independent phases such as pre-processing, similarity search and structural alignment – Each phase is implemented as an independent sub-workflow/software component	– The independent sub-workflows are stored in the PROTEUS workflow meta-data repository, which has been used for the development of overall grid-aware PROuST application

Another related approach is presented in [22] describing a meta-server for *Protein Comparison, Knowledge, Similarity, and Information (ProCKSI),* integrating multiple protein structure comparison methods such as the *Universal Similarity Metric* (USM), the *Maximum Contact Map Overlap* (MaxCMO), and an algorithm for the alignment of distance matrices (DALI), amongst others. Additionally, it produces a consensus similarity profile of all similarity measures employed. The application runs on a mini-cluster and provides a web-based interface (http://www.procksi.net/) for job submission and result visualization. Further details of some grid-enabled applications for protein structure comparison are presented in Table **3**.

3   Grid-Based Data Management Approaches

As important as computational horsepower, data sharing and re-using has become a fundamental aspect of almost all modern applications in the field of life sciences. This is due to the very large size and number of datasets used and the frequency by which these are updated. There have been several contributions targeted at the provision of some universal grid-based data standards, models, tools and technologies. Some of these efforts are summarized in Table **4**.

Table 4. Grid-based data management approaches for structural proteomics

Project/application	Middleware technologies	Databases
ISPIDER [26] *In Silico Proteome Integrated Data Environment Resource*	– *OGSA-DAI:* wrapping databases as web services – *OGSA-DQP:* distributed/parallel query processing – *AutoMed:* global schema transformation	– *gpmDB*: global proteomics machine database – *PEDRo*: Proteome Experimental Data RepOsitory – *PepSeeker*: proteome peptide identification
e-HTPX [27]	– Globus Grid-FTP with web services (SOAP protocols) – Web portal based user interface implemented with Java Server Pages (JSP), Java Beans and Servlets running on Apache Tomcat.	– Automated collection of proteomics data from different academic projects and laboratories and its storage in to public databases such as Macromolecular Structure Database (MSD) and Protein Data Bank (PDB).

4   Conclusions and Future Trends

It has been observed from the reviewed literature that both Grid and distributed public computing schemes have been used successfully in the field of structural proteomics for both compute and data intensive applications. The former is powered by standard grid middleware technologies such as Globus [16,17,25,27], Legion [19], NetSolve [18], Ninf [23,24], myGrid [3], Condor/G [16,17] etc., wheras the latter is powered by BOINC [6,7,8,9], UD MetaProcessor [20] etc. In fact, the diversity of enabling technologies for grid and distributed computing makes it difficult for the developer to select most appropriate technological infrastructure with proven technological standards and tools. Various demonstrations reviewed in this paper are aimed at providing a roadmap in this dilemma. It has been observed that selection of an appropriate grid/distributed computing approach mainly depends on the nature of the application. For example, applications with an independent and parallel nature of jobs are more suitable for distributed computing based on publicly-owned resources. On the other hand, if the application requires some pre-determined and controlled quality of service in terms of data and process management with enhanced reliability and security, then organizational or cross-organizational grid infrastructure with standard middleware would serve in a better way. Furthermore, some middleware technologies such as Nimrod and Legion are considered as best middleware choices for applications with adjustable parametric data values. Similarly Condor/G and Proteus based grid workflow environments provide the highest level of abstraction needed for an easy and efficient exploitation of grid resources from an ordinary user's point of view. However, in order to further extend the level of this abstraction, the future intake of proper grid infrastructure for structural proteomics should move towards the development of more interactive user interfaces and high level services in terms of portals, problem solving environments and workflow management systems. A more comprehensive and detailed review of web and grid technologies in the life sciences can be found in [10].

Acknowledgements. N. Krasnogor acknowledges the BBSRC for funding project BB/C511764/1 and the EPSRC for project GR/T07534/01. A.A Shah acknowledges University of Sindh, Pakistan for scholarship FSCH/ SU/PLAN/F.SCH/794/2006.

References

1. http://en.wikipedia.org/wiki/Biological_databases
2. Rice, P., Longden, I., Bleasby, A.: EMBOSS: The European Molecular Biology Open Software Suite. Trends in Genetics 16, 276–277 (2000)
3. Stevens, R.D., Robinson, A.J., Goble, C.A.: MyGrid: Personalized bioinformatics on the information grid. Bioinformatics 19, 302–304 (2003)
4. Gagliardi, F., Jones, B., Grey, F., Begin, M.E., Heikkurinen, M.: Building an infrastructure for scientific Grid computing: status and goals of the EGEE project. Philosophical Transactions: Mathematical, Physical and Engineering Sciences 363, 1729–1742 (2005)
5. Michael, P., Sergio, M., Peter, K.: The SwissBioGrid Project: Objectives, Preliminary Results and Lessons Learned. In: 2nd IEEE International Conference on e-Science and Grid Computing (e-Science 2006) - Workshop on Production Grids, IEEE Computer Society Press, Amsterdam, Netherlands (2006)
6. World Community Grid: Technology Solving Problems,
   http://www.worldcommunitygrid.org/
7. Pande, V.S., Baker, I., Chapman, J., et al.: Atomistic Protein Folding Simulations on the Submillisecond Time Scale Using Worldwide Distributed Computing. Biopolymers 68, 91–109 (2003)

8. Taufer, M., An, C., Kerstens, A., Brooks, C.L.: Predictor@Home: a protein structure prediction supercomputer based on public-resource computing. In: Proceedings of 19th IEEE International Parallel and Distributed Processing Symposium, IEEE Computer Society Press, Los Alamitos (2005)
9. Rosetta@Home: Protein Folding, Design and Docking, http://boinc.bakerlab.org/rosetta/
10. Shah, A.A., Barthel, D., Lukasiak, P., Blacewicz, J., Krasnogor, N.: Web & Grid Technologies in Bioinformatics, Computational Biology and Systems Biology. Current Bioinformatics (submitted)
11. BioSimGrid: A distributed database for biomolecular simulations, http://www.biosimgrid.org/#about
12. Zhang, Y., Skolnick, J.: The protein structure prediction problem could be solved using the current PDB library. Proceedings of US National Academy of Science 102, 1029–1034 (2005)
13. Susumu, D., Kazutoshi, F., Hideo, M., Haruki, N., Shinji, S.: An Empirical Study of Grid Applications in Life Science Lesson learnt from Biogrid project in Japan. International Journal of Information Technology 11, 16–28 (2005)
14. Chikenji, G., Fujitsuka, Y., Takada, S.: A reversible fragment assembly method for De Novo protein structure prediction. Journal of Chemical Physics 119, 6895–6903 (2003)
15. Birnbaum, A., Hayes, J., Wilfred, W., et al.: Grid Workflow Software for a High-Throughput Proteome Annotation Pipeline. In: Konagaya, A., Satou, K. (eds.) LSGRID 2004. LNCS (LNBI), vol. 3370, pp. 68–81. Springer, Heidelberg (2005)
16. Herrera, J., Huedo, E., Montero, R.S., Lorente, I.M.: Benchmarking of a joint IRISGrid/EGEE Testbed with a Bioinformatics Application. Scalable Computing: Practice and Experience 7, 25–32 (2006)
17. Huedo, E., Ruben, S.M., Ignacio, M.L.: Adaptive Grid Scheduling of a High-Throughput Bioinformatics Application. In: Wyrzykowski, R., Dongarra, J.J., Paprzycki, M., Waśniewski, J. (eds.) Parallel Processing and Applied Mathematics. LNCS, vol. 3019, pp. 840–847. Springer, Heidelberg (2004)
18. Tanimura, Y., Aoi, K., Hiroyasu, T., Miki, M., Okamoto, Y., Dongarra, J.: Implementation of Protein Tertiary Structure Prediction System with NetSolve. In: Proceedings of the High Performance Computing and Grid in Asia Pacific Region, Seventh International Conference on (HPCAsia'04) (2004)
19. Natrajan, A., Crowley, M., Wilkins, D.N., Humphrey, M.A., Fox, A.D., Grimshaw, A.S., Brooks, C.L.: Studying Protein Folding on the Grid: Experiences using CHARMM on NPACI Resources under Legion. In: Proceeding of the HPDC Conference, San Francisco, CA, USA (2001)
20. UK, B., Taufer, M., Stricker, T., Settanni, G., Cavalli, A.: Implementation and characterization of protein folding on a desktop computational grid - is CHARMM a suitable candidate for the united devices metaprocessor? In: Technical Report 385, ETH Zurich, Institute for Computer systems (2002)
21. Ferrari, C., Guerra, C., Zanotti, G.: A grid-aware approach to protein structure comparison. Journal of Parallel Distributed Computing 63, 728–737 (2003)
22. Barthel, D., Hirst, J.D., Blacewicz, J., Krasnogor, N.: Procksi: a metaserver for protein comparison using kolmogorov and other similarity measures. In: Late Breaking Papers. European Conference on Computational Biology, Eilat, Israel (2006)
23. Park, S.J., Yamamura, M.: FROG (Fitted Rotation and Orientation of protein structure by means of real-coded Genetic algorithm): Asynchronous Parallelizing for Protein Structure-Based Comparison on the Basis of Geometrical Similarity. Genome Informatics 13, 344–345 (2002)

24. Park, S., Yamamura, J.: Two-layer Protein Structure Comparison. In: Proceedings of the 15th IEEE International Conference on Tools with Artificial Intelligence (ICTAI'03) (2003)
25. Cannataro, M., Comin, M., Ferrari, C., Guerra, C., Guzzo, A., Veltri, P.: Modeling a Protein Structure Comparison Application on the Grid Using PROTEUS. In: Herrero, P., Pérez, M.S., Robles, V. (eds.) SAG 2004. LNCS, vol. 3458, pp. 75–85. Springer, Heidelberg (2005)
26. Zamboulis, L., Fan, H., Belhajjame, K., Siepen, J., et al.: Data Access and Integration in the ISPIDER Proteomics Grid. In: Leser, U., Naumann, F., Eckman, B. (eds.) DILS 2006. LNCS (LNBI), vol. 4075, pp. 3–18. Springer, Heidelberg (2006)
27. Allan, R., Keegan, R., Meredith, D., Winn, M., Winter, G.: e-HTPX– HPC, Grid and Web-Portal Technologies in High Throughput Protein Crystallography. In: Proceedings of the UK e-Science All Hands Meeting, Nottingham, UK (2004)

Distributed Processing of Clinical Practice Data in Grid Environment for Pharmacotherapy Personalization and Evidence-Based Pharmacology

Alexey Zhuchkov[1], Nikolay Tverdokhlebov[2], Boris Alperovich[3], and Alexander Kravchenko[1]

[1] Telecommunication Centre UMOS, Kosygina str. 4, Moscow, 119991 Russia
`alex@umos.ru, kav_@bk.ru`
`http://rgrid.ru`
[2] Institute of Chemical Physics, Kosygina str. 4, Moscow, 119991 Russia
`nickhard@chph.ras.ru`
[3] Moscow Medical Academy, Trubeckaya str. 8, bld. 2, Moscow, 119992 Russia
`borisalp@mail.ru`

Abstract. The paper describes XML-based information structures (meta-models) and software services both developed to search, collect and aggregate data of drug clinical usage and represent the information to users in a comprehensible way. These tools provide biomedical professionals with more complete, detailed and actual information on possible adverse events related to drug administration and thus support the evidence-based pharmacology and more personalized healthcare. Grid provides implementation of these tools on base of multi-agent system technology enabling information processing in loosely coupled data space.

1 Introduction

Total computerization has considerably changed the Health Care industry in the last years. Information processing became now an important component of any health care organization. The Health Care depends on information and communication technologies in an increasing degree. Information technologies are crucial now for progress in medical research, better management and diffusion of medical knowledge, shifting health care towards evidence-based medicine and evidence-based pharmacology. [1]. At present time more than 4 millions scientific articles are being published a year in more than 20 thousands medical journals. However, limitations that take place in the modern information support services cause difficulties for physicians and pharmacists in getting considerable part of actual achievements of medical sciences and clinical practice. In result, improper drug prescription is widespread all over the world. WHO reporting that 30% - 60% of patients have been prescribed antibiotics (perhaps twice) at the primary level, 25% - 75% of antibiotics are used in inappropriate way in hospitals, and every year about 15 millions injections are being made while about a half of which are not sterilized. This healthcare practice is resulted in virus resistance, adverse complications and harms patients health.

P. Thulasiraman et al. (Eds.): ISPA 2007 Workshops, LNCS 4743, pp. 435–443, 2007.

Besides, unreasonable treatment increases expenses of the patient, the insurance company, the state. Considering this situation WHO/GPP [2] and also European GPP [3] suggest that any pharmacist should be able to access literature which contains all important information on therapeutic efficiency of drugs as well as on their pharmacological properties. The same document recommends create on local, state and international level special databases to provide fast and reliable access to information needed for medical professionals in their everyday professional activity.

Numerous biomedical databases and other information resources are being created now everywhere, including a lot of web-pages. Rational use of these data sources and healthcare process personalization on base of this information could be an effective way to decrease risks associated with inadequate treatment and to increase the safety of patient health. For this purpose the powerful tools are needed which could enable computerized preliminary analysis and selection of data, integration and consistent data management, data mining and others. Besides, the tools should provide maintenance of information safety at teamwork in the environment of distributed resources [4]. We believe that these tools should be intellectual software services based on appropriate information structures (meta-models). Grid provides the secure distributed environment to implement the multitude of interacting services.

2 Management of Clinical Practice Information in Data Space

Information about drug usage in clinical practice should be delivered to users in a comprehensible form (i.e., concentrated and convenient) so that the biomedical researcher or the healthcare professional could concentrate on the research subject or the medical aid process, instead of excavating the necessary information from huge number of publications behind the references found by a search machine in the Internet. For example, in December 2006 the Google answered to the query "warfarin adverse" with more than one million references, for «warfarin adverse reaction» it reacted with 650 000 references. The same time the key words «warfarin complications» produced more than 900 references in PubMed. These references are not the final information but require the thorough work with referred documents in order to extract information that is needed indeed.

Besides, modern conception of healthcare assumes informed, active and responsible participation of patients and their informal careers (family/friends) [1]. Hence, appropriate part of information should be accessible for patients too, who are not medical professionals though they are usually well informed about their own illness.

The effective information support of biomedical research and healthcare process requires new information structures and services, which will provide the opportunity to deliver from different sources to the physician, pharmacist or patient the information that is being:

- permanently added and updated;
- aggregated from different sources considering the data semantics;
- filtered by criteria which user set up;
- represented in a convenient and comprehensible way.

Some problems originate in the fact that the modern technology of accumulation of scientific research information and clinical pharmacology practice data results in dynamic nature of medical knowledge which change and develop permanently. These data are heterogeneous and loosely coupled, many important links are not fixed. It is impossible to create "The General Biomedical Database" but we have to talk rather about loosely coupled Data Space [5]. There are the very different database schemas and data types even if the data are already digital and accessible via network. The data can be in the form of texts, diagrams, tables, pictures and so on. This is why there is not only problem of data mining but also the problem of a representation of these data in the form suitable for automated analysis as well the problem of the comprehensible data representation to the medical professional or patient.

We assume that the key to overcome these problems is the development of service-oriented solutions aimed to operate with Data Space. This requires developing the follow:

- flexible information structures which enable systematic accumulation and integration of heterogeneous loosely coupled data using semantic properties of data;
- intellectual services for search, analysis, integration and comprehensible representation loosely coupled data in order to extract from the Data Space the information which is needed to biomedical researchers and healthcare professionals to provide the patient with personalized medical aid.

The implementation of these information structures and services will enable wider *in silico* investigation of drugs as well as accumulation and dissemination knowledge on clinical usage of drugs. This will result in expanding and strengthening of information base of evidence-based medicine and evidence-based pharmacology which will promote medical errors risk reducing and healthcare efficiency increasing. There are two known technologies which provide us with keys to achieve these goals – XML and multi-agent system technologies.

3   Meta-Models for Accumulating Data of Clinical Usage of Drugs

Clinical experience of drugs usage is accumulating in numerous information sources all over the world. The high interest to this information is proved to be true by the fact that the www-site ClinicalTrials.gov receives over 12 million page views per month and hosts approximately 31,000 visitors daily [6].

The basic sources of clinical drug usage information are scientific journals, many of which are presented also in electronic versions and are accessible on the Web. There is also a lot of the very important information in databases of information systems of hospitals as well as in databases of pharmaceutical companies and universities. Sometimes, physicians and researchers can access these sources also while they participate in Virtual Organization (VO) carrying some biomedical project on. Structured accumulation and comprehensible representation of such information to physicians and pharmacists could advances the knowledge about all *pro* and *contra* in administering drugs to patients.

However, in actually existing electronic resources the accumulation and representation of these data is based on the information structures (Meta-models) which are indeed digital replicas of paper-based documents which delineate the content, structure and format of Summary Product Characteristics and Clinical Guidelines. Considering the latter we can see that there are already some standards of an XML-representation of this sort of documents [7], [8]. The ASTM E2210-02 is standard is a result of the <GEM> - project [9] and serves at present as the solid basement of information support of evidence-based medicine. The same time there is no such a standard in evidence-based pharmacology yet despite considerable amount of papers dedicated to XML-representation of pharmaceutical information. The Structured Product Labeling Standard [8] is not quite adequate for this purpose in our opinion because if is based mainly on a list of *pro forma* headings. This structure is well suited to integrate the final information on drug properties in order to produce a Drug Application to FDA, for example. For goals of the evidence-based pharmacology the scheme of data accumulation of clinical usages of a drug should provide flexible and extendable all-round description of the drug as well as the ability to use this description by different services – data search, information integration and representation to users and so on. We suppose that these data should be accumulating as collections of digital Information Objects (IO) using the Repository of Meta-Descriptions (RMD) [10]. In this way the advantages of Service-Oriented Architecture and the OGSA-DAI could be used to provide transparency of Data Space for both users and mentioned software services.

Considering FP7 schedule related to Information Technology applications in the Health Care [11] the most valuable goals of it are Risk Assessment and Patient Safety, including Adverse Drug Events (3.5 Challenge 5: Towards sustainable and personalized healthcare Objective ICT-2007.5.2). Taking this into account we chose the following set of terms (concepts) used as key tag names in XML-descriptions of clinical usage of drugs:

– Drug Name – defines to what the definite drug the clinical practice information is related which is stored in the IO;
– Adverse Event – defines to what the definite adverse event of the drug clinical usage the information is related which is stored in the IO;
– Risk Factor – defines what the definite sort of reasons of risk is related to the adverse event described in the clinical practice information stored in the IO;
– Risk Probability – defines the block of data which represent in figures the dependences between the probability of the risk of the adverse event and patient data.
– Patient Data – defines the block of data which represent facts about patient parameters which correlated to the risk factor (age, weight, arterial pressure, concurrent pathology, etc.).

The most appropriate base of this scheme is an XML-representation of information structures which arrange semantic relations of data and metadata on drugs. Usually, the XML-descriptions such sort of include numerous tags which are defined in a correspondent DTD [12]. In this paper we consider a limited example that shows mentioned five basic elements that form the core of an IO and which are needed for services of search, analysis and integration of loosely-coupled data in order to take information of Data Space. Namely, we mean here the information that is needed for a biomedical researcher to advance SPL and for a physician to make decision about drug therapy tactics taking into account possible adverse events.

The Fig. 1 shows an XML-structure (Meta-model) which forms a core of an IO in which drug clinical usage data could be stored in RMD. This Meta-model of data storing allows integrating numerous data from different information sources expanding the IO by adding new data structured by tags. The same time this Meta-model allows the semantic search by software services through all IOs which are stored in RMD. We do not fix intentionally the list of tags of possible types of patient data like age, weight, arterial pressure and so on because it is a subject of expansion and besides, there is the problem of different languages which can be solved by using data semantics.

```
<Drug Name>
        <Adverse Event>
             <Risk Factor >
                  <Risk Probability >
                  <Patient Data>
                       ...
                  </Patient Data >
             </Risk Probability >
             </Risk Factor >
        </Adverse Event>
     <URI > http://www....  </URI >
     </Drug Name>
```

Fig. 1. The Meta-model of a description of a drug adverse event risk factor

The Fig. 2 shows an example of the IO that includes multi-parameter data which are found in an analysis of several scientific papers dedicated to age related risk investigation by antithrombosis therapy by using warfarin. The IO on Fig. 2 includes patient data as well as the probability of the risk of hemorrhagic complications different sort of which related to clinical application of warfarin.

The example on Fig. 2 demonstrates abilities of XML-technology and Meta-model presented on Fig. 1 for creating meta-description of semantically linked data which is suitable for automated processing by software services in order to search, integrate and filter data as well as represent data to a user in a comprehensible way. To provide this information processing we need a multitude of appropriate software services. These services should be intellectual enough to process semantics of data. Besides, the set of services should provide interaction with distributed heterogeneous information warehouses with different internal structures because the Data Space has essential intrinsic heterogeneity. To achieve this we use the Grid technology, namely OGSA-DAI and Intermediate services of data management [10].

At last, it is preferable that the different services would be quite intellectual and could interact while processing the same piece of information. Fortunately, there is

```
<Drug Name> warfarin
    <Adverse Event> Hemorrhagic stroke

<Risk Factor> Age <Risk Probability> 40%
<Patient Data> over 70 </Patient Data>
</Risk Probability> </Risk Factor>

<Risk Factor> Arterial Hypertension
    <Risk Probability> 50%
<Patient Data> over 180 Hg mm </Patient Data>
    </Risk Probability> </Risk Factor>

</Adverse Event><URI> http://www.... </URI>
</Drug Name>
```

Fig. 2. The multi-parameter XML-structure of the description of possible adverse drug event

already for our service the quite well developed subject area – multi-agent systems technology.

4 Multi-agent Services of Evidence-Based Medicine in the Grid

The huge amount of data distributed across the global network requires simultaneously acting intellectual tools for automated search, accumulation and primary analysis of data which are being collected to provide a response of a query to Data Space and which should fill information structures of IOs with facts. Another side of the problem originates in the mentioned heterogeneity of information sources. Grid-technology provides us with new abilities that are impossible in the networks which are built using peer-to-peer and client-server technology. That is the ability of full-scale implementation of the technology of the multi-agent systems. The roles of intellectual agents are played here by web- and grid-services. The latter are preferable here due to a number of serious advantages besides web-services.

The first advantage is an ability to use as intellectual agents the grid-services that provide data search functionality which are not restricted by a set of procedures implemented in the data warehouse server. Such a possibility could be provided on any resource that is a part of the grid segment accessible to appropriate virtual organization. From a user's point of view (and also for the RMD service) this ability allows to virtualize the data search service. In addition, for high logical level of the information system the application of the OGSA-DAI services allows to hide where and by which services namely the data was found and collected.

Considering clinical data processing the second advantage of grid-technology is an ability to delegate data access rights from the user to the full sequence of grid-services by using the digital certificate. In this way data access rights are under permanent control in the process of the search and accumulation of data by any grid-service that is started in order to perform a part of the user query. It is very important for any e-Health application due to the very high sensibility of the most of biomedical data [13].

The third advantage of grid-technology is an ability to perform search in the Data Space and to accumulate data by grid-services which could run in the Grid environment even after they had fulfilled the initial user query. The query parameters are being stored in the RMD, besides, the Data Space content permanently increases and actualizes. Hence, in case of presence of appropriate grid-resources (computational power and data warehouse access) the grid-services – intellectual agents of data searching and collecting are able to continue to increase and actualize the knowledge which was constructed in the process of the initial query performing. In this process all access rights are kept (both to data and to computational resources) that have been defined by digital certificates of these services while the query semantic is defined by an ontology which was a base by the query construction and response representation and which was stored in RMD.

At last, we should say that the Grid provides computational power of all cyber-resources of the VO. There is permanent need to apply more and more complicate algorithms, which are used to process primary medical data (e.g., X-ray or ultrasound images) and extended metadata in order to find implicit signs of pathologic processes. Virtualization of computational resources of the VO enables possibility to run data-intensive applications not only at the place where data are stored but at any most powerful computer of VO which is not loaded enough.

It is important that data and metadata which have been accumulated are accessible not only to primary users – physicians and pharmacists, but also to other participants of the VO, namely to specialists in knowledge management. These experts by using the same set of services are able (and are in duty) to check consistency of information as well as produce more adequate formalization of accumulated meta-descriptions (ontologies and metadata). The wide usage of the Grid technology allows the implementation of self-developing information infrastructure that is aimed to provide actual and complete biomedical information which is needed to personalize the healthcare process.

5 Clinical Data Management Services of the Russian ChemBioGrid

In order to provide powerful information support in the research on new vaccines development, including *in silico* investigations, several grid-services have been created and implemented in the environment of Russian ChemBioGrid and are now accessible to users to operate with loosely coupled Data Space:

- The service of constructing of information structure of queries to search data in the Data Space of loosely linked data.
- The services of the data search and aggregation, with ability to access data from warehouses outside the VO resources. These services allow constructing a snapshot all over linked data in accordance with criteria of data filtration and aggregation.

- The services of data filtration, which are able to use semantic criteria in order to grasp from the Data Space the information needed for the user.
- The services of semantic linking of data. These services allow to find links between data and to arrange these links in a formal way, thus forming integrated XML-structures which are being represented to users in the form of subject-oriented ontologies.
- The services of data representation to users. These services allow representing structured data in various form providing different levels of comprehensibility.

The services can be organized into some compositions to provide complex solutions of the information support. It is provided in Russian ChemBioGrid by the implementation of the mentioned above services on base of multi-purposed Intermediate services which have been developed early – services of RMD, ontology and data collections [10]. Information Objects, which describe links between drug clinical application, adverse event risks and patient (population) parameters, are being formed in the RMD as data collections indeed by using the following:

- Service of Repository of Meta-Descriptions;
- Services of data search in loosely coupled Data Space, which use intellectual multi-agent system technology;
- Services of the lexical text analyses that take out drug clinical usage data from plain texts following criteria which are set by users, e.g., patient data related with risk factor for a definite drug.

To represent the complicate structured information, which is full of numerous semantic links, the GUI of Ontology Services is used that was developed early [14].

6 Conclusion

XML-technology provides powerful possibilities to manage implicitly structured data distributed in Data Space. Grid-technology provides operational integrity of heterogeneous distributed cyber-resources and enables the possibility to use advancements of multi-agent technology to develop and deploy sets of intellectual services which should perform search, primary analysis and integration of dispersed data. This couple of technologies constitutes an environment which we should fill up with appropriate web/grid-services and XML-based information structures to provide the new level of information support in e-Health.

XML-structures and grid-services that are developed in Russian ChemBioGrid to provide information support of scientific investigation of new vaccines can also serve as effective tools to search, collect and represent information for evidence-based medicine and evidence-based pharmacology. The usage of the most actual, complete, detailed and comprehensible-represented biomedical information will enable more personalized care solutions and higher patient safety by optimizing medical interventions and preventing errors.

References

1. e-Health - making healthcare better for European citizens: An action plan for a European e-Health Area. SEC(2004)539. Communication from the Commission to the Council, the European Parliament, the European economic and social Committee and the Committee of the regions. COM-2004/356 final. Commission of the European Communities, Brussels (2004)
2. Good pharmacy practice (GPP) in community and hospital pharmacy settings. Geneva, WHO, WHO/PHARM/DAP/96.1 (1996)
3. Good pharmacy practice in Europe. Pharmaceutical Group of the European Union PGEU, Community pharmacists (1998)
4. Peitsch, M.C., et al.: Informatics and Knowledge Management at the Novartis Institutes for BioMedical Research. SCIP-online 46, 1–4 (2004)
5. Franklin, M., Halevy, A., Maier, D.: From databases to dataspaces: a new abstraction for information management. ACM SIGMOD Record 34(4), 27–33 (2005)
6. ClinicalTrials.gov: A service of the U.S. National Institutes of Health, U.S. National Library of Medicine, http://clinicaltrials.gov
7. ASTM E2210-02. Standard Specification for Guideline Elements Model (GEM)-Document Model for Clinical Practice Guidelines, http://www.astm.org
8. Structured Product Labeling. ANSI/HL7 SPL, R1.0-2004. HL7 ANSI-Approved Standards, http://www.hl7.org
9. <GEM> - Guideline Elements Model, http://gem.med.yale.edu
10. Zhuchkov, A., et al.: Advancing of Russian ChemBioGrid by bringing Data Management tools into collaborative environment. In: Hernandes, V., et al. (eds.) Challenges and Opportunities of HealthGrids. Studies in Health Technology and Informatics, vol. 120, pp. 179–186. IOS Press, Amsterdam (2006)
11. Seventh Research Framework Programme. FP7-ICT-2007-1. European Commission, Brussels (2006)
12. ASTM E2183, -02. Standard Guide for XML DTD Design, Architecture and Implementation, http://www.astm.org
13. Breton, V., et al.: The Healthgrid White Paper. In: Solomonides, T., et al. (eds.) From Grid to Healthgrid. Studies in Health Technology and Informatics, vol. 112, pp. 249–321. IOS Press, Amsterdam (2005)
14. Joutchkov, A., et al.: Grid-based Onto-Tecnologies provide an effective instrument for Biomedical research. In: Solomonides, T., et al. (eds.) From Grid to Healthgrid. Studies in Health Technology and Informatics, vol. 112, pp. 37–46. IOS Press, Amsterdam (2005)

Fault Tolerance of Connectivity Performance in CDMA-Based Wireless Sensor Networks

Yung-Fa Huang[1], Ching-Mu Chen[2], Tsair-Rong Chen[2],
Jong-Shin Chen[1], and John Sum[3]

[1] Graduate Institute of Network and Communication Engineering
Chaoyang University of Technology,
Taichung County 41349, Taiwan, R.O.C.
yfahuang@mail.cyut.edu.tw
[2] Department of Electrical Engineering
National Changhua University of Education
Changhua County 500, Taiwan, R.O.C.
abc@abc.ncue.edu.tw
[3] Institute of Electronic Commerce, National Chung Hsing University
Taichung 401, Taiwan, R.O.C.
pfsum@csmu.edu.tw

Abstract. In this paper, we investigate the fault tolerance of connectivity probability for CDMA-based wireless sensor networks with variations of nodes deployment. The variations of deployment are modeled by 2D Gaussian distribution with zero-mean for the triangle, grid and hexagon topologies. Thus, the k-connectivity performance is studied through the outage probability of CDMA signal links. We evaluate the connectivity performance with $SIR_{0,3\text{-con}}$, the minimum requirement of SIR, SIR_0 for the 3-connectivity, when the nodes suffer a failure rate P_f. Simulation results show that the hexagonal and grid topologies suffer a degradation of -2.4 and -0.5 dB, respectively, when the failure rate P_f equals 0.1. However, the triangular topology shows robust fault tolerance with the failure rate P_f below 0.5 and moderate variations of deployment.

1 Introduction

The wireless sensor networks (WSN) consisted of many tiny nodes with sensing, storing and communicating capability have recently emerged as a hot research topic [1]. In the WSN, the data is collected by spreading the sensing nodes into a wide area, then the routing to the sink by multi-hop communications [2]. The code-division multiple-access (CDMA) technology is adopted to perform the 3G mobile communication systems with its high capacity potentials [3]. In CDMA systems, the spreading spectrum is performed to anti-interference. However, the multiple access interference (MAI) degrades the BER performance of multiuser environments [3].

In WSN, the deployment of sensor nodes is an important topic. The proper deployment can make good connectivity and high coverage in the area [4]. Thus, the connectivity performance of WSN obtains large attention [4-5]. In order to cover the entire area, three network topologies, hexagon, grid and triangle, have been proposed in [6] and then the performance with fixed deployment is investigated. However, in

P. Thulasiraman et al. (Eds.): ISPA 2007 Workshops, LNCS 4743, pp. 444–454, 2007.

practical, the fixed node deployment is not easy. Contrarily, there exists some variations in node deployment. Therefore, the connectivity performance of different topologies with deployment variations was investigated in previous works [7]. However, the sensor nodes deployed in the adverse or inaccessible circumstances could be easily destroyed or out of order to be failure. Thus, how to remain the network connectivity even in fault-induced environments is an important issue [8-9]. Therefore, in fault-induced environments, the fault tolerance performance which to keep the WSN 3-connectivity with the deployment variations will be studied in this paper.

2 Network Models

In [6], three topologies are compared with fixed deployment. For easy analysis, the distance between the nodes is set to be constant in [6]. However, for cost fairness, we set the constant node density for three topologies. Thus the distance between the nodes are different with each other. It is easy to know that the nodes' distance of hexagon is the shortest, then grid. The nodes' distance of triangle is the longest. There are 3, 4 and 6 shortest links for hexagon, grid and triangle, respectively.

Due to the obstacles or the placement methods, the deployed node position is difficult to be fixed. Moreover, to be generalized and simplified, the position variation of deployment is modeled as zero-mean Gaussian distribution [10]. Thus, the distribution function of the position of the n-th node can be expressed by

$$Z_n(x_n, y_n) = \frac{1}{2\pi\sigma_x\sigma_y} \times \exp\left\{-\frac{1}{2}\left(\frac{\left(x_n - \eta_{x_n}\right)^2}{\sigma_x^2} + \frac{\left(y_n - \eta_{y_n}\right)^2}{\sigma_y^2}\right)\right\},\qquad(1)$$

where x_n and y_n are the disjoint x-axis and y-axis random variables for the n-th node respectively, η_{x_n} and η_{y_n} are the x-axis and y-axis of the n-th node of the fixed topology respectively. The parameters σ_x^2 and σ_y^2 are the variance of x-axis and y-axis of node deployment respectively. In different topologies, the distances between the nodes are not equal. Hence, to compare the performance of topologies, we define the normalized standard deviation of deployment variation in WSN as

$$\sigma_N = \frac{\sigma_t}{d_t},\qquad(2)$$

where σ_t is the standard deviation of deployment variation of the topology in WSN, and d_t is the distance between the nodes of the fixed deployment topology.

When we consider the network connectivity for the fixed deployment topology, it is easy to know that there are 6, 4 and 3 available links for the triangle, grid and hexagon topologies respectively with sufficient transmitting power in the links. However, when the distance is varied, the available links of each node could be less than 3. Then some nodes become isolated as shown in Fig. 1(a). If we increase the transmitting power, the links can increase to 3 or above. Then, the network can reach well connectivity performance as shown in Fig. 1(b).

In wireless communication channels, the transmitting signals suffer fading effects due to the multipath propagation. For simplicity, with assuming the stationary systems, the short-term fading and shadow fading are ignored. Thus the received signal strength is defined by the path loss of channels as

$$P_r = c \frac{P_t}{d^\alpha},$$

(3)

where d is the distance between the transmitter and receiver, P_t is the transmitting power of transmitter and c is the propagation coefficient. The attenuation exponent α is between 2 and 6 [7]. We assumed in free space, then $\alpha = 2$. That is, the consumed communication power is proportional to d^2. In this paper, the simulation area of WSNs is set to a rectangular area as in [7]. However, to be equally densely deployed for different topologies, the distances between nodes are set 26.4 m, 25 m and 21.486 m for triangle, grid and hexagon topologies respectively.

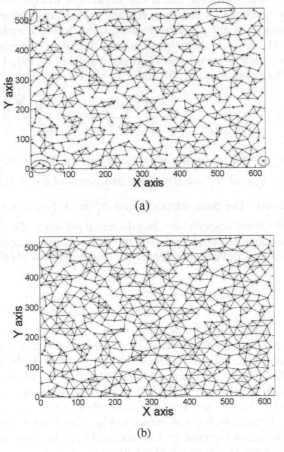

(a)

(b)

Fig. 1. The connectivity performance of networks: (a) poor (b) well

3 Connectivity Performance

In wireless CDMA systems, the MAIs limit the signal capacity of the links. That is, with the design on the length of spreading code, the link is qualified based on the signal-to-interference ratio (SIR) defined by

$$SIR = 10\log_{10}\frac{P_r}{P_i} \text{ (dB)}, \tag{4}$$

where P_r is the received signal strength at receiver, P_i is the interfering power at receiver. We can design the spreading codes to perform a minimum required SIR, SIR_0. When SIR of the link is lower than SIR_0, the link's signal strength is too weak to suppress the MAIs. Then the link suffers failure. We give the probability of outage by

$$P_{outage} = P[SIR < SIR_0], \tag{5}$$

The connectivity probability of networks is defined by the probability of k-connectivity P_{k-con} [5] as

$$P_{k-con} = 1 - P_{k-outage}, \tag{6}$$

where $P_{k-outage}$ is the outage probability of the k-th high SIR link. Then, P_{k-con} expresses the probability of that there are more links than k links in the networks. Moreover, we define that the network performs k-connectivity when

$$P_{k-con} \geq 0.99. \tag{7}$$

To investigate the fault tolerant performance of network connectivity, we set the node failure rate P_f by 0.1, 0.3 and 0.5 which is uniformly distributed in the sensing area.

4 Simulation Results and Discussions

In the simulation, we performed the varied topologies with σN =0.05 and 0.07 respectively. The received signal strength and the MAIs are compared for the topologies. The simulation area are placed an area A. We deployed 576, 572 and 578 sensor nodes in the triangle, grid and hexagon fixed topologies, respectively. For generalization, we compute the results of inner nodes, 371, 320 and 350 nodes for triangle, grid and hexagon fixed topologies, respectively. Then, for simplicity, we assumed that Pt=20dBm, c=1 m2/mW and A=350000 m2. We neglected the MAIs from the areas where the distance is more far than 56 meters due to the negligible interference comparing to the near area.

Since the k-connectivity performance P_{k-con} of the networks should be on $k \geq 3$, we let $P_{3-con} > 0.99$. In other words, the number of connectable links should be 3 or more [5]. Therefore, in this paper the three strongest links, L_1, L_2 and L_3 of the nodes is focused in our investigation. Moreover, the normalized variance σ_N is set 0.05 and 0.7, which are corresponding to the scales of 1 and 1.5m, respectively.

448   Y.-F. Huang et al.

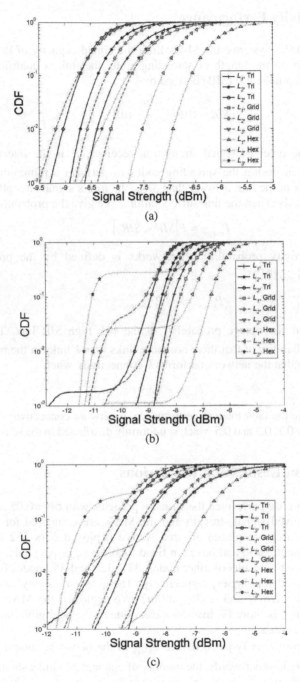

(a)

(b)

(c)

Fig. 2. Comparisons of the RSS of three strongest links for three topologies with the normalized variation σ_N =0.05 for different failure rate (a) no failure (b)P_f=0.1, σ_N =0.05 (c)P_f=0.1, σ_N =0.07

In Fig. 2, we compare the cumulative distribution functions (CDF) of the RSS of the nodes for three topologies with deployment variation and different failure rates. From Fig. 2(a) of no failure, it is observed that with σ_N =0.05 the RSS of three links in hexagon (Hex) is stronger than that of both grid and triangle (Tri) due to its shortest distance between the neighbor nodes. Similarly, the RSS of L_1 and L_2 in grid is stronger than that of triangle. However, the RSS of L_3 in grid is weaker than that of triangle. The reason is that the number of links in triangle is six which is more than the four in grid. Then the probability of the distance between the nodes becoming closer is higher than that of grid. Moreover, when parts of nodes suffer failure, then the RSS of three links in three topologies would suffer degradations as shown in Figs. 2.(b)-(c). In a slight failure rate P_f=0.1, the third strongest link of hexagon is degraded first and the most severe as shown in Fig. 2(b). Then, the third strongest link of grid suffers and then the second strongest link of hexagon is the next one. The last sufferer, the third strongest link of triangle is afflicted comparatively minor. However, in a moderate failure rate P_f=0.3 to 0.5, both the third strongest links of grid and triangle topologies suffer more than that of hexagon due to the shorter distance between nodes as shown in Fig. 2(c).

The CDF of the power of interference (MAI) of the nodes for different topologies can be obtained and compared in Fig. 3. From Figs. 3(a) and 3(b), for the first two strongest links, L1 and L2, with different failure rate and variation of σN =0.05, among the three topologies the power of MAIs in Tri is strongest and the weakest is in Hex. However, for the third strongest links, L3, among the three topologies the power of MAIs in Hex becomes higher than that of Grid for failure rate P_f =0.1 and is the strongest for failure rate P_f =0.3, 0.5 as shown in Fig. 3(a). Moreover, with the larger the variation of σ_N =0.07, for the third strongest links, L_3, among the three topologies the power of MAIs in Hex is the strongest no matter which failure rate P_f =0.1, 0.3 or 0.5 as shown in Fig. 3(b).

Fig. 4 shows the CDFs of SIR of the three strongest links L_1, L_2 and L_3 of the nodes for different topologies with variation σ_N = 0.05 and 0.07. From Fig. 4(a), it can be observed that with P_f =0.1 the third strongest link of hexagon topology exhibits the worst link quality due the most fragile with only three neighbor node in hexagon topology. While both the third strongest link of Tri and Grid topologies exhibit fault tolerance with P_f =0.1 as shown in Fig. 4(a). However, when the failure rate increases by P_f =0.5, the SIR of the third strongest link of Tri topology is degraded more than the other two topologies due its most severe MAI. Moreover, when the failure rate increases to P_f =0.5, the link quality of the third strongest link of Grid topology is degraded to slightly better than the other two as shown in Fig. 4(b). Besides, from the results with higher variations of σ_N =0.07 as shown in Fig. 4(c), it can be observed that the hexagon topology still exhibits worst link quality of L_3 and L_2 than both triangle and grid topologies with moderate failure rates P_f=0.3.

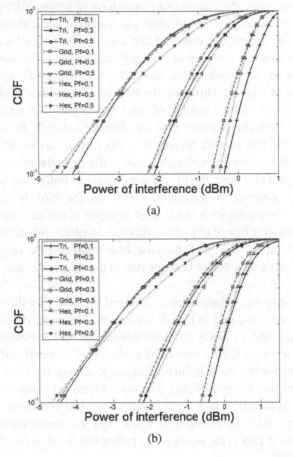

(a)

(b)

Fig. 3. The comparison of CDF of the power of MAIs of the nodes for different topologies with variations: (a) σ_N =0.05, (b) σ_N =0.07

In order to easily find the SIR_0 performed the network 3-connectivity, $SIR_{0,3\text{-con}}$, we transfer the CDFs of SIR of the links to the $P_{k\text{-con}}$ for k=1,2 and 3 in fault environments as shown in Fig. 5. Moreover, in CDMA systems the longer PN sequence obtains higher processing gain and suppresses MAIs. If the minimum SIR requirement SIR_0 is obtained, the useful length of PN codes can be designed to perform required network connectivity. Thus, the connectivity performance in deployment variation is investigated. We depicted the comparison for the three topologies as shown in Fig. 5.

When the variation is small with σ_N=0.05 and the failure rate is minor with P_f=0.1 as shown in Fig. 5(a), the SIR_0 to reach 3-connectivity is -11.4, -10 and -9.8dB for hexagon, grid and triangle topologies respectively. Moreover, when the failure rate increases to P_f=0.5 as shown in Fig. 5(b), the SIR_0 for the three topologies to reach 3-connectivity are almost the same and about -11dB.

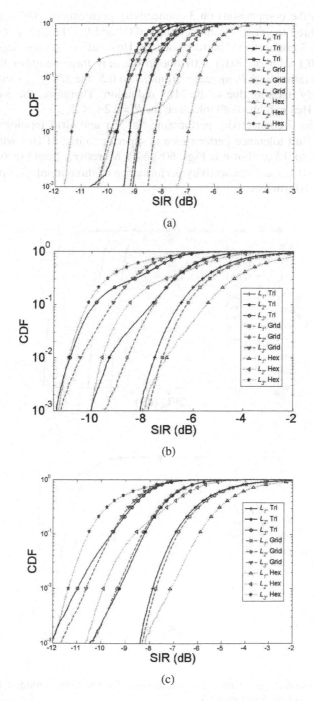

Fig. 4. The CDFs of SIR for the three strongest links in three different topologies with σ_N =0.05: (a) P_f=0.1 (b) P_f=0.5 and σ_N =0.07: (c) P_f=0.3.

Fig. 6 shows the comparisons on 3-connectivity performance $SIR_{0,3\text{-con}}$ vs. failure rate P_f for the three topologies with σ_N =0.05, 0.07 and 0.1. From Fig. 6(a), it is observed that the 3-connectivity performance of Hex suffers severe degradation for failure rate P_f=0.1 with σ_N =0.05, 0.07 due to the only three neighbor links in Hex. However, when failure rate P_f increases from 0.1 to 0.5, the $SIR_{0,3\text{-con}}$ seem not falling down but slightly uprising due to the MAI reduction. Therefore, the 3-connectivity performance of Hex exhibits fault tolerance for P_f =0.2 to 0.5.

As regards the 3-connectivity performance of Tri and Grid topologies, it is observed that the fault tolerance performance is superior to that of Hex with σ_N =0.05, 0.07 and P_f =0.1 to 0.5 as shown in Figs. 6(b)-6(c). Moreover, from Fig. 6, with larger variation of σ_N =0.1, the 3-connectivity performance of three topologies possess good fault tolerance performance.

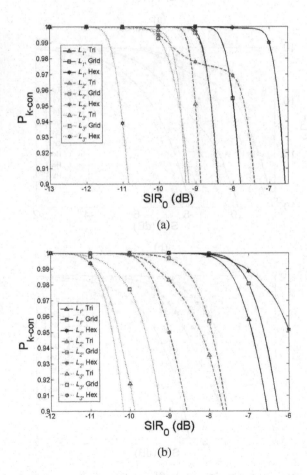

(a)

(b)

Fig. 5. The comparison on connectivity performance for the three strongest links with σ_N =0.05: (a) P_f=0.1 (b) P_f=0.5 and σ_N =0.07

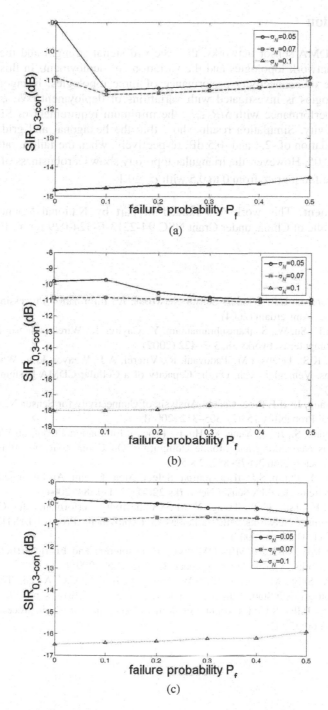

Fig. 6. The comparison on fault tolerance of 3-connectivity with $SNR_{0,3\text{-con}}$ for (a)Hex, (b)Tri, (c) Grid topologies with σ_N =0.05

5 Conclusion

In wireless CDMA sensor networks, the received signal strength and the MAIs depend on the network topologies and the variations of deployment. In this paper, the fault tolerance of connectivity performance of three topologies, hexagon, grid and triangle topologies is investigated with variations of deployment. We evaluate the connectivity performance with $SIR_{0.3\text{-con}}$, the minimum requirement of SIR, SIR_0 for the 3-connectivity. Simulation results show that the hexagonal and grid topologies suffer a degradation of -2.4 and -0.5 dB, respectively, when the failure rate from 0 to 0.1 with $\sigma_N = 0.05$. However, the triangular topology shows a robustness of fault tolerance, when the failure rate from 0 to 0.5 with $\sigma_N \le 0.1$.

Acknowledgment. This work was funded in part by National Science Council, Taiwan, Republic of China, under Grant NSC 94-2213-E-324-029 for Y.-F. Huang.

References

1. Zhao, F., Guibas, L.J.: Wireless Sensor Networks. An Information Processing Approach. Elsevier Inc., Amsterdam (2004)
2. Akyildiz, I.F., Su, W., Sankarasubramaniam, Y., Cayirci, E.: Wireless Sensor Networks. A Survey, Computer Networks 38, 393–422 (2002)
3. Gilhousen, K.S., Jacobs, I.M., Padovani, R., Viterbi, A.J., Weaver, L.A., Wheatley, C.E.: IEEE Trans. Vehicular Tech. On the Capacity of a Cellular CDMA System 40(2), 303–312 (1991)
4. Jia, W., Wang, J.: IEE Proc.-Comm. Analysis of Connectivity for Sensor Networks Using Geometrical Probability 153(2), 305–312 (2006)
5. Liu, K., Wang, S., Ji, Y., Yang, X., Hu, F.: Proc. of International Conf. on Wireless Communications Networking and Mobile Computing. On Connectivity for Wireless Sensor Networks Localization 2, 879–882 (2005)
6. Chatterjee, M., Philip, S.J.: IEEE Journal Select. Areas Comm. An Integrated Cross-layer Study of Wireless CDMA Sensor Networks 22(7), 1271–1284 (2004)
7. Huang, Y.-F., Tsai, C.-C, Tseng, Y.-M.: Connectivity Performance for CDMA-based Wireless Sensor Networks with Variations of Deployment. Proc. of IASTED AsiaCSN 2007. Phuket, Thailand (2007)
8. Liang, Q.: Proc. of IEEE MILCOM 2005. Fault-tolerant and Energy Efficient Wireless Sensor Networks: A Cross-layer Approach 3, 1862–1868 (2005)
9. Khadivi, A., Shiva, M.: Proc. of IEEE WiMob'2006. In: FTPASC: A Fault Tolerant Power Aware Protocol with Static Clustering for Wireless Sensor Networks, pp. 397–401 (2006)
10. Papoulis, A., Pillai, S.U.: Probability, random variables and stochastic processes. McGraw Hill, New York (2002)

Lifetime Performance of an Energy Efficient Clustering Algorithm for Cluster-Based Wireless Sensor Networks

Yung-Fa Huang[1], Wun-He Luo[1], John Sum[2],
Lin-Huang Chang[3], Chih-Wei Chang[1], and Rung-Ching Chen[4]

[1] Graduate Institute of Networking and Communication Engineering
Chaoyang University of Technology, Taichung 41349, Taiwan
yfahuang@cyut.edu.tw
[2] Department of Information Management
Chung Shan Medical University, Taichung 405, Taiwan
pfsum@csmu.edu.tw
[3] Graduate Institute of Networking and Communication Engineering
Chaoyang University of Technology, Taichung 41349, Taiwan
lchang@mail.cyut.edu.tw
[4] Department of Information Management
Chaoyang University of Technology, Taichung 41349, Taiwan
crching@cyut.edu.tw

Abstract. This paper proposes a fixed clustering algorithm (FCA) to improve energy efficiency for wireless sensor networks (WSNs). In order to reduce the consuming energy of sending data at each sensor, the proposed algorithm uniformly divides the sensing area into clusters where the cluster head is deployed in the center of the cluster area. Simulation results show that the proposed algorithm definitely reduces the energy consumption of the sensors and extends the lifetime of the networks nearly more 80% compared to the random clustering (RC).

1 Introduction

Recently, the rapidly developed technologies of microelectro-mechanical systems and telecommunication battery make the small sensors comprise the capabilities of wireless communication and data processing [1]. These small sensors could be used as the surveillance and the control capability under a certain environment. Specially, the location of wireless sensor network (WSN) could be a region where people could not easily reach and there is a difficulty to recharge the device energy. Therefore, the energy efficiency of the sensor networks is an important research topic and the lifetime of WSNs could be considered as the most significant performance in the WSN [2]. Moreover, there are two main issues in the lifetime prolong problems. One is to minimize the energy dissipation for all energy constrained nodes. The other one is to balance the energy dissipation of all nodes [2].

The energy in WSN is mainly consuming on the direct data transmission [2]. Firstly, each sensor collects data and delivers the data to the base station directly, called as "sink". Applying this mode, the sensor will have quick energy exhaustion if

P. Thulasiraman et al. (Eds.): ISPA 2007 Workshops, LNCS 4743, pp. 455–464, 2007.

it is apart from the base station. Thus, this kind transmission scheme is not suitable in a large area [2]. Then, secondly, to enable communication between sensors not within each other's communication range, the common multi-hop routing protocol is applied in the ad hoc wireless sensors communication networks [3]-[5]. In this scheme, several multi-hop paths exist to perform the network connectivity. Each path in the configuration will have one link head to collects data from sensors.

Every sensor node in the WSN sends both the sensing data of itself and the receiving data from previous nodes to its closer node. Then, the destination node delivers the data collection in the path to the base station [4]. The nodes closer to the base station need more energy [4] to send data because the scheme uses hierarchy transmission. However, due the highly complexity in routing protocols and the most likely heavy load on the relaying nodes, this scheme is not suitable for the highly densely WSNs.

The third scheme is the cluster-based one that those closer sensors belong to their own clusters. One of sensors, called "cluster head," in each cluster is responsible for delivering data back to the base station. In this scheme, the cluster head performs data compressing and sending back to the base station. Thus, the lifetime of cluster head may be shorter than that of other sensors [5-7]. Therefore, for WSNs with a large number of energy-constrained sensors, it is very important to design an algorithm to organize sensors in clusters to minimize the energy used to communicate information from all nodes to the base station. Moreover, if the cluster head has more energy, the cluster can prolong the life time. Therefore, in this paper, we would like to propose a fast, centralized algorithm for organizing the sensors in a wireless sensor network into clusters with an objective of minimizing the energy dissipated in communicating the information to the cluster head and prolong the lifetime of the WSN. Furthermore, the energy efficiency of heterogeneous networks with different amount energy at the normal sensors and cluster heads is investigated in this paper.

2 Network Models

In practical, the geometry of the WSN is non-regular. However, the square is a basic area to be consisted of non-regular area. Thus, for simplification, in this paper we adopt a square area with the length D. The sensor area is with a uniformly distributed cluster heads and is shown in Fig. 1. In Fig. 1, the symbol "+" is represented as a location of cluster head whereas the symbol "o" is represented as a location of the sensing node. When the cluster area is of random distributed, the energy efficiency of sensor nodes on data transmitting is terrible [3]. Therefore, the FCA is proposed to divide the sensor area into clusters and to deploy cluster heads uniformly over the network area. Based on the configuration of square area, the sensors are supposed to be spread out uniformly to the whole area. The data from each cluster will be collected by the cluster head and these data will be sent back to the base station located at the point $(0, -B)$.

In wireless communication, the channel models are modeled by

$$P_r = c \frac{P_t}{d^\alpha},$$

(1)

where P_r and P_t are the received power at receiver and the transmitted power at transmitter respectively, c is the propagation coefficient, and α is the path loss exponent, $2 \leq \alpha < 6$. For s free space area, the path loss exponent is set by $\alpha = 2$. The location of the nodes is assumed to be known to base station by GPS.

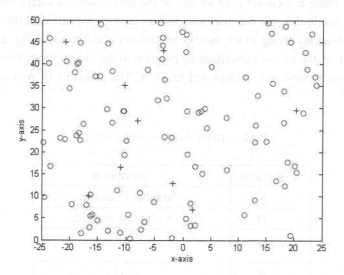

Fig. 1. Random clustering deployment sensor network

In Mac layer, the sensing nodes are assumed to know the belonging cluster head by centralized based station broadcasting. Based on the configuration of square area, Fig. 1 shows the investigated environment in this paper. In Fig. 1, the total Q sensors are supposed to be spread out uniformly to the whole area where is divided into q clusters. The data from each cluster will be collected by the cluster head and these data will be sent back to the base station located at the point $(0, -B)$.

To evaluate the lifetime of the network, one round is defined as a cycle in which the base station receives data from the sensor node. In one round, it contains the time from the data collected at sensor to the corresponding cluster head and the time from the cluster head to the base station.

Thus, the total energy of networks in one round can be expressed by

$$E_T = \sum_{i=1}^{q} \left(\eta_i \cdot E_{ch,i} \cdot \frac{Q}{q} \right) + \sum_{j=1}^{Q-q} E_{n,j} \tag{2}$$

where η_i is a data compressing factor for the ith cluster with $0 < \eta_i < 1$, $E_{ch,i}$ and $E_{n,j}$ are the transmission energy of one packet for the ith cluster head and the jth normal sensor, respectively. Moreover, the dissipation energy of nodes depends on the path loss.

3 Fixed Clustering Algorithm

In order to minimize the energy dissipation of the sensor nodes, an FCA is proposed to normalize the clustering region. The defined parameters for the FCA are depicted in Table 1. There is a cluster head located at the area centric of each clustering area. In order to divide the area into uniform clusters in size, we calculate the location of the cluster head according to the number of clusters q as shown in Fig. 2. In Fig. 2, $x(i)$ and $y(i)$ are the axis of corresponding position of the cluster head. Then, the fixed cluster sensor network can be deployed by FCA. The proposed FCA is described as followings.

Table 1. Definition of variables in FCA

Variable	Description
q	Number of clusters
D	Length of sensing area
p	$\sqrt{q}$
n	$\lceil p \rceil$
k	$\mathrm{mod}\left(\dfrac{q}{n}\right)$
s	$\left\lfloor \dfrac{q}{n} \right\rfloor$
l	$\dfrac{D_1(n-1)}{q}$

Class A: When the number of clusters equals to $p \times p$, that is, the clusters in row and those in column are the same. For example, when the number of clusters is equal to 9, the positions of the cluster heads exhibit a square matrix form by three-row and three-column.

Class B: Depending on the parameter k, if $k = 0$, the clustering is performed by Class B. Otherwise, Class C will be applied in the clustering. In Class B, the number of clusters are with 1×2, 2×3, 3×4, 4×5, ..., $M \times (M+1)$, $M \in \mathbb{N}$. The axes of cluster heads are obtained as shown in Fig. 2 by applying class B.

Class C: When the number of clusters does not fit in Class A or B, then the clustering algorithm is classified to class C. In Class C, we first compare the values between s and $(n-1)$. Then, there are two sub-classes C1 and C2 for the conditions $s<n-1$ and $s \geq n-1$, respectively, as shown in Fig. 2.

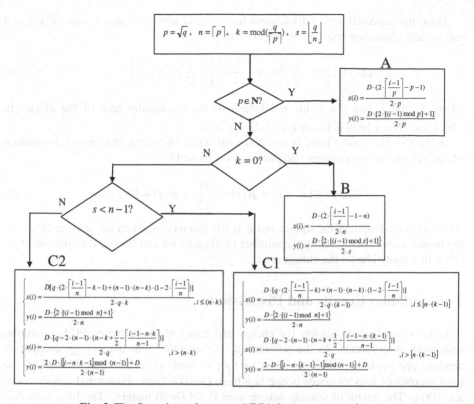

Fig. 2. The flow chart of proposed FCA for a square sensing area

In FCA, we assume that the sensor nodes are uniformly distributed in the area of the cluster. Therefore, the power dissipation of a cluster head to relay the information of the cluster in one round can be obtained by

$$E_{ch,i} = \eta_i \cdot e_l \cdot W_i \cdot \frac{Q}{q}, \qquad (3)$$

where e_l is the energy dissipation sending one packet per square meters, the energy dissipation due to the path loss of a distance between the ith cluster head and the base station is expressed by

$$W_i = d_i^\alpha/c = d_i^2 = x^2(i)+[y(i)+B]^2, \qquad (4)$$

where $a = 2$ and $c = 1$. Moreover, the energy dissipation for a sensor node to transmit one packet in a clustering area can be obtained by

$$E_{n,j} = e_l \cdot Z_j, \qquad (5)$$

where $Z_j = d_j^2$ is the random variable of the rectangular square of the distance between the jth normal sensor node and the cluster head of the cluster.

Thus, the expected power dissipation for a sensor node to transmit one packet in a rectangular clustering area can be obtained by

$$E[Z] = E\left[(x - \frac{L_1}{2})^2 + (y - \frac{L_2}{2})^2 \right] = \frac{1}{12}\left(L_1^2 + L_2^2 \right), \tag{6}$$

where L_1 and L_2 are the width and length of the rectangular area of the cluster in which the cluster head is located at $(L_1/2, L_2/2)$.

In the RC, the cluster head is selected randomly. Therefore, the energy dissipation of each cluster in transmitting one packet is expressed by

$$E[Z] = E[x^2 + (y + B)^2] = \frac{5D^2}{12} + B \cdot D + B^2, \tag{7}$$

where D is the length of the square and B is the distance between the sensing field and the base station. Therefore, by the number of clusters we can choose the suitable algorithm to equally cluster the cluster area.

4   Simulation Results and Discussions

In order to verify and compare the energy efficiency of the proposed FCA, a simulation work is presented. In the simulation, we assumed that the energy dissipation sending one packet by each sensor is $e_l = 5 \times 10^{-7}$ Joule (J)/m^2. In our simulation, the total number of sensors nodes is one hundred, $Q=100$. Then, the normal sensor nodes are 100-q. The length of sensing square area is set $D=50$ meters. The base station is deployed at $(0, -B) = (0, -10)$. To be generalization, the worst case in data fusion with data compressing factors for all clusters $\eta_i = 1$ is performed in the simulations.

Firstly, we compare the energy efficiency between the performance of the proposed FCA and the random clustering (RC) in which the cluster heads are randomly selected to perform clustering [3]. The performance of RC had been analyzed in [3]. Fig. 3 shows the energy consumption of one round vs. the number of clusters. It depicts that the consuming energy of the normal sensor nodes denoted by NS is getting less when number of clusters increases. The reason is that when cluster region gets smaller, the distance from sensor node to cluster head gets shorter. Contrarily, when the number of cluster increases, the energy consumed in cluster heads (CH) increases. Therefore, from Fig. 3, it is observed that the energy dissipation of proposed FCA is more efficient than that of the RC scheme with the number of cluster 1 <q<20.

We assumed that the life time is time duration of WSN working until the energy of any one node runs out. With the assumption of perfect energy distribution on the nodes and the total energy of all nodes $E_T = 100$J, Fig. 4 thus depicts the comparison of lifetime of WSN for FCA and RC. It is obvious that the lifetime with FCA is almost more 50% to 20% than that with RC while q is increased from 1 to 5. When the number of cluster increases, the lifetime with FCA is always longer than that of RC due to the energy efficiency of normal sensor nodes.

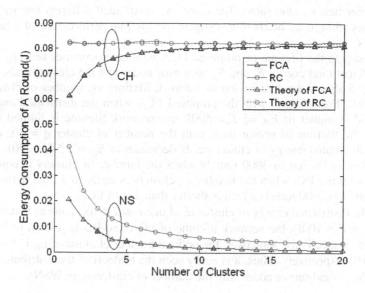

Fig. 3. Energy consummation in one round for FCA and RC

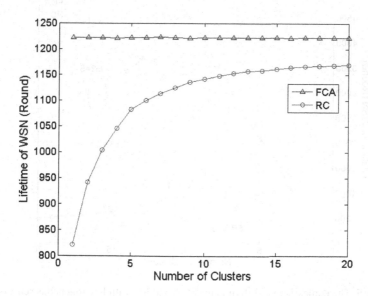

Fig. 4. Lifetime comparison of FCA and RC withop optimal energy distributed sensors

In Fig. 4, the network lifetime is evaluated based on perfect energy distribution for all sensor nodes and cluster heads. In reality, the distributed energy for every sensor node is almost the same. Moreover, when number of cluster is small ($q<10$), cluster head should be distributed more energy in order to send more data. Similarly, energy for all cluster heads is the same. Therefore, we distributed different energy to both sensor nodes and cluster heads to investigate the lifetime performance of a heterogeneous WSN.

To investigate the lifetime of proposed FCA with heterogeneous sensors, we distribute different total energy E_n and E_{ch} to sensor nodes and the cluster heads, respectively. Fig. 5 shows the comparison of network lifetime vs. number of clusters for FCA and RC. From Fig. 5, with the proposed FCA when the distributed energy for cluster head is higher of E_{ch} =5 E_n= 500J, the network lifetime is limited to 4500 rounds by the lifetime of sensor node with the number of cluster q = 10. Besides, when the distributed energy of cluster heads decreases to E_{ch} = 2.5E_n= 250J, the network lifetime is limited to 3000 rounds when the number of clusters is equal to 8. However, with the RC, when the number of clusters is equal to 12 the network lifetime is limited to 2000 rounds which is shorter than that of FCA.

When the distributed energy of cluster head decreases to the same as that of sensor nodes (E_{ch} = E_n= 100J), the network lifetime of FCA and RC is limited to 2000 and 1100 rounds respectively. Moreover, the optimal number of clusters q_{opt} is 5 and 8 for FCA and RC respectively. Thus, it is easily seen the tradeoff of the distributed energy of cluster heads and sensor nodes with the number of clustering in WSNs.

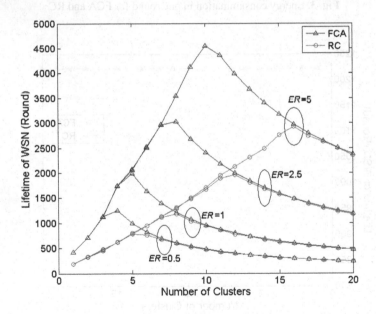

Fig. 5. The comparison of Lifetime for FCA and RC with heterogeneous sensors

Besides, the rising curve in Fig. 5 depicts the energy dissipation of sensor nodes is decreased with the increasing number of clusters. But contrarily the curve going down illustrates that the consuming energy of cluster head increases with the increasing number of clusters. To compare the energy efficiency of WSNs, we further define the energy efficiency (*EE*) as the ratio of total consumed energy to the network lifetime by

$$EE= \text{Lifetime}/(E_{ch} + E_n). \tag{8}$$

Moreover, the energy ratio (ER) of energy of cluster heads to distributed energy of cluster heads and distributed energy of sensor nodes is defined by

$$ER= E_{ch} / E_n \tag{9}$$

for the WSNs. Therefore, we can maximize the life time of WSN by deploying adequate number of clusters according to the ER and EE as shown in Table 2. From Table 2, it is obviously that the proposed FCA outperforms the RC scheme. Moreover, the FCA and RC perform the highest energy efficiency at $q=5$ and $q=8$ respectively.

Table 2. The comparison of energy efficiency and optimal number of clusters for FCA and RC with heterogeneous sensors

	ER	0.5	1	2.5	5
FCA	EE	8.34	9.935	8.66	7.58
	q_{opt}	4	5	8	10
RC	EE	5.21	5.92	5.61	4.87
	q_{opt}	5	8	12	16

5 Conclusions

In this paper, an energy efficient clustering algorithm is proposed to prolong the lifetime of cluster-based WSN. The proposed FCA gives uniform area of cluster area for the WSN and save the energy dissipation of normal senor nodes in the cluster. Simulation results show that the FCA outperforms the RC with more 80% energy efficiency and prolong the life time for both homogeneous and heterogeneous WSNs. Moreover, the FCA and RC perform the highest energy efficiency at number of clusters $q=5$ and $q=8$ respectively.

Acknowledgment. This work was funded in part by National Science Council, Taiwan, Republic of China, under Grant NSC 94-2213-E-324-029 for Y.-F. Huang.

References

1. Culler, D., Estrin, D., Srivastava, M.: Overview of Sensor Networks. IEEE Computer 37(8), 41–49 (2004)
2. Akyildiz, I.F., Su, W., Sankarasubramaniam, Y., Cayirci, E.: Wireless Sensor Network: A Survey. Computer Networks 38, 393–422 (2002)

3. Duarte-Melo, E.J., Liu, M.: Analysis of Energy Consumption and Lifetime of Heterogeneous Wireless Sensor Networks. In: Proc. of IEEE Globalcom 2002, pp. 21–25 (2002)
4. Younis, O., Fahmy, S.: HEED: a Hybrid, Energy-Efficient, Distributed Clustering Approach for Ad Hoc Sensor Networks. In: IEEE Trans. Mobile Computing., pp. 660–669 (2004)
5. Zhu, J., Papavassiliou, S.: On the Energy-Efficient Organization and the Lifetime of Multi-hop Sensor Networks. IEEE Commun. Letters 7(11), 537–539 (2003)
6. Raghunathan, V., Schurgers, C., Park, S., Srivastava, M.B.: Energy-Aware Wireless Microsensor Networks. IEEE Signal Processing Magazine 19(2), 40–50 (2002)
7. Schurgers, C., Srivastava, M.B.: Energy Efficient Routing in Wireless Sensor Networks. In: Proc. of IEEE Military Commun. Conf. 1, 357–361 (2001)

Balancing Energy Dissipation in Clustered Wireless Sensor Networks

Nauman Aslam[1], William Phillips[1], William Robertson[1], and Shyamala C. Sivakumar[2]

[1] Deptartment of Engineering Mathematics & Internetworking
Dalhousie University, Halifax, NS, Canada
[2] Sobey School of Business, Saint Mary's University, Halifax, NS, Canada

Abstract. In wireless sensor networks, unbalanced energy dissipation is one of the major causes for hot spots. The many-to-one communication pattern used by sensor nodes in most of the data gathering applications leads to such unbalanced energy consumption. Cluster-based protocols attempt to solve this problem by load balancing within the cluster and rotating the job of cluster head every few rounds. However, the energy consumption still remains unbalanced because the cluster formation process does not include all the parameters required for balanced energy consumption in the network. Therefore, an optimized cluster formation process which considers the overall network metrics for energy consumption is highly desirable in solving such problems. We introduce an approach to determine the energy dissipation behavior in the sensor deployment area and present results and analysis from our novel multi-criterion cluster formation technique. Simulation results and statistical analysis verify that our technique achieves balanced energy dissipation in the network.

1 Introduction

Wireless Sensor Networks have emerged as the-state-of-the-art technology in data gathering from remote locations by interacting with physical phenomena and relying on collaborative efforts by large number of low cost devices [1]. Typically, a wireless sensor network (WSN) comprises of hundreds or thousands of low cost sensor nodes. Each sensor node has an embedded processor, a wireless interface for communication, a non replenishable source of energy, and one or more onboard sensors for parameters such as temperature, humidity, motion, speed, photo, and piezoelectric detectors. Sensor nodes are significantly constrained in the amount of available resources including storage, computational capacity and specifically energy, which is the most restrictive of these factors because it affects the operational life time of sensor networks [2]. Once deployed, sensor nodes collect the information of interest from their on board sensors, perform local processing of these data including quantization and compression, and forward the data to a base station (BS) directly or through a neighboring relay node. Energy conservation is one of the fundamental challenges in WSNs. In a sensor node, energy is consumed in sensing, computation, and processing. However, the wireless transceiver consumes a significant amount of energy as compared to all other sources. Most of the WSN deployments are based on

P. Thulasiraman et al. (Eds.): ISPA 2007 Workshops, LNCS 4743, pp. 465–474, 2007.

application specific data gathering i.e. a large number of sensor nodes send their data to the base station (BS). Since the information flow follows a many-to-one or converge cast pattern, it is extremely important to balance energy dissipation in the network [3].

In clustered topologies, the energy dissipation for a given sensor node is governed by two main factors, the role that a sensor node takes during each round and the location of a sensor node. Naturally, as a cluster head, a sensor node consumes much more energy than a non cluster head node because of the additional work that it has to do on behalf of its member nodes. In addition, if the cluster head is located far from the sink, its energy consumption would be greater than the energy of a sensor node located closer to the sink. Therefore, if the clustering process is not optimized, unbalanced energy consumption could happen. In addition to the above factors the communication approach used by cluster heads also effects energy dissipation. In the first approach, cluster heads use direct communication for data transmission to the base station. In the second approach a next hop cluster head/relay is used to forward the data to the sink. In the former approach, if the load is not properly balanced, the nodes located far away from the sink consume their energy at a faster rate as compared to the other nodes located closer to the sink, resulting in a hot spot. In the later case, nodes use a next hop cluster head/relay node to forward their data. In this case, since the selection of relay nodes in favored for those located close to the sink we see a dissipation pattern where nodes closer to the sink become inactive at an early stage rendering hot spots or partitions of network. Therefore, performance analysis of all energy efficient protocols must include measures to estimate the energy dissipation pattern. Clearly, all the above factors dictate how the energy is dissipated in clustered WSNs. In this paper we propose a simple approach to model the energy dissipation behavior by monitoring the residual energies of sensor nodes. We also investigate our novel multi-criterion cluster formation algorithm for achieving balanced energy consumption in the network.

The rest of the paper is organized as follows. Section 2 presents an approach to determine the energy dissipation pattern. Section 3 presents a discussion on cluster formation and energy imbalance followed by an overview of our cluster formation technique in Section 4. Simulation results are discussed in Section 5. Finally, our main conclusions and future research directions are highlighted in Section 6.

2 Approach for Determining Energy Dissipation

In order to determine the energy dissipation behavior in the sensor deployment region it is of interest to know at what rate sensors exhaust/consume their energy by estimating the network's energy dissipation pattern. Finding the latter by estimating the energy dissipation of individual sensors is a very complex problem due to the converge-cast communication pattern and the different transmit power levels. However, when sensors are deployed for collaborative information gathering, as is the case in a number of applications, sensors' data are aggregated.

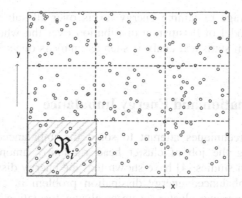

Fig. 1. Sensor deployment area and sub regions

Considering this type of application it makes sense to investigate the average energy dissipation within multiple sub regions. Therefore the total deployment area can be subdivided into small coverage regions. Consider a network consisting of n sensor nodes deployed in area A as shown in Figure 1. The deployment area A can be divided into m non overlapping sub regions.

$$A = \bigcup \mathfrak{R}_i \quad for \ i=1,2,3....m \tag{1}$$

If we assume that sensors were dropped into the deployment area following a uniform distribution, an assumption can be made that the expected number of sensors in each sub region is approximately the same. Let 'X' be a random variable representing a number of sensor nodes in one sub region and m be the number of sub regions in the deployment area, then the expected number of sensor nodes in each box is given by,

$$E[X] = \frac{n}{m} \tag{2}$$

The problem of determining a balanced energy dissipation across the sub regions can also be investigated in the context of monitoring the residual energies of nodes in the sub regions. That is, if the average residual energy of senor nodes within a region is similar to the values in other regions, a statistical analysis can be performed to estimate balanced energy consumption throughout the network. In other words, the similar residual energy levels in all sub regions signify that energy dissipation is independent of sensor location.

Let ξ_j be the residual energy level of a given sensor node. The average residual energy level of a sub region can be represented by,

$$\varepsilon_i = \frac{\sum\limits_{j}^{E[X]} \xi_j}{E[X]} \tag{3}$$

Monitoring the average remaining energy levels over all sub regions allows us to build an abstract model of dissipation distribution over the whole deployment area. We can then perform statistical analysis such as analysis of variance (ANOVA) and draw inferences.

3 Cluster Formation and Energy Imbalance

The cluster based techniques attempt to solve the unbalanced energy dissipation problem by rotating the job of cluster head randomly among the active nodes. However, simulation studies [4] have shown that the energy dissipation still remains unbalanced. The unbalanced energy dissipation problem in clustered networks is caused mainly by improper cluster set up or cluster formation. By improper cluster formation we mean that non cluster head nodes do not consider some significant network parameters when forwarding data to the sink. These parameters include communication costs for forwarding the data to the sink and an estimate of node degree or residual energy. For a sensor node, selecting the cluster head based on a single objective can lead to poor energy dissipation because the nearest cluster head may be located at a greater distance from the base station than the other cluster heads. Thus for that particular node this may not be the best choice. Also, additional factors like residual energy and node degree may be of importance when making a decision. For example, as shown in Figure 2, a sensor node i receives advertisement messages from three different cluster heads A, B and C. The parameters important to the choice of cluster head are included in the advertisement message. Now if node i were to

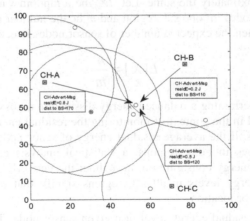

Fig. 2. Example of available choices for cluster head selection in cluster formation

make a decision based on a single parameter it could result in a bad choice overall. For example, selecting based on highest residual energy will lead to choice A which is at a greater distance from the base station as compared to B and C, thus resulting in more energy expenditure. Similarly, making a choice based on the shortest distance to self results in B which has the least residual energy. Hence, it is necessary that, when a node makes a decision about associating with the cluster head all such parameters of local and global significance should be considered. Such a situation forms the basis of our work in tackling the multiple criteria, each of which influences the energy efficiency. We use a multi-criterion optimization technique in this decision process to minimize the energy used both in control and data transmission phases.

4 Multi Objective Cluster Formation

This section describes our novel strategy for cluster formation [5] based on a multi-objective optimization technique. The core of most clustering algorithms for WSNs employs techniques that attempt to maximize the energy efficiency. In our technique the prime focus is on cluster formation i.e. the decision process used by a sensor node to associate itself with a cluster head. Many previously proposed clustering algorithms have attempted to exploit cluster formation in various ways. For example, in [6] the sensor nodes select their cluster head based on the strongest signal strength. In [7] the authors have tackled the problem of unbalanced energy consumption by using a weighted cost function. This cost function takes into account factors such as the distance of a node to the base station, distance of the node to cluster head, and distance of cluster head to base station to produce a composite cost metric which load balances the energy consumption. We argue that the same problem can also be tackled by applying the multi-objective optimization technique. Our technique uses multiple metrics for cluster formation which is critical for well balanced energy

---

Algoithm-1

Notations:
 S: Set of sensor nodes
 OM: Options matrix
 DM: Decision matrix
 P: Preference vector
 W: Weight vector

Cluster Formation:
1. $\forall\ s_i \in S$
2.   While Timer 'T' is valid, do
3.   receive.msg(CH_ADV_MSG)
4.   Extract id, residual energy and
                distance to BS from the message
5.   end While
6.   Build Options matrix (OM) and Decision
        matrix (DM)
7.   Obtain Weight vector (W) by multiplying
        OM to Preference Vector (P)
8.   Select the CH with maximum weight in W
9.   Send CH_JOIN_MSG to the cluster head
        with maximum weight in W

---

dissipation of the system. For completeness and clarity, we now present the algorithm together with an explanation of the steps involved. Interested readers are referred to [5] for further details.

The algorithm is executed by each non-cluster head node in the cluster set up phase. Time 'T' is used to ensure that each non-cluster head node receives the cluster head advertisement messages from one or more elected cluster heads. As outlined in step 3, the information of interest is extracted from each message and used to build the options matrix (*OM*). The options matrix *OM is of the order* (*k* x *n*), where *k* is equal to the number of cluster heads in a node's radio range and *n* is equal to the number of parameters important to the decision criterion. Each element $x_{i,j}$ in the options matrix represents the jth parameter for the ith cluster head. To elaborate, the rows of the option matrix represent the cluster heads, which are in sensor node's radio range. Each element in the ith row represents a parameter important to the decision criteria such as the node's distance to i^{th} cluster head, the distance of the ith cluster head to the base station and the residual energy of the ith cluster head. We assume that after election each potential cluster head broadcasts its willingness to act as a cluster head in a *CH_ADV_MSG* message with the information about its distance to the base station and its residual energy. Nodes record this information for each cluster head from which they receive the *CH_ADV_MSG* message and build the options matrix. The options matrix is converted into a decision matrix (DM) by scaling all elements to the range between 1 and -1. Each element in the DM is found as follows;

$$S_{i,j} = 2\frac{(x_{i,j} - b_j)}{(a_j - b_j)} - 1 \qquad (4)$$

Where a_j equals the best value of $x_{h,j}$ for *h=1,2,3...k* and b_j is the worst value of $x_{h,j}$ for *h=1,2,3...k*. The best and worst values used for calculation in (4) are unique to each parameter. For example, for an arbitrary sensor node the best value for residual energy is represented by the maximum value in the column of the *OM* containing the residual energy values for cluster heads which are in the sensor node's range. In the case of the distance of the sensor node to the cluster head, the best value will represent the minimum value in the corresponding column (distance of closest cluster head to the sensor node). Finally, the weight vector *W* is obtained by multiplying the decision matrix *DM* with the preference vector. The preference vector consists of pre-defined scaled weighted values, chosen by the system designer, involved in the decision process. The best choice for cluster head with for a sensor node is given by the maximum weight in the weight vector. For the present framework we are using only three parameters i.e. the distance from a node to the cluster head, the distance from a cluster head to the sink, and the residual energy of the cluster head.

5   Simulation Results

This section presents the performance analysis of our protocol as presented in this paper. We assume ideal conditions at the physical level such that the probability of wireless interference is negligible. We use the energy model presented in [6] and the assumptions for the system model are the same as presented in [5]. The network simulation model was built using MATLAB. Each simulation experiment is performed on a unique topology and consists of several rounds of cluster set up phase and data transmission phase. We simulated 100 different topologies for the results presented in this section. In each round a set of new cluster heads is elected and the non-cluster head nodes send one data packet to their associated cluster head. We also assume that the cluster head is capable of data aggregation and data received from member nodes is therefore sent in aggregated form. Table 1 summarizes the important simulation parameters used.

Table 1. Simulation Parameters

Sensor Deployment Area	100 x 100 m
Base Station Location	(50,175) m
Number of Nodes	200
Data Packet Size	500 bytes
Control Packet Size	25 bytes
Initial Energy	0. 5 J
E_{elect}	50 nJ/bit
ε_{fs}	10 pJ/bit/m^2
ε_{mp}	.0013 pJ/bit/m^4

For the current paper, our analysis focus remains on measuring the energy dissipation pattern over the deployment area. Therefore as outlined in Section 2, we divide the sensor deployment area A into nine sub regions. The energy dissipation pattern for sensor nodes in each sub region can be estimated by performing an analysis of variance test on the residual energy level of sensor nodes. One of the questions that arises here is "at what point in the network operation should we perform this test?" We argue that the first node death in the network is a critical stage. If the energy consumption is not following a balanced pattern then nodes is a certain region will have residual energy levels significantly different than the overall average. Hence, we can possibly estimate the potential for hot spots in the regions where senor nodes exhibit very low residual energies.

Figure 3a shows the individual value plot and 95% confidence interval for average residual sensor energy in all sub regions (R denotes a sub region). Figure 3b presents the standard deviation and variance for sensor residual energy in each sub region recorded over 100 different topologies. It is obvious that there is no significant difference in the remaining energy levels of sensors in all regions. The results in Figure 3 are further justified by performing the analysis of variance (ANOVA) test.

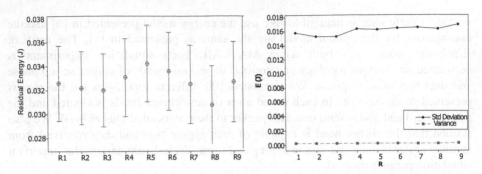

Fig. 3. (a) Average residual sensor energy in sub regions, b) Variance and standard deviation of residual sensor energy in each sub region

Let μ_{ε_i} represent the mean sensor energy in a sub region i, then we wish to test

$$H_o = \mu_{\varepsilon_1} = \mu_{\varepsilon_2} \dots \mu_{\varepsilon_9}$$

H_a = At least two of means are not equal

Figure 4 shows the results obtained from Minitab. It can be seen that the test reports a very high P-value of .937 which means that there is sufficient evidence to believe that we cannot reject H_o.

One- way ANOVA :R1 , R2 , R3 , R4 , R5 , R6 , R7 , R8 , R9

Source	DF	SS	MS	F	P
Factor	8	0.000777	0.000097	0.37	0.937
Error	891	0.233812	0.000262		
Total	899	0.234588			

S = 0.01620 R- Sq = 0.33 % R-Sq(adj) = 0.00%

Fig. 4. ANOVA results output sensor energies in sub regions

We also compare the energy dissipation behavior of sensor nodes in our technique to those using the LEACH protocol. Figure 5 shows the residual energies of sensor nodes along with their x and y coordinate for LEACH. In LEACH the function of cluster head is rotated every few rounds to ensure that the energy dissipation rate is balanced, however it is evident that the rotation of cluster heads alone does not help to avoid the unbalanced energy consumption problem. Therefore, in LEACH an unbalanced energy gradient is setup in the direction of the sink. In contrast, our technique uses the optimized combination of multiple factors that contribute to achieve balanced energy dissipation throughout the sensor deployment area. Figure 5 (c) and (d) show the contour and surface plot for residual energies for our technique. It is clearly observed that that there are no distinct bands of different energy level as compared to LEACH.

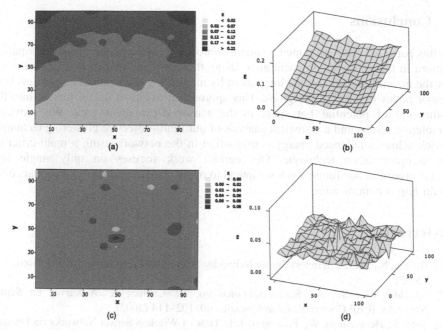

Fig. 5. (a) contour plot for sensor residual energy levels in LEACH, (b) surface plot for sensor residual energy levels in LEACH, (c) contour plot for sensor residual energy levels in our clustering scheme, (d) surface plot for sensor residual energy levels in our scheme

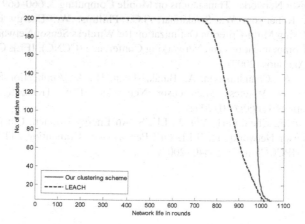

Fig. 6. Network life vs. number of rounds

Figure 6, shows the network life measured as the number of active nodes plotted against the number of rounds. We observe that our technique enhances the life time significantly (about 27% to the death of first node) as compared to LEACH. In addition, the sharp slope observed in our case verifies that energy consumption is indeed well balanced in our technique.

6 Conclusions

In this paper we have presented a simple approach to evaluate the energy dissipation pattern in the sensor deployment area. Using this approach an estimate can be made for the network energy dissipation pattern by monitoring the residual energy levels of sensor nodes in small sub regions. This approach provides a useful insight into the estimation of potential hot spots in the sensor deployment area. We provided simulation results and a statistical analysis of our multi-objective clustering technique which achieves balanced energy consumption in the network using a multi-criterion based optimization technique. Our current work focuses on only single hop architectures. In our future work we intend to investigate our model's performance for multi-hop communication.

Reference

[1] Bulusu, N., Jha, S.: Wireless Sensor Networks: A Systems Prespective: Arctech House Inc. (2005)
[2] Akyildiz, I.F., Su, W., Sankarasubramaniam, Y., Cayirci, E.: A Survey on Sensor Networks. IEEE Communications Magazine 40, 102–114 (2002)
[3] Soro, S., Heinzelman, W.: Prolonging Life Time of Wireless Sensor Networks via Unequal Clustering. In: Proc. of the 19th IEEE International Parallel and Distributed Processing Symposium IPDPS, IEEE, Los Alamitos (2005)
[4] Younis, O., Fahmy, S.: A Hybrid, Energy-Efficient, Distributed Clustering Approach for Ad Hoc Sensor Networks. Transactions on Mobile Computing 3, 660–669 (2004)
[5] Aslam, N., Robertson, W., Sivakumar, S.C., Phillips, W.: Energy Efficient Cluster Formation Using Multi-Criterion Optimization for Wireless Sensor Networks. In: 4th IEEE Consumer Communications and Networking Conference (CCNC), IEEE Computer Society Press, Los Alamitos (2007)
[6] Heinzelman, W., Chandrakasan, A., Balakrishnan, H.: An Application-Specific Protocol Architecture for Wireless Microsensor Networks. IEEE Transactions on Wireless Communications 1, 660–670 (2002)
[7] Ye, M., Li, C.F., Chen, G.H., Wu, J.: EECS: An Energy Efficient Clustering Scheme in Wireless Sensor Networks. In: IEEE Int'l Performance Computing and Communications Conference (IPCCC), pp. 535–540 (2007)

Dynamic Key Management Schemes for Secure Group Communication Based on Hierarchical Clustering in Mobile Ad Hoc Networks*

Woei-Jiunn Tsaur and Haw-Tyng Pai

Department of Information Management
Dayeh University, Changhwa, Taiwan, R.O.C.
{wjtsaur,paioknol_27}@yahoo.com.tw

Abstract. In Mobile ad hoc networks (MANETs), most of current research works in key management can efficiently handle only limited number of nodes. When the number of nodes is gradually increasing, they will become either more inefficient or more insecure. Therefore, how to develop key management schemes for efficiently and securely satisfying the dynamic property of MANETs is a crucial issue. In this paper, by combining the efficient elliptic curve cryptosystem, secure self-certified public key cryptosystem and secure filter technique, we construct dynamic group key management schemes based on hierarchical clustering in MANETs. Specifically, the proposed schemes will effectively renew the group key of intra-cluster or inter-cluster to achieve the forward secrecy and backward secrecy when a node/cluster-head joins or leaves a cluster/cross-cluster. In such a new way, we affirm that the proposed group key management schemes can be very useful for securing practical applications in MANETs.

1 Introduction

With the rapid development of wireless lightweight devices such as mobile phones, PDAs, laptops and wireless equipment, the potential and importance of ubiquitous computing, and particularly mobile ad hoc networking, have become visible. Some applications of mobile networks could not support the dependence on any fixed infrastructure. This infrastructure independency requirement leads to a new kind of network, namely, mobile ad hoc networks (MANETs) [1]. MANETs are an occasional infrastructureless network, formed by a set of wireless mobile hosts that dynamically establish their own network on the fly, without relying on any central administration. In other words, MANETs dynamically handle the joining or leaving of nodes in the network by self-organizing. This is a challenging task [2], since these devices have limited resources (CPU, storage, energy, etc.). Moreover, the network's environment has some features that add extra complications, such as the nodes' mobility bringing about frequent topology changes, as well as the unreliability and the limited

---

* This work was supported by the National Science Council of Republic of China under contract numbers NSC 95-2219-E-212-001 and NSC 95-2218-E-212-008.

P. Thulasiraman et al. (Eds.): ISPA 2007 Workshops, LNCS 4743, pp. 475–484, 2007.

bandwidth of wireless channels. Therefore, the security services of MANETs have a little bit different from other networks [3]. The goal of these services is to protect information and resources from attacks like hijacking, sleep deprivation torture, denial of service, and misbehavior (unauthorized or self-centered behavior).

Group communication applications can use IP multicast to transmit data to all group members using minimum resources [4]. However, Mohapatra et al. [5] stated that the dynamic characteristics of MANETs cause these extra challenges in secure group communication. Moreover, Hegland et al. [6] proposed a survey of key management in MANETs. They stated that none of the currently proposed key management schemes for MANETs are truly effective for all MANET scenarios. They further emphasize secure and efficient key revocation remains an open challenge in MANETs. Therefore, in this paper by combining the elliptic curve cryptosystem (ECC) [15], self-certified public key cryptosystem [17], and secure filter technique [9, 10], we construct dynamic group key management schemes based on hierarchical clustering [7] in MANETs. Specifically, the proposed schemes will effectively renew the group key of intra-cluster or inter-cluster to achieve the forward secrecy and backward secrecy, when a node/cluster-head joins or leaves a cluster/cross-cluster. In summary, our proposed approaches in this paper possess the following advantages:

(1) Because in this paper we adopt the secure filter technique instead of the (k, n) secret sharing scheme [14], and malicious cluster heads/nodes cannot derive any other nodes' secret keys, our proposed dynamic group key distribution is securer than the previously proposed well-known schemes [13, 16].
(2) A joining/leaving member cannot derive the original/latest group key; that is, the forward secrecy and backward secrecy can be accomplished in the proposed schemes.
(3) Since the trust management in this paper is based on the hierarchical clustering instead of the certification authority (CA) and k 1-hop neighbors, it is quite useful for securing practical applications in MANETs.

The rest of this paper is organized as follows. In Section 2, we first describe a hierarchical-clustering-based structure, then construct a group key distribution scheme, and finally propose the dynamic group key management schemes. In Section 3, we analyze the security of the proposed schemes. Finally, some concluding remarks are presented in Section 4.

2 Proposed Dynamic Group Key Management Schemes

In this section, we present secure dynamic key management schemes which combine the ECC-based self-certified public key cryptosystem [8] and the secure filter technique [9, 10] for secure group communication based on hierarchical clustering in MANETs. This paper mainly focuses on proposing the new dynamic group key management schemes, and consequently don't discuss how to construct clusters and to choose cluster heads. A survey of clustering schemes for MANETs can be found in [11].

2.1 Group Key Distribution Scheme

2.1.1 Initialization

To begin with, we describe some terms in hierarchical-clustering-based MANETs, and illustrate them with Figs. 1 and 2.

(1) Nodes: In MANETs each equipment is a node, and we denote it as αi_j, where $\alpha \in \{$ A ~ Z $\}$ and i and j are integers larger than zero. For example, $A1_1$, $B2_3$, $N3_2$, etc are nodes in Fig. 1.

(2) Cluster member: Several nodes αi_j may be classified into a group to form a cluster αi, e.g. in Fig. 1 $A1_1$, $A1_2$, $A1_3$, and $A1_4$ belong to cluster A1.

(3) Cluster head and cross-cluster head: Every cluster head is chosen from all nodes in a cluster, and it can control the cluster. We denote a cluster head as αi_1, e.g. in Fig. 1, $A1_1$, $H16_1$, $G2_1$, etc. As to the cross-cluster head, it is selected from several cluster-head nodes in order to coordinate these cluster heads, e.g. in Fig. 1, $M5_1$, $N3_1$, and $O5_1$ are cross-cluster heads.

(4) The root of cluster heads: It is selected from all of cross-cluster heads to manage them, e.g. in Fig. 2, $N3_1$ is the root of cluster heads.

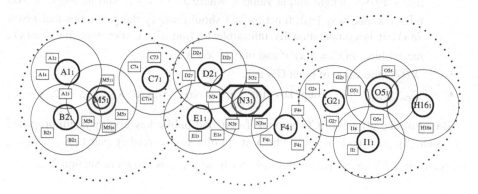

Fig. 1. An example of the nodes relationship in MANETs

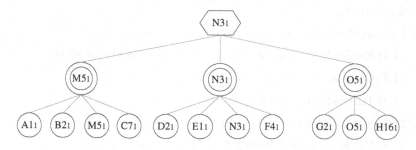

Fig. 2. An example of the cluster heads relationship

Then we define the notations used in the proposed schemes as follows:

[System Notations]

- $ID_{\alpha i_j}$: the identity of node αi_j.

- p : a field size, where p is typically either an odd prime or a power of 2 in general applications, and its length is about 160 bits.

- an elliptic curve E over F_p :

- $E : y^2 = x^3 + ax + b \pmod{p}$, where the two field elements a, $b \in F_P$ and $4a^3 + 27b^2 \pmod{p} \neq 0$, and all the points (x, y), $x \in F_P$, $y \in F_P$, on E form the set of $E(F_p)$ containing a point O called the point at infinity.

- B : a base point of order n over $E(F_p)$, where n is a large prime (160 bits), and the number of F_p -rational points on E denoted by $\# E(\ )$ is divisible by n.

- $PK_{\alpha i_j} / sk_{\alpha i_j}$: node αi_j's public key /secret key.

- $w_{\alpha i_j}$: the witness of $PK_{\alpha i_j}$.

- $h(.)$: a one-way hash function that accepts a variable length input and produces a fixed length output value x, where $x \in [2, n-2]$ and its length is 160 bits. The one-way hash function $h(.)$ should satisfy the properties that given $h(x)$, it is computationally infeasible to find $x' \neq x$ such that $h(x') = h(x)$, meanwhile, $h(x') \neq h(x)$ if and only if $x' \neq x$.

- $X(G)$: the value of point G's axis.

- $K_{Group-\alpha i}$: the group key for cluster αi , where $K_{Group-\alpha i} \in [2, n-2]$.

Based on the efficient ECC-based self-certified public key cryptosystem proposed by Tsaur [8], each node αi_j can obtain its public-key/secret-key pair ($PK_{\alpha i_j}$, $sk_{\alpha i_j}$), respectively, after registering with its cluster head αi_1, as shown in Section 2.1.2.

2.1.2 Node Registration

In the following, each node αi_j registers with its cluster head αi_1 to get its key pair $PK_{\alpha i_j}$ and $sk_{\alpha i_j}$:

Step 1 αi_j performs the following tasks:

(1.1) Randomly select an integer $x_{\alpha i_j} \in [2, n-2]$ as the master key.

(1.2) Compute $V_{\alpha i_j} = h(x_{\alpha i_j} \| ID_{\alpha i_j}) \cdot B$.

(1.3) Transmit $ID_{\alpha i_j}$ and $V_{\alpha i_j}$ to αi_1.

Step 2 αi_1 executes the following tasks:

(2.1) Randomly choose an integer $c_{\alpha i_j} \in [2, n-2]$.

(2.2) Compute a public key $PK_{\alpha i_j}$ and its witness $w_{\alpha i_j}$ for αi_j, where

$$PK_{\alpha i_j} = (c_{\alpha i_j} - h(ID_{\alpha i_j})) \cdot B \, ,$$

$$w_{\alpha i_j} = c_{\alpha i_j} + sk_{\alpha i_1} \cdot (X(PK_{\alpha i_j}) + h(ID_{\alpha i_j})) \pmod{n} \, .$$

(2.3) Return $PK_{\alpha i_j}$ and $w_{\alpha i_j}$ to αi_j.

Step 3 αi_j then executes the following tasks:

(3.1) Derive a secret key $sk_{\alpha i_j} = w_{\alpha i_j} + h(x_{\alpha i_j} \| ID_{\alpha i_j}) \pmod{n}$.

(3.2) Verify the authenticity of $PK_{\alpha i_j}$ by testing if

$$sk_{\alpha i_j} \cdot B = PK_{\alpha i_j} + h(ID_{\alpha i_j}) \cdot B + \left[(X(PK_{\alpha i_j}) + h(ID_{\alpha i_j})) \bmod n\right] \cdot PK_{\alpha i_1} \quad (1)$$

If the secret key $sk_{\alpha i_j}$ (derived by αi_j) and the public key $PK_{\alpha i_j}$ (issued by αi_1) satisfy Eq. (1), then αi_j's public key and secret key are exactly $PK_{\alpha i_j}$ and $sk_{\alpha i_j}$, respectively.

2.1.3 Group Key Distribution

In the proposed group key distribution scheme, the procedures of intra-cluster and inter-cluster group key distribution are similar. For simplicity, we describe only intra-cluster group key distribution for cluster αi in the following.

Step 1 In cluster αi, node αi_j sends to its cluster head αi_1 the identification information $ID_{\alpha i_j}$ and public key $PK_{\alpha i_j}$.

Step 2 αi_1 computes

$$V_{\alpha i_j} = PK_{\alpha i_j} + h(ID_{\alpha i_j}) \cdot B + \left[(X(PK_{\alpha i_j}) + h(ID_{\alpha i_j})) \bmod n\right] \cdot PK_{\alpha i_1} \, . \quad (2)$$

Step 3 αi_j randomly chooses an integer $r_{\alpha i_j} \in [2, n-2]$ to compute $T_{\alpha i_j} = r_{\alpha i_j} \cdot B$, and then transmits $T_{\alpha i_j}$ to αi_1.

Step 4 αi_1 randomly chooses an integer $r_{\alpha i_1} \in [2, n-2]$, and returns it to αi_j.

Step 5 αi_j uses its secret key $sk_{\alpha i_j}$ to compute

$$l_{\alpha i_j} = r_{\alpha i_j} + sk_{\alpha i_j} \cdot r_{\alpha i_1} \pmod{n}, \text{ and sends } l_{\alpha i_j} \text{ to } \alpha i_1.$$

Step 6 αi_1 verifies the identity of αi_j by testing if

$$l_{\alpha i_j} \cdot B - r_{\alpha i_1} \cdot V_{\alpha i_j} = T_{\alpha i_j} \, . \quad (3)$$

If Eq. (3) holds, then αi_1 accepts the identity αi_j claims; otherwise, αi_1 rejects its claim. In the following, we demonstrate why the verification procedure described in Eq. (3) works correctly:

$$l_{\alpha i_j} \cdot B - r_{\alpha i_1} \cdot V_{\alpha i_j} = \left(r_{\alpha i_j} + sk_{\alpha i_j} \cdot r_{\alpha i_1} \right) \cdot B - r_{\alpha i_1} \cdot V_{\alpha i_j}$$

$$= r_{\alpha i_j} \cdot B + sk_{\alpha i_j} \cdot r_{\alpha i_1} \cdot B - sk_{\alpha i_j} \cdot r_{\alpha i_1} \cdot B \quad \text{(from Eqs. (1) and (2))}$$

$$= r_{\alpha i_j} \cdot B = T_{\alpha i_j} \qquad \qquad \qquad \square$$

Step 7 In order to make αi_1 acquire the valid $h(sk_{\alpha i_j})$ from each member αi_j, the following sub-steps will be executed:

(7.1) αi_j randomly chooses an integer $k \in [2, n-2]$, and computes $k \cdot B = (X_{\alpha i_j}, Y_{\alpha i_j})$.

(7.2) αi_j computes $y_{\alpha i_j} = X_{\alpha i_j} (\bmod\ p)$.

(7.3) αi_j computes $z_{\alpha i_j} = k + sk_{\alpha i_j} \cdot h(h(sk_{\alpha i_j}) \| y_{\alpha i_j})\ (\bmod\ n)$.

(7.4) αi_j transmits the signature ($y_{\alpha i_j}, z_{\alpha i_j}$) and $h(sk_{\alpha i_j})$ to αi_1.

(7.5) αi_1 computes
$$z_{\alpha i_j} \cdot B - V_{\alpha i_j} \cdot h(h(sk_{\alpha i_j}) \| y_{\alpha i_j})$$
$$= k \cdot B + (sk_{\alpha i_j}(h(sk_{\alpha i_j}) \| y_{\alpha i_j}) \bmod\ n) \cdot B - (sk_{\alpha i_j} \cdot B) \cdot (h(sk_{\alpha i_j}) \| y_{\alpha i_j})$$
$$= k \cdot B = (X_1, Y_1).$$

(7.6) If $x_1 = y_{\alpha i_j} (\bmod\ p)$ holds, then the signature is valid.

After the above sub-steps have been completed, αi_1 can obtain the valid $h(sk_{\alpha i_j})$ from each member αi_j.

Step 8 αi_1 selects a group key $K_{Group-\alpha i}$ shared among it and the remaining members $\alpha i_2, \alpha i_3, \ldots, \alpha i_m$, and generates the secure filter $f_{\alpha i}(x)$ as follows:
$$f_{\alpha i}(x) = (x - h(sk_{\alpha i_2}))(x - h(sk_{\alpha i_3})) \cdots (x - h(sk_{\alpha i_m})) + K_{Group-\alpha i}\ (\bmod\ n).$$
αi_1 then multicasts $f_{\alpha i}(x)$ to its members αi_j.

Step 9 By employing the secret key $sk_{\alpha i_j}$, each αi_j can obtain the $K_{Group-\alpha i}$ by computing $f_{\alpha i}(h(sk_{\alpha i_j}))$.

2.2 Dynamic Group Key Management

We further describe how the proposed dynamic group key management scheme operates, including node joining and node leaving.

(1) Node joining

"Node joining" means that a new node wants to participate in a cluster to become a new member of the cluster, or a new cluster head wants to cooperate with other cluster heads. We describe the two cases in the following.

(a) Intra-cluster

For instance in Fig. 1, when a new node $A1_7$ wants to join cluster A1, the new intra-cluster group key $K'_{Group-A1}$ can be distributed to all the members by $A1_1$ as follows:

Step1 Following Steps 1-7 in Section 2.1.3, the cluster head $A1_1$ will verify the identify of $A1_7$, and obtain the valid $h(sk_{A1_7})$.

Step 2   If $A1_7$ has passed the verification, then $A1_1$ will select $K'_{Group-A1}$ and construct the new secure filter

$$f'_{A1}(x) = (x - h(sk_{A1_2}))(x - h(sk_{A1_3}))(x - h(sk_{A1_4}))(x - h(sk_{A1_7}))$$

$$+ K'_{Group-A1} \pmod{n},$$

and re-multicast $f'_{A1}(x)$ to all the members of A1.

Step 3   Nodes $A1_2$, $A1_3$, $A1_4$, and $A1_7$ can derive the new group key $K'_{Group-A1}$ by employing their secret keys sk_{A1_2}, sk_{A1_3}, sk_{A1_4}, and sk_{A1_7} to compute $f'_{A1}(h(sk_{A1_2}))$, $f'_{A1}(h(sk_{A1_3}))$, $f'_{A1}(h(sk_{A1_4}))$, and $f'_{A1}(h(sk_{A1_7}))$, respectively.

In summary, the above three steps can prevent node $A1_7$ from deriving the original intra-cluster group key $K_{Group-A1}$, and thus achieve the backward secrecy.

(b) Inter-cluster

As illustrated in Figs. 1 and 2, we can find that an original inter-cluster is formed by clusters A1, B2, C7, and M5, and $M5_1$ is the cross-cluster head of the inter-cluster. When a new cluster J1 wants to join the inter-cluster, the new inter-cluster group key $K_{Group-A1,B2,C7,M5,J1}$ can be distributed to all the members to fulfill the backward secrecy by executing the following steps:

Step 1 Similarly following Steps 1-7 in Section 2.1.3, the cross-cluster head $M5_1$ will verify the identify of $J1_1$, and obtain the valid $h(sk_{J1_1})$.

Step 2 If $J1_1$ has passed the verification, $M5_1$ will choose $K_{Group-A1,B2,C7,M5,J1}$ and construct the new secure filter

$$f_{A1,B2,C7,M5,J1}(x) = (x - h(sk_{A1_1}))(x - h(sk_{B2_1}))(x - h(sk_{C7_1}))(x - h(sk_{J1_1}))$$

$$+ K_{Group-A1,B2,C7,M5,J1} \pmod{n},$$

and re-multicast $f_{A1,B2,C7,M5,J1}(x)$ to all the members of the new inter-cluster.

Step 3   By using the same method stated above, members $A1_1$, $B2_1$, $C7_1$, and $J1_1$ can derive the new group key $K_{Group-A1,B2,C7,M5,J1}$ by using its secret key, respectively.

(2) Node deleting

A deleting procedure will be executed when a node leaves the cluster or a cluster head logs off the system. Such two kinds of procedures are described as below:

(a) Intra-cluster

By the following example, we demonstrate each remaining node αi_j in cluster αi is how to get the renewed $K'_{Group-\alpha i}$. As illustrated in Fig. 1, when a node $A1_3$ leaves cluster A1, the original secure filter $f(x)$ must be renewed by $A1_1$ as

$$f'_{A1}(x) = (x - h(sk_{A1_2}))(x - h(sk_{A1_4})) + K'_{Group-A1} \pmod{n}.$$

Each existing members in cluster A1 will gain the new intra-cluster group key $K'_{Group-\alpha i}$ by computing $f'_{A1}(h(sk_{A1_2}))$ and $f'_{A1}(h(sk_{A1_4}))$, respectively. In such a way, the aforementioned scheme can prevent node A1$_3$ from deriving the renewed group key $K'_{Group-\alpha i}$, and therefore fulfill the forward secrecy.

(b) Inter-cluster
Similar to node deleting in an intra-cluster, when a cluster head leaves an inter-cluster, the cross-cluster head can also renew the original inter-cluster group key to accomplish the forward secrecy. As illustrated in Fig. 2, when a cluster head A1$_1$ leaves the system, the secure filter will be renewed by cross-cluster head M1$_1$ as

$$f_{B2,C7}(x) = (x - h(sk_{B2_1}))(x - h(sk_{C7_1})) + K_{Group-B2,C7} \pmod n.$$

B2$_1$ and C7$_1$ then gain the new inter-cluster group key $K_{Group-B2,C7}$ by computing $f_{B2,C7}(h(sk_{B2_1}))$ and $f_{B2,C7}(h(sk_{C7_1}))$, respectively.

3 Security Analysis

The security of the proposed dynamic group key distribution schemes is based on the following two well-known cryptographic assumptions:

(1) One-way hash function (OWHF) assumption: Let h be a one-way hash function. Given $h(M)$, it is computationally infeasible to find M. Furthermore, given M, $h(M)$ and $h(M')$, it is computationally infeasible to obtain M'. For theoretical analysis, sometimes it is assumed that finding two different values M and M' such that $h(M) = h(M')$ is computationally infeasible.

(2) Elliptic curve discrete logarithm (ECDL) assumption: If P is a point with order n on an elliptic curve, and Q is some other point on the same curve, then the elliptic curve discrete logarithm problem is to determine an l such that $Q = l \cdot P$ and $0 \le l \le n-1$ if such an l exists. As long as n and p are large enough, it is computationally intractable to find l with knowing E, Q, and P.

We then analyze the security of the proposed dynamic group key distribution schemes as follows:

(1) The secret keys used in the proposed schemes include each node αi_j's master key and derived (personal) secret keys. In the following, we discuss the security of the secret keys used in the proposed schemes.

(a) *Revealing any registering node αi_j's master key $x_{\alpha i_j}$*

As one can see that the registering node αi_j's master key $x_{\alpha i_j}$ is protected by the intractability of the ECDL and the OWHF problems. Even in the worst case that node αi_j's derived secret key $sk_{\alpha i_j}$ has compromised due to some unpredictable human factors, e.g., accidentally present to a unauthorized node, αi_j's master key $x_{\alpha i_j}$ is still protected under the OWHF assumption.

(b) *Revealing any registering node αi_j's derived secret key $sk_{\alpha i_j}$*

During the node registration phase, the registering node αi_j's derived secret key $sk_{\alpha i_j}$ is protected by the master key $x_{\alpha i_j}$ that is protected under the OWHF and the ECDL assumptions as discussed above. On the other hand, although αi_j must transmit $h(sk_{\alpha i_j})$ to αi_1 for group key generation at the group key distribution stage, this does not lead into exposing αi_j's secret key $sk_{\alpha i_j}$ due to the intractability of the OWHF problem. Therefore, cluster head αi_1 never knows the registering node αi_j's derived secret key $sk_{\alpha i_j}$.

(2) If an attacker wants to get the group key $K_{Group-\alpha i}$, the only way is to try to derive it via the secure filter $f_{\alpha i}(x)$. Because each member's secret key $sk_{\alpha i_j}$ is protected by a one-way hash function $h(.)$, he/she cannot calculate $f_{\alpha i}(h(sk_{\alpha i_j}))$ to obtain $K_{Group-\alpha i}$ without knowing $sk_{\alpha i_j}$.

(3) In the proposed dynamic group key distribution schemes, by using the secure filter technique, each legal member αi_j in a intra-cluster/inter-cluster can absolutely derive its required group key $K_{Group-\alpha i}$ by computing $f_{\alpha i}(h(sk_{\alpha i_j}))$. Emphatically, in dynamic MANETs environments that the number of nodes is changed constantly, the group key distribution schemes still can work unaffectedly.

(4) In Section 2.2, it is obvious that the proposed schemes will effectively renew the group key of intra-cluster or inter-cluster, when a node/cluster-head joins or leaves a cluster/cross-cluster. In such a way, we can find a joining/leaving member cannot derive the original/latest group key absolutely. Hence, the proposed dynamic group key distribution schemes can achieve the forward secrecy and backward secrecy.

4 Conclusion

Our proposed dynamic hierarchical-clustering-based key management schemes combine the efficient elliptic curve cryptosystem, self-certified public key cryptosystem, and secure filter technique to secure group communication in MANETs. Each cluster head is responsible for coordinating a group key for all members of the cluster, and further managing the dynamic group key distribution; even so, it has no capability to derive its members' secret keys owing to facing the intractability of solving the elliptic curve discrete logarithm and one-way hash function problems. In addition, the proposed schemes are able to securely revoke the group keys of original clusters and further update the group keys of new formed clusters, after clusters are dynamically changed, including node joining/deleting. That is, the proposed schemes can securely renew the group keys of clusters to achieve the forward secrecy and backward secrecy. Therefore, we affirm that the proposed group key management schemes can be very useful for securing practical applications in MANET.

References

1. Wu, J., Stojmenovic, I.: Ad hoc networks. Computer 37(2), 29–31 (2004)
2. Yang, H., Luo, H., Ye, F., Lu, S., Zhang, L.: Security in mobile ad hoc networks challenges and solutions. IEEE Wireless Communications 11(1), 38–47 (2004)
3. Djenouri, D., Khelladi, L., Badache, N.: A survey of security issues in mobile ad hoc and sensor networks. IEEE Communications Surveys & Tutorials 7(4), 2–28 (2005)
4. Rafaeli, S., Hutchison, D.: A survey of key management for secure group communication. ACM Computing Surveys 35(3), 309–329 (2003)
5. Mohapatra, P., Gui, C., Li, J.: Group communications in mobile ad hoc networks. Computer 37(2), 52–59 (2004)
6. Hegland, A.M., Winjum, E., Mjolsnes, S.F., Rong, C., Kure, O., Spilling, P.: A survey of key management in ad hoc networks. IEEE Communications Surveys & Tutorials 8(3), 48–66 (2006)
7. Sucec, J., Marsic, I.: Clustering overhead for hierarchical routing in mobile ad hoc networks. Proceedings of IEEE INFOCOM 3, 1698–1706 (2002)
8. Tsaur, W.J.: Several security schemes constructed using ECC-based self-certified public key cryptosystems. Applied Mathematics and Computation 168(1), 447–464 (2005)
9. Wu, K.P., Ruan, S.J., Tseng, C.K., Lai, F.: Hierarchical access control using the secure filter. IEICE Transactions on Information and Systems E84-D(6), 700–708 (2001)
10. Jeng, F.G., Wang, C.M.: An efficient key-management scheme for hierarchical access control based on elliptic curve cryptosystem. Journal of Systems and Software 79(8), 1161–1167 (2006)
11. Yu, J.Y., Chong, P.H.J.: A survey of clustering schemes for mobile ad hoc networks. IEEE Communications Surveys & Tutorials 7(1), 32–48 (2005)
12. Kanayama, N., Kobayashi, T., Saito, T., Uchiyama, S.: Remarks on elliptic curve discrete logarithm problems. IEICE Transactions on Fundamentals of Electronics, Communications and Computer Sciences E83-A(1), 17–23 (2000)
13. Zhu, B., Bao, F., Deng, R.H., Kankanhalli, M.S., Wang, G.: Efficient and robust key management for large mobile ad hoc networks. Computer Networks 48(4), 657–682 (2005)
14. Shamir, A.: How to share a secret. Communications of the ACM 22(11), 612–613 (1979)
15. Lauter, K.: The advantages of elliptic curve cryptography for wireless security. IEEE Wireless Communications 11(1), 62–67 (2004)
16. Zhang, Y., Liu, W., Lou, W., Fang, Y.: Securing mobile ad hoc networks with certificateless public keys. IEEE Transactions on Dependable and Secure Computing 3(4), 386–399 (2006)
17. Girault, M.: Self-certified public keys. In: Davies, D.W. (ed.) EUROCRYPT 1991. LNCS, vol. 547, pp. 490–497. Springer, Heidelberg (1991)

Privacy Preserving Monitoring and Surveillance in Sensor Networks

Vladimir A. Oleshchuk

Department of Information and Communication Technology
Agder University
Servicebox 509, N-4898 Grimstad, Norway
vladimir.oleshchuk@hia.no

Abstract. In this paper we consider a problem of privacy preserving surveillance and monitoring in sensor networks. We propose a framework and a solution of the problem based on multi-party computations. Our approach use pattern matching on data streams from sensors in order to monitor and detect events of interest.

We study a privacy preserving pattern matching problem where patterns are defined as sequences of constraints on input data items. We describe a new privacy preserving pattern matching algorithm over an infinite alphabet A where a pattern P is given as a sequence $\{p_{i_1}, p_{i_2}, ..., p_{i_n}\}$ of predicates p_{i_j} defined on A. The algorithm addresses the following problem: given a pattern P and an input sequence t, find privately all positions in t where P matches t. The privacy preserving in the context of this paper means that sensor measurements will be evaluated as predicates $p_i(e_j)$ privately, that is, sensors will not need to disclose the measurement values to the monitor.

1 Introduction

When sensor networks are used for monitoring and surveillance they should support distributed sensing of physical environment through measuring and aggregation of data in order to create the dynamic global view of the environment. These tasks generate various streams of measurement data within the networks. However, the data streams from sensors, further referred as sequences of events, are only useful if they can be used to monitor and detect events of interest [6,14].

In the context of this paper we abstract from the physical structure of the sensor networks and consider a simplified model representing a set of sensors and the base station the sensors send measurement data to. In the paper we assume that there are n sensors, denoted $s_1, s_2, ..., s_n$ connected to the base station B. If $x_i^{(t)}$ denotes a measurement value received at a time slot t from sensor s_i then n-tuple $\left\langle x_1^{(t)}, x_2^{(t)}, ..., x_n^{(t)} \right\rangle$ is an event that represents state of monitored sensors at the time slot t.

In this paper we analyze sequences of events in order to detect those subsequences of events that may indicate some predefine activities of interest, for

P. Thulasiraman et al. (Eds.): ISPA 2007 Workshops, LNCS 4743, pp. 485–492, 2007.

example such as fire development in some areas of a monitored building. Detecting subsequence patterns in a sequences of events is an example of the pattern matching problem. The problem is an important component of many applications including real time monitoring and events detection in manufacturing processes by examining noisy sensor data [8].

Formally, the pattern matching problem means finding one, or more generally, all occurrences of some pattern inside sequential raw data. Generally, raw data can be seen as a sequence over a finite or even an infinite alphabet. For example, in the case of sensor networks used for environmental and health monitoring of buildings many measurements such as temperature, humidity, sound level etc. are continuous by their nature. They need to be discretized in some way to be presented in computers due to the finite presentation restrictions of computer representations. Discretizing is one-to-many process, that is, the same continuous object of real world may correspond to many discretized presentation due to, for example, limited equipment resolution, noise or precision measurement problems. Since digitized presentations are approximate representations of continuous objects, the traditional algorithms developed for discrete objects, for example texts, are either unusable by design or inefficient [2,7]. Therefore, it is important to develop new algorithms that are fast, require little memory and limited buffering and can operate in real-time on digitized presentations of continuous objects.

Another important aspect of monitoring sequences of events as described above is their sensitivity with respect to privacy and security. Some measurements can be very sensitive by their nature. However, they are necessary in order to perform monitoring and detection.

In this paper we focus on privacy preserving aspects of pattern matching of in event sequences. That is on the way to perform monitoring and detection without privacy violation.

The paper is organized as follows. In Section 2 we provide necessary definitions and notations. The general pattern matching algorithm (without privacy considerations) is presented in Section 3. The privacy preserving protocol is presented in Section 4. Finally, concluding remarks are made in the last section.

2   Pattern Matching on Sequences

When raw data are texts over finite alphabets the pattern matching problem is known as the string-matching problem. Many different variations of the string-matching problems have been proposed and studied. Efficient solutions proposed in the literature [1,2,3] are based either on the use of automata or on combinatorial properties of strings over finite alphabets. These problems and the proposed solutions are heavily depend on finiteness property of the underlying alphabets and cannot be applied directly to solve the similar problems in the continuous setting where alphabets are infinite or very large and when a precise matching, as in digitized presentations, is often unnecessary, meaningless or even impossible.

In this paper we deal with pattern matching problems applied to sequences of events representing n-tuples of unconventional data as, for example, digitized measurement data [11,12]. Since under digitization both a single pattern and the raw data can map into one-of-many digitized patterns and digitized raw sequences (as explained above) it is unlikely that an exact match can always be achieved. We present an on-line algorithm that solves the problem in general, and then modify it to develop a more efficient privacy-preserving version for some classes of patterns.

Let us consider events as elements of an infinite set A, that is, $A = \{a_1, a_2, ...\}$. Let A^* denote the set of all finite-length sequences of elements from A. The length of a finite sequence $e_n = a_1 a_2 ... a_n$ is denoted as $|e_n|$, that is, $|e_n| = n$. We assume that $e_0 = \epsilon$ where ϵ denotes the empty sequence. Let A^m denote the set of all sequences of length m formed by using elements from A. We say that a sequence w is a prefix of a sequence t if $t = wy$ where $y, w, t \in A^*$. Similarly, we say that a sequence w is a suffix of a sequence t if $t = xw$ where $x, w, t \in A^*$. A sequence w is a subsequence of a sequence t if $t = xwy$ for some $x, y, w, t \in A^*$.

Let $\Omega = \{p_1, p_2, ...\}$ be a set of predicates defined on A, that is, $p_i : A \rightarrow \{true, false\}$ for any $p_i \in \Omega_A$. A pattern P of length m is a sequence $\langle p_{i_1}, p_{i_2}, ..., p_{i_m} \rangle$ of predicates from Ω_A. The pattern $P = \langle p_{i_1}, p_{i_2}, ..., p_{i_m} \rangle$ represents a subset Q_P of sequences from A^m defined as

$$Q_P = \{a_{i_1} a_{i_2} ... a_{i_m} \mid \wedge_{j=1}^m p_{i_j}(a_{i_j}) = true\}$$

where $a_{i_j} \in A$.

We say that a pattern $P = \langle p_{i_1}, p_{i_2}, ..., p_{i_m} \rangle$ from Ω_A matches a sequence $e = a_1 a_2 ... a_n$ from A^*, if a sequence $y_1 y_2 ... y_m$ from Q_P occurs as a subsequence of e, that is, if $e = u y_1 y_2 ... y_m v$ for some $u, v \in A^*$. The pattern P occurs at position $k + 1$ in sequence $e = a_1 a_2 ...$ or matches e in position $k + 1$ if

$$\wedge_{j=k+1}^{k+m} p_{i_j}(a_j) = true$$

where $0 \leq k \leq n - m$.

Thus the pattern matching problem we deal with in this paper can be formulated as following: Given a pattern P from Ω_A and a sequence e of events from A^*, find all positions in e where P matches e.

The efficient algorithm that solves the problem has been proposed in [9]. In the following section for the sake of clarity we give a short presentation of the algorithm. The readers can find the correctness proof and efficiency evaluation of the algorithm in [11].

3   Pattern Matching Algorithm

Let t_k be a string $a_1 a_2 ... a_k$ from A^*, and P be a pattern $\langle p_{i_1}, p_{i_2}, ..., p_{i_m} \rangle$ from Ω_A. Let S_k^P denote a set of lengths of all prefixes of P matching some suffix of t_k, that is, $j \in S_k^P$ if and only if

$$p_{i_1}(a_{k-j+1}) \wedge p_{i_2}(a_{k-j+2}) \wedge \cdots \wedge p_{i_j}(a_k) = true$$

Therefore, P matches t_k if and only if $m \in S_j^P$ for some $j \leq k$. Thus, in order to perform pattern matching based on this idea, we have to construct a sequence of sets $S_0^P, S_1^P, \ldots, S_k^P, \ldots$ for a given pattern $P = \langle p_{i_1}, p_{i_1}, \ldots, p_{i_m} \rangle$ and an input sequence $t = a_1 a_2 \cdots a_k \cdots$, and check whether m is in S_k^P for some $k > 0$. Then, for any S_k^P such that $m \in S_k^P$ we report that P matches t in position $(k - m + 1)$.

The algorithm MATCH, based on the above idea, is presented in Fig. 1. The output of the algorithm MATCH(t, P) is the set of all positions where P occurs in t. The algorithm uses the procedure UPDATE(S^P, x, P) to construct S_i^P based on previously constructed S_{i-1}^P and x, where x is a new input element of sequence t.

```
Input: a sequence of data t and a pattern P = ⟨p_{k_1}, p_{k_2}, ..., p_{k_m}⟩
Output: occurrences of all matching patterns.

Algorithm MATCH(t, P)
S ← {0};
pos ← pos + 1;
while input is not empty do
      x ← read next element from t;
      pos ← pos + 1
      S ← UPDATE(S, x, P);
      if m ∈ S then matching found at position (pos − m + 1)
      S ← S − {m}
end
```

Fig. 1. Algorithm MATCH

Let us explain in details how the algorithm UPDATE works. As it was mentioned above the main purpose of UPDATE is to construct the sets $S_0^P, S_1^P, \ldots, S_k^P, \ldots$ for a given pattern $P = \langle p_{k_1}, p_{k_2}, \ldots, p_{k_m} \rangle$ and an input sequence $t = a_1 a_2 \cdots a_k \cdots a$. The algorithm UPDATE is presented on Figure 2. According to Figure 2, the

```
Input: Set S^P such that S^P ⊆ {0, 1, ..., m − 1}, pattern P =
⟨p_{k_1}, p_{k_2}, ..., p_{k_m}⟩ from Ω_A, and x from A.
Output: Set S^P such that S^P ⊆ {0, 1, ..., m}

Algorithm UPDATE(S^P, x, P)
S ← ∅
for each j from S^P do
      S^P ← S^P − {j}
      if p_{i_{j+1}} = true then S ← S ∪ {j + 1}
S^P ← S ∪ {0}
return S^P
```

Fig. 2. Algorithm UPDATE

algorithm UPDATE computes S_{i+1}^P based on S_i^P, the next input element x and the length of the prefix of P that has been already matched.

The difference between the algorithm UPDATE and a naive brute-force algorithm is that UPDATE is optimized in the sense that for each input element x of input t, UPDATE considers only those predicates of the pattern P that still may be a part of some occurrences of P in t. When an input of length i has been analyzed, UPDATE contains in S_i^P references only on those predicates that need to be evaluated on the next input x, that is, $j \in S_i^P$ represents p_{i_j} from P. However, the time complexity of UPDATE depends on properties of the pattern P, that is, both on complexity of evaluation of predicates from P and on their interdependencies. The interdependency presents the knowledge of how truth values for some predicates of P can be found without their explicit evaluation but based only on truth values of some already evaluated predicates of P. The time complexity of algorithm MATCH is linear of the length of input plus the time complexity of all UPDATE's calls. (Detailed proof can be found in [9].)

4   Privacy Preserving Matching

In this section we show how algorithm from previous section can be modified to perform privacy-preserving detection of activities in sensor networks based on pattern matching over infinite alphabets.

As we can see from the pattern matching algorithm above (Fig. 1), evaluation of predicates $p_i(a_j) = p_i(x_1^{(j)}, x_2^{(j)}, \ldots, x_n^{(j)})$ is an essential part of the algorithm.

Privacy-preserving in the context of this paper means that the base station conducts evaluation of predicates $p_i(e_j)$ on *private inputs* from sensors, that is, sensors will not need to disclose the measurements $x_1^{(j)}, x_2^{(j)}, \ldots, x_n^{(j)}$ to the base station B. In addition, we want to protect the base station from revealing to the sensors both the results of evaluations and the descriptions of predicates. We propose a solution of this problem based on secure multi-party computation approach similar to the approach described in [4,5].

Our solution can be seen as a solution of well known Yao's Millionaire problem [15] that is formulated as a comparison of two private numbers in order to decide which is larger. However, in context of this work it is more convenient to see this problem as a simplified version of the point inclusion problem, namely, a point inclusion in an interval. We want to evaluate privately whether a number x is within a given interval $[\alpha, \beta]$.

In the case when only a finite number of elements can occur in the interval, the solution of Yao's Millionaire problem given in [15] can be used. However, in the case when the number of elements from $[\alpha, \beta]$ is large the solution is not efficient in the terms of communication complexity. Therefore we need to find a new more efficient solution that matches better our problem setting.

We need to find a way to evaluate whether x in $[\alpha, \beta]$ without discloser sensor's measurement x to the base station and without discloser the base station's interval $[\alpha, \beta]$ to the sensor. It means that we need to evaluate the function $f(x) = (x - \alpha)(x - \beta)$ privately. It is easy to see that $x \in [\alpha, \beta]$ if and only if $f(x) \leq 0$. Similarly, by choosing z such that $z \geq (\frac{\alpha+\beta}{2})^2$ we can see that $f(x) + z \geq 0$ for all possible x. Defining $g(x) = f(x) + z$ we can write that $x \in [\alpha, \beta]$ if and only if $g(x) \leq z$. Note that we assume that all possible measurement values that can be received from the sensor (defined by the physical nature of the measurement and the sensor itself) are always within $[\alpha, \beta]$.

In the following presentation we assume that Alice represents a sensor and Bob represents a base station.

We use a public-key cryptosystem with homomorphic property where encryption and decryption are denoted as $E(\bullet)$ and $D(\bullet)$ respectively. The homomorphic property means that there is an operation on encrypted data, denoted $\oplus$, that can be used to perform addition of the encrypted data without their preliminary decryption. That is, we assume that $E(x) \oplus E(y) = E(x + y)$. Many such systems have been proposed in the literature [9,10,13]. Such public key cryptosystems are based on computational number theory where encryption/decryption computations are performed modulo some public number n. Therefore $x - y \equiv x + (n - y) \bmod n$ we can write that $E(x - y) = E(x + (n - y)) = E(x) \oplus E(n - y)$. Furthermore, since $E(x) \oplus E(y) = E(x+y)$, then $E(x) \oplus E(x) = E(x+x) = E(2x)$ denoted as $2 \otimes E(x)$ and

$$k \otimes E(x) = E(kx) = E(\underbrace{x + x + \cdots + x}_{k}) = \underbrace{E(x) \oplus E(x) \oplus \cdots \oplus E(x)}_{k}$$

It means that we can multiply encrypted data if one of the multipliers is known (that is unencrypted).

This is the property we use in the protocol described later in this section. To simplify further notation and make our protocol independent of particular selected homomorphic public-key cryptosystem we assume that there are operations $\otimes$ and $\oplus$ on encrypted data defined as described above.

The description of the protocol for privacy preserving predicates evaluation is presented on Figure 3.

The protocol shows how we can evaluate privately predicate defined as a point inclusion in an interval. The privacy preserving properties of the protocol are based on the fact that the base station (Bob) will never get access in clear text either to the sensor measurement value x or to the value of $f(x)$. Alice sees values of both $f(x) + z$ and z but without being able to identify what is what. From the other side, Alice will never see values of α and β.

Combining the protocol with the pattern matching algorithm presented in Section 3 gives us a privacy preserving pattern matching algorithm.

In the sense of practical applicability of the protocol it is important that the base station (Bob) will do as much computations as possible since sensors are usually small devises with limited resources. Considering the proposed protocol we can see that Step 1 will be performed only on the key establishment phase. This step will be repeated only occasionally when the sensor needs to re-establish keys. The other steps that the sensor must do are Step 2 and Step 5. Together they contain three encryptions, two decryption and one comparison. All other computations are allocated to the base station. Assuming that encryption and

Protocol: Privacy preserving predicate evaluation.
Input: Alice has a homomorphic public key cryptosystem where $E(\bullet)$ is an encryption function and $D(\bullet)$ is a corresponding decryption function (modulo n); Alice (a sensor) has a measurement value x; Bob (a base station) has an interval $[\alpha, \beta]$.
Output: Bob leans whether $x \in [\alpha, \beta]$ is true or false without learning x, and without revealing $[\alpha, \beta]$ to Alice.

Step 1: Alice (sensor) generates a key pair for a homomorphic public key system and sends the public key to Bob (base station).

Step 2: Alice encrypts x, $n - x$ and x^2 using her public key and sends $E(x)$, $E(n - x)$ and $E(x^2)$ to Bob.(Note that n is a large public number generated by Alice at Step 1.)

Step 3: Bob computes the encrypted value $E(g(x))$ (without be able to learn $f(x)$ and x) as following:

(a) Based on the homomorphic property of Alice's public key cryptosystem

$$E(f(x)) = E(x^2 - (\alpha + \beta)x + \alpha\beta) = E(x^2) \oplus (\alpha + \beta) \otimes E(n - x) \oplus E(\alpha\beta)$$

(b) Note that since α and β are known to Bob (but not to Alice), he can compute $\alpha \otimes E(n - x)$ as

$$E(\underbrace{(-x) + (-x) + \cdots (-x)}_{\alpha}) = \underbrace{E(n - x) \oplus E(n - x) \oplus \cdots \oplus E(n - x)}_{\alpha}$$

Step 4: Bob generates a random numbers z, such that $z \geq (\frac{\alpha+\beta}{2})^2$ and sends two pairs (u, v) and (v, u) to Alice in random but known to Bob order where $v = E((f(x) + z)) = E(f(x)) \oplus E(z)$ and $u = E(z)$ to Alice.

Step 5: Alice finds $(f(x) + z)$ and z by using her private key, that is $f(x) + z = D(v)$ and $z = D(u)$, and evaluates truthfulness of the predicate $(D(u) \geq D(v))$ and $D(v) \geq D(u)$. Note that Alice does not know which value of the pairs represent z and which of them represent $f(x) + z$. Alice sends truthfulness results of evaluation to Bob (at the same order the pairs were received from Bob).

Step 6: Based on the received from Alice evaluation result, Bob can see without knowing $f(x)$ whether $f(x) \geq 0$ or not, and consequently decide whether $x \in [\alpha, \beta]$.

Fig. 3. Protocol: Privacy-preserving predicate evaluation

decryption are standard operations required almost always to enforce security in any distributed system, we always would expect at least one encryption in addition to key generation. Therefore those additional encryption and decryption operations can be seen as the price we have to pay for privacy protection.

5   Conclusion

We have proposed a solution of privacy preserving event detection problem based on privacy preserving pattern matching algorithm. The algorithm can be used to implement monitoring and detection events in sensor networks without violating privacy of objects under observation.

References

1. Crochemore, M., Rytter, W.: Text Algorithms. University Press (1994)
2. Crochemore, M., Hancart, C.: Pattern Matching in Strings. In: Atallah, M.J. (ed.) Handbook of Algorithms and Theory of Computation, CRC Press, Boca Raton (1996)
3. Crochemore, M., Lecroq, T.: Pattern Matching and Text Compression Algorithms. In: Tucker, A.B. (ed.) The Computer Science and Engineering Handbook, CRC Press, Boca Raton, USA (1997)
4. Du, W., Atallah, M.J.: Secure Multi-Party Computation Problems and Their Applications: A review and Open Problems. In: Proc. of New Security Paradigms Workshop, pp. 13–22 (2001)
5. Du, W., Zhan, Z.: A practical Approach to Solve Secure Multi-Party Computation Problems. In: Proc. of New security paradigms, pp. 127–135 (2002)
6. Gwadera, R., Atallah, M.J., Szpankowski, W.: Reliable Detection of Episodes in Events Sequences. In: Proc. of the Third IEEE Intern. Conf. on Data Mining (ICDM'03), IEEE Computer Society Press, Los Alamitos (2003)
7. Knuth, D.E., Morris, J., Pratt, V.: Fast Pattern Matching in Strings. SIAM Journ. on Comp. 6, 323–350 (1977)
8. Morrill, J.P.: Distributed Recognition of Patterns in Time Series Data. Comm. of the ACM 41, 45–51 (1998)
9. Naccache, D., Stern, J.: A New Cryptosystem Based on Higher Residues. In: Proceedings of the 5th ACM Conf. on Computer and Communication Security, pp. 59–66. ACM Press, New York (1998)
10. Okamoto, T., Uchiyama, S.: An Efficient Public-Key Cryptosystem as Secure as Factoring. In: Nyberg, K. (ed.) EUROCRYPT 1998. LNCS, vol. 1403, pp. 308–318. Springer, Heidelberg (1998)
11. Oleshchuk, V.A.: On-line Constraint-based Pattern Matching on Sequences. In: Ding, C., Helleseth, T., Niederreiter, H. (eds.) Sequences and Their Applications - Proc. of SETA '98, pp. 330–342. Springer, Heidelberg (1999)
12. Oleshchuk, V.A.: On-line Fuzzy Pattern Matching on Sequences. In: Mastorakis, N.E. (ed.) Advances in Fuzzy Systems and Evolutionary Computation, pp. 144–149 (2001)
13. Paillier, P.: Public-Key Cryptosystems Based on Composite Degree Residuosity Classes. In: Stern, J. (ed.) EUROCRYPT 1999. LNCS, vol. 1592, pp. 223–238. Springer, Heidelberg (1999)
14. Wagner, D.: Resilient aggregation in sensor networks. SASN '04: Proc. of the 2nd ACM workshop on Security of ad hoc and sensor networks, 78–87 (2004)
15. Yao, A.C.: Protocols for Secure Computations. In Proc. of the 23th IEEE Symp. on Foundations of Computer Science (1982).

A Distributed Clustering Algorithm
for Fault-Tolerant Event Region Detection
in Wireless Sensor Networks*

Ali Abbasi[1], Euhanna Ghadimi[1], Ahmad khonsari[1,2], Naser Yazdani[1],
and Mohamed Ould-Khaoua[3]

[1] Department of Electrical and Computer Engineering,
University of Tehran, Tehran, Iran
[2] IPM, School of Computer Science, Tehran, Iran
[3] Department of Computer Science, University of Glasgow, Glasgow, UK
{a.abbasi,e.ghadimi}@ece.ut.ac.ir ak@ip.ir
n.yazdani@ut.ac.ir mohamed@dcs.gla.ac.uk

Abstract. Wireless sensor networks which are envisioned to consist of many
simple processing, storage, sensing, and communication capabilities are
believed to open the doors to a plethora of new applications. Efficient robust
data aggregation is a key feature in information processing in wireless sensor
environments, especially in the presence of faulty sensor nodes which arise due
to harsh environments or manufacturing reasons. These conditions highly affect
the quality of gathering data in different locations and times. In this paper we
propose a distributed localized method for detecting regions that are susceptible
to message loss above a given threshold, and then based on this method we
suggest an algorithm for clustering nodes in that region which proportionally
adapts based on message loss. Simulation experiments confirm the validity of
the proposed algorithm with a high degree of accuracy.

1 Introduction

Wireless sensor networks have revolutionized the way of getting knowledge about our
environment. These networks consist of several nodes that are able to interact with
their environment by sending or controlling physical parameters; these nodes have to
collaborate to fulfill their tasks that usually a single node is incapable of doing so; and
they use wireless communication to enable this collaboration. Usually, the nodes
within such a network contain at least some computation, wireless communication,
and sensing or control functionalities. Wireless sensor networks are powerful since
they are amenable to support a lot of very different real world applications [5].

Sensor networks may be asked to answer any number of queries about the
environment. Existing approaches to in-network query processing and aggregation in
sensor environments can be classified into three classes; Tree-based, multipath-based,

---

* This work is partially supported by Iran Telecommunication research Center (ITRC).

P. Thulasiraman et al. (Eds.): ISPA 2007 Workshops, LNCS 4743, pp. 493–502, 2007.

and hybrid. An approach used in TinyDB [10,11] construct a spanning tree in the network, with the base station as root. Because of high message loss in these environments (up to 30% is frequent [15]) loosing 80% of sensor values is a common case, which results high inaccuracy in query answers.

Multipath-based approaches are designed to conquer non-robustness of tree-based approach. These approaches decouple aggregation and routing, therefore in these approaches, any robust routing can be used. Two disjoint works by Nath et al [13] and Considine et al [2] proposed using multipath routing and DOI (Duplicate and Order Insensitive) data structures for duplicate elimination. Multipath routing may results receipt of messages by multiple parents. To prevent double counting values, DOI structures are used. Due to the probabilistic nature of these structures, we will have an approximation error in the results.

Manjhi et al [12] proposed Tributaries and deltas architecture that combines the benefits of both methods by adaptively using both methods based on network conditions. At the same time tree-based method is used in some portion of network and multipath in other part. Tributary-deltas [12] use one multipath region around the base station. One disadvantage of Tributary-Deltas arises in environment which the probability of regions with high loss rate is high. In such environment there may be regions with high loss rate distributed unevenly in wireless sensor networks and these regions are separated from each other. Tributary-deltas tries to scale multipath region around the base station in a manner to cover other high loss rate regions which are distributed in the network. This method clearly is inefficient when the diameter of the network is large which requires a large number of steps to cover, which increases aggregated approximation errors. Another disadvantage relates to fast power depletion of nodes in the proximity of the base station. Multipath computation requires DOI to repropagate among the collaborating nodes which consumes more power for nodes that are closer to the base station. As a secondary result, the power depletion of nodes may produce a more disconnected network. So this architecture is not suitable for non-uniform network conditions. Our proposed method tries to consider the two problems discussed above. Instead of expanding multipath region around the base station, it is suitable to use multipath routing and computation in every high loss rate regions, then, propagate the query responses from these high loss rate regions to the base station using tree based method.

The base of clustering is that a node can detect which is located in a high loss rate region or not. It can be seen as an event detection process. Krishnamachari et al [6] provides a Bayesian approach for distributed fault-tolerant event region detection. Their work is based on the fact that there is a correlation among near sensors' measurements but faults are likely to be stochastically uncorrelated. Luo et al [9] extends their work to a more general class considering the probability of occurrence or non-occurrence of the event may not be equal. We use a distributed localized event detection algorithm as the base of detecting high loss rate condition at nodes.

The remainder of the paper is organized as follows. Section 2 provides briefly some preliminaries to event detection, and then the suggested method for event detection. Section 3 outlines the clustering algorithm proposed and border node detection method we used. Section 4 presents the simulation experiments and validation of the proposed algorithm. Finally Section 5 concludes this study and presents some future directions.

2   Modified Fault-Tolerant Event Detection Method and Some Preliminaries

In the following section we present some preliminaries on event detection method and then we provide our modified detection method.

2.1   Preliminaries

In detection applications, a sensor network is deployed over an area to detect events of interest. A sensor makes a binary decision on incidence of interested event independent of others based on its own measurement. Incorrect measurement due to noise or faulty sensing devices can lead to wrong event reports, i.e. a sensor reports "no event" when it is in an event region or vice versa. An approach to cope with unreliability of individual sensor's detection is to use a two-layer detection system which consists of a set of sensors as detectors and a fusion sensor [9]. Preliminary decisions concerning to unknown hypothesis (H_0 or H_1) at detectors are sent to fusion sensor at which they are combined to make ultimate decision.

We assume that sensors are densely deployed therefore an event covers multiple sensors. Measurements of the sensors in an event region are highly correlated to each other but this is not the case for faults in these sensors, therefore when faults are not so common, majority of sensors in the event region correctly report "event". As a result, by combining all the decisions through majority voting process, we expect to reach a correct final answer. There are two possibilities for declaring an event occurrence as given in [9]:

$P_F = P(u_i = 1 | H_0)$ Probability of detection of event when there is no event

$P_D = P(u_i = 1 | H_1)$ Probability of detection of event when there is an event

Each node which detects an event locally acts as a fusion sensor and uses its neighbors' decision to correct its own. The node broadcasts a message to its neighbors asking their decisions regarding to event. u_i denotes the binary decision of i'th neighbor. Subsequent to receiving neighbor's decisions a majority voting is done to find the final decision (u_0). If the sum of neighbors' values is above some predefined threshold value, the event is occurred. Otherwise, event does not occur.

$$u_0 = \begin{cases} 1, & u_1 + u_2 + ... + u_n \geq k \\ 0, & u_1 + u_2 + ... + u_n \leq k \end{cases} \qquad [9]$$

2.2   Modified Event Detection Method

We modified the fault-tolerant detection discussed so far slightly. Our aim was to reduce the impact of faulty nodes in final decision making process. To do this, we assign weights to sensor decisions based on correctness of their past history of decisions. Correctness of a local decision is evaluated based on its difference to final decision that we assume shows the real state of environment.

The suggested method is an extension to majority voting process to lessen its limitations. Majority voting procedure as used in the previous work [9], has some limitations: 1- each sensor provides a binary value indicating occurrence of event, not it's level of confidence to the event, 2- each neighbor sensor has the same weight as others, although it is likely that closer neighbors have more correlation with fusion sensor and also some sensors may be pearmanently faulty or their detection always have little correlation with fusion sensor.

In the proposed method, each sensor instead of providing its binary decision sends a value indicating its confidence to event occurrence. Then a weighted averaging process is done at the fusion sensor. As the following (1):

$$avg = \sum_{i=1}^{n} w_i \times p_i \qquad \sum_{i=1}^{n} w_i = 1 \tag{1}$$

Weight w_i in equation (1) has a linear relation to confidence on the operation of the sensor that we denote it by c_i. Fusion sensor assigns confidences to detectors; after each round of decision making process, fusion sensor reevaluates these confidences. The confidence to sensor will be increased if it has large correlation with final answer in this round and vice versa if it has not. As s result of this adaptation process larger weights are assigned to sensors which their history of decisions shows more correlation to the decisions of fusion sensor. So nodes that recently had closer values to the average value, receive more weights in comparison to other nodes. Adaptation mechanism is the same as the method used in TCP for estimating round trip time based on the feedback received from the network [4].

Total detection and adaptation procedure is as follows: fusion sensor n initiates the process. In response, each node in neighbor (n) provides the probability that assigned to the event occurrence. Averaging is done next. Afterward the maximum distance of the values to the average is computed (3). Then, this value is used to compute dissimilarity of each node value from the average, see (4). Formula (4) typically used in clustering algorithms to find distance of two objects [1].

$$m = max(\{|avg - p_i|, \forall i \in neighbor(n)\}) \tag{2}$$

$$D(p_i, avg) = cos([1 - \frac{|avg - p_i|}{m}] \times \frac{\pi}{2}) \tag{3}$$

The current confidence value to each node has an inverse relation to the dissimilarity of node to the average. In other words, if dissimilarity is large, confidence is low and if it is low, the confidence is large. We use (5) to get current confidence to each node.

$$c_{i-cur} = 1 - D(p_i, avg) \tag{4}$$

Then, the adaptation of confidence by the current confidence is done via (6).

$$c_i = \alpha \times c_{i-old} + (1 - \alpha) \times c_{i-cur} \qquad \alpha \in [0,1) \tag{5}$$

Through this process, nodes that are faulty get less and less weighted so their decisions get less effective. At first, the confidence values for all neighbor sensors are equal. We can use confidence values as weights in the averaging process. However, we expect nearer sensors show more correlation with fusion sensor, so we can consider a distance factor that is a decreasing function of distance and obtain weights through below formula (7) and (8).

$$df_i = g(d_i) \tag{6}$$

$$w_i = c_i \times df_i \tag{7}$$

The distance factor, in general, can be dependent on sensors and events they want to detect and can be different for sensors in various modals. For instance, for two sensors detecting humidity in the air distance may not be an important issue but detecting some chemical might be important. So we must use different functions in different scenarios.

3   Clustering Algorithm

The aim of clustering algorithm is grouping all the nodes which located in a region in which message packets are susceptible to loss with high probability. We term such a region "high loss rate region". The algorithm works based on localized high loss rate region detection of each sensor. First part of the clustering algorithm is detecting high loss rate condition around a node and for this purpose we used the method introduced in section 2. For triggering local detection procedure we use information that query processing architecture provides for us.

A spanning tree with the base station as root is a common construct for query processing in sensor networks. Such a tree and query timing impose a specified interval in which a parent node listens to its children messages; performs some computation on them and sends the result to its parent [10]. We use message receipt of children to trigger high loss rate condition detection process. We assume that such a tree is constructed and is fixed for a long time. Another assumption is that the network is used for monitoring applications which provides us long running queries with discussed timing.

Figure 1 provides an instance, which shows a parent (A) and its three children (B,C,D). The parent expects three messages in a specified interval from each of its children. If the number of received messages is below the expected number for consecutive intervals it may be located in a high loss rate region and this triggers high loss rate region detection process (asking assurance values of all neighbors; B,C,D,E,F – figure 2).

Due to the hardware or software faults in sender or receiver, the message may not be transmitted reliably and, mistakenly, it is considered as a high loss rate condition. In our clustering, we want to cluster nodes that operate correctly and have useful data but cannot communicate efficiently because of noise and other conditions. Therefore we must separate a high loss rate condition from a fault occurring condition due to the hardware or software malfunctioning. So using a technique like the method of section 2 is necessary.

After detecting high loss rate condition, a node must structure a cluster or join to an existing cluster. Clustered regions in our application are high loss rate regions that

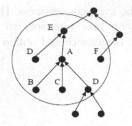

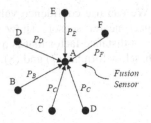

Fig. 1. data aggregation tree, all nodes in the circle are within transmition range of A

Fig. 2. sensor A obtains assurance value of each neighbor to the event occurrence

need more robust approaches for communication. These approaches usually incorporate some redundancy (e.g. multipath routing) that may not be required under normal conditions. Method of communication affects on the nodes processing schemes (e.g. synopses diffusion [12]). As a results, network is partitioned into clustered and unclustered regions each uses individual method of communication and processing. Furthermore, in a cluster all the members should use the same method. Consequently, the created cluster should be a seamless region in which have no node surrounded with the cluster border and is not a member of cluster.

As another issue, we need that all the communications between cluster border nodes and their neighbors is also obedient of cluster communication scheme. This is due to that these communications may be partially affected by high loss rate event. So the set of final cluster members is a superset of nodes located in high loss rate region. Thus we use one layer of sensors more than nodes that actually located in the high loss rate region (see figure 2). Following above discussion, Sensor nodes are classified into three types:

- M node: node located in high loss rate region.
- E node: node that not located in high loss rate region but has an M node neighbor.
- T node: node that not located in high loss rate region but doesn't have an M node neighbor.

As discussed above, a cluster must be a continuous region with no inside node operating differently. One way of ensuring this property is to shrink the cluster solely through the border nodes. This means that if a node inside the cluster detects that a high loss rate property is not satisfied any more, it cannot leave the cluster. By border node, we mean M node located in the border of cluster.

To implement this, nodes must be able to detect if they are located in the border of cluster or not. There are three cases that a node can become a border node or lose this property:

- When node joins to cluster it can be a border node.
- When node is a border node and a neighboring node joins cluster it can lose this property.
- When node is an inside node of cluster and a neighboring border node leaves the cluster it can become a border node.

So at these times, node must check this property. These situations are shown in figure 3. First node **b** is not part of the cluster and node **a** is a border node. After node **b** joined cluster it becomes a border node and node **a** becomes an inside node. In this process both nodes must perform border detection process. If node **b** leaves cluster, again node **a** becomes a border node. In this situation node **a** must perform border detection.

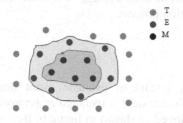

Fig. 3. Different types of nodes in a cluster   **Fig. 4.** Joining and leaving cluster

3.1 Border Node Detection

Boundary Recognition is a well studied problem in sensor networks (e. g., [7, 14]). We assume that sensor node know their location. This information can be obtained using GPS or some localization technique (e. g. [3, 8]). We used the method provided by zhang et al [14] for border node detection. In the process of boundary node detection of cluster only M nodes are considered.

Joining
1. Check for event: a window of measures of loss rate is retained
2. if (average of all the window measures is above Max-Threshold)
   a. Get the measures of neighbors
   b. Compute the weighted average and update confidences to neighbors
   c. If (avg > event-threshold)   // high loss rate event occurred
      i.   Send to all neighbors a message indicating it has changed status to M node
      ii. All nodes that receive message and are T node change type to E
      iii. Node performs border node detection algorithm

Leaving
1. All M border nodes check for event : a window of measures of loss rate is retained
2. if (average of all window measures is below Min-Threshold)
   a. Get the measures of neighbors
   b. Compute the weighted average and update confidences to neighbors
   c. If (avg < event-threshold)   // low loss rate
      i.   Send a message to all neighbors indicating it will change state to T node
      ii. All neighbors that receive message and are of E type because of that node change state to T
      iii. All neighbors that receive message and are of M type perform border node detection algorithm

---

Fig. 5. Clustering Algorithm

The complete algorithm is shown in figure 5. With this process it is possible that we have high oscillation in node type changing. A node maybe repeatedly enters and leaves cluster, so we consider two different thresholds [Min-Threshold...Max-Threshold].

- Max-Threshold: is a value that if the average of window values is higher than it, node enters event detection process.
- Min-Threshold: is a value that if for an M node average of window values is lower than it, node enters event detection process.

4 Experimental Results

In this section we provide our simulation results to evaluate event detection mechanism. The simulator is written in C. We consider a rectangular network with size 50×50 units that nodes are randomly deployed as shown in figure 6. Base station is located in the center of the network. In different runs number of nodes was between 1240 and 1270. Also transmission range was chosen to ensure that sensors have the average number of neighbors in simulation runs.

In each experiment we picked the averages of five runs of our algorithm as the output result. Event-Threshold is the other parameter of our algorithm that determines the minimum value for detecting event. We set Event-Threshold to the 0.35 for the simulation. Rectangular area with the size 11×11 units which contains almost 60 nodes via different simulation runs is high loss rate region as shown in figure 6. In this region each messages is lost with the probability of 0.7. We choose faulty nodes with the fault probability in a range of 0.01 to 0.5. We assume that a faulty node can not receive and send messages properly.

In the first experiment, we calculate the average confidence assigned to the faulty nodes by their neighbors in a long run. We expect that if there is low loss rate in an environment, faulty nodes show a distinguishable behavior from others. Because of the adapting mechanism incorporated in event detection (section 2.1), faulty nodes are assigned lower weights. If fault probability in sensor network increases, or in other words, the number of faulty sensors increases, average weight in every fusion sensor will be highly dependent on faulty sensors. As a consequence, difference between average value and faulty sensor value decreases, therefore the confidence assigned to the faulty sensors will be increased.

In the figure 7 we have depicted the average confidence assigned to the faulty sensors by their neighbors in increasing magnitude of fault probability. Simulation is done with different average number of neighbors. We expect that if the number of neighbors increased, then the number of nodes that participating in decision making increases. Therefore detection will be more accurate. Figure 7 validates this issue. As depicted in this figure the effects of faulty nodes in decision making process in the case of reasonable fault probability (< 0.1) and dense networks are eliminated.

In the second experiment, we assigned a rectangular region of network as a high loss rate region. In this region every message will be dropped with specified probability (0.7). The figure 8 shows detection probability as the ratio of nodes in region that detect high loss rate to the total number of nodes in the event region. As we expect, with increase in faulty nodes an augment in detection probability will be

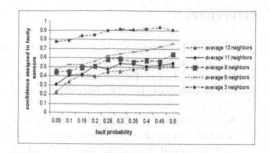

Fig. 6. 50×50 Network with randomly deployed nodes

Fig. 7. Average confidence assigned to the faulty sensors by their neighbors

seen. This is because of the inherent effect of faulty nodes which is similar to the event we want to detect (high loss rate).

In the third experiment, we evaluate the suggested method in terms of false alarm probability. False alarm probability is calculated as the ratio of nodes not located in high loss rate region but report high loss rate condition. The graph is shown in figure 9. As we expect, with growth in fault probability we have higher false alarm probability. But for realistic values of fault probability, false alarm probability is very low.

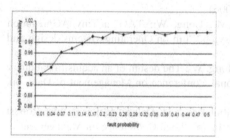

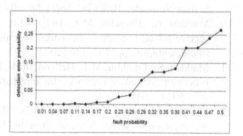

Fig. 8. Detection error probability

Fig. 9. Loss rate detection probability

5   Conclusion and Future Works

In this paper, we proposed a distributed message loss event detection method in high loss rate environments. Such environments are highly vulnerable to message loss events. The main advantage of the proposed method is to mitigate the effect of faulty nodes which arise due to harsh environments or manufacturing reasons. Based on the developed method and using local information an adaptive algorithm for clustering of nodes in high loss rate regions presented. Simulation experiments reveal that suggested algorithm is able to detect high loss rate event with probability over than 95% in most cases where there exists event. Our ongoing study focuses on proposing a method for robust data aggregation based the proposed algorithm of this paper.

References

1. Chidananda Gowda, K., Diday, E.: Unsupervised learning through symbolic clustering. Pattern Recognition Letters 12(5), 259–264 (1991)
2. Considine, J., Li., F., Kollios, G., Byers, J.: Approximate Aggregation techniques for sensor databases. In: 20th International Conference on Data Engineering, pp. 449–460 (2004)
3. He, T., Huang, C., Blum, B., Stankovic, J., Abdelzaher, T.: Range-free localization Schemes for large scale sensor networks. In: 9th international Conference on Mobile Computing and Networking, pp. 81–95 (2003)
4. Jacobson, V.: Congestion avoidance and control. In: Symposium Proceedings on Communication architectures and protocols, pp. 314–329 (1988)
5. Karl, H., Willig, A.: Protocols and Architectures for Wireless Sensor Networks. John Wiley, New York (2005)
6. Krishnamachari, B., Iyenger, S.: Distributed Bayesian Algorithms for Fault-Tolerant Event Region Detection in Wireless Sensor Networks. IEEE TC. 53(3), 241–250 (2004)
7. Kroller, A., Fekete, S.P., Pfisterer, D., Fischer, D.: Deterministic boundary recognition and topology extraction for large sensor networks. In: 7th annual ACM-SIAM symposium on Discrete algorithm, pp. 1000–1009. ACM Press, New York (2006)
8. Langendoen, K., Reijers, N.: Distributed localization in wireless sensor networks: a quantitative comparison. J. Com. Net. 43(4), 499–518 (2003)
9. Luo, X., Dong, M., Huang, Y.: On Distributed Fault-Tolerant Detection in Wireless Sensor Networks. IEEE TC. 55(1), 58–70 (2006)
10. Madden, S., Franklin, M.J., Hellerstein, J.M., Hong, W.: TAG: a Tiny AGgregation service for ad hoc sensor networks. In: 5th symposium on Operating systems design and implementation, pp. 131–146 (2002)
11. Madden, S., Franklin, M.J., Hellerstein, J., Hong, W.: The design of an acquisitional query processor for sensor networks. In: International Conference on Management of Data, pp. 491–502 (2003)
12. Manjhi, A., Nath, S., Gibbons, P.B.: Tributaries and Deltas: Efficient and Robust Aggregation in Sensor Network Streams. In: International Conference on Management of Data, pp. 287–298 (2005)
13. Nath, S., Gibbons, P.B., Seshan, S., Anderson, Z.: Synopsis diffusion for robust aggregation in sensor networks. In: 2nd international conference on Embedded networked sensor systems, pp. 250–262 (2004)
14. Zhang, C., Zhang, Y., Fang, Y.: Localized coverage boundary detection for wireless sensor networks. In: 3rd international conference on Quality of service in heterogeneous wired/wireless networks (2006)
15. Zhao, J., Govindan, R.: Understanding packet delivery performance in dense wireless sensor networks. In: 1st international conference on Embedded networked sensor systems, pp. 1–13 (2003)

Optimal Multicast Multichannel Routing in Computer Networks

Mohsen Heydarian[1], Ayaz Isazadeh[2], and Hosein Isazadeh[3]

[1] Faculty of Computer Engineering, Islamic Azad University Miyaneh-Branch,
Miyaneh, Iran
Mohsen_i2003@yahoo.com,
[2] Faculty of Mathematical Sciences, Tabriz University, Tabriz, Iran
[3] Savalon Information Technology Inc. 79 Queensway, Ontario Canada
hi@savalon.com

Abstract. This paper presents a new method for *optimal routing and transmitting data* in networks with multicast services environment. End to end delay is minimized by the new approach across channels. We entitle this method as ***Optimal Multicasting Multichannel Routing Algorithm (OMMRA)***. The new method transfers data from a sender node to the group of receivers using multichannel paths in minimal time. The new method is extention of an available unicast method. Computer examples will show that the new method is more efficient than unicast method.

1 Introduction

Two major problems that appear in data communication networks, such as Internet, are *multicasting provisioning* and *reducing delay* [1]. Multicast services provide efficient packet delivery to a number of group members, minimizing the total consumption of bandwidth [2,3,4,5].

The delay a packet experiences has three components: propagation delay, transmission delay, and queuing delay. [1]. Network manufactures use various techniques for reducing different components of delay. These techniques include Optimized Routing [6,7,8], Congestion Control [9], Traffic Management [10], Real Time Methods, Buffer Management [2,11,12,13], MPLS [1], and Linear Programming (LP) [14,15,16]. The LP method formulates the resources of the network in terms of a *Linear Programming* system of equations or inequalities. Consequently, network agent can solve this problem and control the delay appropriately [14,17,18].

G. L. Xue has presented a method based on LP modeling [15]. Its algorithm transfers data from a source to a destination using a unicast multichannel path in minimal time. This method is called *Optimal Unicast Multichannel Routing Algorithm (OUMRA)*. We extend the unicast method to the multicasting provisioning and establish the new method. The new method is based on the LP modeling and transfers data from a sender node to the group of receivers using a multicast multichannel path in minimal time. The new method is celled *Optimal Multicast Multichannel Routing Algorithm* or briefly OMMRA.

P. Thulasiraman et al. (Eds.): ISPA 2007 Workshops, LNCS 4743, pp. 503–512, 2007.

2   The New Method

The new method gives solution for the following problem: Let $\sigma > 0$ be the size of the message to be transmitted from source node s to destination nodes $t_1, t_2, \ldots, t_n$,, whereas each $s - t_i$, $i = 1, 2, \ldots, n$ path is a multichannel path, then determine minimum number of the time units in this transmission. We call this problem "Optimal Multicast Multichannel Routing problem".

A computer network is modeled by $N = (V, E, b, p, q)$, where $G = (V, E)$ is a directed simple graph with vertex set V, edge set E, and integer weighting functions $b(\bullet)$, $p(\bullet)$ and $q(\bullet)$: $b(u, v) > 0$ and $p(u, v) \geq 0$ are the bandwidth and propagation delay for a (directed) edge $e = (u, v) \in E$, and $q(u) \geq 0$ is the queuing delay at a vertex $u \in V$. Let s be a source vertex and t a destination vertex, OURMA is interested in routing a message of size σ from s to t as fast as possible while satisfying certain delay constraints .

Let $\pi = \langle v_1, v_2, \ldots, v_k \rangle$ be $v_1 - v_k$ path. The delay of path π is: $D(\pi) = \sum_{1 < j \leq k} p(v_{j-1}, v_j) + q(v_j)$. The maximum usable bandwidth of path π is $B(\pi) = \min_{1 < j \leq k} b(v_{j-1}, v_j)$. The time required to route a massage of $\sigma > 0$ along path π using a bandwidth of $\mathbf{b} \leq B(\pi)$ is $T(\pi, \mathbf{b}, \sigma) = D(\pi) + \lceil \frac{\sigma}{\mathbf{b}} \rceil - 1$ [15].

Definition 2.1. To facilitate the presentation of the OMMR Algorithm, we require to define below notation:

1. **Unicasting node:** This node should send input data only to one destination node. It is a intermediate node so can not be a destination node.
2. **Multicasting node:** This node should send input data to more than one destination node. It receives input data and for each of destination nodes, provides a copy of input data and sends it. The set of multicasting nodes is shown by "Multicast". It is a intermediate node so can not be a destination node.
3. **Multiplication:** It means data duplication in each multicasting node. Available maximum capacity of multiplication in a multicasting node $v \in V$ is shown by "Capacity(v)". Also $dup(v)$ shows that how much should multicasting node $v \in V$ multiplicate input data until data required for destination nodes to be provided.
4. **Multiplication Delay:** It is time units required for multiplication of input data in a multicasting node $v \in V$. It is shown by $c(v) \geq 0$. If v is a unicasting node or $dup(v) = 0$ then $c(v) = 0$.

Definition 2.2. Let n be number of destination nodes t_i, $i = 1, 2, \ldots, n$. Suppose from source s to each destination t_i there are k_i single path π_{ij}, $j = 1, 2, \ldots, k_i$. Furthermore, $\sigma > 0$ be the size of the message to be transmitted from s to each destination t_i and positive integer τ be number of consumed time unites in this transmission. The multicast multichannel routing decision problem asks the existence of a decomposition

$$\sigma = \sum_{1 \leq i \leq n, \ 1 \leq j \leq k_i} \sigma_{ij}, \quad (\sigma_{ij} \geq 0) \tag{1}$$

that part σ_{ij} must be transmitted along path π_{ij} from s to t_i. Also bandwidth of edge $(u, v) \in pi_{ij}$ must be decomposed as

$$b(u, v) = \sum_{1\leq i\leq,\ n,\ 1\leq j\leq k_i} b_{ij}(u, v) \quad (b_{ij}(u, v) \geq 0). \tag{2}$$

Furthermore for each multicasting node $v \in \pi_{ij}$, $dup_{ij}(v)$ to be computed until the following result to be obtained:

$$\max_{1\leq j\leq k_i,\ 1\leq i\leq n} T(\pi_{ij}, B_{ij}(\pi_{ij}), \sigma_{ij}) \leq \tau. \tag{3}$$

Linear Programming Formulation. Now we present the constrained-based routing model for the new method. This model is established by LP formulation. In Theorem 2.1, we will proved that there is always an optimal solution to the multicast maximal dynamic flow problem which can be decomposed into a set of $s - t_i$ arc chain flows. This should be proved.

Theorem 2.1. *The malticast maximal dynamic flow problem or briefly M_ MDF(τ) for τ periods can be computed by solving the following minimum cost static flow problem:*

(1) $M\_MDF(\tau):$ $\min \sum_{(u,\ v)\in E} d(u, v)f(u, v) + \sum_{v\in V} c(v)dup(v) - (\tau+1)n\phi$
s.t.

(2) $\sum_{(s,\ v)\in E} f(s, v) - \phi = 0$

(3) $\sum_{v\in E} f(v, t_i) - \phi = 0$ (i=1, 2, ..., n)

(4) $\sum_{(u,\ v)\in E} f(u, v) + dup(v) - \sum_{(v,\ u)\in E} f(v, u) = 0$, $(u \neq s, t)$

(5) $\sum f(s, v) = \sum f(u, t_i)$, $v \in V$, $\{(s, v), (u, t_i)\} \in \pi_{ij}, j \in \{1, 2, ..., k_i, \}$

(6) $(m-1)\sum f(u, v) \geq dup(v)$, $v \in Multicast$, m is number of outputs of v.

(7) $\sum_{(u,\ v)\in E} f(u, v) \geq f(v, u)$, $v \in V$.

(8) $0\leq f(u, v) \leq b(u, v)$, $(u, v) \in E$.

(9) $0\leq dup(v) \leq Capacity(v)$, $(v) \in V$.

Let (ϕ, f, dup) be an optimal solution to the above LP problem. Then the flow f can be decomposed into a set of $s - t_i$ arc-chain flows $i = 1, 2, ..., n$; for each malticasting node $v \in V$, $dup(v)$ can be distributed along $v - t_i \in \pi_{ij}$ paths; and the maximum amount of data from s to all of the destination nodes t_i in τ time units is:

$$\chi(\tau) = (\tau + 1)n\phi - \sum_{(u,\ v)\in E} d(u, v)f(u, v) - \sum_{v\in V} c(v)dup(v) \tag{4}$$

Corollary 2.1. *The multicast multichannel routing decision problem for τ periods can be computed by solving a corresponding Multicast_ Maximum Dynamic Flow problem._ Should be proved.*

Note that the maximum amount of data to be transmitted from s to a destination node t_i in τ time units is shown by $\chi(\tau, t_i)$ and we have: $\chi(\tau, t_i) \geq \frac{1}{n}\chi(\tau) \geq \sigma$. Let $\chi(\tau, t_i)$ be the maximum amount of data that to be transmitted from s to t in τ time units. The answer to the multicast multichannel routing decision problem is **YES** if $\chi(\tau, t_i) \geq \sigma$ and **NO** Otherwise.

Definition 2.3. The Optimal Multicast Multichannel Routing problem is solving the multicast multichannel routing decision problem as time units τ to be minimized and **YES** answer to be guaranteed.

We present Algorithm OMMR to solving the Optimal Multicast Multichannel Routing problem. Algorithm OMMR solves a sequence of $M\_MDF(\tau)$ problems to find the smallest τ which guarantees an **YES** answer to the multicast multichannel routing decision problem.

Algorithm OMMR:

(1) Let $\alpha :=0$ and $\beta := \sigma + D(\pi^*)$.

(2) If $\beta = \alpha+1$ goto Step-5.

(3) Let $\gamma := \lfloor (\alpha + \beta)/2 \rfloor$ and solve the γ-periods maximal dynamic flow problem. Let $\chi(\gamma)$ be the maximum amount of data that can be transmitted from s to all of the t_i in γ units of time.

(4) If $\lfloor (\chi(\gamma))/n \rfloor \geq \sigma$ then $\beta := \gamma$ else $\alpha := \gamma$ endif; goto Step-2.

(5) Let $\tau := \beta$ and solve the minimum cost flow problem $M\_MDF(\tau)$ to obtain flow value ϕ and edge flow assignments f. Let i:=0. goto Step-6.

(6) Let $i = i+1$, $k_i = 0$, $j = k_i$; if $i > n$ goto step-11, else goto Step-7; endif.

(7) $k_i = k_i+1$, $j = k_i$; Compute an $s - t_i$ path π_{ij} in G(V, E, b, d) to maximize $B_{ij}(\pi_{ij}) = min_{(u,\ v) \in \pi_{ij}} f(u,\ v)$;

if π_{ij} is marked path then let $k_i = k_i$-1, $j = k_i$; goto Step-6

else if

$B_{ij}(\pi_{ij})=0$ then let $k_i = k_i$-1, $j = k_i$; goto Step-9

else

goto step-8

endif;

(8) Choose the node $v_m \in Multicast$ which it is closest multicasting node to t_i and $dup(v_m) > 0$, $(v_m \in \pi_{ij})$.

(a): if $v_m \neq s$ then

Compute the single $v_m - t_i$ path and call it π, $(\pi \in \pi_{ij})$. Compute $less = min_{(u,\ v) \in \pi}\{dup(v_m), f(u,\ v)\}$.

if $less =0$ then goto Step-9. endif;

$dup(v_m) = dup(v_m) - less$

$dup_{ij}(v_m) = less$

for each $e \in E$ do

if $e \in \pi$ then

$b_{ij}(e) = b_{ij}(e) + less$

$f(e) := f(e) - less$

else

$b_{ij}(e) = 0$

endif; endfor; endif; goto step-8

(b): if $v_m = s$ then

Compute $less = min_{(u,\ v) \in \pi_{ij}} f(u,\ v)$.

if $less = 0$ then goto Step-9.endif;

for each $e \in E$ do

if $e \in \pi_{ij}$ then

$b_{ij}(e) = b_{ij}(e) + less$

$f(e) := f(e) - less$

else

$b_{ij}(e) =0$

endif; endfor; endif;

(9) Let $D(\pi_{ij}) = c(v) + \sum d(u,\ v)$. Notice that v is a multicasting node and it is closest node to t_i and $dup_{ij}(v) > 0$. The location of the edge $(u,\ v)$ is after the multicasting node v on the π_{ij}. $B^*(\pi_{ij}) = max_{(u,\ v) \in \pi_{ij}} f(u,\ v), j = 1, 2, \ldots, k_i$. Goto Step-10.

(10) Mark π_{ij}; goto Step-7.

(11) Compute a positive integer decomposition σ. $\sigma = \sum_{1 \le j \le k_i} \sigma_{ij}$, $(\sigma_{ij} \ge 0$ and $i \in \{1, \ldots, n\})$ such that $(\tau - D(\pi_{ij}))B^*(\pi_{ij}) \le \sigma_{ij} \le (\tau - D(\pi_{ij}) + 1)B^*(\pi_{ij})$.

Theorem 2.2. *The input size of the optimal multicast multichannel routing problem is:*
$$\Theta(n + m + \sum_{(u,\ v) \in E}(\lfloor \log_2 b(u,\ v) \rfloor + 1 + \lfloor \log_2 d(u,\ v) \rfloor + 1 + \lfloor \log_2 c(v) \rfloor + 1 + \lfloor \log_2 Capacity(v) \rfloor + 1)).$$

Prof: Is under research these days.

Theorem 2.3. *The worst-case time complexity of the Algorithm OMMR is polynomial in the input size.*

Prof: Is under research these days.

Theorem 2.4. *Algorithm OMMR computes an optimal solution to the multicast multichannel routing problem. The optimal routing consists of transmitting σ_{ij} units of data along path π_{ij} at a rate of $B_{ij}(\pi_{ij})$ units of data per time unit for $i = 1, 2, \ldots, n$ and $j = 1, , 2, \ldots, k_i$._ Should be proved.*

Let $\tau(\sigma)$ be the minimum number of time units required to transmit a message of size σ from s to destination nodes t_i. Let π_{ij}^* be an $s - t_i$ path with minimum delay. Then $\tau(\sigma) \le \sigma + D(\pi_{ij}^*)$ [15].

3 Example and Numerical Results

For describing Algorithm OMMR we select simple network in Fig. 1. The node s is a source node, whereas two nodes t_1 and t_2 are destination nodes. Two intermediate vertexes v_1 and v_2 are multicasting vertexes. Also, two vertexes v_3 and v_4 are unicasting vertexes. To simplify notation, we will assume $e_1 = (s,\ v_1)$, $e_2 = (s,\ v_3)$, $e_3 = (v_1,\ t_2)$, $e_4 = (v_1,\ v_2)$, $e_5 = (v_2,\ t_2)$, $e_6 = (v_2,\ t_1)$, $e_7 = (v_3,\ t_1)$, $e_8 = (v_3,\ v_4)$, $e_9 = (v_4,\ t_1)$. In the Fig. 1, each edge $e_i \in E$ has been labeled by $f(e_i)$ $(b,\ d)$, and also each node $v \in V$, has been labeled by $dup(v)$ $[Capaciyt(v),\ c(v)]$. Note that both $f_i = f(e_i)$ and $dup(v)$ are computed by M_MDF(τ) problem. Figures Fig. 2 through Fig. 6 show applying step 6 through step 10 of the Algorithm OMMR to the Fig. 1. Note that $\pi^* = < s,\ v_1,\ t_2 >$ is the unique shortest delay $s - t_i$ path with a delay of $D(\pi^*) = 5$. We assume that amount of data to be transmitted from s to each t_i is $\sigma = 54$. Therefore at the start of the execution of Algorithm OMMR we have $\alpha = 0$, $\beta = 54 + 5 = 59$, and $\gamma = \lfloor (\alpha + \beta)/2 \rfloor = 30$. We proceed by step 3 to solve M_MDF(30), which produces a solution with $\lfloor \chi(30)/2 \rfloor = 273$, $\phi = 9$, $f_1 = 9$, $f_2 = 0$, $f_3 = 7$, $f_4 = 9$, $f_5 = 2$, $f_6 = 9$, $f_7 = 0$, $f_8 = 0$, $f_9 = 0$. Since $\lfloor \chi(30)/2 \rfloor = 273 \ge \sigma = 54$, β and γ are set to 30 and 15 by step 3.

In this stage the first iteration is ended and Algorithm OMMR jumps to step 2. Second iteration proceeds to solve M_MDF(15). The resultant values of carrying out seven iterations of step 2 through step 4 are given in Table 1. The

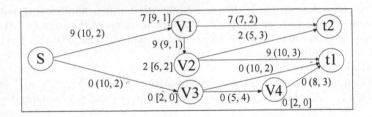

Fig. 1. A simple network with $f(c_i)(b, d)$ for each edge e and $dup(v)[capacity(v), c(v)]$ for each node e

seventh iteration satisfies the condition $\beta = \alpha + 1$, consequently, $\tau = 10$ and Algorithm OMMR jumps to step 5. It solves $M\_MDF(10)$ again and obtains optimal solution (ϕ, f, dup) with $\lfloor \chi(10)/2 \rfloor = 57$, $\tau = 10$, $\phi = 9$, $f_1 = 9$, $f_2 = 0$, $f_3 = 7$, $f_4 = 9$, $f_5 = 2$, $f_6 = 9$, $f_7 = 0$, $f_8 = 0$, $f_9 = 0$, $dup(v_1) = 7$, $dup(v_2) = 2$. Total time computation for above iterations is equal to 1.212

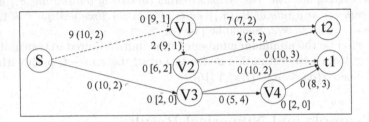

Fig. 2. Choosing and Marking π_{11}

After step 5, steps 6 through 10, compute delay, f_i, $dup(v_i)$ in the each path π_{ik_i}, $i = 1, 2$, $k_1 = 1, 2$, $k_2 = 1, 2, 3$. Note that there are two $s - t_1$ paths and three $s - t_2$ paths from s to destinations t_1 and t_2. As mentioned above, s is multicasting node and $dup(s) > 0$, $c(s) = 0$. In step 6, $i = 1$, $j = 0$. In step 7, we have $j = 1$ and the path $\pi_{11} = < s, v_1, v_2, t_1 >$ is chosen that $B_{11}(\pi_{11}) = 9$. Since π_{11} has not been marked yet and $B_{11}(\pi_{11}) \neq 0$, the Algorithm OMMR jumps to step 8. Note that when a path π_{ij} is marked, it will not be employed by

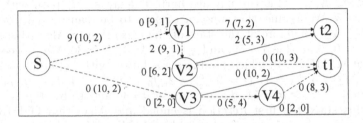

Fig. 3. Choosing and Marking π_{12}

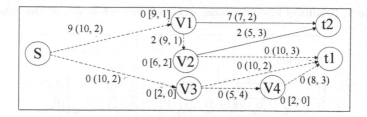

Fig. 4. Choosing and Marking π_{13}

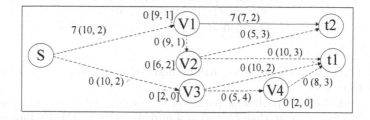

Fig. 5. Choosing and Marking π_{21}

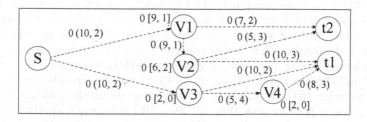

Fig. 6. Choosing and Marking π_{22}

Algorithm OMMR in the next computations. If all of the paths have been marked then Algorithm OMMR will be finished. Since the nearest multicasting node to t_1 is v_2 ($v_m = v_2$) and $dup(v_2) = 2 \neq 0$, the path $\pi = <v_2, t_1>$ is chosen. In this path, step 8(a) computes $less = 2$ and the following results are obtained: $dup(v) = 2 - 2 = 0$, $dup_{11}(v) = 2$, $f_6 = 9 - 2 = 7$, $b_{11}(v_2, t_1) = b_{11}(e_6) = 2$, (the flows assigned to other edges will be zero).

This time, Algorithm OMMR jumps to step 8 again. Step 8 computes ($v_m = v_1$) and $\pi = <v_1, v_2, t_1>$. Step 8(a) computes $less = 7$ and the following results are obtained: $b_{11}(e_6) = 2 + 7 = 9$, $f_6 = 7 - 7 = 0$, $b_{11}(e_4) = 7$, $f_4 = 9 - 7 = 2$, $dup_{11}(v_1) = 7$,, $dup(v_1) = 7 - 7 = 0$, (assigned flows to other edges will be zero). Now, Algorithm OMMR jumps to step 8 and $\pi = \pi_{11}$ and $v_m = s$ are selected. Step 8(b) computes $D(\pi 11) = c(v_2) + d(e_6) = 3 + 2 = 5$. In continuation, at first step 10 marks π_{11} next Algorithm OMMR jumps to step 7. The marked path π_{11} has been shown as dash marks in Fig. 2. Fig. 2 shows residual flow in marked path π_{11}. In the step 7 we have $j = 2$ and path $\pi_{12} = <s, v_3, v_4, t_1>$ will be chosen. Since $B(\pi_{12}) = 0$, Algorithm OMMR goes to step 9 and $D(\pi_{12}) = 9$

Table 1. Results of seven iterations of step 2 through step 4 of Algorithm OMMR

Iteration	α	β	γ	$M\_MDF(\gamma)$	Time Computation	$\lfloor \chi(\gamma)/2 \rfloor$
1	0	59	30	$M\_MDF(30)$	0.210	273
2	0	30	15	$M\_MDF(15)$	0.171	102
3	0	15	8	$M\_MDF(\ 8\ )$	0.170	39
4	8	15	12	$M\_MDF(12)$	0.160	75
5	8	12	10	$M\_MDF(10)$	0.170	57
6	8	10	9	$M\_MDF(\ 9\ )$	0.162	48
7	9	10	10	$M\_MDF(10)$	0.170	57

will be computed. The path π_{12} will be marked as Fig. 3 and Algorithm OMMR jumps to step 7.

As mentioned for path π_{12}, path $\pi_{13} =< s,\ v_3,\ t_1 >$ first is chosen then is marked as Fig. 4. Note that $D(\pi_{13}) = 4$ and Algorithm OMMR jumps to step 7. Since all of the ended paths to the destination t_1 have been marked, Algorithm OMMR jumps to step 6. Now, Algorithm OMMR analysis all of the paths that are ended to the destination t_2. In this stage i is set to 2 and we proceed to steps 7 and 8. The path $\pi_{21} =< s,\ v_1,\ v_2,\ t_2 >$ is chosen and we have $less = 2$. After reducing the flow on π_{21} by $less = 2$, we obtain the residual flow shown in Fig. 5. In continuation step 9 computes $D(\pi_{21}) = 6$ and step 10 marks π_{21} by dash marks (Fig. 5)). Now, Algorithm OMMR jumps to step 7. Step 7 sets j to 2 and chooses $\pi_{22} =< s,\ v_1,\ t_2 >$. Considering step 8(b) we have $less = 8$. After reducing the flow on π_{22} by $less = 8$, we obtain the residual flow in which no edge has a positive flow (Fig. 6). Step 10 marks π_{22} and Algorithm OMMR jumps to step 11. Briefly the results of step 6 through step 10 are : $b_{11}(e_4) = 7$, $b_{11}(e_6) = 9$, $b_{21}(e_1) = 2$, $b_{21}(e_4) = 2$, $b_{21}(e_5) = 2$, $b_{22}(e_1) = 7$, $b_{22}(e_3) = 7$, $dup_{11}(v_1) = 7$, $dup_{11}(v_2) = 2$, $dup(v_1) = 0$, $dup(v_2) = 0$.

After to mark all of the path $s - t_i$, $i = 1, 2$, Algorithm OMMR jumps to step 11. Now we proceed to choose σ_{11}, σ_{12}, σ_{13}, σ_{21}, σ_{21} such that $\sigma_{11} + \sigma_{12} + \sigma_{13} = 54$, $\sigma_{21} + \sigma_{21} = 54$ and $(\tau - D(\pi_{ij}))B^*(\pi_{ij}) \leq \sigma_{ij} \leq (\tau - D(\pi_{ij}) + 1)B^*(\pi_{ij})$. Consequently, we have $45 \leq \sigma_{11} \leq 54$, $0 \leq \sigma_{12} \leq 0$, $0 \leq \sigma_{13} \leq 0$, $8 \leq \sigma_{21} \leq 10$, $42 \leq \sigma_{22} \leq 49$. Therefore we can choose $\sigma_{11} = 54$, $\sigma_{12} = 0$, $\sigma_{13} = 0$, $\sigma_{21} = 8$, $\sigma_{22} = 46$. Algorithm OMMR transmits 54 units of data from s to each destination t_i in 10 time units. In this case note that 108 units of data have been transmitted from s to all of the destination and total transmission time is also 10.

Now we compute time transmission that Algorithm OUMR needs for transmitting 54 units of data from s to destinations t_1 and t_2. First we consider destination t_1. The paths π_{11}, π_{12}, π_{13}, are ended to t_1. The optimal solution $(\phi,\ f)$ is obtained as : $\phi = 19$, $f_1 = 9$, $f_2 = 10$, $f_3 = 0$, $f_4 = 9$, $f_5 = 0$, $f_6 = 9$, $f_7 = 10$, $f_8 = 0$, $f_9 = 0$, $\tau = 7$, $\chi(7) = 67$. Also total time transmission is 0.791. If σ_1, σ_2, σ_3 be amount of data that must be transmitted from π_{11}, π_{12}, π_{13} respectively, then we have $\sigma_1 + \sigma_2 + \sigma_3 = 54$, $9 \leq \sigma_1 \leq 18$, $0 \leq \sigma_2 \leq 0$, $30 \leq \sigma_3 \leq 40$. Consequently we choose $\sigma_1 = 14$, $\sigma_2 = 0$, $\sigma_3 = 40$. After finishing data transmitting from s to destination t_1, we consider destination t_2. As mentioned for destination t_1, for destination t_2 we will obtain the optimal solution (ϕ, f): $\phi = 10$, $f_1 = 9$, $f_2 = 0$, $f_3 = 7$, $f_4 = 3$, $f_5 = 3$, $f_6 = 0$, $f_7 = 0$, $f_8 = 0$, $f_9 = 0$, $\tau = 9$, $\chi(9) = 54$. Also total transmission is 0.570. If σ_1, σ_2, be amount of data that must be transmitted from π_{21}, π_{22} respectively, then we have $\sigma_1 + \sigma_2 = 54$, $9 \leq \sigma_1 \leq 12$, $35 \leq \sigma_2 \leq 42$. Consequently we choose $\sigma_1 = 12$, $\sigma_2 = 42$. Note that Algorithm OUMR transmits 108 units of data to destinations t_1 and t_2 at two different stages.

4 Comparison Between Two Algorithms OMMR and OUMR

Now we compare Algorithm OMMR (the new method) with Algorithm OUMR (the exist method). This comparison will shows advantages of our algorithm.

1. *Total Time of the Data Transmission:* As mentioned above, Algorithm OMMR transmits 108 units of data in $\tau = 10$ time units, whereas Algorithm OUMR transmits them in $\tau = 9 + 7 = 16$ time units. whereupon we obtain Algorithm OMMR as compared to Algorithm OUMR reduces time of transmission by 6 time units (or %37).
2. *Data Rate:* Data rate for Algorithms OUMR and 2 is $\frac{108}{10} = 10.8$ and $\frac{108}{16} = 6.75$, respectively. Therefore, Algorithm OMMR as compared to Algorithm OUMR improves data rate by 4 data units per time unit.
3. *Total Consumption of Bandwidth:* Suppose that bandwidth used for each Algorithm in a transmission be $\sum_{1 \leq i \leq 9} f_i$. Thus bandwidths used for both Algorithms OUMR and OMMR are 69 and 32 data units per time unit, respectively. Therefore Algorithm OMMR considers both the efficient routing by transmitting the multicast packets across as few links as possible, and the minimized used of the bandwidth by duplicating the packets in the multicasting nodes. This means Algorithm OMMR can reduce congestion.
4. *Time Computation of algorithm:* As mentioned above, time computations of Algorithms OUMR and OMMR are $0.570 + 0.791 = 1.361$ and 1.212 of second, respectively. Therefore Algorithm OMMR as compared to Algorithm OUMR reduces time computation by 0.149 of second.

5 Conclusion

In this paper the Unicasting Multichannel Routing Algorithm (OUMRA) has been extended to Multicasting Multichannel Routing Algorithm (OMMRA) and new Algorithm has been established. The new Algorithm transmits a message from a source node to more than one destination nodes in the minimum time. In fact we have presented a new algorithm based on the routing for multicast multichannel data transmission within QoS framework. The new algorithm is polynomial time of complexity. Obtained numerical results displayed OMMRA as compared to OUMRA improves *the rate of data transmission, efficiency of network and reduces the time of computation, total consumption of bandwidth, propagation delay, transmission delay, queuing delay and loss rate.*

References

1. Wang, Z.: Internet QoS: Architectures and Mechanisms for Quality of Service. In: Networking, Morgan Kaufmann, BellLabs, Lucent Technology, San Francisco (2001)
2. Matrawy, A.: A rate adaption algorithm for multicast sources in priority-based ip networks. IEEE Communication Letters 7 (2003)
3. Elwalid, A., Jin, C.: Mate: multipath adaptive traffic engineering. Computer Networks 40, 695–709 (2002)
4. Wang, C.F., Liang, C.T., Jan, R.H.: Heuristic algorithms for packing of multiple-group multicasting. Computers & Operations Research 29, 905–924 (2002)
5. Wang, C.F., Lai, B.R., Jan, R.H.: Optimum multicast of multimedia streams. Computers & Operations Research 26, 461–480 (1999)
6. Oliveira, C.A.S., Pardalos, P.M.: A survey of combinatorial optimization problems in multicast routing. Computers & Operations Research 32, 1953–1981 (2005)
7. Wang, B., Hou, J.C.: An efficient qos routing algorithm for quorumcast communication. Computer Networks 44, 43–61 (2004)
8. Lim, T.K., Praeger, C.E.: Finding optimal routings in hamming graphs. European Journal of Combinatorics 23, 1033–1041 (2002)
9. Zhu, X., Setton, E., Girod, B.: Congestion-distortion optimized video transmission over ad hoc networks. Signal Processing: Image Communication 20, 773–783 (2005)
10. Matrawy, A., Lambadaris, I., Huang, C.: Mpeg4 traffic modeling using the transform expand sample methodology. In: proc. 4th IEEE Int. Workshop on Networked Applications, pp. 249–256. IEEE Computer Society Press, Los Alamitos, amatrawy@sce.carleton.ca (2002)
11. van Lunteren, J., Engbersen, T.: Fast and scalable packet classification. IEEE Communication 21, 560–570 (2003)
12. Khan, S., Watson, R., Shoja, G.C.: Optimal quality of service routing and admission control using the utility model. Future Generation Computer Systems 19, 1063–1073 (2003)
13. Cova, T.J., Johnson, J.P.: A network flow model for lane-based evacuation routing. Transportation Research Part A: Policy and Practice 37, 579–604 (2003)
14. Xue, G.L., Sun, S.Z., Rosen, J.B.: Fast data transmission and maximal dynamic flow. Information Proceeding Letters, 127–132 (1998)
15. Xue, G.L.: Optimal multichannel data transmission in computer networks. Computer Communications 26, 759–765 (2003)
16. Ford, L.R., Fulkerson, D.R.: Constructing maximal dynamic flows from static flows. Operation Research 6, 419–433 (1958)
17. Parsa, M., Zhu, Q.: An iterative algorithm for delay-constrained minimum-cost multicasting. IEEE ACM Transactions on Networking, 127–132 (1998)
18. Simha, R., Narahari, B.: Single path routing with delay considerations. Computer Networks and ISDN Systems 24, 405–419 (1992)

A Secure On-Demand Source Routing Scheme Using Hierarchical Clustering in Mobile Ad Hoc Networks[*]

Woei-Jiunn Tsaur and Haw-Tyng Pai

Department of Information Management
Dayeh University, Changhwa, Taiwan, R.O.C.
{wjtsaur,paiokno1_27}@yahoo.com.tw

Abstract. In mobile ad hoc networks (MANETs), since all of the nodes communicate each other based on the routing protocol, and an attacker could manipulate a lower-level protocol to interrupt a security mechanism in a higher-level one, securing routing protocol is an important issue in MANETs. Recently, there exist several proposals that attempt to develop a secure routing protocol for MANETs. However, those methods are not actually secure against a variety of attacks, including the Sybil, wormhole, black hole, replay, blackmail, denial of service, and routing table poisoning attacks. Therefore, in this paper we design a secure hierarchical-clustering-based routing scheme using the self-certified public key cryptosystem, elliptic curve cryptosystem, pre-hashing, and nonce techniques against such attacks. Finally, we also analyze the advantages of our proposed scheme in terms of security and superiority.

1 Introduction

Mobile ad hoc networks (MANETs) [1] are an occasional infrastructureless network, formed by a set of wireless mobile hosts that dynamically establish their own network on the fly, without relying on any central administration. In other words, MANETs dynamically handle the joining or leaving of nodes in the network by self-organizing. This is a challenging task [2], since these devices have limited resources (CPU, storage, energy, etc.). Moreover, the network's environment has some features that add extra complications, such as the nodes' mobility bringing about frequent topology changes, as well as the unreliability and the limited bandwidth of wireless channels.

Most of the existing routing protocols follow two different design approaches [3] to confront the inherent characteristics of MANETs: the table-driven and the source-initiated on-demand approaches. Owing to limited bandwidth and power in MANETs, the source-initiated on-demand routing protocols are more suitable for such features. Moreover, securing routing protocol is an important issue in MANETs [2-3, 5-9]. In the cause of maintaining connectivity in MANETs, all participating nodes have to perform routing of network traffic. However, the previous research trust all the

---

[*] This work was supported by the National Science Council of Republic of China under contract numbers NSC 95-2219-E-212-001 and NSC 95-2218-E-212-008.

P. Thulasiraman et al. (Eds.): ISPA 2007 Workshops, LNCS 4743, pp. 513–522, 2007.

participants to correctly forward routing and data traffic [4]. Furthermore, an attacker could manipulate a lower-level protocol to interrupt a security mechanism in a higher-level.

Recently, there exist several proposals [3] that attempt to develop a secure routing protocol for MANETs. Each proposal has a different set of operational requirements and provides protection against different attacks by utilizing particular approaches. Ariadne [10] is the flagship protocol for securing dynamic source routing (DSR) [11]. It can defend against the alteration of route message and prevent various types of denial of service (DoS) attacks. Unfortunately, Acs et al. [12] stated Ariadne will suffer from a new attack, and proposed a provably secure on-demand source routing protocol, called ENDAIRA, against such an attack. However, they must assume (1) nodes are identified by identifiers in the neighbor discovery protocol and in the routing protocol. The identifiers are authenticated during neighbor discovery; (2) nodes that are not within each other's radio range are not able to run the neighbor discovery protocol successfully. In other words, the Sybil attack [13] and wormhole attack [14] will occur in ENDAIRA unless the above two assumptions are actually achieved. The Sybil attack exists if a single faulty entity can present multiple identities. Such attackers can control a substantial fraction of the system, and then causing a serious damage in MANETs. In the wormhole attack, an attacker records packets (or bits) at one location in the network, tunnels them to another location, and retransmits them there into the network. Due to most existing ad hoc network routing protocols without some mechanism to defend against the wormhole attack, it would be unable to find routes longer than one or two hops, severely disrupting communication. The wormhole attack can also form a serious threat in wireless networks, especially against many ad hoc network routing protocols.

Therefore, Argyroudis et al.'s [3] affirmed that there is a need for a solution that offers a lightweight approach to the problem of secure ad hoc routing, while taking into account the security prerequisites of different application scenarios, offering a flexible approach to the required security-performance balance. On the other hand, Yu and Chong [15] survey that clustering is an effective technique for regulating nodes in MANETs. It is because clustering makes it possible to guarantee basic levels of system performance [16], such as throughput and delay, in the presence of both mobility and a large number of mobile terminals. Hence, using the self-certified public key cryptosystem, elliptic curve cryptosystem, pre-hashing, and nonce [17] techniques, we propose a hierarchical-clustering-based secure and available routing scheme to actually overcome the above weaknesses in MANETs.

The rest of this paper is organized as follows. In Section 2, we propose a new hierarchical-clustering-based secure on-demand source routing scheme. Then in Section 3, the advantages of our proposed scheme will be analyzed in terms of security and superiority. Finally, some concluding remarks are presented in Section 4.

2   The Proposed Hierarchical-Clustering-Based Secure Routing Scheme

Inspired by Acs et al.'s solution [12], we comprehend a digital signature scheme that can avoid malicious nodes to fake route messages. However, the limited resources of power and computation are inherent in MANETs, and hence it is necessary to design an efficient digital signature schemes. Lauter [18] demonstrated elliptic curve cryptography is quite suitable for securing wireless networks with the point of view on security and performance. Moreover, Tsaur [19] further proposed the ECC-based self-certified public key cryptosystems to contribute that, verifying both a signature and the validity of public key can be concurrently accomplished in a logically single step. Therefore, our proposed secure routing scheme will be based on Tsaur's proposed cryptosystem. In the following, we first propose digital signature scheme for MANETs in Section 2.1, and then describe the proposed new hierarchical-clustering-based route discovery schemes using the proposed digital signature scheme in Section 2.2.

2.1 Initialization

Based on the efficient public key cryptosystem proposed by Tsaur [19], each node i can obtain its public-key/private-key pair ($PK_{\alpha i_j}, sk_{\alpha i_j}$), respectively. To begin with, we describe some terms in hierarchical-clustering-based MANETs, and illustrate them with Fig. 1. Moreover, the notations used in the proposed schemes also be depicted as follows.

[Notations]

*   Node: In MANETs each equipment is a node, and we denote it as αi_j, where $\alpha \in$ { A ~ Z } and i and j are integers larger than zero. For example, $A1_1$, $B2_3$, $N3_2$, etc are nodes.
*   Cluster member: Several nodes αi_j may be classified into a group to form a cluster αi, e.g., members $A1_1$, $A1_2$, $A1_3$, and $A1_4$ belong to cluster A1.
*   Cluster head and cross-cluster head: Every cluster head is chosen from all nodes in a cluster, and it can control the cluster. We denote a cluster head as αi_1, e.g., in Fig. 1, all leaf nodes $A1_1$, $B2_1$, $C7_1$, etc. As to the cross-cluster head, it is selected from several cluster-head nodes in order to coordinate these cluster heads, e.g., $M5_1$, $N3_1$, and $O5_1$ are cross-cluster heads in Fig. 1.
*   The root of cluster heads: It is selected from all of cross-cluster heads to manage them, e.g., $N3_1$ is the root of cluster heads in Fig. 1.
* $ID_{\alpha i_j}$: the identification of node αi_j .
* id: an identifier for route discovery
* p : a field size, where p is typically either an odd prime or a power of 2 in general applications, and its length is about 160 bits.
* E : an elliptic curve E over F_p , $E: y^2 = x^3 + ax + b \pmod{p}$, where the two field elements a, $b \in F_P$ and $4a^3 + 27b^2 \pmod{p} \neq 0$, and all the points (X, Y), $X \in F_P$, $Y \in F_P$, on E form the set of E (F_p) containing a point O called the point at infinity.
* B : a base point of order n over $E(F_p)$, where n is a large prime (160 bits) and the number of F_p -rational points on E denoted by #$E(F_p)$, is divisible by n.

- $X(G)$: the x-coordinate of point G
- M : a routing message to be signed.
- αi_1: the cluster head for issuing nodes' public keys, where the αi_1 can be generated by Chatterjee *et al.*'s proposed on-demand weighted clustering algorithm [20].
- $h(.)$: a one-way hash function [21] that accepts a variable length input and produces a fixed length output value x, where $x \in [2, n-2]$ and its length is 160 bits. The one-way hash function $h(.)$ should satisfy the properties that given $h(x)$, it is computationally infeasible to find $x' \neq x$ such that $h(x') = h(x)$, meanwhile, $h(x') \neq h(x)$ if and only if $x' \neq x$.
- $E(\ )/D(\ )$: the encryption / decryption function.
- $K_{Group-\alpha i}$: the group key for cluster αi , where $K_{Group-\alpha i} \in [2, n-2]$ and is generated by employing the group key generation scheme [22].

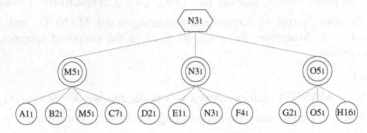

Fig. 1. An example of the cluster heads relationship

[Signature Generation]

Step 1. A node αi_j randomly selects a time-variant integer $k \in [2, n-2]$, and computes $k \cdot B = (X_{\alpha i_j}, Y_{\alpha i_j})$.

Step 2. αi_j computes $r = X_{\alpha i_j} \pmod{p}$ and $s = k + sk_{\alpha i_j} h(M \parallel r) \pmod{n}$.

Step 3. αi_j transmits the signature (r, s) and M to $\alpha i_j'$.

[Signature Verification]

Step 1. A node $\alpha i_j'$ computes

$$V_{\alpha i_j} = PK_{\alpha i_j} + h(ID_{\alpha i_j}) \cdot B + \left[(X(PK_{\alpha i_j}) + h(ID_{\alpha i_j})) \bmod n \right] \cdot PK_{\alpha i_1} \text{ and}$$

$$s \cdot B - h(M \parallel r) \cdot V_{\alpha i_j} = k \cdot B + sk_{\alpha i_j} h(M \parallel r) \cdot B - h(M \parallel r)(sk_{\alpha i_j} \cdot B)$$

$$= k \cdot B = (x_1, y_1) ,$$

where why $V_{\alpha i_j} = sk_{\alpha i_j} \cdot B$ can be found in [19].

Step 2. If $x_1 = r \pmod{p}$ holds, then the signature is valid.

2.2 The New Route Discovery Schemes

In the procedure of route discovery, we first employ the pre-hashing technique to ensure the initiator and target not to be tampered by malicious nodes during the route request process. Next, we use the nonce technique against the replay attack, where the nonce is chosen randomly. Finally, we use the group key and the proposed digital signature scheme as shown in Section 2.1 to protect the route request and reply processes in the two cases of intra-cluster and inter-cluster. The proposed new schemes are described as below.

Fig. 2. The new route discovery example

2.2.1 Intra-cluster

In Fig. 2, when node $A1_2$ initiates a route discovery toward $A1_5$, the intra-cluster route discovery process will be executed.

[Route request phase]

• **Source node** $A1_2$

Step 1. $A1_2$ computes the pre-hashing F, nonce r_{A1_2}, and RM_{A1_2}, where

$F = h(\text{REQUEST}, A1_2, A1_5, id)$, $r_{A1_2} = h(x_{A1_2})$ (x_{A1_2} is a randomly chosen parameter), and $RM_{A1_2} = E_{K_{Group-A1}}(F)$.

Step 2. $A1_2$ sends F, r_{A1_2}, RM_{A1_2} and $msg\text{-}A1_2 = (\text{REQUEST}, A1_2, A1_5, id, ti, ())$ to its cluster head $A1_1$, where ti is the TESLA time interval [23] at the pessimistic expected arrival time of the request packet at the target.

• **Cluster head** $A1_1$

Step 1. $A1_1$ receives F, r_{A1_2}, RM_{A1_2} and $msg\text{-}A1_2$ from $A1_2$.

Step 2. $A1_1$ verifies whether $F = h(\text{REQUEST}, A1_2, A1_5, id)$ and $D_{K_{Group-A1}}(RM_{A1_2}) = F$ hold, and then $A1_1$ stores r_{A1_2} if the result of verification is positive.

Step 3. $A1_1$ computes $r_{A1_1} = h(x_{A1_1})$ and then multicasts F, r_{A1_1}, RM_{A1_2}, and $msg\text{-}A1_1 = (\text{REQUEST}, A1_2, A1_5, id, ti, (A1_1))$ to the neighbor nodes, e.g., $A1_5$.

[Route reply phase]

• **Target node** $A1_5$

Step 1. $A1_5$ receives F, r_{A1_1}, RM_{A1_2} and $msg\text{-}A1_1$ from $A1_1$.

Step 2. $A1_5$ verifies whether $F = h(\text{REQUEST}, A1_2, A1_5, id)$ and $D_{K_{Group-A1}}(RM_{A1_2}) = F$ hold, and then $A1_5$ stores r_{A1_1} if the result of verification is positive.

Step 3. $A1_5$ computes the pre-hashing $F' = h(\text{REPLY}, A1_2, A1_5, id)$, $r_{A1_5}' = h(x_{A1_5}')$, and digital signature $S_{Intra-A1_5} = E_{sk_{A1_5}}(A1_5)$.

Step 4. $A1_5$ forwards $(F', r_{A1_5}', msg\text{-}A1_5')$ to $A1_1$, where
$$msg\text{-}A1_5' = (\text{REPLY}, A1_5, A1_2, ti, (A1_1), (S_{Intra-A1_5})).$$

• **Cluster head** $A1_1$

Step 1. $A1_1$ receives F', r_{A1_5}', and $msg\text{-}A1_5'$ from $A1_5$.

Step 2. $A1_1$ verifies F' and $S_{Intra-A1_5}$. If both $F' = h(\text{REPLY}, A1_2, A1_5, id)$ and $D_{PK_{A1_5}}(S_{Intra-A1_5}) = A1_5$ hold, then $A1_1$ stores r_{A1_5}', where $D_{PK_{A1_5}}(S_{Intra-A1_5})$ denotes the digital signature $S_{Intra-A1_5}$ is verified by employing PK_{A1_5}.

Step 3. $A1_1$ computes $r_{A1_1}' = h(x_{A1_1}')$ and $S_{Intra-A1_1} = E_{sk_{A1_1}}(A1_1)$, where $S_{Intra-A1_1}$ represents $A1_1$ is signed by its private key sk_{A1_1}.

Step 4. $A1_1$ forwards $(F', r_{A1_1}', msg\text{-}A1_1')$ to $A1_2$, where $msg\text{-}A1_1' = (\text{REPLY}, A1_5, A1_2, ti, (A1_1), (S_{Intra-A1_5}, S_{Intra-A1_1}))$.

• **Source node** $A1_2$

Step 1. $A1_2$ receives F', r_{A1_1}', $msg\text{-}A1_1'$ from $A1_1$.

Step 2. $A1_2$ verifies F' and $S_{Intra-A1_1}$. If both $F' = h(\text{REPLY}, A1_2, A1_5, id)$ and $D_{PK_{A1_1}}(S_{Intra-A1_1}) = A1_1$ hold, then $A1_2$ stores r_{A1_1}' and accepts $msg\text{-}A1_1' = (\text{REPLY}, A1_5, A1_2, ti, (A1_1), (S_{Intra-A1_5}, S_{Intra-A1_1}))$.

2.2.2 Inter-cluster

In Fig. 2, the inter-cluster route discovery process will be performed when node $A1_2$ initiates a route discovery toward $B2_3$.

[Route request phase]

• **Source node** $A1_2$

Step 1. $A1_2$ computes the pre-hashing F, a nonce r_{A1_2}, and RM_{A1_2}, where $F = h(\text{REQUEST}, A1_2, B2_3, id)$, $r_{A1_2} = h(x_{A1_2})$ (x_{A1_2} is a randomly chosen parameter), and $RM_{A1_2} = E_{K_{Group-A1}}(F)$.

Step 2. $A1_2$ sends F, r_{A1_2}, RM_{A1_2}, and $msg\text{-}A1_2 = (\text{REQUEST}, A1_2, B2_3, id, ti, ())$ to its cluster head $A1_1$.

- **Source cluster head** $A1_1$

Step 1. $A1_1$ receives F, r_{A1_2}, RM_{A1_2}, and msg-$A1_2$ from $A1_2$.

Step 2. $A1_1$ verifies whether $F = h(\text{REQUEST}, A1_2, B2_3, id)$ and $D_{K_{Group-A1}}(RM_{A1_2}) = F$ hold, and then $A1_1$ stores r_{A1_2} if the result of verification is positive.

Step 3. $A1_1$ computes $r_{A1_1} = h(x_{A1_1})$, digital signature $S_{Inter-A1_1} = E_{sk_{A1_1}}(A1_2)$ and msg-$A1_1 = (\text{REQUEST}, A1_2, B2_3, id, ti, (A1_1), (S_{Inter-A1_1}))$, and then multicasts F, r_{A1_1}, RM_{A1_2} and msg-$A1_1$ to the neighbor nodes, e.g., $A1_5$.

- **Intermediate node** $A1_5$

Step 1. $A1_5$ receives F, r_{A1_1}, RM_{A1_2}, and msg-$A1_1$ from $A1_1$.

Step 2. $A1_5$ verifies whether $F = h(\text{REQUEST}, A1_2, B2_3, id)$ and $D_{K_{Group-A1}}(RM_{A1_2}) = F$ hold, and then stores r_{A1_1} if the result of verification is positive.

Step 3. $A1_5$ computes $r_{A1_5} = h(x_{A1_5})$ and msg-$A1_5 = (\text{REQUEST}, A1_2, B2_3, id, ti, (A1_1, A1_5), (S_{Inter-A1_1}))$, and then multicasts F, r_{A1_5}, and msg-$A1_5$ to the neighbor nodes, e.g., $B2_3$.

- **Target node** $B2_3$

Step 1. $B2_3$ receives F, r_{A1_5}, and msg-$A1_5$ from $A1_5$.

Step 2. $B2_3$ verifies whether $F = h(\text{REQUEST}, A1_2, B2_3, id)$ holds, and then $A1_5$ stores r_{A1_1} if the result of verification is positive.

Step 3. $B2_3$ computes $r_{B2_3} = h(x_{B2_3})$, $RM_{B2_3} = E_{K_{Group-B2}}(F)$ and msg-$B2_3 = (\text{REQUEST}, A1_2, B2_3, id, ti, (A1_1, A1_5, B2_3), (S_{Inter-A1_1}))$, and then sends r_{B2_3}, RM_{B2_3} and msg-$B2_3$ to $B2_1$ for verifying the validity of $S_{Inter-A1_1}$.

- **Target cluster head** $B2_1$

Step 1. $B2_1$ receives r_{B2_3}, RM_{B2_3} and msg-$B2_3$ from $B2_3$.

Step 2. $B2_1$ verifies whether $F = h(\text{REQUEST}, A1_2, B2_3, id)$, $D_{K_{Group-B2}}(RM_{B2_3}) = F$, $D_{PK_{A1_1}}(S_{Inter-A1_1}) = A1_1$ hold, and then $B2_1$ stores r_{B2_3} if the result of verification is positive.

Step 3. When the result of verification is positive, $B2_1$ computes $r_{B2_1} = h(x_{B2_1})$, digital signature $S_{Inter-B2_1} = E_{sk_{B2_1}}(B2_3)$ and msg-$B2_1 = (\text{REPLY}, B2_3, A1_2, id, ti, (A1_1, A1_5, B2_3, B2_1), (S_{Inter-B2_1}))$, and then returns msg-$B2_1$ and r_{B2_1} to $B2_3$. Otherwise, $B2_1$ discards $B2_3$'s request.

[Route reply phase]
The operation of the route reply phase is similar as the one in intra-cluster as stated in Section 2.2.1. Each intermediate node signs the route reply, and then verifies the signature generated from its foregoing node. If the result of verifycation holds, the nonce will be stored, and then the route reply will be forwardded to source cluster head $A1_1$; otherwise, the route reply will be discarded. When $A1_1$ receives the route reply from intermediate node $A1_5$, it first verifies whether $D_{PK_{B2_1}}(S_{Inter-B2_1}) = B2_3$ and $D_{PK_{A1_5}}(S_{Intra-A1_5}) = A1_5$ hold, and then $A1_1$ stores r_{A1_5}' if the result of verification is positive. Second, $A1_1$ computes $r_{A1_1}' = h(x_{A1_1}')$, $S_{Intra-A1_1} = E_{sk_{A1_1}}(A1_1)$ and $msg\text{-}A\,1_1' = $ (REPLY, $B2_3$, $A1_2$, ti, ($A1_1$, $A1_5$, $B2_3$, $B2_1$), ($S_{Inter-B2_1}$, $S_{Intra-B2_3}$ $S_{Intra-A1_5}$, $S_{Intra-A1_1}$)). Afterward, $A1_1$ returns r_{A1_1}' and $msg\text{-}A\,1_1'$ to the source node $A1_2$. When $A1_2$ receives r_{A1_1}' and $msg\text{-}A\,1_1'$ from $A1_1$, it will verifie whether $D_{PK_{A1_1}}(S_{Intra-A1_1}) = A1_1$ holds. If the result of verification is positive, $A1_2$ stores r_{A1_1}', and therefore the inter-cluster route discovery process has been accomplished.

3 Discussion

The advantages of our proposed scheme will be analyzed in terms of security and superiority as follows:

(1) Security
Based on the computational intractability of a one-way hash function, because our proposed scheme uses the pre-hashing technique before broadcasting route request, no malicious nodes can tamper the REQUEST and identity of initiator and target to cause DoS attacks. Moreover, we also employ the nonce technique to avoid malicious nodes to paralyze the routing service. In addition, due to the difficulty of solving the elliptic curve discrete logarithm problem (ECDLP) [24], malicious nodes have no ability to fake any node's digital signature without its private key. Hence, each route reply must be valid and no one is able to possess multiple identities. On the other hand, our proposed scheme can prevent from the Sybil attack and wormhole attack (when only one pair of malicious nodes) owing to the fact that our proposed scheme actually makes nodes identified by identifiers in the procedure of the neighbor discovery. In addition, like the route request steps, the route reply steps also avoid DoS attacks by using the pre-hashing and nonce techniques.

(2) Superiority
There are several crypto-theories for securing routing protocols in MANETs [2-3, 6-9]. Even though the ID-based cryptosystem is efficient methods to secure routing protocols, it knows all users' private keys after user registration. Hence, the system authority may have the opportunity to masquerade as any legitimate user by generating a valid public-key/private-key pair for the user without being detected. Besides, the threshold scheme [25, 26] is also a solution for securing routing protocols in

MANETs, but it cannot actually satisfy MANETs' dynamic environments. This is because the threshold-based mechanisms cannot be achieved when the number of members is not up to the threshold value. Furthermore, the certificate revocation in the threshold solution must assume that each node is capable of monitoring the behavior of all its one-hop neighbors. This assumption, however, must be unreasonable in MANETs. Thus, as compared with the aforementioned two solutions, the proposed hierarchical-clustering-based secure routing scheme using the filter-based group key generation technique [22] and ECC-based self-certified digital signature scheme [19] will not suffer from the above problems, and is quite appropriate for MANETs.

4 Conclusion

In this paper, we propose a new hierarchical-clustering-based secure routing scheme by using the self-certified public key cryptosystem, elliptic curve cryptosystem, pre-hashing, and nonce techniques. It is extremely apparent that an attacker is unable to tamper any message of route request and route reply due to the difficulty of solving the elliptic curve discrete logarithm problem. Thus, the proposed routing scheme can be actually secure against a variety of attacks in MANETs. Moreover, in terms of superiority, the proposed scheme is also better than these based on the well-known ID-based cryptosystem or threshold scheme. In summary, the proposed scheme is quite suitable for securing routing in MANETs.

References

1. Wu, J., Stojmenovic, I.: Ad hoc networks. Computer 37(2), 29–31 (2004)
2. Yang, H., Luo, H., Ye, F., Lu, S., Zhang, L.: Security in mobile ad hoc networks challenges and solutions. IEEE Wireless Communications 11(1), 38–47 (2004)
3. Argyroudis, P.G., O'Mahony, D.: Secure routing for mobile ad hoc networks. IEEE Communications Surveys & Tutorials 7(3), 2–21 (2005)
4. Royer, E.M., Toh, C.K.: A review of current routing protocols for ad hoc mobile wireless networks. IEEE Personal Communications 2(6), 46–55 (1999)
5. Djenouri, D., Khelladi, L., Badache, N.: A survey of security issues in mobile ad hoc and sensor networks. IEEE Communications Surveys & Tutorials 7(4), 2–28 (2005)
6. Deng, H., Li, W., Agrawal, D.P.: Routing security in wireless ad hoc networks. IEEE Communications Magazine 40(10), 70–75 (2002)
7. Milanovic, N., Malek, M., Davidson, A., Milutinovic, V.: Routing and security in mobile ad hoc networks. Computer 37(2), 61–65 (2004)
8. Zhang, C., Zhou, M.C., Yu, M.: Ad hoc network routing and security: a review. In: International Journal of Communication Systems (in press, 2006)
9. Hu, Y.C., Perrig, A.: A survey of secure wireless ad hoc routing. IEEE Security and Privacy 2(3), 28–39 (2004)
10. Hu, Y.C., Perrig, A., Johnson, D.B.: Ariadne: A secure on-demand routing protocol for ad hoc networks. Wireless Networks 11(1-2), 21–38 (2005)
11. Johnson, D.B., Maltz, D.A., Hu, Y., Jetcheva, J.G.: The dynamic source routing protocol for mobile ad hoc networks (DSR). In: IETF Internet Draft (2002), http:// www.ietf.org/ internet-drafts/draft-ietf-manet-dsr-07.txt

12. Acs, G., Buttyan, L., Vajda, I.: Provably secure on-demand source routing in mobile ad hoc networks. IEEE Transactions on Mobile Computing 5(11), 1533–1546 (2006)
13. Douceur, J.R.: The Sybil attack. In: Druschel, P., Kaashoek, M.F., Rowstron, A. (eds.) IPTPS 2002. LNCS, vol. 2429, pp. 251–260. Springer, Heidelberg (2002)
14. Hu, Y.C., Perrig, A., Johnson, D.B.: Wormhole attacks in wireless networks. IEEE Journal on Selected Areas in Communications 24(2), 370–380 (2006)
15. Yu, J.Y., Chong, P.H.J.: A survey of clustering schemes for mobile ad hoc networks. IEEE Communications Surveys & Tutorials 7(1), 32–48 (2005)
16. Belding-Royer, E.M.: Multi-level hierarchies for scalable ad hoc routing. Wireless Networks 9(5), 461–478 (2003)
17. Keung, S., Siu, K.Y.: Efficient protocols secure against guessing and replay attacks. In: Proceedings of the International Conference on Computer Communications and Networks, pp. 105–112 (1995)
18. Lauter, K.: The advantages of elliptic curve cryptography for wireless security. IEEE Wireless Communications 11(1), 62–67 (2004)
19. Tsaur, W.J.: Several security schemes constructed using ECC-based self-certified public key cryptosystems. Applied Mathematics and Computation 168(1), 447–464 (2005)
20. Chatterjee, M., Das, S.K., Turgut, D.: On-demand weighted clustering algorithm (WCA) for ad hoc networks. In: Proceedings of IEEE Global Telecommunications Conference, pp. 1697–1701. IEEE Computer Society Press, Los Alamitos (2000)
21. Merkle, R.: One way hash functions and DES. In: Advances in Cryptology CRYPTO'89. LNCS, pp. 428–446. Springer, Heidelberg (1990)
22. Tsaur, W.J., Pai, H.T.: Dynamic Key Management Schemes for Secure Group Communication Based on Hierarchical Clustering in Mobile Ad Hoc Networks. In: Proceedings of the 2nd International Workshop on Intelligent Systems Techniques for Ad Hoc and Wireless Sensor Networks, in Conjunction with The Fifth International Symposium on Parallel and Distributed Processing and Applications (ISPA '07), Canada (August 2007)
23. Perrig, A., Canetti, R., Tygar, J.D., Song, D.: Efficient authentication and signing of multicast streams over lossy channels. In: Proceedings of the IEEE Symposium on Security and Privacy, pp. 56–73. IEEE Computer Society Press, Los Alamitos (2000)
24. Kanayama, N., Kobayashi, T., Saito, T., Uchiyama, S.: Remarks on elliptic curve discrete logarithm problems. IEICE Transactions on Fundamentals of Electronics, Communications and Computer Sciences E83-A(1), 17–23 (2000)
25. Wu, B., Wu, J., Fernandez, E.B., Ilyas, M., Magliveras, S.: Secure and efficient key management in mobile ad hoc networks. Journal of Network and Computer Applications 30(3), 937–954 (2007)
26. Zhang, Y., Liu, W., Lou, W., Fang, Y.: Securing mobile ad hoc networks with certificateless public keys. IEEE Transactions on Dependable and Secure Computing 3(4), 386–399 (2006)

A Hybrid Location-Semantic Approach to Routing Assisted by Agents in a Virtual Network

Nafaâ Jabeur and Phil Graniero

University of Windsor, Department of Earth and Environmental Sciences, 401 Sunset
Ave., Windsor, Ontario, Canada, N9B 3P4
{jabeur,graniero}@uwindsor.ca

Abstract. Routing in Ad-hoc Wireless Sensor Network (AWSN) has been
addressed by several research works which can basically be divided into flat-
based, hierarchical-based, and location-based routing depending on the network
structure. Despite advances in these interesting works, straightforward
messages routing is still extremely difficult. We still seek a flexible approach
that provides sensors with enough autonomy and processing capabilities to
determine secure, lower-cost, and reliable routes while preventing the routing of
unused data that burdens sensors. To meet this goal, we propose a requirement-
driven approach that uses geographic-based routing to focus sensing efforts
in areas of interest, plus semantic-based routing to determine and use relevant sensors semantically connected with respect to current monitoring
requirements. By moving most intensive processing into a virtual network
running in parallel to the physical AWSN, our approach uses software agents to
reduce network resource consumption and find enhanced routing pathways.

1 Introduction

Spatially distributed monitoring systems have been used in a wide variety of
applications over several decades. Conventional systems are structured as a collection
of stationary nodes; and where short-range, self-managed wireless communication is
used, the problem of setting up the communication network is relatively
straightforward. Once the network is deployed some adjustments may be made to
improve communication, but once communication is reliably established, things don't
really change much after that. For AWSN, in contrast, a 'deploy and ignore' approach
is no longer possible. Indeed, the conventional 'built-in' station is replaced by a large
number of lower-power motes which often conserve their resources by having
sleep/wake cycles and therefore communication pathways and network topologies
regularly change. Addition of mobile data collectors to monitoring systems creates a
similar challenge. Thus, especially in remote areas, sensors must be able to establish
and maintain routing pathways in order to collect and forward data to target sinks or
gateways. This routing task is particularly complex due to limited processing
capabilities and context awareness of sensors, large potential for data collisions, and
instability of the network topology; thus predefined paths become infeasible.

Routing in AWSN has attracted much attention during recent years [e.g. 1, 3, 5,
6, 9, 4, 8]. However, despite the existence of several approaches, straightforward

P. Thulasiraman et al. (Eds.): ISPA 2007 Workshops, LNCS 4743, pp. 523–533, 2007.

message routing is still extremely difficult. We still seek a flexible approach that provides sensors with enough autonomy and processing capabilities to determine secure, lower-cost, and reliable routes while avoiding message collisions and solving the problems resulting in transient or localized 'holes' during transmission. In addition, it is highly helpful to reduce network resource consumption by preventing the routing of insignificant data that burdens sensors. Indeed, current AWSNs gather huge amounts of data which are not always relevant to current monitoring requirements. To this end, we propose a conceptual hybrid approach that uses geographic-based routing to focus sensing efforts in areas of interest, plus semantic-based routing to determine and use relevant sensors semantically connected with respect to current monitoring requirements. Our approach is aided by software agents located on a virtual network running in parallel to the physical AWSN. In the remainder of this paper, Section 2 connects current works that address the topic of routing in AWSN. Section 3 outlines the fundamental ideas of our proposed solution. Section 4 presents the setup of initial sensing requirements for present data acquisition. Finally, Section 5 explains our proposed routing structure.

2 Related Works

The establishment and maintenance of lower-cost, secure, and reliable communication pathways considerably affects the efficiency of AWSN by minimizing message exchanges between sensors. This challenge has been addressed using three general approaches depending on the network structure [4]: flat-based [e.g. 1], hierarchical-based [e.g. 3], and location-based routing [e.g. 5, 6, 9]. In flat-based routing, equal roles or functionality are typically assigned to all nodes. In hierarchical-based routing, nodes will play different roles in the network. In location-based routing, the positions of sensors are exploited to route data in the network.

In the context of location-based routing, the ALS protocol [5] constructs a grid for forwarding data towards a target sink. This grid, used to define the naming system and assign roles to sensors, is set up by sensors once they are deployed. The TTDD routing protocol [7] constructs a grid during the data advertisement phase and uses dissemination nodes to forward the queries from the sink and to move data using a simple geographic forwarding process. [6] proposes a geographic grid routing (GGR) protocol that constructs a grid rooted at the data sink rather than the data source, as done by TTDD. [9] proposes a mesh-based routing approach that divides the environment under investigation into several regions. In each region, considered as a node in a mesh topology, a group of sensors called GoL (Group of Leaders) is constructed in order to increase the fault tolerance. The addition of mobile hosts complicates the location-based routing. Some approaches [e.g. 10] use mobile agents that move from one node to another, giving and taking relevant information. Recent research works [e.g. 1, 8] proposed semantic-oriented routing where sensors analyze the content of incoming messages and make associated decisions. In this respect, [8] enables some sensors, called semantic routers, to choose the right naming system to forward data through different sensor networks.

In spite of the intensity of research that has addressed the routing problem in AWSN, no complete solution is yet available. This is particularly due to the limited capabilities of remote sensors, their tendency to failure, and tendency to have sleep/wake cycles in order to conserve their resources. We believe that an approach driven by monitoring requirements and simultaneous use of geographic and semantic routing could improve the establishment and maintenance of more secure, reliable, and lower-cost communication pathways. We also believe that if this solution is able to acquire the right data from the right subspace using the right sensor subnets, then it should lengthen sensors' lifetimes and preserve their capabilities, which in turn better maintains routing pathways. Due to current limited hardware capabilities of sensors, we expect that realizing this solution will take further development into the future, but the conceptual approach we outline here begins this new avenue of investigation.

3 Fundamental Ideas of Our Solution

Since current sensors' hardware capabilities prevent large improvements in the efficiency of 'intelligent' routing approaches, we propose to virtually manage the AWSN by moving most intensive processing out of the physical network and into a parallel "Virtual" AWSN (VAWSN) operating on a base station or remote server. Using a multiagent system, our VAWSN provides sensors with more complete data and enhances their context awareness. Thus, sensors can improve their decision-making process and cope with frequent changes in communication pathways. In order to reduce the resource consumption of the AWSN, a Sensor Management Agent (SMA) manages the VAWSN and identifies the areas of interest where data will be acquired using a spatial grid. This agent identifies the minimal subset of sensors currently able to collect data from the areas of interest. We assign software agents to manage and control these sensors. Our agent architecture encompasses a *knowledge unit* (containing updated information and knowledge held by the agent), a *processing unit* (containing the analysis, planning, and execution layers of the agent), and a *working space* (containing current running threads of the agent). During processing, our agents self-organize into logical clusters, then instruct their sensors to self-configure into physical clusters, forming a Physical Management Network (PMN). Using their easy access to available information, agents actively and continually update communication pathways for task dissemination and data forwarding.

4 Setup of Initial Sensing Requirements

4.1 Reducing Sensing Scope

Generally, currently targeted data does not necessarily span the network's entire geographic space. Thus, it is relevant to focus the sensing efforts on areas of interest where data will be collected. These areas are determined according to their contents (targeted data, sensors) and locations (position regarding targets and tasks/data communication pathways). In order to locate them quickly, the SMA marks off these areas using a spatial grid that divides the space into tiles, the sizes of which depend on the density of sensors, the repetition and frequency of the measured phenomena, as well the required accuracy of processing. Several grids may be set up beforehand and used by the SMA according to current context and requirements. In the spatial database, relevant objects are linked to the tiles in which they are located. Moreover, the SMA categorizes the content of the space in accordance with the importance of spatial objects to current data acquisition. In this respect, an object of interest may have several semantics and sensitivity levels. Sensitivity refers to how much the object may be affected by or affect current data gathering or phenomenon tracking. Like sensitivity, 'semantics' is a subjective notion that depends on the intended use of the network. For example, if pollution is detected in a given water stream, the SMA examines the spatial database in order to locate factories that have been identified as potential sources of this pollution. The SMA also locates any object considered as sensitive to this pollution, such as lakes and farms. The use of several degrees of importance for spatial objects and targeted data enables us to set up priority orders between the areas of interest, use of network capabilities, and routing activities.

4.2 Identifying Relevant Sensor Subnets

After determining the tiles that mark off the areas of interest, the SMA determines the sensors that are potentially able to collect the required data from these areas. Only the minimal subset of these sensors will be used to achieve data acquisition. Some sensors may be eliminated for several reasons such as current capability (e.g. power), involvement in other ongoing processing, or low observed reliability. This task is done using stored information about the present state of the network, including its sensors' capabilities and topology, ongoing processing, and neighborhood relationships. Due to frequent changes in network topology, this information is updated on a predefined schedule or when there is a specific need (Figure 1).

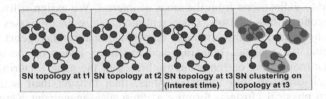

Fig. 1. Sensor network topology changes (shading indicates areas of interest)

Once relevant sensors are identified for current data gathering, the SMA categorizes them into clusters according to their geographic locations regarding the areas of interest. These clusters help improve query dissemination and in-network processing. In addition, they create data-gathering points and introduce new decisional levels at lower ranks than the SMA. Indeed, in accordance with their current capabilities and neighborhood relationships, the SMA appoints one of the sensors in each ad-hoc cluster as a leader. This leader manages the cluster and has authority to change the behaviors, processing priorities, and roles of its sensors. Since the AWSN may be used simultaneously for more than one data acquisition mission, sensors may have several roles. Therefore, in addition to physical connections, sensors and subnets are tied with semantic connections.

4.3 Setting Up the Agent-Based Virtual Network

In the VAWSN, we assign software agents to the sensors identified by the SMA as relevant to current data acquisition. Basically, we call every sensor a PS (Physical

Sensor) and its manager agent a VSA (Virtual Sensor Agent). Just like sensors gathered into physical clusters, agents group together into logical clusters. We call PLS (Physical Leader Sensor) and VLA (Virtual Leader Agent) the leader sensor of a given ad-hoc cluster and its manager agent respectively. Agents appointed as leaders notify their leading roles to each other within the virtual network. Close logical clusters may be disconnected if their physical clusters are not sufficiently close to communicate. In this case, their virtual leaders negotiate in order to connect their clusters. The parameters of the connecting configuration (Figure 2) are then sent to the physical leaders. In this configuration, several sensors with different roles may be used. Indeed, if two nearby clusters wish to use a sensor belonging to neither of clusters, we call the sensor a PBS (Physical Bridge Sensor). We assign a VBA (Virtual Bridge Agent) to the management of this PBS. If the sensor already belongs to one of the two clusters, we call it a PRS (Physical Relay Sensor) to which we assign a VRA (Virtual Relay Sensor). The sensor connecting two nearby clusters may also be a gate connecting the virtual and physical networks. In this case, we call this sensor a PGS (Physical Gate Sensor) and assign to it management a VGA (Virtual Gate Agent). These gates are the targets towards which our sensors forward their data, rather like the sinks in existing routing solutions.

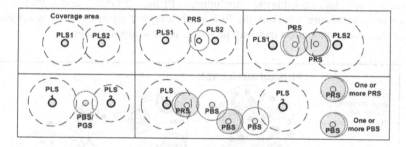

Fig. 2. Connection types between two neighboring PLSs

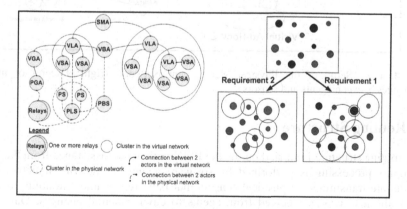

Fig. 3. (left) Agent-based architecture forming the Virtual Management Network, (right) Dependence of the Physical Management Network topology on requirements

The VLA, VSA, VBA, VRA, and VGA agents (Figure 3, left) form the Virtual Management Network (VMN) that will be used to control the current data acquisition and routing. Data acquisition is carried out by the Physical Management Network (PMN) consisting of PLS, PS, PBS, PRS, and PGS sensors. Since several simultaneous data- gathering missions may run at the same time, more than one PMN may coexistent within the same AWSN. These PMNs may have different topologies (Figure 3, right) according to current requirements and transmission ranges used by sensors to maintain the connectivity of the network.

4.4 Setting Up the Physical Management Network

Before data acquisition begins, agents test the connectivity of the PMN (Figure 4, left) and make sure that communication is flowing between the virtual and physical networks. To this end, they send *setup messages* to their sensors. These messages contain sensors' roles, neighbors, transmission ranges, locations of gates and relays, processing schedules (including wake/sleep cycles), and lowest-cost paths to send data to the VMN. Using this information that may change as time goes by, sensors self-configure to create physical clusters and set up the PMN. Every PLS tests the connectivity of its cluster by sending *ping messages* to its sensors. It sends similar messages to its neighbors, including PLSs, PGSs, and PRSs. When *acknowledgements* are received, the PLS sends a *report message* to its agent using the lowest-cost communication pathway provided in its setup message.

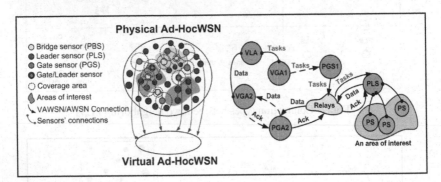

Fig. 4. (left) Setup of the Physical Management Network, (right) Excerpt of message exchanges between agents and sensors

5 Routing Structure

Our routing structure is carried out by the PMN with active assistance from the VMN. Complex processing is performed by software agents in the virtual network then results are transmitted to physical sensors that have reasonable autonomy to further adapt the instructions received from agents to environmental changes. Our routing approach is requirement-driven since it is built upon current requirements and priorities set up between collected data and areas of interest. From one perspective, our approach is location-based since we exploit the position of sensors to route data in the network. From another perspective, it is semantic-based since routing decisions may be based upon the content of messages and using semantic connections with neighboring sensors. For example, if new measurements show that water levels are rising enough to flood some areas, a given sensor may change its communication range in order to speed up the delivery of new information to suitable sensors. From a physical network perspective, semantic routing is difficult to realize due to limited processing capabilities of sensors. However, from a virtual network perspective, this routing is straightforward since agents have enough capabilities to analyze data and extract relevant information for pulling/pushing data towards suitable sensors. In this section, we break the routing effort into three stages as proposed by [6]: task dissemination, data forwarding, and maintenance. Before discussing these stages, we present the different messages exchanged between the actors (i.e. agents and sensors) of our system involved in the current data acquisition and outline their routing tables.

5.1 Proposed Messages

In the virtual network, messages are exchanged between agents without any difficulty. However, due to several constraints affecting the network topology and sensors' capabilities, this exchange (Figure 4, right) becomes hard to ensure between sensors. In order to support this exchange, we propose the following messages:

- TASK: message containing a new task, sent by an actor to another actor upon which it has authority. For example, a VLA may send TASK messages to the PSAs of its subnet, available VGAs, and connected VBAs.
- UCS (Update Current State): message sent by a given sensor to its agent or by a VLA to the SMA. This message contains new sensor's or subnet's state.
- DATA: message exchanged between actors and containing new or requested data.
- SETUP: message sent by an actor to another actor upon which it has authority. It specifies new parameters, such as role, neighbours, and processing priorities.
- REQR (REQuest Relay): message sent by a given VLA to a neighbour VLA asking it to propose a VRA from its subnet.
- REQB (REQuest Bridge): message sent by a given VLA to another VLA asking it to provide a VBA for making connection with a third VLA.
- CoP (Connection Proposal): message answering a previous REQR/REQB. It proposes a relay/bridge (as well its communication range). This message enables two neighbouring VLAs to negotiate the use of their resources. It is particularly interesting when concurrent tasks are running in the same network.
- CoC (Confirm Connection): message confirming a connection (relay or bridge) between two VLSs that previously exchanged CoP messages.
- PING: message exchanged between sensors in order to test their connections.
- NOTIFY: message used by every VLA, VBA, and VGA agent to confirm its role to its neighbours or to the SMA. It is also used by every PLS, PBS, and PGS sensor to confirm its role to its neighbours.
- REPORT: message sent by a given sensor to its agent during the setup phase reporting the course of its initialization process.
- PTD (Path To Destination): message sent by a given PLS to one of its PSs or to a connected PBS. It specifies a path to send messages to a specific destination.
- ACK (ACKnowledgment): After receiving a DATA message, a sensor sends an acknowledgment to the issuer of the message.

5.2 Routing Tables

In order to route task and data messages, our agents prepare and send routing tables to their sensors. These tables contain entries associated with each neighbor located in predefined communication ranges. These ranges are determined by agents according to the roles and current capabilities of their sensors. Particularly due to their roles, sensors have distinct types of routing tables. As for example, a given PLS has a routing table containing information about several actors (e.g. the PSs of its subnet, available PGSs, connected PBSs, and neighbor PLSs), a chain of relays to reach them, and estimated costs of any communication with them. The same sensor may have another routing table if it is involved in another PMN as a simple PS. In Table 1, PLS7 has a connection with the gate PGS10 through the neighbor PLS5. The path to PLS5 ("PRS71/PRS73/PBS1/PBS5/PRS54") costs 10. In contrast with the other sensors, a PGS does not need a routing table. Indeed, messages coming from the virtual network already contain the destination. If this destination does not acknowledge the reception of its message, a PGS contacts its VGA for an alternative. However, messages coming from sensors are simply routed to the VGA thanks to the direct connection with the PGS. The routing table of every sensor is updated in order to adapt to new events, such as breaking down or addition of new sensors. Basically, these updates are carried out by agents. They may also be carried out by sensors if an immediate decision must be taken after a sudden change in their environment.

Table 1. Routing table of a Physical Leader Sensor (PLS7)

Connection	Position	Relay	Chain	Cost
PLS10	NE	PS78	...	5
...	...	...	...	...
PGS10	S	PLS5	...	20
PLS5	N	...	PRS71/PRS73/PBS1/PBS5/PRS54	10

The routing processes of agents and sensors are aided by routing rules that capture decisions associated with incoming messages. For example, a PLS may ask one of its PS to collect data and forward it to a specific destination. If this destination does not acknowledge its data message, the PS sends the data to its PLS. If the PS is no longer able to contact its PLS, it increases its communication range. The solution of increasing communication range is used (if possible) by any PLS in order to speed up the gathering and forwarding of specific data which priority was recently increased. The decision-making processes of sensors and agents are based upon rule engines. In this respect, when an agent receives a new message, it analyzes the message's content and plans its actions using routing rules and available information (held by the agent or requested from other agents). As a result, the agent is able to continually update its rule engine and improve its decision-making process. Unlike agents, sensors cannot easily update their rule engines. They have access to limited information which is explicitly updated by agents or by sensors based upon detected events or information received from neighboring sensors.

5.3 Dissemination Task

The dissemination task process aims at communicating a new TASK message to concerned sensors. This process is straightforward between agents, but more complicated between sensors. In contrast with several existing solutions (e.g. [7, 6, 9]) that allow their sensors (sink or data source) to set up a grid/mesh for the dissemination of their tasks, our proposed approach identifies the locations of data sources using agents in the virtual network. These agents, which have free access to the spatial partitioning of the network, process and transmit required information to their sensors. Unlike existing solutions, a part of our communication pathway is done in the virtual network. Every agent sends its tasks to its sensor using the most appropriate gate based upon its availability (the agent tries to avoid busy gates), its geographic location with respect to the targeted sensor, and offering lower communication costs. The agent also identifies the required relay sensors that will be used in order to forward its TASK message to its sensor. Since some relays may be busy or committed, agents may negotiate in order to find an appropriate solution using the priority of ongoing and required processing tasks.

Once the TASK message reaches the physical network, it is forwarded to the sensor according to the path already identified by the agent. Since the network topology may change suddenly, a relay can update the forwarding path. If this relay is unable to carry out this task, it sends back the TASK message to the previous relay. Relays keep trying to find a new communication pathway during this backward chaining until the forwarding is successful. If the TASK message is received by a gate, it is sent to its issuer agent that will set up a new communication pathway.

5.4 Data Forwarding

Once data is gathered by a given sensor, it is formatted into a DATA message. Some approaches to forwarding this message have been proposed by others. In [6], this message is sent to the sink using intermediate and dissemination nodes. These nodes, which were identified during the advertisement phase, exchange DATA and ACK messages during the data forwarding process. In [5], the data source registers itself with the nearest grid node which is known as the source agent. The source agent finds the location of the sink agent and forwards it to the data source. The data source sends data packets to the sink agent using any existing location-based routing protocol.

Unlike the approaches mentioned above, our sensors target the gates connecting the virtual and physical networks. Their agents supply them with knowledge about the locations, roles, and costs relative to relays that could be used to reach the gates. They may ignore this information available in their routing tables if explicit routing orders are sent to them by agents/sensors having higher ranks. For example, PSs basically send their collected data to their PLSs. However, in some conditions, they may receive the order to forward the data to specific destinations. If a given PS cannot reach this destination, it sends its data to its PLS. Once data are received by a gate sensor, they are easily forwarded to the sink agent. This agent processes the content of the DATA message, updates its knowledge, and forwards relevant information to the SMA, its sensor, or other agents.

5.5 Communication Pathway Maintenance

Due to network topology changes and variable availability of sensors, maintenance of communication pathways is important in order to keep reliable message exchanges flowing. It is also important for sensor replacement since new sensors may be added to the network while others are sleeping, broken, or simply stolen. Despite its importance, some research works (e.g. [7, 8]) do not include mechanisms to support pathway maintenance. In [9], there is no specific focus on maintenance. Instead, GoL sensors and the sensors with higher energy resources are used to lengthen the lifetime of the network. This approach gives only minor benefit since the lifetimes of current sensors cannot be lengthened considerably. In [6], updates may be triggered by information carried in DATA messages or by the diminishment of sensors' capabilities. In this case, a new grid is rebuilt using a different cell size. In [10], communication pathway maintenance is carried out using new information brought to sensors by mobile agents. Like in [6], our updates may be triggered by the content of DATA messages or the availability of sensors. In addition, they may also be triggered by a change in processing priority and semantic connections between sensors. For example, in a water monitoring application, an increase in water level in some rivers upstream from a given lake may trigger a need for more frequent or accurate water level or water quality information from sensors monitoring that lake. Moreover, our sensors have reasonable autonomy to maintain and update their own communication pathways, particularly when sudden events occur. Maintenance decisions will be later reviewed by agents once they receive update notification from their sensors.

6 Conclusion

In this paper, we have described a conceptual approach that uses both location and semantics in order to improve routing in AWSN. Our approach is based upon the use of software agents, located on a virtual network running in parallel to the physical network. In order to reduce the routing of insignificant data that consumes the limited resources of sensors, our agents focus the sensing efforts on the current areas of interest, using the minimal sensors currently able to respond to new requirements. Moreover, they carry out most intensive processing and transfer decisions and more accurate data to their sensors in order to adapt to network topology changes and set up reliable communication pathways. These pathways are short-circuited since some messages are exchanged between agents. In this case, the routing approach may avoid the costly identification and use of several relay sensors, as well some of the communication pitfalls which exist with AWSN. The conceptual and architectural designs are complete, and implementation experiments are underway. Our future work will particularly focus on the development of a rule engine to support the decision-making process of agents and sensors. Meanwhile, ontologies are being developed for geographic space and AWSN in order to speed up the identification of areas of interest and the sensors relevant to the current processing needs.

References

1. Intanagonwiwat, C., Govindan, R., Estrin, D.: Directed Diffusion: a scalable and robust communication paradigm for sensor networks. In: Proceeding of the ACM MobiCom 2000, Boston, MA, pp. 56–67. ACM, New York (2000)
2. Kulik, J., Heinzelman, W.R., Balakrishnan, H.: Negotiation-based protocols for disseminating information in wireless sensor networks. Wireless Networks 8, 169–185 (2002)
3. Lindsey, S., Raghavendra, C.: PEGASIS: Power-efficient gathering in sensor information systems. In: Proceeding of the IEEE Aerospace Conf., vol. 3, pp. 25–30 (2002)
4. Al-Karaki, N., Kamal, A.E.: Routing Techniques in Wireless Sensor Networks: A Survey. IEEE wireless communications 11(6), 6–28 (2004)
5. Zhang, R., Zhao, H., Labrador, M.A.: A Grid-based Sink Location Service for Large-scale Wireless Sensor Networks. In: Proceedings of ACM International Wireless Communications and Mobile Computing Conference (IWCMC 2006), Vancouver, Canada (July 2006)
6. Hornsberger, J., Shoja, G.C.: Geographic Grid Routing: Designing for Reliability in Wireless Sensor Network. In: Proceedings of 2006 International Wireless Communication and Mobile Computing Conference, Vancouver, BC (July 3-6, 2006)
7. Ye, F., Luo, H., Cheng, J., Lu, S., Zhang, L.: A two-tier data dissemination model for large scale wireless sensor networks. In: Proceedings of the 8th ACM International Conference on Mobile Computing and Networking, number 8 in MobiCom, Atlanta, GA, USA, pp. 585–594. ACM Press, New York (2002)
8. Wang, K., Ayyash, S.A., Little, T.D.C.: Semantic Internetworking for Sensor Systems. In: proceedings of 1st IEEE International Conference on Mobile Ad-hoc and Sensor Systems, Fort Lauderdale, FL, pp. 484–492 (October 2004)
9. Lotfifar, F., Shahhoseini, H.S.: A mesh-based routing protocol for wireless ad-hoc sensor networks. In: Proceedings of the 2006 international conference on communications and mobile computing, Vancouver, Canada (July 2006)
10. Choudhury, R., Paul, K., Bandyopadhyay, S.: MARP: A multi-agent routing protocol for mobile wireless ad hoc networks. Autonomous Agents and Multi-Agent Systems 8(1), 47–68 (2004)

Author Index

Lecture Notes in Computer Science

For information about Vols. 1–4409

please contact your bookseller or Springer

Vol. 4546: J. Kleijn, A. Yakovlev (Eds.), Petri Nets and Other Models of Concurrency – ICATPN 2007. XI, 515 pages. 2007.

Vol. 4545: H. Anai, K. Horimoto, T. Kutsia (Eds.), Algebraic Biology. XIII, 379 pages. 2007.

Vol. 4533: F. Baader (Ed.), Term Rewriting and Applications. XII, 419 pages. 2007.

Vol. 4528: J. Mira, J.R. Álvarez (Eds.), Nature Inspired Problem-Solving Methods in Knowledge Engineering, Part II. XXII, 650 pages. 2007.

Vol. 4527: J. Mira, J.R. Álvarez (Eds.), Bio-inspired Modeling of Cognitive Tasks, Part I. XXII, 630 pages. 2007.

Vol. 4525: C. Demetrescu (Ed.), Experimental Algorithms. XIII, 448 pages. 2007.

Vol. 4514: S.N. Artemov, A. Nerode (Eds.), Logical Foundations of Computer Science. XI, 513 pages. 2007.

Vol. 4513: M. Fischetti, D.P. Williamson (Eds.), Integer Programming and Combinatorial Optimization. IX, 500 pages. 2007.

Vol. 4510: P. Van Hentenryck, L.A. Wolsey (Eds.), Integration of AI and OR Techniques in Constraint Programming for Combinatorial Optimization Problems. X, 391 pages. 2007.

Vol. 4507: F. Sandoval, A. Prieto, J. Cabestany, M. Graña (Eds.), Computational and Ambient Intelligence. XXVI, 1167 pages. 2007.

Vol. 4501: J. Marques-Silva, K.A. Sakallah (Eds.), Theory and Applications of Satisfiability Testing – SAT 2007. XI, 384 pages. 2007.

Vol. 4497: S.B. Cooper, B. Löwe, A. Sorbi (Eds.), Computation and Logic in the Real World. XVIII, 826 pages. 2007.

Vol. 4494: H. Jin, O.F. Rana, Y. Pan, V.K. Prasanna (Eds.), Algorithms and Architectures for Parallel Processing. XIV, 508 pages. 2007.

Vol. 4493: D. Liu, S. Fei, Z. Hou, H. Zhang, C. Sun (Eds.), Advances in Neural Networks – ISNN 2007, Part III. XXVI, 1215 pages. 2007.

Vol. 4492: D. Liu, S. Fei, Z. Hou, H. Zhang, C. Sun (Eds.), Advances in Neural Networks – ISNN 2007, Part II. XXVII, 1321 pages. 2007.

Vol. 4491: D. Liu, S. Fei, Z.-G. Hou, H. Zhang, C. Sun (Eds.), Advances in Neural Networks – ISNN 2007, Part I. LIV, 1365 pages. 2007.

Vol. 4490: Y. Shi, G.D. van Albada, J. Dongarra, P.M.A. Sloot (Eds.), Computational Science – ICCS 2007, Part IV. XXXVII, 1211 pages. 2007.

Vol. 4489: Y. Shi, G.D. van Albada, J. Dongarra, P.M.A. Sloot (Eds.), Computational Science – ICCS 2007, Part III. XXXVII, 1257 pages. 2007.

Vol. 4488: Y. Shi, G.D. van Albada, J. Dongarra, P.M.A. Sloot (Eds.), Computational Science – ICCS 2007, Part II. XXXV, 1251 pages. 2007.

Vol. 4487: Y. Shi, G.D. van Albada, J. Dongarra, P.M.A. Sloot (Eds.), Computational Science – ICCS 2007, Part I. LXXXI, 1275 pages. 2007.

Vol. 4484: J.-Y. Cai, S.B. Cooper, H. Zhu (Eds.), Theory and Applications of Models of Computation. XIII, 772 pages. 2007.

Vol. 4475: P. Crescenzi, G. Prencipe, G. Pucci (Eds.), Fun with Algorithms. X, 273 pages. 2007.

Vol. 4474: G. Prencipe, S. Zaks (Eds.), Structural Information and Communication Complexity. XI, 342 pages. 2007.

Vol. 4459: C. Cérin, K.-C. Li (Eds.), Advances in Grid and Pervasive Computing. XVI, 759 pages. 2007.

Vol. 4449: Z. Horváth, V. Zsók, A. Butterfield (Eds.), Implementation and Application of Functional Languages. X, 271 pages. 2007.

Vol. 4448: M. Giacobini (Ed.), Applications of Evolutionary Computing. XXIII, 755 pages. 2007.

Vol. 4447: E. Marchiori, J.H. Moore, J.C. Rajapakse (Eds.), Evolutionary Computation, Machine Learning and Data Mining in Bioinformatics. XI, 302 pages. 2007.

Vol. 4446: C. Cotta, J. van Hemert (Eds.), Evolutionary Computation in Combinatorial Optimization. XII, 241 pages. 2007.

Vol. 4445: M. Ebner, M. O'Neill, A. Ekárt, L. Vanneschi, A.I. Esparcia-Alcázar (Eds.), Genetic Programming. XI, 382 pages. 2007.

Vol. 4436: C.R. Stephens, M. Toussaint, D. Whitley, P.F. Stadler (Eds.), Foundations of Genetic Algorithms. IX, 213 pages. 2007.

Vol. 4433: E. Şahin, W.M. Spears, A.F.T. Winfield (Eds.), Swarm Robotics. XII, 221 pages. 2007.

Vol. 4432: B. Beliczynski, A. Dzielinski, M. Iwanowski, B. Ribeiro (Eds.), Adaptive and Natural Computing Algorithms, Part II. XXVI, 761 pages. 2007.

Vol. 4431: B. Beliczynski, A. Dzielinski, M. Iwanowski, B. Ribeiro (Eds.), Adaptive and Natural Computing Algorithms, Part I. XXV, 851 pages. 2007.

Vol. 4424: O. Grumberg, M. Huth (Eds.), Tools and Algorithms for the Construction and Analysis of Systems. XX, 738 pages. 2007.

Vol. 4423: H. Seidl (Ed.), Foundations of Software Science and Computational Structures. XVI, 379 pages. 2007.

Vol. 4422: M.B. Dwyer, A. Lopes (Eds.), Fundamental Approaches to Software Engineering. XV, 440 pages. 2007.

Vol. 4421: R. De Nicola (Ed.), Programming Languages and Systems. XVII, 538 pages. 2007.

Vol. 4420: S. Krishnamurthi, M. Odersky (Eds.), Compiler Construction. XIV, 233 pages. 2007.

Vol. 4419: P.C. Diniz, E. Marques, K. Bertels, M.M. Fernandes, J.M.P. Cardoso (Eds.), Reconfigurable Computing: Architectures, Tools and Applications. XIV, 391 pages. 2007.

Vol. 4416: A. Bemporad, A. Bicchi, G. Buttazzo (Eds.), Hybrid Systems: Computation and Control. XVII, 797 pages. 2007.

Vol. 4415: P. Lukowicz, L. Thiele, G. Tröster (Eds.), Architecture of Computing Systems - ARCS 2007. X, 297 pages. 2007.